Monasticism in Ireland, AD *900–1250*

Monasticism in Ireland, AD 900–1250

Edel Bhreathnach

FOUR COURTS PRESS

Set in EhrhardtMTPro 10.5pt on 12.5pt by
Carrigboy Typesetting Services for
FOUR COURTS PRESS LTD
7 Malpas Street, Dublin 8, Ireland
www.fourcourtspress.ie
and in North America for
FOUR COURTS PRESS
c/o IPG, 814 N Franklin St, Chicago, IL 60610.

A catalogue record for this title is available
from the British Library.

ISBN 978-1-80151-117-9

SPECIAL ACKNOWLEDGMENT

This publication has been financially supported by The Discovery Programme; Meath County Council; The National Monuments Service of the Department of Housing, Local Government and Heritage; Offaly County Council; and Wicklow County Council.

Comhairle Chontae Uíbh Fhailí
Offaly County Council

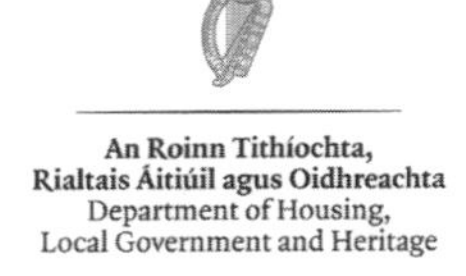

Printed in England
by CPI Antony Rowe Ltd, Chippenham, Wilts.

Contents

Illustrations

appear between pp 140 and 141, and pp 300 and 301.

Abbreviations

AC	*Annála Connacht: The Annals of Connacht* A.D. *1224–1544*, ed. and trans. A. Martin Freeman (Dublin, 1944; repr. 1996)
Adomnán, *VSC*	*Adomnán's Life of Columba*, ed. and trans. A.O. Anderson and M.O. Anderson [ed., rev.], Oxford medieval texts (Oxford, 1961; revised ed. 1991)
AFM	*Annala rioghachta Eireann: Annals of the kingdom of Ireland by the Four Masters, from the earliest period to the year 1616*, ed. and trans. John O'Donovan, 7 vols (Dublin, 1848–51; repr. 1990)
AI	*The Annals of Inisfallen (MS Rawlinson B.503)*, ed. and trans. Seán Mac Airt (Dublin, 1951; repr. 1988)
ALC	*The Annals of Loch Cé: a chronicle of Irish affairs from* AD *1014 to* AD *1590*, ed. and trans. William M. Hennessy, 2 vols (London, 1871; repr. 2000)
ATig	'The Annals of Tigernach', ed. and trans. Whitley Stokes, *Revue celtique* 16 (1895), 374–419; 17 (1896) 6–33, 116–263, 337–420; 18 (1897), 9–59, 150–303 (repr. 2 vols, Felinfach 1993). Electronic version trans. Gearóid Mac Niocaill https://celt.ucc.ie/published/T100002A/index.html
AU	*The Annals of Ulster (to* AD *1131)*, ed. and trans. Seán Mac Airt and Gearóid Mac Niocaill (Dublin, 1983); *Annala Uladh: Annals of Ulster, otherwise Annala Senait, Annals of Senat; a chronicle of Irish affairs* AD *431 to* AD *1540*. 4 vols, ed. and trans. W.M. Hennessy and B. Mac Carthy (Dublin, 1887–1901; repr. 1998)
CDI	*Calendar of documents relating to Ireland, 1171–1307*, ed. H.S. Sweetman, 5 vols (London, 1875–86)
CHMM	*The Cambridge history of medieval monasticism in the Latin west*, vols 1 and 2, ed. Alison I. Beach and Isabelle Cochelin (Cambridge, 2020)
CLH	Donnchadh Ó Corráin, *Clavis litterarum Hibernensium: medieval Irish books and texts (*c.*400–*c.*1600)*, 3 vols (Turnhout, 2017)
CPR	*Calendar of the patent and close rolls of chancery in Ireland, of the reigns of Henry VIII., Edward VI., Mary, and Elizabeth*, vol. 1, ed. James Morrin, (Dublin, 1861)

CS	*Chronicum Scotorum: A chronicle of Irish affairs, from the earliest times to AD 1135, with a supplement containing the events from 1141 to 1150*, ed. and trans. William M. Hennessy (London, 1866)
DIB	*Dictionary of Irish biography*: www.dib.ie
DIL	*Dictionary of the Irish language*: www.dil.ie
DIS	Pádraig Ó Riain, *A dictionary of Irish saints* (Dublin, 2011)
FAIre	*Fragmentary Annals of Ireland*, ed. and trans. Joan Newlon Radner (Dublin, 1978)
Heist, *VSH Salm.*	*Vitae sanctorum Hiberniae: ex codice olim Salmanticensi, nunc Bruxellensi. Lives of the saints of Ireland, from the Salamanca manuscript now of Brussels*, ed. W.W. Heist (Brussels, 1965)
Kenney, *Sources*	James F. Kenney, *The sources for the early history of Ireland: an introduction & guide. Volume 1: ecclesiastical* (New York, 1929; repr. Dublin, 1979)
MRHI	Aubrey Gwynn and R.N. Hadcock, *Medieval religious houses: Ireland* (London, 1970; repr. Dublin, 1988)
Ó Riain, *CGSH*	*Corpus genealogiarum sanctorum Hiberniae*, ed. Pádraig Ó Riain (Dublin, 1985)
Plummer, *BNnÉ*	*Bethada náem nÉrenn. Lives of the Irish saints*, 2 vols, ed. and trans. Charles Plummer (Oxford, 1922; repr. 1968)
Plummer, *VSH*	*Vitae sanctorum Hiberniae, partim hactenus ineditae*, 2 vols, ed. Charles Plummer (Oxford, 1910)
RB	*Sancti Benedicti regula* http://www.intratext.com/IXT/LAT0011/ Timothy Fry (trans.), *The Rule of St Benedict in English with notes* (Collegeville, 1981; repr. 2018)
RM	Luke Eberle (trans.), *The Rule of the Master* (Kalamazoo, 1977)
Sheehy, *Pont. Hib.*	*Pontificia Hibernica: medieval papal chancery documents concerning Ireland, 640–1261*, 2 vols, ed. Maurice P. Sheehy (Dublin, 1962)
Vanderputten, *Medieval monasticisms*	Steven Vanderputten, *Medieval monasticisms. Forms and experiences of the monastic life in the Latin west* (Berlin and Boston, 2020)

Glossary

This glossary provides definitions of common monastic terminology as used in the context of this volume. Middle Irish terms are in italics. The Latin terms included in this list have specific meanings in an Irish context.

ABBESS (*banabb*, *banchomarbae*): the head of a female community and successor of a church or monastery's founder. Abbesses may have followed a committed religious life or in many instances were lay heads belonging to hereditary families or royal dynasties.

ABBOT (*abb/ap*, *airchinnech*, *comarbae, princeps*, *principatus*): the Irish terms are interchangeable in their usage and in their meanings. Depending on the source and the particular individual, they mean the superior of a monastic community following a committed religious life, the founder's successor who can be an avowed monk, a cleric or a lay person presiding over all aspects of a MONASTERY's life.

ANCHORITE (*ancharae*)/HERMIT (*dísertach*, *díthrubach*, *mog Dé*, *trúag(án)*): These words are variously translated as 'anchorite' or 'hermit' and it is difficult to distinguish them in the sources. It would appear that they describe monks and clerics who withdrew from the world to a hermitage (*dísert*) or the wilderness as a penitential exercise for a period. Permission to withdraw was regulated by an individual's superior. Communities of anchorites/hermits were common, especially along the western seaboard. They withdrew permanently to hermitages but were supported materially by ecclesiastical or lay patrons. Many of these individuals' obits are recorded in the annals and on inscribed grave slabs and in most cases they were senior ecclesiastics and renowned for their learning and piety.

ASCETIC: In common with universal monastic tradition, this term relates to the pursuit of Christian perfection, purity and virtue. A particularly strict regime was undertaken by ANCHORITES and HERMITS and during the eighth and ninth centuries by the CÉLI DÉ whose regulations continued in use in subsequent centuries. This tradition viewed the monk as a *miles Christi/Dei* (*míl Chríst/Dé*) 'soldier of Christ/God' on life's pilgrimage fighting off the challenges of the world and enemy demons in pursuit of Paradise.

CANONICAL HOURS/DIVINE OFFICE (*trátha*): The liturgy that divided the clerical and monastic day into eight hours (prime, terce, sext, none(s), vespers, compline, nocturns/matins, lauds). In some instances, especially among the non-monastic clergy, only the major hours, matins, lauds and vespers, were celebrated. This liturgy consisted of psalms, hymns, antiphons, canticles, prayers, biblical and spiritual readings chanted or recited.

CÉLI DÉ: The form 'Culdee' is used in later sources. Meaning 'clients of God', the *céli Dé* movement appears in eighth-century Ireland associated with certain monasteries, some of them new foundations. They included Armagh, Tallaght, Finglas and Clondalkin (Co. Dublin) and Lorrha and Terryglass (Co. Tipperary). The most prominent among them were often bishops and they produced monastic and other ecclesiastical regulations, martyrologies and tracts on the Mass and Sunday observance. Their texts remained in circulation for many centuries after their heyday and the term *céli Dé* was used subsequently to describe a range of communities, including a religious community of either monks or priests and a community in charge of a hospice. Such communities survived in Ireland and Scotland as late as the sixteenth-century reformation although many were absorbed or forced into communities of regular canons and collegiate churches during the late medieval period.

CLERGY (*cléirech, deochain, epscop, sacart*): The clergy consisted of those who were ordained, deacons, priests and bishops along with those in minor orders. Some holding these offices in Ireland were also monks but it is difficult to estimate prior to the twelfth century how common it was for monks to be ordained.

CONFESSOR, SPIRITUAL DIRECTOR (*anmcharae*): Many senior ecclesiastics whose obits are recorded in the annals held the office of *anmcharae* and the early laws suggest that they interpreted canon law for religious communities. As they were confessors to the laity, and especially royal men and women, their influence was potentially significant. As a result they were warned in regulatory texts not to exploit their position to gain worldly possessions.

EREMITIC: living a contemplative life as a HERMIT either alone or in a small select community. See ANCHORITE.

HEAD OF SCHOOL (*fer léiginn*): The term literally means 'man of learning' but given that all obits are of those associated with monasteries, most were in charge of monastic schools. This does not mean that they were monks or teaching novices only. Many belonged to hereditary families and are known to have been experts in *senchas*, 'vernacular history, traditional lore'. Others undoubtedly were experts in scripture and canon law, chant and music while many were scribes (*ecna*, *scríbnid*, *suí*). The obits of *fir léiginn* occur in most major monasteries but these are sporadic with the exceptions of Armagh, Clonard, Clonmacnoise, Derry, Emly, Kells and Kildare where holders of this office occur frequently.

From the mid-twelfth century, they disappeared and the last obit recorded in the annals was in Derry in 1189.

HERMITAGE (*dísert*, *díthrub)*: *Dísert* derived from Latin *desertum* in an Irish context usually associated with bogs, coastal and lake islands. The most famous hermitages located in such places include Sceilig Mhichíl (Skellig, Co. Kerry), Inismurray (Co. Sligo) and Monaincha (Co. Tipperary). Many hermitages were also located within or close to large monasteries, as was the case in Glendalough (Co. Wicklow) and Kells (Co. Meath). *Dísert* (anglicized to *dysart*, *desert*) occurs as a place-name element scattered throughout Ireland.

MONASTERY (*civitas*, *cathair*, *locán*, *mainister*, *rúam*): Use of the term 'monastery' is complicated in Ireland. Every medieval church ruin, no matter its age or size, is described incorrectly as a monastery. These sites range from large complexes, which did indeed house monastic communities, to pre-Norman proprietary churches, hermitages and later parish churches. In an effort to distinguish between the various sites, scholars use the terms '*civitates*' and 'ecclesiastical complexes' and more controversially 'monastic towns' to describe the larger sites, the middle-sized and lesser sites usually covered by a variety of terms. The most detailed and accurate classification, based on archaeological, architectural and historical evidence, is contained in the National Monument Service's Historic Environment Viewer (www.archaeology.ie). The term MONASTERY is used throughout this volume although with qualifications. Larger monasteries such as Armagh and Clonmacnoise consisted of diverse populations and hierarchical structures, clerical, monastic and lay. They were significant landholders and deeply embedded in dynastic and territorial politics. Middle and smaller sites are more difficult to define and with little or no historical evidence, the existence of monastic communities living in them is open to question. Some, of course, were hermitages and many probably housed very small communities or individual priests who followed a basic regulated life (e.g. celebrating the major canonical hours) and served a local dynasty and population.

MONASTIC COMMUNITY (*manaig*, *fír-manaig*, *boicht*, *cráibdig*, *deorada Dé*, *muinter*, *familia*): The term COENOBITIC COMMUNITY is also used in monastic scholarship. In this volume a monastic community is confined to a group of individuals and solitaries who live a committed religious life under the direction of a superior (abbot) either within a greater monastery, in hermitages or in smaller communities. They were intentional communities distinguished from other inhabitants by their dedication to *opus Dei*, namely, constant prayer, penitential exercises and following the canonical hours and liturgical calendar. Humility and obedience were central to their lives while chastity, although practised by many, was required mainly of those who were ordained. They remained silent at certain times, chanted the liturgy, processed and prostrated themselves as part of their daily regime. They confined their normal activities to teaching, learning and writing and household tasks such as cooking, sewing and caring for guests, penitents and the sick. They were subject to a special diet that was imposed especially during seasons such as Lent or as part of an individual's penance. They were not totally enclosed and at least some senior monks moved from one community to another. Their involvement in pastoral care among the laity varied. Some were confessors to the ecclesiastical and lay nobility while others in smaller communities probably served the laity around them. Members of a monastic community were ordained but it is not clear how common this was until the twelfth century when canons and monks were ordained in increasing numbers.

MONK (*macc bethaid*, *macc eclaise*, *manach*, *cráibdech*, *deorad Dé*): In the context of this volume, the Irish term *manach* is understood as a monk living in a monastic or eremitical community. *Manach* is used also to describe a tenant living on monastic estates who was subject to those in a monastery administering its temporal possessions.

NUN, VOWESS, FEMALE PENITENT (*caillech*): The term *caillech* has a wide range of meanings both lay and religious. *Caille* 'veil' is derived from Latin *pallium* and hence the interpretation of *caillech* as 'a veiled one' or nun. *Caillech*, however, can mean 'a spouse, married woman', 'a spouse of Christ, virgin, nun', 'an old woman', 'a supernatural being' and 'a housekeeper'. In addition, *caillech aithrige* means 'a penitent spouse' (Latin *clientella*), *caillech ailithre* 'a penitent, penitent spouse'. *Fedb*, from Latin *uidua* 'a widow', can be a synonym for *caillech aithrige*.

PILGRIM (*ailithir*, *deorad*)/PILGRIMAGE (*ailithre*): The pilgrims discussed in this volume were confined to a restricted group in society, namely, the monk on his journey to Paradise, ecclesiastics taking on a deliberate exile or journey to Rome, and lay people who travelled to Rome or who ended their lives in penance in monasteries. Popular pilgrimages were a phenomenon of the later medieval and early modern periods.

REICLÉS: A free-standing chapel dedicated to a particular saint, possibly housing a relic. These chapels often had specific custodians in charge of them and presumably controlling who entered them, ceremonies conducted in them (e.g. on a saint's feast day) and collecting any income due to the chapel. The custodians may have resided in them during certain periods but it is unlikely that they were permanent residences. The term is also used to describe the section in a greater monastic settlement where a coenobitic community lived.

RULE (*recht*, *ríagail*): Irish vernacular rules are advisory handbooks or compendia aimed at all levels of ecclesiastics including bishops, monks and the laity. They are exhortations in metre and prose and some, especially those attributed to the *céli Dé*, include elements of the customaries of particular monasteries. Although different in language and style to well-known rules such as the Rule of Benedict, they include all the fundamentals and ideals of monastic life and can be shown to have drawn on a variety of monastic traditions.

SCHOLARS (*fer léiginn*, *ecnae*, *senchaid*, *suí*, *scríbnid* (*scriba*)): These terms relate to the range of officials who were involved in learning, teaching and intellectual activities, mainly, but not always, in a monastic setting. The *fer léiginn* could be the head of a school catering for monastic and clerical novices, and in some instances members of the nobility. The *ecnae* and *suí* were experts in subjects including scripture, canon law and occasionally secular law. The *senchaid* was an historian learned in biblical and native history, a combination of learning essential to the Irish view of their own history.

***

Useful general glossaries for monasticism: https://religiouslife.com/glossary; Janet Burton and Julie Kerr, *The Cistercians in the Middle Ages* (Woodbridge, 2011), pp 203–8.

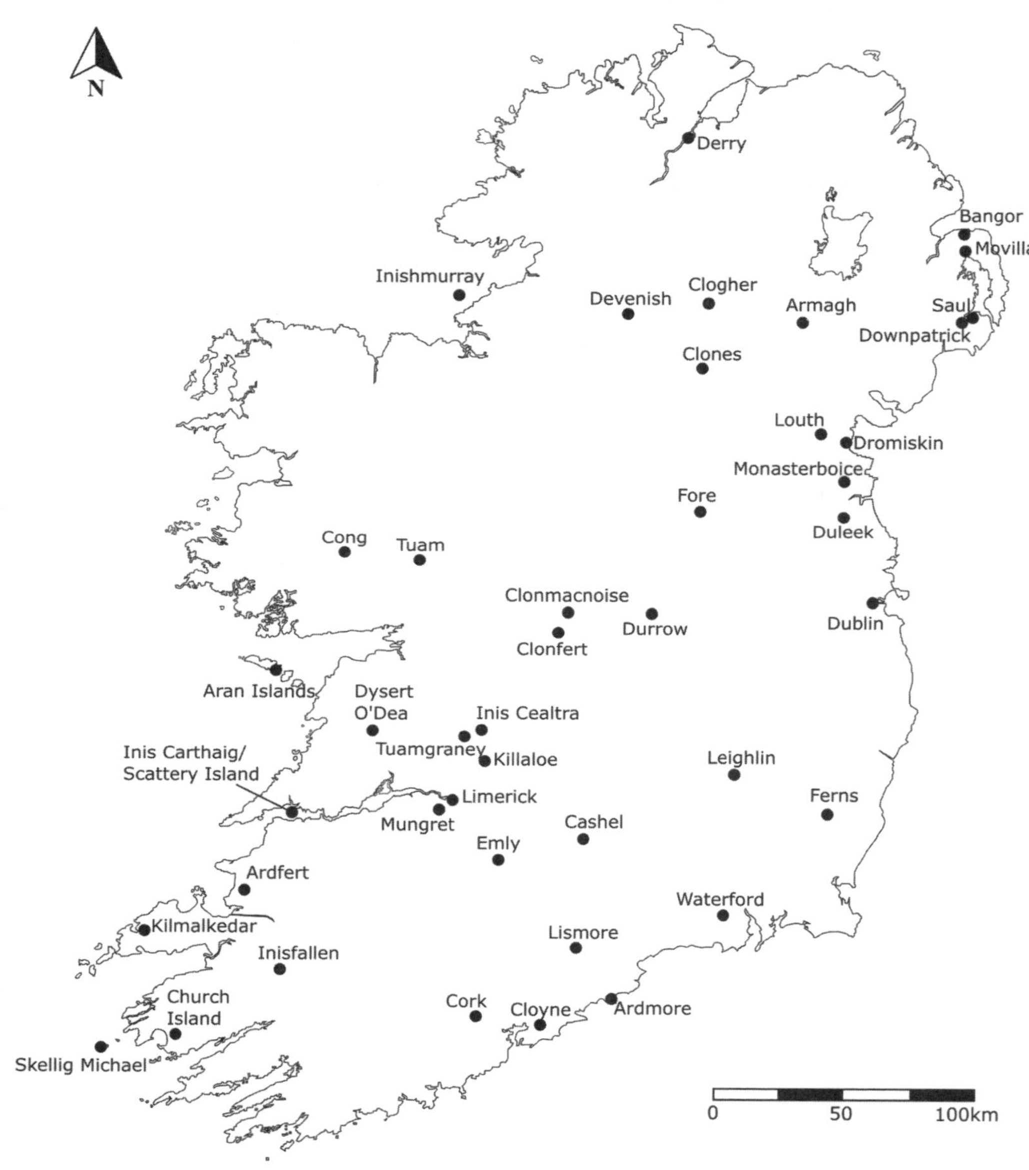

Map 1: Monasteries and churches in Ireland, AD 900–1250.

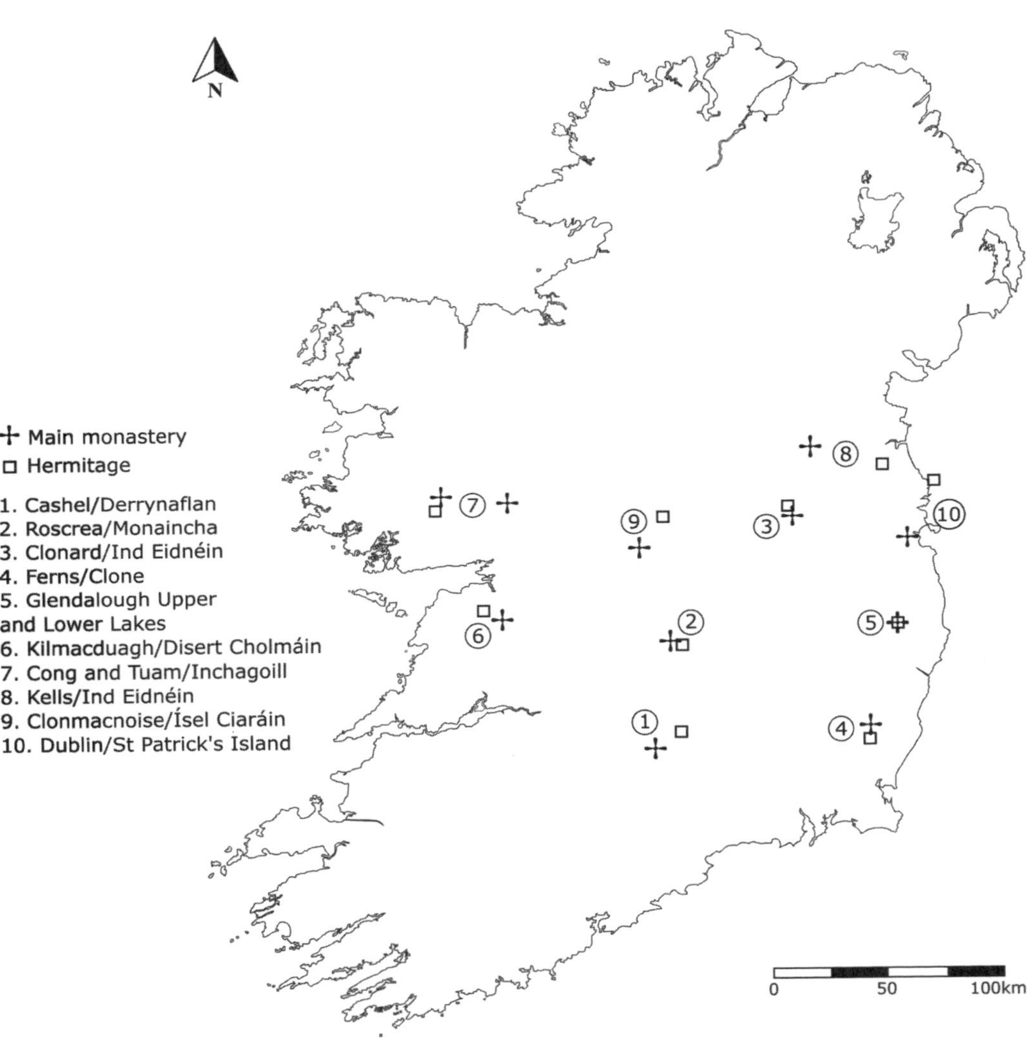

Map 2: Monasteries and their hermitages.

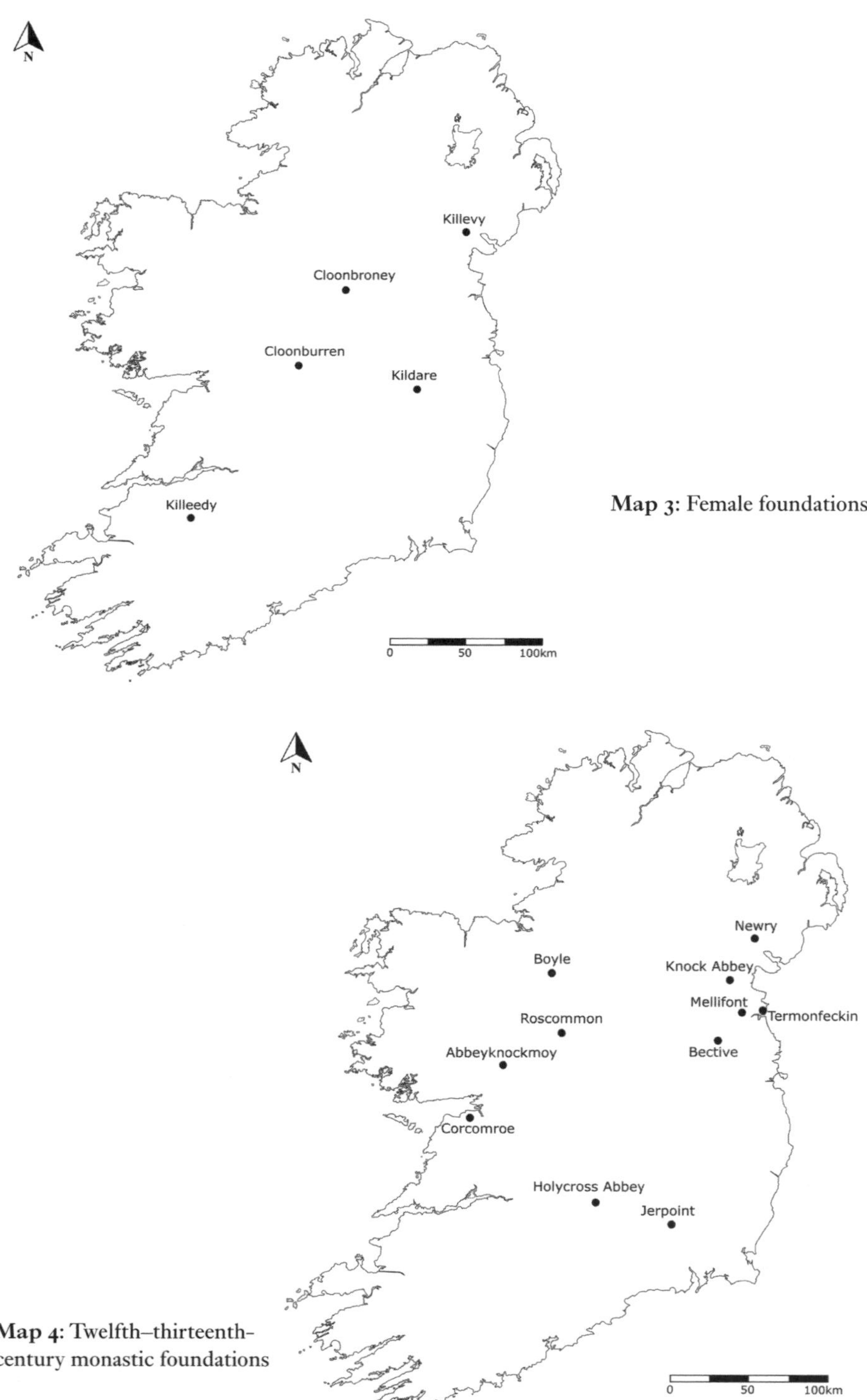

Map 3: Female foundations

Map 4: Twelfth–thirteenth-century monastic foundations

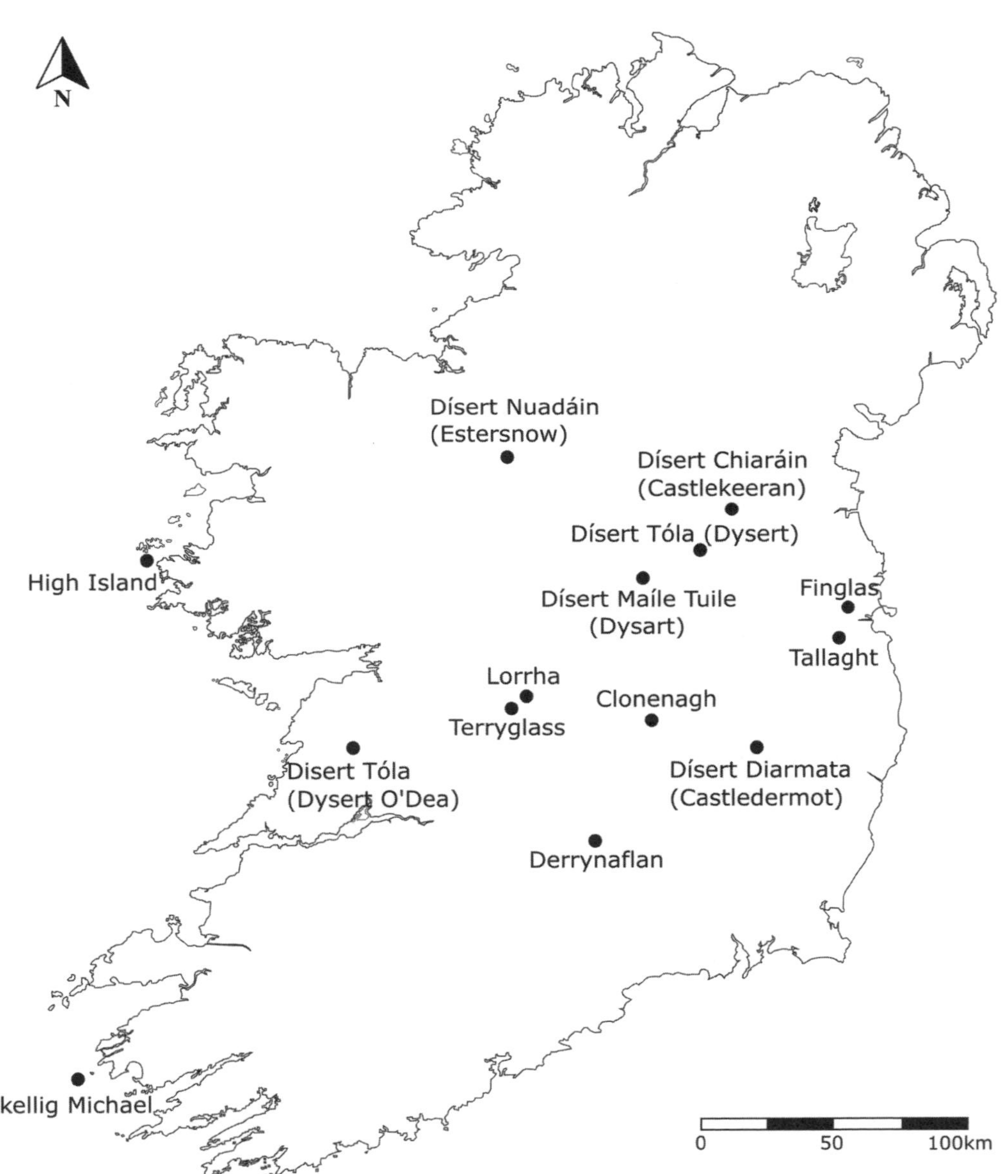

Map 5: *Céli Dé* and *dísert* foundations

Acknowledgments

This volume is part of the *Monastic Ireland* project that has gone through various iterations since I initiated it in 2011. It is a sequel to the volume *Monastic Europe: medieval communities, landscapes, and settlements,* which I co-edited with my colleagues Małgorzata Krasnodębska-D'Aughton and Keith Smith. I am grateful to many colleagues and institutions who supported me as I researched and wrote the volume, especially during the Covid lockdowns. The peer reviewer assigned by Four Courts Press to read the first draft undertook their task with diligence and provided me with clear directions towards improving the text's structure and many other details. Martin Fanning and the team at Four Courts Press guided me with their usual efficiency and graciousness from peer review to publication.

I owe my greatest debt to my friends Cormac Bourke and Colmán Ó Clabaigh, and to my husband Raghnall Ó Floinn, all of whom carefully read every page of the draft text and shared their own extensive knowledge with me, as well as applying their considerable editorial skills to improve and correct the text. Janet Burton read the final chapter and shared her expertise on twelfth-century monasticism with me. What errors are now in the text are mine alone.

While writing I mulled over on how best to illustrate the volume with engaging images. I discovered two wonderful illustrators among my immediate family and friends. Rosie Mears painted the Lismore figure for the front cover and the Ballyvourney cross slab for the back cover, two striking images executed with minute attention to detail. Yvonne McDermott accepted the challenge to produce a series of beautiful and unusual ink and watercolour drawings of monuments and objects that I suggested to her as I wrote the book. Annejulie Lafaye created the clear distribution maps.

I am grateful to the librarians and staff of All Souls College Oxford, Bibliothèque nationale de France, British Library, Corpus Christi College, Oxford, the Dublin Institute for Advanced Studies (School of Celtic Studies), Jesus College Oxford, National Gallery of Ireland, National Library of Ireland, National Museum of Ireland, Royal Irish Academy, Royal Society of Antiquaries of Ireland and University College Dublin (Archives) for providing me with material during Covid lockdowns and also permission to reproduce images in their care.

Financial support was generously granted by the National Monuments Service (Michael MacDonagh, Chief State Archaeologist), Discovery

Programme (John O'Keeffe, CEO), Meath County Council (Loreto Guinan, Heritage Officer), Offaly County Council (Amanda Pedlow, Heritage Officer) and Wicklow County Council (Deirdre Burns, Heritage Officer).

I am grateful to many other colleagues for their assistance: Saskia Dade, Wendy Davies (Oxford Centre for Late Antiquity), Lisa Gotthard (University of Edinburgh), Alyssa Izzo, Catherine McKenna (Harvard University), Emer Purcell (National University of Ireland), John Waddell (University of Galway) and Richard Warren. The Warden and Fellows of All Souls College Oxford afforded me a Visiting Fellowship in Michaelmas Term 2016, a period of research that opened up so many new perspectives on monasticism for me that it completely changed the path I finally took in writing the volume. I wish to thank Julia Smith, Chichele Professor of Medieval History, and remember her late husband Professor Hamish Scott, Senior Research Fellow, Jesus College for their friendship and generosity. Janet Burton and William Marx, Peregrine Horden (All Souls) and Jane Baun (Wadham College) and Bridget Riley all welcomed me and became close friends. Professor Thomas Charles-Edwards, Corpus Christi College and Jesus College Oxford, continued in his long-standing role as mentor and *anmcharae*.

This volume is dedicated to the memory of Joseph MacMahon OFM, friar, scholar and kindly friend. Joe was an inspiration to so many of us who worked with him and who encouraged me to persevere with the *Monastic Ireland* project.

Ní bheadh aon leabhar ann murach an síor-thacaíocht óm chlann, Raghnall, Sorcha agus Muiris maraon le Rosie agus Thomas. Tógfad sos ós na manaigh ar feadh tamaill agus fágfad faoi na léitheoirí a dtuairimí féin a chur in iúl anois!

Na Déise
31ú Nollaig 2023

Conventions

Many early Irish texts cannot be dated precisely. The standard designations used for periods of the Irish language provide a general framework for the chronology of texts referred to in this volume: 'Old Irish' covers *c*.700 to *c*.900; 'Middle Irish' covers *c*.900 to *c*.1200. The original versions of most Old and Middle Irish and Latin extracts are provided in the footnotes.

Irish personal names are normalized as far as possible with the designations *mac* 'son of' and *ua* 'grandson of' used where this refers to a genuine son/grandson relationship and *Mac/Ua* 'descendants of' refers to a familial/dynastic surname that became more prevalent from the eleventh century onwards. In general, the forms of personal names used in the *New history of Ireland* volume I are followed.

Irish place-names that cannot be identified are italicized.

Introduction

Benedictus caput monachorum totius Europae. Fintan Cluana Eidnig caput monachorum totius Hiberniae[1]

'Benedict head of the monks of all Europe. Fintan of Clonenagh head of the monks of all Ireland'

This quote from a compilation of Irish saints' genealogies, probably collated into one text during the eleventh and twelfth centuries, encapsulates the essence of this present volume on Irish monasticism. Benedict of Nursia (d. 547) was known in early medieval Ireland as a leader of monks on the Continent, more so than Columbanus of Bobbio (d. 615), a native of Ireland, who was an influential monastic founder in Burgundy and Lombardy. The Irish had their own monastic founders, the most renowned being Finnian of Clonard and Columba of Iona. In the genealogical list, Benedict is equated to a lesser-known, although important, saint, Fintan of Cluain Eidnech (Clonenagh, Co. Laois). Monasticism emerged as a prominent movement in Ireland during the mid-sixth century. Its transference to the island was mainly from Britain and Gaul and once established, through the foundation of numerous monasteries, it maintained strong links with both regions and extended its influence beyond them to Lombardy and the greater Frankish Empire. Most scholarship relating to monasticism in Ireland deals with its emergence and early successful flourishing, and its increasing influence elsewhere during the sixth to ninth centuries. There is a gap from then until the late eleventh century when the growing effect of the transformation of western Christendom is viewed as reaching the Irish church, and 'new' monastic orders are seen to 'reform' monasticism in Ireland at a time when it was perceived to have declined from its 'golden' age. This standard narrative was the basis of Fr John Ryan's *Irish monasticism. Origins and early development*, published in 1931, which became the cornerstone of the subject during the twentieth century.[2] In recent decades, scholars have reassessed many elements of Ryan's work especially around the idea of the so-called twelfth-century reform. Notable among these works is Marie Therese Flanagan's *The transformation of the Irish church in the twelfth century*, which places the changes in the Irish church of the period in the wider context of western Christendom,

1 Pádraig Ó Riain (ed.), *Corpus genealogiarum sanctorum Hiberniae* (Dublin, 1985), p. 162 § 712.34. 2 John Ryan, *Irish monasticism. Origins and early development* (Dublin, 1931; repr.

and in doing so, determines that Ireland's position was not that dissimilar from many other regions.[3] There have been many other debates, as will be clear from the secondary sources quoted in this volume, regarding the nature of the Irish church in the centuries before this transformation, covering topics such as its organization, its wealth, its system of pastoral care, the influence of the Vikings, levels of literacy, the archaeology of the early Irish church, the archaeology, history and landscape of specific monasteries and so forth. While monasticism often features in these studies, it is rarely the sole focus, or the definition of monasticism is very broad and not confined to communities committed to a religious life. The aim of this volume is to attempt to identify those specific communities living in Irish monasteries between the ninth and twelfth centuries which the quote from the saints' genealogies regarded as being under the leadership of Fintan of Clonenagh and equivalent to those understood to be following Benedict's direction.

Canon 13 of the Fourth Lateran Council of 1215 is adopted here as a pivotal decree insofar as Pope Innocent III (d. 1216) sought to regulate corporate religious ways of life (*religiones*) by advising that already approved institutions and rules should be followed.[4] While this canon was a response to the proliferation of various types of religious communities throughout Europe and did not necessarily reflect the situation in Ireland, nevertheless, from the mid-thirteenth century onwards, monasticism in Ireland was mainly confined to the major monastic and mendicant orders (Augustininans, Benedictines, Cistercians, Dominicans, Franciscans and Premonstratensians). The monastic tradition as lived prior to that period had undergone an almost complete transformation. A starting point is far more difficult to determine. The volume does not deal with the early centuries of monasticism in Ireland although at times the narrative is drawn back into these centuries. One significant reason for this less defined beginning relates to the *céli Dé* ('clients of God'), an elite religious movement that was concerned with the regulation of religious life, the church's relationship with lay penitents, and the enhancement of liturgy in general. Although the *céli Dé* were most active during the late eighth and early ninth centuries, their texts and dictums circulated and were revised during later centuries and remained relevant to monastic life until the twelfth century.[5] Hence I have tried to work mainly from AD 900 while not at all ignoring the monastic tradition that existed prior to that date.

1992). 3 Marie Therese Flanagan, *The transformation of the Irish church in the twelfth century* (Woodbridge, 2010). 4 The common perception is that this canon forbade the establishment of new orders (*ordo*, *religio*) but for a more nuanced interpretation of Canon 13 see Elizabeth Freeman, 'The Fourth Lateran Council of 1215, the prohibition against new orders, and religious women', *Journal of Medieval Religious Cultures* 44:1 (2018), 1–23. 5 Peter O'Dwyer, *Céli Dé. Spiritual reform in Ireland, 750–900* (Dublin, 1981); Westley Follett, *Céli Dé in Ireland. Monastic writing and identity in the early Middle Ages* (Woodbridge, 2006).

Terminology represents a challenge for scholars of early Irish monasticism, for as Colmán Etchingham demonstrated in his study of the early Irish church, standard monastic terms were used beyond their basic meaning.[6] The most obvious challenge relates to the word *manach* (from Latin *monachus*) 'monk' which also came to mean 'monastic tenant'. The shift became so pervasive that the term *fír-manach* 'true monk' was coined. The complexity of monastic institutions in Ireland is reflected in the range of titles accorded to superiors of monasteries, the most common being *abbas/abb*, *airchinnech*, *comarbae*, *princeps*, *principatus*. Any of these could refer – depending on a particular source's usage at a given time – to the religious superior of a monastic community living a religious life or to the often lay superior in charge of the temporal affairs of a large monastic settlement and its lands. The latter might hold an office similar to advocates elsewhere, not be in orders or be in minor orders, be married and often be a member of a hereditary ecclesiastical family. A *comarbae*, fully monastic or not, was defined as the successor of a monastery's founder saint. Recent studies have very much focused on the latter and their temporal power, along with two key issues, the provision of pastoral care to the laity and the hierarchical structure of the church in general and whether it was primarily a monastic organization, an episcopal organization or a combination of both. There is general agreement now that it was the latter but the challenge has been to identify monasticism, *fír-manaig* 'true monks', in this complex organization. The other related issue yet to be fully addressed is whether it is valid to regard Ireland's monastic tradition as an aberration, an outlier with Scotland and Wales, similar in ways to Scandinavia, and impervious to developments in England and on the Continent.[7] Evidence emerging for the eleventh century and later suggests that this was not so. The situation prior to that requires greater attention.

The term 'monastery' is used throughout this volume although this causes considerable problems. In modern popular literature most early medieval ecclesiastical sites in Ireland, even the smallest, are described as monasteries. As shown by Tomás Ó Carragáin in his study of churches in the Irish landscape, there was a hierarchy of ecclesiastical settlements from large-scale sites such as Armagh, Clonmacnoise, Glendalough and Kells to small churches dotted throughout Ireland.[8] Not all of them housed monastic communities or even individuals committed to a monastic or religious life. Some were monastic, while most others simply maintained priests who provided pastoral care to the

6 Colmán Etchingham, *Church organisation in Ireland AD 650 to 1000* (Naas, 1999), p. 319. 7 A similar discussion, although in a different context, is taking place about monasticism in Iceland. See, for example, Steinunn Kristjánsdóttir, 'No society is an island: Skriðuklaustur monastery and the fringes of monasticism', *The Journal of Medieval Monastic Studies* 4 (2015), 153–72; Steinunn Kristjánsdóttir, *Monastic Iceland* (Abingdon, 2022). 8 Tomás Ó Carragáin, *Churches in the Irish landscape AD 400–1100* (Cork, 2021).

surrounding population and while not monastic in their lifestyle would have followed some form of the Divine Office. Ó Carragáin uses the term *civitates* for larger monasteries to distinguish them from other churches. In the background is use of the term 'monastic town', which has been the source of a long-standing controversy since the 1980s.[9] These places are also designated as 'ecclesiastical complexes' and 'ecclesiastical settlements', mainly in archaeological literature, but they were more than that given their varied functions and populations. The term 'monastery' is adhered to throughout as it has an international validity and in a sense, as the volume's objective is to concentrate on committed religious communities, it is the appropriate term, no matter what other activities occurred around these communities.

The nine chapters in this volume follow one approach of many that were tried in preparing the text and that might be taken by other scholars. To a certain extent, this is an experiment that if it succeeds in any of its purposes, might at least open up further avenues of research. Fundamental to its approach is that the Irish monastic tradition was not an aberration but was one of many 'monasticisms' in existence throughout the eastern and western churches in the early medieval world.[10]

To understand the history of the view that early Irish monasticism was different, that it was a 'Celtic' deviation, it was necessary to narrate the subject's historiography from the seventeenth century onwards when it became entangled in the debates of confessional historians, Catholic and Protestant, who sought to appropriate the early Irish church for their own political and religious motivations. This conflict continued through the centuries, but especially with the rise of Catholic nationalism during the nineteenth century. This movement adopted many material elements of early Irish monasticism – the high cross and round tower being the most evident – as symbols of its ancient roots. The late twentieth century heralded serious interrogation of this narrative although this questioning, as previously noted, tended to concentrate on the early monastic period and the twelfth century. Chapter 1 deals with this historiographical narrative and while some might question the value of this preliminary discussion, given that there is a considerable corpus of recent scholarship in the field, the focus on monasticism has not been to the fore to date. This chapter is thus an essential guide to an international readership that may have only encountered medieval Irish monasticism in the guise of 'Celtic' monasticism.

9 To gain a sense of this debate see Catherine Swift, 'Religion (as a factor in Irish town formation)' in Howard B. Clarke and Sarah Gearty (eds), *More maps and texts. Sources and the Irish Historic Towns Atlas* (Dublin, 2018), pp 67–86. **10** The term 'monasticisms' has been used by Steven Vanderputten in his studies. See Vanderputten, *Medieval monasticisms. Forms and experiences of the monastic life in the Latin west* (Berlin and Boston, 2020); Alison I. Beach and Isabelle Cochelin (eds), *The Cambridge history of medieval monasticism in the Latin West* [*CHMM*] (Cambridge, 2020).

One reason why Ireland has been regarded as different relates to the type of sources produced in medieval Ireland and also to the survival of sources. In the case of survival of sources from the period under consideration, there is a dearth of monastic books, especially liturgical books such as antiphonaries, hymnals and missals, although those that survive when analysed from a monastic perspective offer much material that has hitherto gone unnoticed. Many other sources for the period are in the vernacular and while they were often transcribed from their manuscript sources during the nineteenth and twentieth centuries, have lain unedited and untranslated or infrequently used by many scholars. In addition, those who can read them have not often used them as sources that might deepen our understanding of monasticism. Chapters 2 and 3 examine a number of texts of various dates as case studies with the intention of demonstrating how sources can be quarried for evidence.[11] These are divided between sources of the foundational period, pre-900 and those dating to post-900. The later period cannot be understood without knowledge of the direction monasticism took in Ireland from as early as the fifth century onwards.[12] The sources interrogated include the Irish canon laws, vernacular laws, Adomnán of Iona's *Vita Sancti Columbae*, the *Regula Choluimb Chille*, a series of adages in Old Irish on living as an anchorite attributed to St Columba (d. 597), a similar set of adages known as the *Apgitir Chrábaid* 'The Alphabet of Devotion', and early kalendars and martyrologies. Martyrologies and kalendars were part of the church's apparatus in following the liturgical year. In this study they are represented by the *céli Dé* early ninth-century martyrology *Félire Óenguso* which is here compared to the twelfth-century *Félire Uí Gormáin*, compiled by Máel Muire Ua Gormáin in the Arrouaisian foundation of Knock, Co. Louth, both of which were primarily monastic in their function.

The sources of the post-900 period are mainly in the vernacular and are more diverse. Hagiographical texts in particular begin to mirror developments in monasticism and the concerns of monasteries for their own economic and political power in a changing world. The homiletic preface to the twelfth-century Irish life of Columba, likely to have been preached to a religious community and lay penitents on the saint's feast day, is contrasted with the twelfth-century Irish life of St Colmán mac Luacháin of Lynn, Co. Westmeath, composed to defend the monastery's estates and landowners from episcopal control and potential land transfers by patrons to new foundations. The Gospel Book BL Harley 1802 compiled by a young scholar Máel Ísu Ua Máel Uanaig in Armagh in 1138, the so-called Corpus Gospel Book (Bodleian Library Oxford MS CCC 122) and the

11 Specific references to editions and secondary sources commenting on these texts are provided in detail in the various chapters. 12 In his *Confessio* St Patrick mentions that young men and women in Ireland were being called to become monks and virgins of Christ. See Ludwig Bieler, *Libri epistolarum sancti Patricii episcopi*. Clavis Patricii II (Dublin, 1993), pp 1, 85 §§41–2, 49. For access online to the Latin text and translation see www.confessio.ie.

Corpus Missal (Bodl. MS CCC 282), all probably produced by monastic communities in large monasteries, are compared. They reflect a common trend both in their contents, commentaries and decoration, of adherence to long-established norms while being cautiously receptive to new influences. The importance of the psalter to monastic life occurs throughout this volume, not unexpected given the centrality of the psalms to the Divine Office for both monks and other clerics. The vernacular didactic poems on the psalms composed by Airbertach mac Coisse Dobráin of Ros Ailithir (Rosscarbery, Co. Cork) (d. 1015/16) provide an insight into the teaching methods used in monastic schools, the constant question here being whether his pupils were monastic novices only, or if clerical and lay students were among them. Records of land grants to monasteries were not preserved in charters in Ireland until the twelfth century when Irish kings adopted the practice of registering endowments to the 'new' orders.[13] Prior to that, the main mode of confirmation was through hagiographical texts where larger monasteries incorporated records of subject churches and their estates. A small number of eleventh- and twelfth-century memoranda were written into the Book of Durrow and the Book of Kells which record land transactions for the monasteries of Kells (Co. Meath) and Durrow (Co. Offaly). Writing such transactions into these books, which were probably regarded as precious relics, conferred a legal status on the events recorded. Finally, on the question of sources, the evidence used here is not confined to manuscripts and texts. Archaeology, architecture and landscape studies have to be included in any study of Irish monasticism, as the material is so rich. This evidence is cited throughout the volume in the hope that it not alone strengthens the narrative but also imparts a sense of reality to the textual sources.

Throughout the volume, the lives of female religious are woven into the narrative. The names of many women are memorialized in dozens of parishes throughout Ireland and while many of their names are recorded in the saints' genealogies,[14] there is little evidence to suggest that female religious communities were associated with these small churches beyond the seventh century. Discussion of this topic has been dominated for centuries by St Brigit and her foundation at Kildare based on the assumption, which is difficult to substantiate, that a female community lasted there until the twelfth century. In recent decades, however, the story of women religious, apart from Brigit, in early and late medieval Ireland has gained more attention with the publication of subject specific volumes, among them Christina Harrington's *Women in a Celtic church. Ireland 450–1150*, Tracy Collins's volume on the archaeology of female

13 Marie Therese Flanagan, *Irish royal charters. Texts and contexts* (Oxford, 2005). 14 Edel Bhreathnach, 'The saintly mothers and virgins of early Ireland. A diverse group remembered in places, personal names and genealogies' in Alf Tore Hommedal, Åslaug Ommundsen and Alexander O'Hara (eds), *St Sunniva. Irsk dronning, norsk vernehelgen. Irish queen, Norwegian patron saint* (Bergen, 2021), pp 138–53.

communities and the suite of essays in the volume *Brides of Christ. Women and monasticism in medieval and early modern Ireland.*[15] Despite this greater attention, a consistent problem lies in the interpretation of the sources, especially hagiography, which is difficult to date and to relate to the reality of early Irish society. In their enthusiasm to balance the gender narrative, scholars have overestimated the number of female religious houses in medieval Ireland, often due to mis-interpretations of the sources and their given context. Rather than dividing the narrative between female and male religious, the discussion in this volume attempts to include women in the greater narrative of medieval Irish monasticism in the circumstances of their own society.

As previously mentioned, scholars have attempted to tease out the difference between the various officials associated with monasteries, the *abbas/abb*, *airchinnech*, *comarbae*, *princeps*, *principatus* and others such as the *secnap* (*secundus abbas*), *fer léiginn*, *suí ecna* and *senóir*. Less attention has been given to two corporate religious terms, *sámud* and *cráibdig*. Chapter 4 concentrates on these terms and on networks of monastic officials operating locally and nationally. *Sámud* is a collective noun, meaning 'congregation, assembly', which in monastic terms defines a monastic community or an ecclesiastical ruler's household, and specifically its ruling elite. Like the term *comarbae*, the *sámud* is identified with the founder, hence references to *sámud Pátraic*, *sámud Brigte*, *sámud Choluim Chille* and *sámud Chiaráin*. It was the public face of the *muinter* or *familia monastica*. Most references relate to larger monasteries and the power of the *sámud*, which would have been considerable, was often felt beyond the monastic enclosure. There are instances of the community of St Ciarán of Clonmacnoise, *sámud Chiaráin*, for example, fasting against kings. A particularly dramatic event involving the *sámud Pátraic* was the funerary ceremony of Brian Bórama and his son Murchad, killed at the battle of Clontarf in 1014. Their bodies were accompanied from Swords, north of Dublin, to Armagh by *sámud Pátraic* which then waked the king and his allies for twelve nights before their burial in a new tomb in Armagh.[16]

The term *cráibdech* in general means 'pious, devout, faithful' but in many texts is linked to the *deorad Dé* 'exile of God' and *céle Dé* 'client of God'. Individuals are described as *crábud* or *cráibdech* while also holding the office of *fer léiginn* 'head of a monastic school', *suí ecna* 'master in ecclesiastical learning', *anmcharae* 'spiritual guide, confessor' or *sruithsenóir* 'esteemed elder'. The use of *crábud* or *cráibdech* in these instances could have meant simply that these eminent individuals were pious people – hence an adjectival use – but the

15 Christina Harrington, *Women in a Celtic church. Ireland, 450–1150* (Oxford, 2002); Tracy Collins, *Female monasticism in medieval Ireland. An archaeology* (Cork, 2021); Martin Browne, Tracy Collins, Bronagh Ann McShane and Colmán Ó Clabaigh (eds), *Brides of Christ. Women and monasticism in medieval and early modern Ireland* (Dublin, 2023). 16 AU, AFM, ALC.

occurrence of the term *cenn crábuid Érenn* 'head of religious life/piety of Ireland' points towards the existence of a hierarchy among those committed to a religious life in Ireland. Obits of eminent *cráibdig* occur primarily between 1020 and 1172, after which they peter out. There are sufficient time lapses between these entries, especially during the eleventh century, to contend that this was not just a general description used for the saintly religious, but a specific office held either nationally (*cenn crábuid Érenn/na nGaedil*), or provincially and regionally (*cenn crábuid Osraige, Muman, Ulad, Leithe Cuinn, Tuaiscirt Érenn, Airthir Érenn*). The title was held by those associated with specific churches, such as Armagh, Clonard, Emly, Glendalough, Inis Cealtra and Lismore.

The construction of monastic communities committed to a religious life is considered in Chapter 5. The culture of early monastic communities is predominantly identified with Christianity as it emerged in the Middle East and north Africa, particularly in Egypt, Palestine and Syria.[17] Aristocratic Roman ideals of *amicitia* 'close friendship' or of *otium honestum* 'dignified leisure' were social relationships and means of withdrawing from the world that also had an impact on western monasticism, most especially through the works of Augustine composed, for example, when he retreated to an estate at Cassiciacum near Milan.[18] It is evident too that ideals relating to brotherhood and kinship that existed in Irish law and society transferred over to the Irish monastic tradition, although the extent to which these concepts were unambiguously native or greatly influenced by Christianity is subject to debate.[19] A monastic community was based primarily on a scriptural foundation following Christ's words to the apostles: 'Amen, I say to you, there is no one who has given up house or wife or brothers or parents or children for the sake of the kingdom of God who will not receive [back] an overabundant return in this present age and eternal life in the age to come' (Luke 18:29–30). Christ's leadership was emulated by a founder saint. Indeed, the founder saint was the essential persona in a community's history, as they were often described as the saint's *familia* or *muinter*. Saints' lives were the means by which a community's spiritual and temporal interests were communicated. The aims of authors or compilers of saints' lives also varied considerably: some sought to bolster the interests of royal dynasties and hereditary families, some to confirm land-ownership as charters did elsewhere, others to boost their saint's cult in order to gain income from pilgrims, and finally, a small number genuinely reflect an interest in their founder's monastic life. The case studies examined in this chapter analyse the monastic tradition

17 Derwas J. Chitty, *The desert a city. An introduction to the study of Egyptian and Palestinian monasticism under the Christian empire* (New York, 1966; repr. 1995); Peter Brown, *The rise of western Christendom. Triumph and diversity, AD 200–1000* (Chichester, 1996; repr. 10th anniversary revised edition, 2013). 18 Dennis E. Trout, 'Augustine at Cassiciacum: *otium honestum* and the social dimensions of conversion', *Vigiliae Christianae* 42:2 (1988), 132–46. 19 Donnchadh Ó Corráin, Liam Breatnach and Aidan Breen, 'The laws of the Irish', *Peritia*

from different perspectives. The St Brendan dossier, comprising the renowned *Navigatio Sancti Brendani* and later Latin and vernacular texts, range in their presentation of monasticism from the late eighth-century ideal view of the *Navigatio* to the early thirteenth-century Cistercian, Anglo-Norman or Welsh ideal expressed in the text preserved in the *Valle Crucis* manuscript (Bodl. MS 3496 (e Mus. 3)). The dossier of St Darerca or Monenna of Killevy, Co. Armagh, matches the Brendan dossier to a certain degree in that both span a period from the eighth/ninth to the twelfth centuries. Yet they also offer a different perspective. The Monenna texts are all written in fairly scholarly Latin, two of them cover traditions gathered from Ireland, England and Scotland, and their subject is a woman and her life as a *virgo venerabilis* ('a venerable virgin'). The Monenna cycle sheds light on the ideal and institutional attributes of female monasticism with its emphasis on virginity, the capacity of women to be educated in the liturgy, on the dangers of the world to a community of women, and on their sanctity, toughness and virility. The final phase in Irish hagiographical writing, apart from the constant revision of saints' lives that continued in Ireland into the late medieval and early modern eras, became part of the wider western Christian tradition. The lives of Malachy of Armagh and Lorcán Ua Tuathail of Dublin and Glendalough were written on the Continent, one by St Bernard of Clairvaux, the other by a canon of Eu in Normandy as part of the process of Lorcán's canonization. The life of St Flannán of Killaloe, although maintaining many features of the Irish hagiographical tradition, was composed by an Irishman who had been trained on the Continent, possibly in one of the Irish foundations in imperial Germany. This author was more interested in Flannán as the ideal bishop than in his monastic life while Malachy and Lorcán are portrayed as the ideal abbot-bishops.

To prepare a path for the novice and to keep monastic communities on their path to God, all strands of the tradition produced texts on the principles (rules) and practices (customs) governing the ideals and conduct of monastic life, influenced, of course, by the cultures in which they were written. As there were many 'monasticisms', so there were many genres in which monastic ideals, theology and disciplines were expressed while the formats used to convey the parameters of a monastic life were also diverse: questions and answers, words of wisdom spoken by venerable fathers at monastic gatherings, vociferous admonitions, florilegia of older monastic rules and rephrased texts of older rules.[20] All Christian monastic traditions profess core ideals and the Irish tradition is no exception. Hence in their regulatory texts, no matter what type of format or language, the usual monastic precepts are expressed: love and fear of God (*amor et timor Dei*), purity of heart (*puritas cordis*), obedience and

3 (1984), 382–438. **20** Albrecht Diem and Philip Rousseau, 'Monastic rules (fourth to ninth century)' in *CHMM*, pp 162–94, at pp 165–6, 175.

humility, discipleship of Christ (*imitatio Christi*), poverty, spiritual love and communal fraternity lived out under the eyes of God. Such an understanding of the diversity and purpose of regulatory monastic texts is vital to approaching the Irish vernacular texts on monasticism that seem to have been produced mainly during the eighth and ninth centuries, followed by other assorted texts that continued to be composed to the twelfth century, often harking back to earlier material. This subject is covered in Chapter 6. These were not 'rules' in the sense that the Rule of Benedict (*RB*) gradually became a normative text regulating monastic life, but as with all such texts, the fundamental precepts of monasticism formed their core ideals. Vernacular regulatory texts are usually described as *ríagla* 'rules' (Irish *ríagail* deriving from Latin *regula*) of particular saints, most of which are not necessarily genuine historical attributions. They circulated and were revised during later centuries as they functioned as the mainstay of a monastic life until the introduction of new rules during the twelfth century. The most influential of such Irish regulatory texts were those produced by *céli Dé* communities, classified in recent scholarship as the 'Tallaght dossier', referring to the chief foundation of the *céli Dé* in Tallaght, Co. Dublin.[21] These regulatory texts were not only directed at monks. The use of the vernacular, along with their content, suggests that they were composed for three audiences: monastic female and male communities, and especially novices, clergy active in pastoral care, and lay penitents. For example, the metrical rule associated with Mochutu of Rahan (Co. Tipperary) and also attributed to Fothud na Canóine of Fahan (Co. Donegal), addresses all those who held a position of authority in the church or were subject to these authorities: bishops, *céli Dé*, kings, priests, confessors, students and lay tenants. The metrical Rule of Ailbe, the founder saint of the important royal monastery of Emly (Co. Tipperary) is a composite text, the first part of which would seem to address priests involved in pastoral care as much as it does monks, while the second addresses a community headed by an abbot (*ríaglóir*, *cenn manaig*) and prior or *secundus abbas* (*secnap*) with particular advice to an *airchinnech*, understood as the head of a *cathair* (*civitas*). The *airchinnech* is in charge of church tenants – although the verse dealing with *manaig* as church tenants may be an accretion to the original – but his main responsibility was in leading a committed religious community. The context for the 'Tallaght dossier', addressed to the *céli Dé* in particular, presupposes conversations among the leaders of the movement about certain provisions. This model is a less complex version of Cassian's *Conferences* or even the texts known as the *Apophthegmata Patrum* 'The Sayings of the Desert Fathers'. These conversations also signal that varying customs were followed in *céli Dé* foundations, especially with regard to liturgy, food and fasting, and penance, but that the customs of Máel Ruain and his foundation at Tallaght were generally

21 Follett, *Céli Dé in Ireland.*

regarded as superior among other *céli Dé* leaders. A constant theme concerning the avoidance of sin was the suppression of the seven or eight deadly sins and learning how to recognize and avoid them was uppermost in the minds of those instructing the faithful in general, but most especially religious communities.

Penitentials were a long-established genre in the Irish church and their influence can be detected in the 'rules' which deal with penances for monks and laity alike, some of which are lenient, others severe. The fear of the outside world encroaching was always present, be it in the form of violence, seduction or gossip, all of which were countered by restrictions and punishments. Some monks and nuns chose to withdraw further from the world to hermitages, located either close to their monasteries or in isolated places further away, and, if their withdrawal was sanctioned by the authorities, they were expected to remain in contact with their communities. There appear to have been degrees of withdrawal: some monks withdrew during certain liturgical seasons such as Lent, others to expiate their sins, and the most ardent withdrew for good. Chapter 6 also attempts to extract useful information from the 'rules' about daily life in a monastery: diet, fasting, etiquette in the refectory, clothing, hygiene, manual labour and rest. Not a lot of information is forthcoming, not surprising given that rules in general tend not to yield up a full picture of life inside the monastery.

Despite the dearth of functional monastic liturgical books – missals, antiphonaries, hymnals and psalters – surviving from medieval Ireland, there is a wealth of other texts that provide an insight into Irish worship and devotion to Heaven and to 'the end and beyond'.[22] These include a wide range of texts in Irish and in Latin: commentaries on the Bible, specific commentaries on the Psalms, patristics, apocrypha, eschatological texts such as visions and world history wherein the Irish integrated themselves into a biblical and hence Christian schema of the past. Chapter 7 deals with levels of learning and literacy, especially liturgical and spiritual literacy, and devotional practices in Irish monasteries. The many anonymous texts of the period written in Irish and Latin on an extensive range of subjects are interpreted by scholars as reflecting the general levels of literacy, learning and spirituality in the Irish church, including among its monastic communities. This view has merit but it overlooks the devotion to Heaven as understood by less literate, even illiterate, monks, nuns and novices, and does not consider levels of spiritual learning and literacy among the ordinary clergy and their capacity to communicate abstract religious concepts to the laity. Psalm 118 (119), otherwise known as the *Beati*, was regarded as one of the most efficacious of all prayers, and was used to

22 I have taken this all-encompassing phrase from the two volumes *The end and beyond. Medieval Irish eschatology* ed. John Carey, Emma Nic Cárthaigh and Caitríona Ó Dochartaigh, 2 vols (Aberystwyth, 2014).

compensate for liturgical inadequacies in a community by reducing a reliance on the full cycle of psalms and by repeating this psalm over and over again. This was an equivalent to John Cassian's monologistic or repetitive prayer whereby commandments regarding humility, prayer, constant praise of God, the law and many other injunctions were being repeated ceaselessly in an individual's mind, be they monks, nuns or secular priests.[23] At the other end of the spectrum, two characteristics dominated the Irish scholarly approach to interpreting the psalms: their interpretation was primarily literal and historical, as opposed to Christological, mystical and moral, and their exegetical method of commenting and glossing on the whole remained unchanged from the eighth to the twelfth century. In seeking to navigate the substantial amount of material on the psalms, the abundant commentaries and glosses of two psalters are surveyed on the basis of recent expert scholarship. These are the Southampton Psalter (Cambridge, St John's College, MS C 9), probably dated to the eleventh century, and the Psalter of Caimín (UCD-OFM A1), also dated to the eleventh or early twelfth century.[24] Both are most likely to have been produced in monastic scriptoria for monastic communities. And what of devotion and spirituality? The Irish corpus of religious literature is replete with evidence of intellectual monastic spirituality and theology (*summa scientia*) and of the daily practice of *opus Dei*, constant prayer in the guise of the Divine Office focussing on the psalter, penance and hymns, and later in the period under consideration, on the Mass and sacraments, especially the Eucharist. Personal religious experience is best measured by devotional Middle Irish poetry which unfortunately is often anonymous and hence not necessarily composed in a monastic milieu, although the likelihood is that most of it was at least influenced by monastic devotion. The compositions of Máel Ísu Ua Brolcháin of Armagh and Lismore (d. 1086) are exceptional in that the attribution to him is fairly secure, but they are also important as they highlight subjects of concern to a monastic community: avoiding sin in this world to ensure a safe passage to an eternal, heavenly life, seeking the protection of Christ and the saints from the Devil, fasting as penance, and overcoming the eight vices.

There has been much speculation among scholars of liturgy for more than a century as to the structure of monastic liturgy in Ireland, much of it determined by the regime laid down in Columbanian monasteries on the Continent and what can be gleaned from disparate sources such as the Antiphonary of Bangor and the Stowe Missal. Once more the lack of source material has greatly hampered

23 Columba Stewart, *Cassian the monk* (New York and Oxford, 1998), p. 111. 24 Pádraig Ó Néill, 'Glosses to the psalter of St Caimín: a preliminary investigation of their sources and their function' in Pádraig A. Breatnach, Caoimhín Breatnach and Meidhbhín Ní Urdail (eds), *Léann lámhscríbhinní Lobháin. The Louvain manuscript heritage* (Dublin, 2007), pp 21–31; Pádraig P. Ó Néill, (ed.), *Exegetica: Psalterium Suthantoniense*, Corpus Christianorum 240 (Turnhout, 2012).

work on this topic, especially in relation to practices in Ireland itself. Earlier scholars argued for the existence of 'Celtic' as opposed to 'Roman' rites. Frederick Warren in his volume *The liturgy and ritual of the Celtic church*, published in Oxford in 1881, contended that this 'Celtic' church was independent of Rome and a primitive Christian church 'in these islands differing from the Anglo-Roman or Scoto-Roman Church of later days'.[25] However, the diverse features of the liturgy do not mean that the Irish monastic tradition produced a 'Celtic' rite. Instead, it was one of the many regional varieties of liturgy to exist throughout Christendom, as opposed to diverging completely from the 'Roman' rite. The details of the liturgies used in Ireland can be elicited from missals such as the Stowe (RIA MS D ii 3), the Corpus (Corpus Christi College, Oxford MS 282) and Drummond missals (The Morgan Library and Museum, New York MS 6271). The Irish *Liber Hymnorum* [*LH*] is a unique treasury of liturgical materials that until recently has defied precise classification and dating.[26] It is unique in that two relatively contemporary copies exist, TCD MS 1441 [*LH*(*T*)] and UCD-OFM MS A 2 [*LH*(*F*)].[27] Following Susan Boynton's studies on continental missals[28] and Kathryn Izzo's work on the Irish *Liber Hymnorum* (henceforth *LH*)[29] it seems acceptable to classify the manuscripts as glossed hymnals, used as teaching aids that offer a window into liturgical training. The question remains open as to whether *LH* was a strictly monastic compilation or if it was relevant to the wider Christian community. The two manuscripts are the products of ecclesiastical schools of learning and, given our knowledge of learned masters and of similar compilations elsewhere, the likelihood is that many of these masters or *fir léiginn*, led regulated, if not always celibate, lives. Bodily gestures were an integral part of monastic prayer, and indeed remain so in eastern Christian churches (*metanoia*). There are many vernacular terms for kneeling, prostration, making signs of the Cross and praying involving various levels of humility and intensity, some of which were universal customs in societies that valued obedience and honour. These bodily gestures are steeped, consciously or otherwise, in Christian – and many originally Judaic – symbolism. Outstretched hands in the form of the cross meant praying in the posture of Christ crucified, challenging Satan and giving

25 Frederick E. Warren, *The liturgy and ritual of the Celtic church* (Oxford, 1881; repr. 1987), p. 35. 26 John Henry Bernard and Robert Atkinson (eds and trans), *The Irish Liber Hymnorum*. 2 vols. Henry Bradshaw Society 13 and 14 (London, 1898). On the literature to date, see Ó Corráin, *CLH* i, pp 364–85. 27 Digital versions available on https://digital collections.tcd.ie/ and https://www.isos.dias.ie/. 28 Susan Boynton, 'Eleventh-century continental hymnaries containing Latin glosses', *Scriptorium* 53:2 (1999), 200–51; Boynton, 'Latin glosses on the office hymns in eleventh-century continental hymnaries', *Journal of Medieval Latin* 11 (2001), 1–26. 29 Kathryn Alyssa Izzo, 'The Old Irish hymns of the Liber Hymnorum: a study of vernacular hymnody in medieval Ireland' (PhD, Harvard University, 2007). I wish to thank Dr Izzo and Professor Catherine McKenna for granting me permission to consult this thesis.

direction to one's prayers. Lifting one's eyes or face to Heaven recalled the words of the psalms: 'I lift up my eyes to you, to you who sit enthroned in Heaven' (Ps. 123.1). These performative actions are explored through the prism of the 'Tallaght dossier' and other dramatic texts.

Understanding the physical layout of monasteries requires examination of the archaeology, architecture and landscape of ecclesiastical sites. Much has been made of the enclosures that surround many monastic and smaller church sites throughout Ireland. Some were monumental and clearly they represented a variety of functions from delineating the *sanctus*, *sanctior* and *sanctissimus* of an ecclesiastical complex to forming practical and defensive purposes. But these complexes, while often dating back to the sixth and seventh centuries, were not static. There are indications that some of the enclosures, at least the monumental ones, may have been backfilled during the ninth century, which suggests a re-organization of the monastic landscape. This became evident during excavations at Clonmacnoise when the layout of the monastery was possibly re-organized both in the ninth and tenth centuries.[30] A similar pattern can be traced in many major monasteries during the late eleventh and twelfth centuries. Archaeological, architectural and textual evidence suggests that Derry, Ferns, Glendalough, Iona and Tuam were subjected to physical re-organization at that time.[31]

Irish monasteries are viewed as being outside the mainstream when it comes to architecture and layout, regarded as not conforming to the 'normal' pattern such as that depicted in the Plan of St Gall – the ideal monastery – or in or the plan of Cluny III built between 1089 and 1131/2 which illustrate why such places were the *axis mundi* of their regions. In Cluny, monastic life was spatially focused on the monastery church, monastic cloister, refectory, novitiate, dormitory, abbot's chapel and other smaller chapels, chapter house, calefactory and monks' kitchen and monastic cemetery. Monks encountered the laity to various degrees, mainly in the church, in the segregated guest house, hospice, lay kitchen, cellars and bakery. Even if Irish sites do not obviously fall in line with the 'normal' architecture and landscape of medieval monasteries, and there was a diversity of plans elsewhere as well, the activities performed in them were not dissimilar. A potential approach, which is the basis of Chapter 8, is to look

30 Donald Murphy, 'Excavations of an early monastic enclosure at Clonmacnoise' in Heather A. King (ed.), *Clonmacnoise Studies* 2 (Dublin, 2003), 1–33, at p. 19. **31** Tomás Ó Carragáin,'Rebuilding the 'city of angels': Muirchertach Ua Briain and Glendalough, *c.*1096–1111' in John Sheehan and Donnchadh Ó Corráin (eds), *The Viking Age: Ireland and the West. Papers from the proceedings of the fifteenth Viking Congress, Cork, 18–27 August 2005* (Dublin, 2010), pp 258–70; Edel Bhreathnach and Ger Dowling, 'Founding an episcopal see and an Augustinian foundation in medieval Ireland: the case of Ferns, Co. Wexford', *Proceedings of the Royal Irish Academy* 121C (2021), 191–226; Ewan Campbell and Adrián Maldonado, 'A new Jerusalem "at the ends of the earth": interpreting Charles Thomas's excavations at Iona Abbey 1956–63', *The Antiquaries Journal* 100 (2020), 33–85.

for textual, spatial and material evidence of the functions known to have been performed by contemporary monasteries elsewhere in the Irish material. Another approach to the topic is based on defining private and public functions. Monastic spaces might be communal, personal, ascetic, spiritually and physically pastoral, pedagogical, economic and political spaces that were divided between the *domus interior* (the inner house) and the *domus exterior* (the outer house). And even that clear divide was often opaque as some spaces, especially churches, schools and hospices, were shared with many others outside monastic communities. A debate on the concept of the 'monastic town' in early medieval Ireland has persisted ever since Charles Doherty proposed its existence in a series of articles during the 1980s.[32] The main arguments in favour of defining large Irish ecclesiastical complexes – Armagh, Clonmacnoise, Kildare, Kells, Glendalough – as towns has concentrated on economic activity and trade, with less emphasis on the monastic activity in these places.[33] Discussion of their religious and spiritual facets has been confined in general to their status as *civitates refugii*, places of sanctuary, the resting places of founder saints and other holy people, the theological meanings of the three enclosures that often surround these sites,[34] and the perception of them as the New Jerusalem or New Rome.[35] A different approach is required to tease out the spatial divisions in Irish monasteries. Citing early Latin sources, Columba Stewart draws attention to differentiations of space and time fundamental to monasticism.[36] *Functional differentiation* of material space responds to the need to pray, eat, sleep, read, work, receive guests and so on and some spaces can serve both a monastic community and others from outside. Time is apportioned according to various duties and tasks particular to day and night. Functional differentiation of monastic space and time cannot be fully understood without reference to

32 Charles Doherty, 'Exchange and trade in medieval Ireland', *Journal of the Royal Society of Antiquaries of Ireland* 110 (1980), 67–89; Doherty, 'Some aspects of hagiography as a source for Irish economic history', *Peritia* 1 (1982), 300–28; Doherty, 'The monastic town in early medieval Ireland' in Howard Clarke and Anngret Simms (eds), *The comparative history of urban origins in non-Roman Europe. Ireland, Wales, Denmark, Germany, Poland and Russia from the ninth to the thirteenth century*. BAR International Series 255 (Oxford, 1985), i, pp 45–75. 33 Richard Sharpe sought to address the absence of consideration of pastoral activity and religious practices in general from this discussion in his article 'Some problems concerning the organization of the church in early medieval Ireland', *Peritia* 3 (1984), 230–70. 34 Catherine Swift, 'Forts and fields: a study of "monastic towns" in seventh- and eighth-century Ireland', *Journal of Irish Archaeology* 9 (1998), 105–25. 35 Ó Carragáin, *Churches in early medieval Ireland*, pp 57–66; David Jenkins, *'Holy, holier, holiest'. The sacred topography of the early medieval Irish church* (Turnhout, 2010); Melanie C. Maddox, 'Finding the City of God in the lives of St Kevin: Glendalough and the history of the Irish celestial civitas' in Charles Doherty, Linda Doran and Mary Kelly (eds), *Glendalough. City of God* (Dublin, 2011), pp 1–21. 36 Columba Stewart, 'Monastic space and time' in Hendrik W. Dey and Elizabeth Fentress (eds), *Western monasticism* ante litteram. *The spaces of monastic observance in late antiquity and the early Middle Ages* (Turnhout, 2011), pp 43–51, at pp 43–4.

ideological differentiation, which has to do with certain qualities attributed to particular spaces and times. This approach is placed in an Irish context by examining the function and location of the *dísert* 'hermitage', be it a hermitage in the middle of a busy monastery or a hermitage in a perceived desert. Within a complex, a community's private spaces are identified, among them the *reiclés*, refectory and individual cells.

How monks interacted with the world beyond the enclosure is best understood from textual evidence. Their participation in pastoral care is a recurrent theme throughout monastic scholarship and the Irish situation is complicated as it is elsewhere. The wider population was mostly cared for by individual priests or small communities of priests who lived among them and who followed a variety of lifestyles – some monastic, some following the canonical hours, others married yet providing basic pastoral care to their communities. Monks, and especially those who were clerics, were spiritual directors (*anmchairde*) as were bishops, who played a role in pastoral care, although in many instances their attention was directed at the aristocracy and their own pupils. Eminent *anmchairde* were valuable for churches as they probably attracted kings and nobles to spend their final days in their midst, and to grant endowments for care given to them and for the redemption of their souls and those of their families. Certain dynasties show a predictable affiliation to particular churches, the Uí Néill to Armagh, the Meic Lochlainn to Derry and the Uí Briain to Killaloe and Lismore. This included noble women who were also attracted to these places and may have spent their final years as vowesses or nuns under the spiritual guidance of an *anmcharae*.

As to the economy and spatial landscape of Irish monasteries, Tomas Ó Carragáin has made a significant contribution to the subject in his study of the various categories of pre-1100 churches that have physically survived or are known to have existed based on a detailed analysis of the kingdoms of southern Uí Fáeláin (in the east), Mag Réta (in the midlands), Fir Maige (in the south) and Corcu Duibne (in the southwest).[37] As previously alluded to, Ó Carragáin's model distinguishes between large ecclesiastical estates, often consisting of widely dispersed landholdings and mostly owned by large or medium-sized monasteries – the term *civitates* is used – and lesser churches, small ascetic monasteries, churches with or without a resident priest, family and royal churches (*túath* churches). Combining this study with other textual evidence has allowed for a clearer picture to emerge about the economy of monastic communities, whether they were living in large complexes or existing as separate ascetic monastic communities elsewhere. Among Ó Carragáin's conclusions for the period 800–1100 based on archaeology, landscape and textual evidence is that 'monasticism declined, or ceased altogether, at a significant number of

37 Ó Carragáin, *Churches in the Irish landscape*.

substantial *civitates* but continued, or was revived, at others, facilitated it seems by the fact that they often managed to retain the bulk of their landholdings'.[38] This deduction accords well with the thesis of the present study that regulated, ascetic monastic communities were not as numerous as widely believed and that Ó Carragáin's 'middle-tier' churches were more often than not maintained by individual priests and rarely by monastic or even clerical communities. Where a monastic community existed, the likelihood is that it was usually small, even at more extensive ecclesiastical complexes such as Armagh, Clonmacnoise or Glendalough. Donnchadh Ó Corráin's valuable study of the Meic Cuinn na mBocht ('the descendants of Conn of the poor') of Clonmacnoise, a hereditary family of ecclesiastical aristocrats and scholars, points in the direction of the likely regulation and relationships involved within monastic communities and with these powerful families.[39] Whatever material provisions that were needed by the monastic communities of Clonmacnoise, particularly those of Ísel Ciaráin, a settlement dedicated to those following a vow of poverty, were guaranteed by Meic Cuinn na mBocht, probably in return for the salvation of their souls. This is a telling illustration of the workings of Irish monasteries, in which the community committed to a religious life was dependent on and protected by those who governed their monasteries, most likely in the hope of forgiveness of their sins and their future salvation.

Chapter 9 addresses the effect of emerging spiritual and liturgical movements on Irish monasticism during the late eleventh to mid-thirteenth centuries, the consequences of greater institutionalization of the Irish church on monastic offices, the reaction to these changes and the relationship between monasteries and the laity. The most dominant of the 'new' monastic cultures to spread through Ireland during the twelfth century were those of the Arrouasian canons, the Cistercians, and to a lesser extent the Premonstratensians and Benedictines, the first two introduced into the country by Malachy of Armagh. Once more, due to the lack of sources it seemed too difficult to determine how this 'new' monastic culture was received in Ireland, and how it compared with the existing monastic tradition on the island. One approach adopted was to measure the extent of its influence on various aspects of Irish monasticism by identifying themes in the surviving literature and by following the response of leading Irish ecclesiastics. The most obvious example is that of St Bernard's correspondence with and works relating to Malachy. Unfortunately, nothing survives of the Irishman's responses and thoughts. Nevertheless, if Bernard's letters to Malachy and to his brethren in Ireland following the latter's death in Clairvaux are read as written primarily in a monastic and spiritual idiom, even though they

38 Ibid., p. 268. 39 Donnchadh Ó Corráin, 'Máel Muire, the scribe: family and background' in Ruairí Ó hUiginn (ed.), *Lebor na hUidre. Codices Hibernenses Eximii 1* (Dublin, 2015), pp 1–28.

comment on practical issues, then the importance of personal transmission of ideas can be understood. Spiritual friendship was an essential part of twelfth-century Cistercian culture and Bernard's communications with Malachy and his descriptions of him in the *vita* and in his sermons after Malachy's death are replete with the language of loving *amicitia*.[40] To Bernard, Malachy represented a *speculum et exemplum* ('a mirror and example'), a man embodying an ideal of abbatial and episcopal spirituality. Malachy led by example. Leadership was to the fore among the many reformers of the age, the concept of abbots guiding their communities *verbo et exemplo* ('by word and deed') being the fundamental cornerstone of highly influential monasteries such as Bec in Normandy, which boasted such influential abbots as Lanfranc and Anselm. As part of their renewal of the *RB*, they were to be living examples of monastic virtue.[41] That this message was acted on in Ireland is manifest from the calibre of church leaders who emerged during the twelfth century. The transformation was not due to Malachy alone. He could not have succeeded without the many individuals who were already working towards it, who worked with him and who succeeded him after his death in 1148. The narrative of the movement towards the re-organization of the Irish church, as revealed in the affiliations and careers of twelfth-century Irish bishops, was not unusual. Choices were made on the basis of the strong influence of a particular personality and their strategies – mainly prominent abbots, bishops and kings –, external campaigns and orders, regional differences, and existing infrastructures. This was an age of monastic experimentation, and one of the primary instances of such experimentation in Ireland was Malachy's experiment in Louth, whereby the traditional episcopal seat of the diocese of Airgialla was moved from Clogher (Co. Tyrone) to Louth, a venture promoted by an alliance between Malachy, his brother Gilla Críst who was consecrated bishop of the diocese, Gilla Críst's successor Áed Ua Cáellaide and the powerful regional king, Donnchad Ua Cerbaill, king of Airgialla.[42]

The monastic progression of Áed Ua Cáellaide's contemporary, Lorcán Ua Tuathail's career also reflects the narrative of monasticism in twelfth-century Ireland. He was trained in Glendalough by an unnamed bishop who was his master and who taught him *verbo pariter et exemplo*.[43] He became abbot at the age of 25 in 1153 and archbishop of Dublin in 1162. His associations with new

40 Janet Burton and Julie Kerr, *The Cistercians in the Middle Ages* (Woodbridge, 2011), pp 142–3. 41 Steven Vanderputten, 'Custom and identity at Le Bec' in Benjamin Pohl and Laura L. Gathagan (eds), *A companion to the Abbey of Le Bec in the central Middle Ages (11th–13th centuries)* (Leiden and Boston, 2018), pp 228–47. See also Steven Vanderputten, *Imagining religious leadership in the Middle Ages. Richard of Saint-Vanne and the politics of reform* (Ithaca, 2015). 42 Marie Therese Flanagan, 'St Mary's Abbey, Louth, and the introduction of the Arrouaisian observance into Ireland', *Clogher Record* 10:2 (1980), 223–34. 43 Charles Plummer (ed.), 'Vie et miracles de S. Laurent, archevêque de Dublin', *Analecta Bollandiana* 33 (1914), 121–86, at p. 131: lines 16–19.

monasticisms being introduced into Ireland during his career are evident in his witnessing the charters of Diarmait Mac Murchada, king of Leinster and his brother-in-law, granting lands and freedoms to Cistercian monks and Augustinian canons, and also in the building programmes in the Romanesque style undertaken in Glendalough, most notably the priory of St Saviour's which was an Augustinian foundation, at least from the time of Lorcán's elevation as archbishop of Dublin.[44] Once he became archbishop he moved to re-organize the observances of the community in the cathedral of Holy Trinity, which may have transferred from Benedictine monks to secular canons during the twelfth century, to canons following Arrouaisian observances. Finally, the monastic background of Gillebertus (Gille), bishop of Limerick (d. 1145) and author of the only substantial works relating to the twelfth-century re-organization of the Irish church to survive, *De uso ecclesiatico* and *De statu ecclesiae*, is worthy of consideration.[45] While Gillebertus says little about monks, his encounters with monasticism were not dissimilar to those of the other Irish reformers. He corresponded and met with Anselm, and attended the court of Queen Matilda. In such circles, Gillebertus would have encountered highly influential prelates, many of them monks, and perhaps, more significantly, the queen herself who with her husband Henry I was an enthusiastic patron of the Augustinians. As papal legate until the 1130s these various experiences must surely have influenced his guidance of the Irish church. The circumstances in which the second generation of Irish diocesan bishops found themselves could be regarded fairly as more complex than those of the initial generation of reformers.[46] Some were monks, others not. Whether monastic or not, they all had to negotiate their way around multiple networks, be it their own kin, many of whom belonged to hereditary ecclesiastical families, the papacy, a world of increasingly institutionalized international orders, local and provincial Irish kings, recently arrived Anglo-Norman prelates and rulers, and the power of the English crown. The complexity of this world is evident from the many disputes that arose relating to Irish church affairs in the late twelfth and early thirteenth centuries.

The pattern of patronage changed during the twelfth century with Irish kings adopting administrative practices such as recording endowments in charters and Anglo-Norman lords founding monasteries and granting lands already owned by existing monasteries and by Irish kings for their own political gain.[47] There was also a surge in architectural activity, beginning with the Romanesque

44 Flanagan, *Irish royal charters*, pp 37–105, 253–90; Tadhg O'Keeffe, 'Diarmait Mac Murchada and Romanesque Leinster. Four twelfth-century churches in context', *Journal of the Royal Society of Antiquaries of Ireland* 127 (1997), 52–79, at pp 53–4. **45** John Fleming, *Gille of Limerick (*c.*1070–1145). Architect of a medieval church* (Dublin, 2001). **46** Edel Bhreathnach, 'The world of bishops in religious orders in medieval Ireland, 1050–1230' in Karen Stöber, Julie Kerr and Emilia Jamroziak (eds), *Monastic life in the medieval British Isles. Essays in honour of Janet Burton* (Cardiff, 2018), pp 71–88. **47** Flanagan, *Irish royal charters*.

style, and moving on later to Gothic. Stone churches built in the Romanesque style, large and small, urban and rural, are found throughout Ireland with concentrations in the east and south east, along the Shannon and in the Burren (Co. Clare).[48] On the basis of the fairly rare surviving inscriptions, normally carved on and around doorways, this surge in building was the result of an alliance between powerful ecclesiastical and lay lordships. Eleventh- and twelfth-century Ireland saw a consolidation of power in the hands of provincial kings and as the movement towards church re-organization advanced, episcopal power also increased. How did this alliance affect monasticism? Monastic communities, among them eremitical communities, benefited from the surge in Romanesque buildings. Romanesque sculpture occurs on the sites of existing communities and of new foundations of the continental orders. The conflicting strategies of Irish kings, diocesan bishops, new monastic orders, Anglo-Norman adventurers and Angevin kings made for a turbulent twelfth and thirteenth centuries for monasticism in Ireland. Reforming bishops and orders have been portrayed as asset-stripping the existing churches and monasteries, especially of their lands.[49] This conclusion is too simple for what was a constantly changing situation that varied enormously from one locality to the next. In general, both Anglo-Norman and Irish bishops appropriated lands that had been set aside to support monastic communities, and it is likely that individuals who had been attached to these communities were subsumed into the new ecclesiastical structure as canons of emerging cathedral chapters, as regular canons or as monks in new foundations. Some monastic offices such as that of the *fer léiginn* 'head of a monastic school' no longer had a place in the 'new' monasteries, and the vernacular and traditional historical elements of the office were conducted mainly in aristocratic households and in schools of native lawyers, historians and poets. This transformation was not accomplished by the end of the twelfth century and was not as clear-cut as often portrayed, but continued as a highly complex, evolving narrative as late as the seventeenth century.

As to female monasticism during this period, Gwynn and Hadcock's inference in their fundamental work *Medieval religious houses Ireland* that a network of Augustinian nunneries existed in late twelfth-century Ireland needs to be re-evaluated, in parallel with their assumption about the foundation of many houses of regular canons at the same time. What emerges from the evidence is closer to Vanderputten's 'ambiguous identity of female monasticism' than a standard narrative of enclosed women following a rule under the authority of an abbess whose power was contained by an abbot, bishop or prior.[50] That is not to deny the existence of female Augustinian houses – St Mary de Hogges in

48 Tadhg O'Keeffe, *Romanesque Ireland. Architecture and ideology in the twelfth century* (Dublin, 2003), p. 34 (fig. 5). 49 Donnchadh Ó Corráin, *The Irish church, its reform and the English invasion* (Dublin, 2017). 50 Steven Vanderputten, *Dark age nunneries. The ambiguous identity of female monasticism, 800–1050* (Ithaca and London, 2018).

Dublin and Killone, Co. Clare, being the best-known examples – but it demands a more nuanced approach to female monasticism in twelfth-century Ireland.[51]

The mendicants appeared in Ireland during the 1220s and gradually had a huge impact on Irish and Anglo-Norman society. Although a transfer of manpower and lands from early Irish monasteries to these new orders is far from clear, mainly due to a lack of sources and, of course, to the latters' espousal of complete poverty. There are hints that this did happen, and that the Dominicans and Franciscans, once they moved outside the towns, fulfilled many of the roles that had been performed by their monastic predecessors, including embedding themselves in local communities and forming strategic relationships with local magnates.[52] By the end of the thirteenth century, therefore, monasticism had become more regulated, as envisaged by the Fourth Lateran Council, and many older monasteries fulfilled the roles of cathedral or parish churches and a number of them were renewed by the Augustinian canons and other orders. And yet, while the face of monastic regulation had changed, many of those who had ruled and participated in the 'old' monastic tradition remained part of the narrative for the next five centuries.

51 Tracy Collins, '"The other monasticism". Killone nunnery, Co. Clare'. *Archaeology Ireland. Heritage guide* 38 (Dublin, 2007). **52** Colmán Ó Clabaigh, *The friars in Ireland, 1224–1540* (Dublin, 2012).

CHAPTER 1

The origins of modern perspectives

The writing of monastic history through the ages has been subject to a few common characteristics. Since the fourth century, monastic literary endeavours, including the foundational hagiographical text of Athanasius's *Life of Antony*, composed in Greek around 357 and translated into Latin around 373, have been used to characterize the story of monastic traditions.[1] Antony is represented as a father of Christian monasticism and his *vita*, despite evidence to the contrary, 'is still placed at the very beginning of any literary history of the monastic movement'.[2] The popularity of the Latin version of the *Life of Antony* along with that of other saints' lives, especially Sulpicius Severus's *Life of Martin of Tours*, resonated throughout western Christendom, providing both literary templates and ideal role models to many individuals and communities from different cultures attempting to adhere to a committed monastic life. Similarly, the *Dialogues* of Gregory the Great contributed to the shaping of western monasticism. That Antony, Benedict of Nursia, Martin and Gregory the Great were recognized in Ireland as monastic leaders is clear from early medieval texts. The epilogue to the ninth-century martyrology *Félire Óenguso* places Anthony and Martin together, and they are immediately followed by Patrick and Columba as the noble, leading saints of Ireland and Alba respectively, then followed by Brigit as the principal virgin.[3] The earliest hagiographies of SS Patrick, Brigit and Columba, composed during the seventh century respectively by Muirchú moccu Machtheni, Cogitosus and Adomnán, reflect to varying degrees the structure and phraseology of the *Life of Martin*.[4] Although the references to the Rule of St Benedict (*RB*) are fleeting, knowledge of the saint's life was transmitted to Ireland through Gregory the Great's second book of *Dialogues*, the primary source relating St Benedict's life at this time, and some topoi from it were borrowed by Adomnán for his life of Columba.[5] The hagiography of saints whose virtues and miracles were used to create templates for an exemplary

1 Columba Stewart, 'The literature of early western monasticism' in Bernice M. Kaczynski (ed.), *The Oxford handbook of Christian monasticism* (Oxford, 2020), pp 85–100. 2 Roberto Alciati, 'The invention of western monastic literature: texts and communities' in *CHMM*, pp 144–61, at p. 145. 3 Whitley Stokes (ed.), *Félire Óengusso Céli Dé. The martyrology of Oengus the Culdee*, Henry Bradshaw Society 29 (London, 1905; repr., Dublin, 1984), pp 276–7: lines 273–85. 4 Jean-Michel Picard, 'Structural patterns in early Hiberno-Latin hagiography', *Peritia* 4 (1985), 67–82. 5 Colmán Ó Clabaigh, 'The Benedictines in medieval and early modern Ireland' in Martin Browne and Colmán Ó Clabaigh (eds), *The Irish*

form of monasticism often obscured the actual lived monastic life of these model saints, as in the cases of Columba and Columbanus in the *vitae* written during the seventh century by Adomnán of Iona (d. 704) and Jonas of Bobbio (d. 659) respectively.

The pursuit of norms in monastic traditions has led historians of the subject since the medieval period to create an idealized model, often based on perceptions of the existence of a standard Rule of St Benedict, against which all traditions have been measured. This is particularly relevant to histories of the Irish monastic tradition which in its early phase are dominated by Columbanus of Bobbio and how his regulatory texts compare with those of Benedict, how monasticism in Ireland itself deviated from the norm, only to be drawn back into the fold with Malachy of Armagh's reforms in the twelfth century. Before any new study of the Irish monastic tradition can be presented, it seems appropriate to provide a short historiography of the subject to appreciate why historians came to believe that medieval Irish monasticism was a distinct tradition that deviated from the norm. As with all such historiographical narratives, an essential element of the study involves an understanding of the cultural, political, religious and scholarly contexts in which specific histories were written. This chapter chronicles this historiographical narrative from the seventeenth century to the modern period.

DEFINING MEDIEVAL MONASTIC PURITY AND HISTORY: FROM CAROLINGIANS TO MAURISTS

Apart from producing schematic hagiography, monasticism has been subjected regularly to campaigns of so-called 'reform'. While many reform movements were initiated by monks seeking a purer form of monasticism, they were also instigated by papal, episcopal or royal authorities for their own purposes. These campaigns often involved significant historiographical ventures that led not only to the creation of apparently standard monastic rules but also to the gathering of diverse materials from monastic archives and libraries that otherwise might have been lost. The great Carolingian project of 'reform' undertaken by Benedict of Aniane (d. 821) and the French Maurists of the seventeenth and eighteenth centuries, which are separated chronologically by almost a thousand years, are illustrative of this phenomenon. While Benedict of Aniane is associated in monastic histories with the Carolingian codification of rules for canons and monks, one of his greatest legacies was to collect twenty-four rules for monks and six rules for nuns in his *Codex regularum*.[6] As Albrecht Diem and Philip

Benedictines. A history (Dublin, 2005), pp 79–121, at pp 80–4. 6 Diem and Rousseau, 'Monastic rules'. For a list of the various rules see Diem and Rousseau at pp 192–3.

Rousseau observe, Benedict of Aniane's view of pre-Carolingian monastic history as a series of rules that devolved chronologically, finally arriving at a codified *RB*, was in reality far more complex. There was a long-lasting tradition of diverse monasticisms and a confusing variety of textual options to express and enforce ascetic values, monastic practices, and concepts of community.[7] This situation did not end with Benedict of Aniane and the Carolingians for the practical reason that even if the *RB* attained a pre-eminent position among monastic rules, it could not make allowance for the lives of hundreds of monastic communities in western Christendom who lived in such diverse cultures and societies, were subject to various types of crises at different times, and whose physical environs were often so dissimilar to one another. In his re-assessment of medieval monastic history Steven Vanderputten has coined the term 'monasticisms' in an effort to reflect the complexity of the monastic tradition in western Christendom.[8]

Gathering and compiling materials from monasteries and other repositories has always formed an essential part of the writing of monastic history, as has the influence of external discourses and intellectual movements, if only to refute them. While many monastic histories were heroic in their endeavours, an ever-present intellectual objective of historians of monasticism, often monks themselves, was to define monastic purity based on historical sources. Moving from Benedict of Aniane to the other end of the chronological spectrum and to the great historical enterprise of the French Benedictine Maurists – to adopt a designation coined by David Knowles (d. 1974), the English Benedictine monk-historian[9] – theirs was a vast enterprise that spanned the period from *c.*1640 to 1789. Monastic history and the collection and interpretation of historical materials were at the heart of the Maurist project, but it was more than that, as they were deeply involved in contemporary French cultural and religious discourses. The colossal output of Dom Jean Mabillon (d. 1707) is a case in point.[10] Mabillon collaborated in the publication of the works of Bernard of Clairvaux and the *acta sanctorum* of Benedictine saints. He himself produced one of the seminal texts on diplomatics, *De re diplomatica* (1681), in which he described how a document should be evaluated for authenticity, by examination

7 Ibid., p. 188. 8 Vanderputten, *Medieval monasticisms.* For further discussion of approaches to the historiography of monasticism and the challenges faced by historians of the subject, see Emilia Jamroziak, 'The historiography of medieval monasticism: perspectives from northern Europe' in Steinunn Kristjánsdóttir (ed.), *Medieval monasticism in northern Europe. Religions* 12:7 (Basel, 2021), pp 1–13. https://doi.org/10.3390/rel12070552 accessed 4 April 2021. 9 Michael David Knowles, 'Great historical enterprises II. The Maurists', *Transactions of the Royal Historical Society* 9 (1959), 169–87. **10** For a clear overview of Mabillon as a monastic historian and his part in controversies around the writing of critical history see Mette B. Bruun, 'Jean Mabillon's Middle Ages: on medievalism, textual criticism, and monastic ideals' in Alicia C. Montoya, Sophie van Romburgh and Wim van Anrooij (eds), *Early modern medievalisms. The interplay between scholarly reflection and artistic production* (Leiden, 2010),

of style, script, language, seals and other criteria as well as pursuing comparative research that might identify forgeries or re-writing of an original. This work was the result of Mabillon's search through monastic archives and libraries in France, Germany, Austria, Switzerland and Italy for histories of monasteries and for charters. The *De re diplomatica* was a systematic scientific work that was not out of place in the age of enlightenment. Even if Mabillon was a methodical scholar, he was also a Benedictine monk and his monastic life could never be left aside nor could controversies arising from his vows to the Benedictine Congregation of St Maur. This dual – and in Mabillon's mind – indivisible existence is particularly evident in his dispute with the Trappist monk Armand-Jean de Rancé (d. 1700). Having lived as a courtier and having inherited a number of commendatory abbacies, Rancé retreated from the world to become abbot of the Cistercian monastery of La Trappe in Normandy. In doing so, he chose to live as a strict observant and to revert to what he regarded as the original ideals of the *RB*.[11] In his treatise *De la sainteté et des devoirs de la vie monastique* (1683) de Rancé argued that monks should follow a life of extreme austerity and that nominal study of Scripture, the early church fathers, the works of the desert fathers and fundamental texts such as those of John Cassian, and no more intellectual endeavour than that, was true to the original Benedictine ideal. The Maurist response was produced by Mabillon in 1691 at the behest of his own congregation along with other orders. His *Traité des études monastiques* is addressed to the young members of the community for whom he provided a justification from monastic texts and monastic history as to why they should be involved in scholarly pursuits. This is followed by a guide to the various disciplines, authors and works that these novice-scholars should follow, and finally, Mabillon ends with a caution to them that they should not pursue scholarship that cut them off from the search for the spiritual perfection that is the monk's constant goal.[12] Of particular relevance to this chapter were Mabillon's observations on the study of ecclesiastical history.[13] While the study of ecclesiastical history might suit the clergy, it could be argued that it was not fit for monks 'since they must forgo knowing about what happens in the world, they are no less obliged to distance their minds from thoughts of past events'.[14] But it was not to the detriment of monks to be knowledgeable in the affairs of the church: historians were indebted to monasteries for preserving history through their manuscripts, and many monks had written history themselves. There was no issue with knowing the history of their own monastic tradition: 'and that, in fact, is where their study of history should begin'.[15] This latter

pp 427–44. **11** For a summary of the exchanges between Mabillon and Rancé and a translation of Mabillon's *Traité des études monastiques* (1691), see John Paul McDonald, *Treatise on monastic studies – 1691– Dom Jean Mabillon* (Lanham, 2004), pp ix–xvii. **12** McDonald, *Treatise*, p. xii. **13** Ibid., pp 147–57 (Chapter 8 'On studying sacred and profane history'). **14** Ibid., pp 147–8. **15** Ibid., p. 149.

exhortation is key to the tradition of writing monastic history almost to the present day: monks and friars were the custodians of their own histories, and, as with the Maurists and many other such movements, they reflected the values of their own ages and identities.[16] While their *opera* might be criticized by today's standards, their invaluable contribution to monastic scholarship was their sustained effort at preserving and copying historic texts and a mass of other materials in the possession of their own foundations and orders.

WRITING THE HISTORY OF IRISH MONASTICISM

Seventeenth and eighteenth-century confessional historians and antiquaries

The writing of Irish ecclesiastical history from the seventeenth to the twentieth century is inextricably linked to the political history of Ireland and to prevailing confessional perspectives.[17] This is complicated by the constant portrayal of Irish monasticism as particularly distinct, popularly described as 'Celtic monasticism'.[18] In the spirit of the age of the Reformation and Counter-Reformation, a huge effort was made by scholars of both confessions during the seventeenth century to save medieval ecclesiastical materials and to write the religious history of Ireland. There are so many facets to this chapter of Irish ecclesiastical history and its effect on the writing of monastic history that a focus on a number of representative and influential works is the most profitable approach to adopt here. The first to consider is the Irish Franciscan project, conducted in their houses in Donegal, Louvain and Rome, which combined Counter-Reformation-inspired history writing with the collection and compilation of Irish saints' lives and traditional medieval Irish learning (*senchas*). As argued by Bernadette Cunningham in her study of the Annals of the Four Masters:[19]

16 A notable example of another monastic movement of renewal was the revival of the monastery of Solesmes in France during the nineteenth century and the consequent interest in Benedictine monasticism, as seen in the historical works and editions of Dom Paul Delatte, abbot of Solesmes from 1890–1921. See Judith Margaret Bowen, 'Serving the greater cause: aspects of the religious thinking of Prosper Guéranger (1805–75)' (PhD, University of York, 2004) https://etheses.whiterose.ac.uk/21049/1/415181.pdf accessed 7 April 2022.
17 Richard Sharpe, *Medieval Irish saints' lives. An introduction to* Vitae sanctorum Hiberniae (Oxford, 1991), pp 39–74; Nicholas Canny, *Imagining Ireland's pasts. Early modern Ireland through the centuries* (Oxford, 2021).
18 For thoughtful and measured comments on Celtic monasticism, spirituality and theology, see Thomas O'Loughlin, *Celtic theology. Humanity, world and God in early Irish writings* (London and New York, 2000) and his review of Catherine Thom's book *Early Irish monasticism. An understanding of its cultural roots* (London, 2007), *New Blackfriars* 90:1030 (November 2009), 740–1.
19 Bernadette Cunningham, *The Annals of the Four Masters. Irish history, kingship and society in the early seventeenth century* (Dublin, 2010), p. 216.

> history was a tool of the Counter-Reformation and, among the objectives of the Four Masters [compilers of the annals under the direction of the Franciscan lay brother Mícheál Ó Cléirigh (d. 1634)[20]] was to supply a weapon in the armoury of the Catholic Irish scholarly contributors to the debate over the true church.

Medieval Irish monasticism was communicated through a Franciscan lens and focused in particular on the careers of Columbanus of Bobbio and Malachy of Armagh as key phases in Irish ecclesiastical history. The Annals of the Four Masters [AFM] proclaim in Malachy's obit (1148) that he died and was buried at Clairvaux:[21]

> ... after having founded churches and monasteries (for by him were repaired in Ireland every church which had been consigned to decay and neglect, and they had been neglected from time remote); after leaving every rule and every good moral in the churches of Ireland in general ...

John Colgan (d. 1658), Mícheál Ó Cléirigh's confrère and Irish Franciscan hagiographer,[22] included a fairly detailed life of Malachy's successor as archbishop of Armagh Gilla Meic Liac (Gelasius) (d. 1173)[23] in his *Acta Sanctorum Hiberniae* (27 March) lauding him '[for] advancing morals among the clergy and the people and for the transformation of church discipline'.[24] In line with presenting the medieval Irish church as moral and proper, the Four Masters were inclined to omit references to wives, concubines or offspring of regular and secular churchmen that are recorded in other annals. Such 'abuses', common as much elsewhere as in Ireland, did not conform with the value judgment and narrative of Ireland as the ultimate *insula sanctorum* that the Franciscans – and their contemporaries – wished to present to Counter-Reformation Europe and to the 'heretics' of the reformed church active at home.[25] Ironically, many of these friars, including John Colgan and Mícheál Ó Cléirigh, belonged to hereditary families who had held various offices in the late medieval church.

In dealing with Ireland's patron saints, Patrick, Brigit and Columba in his *Triadis Thaumaturgae*,[26] Colgan followed his fellow Irish hagiographers, among

20 https://www.dib.ie/biography/colgan-john-a1835; https://www.dib.ie/biography/o-cleirigh-micheal-oclery-michael-a6307. **21** AFM 1148. Original: ... *iar ffothughadh ceall 7 mainistreach, ar as leisiomh ro hathnuadhaighthe i nErinn, iar na ffailliughadh ó chéin mháir, gach eaglais ro léicthi i faill, 7 i néislis, iar bfághbhail gach riaghla 7 gach soibhésa in eaglaisibh Ereann archeana* ... **22** https://www.dib.ie/biography/colgan-john-a1835. **23** https://www.dib.ie/biography/gilla-meic-liac-gelasius-a3480. **24** John Colgan, *Acta sanctorum veteris et maioris Scotiae sev Hiberniae sanctorum insulae* (Louvain, 1645), p. 778b, § XXX. Original: *promotam in Clero & populo morum & Ecclesiasticae disciplinae reformationem*. My translation. **25** Cunningham, *The Annals of the Four Masters*, passim. **26** John Colgan, *Triadis Thaumaturgæ seu divorum Patricii Columbae et Brigidae ... acta* (Louvain, 1647).

them Thomas Messingham, rector of the Irish College in Paris (d. 1638?)[27] and the Franciscan Robert Rochford,[28] in using the terminology of the Counter-Reformation and early modern hagiography to transform them into modern Catholic saints. Their treatment of St Brigit converted her into what John McCafferty in his study of Robert Rochford's life of Brigit aptly describes as 'the very model of an early modern nun-saint'.[29] Rochford made a point of itemizing what would 'sound very harshly in Protestants eares' from the history of the early Irish church. These features included 'quires of sacred virgins', 'troupes of holy monkes', 'holy vayles', and 'ecclesiasticall tonsure'. Protestants could 'hold no commerce, or society with a Continent and chast monke' as reformed clergymen lay 'immersed in beds of downe, not alone, but embracing their sweet harts'.[30]

More significant in relation to early monasticism, but less well known, was the *Collectanea Sacra* of Patrick Fleming, a Franciscan contemporary of Colgan and the Four Masters from an Old English family in Co. Louth (d. 1631).[31] Having entered the order in 1617, he became one of the leading scholars along with Fr Hugh Ward (d. 1635)[32] in collecting Irish hagiographical manuscripts on the Continent, and as evidenced in his work *Collectanea Sacra*, he placed a particular emphasis on retrieving materials relating to Columbanus. He was appointed Guardian and lecturer in theology in the Irish Franciscan college in Prague in 1631 but within months was murdered in Bohemia. His work was subsequently published in Louvain in 1667 under the direction of another Franciscan, Thomas O'Sherrin (d. 1673).[33] One particular tract provides a detailed insight into Fleming's, and presumably his Franciscan confrères', interpretation of the type of monastic rules that existed in Ireland and that influenced Columbanus's monasticism. This is a long dissertation entitled *Articulus II examinatur an S Columbanus sub regula S Benedicti militaverit*.[34] Its aim was to refute suggestions that Irish monasteries prior to the twelfth century

27 Thomas Messingham, *Florilegium insulae sanctorum, seu vitae et acta sanctorum Hiberniae* (Paris, 1624). https://www.dib.ie/biography/messingham-thomas-a5804. 28 Robert Rochford (Fr B.B.), *The life of the glorious bishop S. Patricke, apostle and primate of Ireland together with the lives of the holy virgin S. Bridgit and of the glorious abbot Saint Columbe, patrons of Ireland* (St Omer, 1625). 29 John McCafferty, 'Brigid of Kildare: stabilizing a female saint for early modern Catholic devotion', *Journal of Medieval and Early Modern Studies* 50:1 (2020), 53–73, at p. 55. https://read.dukeupress.edu/jmems/article-pdf/50/1/53/735141/0500053.pdf accessed 4 February 2020. 30 Salvador Ryan, 'Steadfast saints or malleable models? Seventeenth-century Irish hagiography revisited', *The Catholic Historical Review* 91:2 (2005), 251–77, at p. 262 (quoting Rochford, *The life of glorious bishop S. Patricke &&*, epistle dedicatory p. ix). 31 William Reeves, 'Irish Library – No. 2: Fleming's *Collectanea Sacra*', *Ulster Journal of Archaeology*, 1st series 2 (1854), 253–61; https://www.dib.ie/biography/fleming-patrick-a3286. 32 https://www.dib.ie/biography/mac-bhaird-aodh-buidhe-ward-hugh-vardaeus-hugo-a4989. 33 R.P.F. Patricii Flemingi, *Collectanea Sacra seu S. Columbani Hiberni Abbatis … seu Hibernia antiqorum Sanctorum ACTA ET OPUSCULA & &* (Louvain, 1667). 34 Ibid., pp 406–41.

were subject to the *RB* and assert that Columbanus neither copied the *RB* nor were he or his monks professed as Benedictines. He countered, among others, Ordericus Vitalis's proposition that Columbanus and his monks had followed St Maur – Benedict's successor – and had been professed into his order.[35] Columbanus had devised a monastic rule himself and had brought it to Gaul and particularly to Burgundy. Ireland's monastic rules were varied and emanated from the great monastic founders, among them Finnian of Clonard, Colum Cille (Columba) of Iona, Comgall of Bangor, Cóemgen of Glendalough and Ciarán of Clonmacnoise,[36] and although Fleming had sifted through extensive collections of early Irish texts he claimed that he had not come across any reference to the *RB* or a life of St Benedict. He contended that if Benedictines had been in Ireland at this early time it was a wonder that there was no memory of them.[37] Columbanus was educated as a monk by Comgall in Bangor and it was on the basis of what he had been taught there that he devised his rule. Fleming even argued that Columbanus's foundations, especially Luxeuil, were actually part of the *familia* of Comgall and Bangor.[38] The *RB* had not come to Ireland before the time of St Malachy who described Ireland as being 'a land inexperienced in monastic discipline'.[39] An argument throughout Fleming's tract distinguished Ireland from Britain insofar as he, like many historians, thought that Benedictines had arrived with Augustine of Canterbury (d. 604). Augustine's mission and the *RB* had not spread to Ireland and proof of this was that during the seventh century Ireland had to be brought into line with Rome on matters such as the Paschal cycle and the monastic tonsure. Throughout all of this discourse, Fleming followed the contemporary narrative that a Benedictine order had existed in this early period, an understanding that can no longer be justified. There were monks who followed the Rule of St Benedict, as others followed the directions of Columbanus, but neither were formal orders as defined, for example, by the medieval Benedictine and Cistercian orders.

Despite deviation from the Roman Paschal cycle, Fleming found it necessary to signal that the Irish church had always accepted the norm as laid down by Rome, and that Columbanus was instrumental in confirming its orthodoxy. From a personal perspective, Fleming seems to have adopted Columbanus as a patron and protector as he faced the challenges involved in founding the Irish Franciscan college in Prague. He is said to have recited daily 'the Litany of the Blessed Virgin … with prayers to St Francis, St Patrick, St Columbanus, St Ambrose, St Catherine, and other saints'.[40] All Fleming's work on Columbanus

35 Ibid., p. 418 §58. 36 https://www.dib.ie/biography/finnian-vinnianus-findbarr-a3100; https://www.dib.ie/biography/colum-cille-columba-a1890; https://www.dib.ie/biography/comgall-a1902; https://www.dib.ie/biography/coemgen-kevin-a1789; https://www.dib.ie/biography/ciaran-a1664. 37 Fleming, *Collectanea Sacra*, pp 410–11 §§41–3. 38 Ibid., p. 440 §97. 39 Ibid., p. 409 §38. Original: *terram inexpertam monasticae disciplinae.* 40 Quoted in Myles O'Reilly, *Lives of the Irish martyrs and confessors* (New York, 1878), p. 681; *Collectanea*

was framed in a pan-European and Catholic Counter-Reformation context in which the Irish Franciscans and others wished to place the ecclesiastical history of Ireland, primarily through the lives of its saints. In an exhortation to Fr Hugh Ward (Aodh Mac an Bháird), Fleming asked the question 'Why not give us, in the course of time, a history of the kings of Ireland, *such as other nations have* [my italics]?'[41] And a brief biographical note on Fleming included in the preface to *Collectanea Sacra* expresses concisely the objective of their project 'that, by promoting piety toward those holy men, their example might be imitated by our people, and those golden years be renewed amongst us which shed such lustre and glory on our country'.[42]

Geoffrey Keating's (d. 1644) influence on the writing of Irish ecclesiastical and secular history cannot be underestimated.[43] His seminal history of Ireland, *Foras feasa ar Éirinn*, was widely circulated and transcribed to the point that it became the unofficial popular history of Ireland. But, as noted by Bernadette Cunningham in her detailed study of Keating and his world, he was 'an advocate of a diocesan parochial structure rather than the monastic structure of the religious orders' and as a result he had difficulty in accommodating stories of monastic saints within his vision of the most appropriate structures for the contemporary Irish church.[44] Keating's monastic terminology belongs to a Counter-Reformation church and his depiction of a pure Irish monasticism forms part of his discourse against Protestant and British commentators. His description of the church of Mungret, Co. Limerick, founded by St Nessán is a typically exaggerated mix of old and contemporary terms:[45]

> That church was called the city (*cathair*) of Deacon Neasán. This was the number of monks that inhabited it, namely, five hundred monks learning to preach; six hundred psalmists to service choir; and four hundred elders for keen meditation or contemplation (*ré contemplation* [sic]).

Such descriptions were the source of later fabricated – and often romantic, popular – accounts of early monasteries as universities populated by hundreds

Sacra (preface), *Historia Martyrii Venerabilis Patris Fratris Patricii Flemingi*, [p. 7]. 41 O'Reilly, *Lives of the Irish martyrs*, p. 671. 42 Ibid., p. 661; *Collectanea Sacra* (preface), *Brevis notitia de collectore*, [p. 5]. For an explanation of the context of the Irish Franciscan hagiographical project, see Pádraig Ó Riain, 'The Louvain achievement II: hagiography' in Edel Bhreathnach, Joseph MacMahon and John McCafferty (eds), *The Irish Franciscans, 1534–1990* (Dublin, 2009), pp 189–200. 43 https://www.dib.ie/biography/keating-geoffrey-ceitinn-seathrun-a4417. 44 Bernadette Cunningham, *The world of Geoffrey Keating. History, myth and religion in seventeenth-century Ireland* (Dublin, 2000), p. 170. 45 Patrick S. Dinneen (ed. and trans.), *Foras feasa ar Éirinn le Seathrún Céitinn, DD. The history of Ireland by Geoffrey Keating, DD*, vol. III (London, 1908), p. 198 Original: *Cathair Dheochain Neasáin ghairthear don chill sin. Ag so an líon manach do bhí innte, mar atá cúig céad manach foghlumtha ré seanmóir; sé céad psalmaire ré freastal coradh; is cheithre céad seanóir ré*

of monks. Keating also refuted the history of the Irish church as presented by Protestant historians as part of the seventeenth-century confessional discourse on its origins. He contradicted Meredith Hanmer (d. 1604),[46] a Welsh clergyman who had produced a *Chronicle of Ireland* (published posthumously in 1633) in which, for example, the latter claimed that Comgall of Bangor was British and that his foundation was not only in Bangor, Co. Down, but also in Bangor beside 'west Chester', and hence that the glory of Comgall's monastery in Ireland, which extended throughout Europe, was shared with Britain. In Hanmer's opinion the fame of both monasteries 'should reconcile Britaine and Ireland now being in one, and breed an agreement among Antiquaries'.[47] Keating, a priest active in Ireland during the difficult 1600s who was educated and lectured in France, also challenged the contention in the *Bulla Laudabiliter*, reputed to have been presented to Henry II by Pope Adrian IV in 1155, that the pre-Norman Irish church was corrupt and in need of reform. Among his many arguments against this representation of the Catholic church in Ireland was that Irish kings had taken the initiative to endow many renowned monasteries during the twelfth century prior to the coming of the Anglo-Normans. Hence both the church and native aristocracy benefited from this mutual relationship and monasticism was an important element of this vibrant society.[48] For many generations after him, Keating's work had a lasting impact on the writing of Irish history, greater than others in that his narrative became part of the oral tradition in Ireland, as well as being firmly part of the nationalist history of Ireland.

If the Franciscans and their compatriot Counter-Reformation hagiographers promoted an island of saints whose monastic tradition was distinct from the Benedictine tradition, adherents to the Reformation used early sources to create a pure and Protestant Irish church that had had sporadic links with Rome but had not been bound by papal resolutions. The most authoritative advocate of this thesis was James Ussher, reformed bishop of Armagh, historian and theologian (d. 1656).[49] (Fig. 1) In his treatise *A discourse of the religion anciently professed by the Irish and the British*, published originally in 1622 and reprinted in a revised form in 1631,[50] Ussher compared the purity of the early monks with 'the hypocrisy, pride, idleness and uncleanliness of those evil beasts and slothful

rinnfheitheamh nó ré contemplation. Translation corrected. **46** https://www.dib.ie/biography/hanmer-meredith-a3783. **47** Meredith Hanmer, *The chronicle of Ireland. Collected by Meredith Hanmer in the yeare 1571* (Dublin, 1633; repr. Dublin, 1809), pp 105–7; David Comyn (ed. and trans.), *Foras feasa ar Éirinn le Seathrún Céitinn, DD. The history of Ireland by Geoffrey Keating, DD*, vol. I (London, 1902), pp. 52–3. **48** Dinneen, *Foras feasa* III, pp 350–3. **49** Alan Ford, 'James Ussher and the creation of an Irish protestant identity' in Brendan Bradshaw and Peter Roberts (eds), *British consciousness and identity. The making of Britain, 1533–1707* (Cambridge, 1998), pp 185–212; https://www.dib.ie/biography/ussher-james-a8774. **50** Charles Richard Elrington (ed.), *The whole works of the Most Rev. James Ussher, DD, lord archbishop of Armagh and primate of all Ireland*, vol. iv (Dublin, 1864), pp 235–381.

bellies that afterward succeeded in their room'.[51] He was particularly critical of the four orders of mendicant friars 'a new generation of men, that refuse to eat their own bread, and count it a high point of sanctity to live by begging of other men's bread'.[52] But Ussher argued that the begging friars were 'a kind of creature unknown to the Church for twelve hundred years after Christ'.[53] In contrast, monks in early Ireland and Britain 'got their living by the labour of their own hands'.[54] No more than with Patrick Fleming, Ussher was to rely on the so-called Rule of Columbanus and the Penitential of Columbanus as primary sources to demonstrate the strict discipline imposed as part of this early insular monastic tradition in the realms of obedience, fasting and perpetual virginity. Ussher accepted the three orders of Irish saints devised by the Irish Jesuit Henry Fitzsimon (d. 1643) in his *Catalogus praecipuorum sanctorum Hiberniae*.[55] These orders began with St Patrick, the holiest, then the great monastic founders, and finally, renowned hermits. In his history of the British and Irish church, *Britannicarum ecclesiarum antiquitates*, Ussher explained that four monastic rules had existed in Ireland, had spread to Britain and ultimately to the Continent, those of Columba of Iona, Comgall of Bangor, Mochutu of Lismore and Ailbe of Emly. He argued that in England, Wilfrid of York (d. 709) had replaced the Rule of Columba with *RB*.[56] Thus from opposite sides of the dispute, Fleming and Ussher attempted to set the Irish monastic tradition apart from the Benedictine tradition. The great difference was that Ussher claimed that Irish practices and rites deviated from Rome *ab initio*, further evidence that the early Irish church was closer to the established Church of Ireland than to the Roman Catholic church and the papacy. Of course, this thesis was fraught with ambiguities that reflected 'the wider tensions inherent in his [Ussher's] position as an Irish protestant'.[57] Although Ussher did not characterize the Irish church as a 'Celtic' church or its monasticism as 'Celtic' monasticism, nevertheless this belief in a separate church with its own practices and rites fed into the creation, especially from the nineteenth century onwards, of a discrete tradition that blossomed in the 'Celtic' lands of Cornwall, Brittany, Ireland, the Isle of Man, Scotland and Wales. Acknowledging that this concept originated from a seventeenth-century discourse is essential if there is to be any prospect of understanding early Irish monasticism on the basis of its own direct witness.

For the next two hundred years, the confessional dispute about the origins of the Irish church and its loyalty to Rome continued unabated and every so often

51 Elrington, *James Ussher*, iv, pp 299–300. 52 Ibid., iv, p. 301. 53 Ibid., iv, p. 303. 54 Ibid., iv, p. 301. 55 Henry Fitzsimons, *Catalogus præcipuorum sanctorum Hiberniæ* (Liège, 1619); https://www.dib.ie/biography/fitzsimon-henry-a3249. See also Paul Grosjean, 'Édition du *Catalogus praecipuorum sanctorum Hiberniae* de Henry Fitzsimon' in John Ryan (ed.), *Féil-sgríbhinn Eóin Mhic Néill. Essays and studies presented to Professor Eoin MacNeill on the occasion of his seventieth birthday, May 15th 1938* (Dublin, 1940; repr. 1995), pp 335–93. 56 James Ussher, *Britannicarum ecclesiarum antiquitates* (Dublin, 1639), p. 919. 57 Ford,

aspects of the monastic tradition became entangled in this complex discussion.[58] The seventeenth century also heralded the beginnings of an antiquarian movement in Ireland that was influenced by similar endeavours in Britain. In many instances, British antiquaries included Ireland in their treatises on ancient monuments and objects. Monastic remains, especially round towers, high crosses and inscribed stones, attracted their attention and in the case of round towers generated many fanciful theories as to their function and who built them. The most prominent antiquary to gather together original texts and to write up the histories of Irish monasteries and friaries was the scholarly Sir James Ware (d. 1666) who was a student of Archbishop Ussher in Trinity College Dublin.[59] Apart from gaining his antiquarian interests from Ussher and his scholarly network – which he used to extend across confessional barriers[60] – Ware benefited from access to an extensive range of original records due to his father-in-law Jacob Newman's position as clerk of the rolls in Dublin Castle.[61] As early as 1625 Ware was able to send Ussher a list of manuscripts in his possession. This first list contained the registers of late medieval foundations: St Thomas's Abbey, Dublin; Knockmoy Abbey, Co. Galway; Muckamore Abbey, Co. Antrim; St Mary's Abbey, Dublin; Kilmainham Priory, Co. Meath. The only source associated with an early medieval monastery was the text of the Annals of Inisfallen, which was preserved in a late medieval manuscript (now Bodl. MS Rawl. B503).[62] Ware's catalogue printed in 1648[63] added to the number of late medieval monastic sources that had come into his possession.[64] Far fewer were

'James Ussher and the creation of an Irish protestant identity', 202. **58** Clare O'Halloran, *Golden ages and barbarous nations. Antiquarian debate and cultural politics in Ireland, c.1750–1800* (Cork, 2004), pp 87–92. **59** https://www.dib.ie/biography/ware-sir-james-a8928. **60** Mark Empey, '"Value-free" history? The scholarly network of Sir James Ware', *History Ireland* 20:2 (2012), 20–3. **61** William O'Sullivan, 'A finding list of Sir James Ware's manuscripts', *Proceedings of the Royal Irish Academy* 97 (1997), 69–99, at p. 70. **62** O'Sullivan, 'A finding list', 71. **63** James Ware, *Librorum manuscriptorum in bibliotheca Jacobi Waraei equitis aurati catalogus* (Dublin, 1648); O'Sullivan, 'A finding list', 84–99. **64** These included books and manuscripts from St Mary's Abbey Navan, Co. Meath (martyrology); St Mary's Abbey, Dublin (a life of the BVM); All Saints' Priory, Lough Ree, Co. Longford (annals); St John the Baptist, Dublin (register); Tristernagh Priory, Co. Westmeath (register); Athenry Priory, Co. Galway (register); Lough Key Priory, Co. Roscommon (annals); St Mary's Cong, Co. Mayo (list of benefactors); St John the Evangelist Hospital, Co. Kilkenny (copy of foundation charter); Dunbrody Abbey, Co. Wexford (register excerpts); Ballintober, Co. Mayo (register excerpts); Kilkenny Friary (Annals of John Clyn); Multyfarnham Friary (fragmentary annals); Strade/*Athlethan*, Co. Mayo (fragmentary annals); St Mary's Glascarrig, Co. Wexford (copy of foundation charter); St John the Baptist Ardee, Co. Louth (copy of foundation charter); St Columba's Inistioge, Co. Kilkenny (copy of foundation charter); St Finbar (de antro), Cork (copy of foundation charter); Clare Abbey (de Forgio), Co. Clare (copy of foundation charter); Limerick Priory (excerpt from calendar of saints); Galway Friary (excerpts from Book of Obits); St Wolstan's Priory, Co. Kildare (excerpts from registry); St Mary's Kells, Co. Kilkenny (excerpts from registry); Nenagh Friary, Co. Tipperary (annals); Duiske Abbey, Co. Kilkenny (from register and annals) and associated with earlier foundations.[65] Nevertheless, Ware's two works *De Hibernia et Antiquitatibus ejus, Disquisitiones* (1654) and *De praesulibus Hiberniae commentarius* (1665) had a long-lasting influence on the study of medieval monasticism in Ireland. Ware's authority can be traced in works from Mervyn Archdall's *Monasticon Hibernicum* (1786) to Aubrey Gwynn and R. Neville Hadcock's *Medieval religious houses Ireland* (1970) and through them into modern scholarship.

Cap. XXVI of *De Hibernia* entitled 'Monasteriologia Hibernica' is a list of the main late medieval monasteries of Ireland in which reference is made to earlier monasteries if they existed in the same location.[66] Of particular note is how Ware classified most early monastic foundations as Augustinian, frequently describing their origins as he does in the case of Seir Kieran (Saigir Ciaráin), Co. Offaly:[67]

> St Kieran (Ciarán) the elder built a monastery here during the early infancy of the Irish church, that once blossomed with great honour … The canons of this monastery were of the order of St Augustine.

The impression that most major early foundations adopted the Rule of St Augustine during the twelfth century has lasted among scholars to the present although this view has been questioned in recent times.[68] Ware did not offer any further evidence for the majority of monasteries and founders although he made interesting comments in some cases that suggest that he understood that early foundations were not uniformly Augustinian. Ware classified Durrow, for example, as an Augustinian foundation – which it may have become during the twelfth century – but noted in addition that St Columba and his monks followed a rule similar to those of other early monastic founders such as SS Brendan and Comgall.[69] Yet, Columba was also reputed to have founded a monastery of canons regular on Inchmore Island in Lough Gowna, Co. Longford.[70] Ware's entries on Armagh, Derry and Devenish are indicative of the uncertainty surrounding monastic rules prevailing in Ireland at the time. On Armagh he comments on the foundation dedicated to SS Peter and Paul that Patrick was its original founder and that its second founder was Ímar Ua hÁedacáin, St

Claregalway Friary, Co. Galway (from charters). **65** These included Clonmacnoise, Co. Offaly (annals); Glendalough, Co. Wicklow, or Killeshin, Co. Laois (Bodl. MS Rawl. B502); All Saints' Dublin (register excerpt); St Columba's Kells (gospels?) as well as lives of Irish saints. **66** Ware, *De Hibernia*, pp 140–231. **67** Ibid., pp 161–2. Original: *Sanctus Kiaranus vel Ciaranus senior construxit ibi cœnobium in primâ ecclesiæ Hibernicæ infantiâ, quod magno olim honore floruit … Canonici hujus cœnobii Ordinis fuerunt S. Augustini.* **68** Edel Bhreathnach, 'The *Vita Apostolica* and the origin of the Augustinian canons and canonesses in medieval Ireland' in Martin Browne and Colmán Ó Clabaigh (eds), *Households of God. The regular canons and canonesses of Saint Augustine and of Prémontré in medieval Ireland* (Dublin, 2019), pp 1–27. **69** Ware, *De Hibernia*, pp 160–1. **70** Ibid., p. 171.

Malachy's tutor (d. 1134).[71] The stone church built under the direction of Ímar was consecrated by Cellach, the successor of Patrick in 1126.[72] As Ware claimed in *De praesulibus* that Patrick was not only a canon but that he received his formation in the Lateran in Rome (*in Ecclesia Lateranensi, Canonicus Regularis vixit*),[73] Armagh's new church was simply a reaffirmation of the founding saint's monastic affiliation. Acknowledging that Columba had founded Derry, Ware noted that the church there popularly known as the *Dubreiclés* or *Cella Nigra* 'black chapel' was a house of canons subject to SS Peter and Paul in Armagh.[74] His entry relating to Devenish on Lough Erne highlights the confusion at the time about the monastic rules practised in such places. He claimed that St Molaise, the early founder, had his own rule but that his successors followed the Rule of St Augustine. Commenting on the record in the Annals of Ulster under 1130 that a monastery was established on Devenish, he surmised that the annalist was either referring to the renewal of the earlier monastery or that this related to a new priory that housed the *Colideorum* (*céli Dé*) who in Ware's estimation were secular priests.[75] This assumption fits with Ware's general description of the offices associated with Irish monasteries.[76] He defined the *comarbae* ('heir, successor') as the highest ranking dignity in his position as successor to the founder saint and keeper of a foundation's goods and lands. Often lay and married, their families were entitled to their own lands known as 'termon lands'. Also known as 'erenaghs' (anglicized from the Irish term *airchinnig*) they and their families were free from secular impositions but they were due annual payments from their local bishop, an onerous burden on the latter. The office was often hereditary but an heir had to be sworn into office by the bishop. Ware noted that scholars were given the titles *scriba*, *lector* and *doctor*. In his estimation, the Irish had few ordained priests and some were known as *Colidei*, *Culdei* (*céli Dé*) defined by Ware as *cultures Dei* 'worshippers or supporters of God'. Unlike in Wales, Irish *Colidei* were not monks but in Armagh they were secular priests serving the sanctuary (*choro inservientes*) and the person in charge of them (*praeses*) was the prior of the college of *Colidei* who also acted as *praecentor* of Armagh. A similar 'prior' was at Clones, Co. Monaghan, and at Devenish. In Scotland, *céli Dé* were monks as well as priests and Ware also noted a reference to them existing in St Peter's cathedral in York during the reign of King Æthelstan (d. 939).[77] Ware's description of anchorites or *inclusi* appears to have been influenced by the customs of the late medieval period as he alludes to the Rule of the Anchorite from a manuscript that belonged once to St Thomas's Abbey, Dublin.[78] Apart from references to late medieval foundations for women,

71 Ibid., p. 177. 72 AU. 73 Ware, *De praesulibus*, p. 1. 74 Ware, *De Hibernia*, p. 184. 75 Ibid., p. 188. 76 Ibid., pp 78–84 (CAP. XVII). 77 Ibid., pp 80–1. 78 Colmán Ó Clabaigh, 'Community, commemoration and confraternity: the chapter office and chapter books in Irish Augustinian foundations' in Browne and Ó Clabaigh, *Households of God*,

Ware provides little information about early female foundations, the exceptions being Kildare, Killevy, Co. Armagh, Killaraght, Co. Sligo, and Annaghdown, Co. Galway, the latter reputed to have been founded by St Brendan for his sister Bríg.[79]

Ware's legacy to Irish monastic studies was considerable. He promoted the idea that from the very beginning monastic houses followed the Rule of St Augustine even though he could not offer any certain evidence for the use of this rule in Ireland until the twelfth century. His narrative was coloured by the nature of medieval monastic orders such as the Augustinians, Cistercians and others. He regarded Malachy of Armagh as both an Augustinian canon and a Cistercian monk. Along with other historian-antiquaries, he acknowledged that Irish monasticism, at least at the time of the early founders, may have been subject to the individual rules of authoritative abbots, but that their successors ultimately imposed the canonical rule on their monasteries. His sources for the early period, annals, saints' lives and the witness of later commentators such as Giraldus Cambrensis, Jocelin of Furness and his own contemporary John Colgan, attested to an array of officials existing in monasteries – *coarbs*, *erenaghs*, *colidei*, *seniores* – but Ware wrote of these in the language of the late medieval church. And hence, as well as the huge legacy of source material transmitted by Ware to scholars of Irish monasticism, he framed the narrative of Irish monastic history for many generations after him.

One of the most influential of the scholars to follow Ware was Mervyn Archdall (d. 1791) who published his *Monasticon Hibernicum* in 1786.[80] Archdall's work followed Ware in many details and used the same sources but his list of religious houses included more pre-Norman monasteries, even if in some cases he had nothing to observe beyond a place-name and a local cult. A Church of Ireland clergyman, Archdall was not as virulently confessional as others of the time in his ecclesiastical history writing, although he claimed that the Irish adherence to Catholicism was due to their passive acceptance of papal domination. Monasticism remained strong as it was 'rooted in the affection of the less intelligent natives for the monastic institution'.[81] This was especially true in the case of the Franciscans. He acknowledged that Ware as 'a judicious Antiquary' had composed 'the first idea of an Irish Monasteriology' but had 'contented himself … with an outline, tolerably correct, of our cenobitic establishments, but very imperfect as to their private history and property'.[82] Archdall included detailed information on the possessions, mainly lands, of Irish foundations, and thus his *Monasticon* became an invaluable primary source due

pp 235–51, at p. 247. **79** Ware, *De Hibernia*, p. 216. **80** Mervyn Archdall, *Monasticon Hibernicum. Or, a history of the abbeys, priories, and other religious houses in Ireland* (Dublin, 1786); edited with additional notes by Patrick F. Moran 3 vols (Dublin, 1873); https://www.dib.ie/biography/archdall-mervyn-a0194. **81** Archdall, *Monasticon*, p. xii (1786 edition). **82** Ibid., p. xiii.

to the subsequent loss of Irish records. On the question of the nature of early medieval Irish monasticism, Archdall expressed some doubts about the likelihood that all early foundations followed the Rule of St Augustine as he acknowledged that no such rule existed until the twelfth century and in any case – resorting to a Protestant perspective – the Irish church was not subject to the papacy until that time.[83] St Patrick had established 'the monkish profession' in Ireland which was marked by 'simplicity and purity of manners, and the most rigid mortification … the Irish received, with the rudiments of their faith, a predilection for the monastic state'.[84] The ancient 'orders' of Comgall, Cárthach/Mochutu and Columba were deemed 'heretical' in the twelfth century and were no longer called 'by their old titles, but by new and fashionable names', and 'hence it is, that of the numerous monasteries founded by Columba, not more than the names of three or four are handed down to us, the rest were ranked as Augustinians, and continued to be recorded, as such, by succeeding writers'.[85] While Archdall associated most early saints and their foundations with the canons regular, the uncertainty due to the absence of original records bothered him and he grappled throughout the work with this problem. His comments about the governance of the Priory of the Holy Trinity Dublin before Lorcán Ua Tuathail introduced the Arrouasian rule there in the 1160s testifies to his scholarly doubts:[86]

> … involved in darkness and obscurity, in vain we search for the origin of our religious foundations, the improbabilities and fictions of ancient legends are often our only evidences, and we are frequently obliged to adopt the palpable anachronisms of such writings, in the place of authentic documents and chronological certainty …
>
> … The religious of this community were secular canons, not tied to the observance of strict monastic rules, or belonging to any of the cenobitical orders; yet they were a sort of monks [*sic*] lax in discipline, and bound to such regulations as the bishop prescribed …

In addition to his inclusion of lengthy details about monastic lands and possessions, the significance of Archdall's work lies in his extensive descriptions of the physical remains of medieval monasteries and friaries, especially in the larger foundations such as Armagh, Derry, Clonmacnoise, Devenish, Monaincha and Glendalough. These descriptions were not necessarily first-hand observations but depended on acquaintances who had visited the sites or on other written works. Archdall, for example, describes the landscape of Kilmacduagh, Co. Galway quoting Richard Pococke, antiquary and bishop of

83 Ibid., p. xvii. 84 Ibid., p. x. 85 Ibid., p. xviii. 86 Ibid., i, pp 147–8 (1873 edition).

Ossory and Meath (d. 1765) as his source.[87] Pococke visited Kilmacduagh in 1752 and he described the site in detail. I quote it extensively as it epitomizes accounts of the period:[88]

> I came to Kilmacduagh situated on a rising ground over some *little* Loughs which are to the west. It is the See of an ancient Bishoprick now united to Clonfert and consists only of old buildings and of two or three Cabins … The first building that offers is the ancient Cathedral in the form of a Latin Cross; on the south side of which is an ancient Altar in good taste; under a relief of a Bishop is this inscription 'Sanctus Coloman Patronus Totius Diecesis Duacensis': In the middle is a crucifix and a person on each side with '*Ave Maria*' and some devotion round it … To the west in the church yard is a small cell where they say the Patron Saint was *buried*, and that the body was afterwards *carried* to Agherrim. Between this and the church is Macduagh's Chapel, in which there is a standing large dead Tree, of which they take pieces by way of Relicks; and to the south of this is a raised work of stone, which they call the Saints Bed. In the church yard is one of the round towers, if I mistake not; fifteen feet in diameter: it is finely built of stones well chosen, but do not seem to have been *hammered* and they are not all laid in regular courses … To the east of the church is our Ladies chapel and to the north of it St John Baptist's. To the north of it is the Monastery of Kilmacduagh, said to be of Regular Canons …

To many antiquaries two monuments – the round tower and the high cross – typified an early Irish monastery and these later became visual representations of Irish national identity. That round towers did not look like ecclesiastical towers elsewhere, or could not be equated easily with such buildings elsewhere apart from a few in Scotland, intrigued antiquaries and led to the wildest speculation about their origin and function. The high crosses were noticed because of their monumental size and remarkable ornamentation, and also because they were 'living' monuments, along with holy wells and cemeteries, which drew pilgrims to these early sites. Otherwise, late medieval gothic abbeys and friaries were far more attractive and culturally similar to ruins elsewhere, as well as which they blended into picturesque romantic landscapes.[89] Round towers and high crosses

87 Ibid., ii, p. 220 n. 22 (1873 edition). 88 George T. Stokes (ed.), *Pococke's tour in Ireland in 1752* (Dublin and London, 1891), pp 108–10 accessed https://celt.ucc.ie//published/E750002-001.html 9 March 2020; Jerome Fahey, 'Kilmacduagh and its ecclesiastical monuments', *Journal of the Royal Society of Antiquaries of Ireland* 34 (1904), 220–33, at p. 229. 89 Niamh NicGhabhann, *Medieval ecclesiastical buildings in Ireland, 1789–1915* (Dublin, 2015). Of later medieval monastic foundations of European orders in Ireland, along with contemporary cathedrals and parish churches, Dr NicGhabhann (pp 2–3) succinctly summarizes their role: 'They were seen variously by different people and at different times as symbols of religious persecution, symbols of religious identity and continuity, as picturesque

are also significant as they represented important changes in monastic studies in Ireland during the eighteenth and nineteenth centuries, which saw a gradual shift from antiquarianism to more scientific approaches to monuments. In addition, art and architectural history progressed as did the surveying and recording of early monastic monuments throughout Ireland, and the editing and translation of many original early Irish texts from medieval and later manuscripts.

Advances in scholarship during the nineteenth century

Many individuals contributed to monastic history during this period but a number of scholars were to the forefront of improving the standard of scholarship. Among the most important scholars were Eugene O'Curry (d. 1862), John O'Donovan (d. 1861) and George Petrie (d. 1866), the artist George du Noyer (d. 1869), and art historian Margaret Stokes (d. 1900).[90] And yet despite this progress, wild speculation and confessional debates around early Irish monasticism continued and some, such as Edward Ledwich (d. 1823) and Charles Vallancey (d. 1812),[91] were condemned on a scale similar to the damnation of Giraldus Cambrensis on the subject of Irish monasticism. Ledwich's primary aim in the ecclesiastical history chapter of his work *The antiquities of Ireland* (1790) was to prove that the Irish church was separated from the beginning from Rome. As to monasticism there was no Rule of St Patrick as 'the inferior orders of Columba, Congel and Carthag would never have swallowed up and annihilated every remembrance of that given by our great apostle had it ever existed'.[92] The Culdees, which Ledwich claimed were founded as an order by Columba, eschewed Roman practices and as a result were persecuted for their different ways. Curiously, he argued that 'the Anglo-Saxons accepted the Roman office, but the Britons and Irish retained their primitive forms'.[93] This situation changed when the 'Ostmen' became Christians:[94]

> Instead of uniting in restoring the purity of our church, or of reviving the splendour of our institutions and literary seminaries which their pagan zeal had nearly annihilated, they introduced the Benedictine Order, which sought admiration more from the mummery of external performances than the cultivation of useful literature or substantial piety.

survivals from a long-past era, as areas for potential religious renewal, as an important facet of a shared architectural heritage and as ugly ruins to be removed and replaced as quickly as possible'. **90** https://www.dib.ie/biography/ocurry-curry-o-comhrai-eugene-eoghan-a6664; https://www.dib.ie/biography/odonovan-o-donnabhain-john-sean-a6718; https://www.dib.ie/biography/petrie-george-a7300; https://www.dib.ie/biography/du-noyer-george-victor-a2791; https://www.dib.ie/biography/stokes-margaret-mcnair-a8332. **91** https://www.dib.ie/biography/ledwich-edward-a4751; https://www.dib.ie/biography/vallancey-charles-a8781. **92** Edward Ledwich and James Ford, *The antiquities of Ireland* (Dublin, 1790; repr. 1804), p. 90. **93** Ibid., p. 112. **94** Ibid., p. 121.

In line with other earlier authors, Ledwich believed that the Danes on their conversion, which he thought happened during the ninth century, built round towers, initially as watch towers and later as belfries.[95] This theory about round towers was not as wild as Charles Vallancey's speculation in his *Collectanea de rebus Hibernicis* which claimed that round towers were a feature of the Scytho-Phoenician settlement of Ireland and its archaic Chaldean religion.[96] Although these theories were rebutted during the nineteenth century, they continued to be revived, with Henry O'Neill, well known for his illustrations of high crosses, publishing a volume in 1877 espousing theories of their pagan origin.[97]

All of this unscientific and confessional speculation was countered by George Petrie who approached the subject more scientifically, supported by the serious linguistic and literary scholarship of Eugene O'Curry and John O'Donovan.[98] Petrie's essay on the ecclesiastical architecture of Ireland, including round towers, was a turning point in the study of the early Irish church in that it established that round towers were Christian and ecclesiastical in origin, that they were belfries and used 'as keeps, or places of strength, in which sacred utensils, books, relics, and other valuables were deposited' in times of danger, and were occasionally used as beacons and watch-towers.[99] Petrie extended his study beyond round towers to other ecclesiastical monuments: churches, oratories, belfries, houses, 'erdamhs', kitchens, cashels, well coverings, tombs and mills. He described many surviving examples and provided detailed drawings that brought the subject to another level beyond the reaches of unfounded speculation and out of the arena of what Joep Leerssen has described as 'freewheeling speculation which until then had been the hallmark of Irish antiquaries'.[100] Petrie made clear in his introduction that he did not expect his work to have 'any very immediate effect on the great majority of the middle classes of the Irish people (for the lower or agricultural classes have no ideas upon the subject but the true ones) in changing their opinions as to their

95 Ibid., pp 155–70. **96** Charles Vallancey, *Collectanea de rebus Hibernicis* vol. 3 (Dublin, 1786), pp 193–6; Bernd Roling, 'Phoenician Ireland: Charles Vallancey (1725–1812) and the oriental roots of Celtic culture' in Karl A.E. Enenkel and Konrad Adriann Ottenheym (eds), *The quest for an appropriate past in literature, art and architecture.* (Leiden, 2018), pp 750–70. **97** https://www.dib.ie/biography/oneill-henry-a6925. **98** George Petrie acknowledges Captain Thomas Larcom, Superintendent of the Ordnance Survey of Ireland for his assistance in securing 'local and other necessary information, which his position enabled him to obtain' and his 'warmest and most attached friends' John O'Donovan and Eugene O'Curry for 'lending the weight of their invaluable authority to the translations from Irish MSS. to be found throughout this work'. George Petrie, *The ecclesiastical architecture of Ireland, anterior to the Anglo-Norman invasion; comprising an essay on the origin and uses of the round towers of Ireland* (Dublin, 1845), p. x. **99** Petrie, *Ecclesiastical architecture*, pp 2–3. **100** Joep Leerssen, 'Petrie: polymath and innovator' in Peter Murray (ed.), *George Petrie (1790–1866). The rediscovery of Ireland's past* (Cork, 2004), pp 7–11, at p. 9; Peter Murray, 'The Tara paper controversy and the round towers essay' in Murray, *George Petrie*, pp 103–7.

indefinite antiquity and Pagan uses'.[101] Apart from his contribution to recording so many monuments in detail, Petrie speculated about the layout of early monasteries, and although he incorrectly attributed some buildings and features to the conversion period, his overall conclusions were reasonable. Of larger monastic communities, he hypothesized that[102]

> unlike those in the East, of whom Epiphanius speaks, [the Irish] did not dwell in any single building, but in a multitude of separate cells, arranged in streets in the vicinity of the church … Such communities would, however, require at least one large building, to answer the purpose of a common refectory; and that they had such is proved by innumerable references in the Irish annals … the name of such a building was *Proinnteach*, or dining-house … Such buildings, however, though probably differing in form from the cells – which, as I have already stated, seem to have been of a round figure, while these were probably quadrangular – were, like the smaller houses, generally, if not always, erected of perishable materials, and, would, consequently, leave no vestiges to present times … In these great cœnobitical monasteries, it is probable, also, that the houses of the abbots were of a quadrangular form, and more than the ordinary size.

Petrie was insistent that the Irish had had the capacity to build stone churches prior to the arrival of the Vikings, often citing prehistoric parallels to date surviving stone structures to support his case. He included among them the monuments known as St Columba's House at Kells and St Kevin's Church at Glendalough. He provided detailed surveys of both but erroneously concluded that they were 'erected by the persons whose names they bear, and that they both served the double purpose of a habitation and an oratory'.[103] Petrie was acutely aware of the precarious state of surviving monastic remains and declared that[104]

> by making the age and historical interest of these memorials of our early Christianity more generally known to, and appreciated by my countrymen, some stop might be put to the wanton destruction of these remains, which is now, unhappily, of daily occurrence, and which, if not by some means checked, must lead ere long to their total annihilation.

Petrie's portrayal of early Irish monasticism is most popularly known from his often spectacular landscape watercolours and drawings of monastic sites. The watercolours sometimes depict very dramatic scenes, one of the most expressive

101 Petrie, *Ecclesiastical architecture*, p. ix. **102** Ibid., pp 427–9. **103** Ibid., p. 437. **104** Ibid., pp v–vi.

of which is his *Gougane Barra with the hermitage of St Finbar* described by William Stokes in his life of Petrie [Fig. 2]:[105]

> The subject is the hermitage of St Finbar, situated on a lake between Cork and Bantry. The lake is surrounded by hills, whose apparent height is increased by a shrouding veil of mist while the sky is overcast by dark clouds. There is a partial break in this gloomy canopy overhead through which a single sunray falls perpendicularly on the still waters of the lonely lake, on the ruins, and the wild wood which hangs above them, as if to show that even in its desolation and ruin, and in storm and darkness, some light from Heaven still falls on this old scene of Christian worship.

Petrie painted two watercolours entitled *The last circuit of the pilgrims at Clonmacnoise c.*1828 and *c.*1842.[106] Although similar in subject matter, the second and larger version is more dramatic and distinguishes Petrie as a romantic artist. There is an element of memorialization of Ireland's past through the monastic ruins and the practice of an ancient rite of pilgrimage, an image that became popular [Fig. 3]. He explained:[107]

> It was my wish to produce an Irish picture, somewhat historical in its object, and poetical in its sentiment – a landscape composed of several of the monuments characteristic of the past history of our country, and which will soon cease to exist, and to connect with them the expression of human feelings equally belonging to our history, and which are destined to a similar extinction.

Petrie's own essays and detailed drawings as opposed to his grander watercolours, along with the efforts of individuals such as the artist George du Noyer (d. 1869)[108] (Fig. 4) and antiquary and artist William Wakeman (d. 1900), who published *Archaeologia Hibernica: a hand-book of Irish antiquities* in 1848,[109] went a long way towards recording the physical remains of early Irish monastic art, architecture and landscapes. Their works became fundamental sources for scholarship in the field to the present.

105 William Stokes, *The life and labours in art and archaeology of George Petrie LL.D.* (London, 1868), p. 17; Murray, *George Petrie*, p. 147 catalogue no. GP.76. **106** Murray, *George Petrie*, pp 20, 32 (colour), 144 catalogue no. GP.59, 151 catalogue no. GP.87. **107** Stokes, *Life and labours*, p. 15; Tom Dunne, 'Towards a national art?' in Murray, *George Petrie*, pp 126–36, at pp 129–30. **108** The collection of George du Noyer's watercolours and drawings preserved in the Royal Society of Antiquaries of Ireland is available at http://rsai.locloudhosting.net/exhibits/show/du-noyer-volumes/about accessed 13 March 2020. **109** William Frederick Wakeman, *Archaeologica Hibernica. A hand-book of Irish antiquities, pagan and Christian, especially of such as are of easy access from the Irish metropolis* (Dublin, 1848).

Catholic historians and Celtic scholars

In parallel with antiquarian scholarship, much was produced in the Irish language during this period which Vincent Morley in his studies of this literature cautions against viewing as irrelevant or as the literature of the lower classes.[110] Scribes sustained a manuscript tradition to the beginning of the twentieth century and while monastic texts were not often present in most manuscripts of the era, occasional unusual items crop up, as in RIA MS 23 O 35 compiled by Brian Ó Fearraghail in the 1770s, which contains an Irish translation of John Colgan's lives of Gille Meic Liac (Gelasius) and of Malachy of Armagh.[111] One of the most influential works in English were the four volumes entitled *An ecclesiastical history of Ireland from the first introduction of Christianity among the Irish, to the beginning of the thirteenth century* (Dublin, 1822–9) written by John Lanigan (d. 1828).[112] Lanigan was trained in Rome and became a professor of Hebrew, Sacred Scriptures and Ecclesiastical History in the University of Pavia until he had to leave in 1796 due the French assault on northern Italy. Returning to Ireland he found it difficult to be assigned to a parish and for a while became an assistant librarian in the Royal Dublin Society. He was a founder member in 1807 of the Cumann Gaelach (Irish Language Society) in Dublin.[113] His history of the Irish church was unashamedly Catholic and aimed to be 'a complete refutation of these slanderers of the Irish character, and villifiers of the ancient religion of the *Island of Saints*'.[114] Lanigan included a lengthy discussion on Irish monasticism and monastic rules,[115] mainly the rules of Columbanus, and during this discourse commented on what had been covered by scholars before him: the nature of Irish rules as opposed to others, especially compatibility with the canons regular, the function of *céli Dé*, and the strictness of Irish monasticism. His views are represented in the following observations:[116]

> The transition [to the rule of the canons regular of St Augustine] was not difficult; for the Old Irish rules did not, in substance, differ much from that of said Canons, inasmuch as they were not as strictly monastical as those of the Egyptian, Basilian, or Benedictine monks, and allowed, without particular dispensation, the union of the active service of the Church, such as practised by the secular clergy, with the observance of monastic regulations, which, although varying more or less, were, as I have often remarked, founded on the system, which St Patrick had seen followed in Lerins and at Tours, and which he introduced into Ireland.

110 Vincent Morley, *Ó Chéitinn go Raiftearaí. Mar a cumadh stair na hÉireann* (Baile Átha Cliath, 2011; athchló, 2017). **111** Mághnus Ó Domhnaill (ed.), *Beatha Gillasius Ardmachanus* (Baile Átha Cliath, 1939); Mághnus Ó Domhnaill (ed.), *Beatha Naoimh Maolmhodhaigh* (Baile Átha Cliath, 1940). **112** https://www.dib.ie/biography/lanigan-john-a4675. **113** Morley, *Ó Chéitinn go Raiftearaí*, pp 240–2. **114** Lanigan, *An ecclesiastical history of Ireland*, vol. 1, p. x; Morley, *Ó Chéitinn go Raiftearaí*, p. 241. **115** Lanigan, *An ecclesiastical history of Ireland*, vol. 4, pp 347–69. **116** Ibid., vol. 4, p. 348.

Lanigan relied on all those who went before him – Colgan, Ware, Ussher – and constantly had in mind those whom he sought to counter, Ledwich in particular. His assured narrative reflected an increasingly confident Catholicism, and although Lanigan was no favourite of the Irish hierarchy, the popularity of his volumes as a definitive history of the medieval Irish church ensured that his influence lasted until John Ryan published his volume on Irish monasticism in 1931.

If George Petrie and others in his circle advanced antiquarianism towards a more scientific investigation of Ireland's antiquities – monuments and material objects – and art history, a corresponding advance developed in relation to the transcription, edition and translation of primary sources. Petrie's colleagues John O'Donovan and Eugene O'Curry were particularly active in producing texts, among them O'Donovan's edition of the seventeenth-century Annals of the Four Masters published between 1848 and 1852.[117] From the mid-nineteenth century an assiduous group of scholars concentrated on transcribing, editing and translating martyrologies, liturgical works, hagiography and other texts crucial to understanding monasticism in early Ireland. Among the most productive of these scholars were Whitley Stokes (d. 1845), James Henthorn Todd (d. 1869), William Reeves (d. 1892) and Charles Plummer.[118] Notably, Stokes, Todd and Reeves belonged to the Church of Ireland, Todd and Reeves being clergymen, and all were educated at Trinity College Dublin. Plummer was also an Anglican and chaplain of Corpus Christi College, Oxford. The establishment of the Henry Bradshaw Society, founded in 1890 to publish editions and facsimiles of rare liturgical texts,[119] provided scholars with a dedicated medium for their publications. The commentaries accompanying these editions advanced the narrative on medieval monasticism to a certain degree, the most notable contribution being William Reeves' extensive work on the Culdees of the 'British

117 Patricia Boyne, *John O'Donovan (1806–1861). A biography* (Kilkenny, 1987); Nollaig Ó Muraíle, 'O'Donovan, John (1806–1861)', *Oxford dictionary of national biography* (Oxford, 2004). Online edition (2008) www.oxforddnb.com/view/article/20561) accessed 27 May 2020; John O'Donovan: https://celt.ucc.ie//odonovan.html accessed 27 May 2020.
118 https://www.dib.ie/biography/stokes-whitley-a8334; https://www.dib.ie/biography/todd-james-henthorn-a8577; https://www.dib.ie/biography/reeves-william-a7612.
119 https://henrybradshawsociety.org/history accessed 27 May 2020. Among the volumes published by the Society were Whitley Stokes (ed.), *Félire Huí Gormáin. The martyrology of Gorman*. Henry Bradshaw Society 9 (London, 1895); John Henry Bernard and Robert Atkinson (eds), *The Irish Liber Hymnorum*. Henry Bradshaw Society 13 and 14 (London, 1898); Whitley Stokes (ed.), *Félire Óengusso Céli Dé. The martyrology of Oengus the Culdee*. Henry Bradshaw Society 29 (London, 1905); George F. Warner (ed.), *The Stowe missal. MS D.II.3 in the library of the Royal Irish Academy*, Dublin. Henry Bradshaw Society 31 and 32 (London, 1906, 1915); Charles Plummer (ed.), *Irish litanies. Text and translation*. Henry Bradshaw Society 62 (London, 1925); Richard Irvine Best and Hugh Jackson Lawlor (eds), *The martyrology of Tallaght: from the Book of Leinster and MS 5100–4 in the Royal Library, Brussels*. Henry Bradshaw Society 68 (London, 1931).

Islands' published in 1864 and in 1873.[120] Reeves (d. 1892) was a distinguished scholar, keeper of early books and manuscripts at Armagh Public Library and Church of Ireland bishop of Down, Connor and Dromore.[121] Despite his ecclesiastical background, he was not confessional in his approach to his sources and maintained a high standard of scholarship throughout his works. In his works Reeves extracted all references to *céli Dé* in Ireland, Scotland, England and Wales from early medieval Patrician texts to seventeenth-century documents. Throughout this study, Reeves makes quite perceptive comments, although dressed in the scholarly language of his time, some that remain to be explored properly. Reeves countered the argument that an order bearing the name *céli Dé* existed pointing to the diverse use of the term in the sources:[122]

> sometimes borne by hermits, sometimes by conventuals; in one situation implying the condition of celibacy, in another understood of married men; here denoting regulars, there seculars; some of the name bound by obligations of poverty, others free to accumulate property; at one period high in honour as implying self-denial, at another regarded with contempt as the designation of the loose and worldly-minded.

Quite correctly, although not easily proven, Reeves wondered if external influences had caused the *céli Dé* movement to flourish during the late eighth and ninth centuries in Ireland. Looking to Chrodegang of Metz's drawing up of a rule for canons and to the Council of Aachen in 817, he comments:[123]

> Possibly the institution of Maelruain may have borrowed from, or possessed some features in common with, the order of canons: for certain it is that in after ages both the Keledei of Scotland and the Colidei of Ireland exhibited in their discipline the main characteristics of secular canons.

In Reeves' estimation, the *céli Dé* of Armagh came into their own during the period of most intense Viking attacks on the settlement (830–914) and functioned as 'the most devoted and self-denying ministers' and 'the officiating attendants of the choir and altar, and in close connexion with whom were the receptacles for the sick and poor'.[124] He noted a similar function of ministering

120 William Reeves, *The culdees of the British Islands, as they appear in history, with an appendix of evidences* (Dublin, 1864); William Reeves, 'On the Céli-Dé, commonly called Culdees', *The Transactions of the Royal Irish Academy* 24 (1873), 119–263. **121** John Thompson, 'William Reeves and the medieval texts and manuscripts at Armagh', *Peritia* 10 (1996), 363–80. **122** Reeves, 'On the Céli-Dé', 120–1. It has to be acknowledged, of course, that Westley Follett has advanced our understanding of the *céli Dé* considerably in his volume *Céli Dé in Ireland.* **123** Reeves, 'On the Céli-Dé', 128. **124** Ibid., 129.

to the poor and sick in Clonmacnoise where the family of Conn na mBocht ('Conn of the poor') operated some form of institution at Ísel Ciaráin, some distance away from the main settlement. In this instance, father and son were successively guardians.[125] Along with many scholars well into the twentieth century – as in the case most obviously of John Ryan's treatise on Irish monasticism – Reeves believed that the church both in Ireland and Scotland was monastic and not episcopal:[126]

> And here I may observe, as the principle which, if borne in mind, will solve many enigmas in the ecclesiastical history of Scotland as well as of Ireland, that the distribution of the country into dioceses and parishes was practically unknown in the Scotic Church till the beginning of the twelfth century. The whole ecclesiastical fabric was constructed on the monastic foundation, and its entire economy regulated by the discipline of conventual life. That this was the system which for ages placed the episcopate in a subordinate position, exalting the office of abbot to the pinnacle of church preferment, and subjecting all other relations to its social weight, until, in the lapse of time, it lost much of its sacred character, and became compatible with a secular life.

In the end, in Reeves' estimation, reform was timely whether promoted by St Malachy of Armagh, Turgot of Durham and St Andrews, King Alexander I or David I of Scotland, and as a consequence, the *céli Dé* in all their guises were marginalized.

For the study of Irish monasticism, one of the most significant milestones since the appearance of John Colgan's *Acta Sanctorum* and *Triadis Thaumaturgæ* was the publication of Charles Plummer's *Vitae sanctorum Hiberniae* and *Bethada náem nÉrenn/Lives of the Irish saints*.[127] Plummer (d. 1927) studied early Irish with Sir John Rhys at Jesus College, Oxford (d. 1915) and the eminent German scholar Heinrich Zimmer (d. 1901).[128] His volumes are comprehensive editions of medieval saints' lives in Latin and Irish, most of them purporting to be the biographies of founders of the most important monasteries around Ireland. Plummer's assessment of the lives remains apposite:[129]

> In their present shape none of them are very ancient. But they contain earlier, sometimes primitive, materials. We have seen in many cases the process of composition going on under our eyes: the conflation of two

125 Ibid., 137–8. See Chapter 9 for a different interpretation of the 'poor' of Clonmacnoise. **126** Ibid., 146. **127** Charles Plummer (ed.), *Vitae sanctorum Hiberniae*. 2 vols (Oxford, 1910; repr. 1968) [hereafter *VSH*]; *Bethada náem nÉrenn. Lives of Irish saints.* 2 vols (Oxford, 1922; repr. 1968) [hereafter *BNnÉ*]. **128** Information from ainm.ie: https://www.ainm.ie/Bio.aspx?ID=2165 accessed 28 May 2020. **129** *VSH*, i, pp lxxxix–xc; for a re-assessment see

> different recensions of the same or closely analogous series of incidents … the 'farcing' of an earlier life with scriptural references and religious commonplaces for purposes of edification … the abbreviation of an earlier life to make it more suitable for use as Lections in Choir or Refectory; the translation of an Irish life into Latin.

Plummer viewed the early Irish church as primarily monastic although 'no doubt many of our saints were also bishops, but they exercised their jurisdiction as abbots, not as bishops'.[130] However, his description of a monastic settlement is closer to a genuine layout than had been advanced by previous scholars. It was not influenced by the Plan of St Gall or the claustral arrangement of medieval monasteries and friaries. The basis of Plummer's understanding was his reading of the primary sources and William Reeves' plan devised from Adomnán's life of Columba:[131]

> Within this [the monastic enclosure] were the common buildings, the church or churches, and oratories, the refectory, and, a little apart from the other buildings, the school. Besides these there were the separate cells. We find a special cell for older monks, for ascetics, for a single anchorite … In many cases the cells would be of the beehive type. We seem to have traces of a body of penitents living apart from the rest of the monks.

As will be evident from a consideration of the monastic landscape in Chapter 8, the archaeological and architectural proof for many of these buildings remains minimal, notably the living quarters, guest houses and refectories.

Many other scholars of the period produced transcriptions, editions and translations of texts relevant to Irish monastic studies. The documents of the so-called 'Tallaght dossier' associated with the *céli Dé* were edited and translated primarily by Edward Gwynn, professor of Celtic Languages and provost of Trinity College Dublin (d. 1941).[132] One of the most prolific contributors to this endeavour was the German celticist Kuno Meyer (d. 1919) who in the copious transcriptions under the title 'Mitteilungen aus irischen Handschriften' published significant ecclesiastical texts in the journal *Zeitschrift für celtische Philologie* between 1910 and 1921.[133] These fragmentary texts, published by Meyer in this series and elsewhere, amount to a Middle Irish dossier of monastic texts sufficient to provide a foundation for the study of early monasticism in

Sharpe, *Medieval Irish saints' lives*. **130** *VSH*, i, pp cxii–cxiii. **131** *VSH*, i, p. cxiii and n. 8 on the same page. **132** Edward J. Gwynn and Walter J. Purton (eds), 'The monastery of Tallaght', *Proceedings of the Royal Irish Academy* 29C (1911–12), 115–79; Edward J. Gwynn (ed.), 'The rule of Tallaght', *Hermathena* 44 (1927) (second supplement; https://www.dib.ie/biography/gwynn-edward-john-a3692. **133** https://www.dib.ie/biography/meyer-kuno-a5810.

Ireland. And yet, despite Meyer's many transcriptions and editions, which are rarely prefaced with any comments on monasticism, his views on the subject – in the context of early Irish poetry – were nothing if not romantic, but were influential:[134]

> Religious poetry ranges from single quatrains to lengthy compositions dealing with all the varied aspects of religious life. Many of them give us a fascinating insight into the peculiar character of the early Irish Church, *which differed in so many ways from the rest of the Christian world* [my italics]. We see the hermit in his lonely cell, the monk at his devotions or at his work of copying in the scriptorium or under the open sky; or we hear the ascetic who, alone or with twelve chosen companions, has left one of the great monasteries in order to live in greater solitude among the woods or mountains, or on a lonely island. The fact that so many of these poems are fathered upon well-known saints emphasises the friendly attitude of the native clergy towards vernacular poetry.

The stylized wilderness of the solitary hermit composing nature poetry while meditating and praying 'under the forest trees … listening to the birds' in 'a hut at the lakeside, or within sight of the sea'[135] gained traction among historians as well as in popular literature, and still does to the present day.[136]

As apparent from the narrative to this point, histories of the monastic tradition in Ireland follow similar patterns to elsewhere and need to be contextualized within the wider culture of monastic scholarship and scrutinized for the contemporary perspectives that impinged upon them. Certain tropes recur throughout the literature especially in works dating from the seventeenth century to the present. Since the *RB* seems to be all but missing from medieval Irish literature, there is an assumption that this was a monastic tradition that diverged from Britain and the Continent from the beginning. But despite this, it is constantly repeated that the Irish had their monastic champion in Columbanus whose monasticism not only rivalled so-called Benedictine monasticism but because of its austerity was a purer form of monasticism. The conclusion by John Ryan (d. 1973) – notably a Jesuit priest and not a monk – to his volume on Irish monasticism published in 1931 encapsulates this idea of competing systems:[137]

134 Kuno Meyer, *Selections from ancient Irish poetry* (London, 1911), p. xii. **135** Kathleen Hughes, *The church in early Irish society* (London, 1966; repr. 1980), p. 185. **136** Robin Flower's works were particularly influential and are still quoted: *The Irish tradition* (Oxford, 1947; repr. Dublin, 1993); https://www.dib.ie/biography/flower-robin-ernest-william-a3302. **137** Ryan, *Irish monasticism*, pp 412–13.

> In conclusion, two points of interest may be noted. The older monastic tradition, abandoned by St Benedict, made its influence felt again in the later centuries, when the Benedictine Rule was supreme upon the Continent. The reforms connected with the names of St Benedict of Aniane and the monks of Cluny are very largely a return to the Irish system, though the combination of learning with austerity as a normal feature of the reformed rule is absent. Secondly, the Irish system was sufficiently strong in organization to survive at home for almost seven centuries. When at last it collapsed and an influx of new religious life had to be sought from abroad, it was not the Benedictine Rule but the more austere Rule of the Cistercians that appealed to the Irish churchmen. Thus the fundamental attachment of Irishmen to their old system continued.

That the Rule of Benedict was the cornerstone of Cistercian monasticism was seemingly lost on John Ryan. The above extract is an extreme version of normalization of the monastic tradition and a somewhat triumphal perspective in tune with John Ryan's own views of Irish history and religion. For example, he joined in the debate triggered by Seán Ó Faoláin's *King of the beggars* (1938), a study of the nineteenth-century Irish politician and lawyer Daniel O'Connell who led the campaign for Catholic Emancipation. Ryan, among others, took issue with Ó Faoláin's theories, including on O'Connell's abandoning the masses in favour of a Catholic middle class. In his response he argued that religion embodied the highest cultural achievement of the Irish people and that it would provide Ireland with a direction for the future. He was particularly keen to demonstrate that Ireland, and especially Catholic Ireland, protected the country from English Puritanism and utilitarianism.[138] While Ryan can be easily criticized for allowing his own opinions on morality and society to influence his history writing – describing the story of Brigit being conferred with episcopal orders as 'absurd' on the basis that 'no semblance of an order corresponding to that of priest or bishop was ever conceded to the female sex'[139] – and for accepting his sources at face value, he was proficient in patristic and Hiberno-Latin sources. It is clear, however, that he drew heavily on certain texts, the various regulations associated with Columbanus (the so-called Rule of Columbanus, the Penitential of Columbanus, the *Regula Coenobialis*), Jonas's life of Columbanus and Adomnán's life of Columba, to depict the details of life within an Irish monastery.[140] This section of Ryan's work, the most extensive part, set Columbanus and Columba's monasticism as the standard for Irish monasticism, and created a dichotomy between the Irish and Benedictine

138 Maurice Earls, 'Lost connections', *Dublin Review of Books* 118 (August 2015), https://www.drb.ie/essays/lost-connections accessed 30 January 2020. 139 Ryan, *Irish monasticism*, pp 183–4. 140 Ibid., pp 193–403.

traditions, and between Celtic and Roman cultures. He comments that 'Owing to the Celtic, as distinct from the imperial, character of Irish civilisation, many small features of monastic life in Ireland have no parallels elsewhere'. This, in his view, explained the prominence of abbots as ecclesiastical rulers, 'a development which arose partly from the popularity of the monastic institute and partly, perhaps, from an ascetical fear of the worldly advantages then commonly attached to the episcopal office in Christian lands'.[141]

At the time Ryan was writing, the Benedictine monk Dom Louis Gougaud (d. 1941) was also contributing to the history of the 'Celtic' churches of Brittany (his native land), Ireland and Wales from the perspective of his own order. He applied a continental approach to historiography believing that the history of the Celtic church and its influence on the Continent could not be written until hundreds of detailed points had been properly interpreted. As a result he published numerous notes on aspects of 'Celtic' ecclesiastical history, including monasticism.[142] In an article listing some of the texts known as Irish monastic rules, Gougaud distinguished between texts that were laws to do with exacting tributes (*cána*) and other texts that dealt with monastic discipline.[143] Although versed in dealing thoroughly with his sources, given his background, he nevertheless maintained that it was a flawed approach (*une idée défectueuse*) to compare the Irish 'rules' with those of the great eastern and Latin traditions. Although they provided incidental details on monastic organization, liturgy and monks' lives, in reality they only consisted of disconnected sentences and exhortations and were quite different from continental rules.[144] Gougaud's greatest contribution to monastic studies in Ireland was his editions of dozens of Latin and vernacular texts, the value of which has remained unexplored in modern scholarship. While he did not focus specifically on monastic practices, the Jesuit, Bollandist and Celtic scholar, Paul Grosjean (d. 1964) adopted a similar approach to Gougaud in producing essential editions of hagiographical texts and hagiographical *exempla* that Plummer had not published in his volumes.

The influence of John Ryan's volume on twentieth-century Irish monastic scholarship can be matched only by Aubrey Gwynn and R. Neville Hadcock's *Medieval religious houses Ireland* [*MRHI*] published in 1970, the third volume of a series directed by the English Benedictine monk David Knowles (d. 1974) on the religious houses of England, Ireland, Scotland and Wales. Aubrey Gwynn (d. 1983), a Jesuit originally from a well-established Church of Ireland family and first professor of medieval history in University College Dublin,[145] also

141 Ibid., pp 408–9. **142** John Hennig, 'The historical work of Louis Gougaud', *Irish Historical Studies* 3 (1942), 180–6. **143** Louis Gougaud, 'Inventaire des règles monastiques irlandaises', *Revue Bénédictine* 25 (1908), 167–84, 321–33; 28 (1911), 86–9. **144** Gougaud, 'Inventaire', 168–9. **145** https://www.dib.ie/biography/gwynn-aubrey-osborn-a3690.

contributed many papers on the subject, concentrating most valuably on the Irish church during the eleventh and twelfth centuries.[146] R. Neville Hadcock (d. 1980), an English historian, primarily of ecclesiastical architecture and a map-maker, was involved in all the religious houses' volumes. Gwynn and Hadcock's introductions to their chapters on 'Early Irish monasteries' and 'The Augustinian Canons' provide an insight into their understanding of medieval monasticism in Ireland.[147] Their focus was on explaining the Irish sources and their reliability but their general observations could be perceptive as in the case of the *céli Dé* who they viewed 'as a minority among the monks of their day … they seem to have lived a separate and austere life of their own, often in the midst of a very much larger community which respected their ideals, but did not share their devotions and austerities'.[148] On the introduction of the Augustinian canons to Ireland, Gwynn and Hadcock included many earlier monasteries in their list of canons' houses, not on the basis of definitive evidence but in the belief that although nothing definite was known of the rule initially followed by Malachy of Armagh, 'it seems probable that he had already decided to endeavour to introduce these recognized orders [Augustinians, ?Benedictines] as the best means of instilling new life into Irish monasticism which was then at its lowest ebb and showing no signs of recovery'.[149] Their précis of Irish monasticism from the twelfth century onwards built assumptions into the historiography of the subject that have been very difficult to alter:[150]

> No authentic records exist of the dates when certain early Irish monasteries became Augustinian, nor for new foundations in that order. Most of these probably belong to the period before the arrival of the Anglo-Normans (1166–72), after which such records are usually to be found. In many cases, such monasteries are presumed to date from after 1140, and the foundation date '+1140' in the following list does not necessarily mean that they became Augustinian during Malachy's lifetime. At several of the early monasteries which became houses of regular canons, coarbs or erenaghs continue to be recorded, the titles having become secular or hereditary, though occasionally assumed by the Augustinian superior in the twelfth century. Some of the Irishmen who became Augustinian may have drifted back to earlier Celtic customs for a time, as seems to have happened among some who became Cistercian. Others would not become Augustinian and adhered to their earlier rules and customs, generally under the name 'Culdees'. Such establishments continued side by side with the Augustinian monasteries at Armagh and

146 Aubrey Gwynn [Gerard O'Brien (ed.)], *The Irish church in the eleventh and twelfth centuries* (Dublin, 1992). **147** *MRHI*, pp 20–7, 146–52. **148** *MRHI*, p. 22. **149** *MRHI*, p. 147. **150** *MRHI*, p. 151. For a critique of the spread of the Augustinian canons in Ireland see Bhreathnach, 'The *Vita Apostolica*'.

> Devenish until the sixteenth century, and probably at Monaincha, Clogher and other places till the thirteenth century or later.

While many scholars have steadfastly clung to this narrative, they have not heeded Gwynn and Hadcock's caveat regarding foundation dates of Augustinian houses – both male and female. The idea that earlier monasteries followed 'Celtic' customs, which was not particularly central to Gwynn and Hadcock's narrative, gained potency in the late twentieth century with the popular promotion of Celtic monasticism and spirituality. This was partly due to the relative absence of dedicated studies of monasticism in early Ireland in the context of wider debates on monasticism in western Christendom, especially between its floruit in the sixth and seventh centuries and its 'reform' in the twelfth century.

A more nuanced approach in modern scholarship

Major questions have been debated since Ryan published his *Irish monasticism*, the most important of which have related to the organization of the early Irish church: the dominance of a monastic and/or episcopal structure, the concept of the 'monastic town', and the archaeology and landscape of ecclesiastical settlements. Late twentieth-century scholarship on the early Irish church was invigorated by the works of Kathleen Hughes (d. 1977), a Cambridge historian who taught and influenced many scholars of the next generation.[151] Her seminal works *The church in early Irish society* and *Early Christian Ireland: introduction to the sources* along with the slim, but inspiring, book *Celtic monasticism. The modern traveller to the early Irish church* co-authored with the archaeologist Ann Hamlin, became essential reading for students of the discipline and remains so in many institutions.[152] In all her publications, Hughes took on the challenge of understanding the many facets of an early Irish monastery, in one instance offering the pithy definition that:[153]

> An Irish monastery was not just a place for the pursuit of the religious life: it was also a city, a place where hospitality was dispensed, a school, a penitentiary. And it had *manaig*, 'monks'.

And she compared the Irish *manaig* – not necessarily 'monks' but 'monastic clients/tenants' – with the tenants of Benedictine monasteries:[154]

151 Rosamund McKitterick, 'Kathleen Winifred Hughes 1926–1977' in Dorothy Whitelock, Rosamund McKitterick and David Dumville (eds), *Ireland in early mediaeval Europe. Studies in memory of Kathleen Hughes* (Cambridge, 1982), pp 1–18, at pp 9–12. **152** Hughes, *The church in early Irish society*; *Early Christian Ireland: introduction to the sources* (London, 1972; repr. 2008); Kathleen Hughes and Ann Hamlin, *Celtic monasticism. The modern traveller to the early Irish church* (New York, 1977; repr. Dublin, 2004). **153** Hughes, *Early Christian Ireland*, p. 93. **154** Ibid., p. 94.

> An Irish monastery was a community following its own independent practices, with abbot, men in higher orders, ascetics and scholars; officials like a steward and a cook. There were also the *manaig*, married laymen without whom it could not have survived in prosperity. The tenants of a Benedictine monastery were outside the monastic family, the *manaig* of an Irish monastery were within it. The rules relate mostly to the ascetics, but the *manaig* must not be forgotten, for they are an essential part of the constitution of the Irish Church.

Hughes's interpretation governed subsequent scholarship on Irish monasticism to a significant extent. For example, the existence of *manaig*, monastic lay clients who belonged to the monastic family and worked as tenants on monastic estates led to later hypotheses regarding a para-monastic community and the existence of monastic towns. Hughes, however, adhered to the given trajectory of a golden age of monastic founders (sixth/seventh centuries), the abuse of power and the ascetic 'revival' (eighth/ninth centuries) partly due to the disruption of the Vikings, another renewal after the battle of Clontarf (1014), and a transmutation influenced by outside forces during the eleventh and twelfth centuries. This narrative is most clearly followed in *The church in early Irish society* and is understandable insofar as she was dealing with the church and its relationship with the wider laity. In her estimation of Irish monastic 'rules', she followed the traditional view:[155]

> Anyone who tries to measure Irish monasticism by the standard of the Benedictine Rule will be impatient and bewildered. Irish monasticism had diverged from the common stock before the Benedictine Rule spread, and it is more enlightening to compare it with the very early monasticism of the desert; its asceticism, variety of practice and absence of clear legislation are all similar.

While Hughes divided her narrative into periods, she, and many others before and after her, presumed that Irish monasticism was more-or-less static until 'reformed' during the eleventh and twelfth centuries. It had no semblance of a central organization and varied in its practices from monastery to monastery or within the *paruchiae* of the greater monastic *familiae*. This was also the view of the Irish church expressed by Denis Bethell in his influential article 'English monks and Irish reform in the eleventh and twelfth centuries' where he argued that English 'conservative' Benedictine monks who came in the late eleventh century to Ireland found there (and in Scotland) 'a Church without organisation, a Church which differed in many ways from their own, and, of course, a social

155 Ibid., p. 90.

context entirely outside their experience.'[156] Nevertheless, Bethell's article is valuable as it provided an overview of Irish monastic contacts with England, especially pre-Norman Benedictine England, imperial Germany and Rome. In his opinion, these contacts were strong because the Irish were attracted to the rather conservative intellectual centres of the Roman Empire and that until 1066 the Irish had been admired in England for their sanctity and learning since Bede's time. In 'pre-Conquest' England, contacts with Ireland, and increasingly with the Norse court in Dublin, were strong, a factor, according to Bethell, that played into the question of the extent of *orbis Britanniae*, the rule of English kings, and the ecclesiastical *imperium* of Canterbury. In the end, the English Benedictine influence and Canterbury's claims to primacy were undermined by Malachy of Armagh's friendship with Bernard of Clairvaux and the Cistercian pope, Eugenius III, and also by King David's move towards creating an independent church in Scotland.[157]

In his reassessment of the early Irish church, Richard Sharpe posed the fundamental question concerning the nature of the institution and its relationship with the laity: 'How monastic was the monastic church, and what was its relationship to the church among the laity?'.[158] The response among scholars to date tends to echo Sharpe's own response: 'It is a mistake to treat monasticism as the be-all and end-all of Irish ecclesiastical organization'.[159] Pastoral care functioned under the jurisdiction of bishops and a secular clergy, although diocesan and parish formation was organized to take account of a kin-based society and the interests of large corporate churches.[160] Colmán Etchingham, for example, treated the issue of monasticism in the context of the role and jurisdiction of the various church officials and their dependents especially bishops, abbots and *manaig*, the latter whom he defined in his considerations of the early Irish church as either lay tenants working on monastic estates or as a 'para-monastic' Christian elite who paid their dues in exchange for pastoral care. While Etchingham acknowledged the need for an extensive discussion of the place of monks following a committed religious life, he summarized their monasticism as living 'under a more-or-less conventional regime of self-mortification – including those withdrawing permanently or temporarily to the solitude of a hermitage – headed by an abbot'.[161] In her

156 Denis Bethell, 'English monks and Irish reform in the eleventh and the twelfth centuries' in T. Desmond Williams (ed.), *Historical Studies VIII* (Dublin, 1971), pp 111–135, at p. 128. 157 Bethell, 'English monks and Irish reform', pp 116–8, 126–8, 134–5. 158 Sharpe, 'The organization of the church in early medieval Ireland'. 159 Ibid., 270. 160 Donnchadh Ó Corráin, 'The early Irish churches: some aspects of organization' in Donnchadh Ó Corráin (ed.), *Irish antiquity. Essays and studies presented to Professor M.J. O'Kelly* (Cork, 1981), pp 327–41; Liam Breatnach, *Córus Bésgnai. An Old Irish law tract on the church and society* (Dublin, 2017). 161 Etchingham, *Church organisation*, pp 363–454; Etchingham, 'The organization and function of an early Irish church settlement: what was Glendalough?' in Doherty et al., *Glendalough. City of God*, pp 22–53, at pp 27–8.

monograph *Isle of the saints. Monastic settlement and Christian community in early Ireland*, Lisa Bitel produced an accessible description of evidence for early monasticism based on Old Irish and Latin sources, concentrating on saints' lives and applying anthropological methodology.[162] No more than other narratives, Bitel's survey did not distinguish between the monasticism of different periods or regions and although she examined various *familiae* of monasteries, the narrative of the period covered – from 800 to 1200 – shows little changing during those 400 years.

An exemplary analysis of the Columban *familia*, which continues to be a model for such studies, is Máire Herbert's *Iona, Kells, and Derry. The history and hagiography of the monastic* familia *of Columba* published in 1988.[163] In her introduction Herbert expressed in precise terms the problems with syntheses and the need for closely focused studies, a statement that should be a cornerstone of monastic studies in Ireland. Discussing the problem of the existence of *paruchiae*, Herbert comments:[164]

> There have been, perhaps, too many attempts at synthesis, and too few close studies of particular aspects of the Irish ecclesiastical scene. Thus there has been, on the one hand, a tendency to generalize from the Columban model, and to assign monastic *paruchiae* to other sixth-century Irish saints, while a contrary view is sceptical about the existence of any such structure. Neither view draws on a full range of available sources. The present account of the Columban *familia* is deliberately limited in scope, and does not profess to arrive at any conclusions regarding the nature of Irish monastic organization. It does, however, suggest an approach to the evidence which, in time, should place future works of synthesis on a firmer footing.

Since the publication of Herbert's monograph, Clonmacnoise and Glendalough have been the subject of 'closely focused' studies in monographs by Annette Kehnel and Ailbhe Mac Shamhráin, and in collected essays.[165] Other larger monasteries, most particularly Armagh, have been investigated in some considerable detail but in disparate studies, while others, especially Kildare, await serious analysis.

162 Lisa M. Bitel, *Isle of the saints. Monastic settlement and Christian community in early Ireland* (Ithaca and London, 1990). **163** Máire Herbert, *Iona, Kells, and Derry. The history and hagiography of the monastic* familia *of Columba* (Oxford, 1988; repr. Dublin, 2002). **164** Herbert, *Iona, Kells, and Derry*, p. 5. **165** Annette Kehnel, *Clonmacnois. The church and lands of St Ciarán: change and continuity in an Irish monastic foundation (6th to 16th century)*. Vita regularis 8 (Münster, 1997); Ailbhe Mac Shamhráin, *Church and polity in pre-Norman Ireland. The case of Glendalough* (Maynooth, 1996); Charles Doherty, Linda Doran and Mary Kelly (eds), *Glendalough. City of God* (Dublin, 2011). Ailbhe Mac Shamhráin, Aidan Breen and Nora White also created the Dublin Institute for Advanced Studies (Celtic Studies)

A number of significant textual and period-based studies have advanced aspects of Irish monasticism considerably in recent decades and have introduced scholars elsewhere to the subject beyond Ryan and Gwynn and Hadcock. While Peter O'Dwyer in his study of the *céli Dé*, *Céli Dé. Spiritual reform in Ireland 750–900*, adheres to the view that this was a reform movement 'to counterbalance a tendency towards laxity in the older churches'[166] and the introduction of lay abbacy, nevertheless, his volume is a reliable summary of the *céli Dé* texts and of the available historical evidence for the individuals involved. Westley Follett's *Céli Dé in Ireland. Monastic writing and identity in the early Middle Ages* is a comprehensive reassessment of the historiography and textual tradition of the *céli Dé* in Ireland.[167] In searching for particular *céli Dé* attributes, Follett identifies concern for pastoral care, penance, liturgy and devotion, and asceticism as integral features of their identity. Rather than being a reform movement, an attribute so often associated with them, he argues that their strict observance involved 'a desire for a more personal, spiritually committed relationship with Deity [*sic*], such as implied by their name for one another, *céle Dé*, a 'client of God'.[168] Of greatest significance for the period under consideration in this volume are the works of Marie Therese Flanagan and in particular her monographs, *Irish royal charters. Texts and contexts* and *The transformation of the Irish church in the twelfth century*.[169] Both volumes have lifted debates around the pre-Norman and indeed early Norman church in Ireland out of their introverted conversations. Through the lens of new editions of texts such as the twelfth-century charters of Irish kings in which they endowed the foundations of the new continental orders along with a reappraisal of the Irish church as it restructured itself during the twelfth century, Flanagan has positioned issues about monasticism of the period firmly within western Christendom.

The study of female monasticism in medieval Ireland in its own right has only gradually become part of the wider subject in the last two decades. St Brigit's preeminence has until recently eclipsed other saints and the nature of female monasticism with the assumption that her foundation at Kildare was a double monastery under episcopal control that survived until the twelfth century.[170] That Kildare was unique has not been sufficiently emphasized in the secondary literature, and as a result the fate of the hundreds of smaller churches dedicated to female saints, most of them local family foundations that probably never developed into monastic communities, has been neglected. In recent years, however, in line with explorations of female monasticism elsewhere, a number of key volumes and articles have appeared. The most substantial work on women

Monasticon Hibernicum database (https://monasticon.celt.dias.ie/). **166** O'Dwyer, *Céli Dé*, p. 192. **167** Follett, *Céli Dé in Ireland*. **168** Ibid., p. 214. **169** Flanagan, *Irish royal charters*; Flanagan, *Transformation*. **170** An extensive literature on St Brigit exists (see *CLH* i, pp 274–9).

in the early Irish church is Christina Harrington's *Women in a Celtic church. Ireland, 450–1150*.[171] Harrington used a wide array of sources for her analysis of all forms of women religious, although her definition of such women is too broad and the power that is ascribed to them somewhat overstated. Instead of addressing her subject in a chronological sweep, she divided her study into historically cogent periods: the conversion period, fifth to sixth centuries; the seventh to ninth centuries; and the tenth to twelfth centuries. The main focus of her study was to prove that Irish women played a more powerful role in the church than their counterparts in western Christendom. A secondary theme throughout her volume involves a challenge to 'modern Celtic Christians', the women's or feminist spirituality movement, neo-pagan, modern druids, whose interpretations of the sources Harrington largely blames on academics' failure to communicate scholarly interpretations to a wider public.[172] This discourse drew the ire of these communities as well of feminist historians and Irish academics who regarded her readings of the sources as naive and inaccurate.[173] Many of the topics covered by Harrington are mentioned in this present volume, some of them hopefully enhanced with the advancement of scholarship over the past two decades. While primarily dealing with the late medieval period, Dianne Hall's pioneering book *Women and the church in medieval Ireland,* c.*1140–1540* assembled surviving sources relevant to nunneries and women's piety and patronage.[174] As with male monasticism in medieval Ireland, Hall – along with many other scholars – has little to say about early female communities, regarding the twelfth century as a watershed for women's monasticism in Ireland, as in other parts of medieval Europe: 'Irish women seem to have entered the newly established convents enthusiastically in these heady days of reform'.[175] Studies of saints other than Brigit have expanded our understanding of female sanctity and tackled the ever-present question as to the historicity of these women and their possible mythological origins. The nature of St Íte of Killeedy, Co. Limerick, the *matrona* of her people, who nurtured the infant Jesus on her breast, has been considered by Dorothy Ann Bray and Elva Johnson.[176] Johnson demonstrated that Íte's is a highly gendered traditional image of mother and more commonly foster-mother. Her depiction as a *matrona* may be a deliberate borrowing from a late Roman meaning of the term, that of an unmarried Christian virgin, who cared for and protected her people. The contextualization

171 Harrington, *Women in a Celtic church*. 172 Ibid., pp 9–16. 173 Lisa Bitel, Review of Harrington, *Women in a Celtic church*, *The Catholic Historical Review* 89:4 (2003), 749–51; Catherine Swift, Review of Harrington, *Women in a Celtic church*, *Irish Economic and Social History* 30 (2003), 128–9. 174 Dianne Hall, *Women and the church in medieval Ireland,* c.*1140–1540* (Dublin, 2003; repr. 2008). 175 Ibid., p. 68. 176 Dorothy Ann Bray, '*Secunda Brigida*: Saint Ita of Killeedy and Brigidine tradition', *North American Congress of Celtic Studies* 2 (1992), 27–38; Elva Johnson, 'Íte: patron of her people', *Peritia* 14 (2000), 421–8.

of the hagiography of Irish female saints outside the long-standing scholarly tradition of mythologizing them into Celtic deities is an important step which has enabled comparative studies with female saints elsewhere. In the absence of standard sources, comparative and precise studies can open up new avenues. This is evident in the essays on women listed in early Irish martyrologies and in comparing the characteristics of Brigit and Íte with late antique eastern saints such as St Macrina published in the edited survey *Brides of Christ. Woman and monasticism in medieval and early modern Ireland*.[177] In placing Brigit and Íte in their late antique context, Catherine Swift argues that female religious in early Ireland were integral to the pastoral activities within their local territories under the authority of a bishop, 'providing material support and sustenance, rearing the young, supporting the abandoned, looking after the sick and caring for the old'. She contends that the strongest parallels for this form of religious female life are with 'the more egalitarian and more socially engaged Cappadocian communities of St Macrina'.[178] Swift's comparison proposes a realistic model for early female monasticism in Ireland, one that calls for further investigation. Cross-disciplinary interaction has taken a long time to emerge in medieval Irish scholarship. Chasms between the various disciplines of archaeology, history and language persist to the detriment of the wider subject. The value of such work is evident in Tracy Collins' volume *Female monasticism in medieval Ireland. An archaeology* where the author seeks to find ways into the subject through the surviving architecture and archaeology of female houses, particularly during the late medieval period.[179] This volume is valuable as Collins has catalogued and considered all the archaeological data currently available on female monasticism, a new departure that lays out a fresh landscape for the study of women religious in medieval Ireland. However, as with many studies of this subject, Collins probably overestimates the number of these communities and their archaeological and architectural imprint on the medieval Irish landscape.

Until the 1980s landscape and settlement studies in Ireland promoted ideals of rural pastoralism and tribal nomadism coined in the clichéd definition of the great expert in early Irish law, Daniel A. Binchy that Irish society was 'tribal, rural, hierarchical, and familiar (using this word in its oldest sense, to mean a society in which the family, not the individual, is the unit)'.[180] To be fair to Binchy, his view reflected the common approach of scholars to Ireland: it was

177 Elva Johnson, 'Locating female saints and their foundations in the early medieval Irish martyrologies' in Browne et al., *Brides of Christ*, pp 22–36. 178 Catherine Swift, 'Soul sisters: two Irish holy women in their late antique context' in Browne et al., *Brides of Christ*, pp 37–55, at p. 55. 179 Collins, *Female monasticism in medieval Ireland*. 180 Daniel A. Binchy, 'Secular institutions' in Myles Dillon (ed.) *Early Irish society* (Dublin, 1954), pp 52–65, at p. 54; https://www.dib.ie/biography/binchy-daniel-anthony-a0659.

uninfluenced by Roman urbanization and genuine nucleated settlements only appeared in Ireland with the growth of the Norse coastal towns:[181]

> ... the idea of a town, with a corporate personality distinct from that of the ruler, was quite foreign to the Gaelic mind until the Scandinavians set up their 'cities' in Dublin, Limerick, Waterford, and elsewhere.

The significance of Viking settlements and their development into urban centres became increasingly clear from the large-scale excavations undertaken from the 1960s onwards, firstly in Dublin and subsequently in Waterford and Wexford.[182] But what of the rest of Ireland? Were there no nucleated settlements or trading centres of any note prior to the coming of the Vikings, or developing in parallel to the Norse towns? During the 1980s, Charles Doherty, in ground-breaking studies,[183] proposed the model of the 'monastic town' that was the nucleus of exchange and trade with the growing Norse towns from the tenth century onwards. He argued that 'with the increase of population, the growth of trade, and the growth of administrative authority, we can detect the emergence of a primitive medieval state'.[184] Since he published his proposed model, Doherty's thesis has been the focus of much controversy, mainly arising out of its compatibility with the international definition of cities and towns. Scholars of medieval urbanization have contended that the Irish 'monastic town' does not meet many of the criteria required to be defined as a town (e.g. founding charters, permanent royal residences).[185] Most commentators, however, accept that the Irish interpreted the terms *civitas* and its Irish equivalent *cathair* as sacred loci and in many instances as the equivalent of the celestial city or the 'city of God'.[186] It cannot be denied that the larger monasteries in Ireland – Armagh,

181 Daniel A. Binchy, 'The passing of the old order' in Brian Ó Cuív (ed.), *Proceedings of the International Congress of Celtic Studies held in Dublin, 6–10 July, 1959* (Dublin, 1962), pp 119–32, at p. 122. 182 For comprehensive surveys of the Dublin excavations, see Linzi Simpson, 'Forty years a-digging: a preliminary synthesis of archaeological investigations in medieval Dublin' in Seán Duffy (ed.), *Medieval Dublin I* (Dublin, 2000), pp 11–68; 'Fifty years a-digging: a synthesis of medieval and archaeological excavations in Dublin city and suburbs' in Seán Duffy (ed.), *Medieval Dublin XI* (Dublin, 2011), pp 9–112. 183 Doherty, 'Exchange and trade'; 'The monastic town in Ireland'. 184 Ibid., 85. 185 An extensive literature exists on the subject. Here I cite some of the most important publications: Mary Valente, 'Reassessing the Irish "monastic town"', *Irish Historical Studies* 31 (1998), 1–18; John Bradley, 'Toward a definition of the Irish monastic town' in Catherine E. Karkov and Helen Damico (eds), *Aedificia nova. Studies in honor of Rosemary Cramp* (Kalamazoo, 2008), pp 325–60; Colmán Etchingham, 'The Irish "monastic town": is this a valid concept?', *Kathleen Hughes memorial Lectures* 8 (Cambridge, 2010); Howard B. Clarke, 'Quo vadis? Mapping the Irish "monastic town"' in Seán Duffy (ed.), *Princes, prelates and poets in medieval Ireland. Essays in honour of Katharine Simms* (Dublin, 2013), pp 261–78; Melanie C. Maddox, 'Re-conceptualizing the Irish monastic town', *Journal of the Royal Society of Antiquaries of Ireland* 146 (2016), 21–32. 186 Maddox, 'Re-conceptualizing the Irish monastic town'.

Clonmacnoise, Derry, Glendalough, Kells and Kildare being the most prominent – were significant settlements whose core and estates were populated by a myriad of inhabitants with many skills. Although culturally distinct and much smaller and less wealthy, the function of Irish monasteries for their inhabitants, at the heart of their settlements and in their dispersed estates, was in many ways similar to their great continental counterparts in that they provided leadership, and material and spiritual guidance in return for economic supplies and the products of other skills, both artisan and intellectual. In the context of this volume, the spiritual element of these settlements is paramount.

CHAPTER 2

Reading the primary sources for Irish monasticism: Part I: pre-900 sources

The long-established narrative of monasticism in western Christendom that focused primarily on its normalization around the Rule of Benedict especially from the ninth century onwards, and that viewed other forms of monasticism as 'undisciplined and bizarre anarchy'[1] has been set aside to a certain extent in recent years.[2] This re-evaluation that has evolved elsewhere, however, has not had the same corrective impact on monastic studies in Ireland. One important reason for regarding the Irish monastic tradition as distinct lies in the relative uniqueness of the Irish sources. As they deviate from 'standard' monastic sources, it might be concluded that they reflect a distinctive form of monasticism or are so impenetrable as to render many of them useless. The relative absence of administrative documents (charters, chartularies), liturgical books (missals, antiphonaries etc.), and legislative documents (normalized rules and customaries) in Latin until the twelfth century demands a different approach to the subject. This is compounded by the existence of so much material in the vernacular, often fragmentary and disparate, but clearly emanating from a monastic or other religious milieu. These sources have never been regarded by scholars as a coherent corpus. In addition, since the seventeenth century some texts have been judged to be so fictitious that they hardly rank as historical sources. The lives of many Irish saints fall into this category, criticized as wholly unreliable by Counter-Reformation hagiographers and as folklore in later centuries. The greatest difficulty, however, with the Irish hagiographical tradition, both Irish and Latin lives, lies in tackling the myriad of recensions, the modus operandi of authors and compilers, and the potential dating of each recension. Richard Sharpe's extensive study of the hagiographical manuscript collections advanced the subject by using modern methodology, but as he himself admitted there is more to be accomplished.[3] And not least is the examination of what type of monasticism, if any, the lives reveal.

If the considerable corpus of texts produced during the early medieval period is to yield a fresh appraisal of Irish monasticism, the various categories of sources

1 Felice Lifshitz, 'The historiography of central medieval western monasticism' in *CHMM*, pp 365–81. 2 Vanderputten, *Medieval monasticisms*; Kristjánsdóttir, *Medieval monasticism in northern Europe*. 3 Sharpe, *Medieval Irish saints' lives*.

need to be identified and surveyed as to their value for understanding monastic life. Reading the sources is not a one-dimensional task involving the search for historical 'facts', an approach that has limited their use to date. The sources offer a difficult but rewarding repository for comprehending Irish views on the place of monks in society, monastic community formation, sanctity, poverty, human emotions and many other elements of monasticism. Drawing on all the sources available to establish a holistic study of the topic is also likely to provide a more intimate appreciation of lives regulated by a monastic *cursus*. This chapter and the next introduce a select sample of texts and material objects and aim to show how contrasting sources can be exploited to understand the monastic tradition in Ireland from around AD 900 onwards.[4] This current chapter deals with a number of sources in Irish and Latin dating from the seventh to the tenth century that summarize the essential characteristics of the foundations of Irish monasticism. Chapter 3 moves to the tenth century and later with a view not only to provide a synthesis of the types of sources available but also to trace changes, or otherwise, during this formative period in monasticism throughout western Christendom.

THE INHERITED MONASTIC TRADITION: EARLY SOURCES

Monasticism arrived in Ireland as part of the conversion process. Its origins are obscure although it is most likely that contacts with western Britain and with western Gaul, reflected in the archaeological record,[5] brought various monastic traditions into the country. Patrick alludes to monasticism being part of his mission in the fifth century:[6]

> How has this happened in Ireland? Never before did they know of God except to serve idols and unclean things. But now, they have become the people of the Lord, and are called children of God. The sons and daughters of the leaders of the Irish are seen to be monks and virgins of Christ!

4 The most comprehensive introductory guides to ecclesiastical Irish sources in Irish and Latin are James F. Kenney, *The sources for the early history of Ireland. An introduction and guide* vol. 1 (New York, 1929; repr. Dublin, 1993) and Donnchadh Ó Corráin, *Clavis litterarum Hibernensium. Medieval Irish books and texts (*c.*400–*c.*1600)*, 3 vols (Turnhout, 2017) [*CLH*]. 5 Ian W. Doyle, 'Mediterranean and Frankish pottery imports in early medieval Ireland', *The Journal of Irish Archaeology* 18 (2009), 17–62; Doyle, 'Early medieval E ware pottery: an unassuming but enigmatic kitchen ware?' in Bernice Kelly, Niall Roycroft and Michael Stanley (eds), *Fragments of lives past. Archaeological objects from Irish road schemes* (Dublin, 2014), pp 81–93. 6 Bieler, *Libri epistolarum sancti Patricii episcopi*, p. 81, §41. See also www.confessio.ie. Original: *Unde autem Hiberione qui numquam notitiam Dei habuerunt nisi idola et inmunda usque nunc semper coluerunt quomodo nuper facta est plebs Domini et filii Dei*

It appears that monastic life was so attractive to the Irish in the first centuries of conversion that it became a problem. Writing to Pope Gregory the Great *c.*AD 600, Columbanus of Luxeuil and Bobbio (d. 615)[7] noted that a certain Uinniau *auctor*, possibly a Briton working as a missionary in Ireland and sometimes identified as Finnian of Moville (d. 579) or Finnian of Clonard,[8] had consulted Gildas (d. *c.*570) author of *De excidio et conquestu Britanniae*[9] on the problems resulting from this explosion of monastic life.[10] By the late sixth and early seventh century, the issue had become more pressing as Columbanus asked Gregory:[11]

> In the third part of my inquiry, please tell me now, if it is not troublesome, what is to be done about those monks who, for the sake of God, and inflamed by the desire for a more perfect life, impugn their vows, leave the places of their first profession, and against their abbots' will, impelled by monastic fervour, either relapse or flee to the deserts. Uinniau the writer questioned Gildas about them, and he sent a most polished reply; but yet, through the zeal for learning, anxiety grows ever greater.

This fervent monastic movement led to the establishment of many communities of various sizes and structures in Ireland during the conversion period, often led by charismatic founders whose legacies lasted well into the medieval period. Among the most renowned were Comgall of Bangor, Columba of Iona, Ciarán of Clonmacnoise, Cóemgen of Glendalough and Brigit of Kildare.[12] As demonstrated by recent generations of scholars, the overwhelmingly monastic nature of early sources led to the incorrect belief that monasticism dominated the Irish church and hence hindered the development of episcopal governance. Both existed and were often integrated insofar as many of the larger monasteries – often classified as *civitates* – became important

nuncupantur, filii Scottorum et filiae regulorum monachi et uirgines Christi esse uidentur? **7** https://www.dib.ie/biography/columbanus-colman-columba-a1891. **8** *DIS*, pp 318–24. **9** https://www.dib.ie/biography/gildas-a3471. **10** David N. Dumville, 'The origins and early history of insular monasticism: aspects of literature, christianity, and society in Britain and Ireland, AD 400–600', *Kansai Institutional Repository* 30 (1997), A85–A107, at p. 100. https://www.kansai-u.ac.jp/Tozaiken/publication/asset/bulletin/30/85david.pdf (accessed 10 January 2023). **11** G.S.M. Walker (ed), *Sancti Columbani Opera*. Scriptores Latini Hiberniae 2 (Dublin, 1957; repr. 1970), Letter 1, p. 9, para. 7. Original (following Dumville, 'Insular monasticism'): *Tertio interrogationis loco responde adhuc, quaeso, si non molestum est, quid faciendum est de monachis illis qui pro Dei intuitu et uitae perfectioris desiderio accensi, contra uota uenientes primae conuersionis loca relinquunt et inuitis abbatibus, feruore monachorum cogente, aut laxantur aut ad deserta fugiunt. Uennianus auctor Gildam de his interrogauit, et elegantissime ille rescripsit; sed tamen discendi studio semper maior metus accrescit.* **12** On the earliest phase of monasticism in Ireland, see Dumville, 'Origins and early history of insular monasticism'; T.M. Charles-Edwards, *Early Christian Ireland* (Cambridge, 2000), pp 223–6, 250–64; Marilyn Dunn, *The emergence of monasticism. From the Desert Fathers to the early Middle Ages*

population centres where bishops, abbots, kings and religious communities were active. Many monastic communities, especially female foundations, did not survive beyond the founding generation, and their churches reverted to the founder's kin to serve as local churches or were annexed by larger monasteries.

Monasticism is alluded to in Irish canons, penitentials and early laws, all of which date mainly to a period between the seventh and ninth centuries. A constant obstacle to separating what constituted monasticism in the strict sense, communities or individuals subject to a monastic vow and following a coenobitic or eremitic lifestyle, from the rest of the church, clergy and laity, lies in the practice of the Irish blurring the distinction between the two in their use of terminology. Hence, as previously noted, a *manach* could refer to a monk dedicated to a committed religious life, but more often than not described a lay tenant living on ecclesiastical lands. Yet, there is sufficient material in these early texts to prove the existence of a living monastic tradition in Ireland in the period being considered in this volume. In his study of church organization between AD 650 and 1000, Colmán Etchingham sketches out the likely monastic model followed in Ireland during that period.[13] Essentially monasticism was coenobitic, an abbot and his monks living in a community being the most acceptable form of committed religious life. Some were priests and it appears likely that bishops were often members of monastic communities. Anchorites who were in some way attached to monasteries and regulated were highly regarded in society, while the self-appointed holy man was viewed unfavourably. It was common for monks from a coenobitic community to withdraw temporarily to seclusion, often not far from their monastery. The opposite also occurred when an anchorite could be called upon to assume another ecclesiastical office such as becoming a bishop. One of the most renowned examples of this practice was Brigit's calling of the anchorite Conláed to become her bishop at Kildare.[14] The perennial issue of the extent to which monks and anchorites involved themselves in manual labour and pastoral care surfaces in the early texts. Opinions differed on how the monastic day was structured: it could be divided between prayer, labour and study (*airnaigthe 7 liubair 7 légund*),[15] be even more exclusively contemplative and depend on others for their subsistence, or involve more active labour, either working the land or practising crafts. While participation in active labour may have been undertaken to a greater degree by *manaig* who were lay tenants, archaeological evidence suggests that high-level crafts such as metal-working and sculpture were practised fairly close to the centre of ecclesiastical settlements. Examples of such activity have been discovered at, among other

(Malden, Oxford and Victoria, 2000; repr. 2007), pp 142–57. 13 Etchingham, *Church organisation*, pp 319–62. 14 Seán Connolly and Jean-Michel Picard, 'Cogitosus's *Life of St Brigit*: content and value', *Journal of the Royal Society of Antiquaries of Ireland* 117 (1987), 5–27, at p. 11 §5; Etchingham, *Church organisation*, p. 336. 15 Etchingham, *Church organisation*, p. 346 from Meyer, '*Regula Choluimb Chille*', 29 §16.

sites, Iona, Inis Cealtra on the Shannon,[16] Clonmacnoise,[17] and Clonfeacle, Co. Armagh.[18] A constant, and universal, issue for monks and the church in general concerned the extent to which they were involved in pastoral care among the laity (*cura animarum*). Ireland was no exception in that early canonical and legal texts, and especially the 'Tallaght dossier' compiled during the eighth and ninth centuries by the *céli Dé*, continually stressed the responsibilities of the church, including monks, for the salvation of the laity.[19]

THE MONASTIC TRADITION IN IRISH CANON LAW

The key to understanding the type of monasticism prevalent in Ireland before the tenth century lies in the terminology used to describe various monastic offices and the legal status and obligations accorded to those holding such offices. Legal canons and synods regulate the behaviour of those living a committed religious lifestyle. One of the earliest texts, the *Sinodus episcoporum Patricii Auxilii Issernini*, attributed to Patrick and two other pioneering missionaries in Ireland, warns that:[20]

> A monk (*monachus*) and a nun (*uirgo*), he from here and she from elsewhere, shall not stay together in one guesthouse, nor shall they travel about in one carriage from settlement to settlement, nor shall they engage eagerly in conversation together.

One chapter of the *Collectio canonum Hibernensis* (hereafter *Hibernensis*), a collection of Irish canons probably compiled during the first half of the eighth century,[21] deals specifically with monks (*De monachis*).[22] This is not a monastic rule but is a set of legislative canons drawn from fundamental biblical texts, commentaries, church fathers, rules and synods. Apart from quotations from the New Testament, the authors quoted include Augustine, Isidore of Seville, Jerome, John Cassian, St Patrick, Gildas and Gregory the Great, none particularly unusual in the literature of early canon law. The synods quoted include Irish synods,[23] the fourth- to sixth-century synods of Arles, Nicaea,

16 https://excavations.ie/report/1970/Clare/0000004/ accessed 9 July 2020. **17** https://excavations.ie/report/1996/Offaly/0002455/ accessed 9 July 2020. **18** https://excavations.ie/report/2006/Armagh/0014871/ accessed 9 July 2020; Chris Long, 'Clonfeacle, an early monastic site', *Seanchas Ard Mhacha* 20:2 (2005), 23–33. **19** Follett, *Céli Dé in Ireland*, pp 191–9. **20** David N. Dumville, *Councils and synods of the Gaelic early and central Middle Ages*. Quiggin Pamphlets on the Sources of Mediaeval Gaelic History 3 (Cambridge, 1997), pp 8–9 §7(9). Original: *Monachus et uirgo, unus abhinc et alia ab aliunde, in uno hospitio non conmaneant nec in uno curru a uilla in uillam discurr(e)ant nec adsidue inuicem confabulationem exerceant.* **21** Roy Flechner, *The Hibernensis. A study and edition*. 2 vols. Book 1 (Washington, 2019), pp 59–61. **22** Ibid., Books 1 and 2 §38. **23** The *Hibernensis* suggests that synods were a regular

Chalcedon, Agde and Orléans. The crucial section on the different categories of *monachi* (*De uariis generibus monachorum*)[24] does not deviate from the standard classifications of the early church. Isidore of Seville is quoted as enumerating six kinds of *monachi*: coenobites (monks living in a community); hermits; trained anchorites; independent, arrogant anchorites; wanderers (*circumcilliones*), and sarabaites (recluses who lived together in small communities who were accused of being lax in their lifestyle). Jerome is cited as describing four kinds of monk: hermits, coenobites, vagabonds and sarabaites, which tallies with the classification of monks in *RB*. Notably, *RB* is mentioned in the *Hibernensis* under the annotation 'Jerome says in his letter to Benedict' (*Hironimus in epistola ad Benedictum dicit*) suggesting either that the original Irish compilers were aware of some form of *RB*, or that this passage was added to the text on the Continent at a later stage.[25] It is clear from all authorities, including the authors of the *Hibernensis*, that the coenobite was the most worthy kind of monk who 'soldiers under a rule and an abbot' (*Reuertamur ad optimum genus quod militans sub regula et abate*). It is also evident from the *Hibernensis* that no one rule prevailed – a situation that was also the case elsewhere[26] – but certain universal norms were stipulated. Stability was a priority, no monk should be without an abbot and monks were not to migrate from one community to another without their abbot's permission, unless they were seeking to adhere to a stricter way of life or fleeing a wicked *princeps*.[27] The good *princeps*, an abbot or a bishop, is glowingly presented in the words of a Hibernian synod:[28]

> Every *princeps* ought to be earth for nourishing, a leader for reforming, an anchor for stabilizing, a hammer for striking, tongs for holding, a sun for illuminating, dew for making moist, a slate for writing, a book for reading, a mirror for reflecting, dread for terrifying. His image should be seen in all good things, so that he might be all things to all things.

Wendy Davies rightly compares this description with the portrayal of the righteous king in the seventh-century Irish text *De duodecim abusivis saeculi* 'On the twelve abuses of the world'.[29]

occurrence in Ireland but very few of their enactments survive. See Dumville, *Councils and synods of the Gaelic early and central Middle Ages.* **24** Flechner, *Hibernensis*, Books 1 and 2 §38.3. **25** See Flechner, *Hibernensis*, Book 2, p. 871 nn 375–6 in which he surmises that the *RB* 'might have been known in Ireland in one form or another'. **26** Dáibhí Ó Cróinín, 'A tale of two rules: Benedict and Columbanus' in Browne and Ó Clabaigh, *The Irish Benedictines*, pp 11–24, at p. 19. **27** Flechner, *Hibernensis*, §§38.4–6, 38.9–13, 38.15–16. **28** Ibid., §36.3. Original: *Oportet omnem principem, ut terra sit ad sustinendum, gubernator sit ad corrigendum, anchora sit ad sustendandum, malleus sit ad percutiendum, forceps sit ad tenendum, sol sit ad inluminandum, ros sit ad madeficandum, pugillarius ad scribendum, liber sit ad legendum, speculum sit ad conspiciendum, terror sit ad terrendum, imago sit in omnibus bonis, ut sit omnia in omnibus.* **29** Wendy E. Davies, 'Clerics as rulers: some implications of the terminology of

Throughout the *Hibernensis*, the bishop is the leading authority in the church with power over monasteries. No one could build or found a new monastery without a bishop's approval or command.[30] And following a prohibition from the Council of Orléans (AD 511), no monk could build a cell without the abbot's permission, lest he be driven by ambition or vanity.[31] Monasteries being governed by bishops were a contentious issue in the early church with the Council of Chaledon (AD 451) subjecting monks to episcopal authority on the basis that otherwise they created disorder and needed to be reined in.[32] The distinction between the contemplative (*theorica*) and active (*actualis*) life surfaces, as it does in relation to monasticism universally. Quoting Jerome, the *Hibernensis* defines the church as consisting of three ways of life only – the contemplative, the active and the penitential.[33] The necessity to have a church including contemplative religious was transferred over to the vernacular laws: among the attributes ennobling a church were 'the shrine of a righteous man, the relics of saints, divine scripture, a sinless superior, devout monks'.[34] A debased church was without either a contemplative or an active life, and in one of the rare references to women, it was a church in which a veiled woman summoned people to celebrate the canonical hours.[35]

THE MONASTIC TRADITION IN IRISH VERNACULAR LAW

The truly extensive corpus of early vernacular Irish laws deals with a vast array of legal issues concerning the kin-group, status, clientship, the professional classes – including those in the church – land ownership and inheritance, property, marriage, fosterage, offences, contracts and legal procedure.[36] The fluidity between ecclesiastical canons and the vernacular laws was identified by

ecclesiastical authority in early medieval Ireland' in Nicholas P. Brooks (ed.), *Latin and the vernacular languages in early medieval Britain* (Leicester, 1982), pp 81–97, at pp 84–5. 30 Flechner, *Hibernensis*, §42.1. 31 Ibid., §42.4. 32 Anne-Marie Helvétius et al., 'Re-reading monastic traditions: monks and nuns, east and west, from the origins to *c.*750' in *CHMM*, pp 40–72, at pp 51–2. 33 Flechner, *Hibernensis*, §41.1. 34 Liam Breatnach, 'The first third of *Bretha Nemed Toísech*', *Ériu* 40 (1989), 1–40, at pp 8–9(3): *martarlaic firéoin, reilgi nóeb, scriptuir déodae, airchinnech etail, manaig cráibthig*; Folett, *Céli Dé in Ireland*, p. 79. 35 Breatnach, 'The first third', 10–11(6). Original: *cen achtáil, cen teoir … caillech do fhócru a tráth.* See Folett, *Céli Dé in Ireland*, p. 79 n. 277 on the interpretation of *caillech*. 36 Daniel A. Binchy (ed.), *Corpus iuris Hibernici* 6 vols (Dublin, 1978); Fergus Kelly, *A guide to early Irish law* (Dublin, 1988); Neil McLeod, *Early Irish contract law* (Sydney, 1992); Thomas Charles-Edwards, *Early Irish and Welsh kinship* (Oxford, 1993); Liam Breatnach, *A companion to the Corpus iuris Hibernici* (Dublin, 2005); Robin Chapman Stacey, *Dark speech. The performance of law in early Ireland* (Philadelphia, 2007). An extensive corpus of secondary literature relating to early Irish law, much of it published in the past three decades, delves into this magnificent resource. See the bibliographies https://www.vanhamel.nl/codecs and https://bill.celt.dias.ie/.

scholars during the 1980s.[37] They demonstrated that the professional classes, poets, for example, created a hierarchy of seven grades of their own to mirror the seven grades of the ecclesiastical orders.[38] No more than ecclesiastical canons, the vernacular laws are a view of the world as perceived through the schematic lenses of lawyers. Nonetheless, early Irish lawyers were particularly accomplished at covering every possible situation and, in addition, the original texts were heavily glossed with commentaries. This is not a system based on royal decrees but is a remarkably centralized set of laws that 'distill the legal rules and remedies developed over the centuries by highly trained professional jurists'.[39] As the laws are especially concerned with status, property and contracts, the spiritual aspects of monasticism are secondary to the material interests of the church – land, dignity, status and honour-price, types of churches, vacant churches, the rights of patrons, the obligations of tenants (*manaig*), and many other matters. A few ecclesiastical grades occur throughout the laws, which appear to form the nucleus of coenobitic communities. Apart from the bishop and abbot, the latter at times a spiritual leader, at other times an ecclesiastical administrator, specific groups are regarded as monastic: the *deorad Dé* ('exile of God'), *aíbell téoir/oíbelteóir* (literally meaning 'a spark of contemplation' but alluding to a pious person), *dísertach* ('an anchorite, a hermit'), and in certain contexts the ubiquitous *anmcharae* ('confessor') and *ailithir* ('a pilgrim'). *Córus Bésgnai*, the Old Irish law on the church and society, described by Liam Breatnach as 'the most significant witness to the relationship of Church and laity in early mediaeval Ireland',[40] is an important witness to the role of the *deorad Dé* in society. Discipline and having every individual and institution in their right place was a primary concern for the lawyers, reflected in the statement:[41]

> How are peoples held fast to discipline? Everyone is tied to that which is proper to them. Male ecclesiastics (*clérig*) and nuns (*caillecha*) to a church, under the direction of a confessor (*anmcharae*), with law (*racht*) and rule (*ríagail*), until vow (*gell*) until breaking. A pledge after breaking for the arrangements of a promulgation of the church, under the direction of the head of a church (*abb*) and a proper confessor (*anmcharae*).

In this passage and its accompanying commentary – and indeed the general tenor of the law – all individuals should know their place in society, an essential part of which involves responsibilities and offerings to the church. Hence the

37 Ó Corráin, Breatnach and Breen, 'The laws of the Irish'; Liam Breatnach, 'Canon law and secular law in early Ireland: the significance of *Bretha Nemed*', *Peritia* 3 (1984), 439–59. 38 Liam Breatnach, *Uraicecht na ríar. The poetic grades in early Irish law* (Dublin, 1987), pp 81–9. 39 Neil McLeod, 'Brehon law' in Seán Duffy (ed.), *Medieval Ireland. An encyclopedia* (New York, 2005), p. 42. 40 Breatnach, *Córus Bésgnai*, p. 23. 41 Ibid., pp 134–5 §13. Original: *Coastaidter tuatha imbescna. Adragar cach fria techta. Clerig 7 caillecha fri heclais. Fo*

anmcharae should be teaching clerics and nuns the gospel and law (*racht*) with regard to abstaining from meat on Fridays and Wednesdays, along with the rule (*ríagail*) directing that a single meal should be taken from none to none (*ó nóin do nóin*).[42] Some of these directions, of course, could have been given to the laity as well as to clerics, monks and nuns. When matters went awry, such as vows and pledges not being fulfilled, an abbot or *anmcharae* from outside intervened to deal with the situation. Notably, the word *anmcharae* is glossed as *in aíbell téoir nó in deorad Dé* ('the 'spark of contemplation' or 'the exile of God').[43] The *deorad Dé* was accorded a legal role when all options of finding a person fit to become abbot of the church of the patron saint's kin (*eclais fine érlama*) were exhausted.[44] An abbacy first and foremost belonged to the kin of the patron saint, 'even if there is only a psalmist [available] from them' (*cinco roibe acht sailmcéatluidh díbh*).[45] After that the abbacy was offered in order of precedence, and depending on finding a suitable candidate, to the kin of the land on which the church was located, the kin of the church vassals, to a mother church (*annóit*), a pupil (*dalta*), a confederate church (*compairche*) and a neighbouring church (*cell comfoguis*). If all else failed the abbacy was to be offered to a *deorad Dé*. At all times it was open to the kin of the patron to present a suitable candidate. The impression is given that the *deorad Dé* was the candidate of last resort and the law lays down particular conditions in such circumstances. As noted by Breatnach, the *deorad Dé* was a complete outsider with no prior right to the abbacy and hence the imposition of conditions was essential. He had to come from a church of equal standing and both churches had to enter into a partnership. He was obliged to leave his estate with the new church, and was liable to a substantial fine for any damage caused to the appropriated church.[46] There was a practical reason for resorting to the *deorad Dé*, even if he was an outsider. The *deorad Dé* held an esteemed legal status.[47]

According to the law on distraint *Cetharslicht Athgabála*, there were three ecclesiastics whose evidence could not be overturned, even by a king: a scholar (*suí*), a bishop and a *deorad Dé*.[48] As evident from the annals, many individuals could have held all three positions simultaneously and they would have been respected members of society as in the case, for example, of Ioseph, superior (*princeps*) of Armagh who was also a bishop, a scholar and an anchorite (*episcopus 7 sapiens 7 ancorita*).[49] The law on sick-maintenance *Bretha Crólige* confirms the importance of the *deorad Dé* – and to a lesser extent the *aíbell téoir* – in the eyes of the lawyers. Every *deorad Dé* had the same honour-price (*díre*) as a king and a bishop.[50] He is also listed among those who could not be brought away from

reir anmcarat. Coracht. 7 riagail. Cotarngaire cobrud gell iar mbrud. Fri corus rachtge ecalsa. Fo reir abbad 7 anmcarat techta. **42** Ibid., pp 134–5 nn 6–7. **43** Ibid., pp 134–5 n. 13. **44** Ibid., pp 244–9 §§86–9. **45** Ibid., pp 244–5 §86. **46** Ibid., p. 266 §88. **47** T.M. Charles-Edwards, 'The social background to Irish *peregrinatio*', *Celtica* 11 (1976), 43–59, at pp 53, 58–9. **48** *CIH* 357.25–7; Kelly, *Guide*, p. 41. **49** AU 936. **50** Daniel A. Binchy (ed.),

their residences to be nursed on sick-maintenance because of their high rank (a king, bishop, hospitaller, *deorad Dé*, *aíbell téoir*, scholar learned in canon law, poet, advocate and judge).[51] A gloss to the main text explains that the *deorad Dé*'s high status related to his ability to perform miracles through his prayers.[52] Notably, the *aíbell téoir* is glossed as 'a virgin youth of pious life of his own territory' (*mac óigi co crábud di[a] túaith féin*).[53] In his note on the two terms, Binchy draws attention to a significant reference to them in a legal glossary in relation to a case whereby despite application to a series of judges, there is no decision, and, therefore, 'it shall be brought to an *aíbelltéoir* or a *deorad Dé*, for God will probably reveal it to them'.[54] The text and glosses of *Bretha Crólige* also include important remarks about religious women that are similar to its treatment of the *deorad Dé*. This states that certain women were not nursed away from their homes, among them, 'a woman who turns back the streams of war' glossed 'such as the abbess of Kildare or the female *aíbell teóir*, one who turns back the manifold sins of wars through her prayers' and 'a woman who is abundant (?) in miracles' glossed 'the virgin (*in banógh*) or the female exile of God (*in bandeorad*)'.[55]

The law tract *Coibnes Uisci Thairidne* reinforces the status of the *deorad Dé* as a legal agent. It counts a contract 'for which the men of Heaven and gospel of Christ are invoked [as sureties]'[56] as one of the seven high contracts which are not possible to rescind. A *deorad Dé* is obliged to enforce his suretyship 'as though he himself had been invoked for it or as though his celebration [of religious rites] had guaranteed it'.[57] Such is the *deorad Dé*'s sanctity and devotion to those in Heaven and to the gospels that he and his liturgical rites represent them on earth, even in binding legal contracts. Binchy also notes that the legal glosses attempt to distinguish between the two terms, claiming that the *aíbell téoir* remained in his own territory and was not learned, while the *deorad Dé* was learned and an outsider, as implied in *Córus Bésgnai* on the subject of a vacant abbacy. Such explanations, while possible, are literal and stray away from the monastic ideology behind them of being exiled from the world and on life's pilgrimage and being contemplatives inspiring others to follow a committed religious life. It is understood from the *deorad Dé*'s profile in the laws that society viewed his life as exemplary and that effectively he was God's witness on earth.

'*Bretha Crólige*', *Ériu* 12 (1938), 1–77, at pp 6–7 §4. Original: *Comdire cac deoradh de fri ri[g] 7 espoc.* **51** Ibid., pp 12–13 §12. Persons of unsound mind as well as fools (*druth*) were also nursed at home. **52** Ibid., pp 12–13 §12 n. 5; pp 58–9 notes to §12. **53** Ibid., pp 12–13 §12 n. 6; pp 58–9 notes to §12. **54** Ibid., p. 59 n. §12. Original: *a breith docum aoibhilteora no deoraid de, uair is daigh foillseochaid dia doibh he.* **55** Ibid., pp 26–7 §32 nn 2 and 4. Original: *ut est bancomarba cille dara .i. in banaibellteoir .i. impodus imad peccad na cocad for cula trena hirnaigthi … .i. in banogh .i. in bandeorad de.* **56** Daniel A. Binchy (ed.), 'Irish law tracts re-edited. I. *Coibnes uisci thairidne*', *Ériu* 17 (1955), 52–85, at pp 66–7 §7.8. Original: *ní i n-aiccditer fir nime 7 soscéla[e] críst.* **57** Binchy, '*Coibnes Uisci Thairidne*', pp 66–7 §7.8. Original: *ar dleg[a]ir do cach déorad dé saigid a nadma[e] amal ad-rogesta[e] ind no do-dic[h]sed*

He, and the bishop and canon lawyer, of course, could have been one and the same, and have had experience in imposing canon law, which might be regarded as an additional skill. Hence their reliability as legal agents.

Involvement by individuals dedicated to an ascetic life in worldly affairs such as witnessing contracts, and even taking over a vacant abbacy, may not have always been approved by their fellow ascetics. Máel Ruain, founder of the *céli Dé* ascetic movement, for example, when asked by his disciple Máel Díthruib how he might rule his life, responded that he should stay in his normal abode and not become involved in worldly disputes. He should not go to any law court (*tigh an britheamhnais*) nor an assembly (*aireachtas*) to plead on behalf of anyone, but should pray, study and teach anyone who sought instruction from him.[58] Máel Ruain's desire that the *céli Dé* withdraw from worldly disputes was hardly successful as can be seen from annalistic references to their involvement in political affairs from their first appearance during the eighth century. But his wish articulated an ideal, like so many monastic rules and instructions, that sought to distance monks and nuns from the world beyond the enclosure.

TEXTS OF THE GREAT FOUNDERS: THE IDEAL ABBOT AND HIS MONASTERY

Canon and vernacular laws go some way towards depicting the monastic model known in early Ireland and how monks of various kinds were to behave and fitted into the ecclesiastical and secular law codes. More fundamental values, however, sustained monastic traditions and these values are found in many earlier texts and in the spirituality of eminent monastic founders, Columba and Columbanus being the greatest luminaries of the tradition. Obedience to the *senior/seniores* of a community is evident in the earliest monastic texts from Ireland as it is generally in monastic literature.[59] Columbanus opens his *Regula Monachorum*, 'a treatise on monastic virtues',[60] with a provision on obedience with the implication that obeying a senior was equal to obeying God:[61]

> At the first word of a senior, all on hearing should rise to obey, since their obedience is shown to God, as our Lord Jesus Christ says: *He who hears you hears Me* [Luke 10.16].

a chelebrad aire. **58** Gwynn, 'The rule of Tallaght' contains the 'The rule of the Céli Dé' and the 'The teaching of Mael Ruain'; Gwynn, 'The teaching of Mael Ruain', 8–11 §12. **59** O'Dwyer, *Céli Dé*, pp 107–8; Eoin de Bhaldraithe, 'Obedience: the doctrine of the Irish monastic rules', *Monastic Studies* 14 (1983), 63–84. **60** T.M. Charles-Edwards, 'The monastic rules ascribed to Columbanus' in Sébastien Bully, Alain Dubreucq and Aurélia Bully (eds), *Colomban et son influence: moines et monastères du haut Moyen Âge en Europe* (Rennes, 2018), pp 295–304, at p. 295. **61** Walker, *Sancti Columbani opera*, pp 122–5, 140–3. Original:

> Therefore if anyone hearing the word does not rise at once, he is to be judged disobedient. But he who answers back incurs the charge of insubordination, and thus is not only guilty of disobedience, but also, by opening the way of answering back for others, is to be regarded as the destroyer of many.
>
> Yet if any murmurs, he too, as though not obeying heartily, must be considered disobedient. Therefore let his work be rejected until his goodwill be made known. But up to what measure is obedience laid down? Up to death …
>
> Let him keep silence when he has suffered wrong, let him fear the superior of his community as a lord, love him as a father, believe that whatever he commands is healthful for himself, and let him not pass judgement on the opinion of an elder, to whose duty it belongs to obey and fulfil what he is bidden.

Here Columbanus is relying on Basil of Caesarea, John Cassian and Jerome. His insistence on obedience first and foremost echoes John Cassian's emphatic strictures to novices on the subject:[62]

> Along with this such a great observance is maintained, thanks to the rule of obedience, that the young men do not even presume to attend to their common and natural necessities on their own authority, to say nothing of daring to leave their cells, without the knowledge and permission of their superior.

This strict approach to authority is also characteristic of the Rule of the Master: 'In the monastery their [the monks] will is daily thwarted for the sake of the Lord, and in the spirit of martyrdom they patiently endure whatever commands they receive to test them'.[63] While the opening section on obedience

Ad primum verbum senioris omnes ad oboediendum audientes surgere oportet, quia oboedientia deo exhibetur, dicente domino nostro Iesu Christo: Qui vos audit me audit (*Luc. 10.16*). *Si quis igitur verbum audiens non statim surrexerit inoboediens iudicandus est. Qui autem contradixerit contumaciae crimen incurrit, et ideo non solum inoboedientiae reus est, sed etiam contradictionis aditum aliis aperiens* (Basil. (trans. Rufin.) Interrog. 69) multorum destructor aestimandus est. Si quis vero murmuraverit, et ipse tamquam non ex voto oboediens inoboediens putandus est. Idcirco *opus eius abiiciatur,*" (Basil. Interrog. 71) donec illius bona voluntas cognoscatur. Oboedientia autem usque ad quem modum definitur? *Usque ad mortem*" (Basil. Interrog. 65, Cassian. Inst. xii. 28) … *Passus iniuriam taceat, praepositum monasterii timeat ut dominum, diligat ut parentem, credat sibi hoc esse salutare quicquid ille praeceperit, nec de maioris sententia iudicet, cuius officii est oboedire et implere quae iussa sunt* … (Hieron. Epist. cxxv. 15). **62** Boniface Ramsey, *John Cassian. The institutes* (New York, 2000), p. 81 (Book IV, Chapter X). **63** *RM*, p.123 §VII (obedience). The relationship between Columbanus's prescriptions and the Rule of the Master is a matter of scholarly debate epitomized by the lively conversation between

in the *RB* uses similar phrases to Columbanus regarding abbatial authority,[64] the overbearing character of the abbot is absent from the *RB*, reflecting Augustine's influence on Benedict. In his consideration of Benedict's form of abbatial authority, Conrad Leyser observes that the abbot 'must experience the anxiety of authority – the strain of constantly calculating what he will say to each of his flock, and the possibility that his insight might one day fail him'.[65] Here moderation and humility are to be lauded in a superior:[66]

> He is to distrust his own frailty and remember *not to crush the bruised reed* (Isaiah 42:3). By this we do not mean that he should allow faults to flourish, but rather, as we have already said, he should prune them away with prudence and love as he sees best for each individual. Let him strive to be loved rather than feared.

The ninth abbot of Iona, Adomnán (d. 704) and author of the *Vita sancti Columbae*[67] aimed to depict the ideal abbot and monastery in his work.[68] Columba was an angelic *miles Christi* 'soldier of Christ', living on an earthly island closer to Heaven than the rest of the world, studying the scriptures, church fathers and monastic founders, fasting and praying in vigils, occupied with computistical calculations, and compiling liturgical books. He and his monks were on a life's pilgrimage to a heavenly paradise and perfection. As Katja Ritari explains:[69]

> The exemplary role of the abbot, therefore, explains the emphasis placed on his moral character and purity, since without virtues one cannot gain salvation ... The abbot is thus a teacher and the father or shepherd – like Fintán [of Taghmon] – who tends to the needs of his spiritual sons or flock

Marilyn Dunn and Adalbert de Vogüé in *The English Historical Review* during the early 1990s. See Marilyn Dunn, 'Monastic rules and their authors in the early medieval West', *The English Historical Review* 105 (1990), 567–94; Adalbert de Vogüé, 'The Master and St Benedict: a reply to Marilyn Dunn', *The English Historical Review* 107 (1992), 95–103; Marilyn Dunn, 'The Master and St Benedict: a rejoinder', *The English Historical Review* 107 (1992), 104–11. **64** *RB*: Chap. 5.4–6: 'they carry out the superior's order as promptly as if the command came from God himself. The Lord says of men like this: *No sooner did he hear than he obeyed me* (Ps 17[18]:45]; again, he tells teachers: *Whoever listens to you, listens to me* (Luke 10:16)'. **65** Conrad Leyser, *Authority and asceticism from Augustine to Gregory the Great* (Oxford, 2000), p. 127. **66** *RB*: Chap. 64.13–15. **67** https://www.dib.ie/biography/adomnan-a0032. Alan Orr Anderson and Marjorie Ogilvie Anderson (eds), *Adomnán's life of Columba* (Oxford, 1991 revised ed.); Richard Sharpe (trans.), *Adomnán of Iona. Life of St Columba* (London, 1995). **68** On this subject see Aidan MacDonald, 'Adomnán's monastery of Iona' in Cormac Bourke (ed.), *Studies in the cult of Saint Columba* (Dublin, 1997), pp 24–44, at pp 27–8; Katja Ritari, 'Holy souls and a holy community: the meaning of monastic life in Adomnán's *Vita Columbae*', *Journal of Medieval Religious Cultures* 37:1 (2011), 129–46. **69** Ritari, 'Holy souls and a holy community', pp 133–4.

of sheep. These images emphasize the practical and theological role an abbot plays: he is in charge of the spiritual well-being and instruction of his monks and thus in helping them to reach Heaven.

Obedience and humility were essential virtues in the monastic life lauded by Columba. Once he sent for the monk Cailtan, who was serving a church on the mainland in the kingdom of Dál Riata, and on hearing the saint's request Cailtan hurried to Iona, where he was greeted by Columba:[70]

> 'You have done well, Cailtan, in hastening to me obediently. Rest a little. As one that loves his friend, I have sent to invite you, so that here with me in true obedience you may end the course of your life; for before the end of this week you will pass to the Lord in peace.'

Cailtan died on Iona, one step away from Heaven, as an obedient monk blessed by the model and saintly abbot. Status and humility come together in the episode about bishop Crónán from Munster who visited Iona as a pilgrim concealing his identity 'out of humility' (*in quantum potuit occultabat humiliter*). Knowing who he was, Columba invited him to celebrate the Eucharist with him and as the saint approached the altar he spoke:[71]

> 'Christ bless you, brother; break this bread alone, according to the episcopal rite. Now we know you are a bishop: why until now have you tried to conceal yourself, so that the reverence due to you was not paid by us?'

Here not only was the bishop humble, but so was Columba in acknowledging the superior authority of a bishop and offering him due reverence, despite his own noble and saintly status. As aristocrats no doubt versed in canon and secular laws, Columba and Adomnán would have been acutely aware of the importance of rank and status which made their exercise of humility all the more chastening. Despite evidence of severity and aristocratic haughtiness, a more humble and peaceable approach to leading a community is also evident in the sources, best expressed in the later Rule of Ailbe:[72]

70 Anderson and Anderson, *Life of Columba*, pp 58–9 [i.31]; Sharpe, *Adomnán of Iona*, p. 134 [I 31]. Original (Andersons' ed.): *'O Cailtane, bene fecisti ad me oboedienter festinando; requiesce paulisper. Idcirco ad te inuitandum misi, amans amicum, ut hic mecum in uera finias oboedientia uitae cursum tuae. Nam ante huius ebdomadis finem ad dominum in pace transibis.'* 71 Anderson and Anderson, *Life of Columba*, pp 80–1 [i.44]; Sharpe, *Adomnán of Iona*, p. 147 [I 44]. Original: '*Benedicat té Christus, frater. Hunc solus episcopali ritu frange panem. Nunc scimus quod sis episcopus: quare hucusque te occultare conatus es, ut tibi a nobis debeta non redderetur ueneratio?*' 72 Joseph O Neill, 'The Rule of Ailbe of Emly', *Ériu* 3 (1907), 92–115, at 102–5 §§32–3. Original: *Mad ecnaid int aircinnech a ríagol níb borb,/ amal bies int acnamad bid samlaid int ord. Ná bad rothend, ná bad lax, níp riágol cen fhiss,/ ara rucca cách a mám, ná farcba a liss.*

> If the abbot (*airchinnech*) be wise, his rule (*ríagol*) shall not be harsh; as the food shall be, so will the order (*ord*) be.
>
> Let it not be too strict; let it not be lax; let it not be a rule without knowledge, that each may be able to bear his yoke, that he may not leave his enclosure.

Insofar as this rule can be compared with *RB*, for example, both present the abbot – although in the Rule of Ailbe called an *airchinnech* which is more appropriate to the person in charge of *manaig* 'lay tenants' – as fair and prudent with the spiritual welfare of his community as his first concern. The abbot was shepherd and father, in Christ's place in the monastery.[73] One of the finest, and most gentle, descriptions of an abbot, comes at the end of the late tenth-century life of Adomnán, describing the saint's character:[74]

> A just man, indeed, was this man, with purity of nature like a patriarch. A true pilgrim, like Abraham … A brilliant fire with embers which warm and heat the sons of life, kindling and inspiring charity … Mild, humble, and gentle towards the sons of life (*fri maccu bethadh*) …

This is the perfect abbot, but, as with human nature in all circumstances, the gentleness or severity of the shepherd's rule often depended on the shepherd's own disposition.

Among the many noteworthy aspects of Adomnán's life of Columba is the saint and his monastery's interaction with the laity. Apart from Columba's mission to northern Pictland, and especially to the royal residence of King Bridei, Adomnán describes considerable interaction between lay people and Iona's community. Some visited the island seeking succour from afflictions of body and soul and were sent to do penance; the pains of others were prophesied by Columba and they were usually saved, although not always if they countered the saint's directions. Penance was at the heart of dealing with the laity – and indeed clerics – so much so that penitential communities existed on the island of *Hinba* and on Mag Luinge in Tiree.[75] The story of Neman mac Cathir is representative of how laymen might be treated and the fate awaiting them if they did not follow the great abbot's directions:[76]

73 *RB*: Chap. 2.2. 74 Máire Herbert and Pádraig Ó Riain (eds), *Betha Adamnáin: The Irish life of Adamnán* (Cork, 1988), pp 61–2 §18 (14). Original: *Fer firén trá an fer-so go nglaine aiccnidh amhail uasalathair. Firailither amhail Abram … Tene taídhlech go ngrís goirthige ocus tesaigthe na mac mbethad im annad 7 im ellscoth [n]désherce … Cennais umhal áilghen fri maccu bethadh.* 75 Sharpe, *Adomnán of Iona*, p. 282. For a discussion on the identification of the island of *Hinba* and *Saine*, mentioned below, see Pamela O'Neill, 'When onomastics met archaeology: a tale of two Hinbas', *The Scottish Historical Review* 87:1 (2008), 26–41. 76 Anderson and Anderson, *Life of Columba*, pp 46–9 [i.21]; Sharpe, *Adomnán of Iona*, pp 127–8 [I 21]. Original: *Alio in tempore sanctus ad Hinbinam insulam peruenit; eademque die ut*

> At another time, the saint came to the island of Hinba. And on that day he ordered that some indulgence in food should be allowed, even to the penitents. There was among the penitents there one Nemán, Cather's son, who refused to take at the saint's bidding the proffered consolation. Him the saint addressed in these words:
>
> 'Nemán, you do not accept an indulgence in diet that I and Baithéne have granted. The time will come when in a wood, with thieves, you will chew the flesh of a stolen mare.'
>
> And so afterwards, when he had returned to the world, this same man was discovered, according to the saint's word, in a forest pasture with thieves, consuming such flesh taken from a wooden griddle.

Hinba and Tiree were places of penance separated from the paradisiacal Iona which could only receive those pilgrims who had been cleansed of their sins through penance and prayer.[77] Adomnán himself makes this distinction between Iona and the rest of the world clear when, returning from an Irish synod, he was delayed by winds on the island of *Saine* on the eve of Columba's feast day. He complained to his patron saying:[78]

> 'Does it please you, holy one, that we should pass the day of your festivity tomorrow among laymen and not in your church? In the beginning of such a day it is an easy thing for you to obtain of the Lord that the contrary winds should be turned to favourable ones, and that we should celebrate in your church the solemn rites of masses, on your natal day.'

And, of course, the saint obliged. The wind abated and Adomnán reached Iona in time to celebrate Columba and Baithéne's feast day with the brethren at the hour of sext. The distinction between the inner space of the monastery, where the avowed community lived and prayed, the space for the penitent laity, and the world further outside manifests itself in the multiple enclosures present at numerous ecclesiastical sites in Ireland. As with so many aspects of society, access to the monastery and its environs was regulated, at least in theory.[79] And, yet, on

etiam penitentibus aliqua praecipit cibi consulatio indulgeretur. Erat autem ibi inter penetentes quidam Nemanus filius Cathir qui a sancto iusus rennuit oblatam accipere consulatiunculam. Quem sanctus hiíconpellat uerbís: 'Ó Nemane, a me et Baitheneo indultam non recipis aliquam refectionis indulgentiam. Erit tempus quo cum furacibus furtiuae carnem in silua manducabis equae.' Hic idem itaque postea ad seculum reuersus in saltu cum furibus talem comedens carnem iuxta uerbum sancti de graticula sumtam lignea inuentus est. 77 Ritari, 'Holy souls and a holy community', pp 136–8. 78 Anderson and Anderson, *Life of Columba*, pp 176–7 [ii.45]; Sharpe, *Adomnán of Iona*, p. 202 [II 45]. Original: '*Placetne tibi sancte crastinam tuae festiuitatis inter plebeos et non in tua eclesia transigere diem? Facile tibi est talis in exordio diei a domino inpetrare, ut contrarii in secundos uertantur uenti, et in tua celebremus eclesia tui natalis misarum sollemnia.*' 79 Swift, 'Forts and fields'.

the other hand, the sources suggest that throughout the early medieval period, monastic communities only detached themselves fully from lay society when they, usually as individuals or in small numbers, chose to withdraw to a hermitage with the intention of not interacting with the wider world.

RELIGIOUS WOMEN IN THE EARLY SOURCES

The mid seventh-century text known as the *Liber Angeli* 'The Book of the Angel', composed to secure the church of Armagh's primacy over the whole of Ireland and to confirm Patrick's role as the apostle of the Irish, includes a rare topographical description of the sacred *urbs* and its inhabitants:[80]

> In the city of Armagh Christians of both sexes are seen to live together in religion from the coming of the faith to the present day almost inseparably, and to this aforesaid (city) also adhere three orders: virgins and penitents, and those serving the church in legitimate matrimony. And these three orders are allowed to hear the word of preaching in the church of the northern district on Sundays always; in the southern basilica, however, bishops and priests and anchorites and the other religious offer pleasing praises.

This passage either truly reflects the topography of Armagh or is an image of the celestial city, which could be the heavenly Jerusalem or Rome. If the latter, the Irish author may have had an image of the layout of Christian Rome in mind: the *urbs* on a hill with its various churches, including a basilica, and its orders of inhabitants. Hence the deliberate use of the term *urbs* for Armagh. Whether a fictional topography or otherwise, a female community of virgins inhabited the *urbs*, one element of three 'orders' – the others being penitents and those living in Christian marriage while serving the church – whose worship was assigned to a particular church on the hill. Their superiors, bishops, priests, anchorites and other religious – presumably abbots and committed monks – worshipped in the southern basilica. From the perspective of female monasticism, the arrangement that included a community of women living inside or close to a large monastery was replicated elsewhere, if only at a small number of sites. The community at Armagh may have continued to exist to a later period as *Cell na n-Ingen* 'the

80 Bieler, *Patrician texts*, pp 186–7 (15)–(16). Original: *In ista uero urbe Alti Machæ homines Christiani utriusque sexus relegiossi ab initio fidei hucusque pene insepabiliter commorari uidentur, cui uero praedictae tres ordines adherent uirgines et poenitentes* <*et*> *in matrimonio ligitimo aeclessiae seruientes. Et his tribus ordinibus audire uerbum praedictationis in aeclessia aquilonalis plagae conceditur semper diebus dominicis, in australi uero bassilica aepiscopi et praesbiteri et anchoritae aeclessiae et caeteri relegiossi laudes sapidas offerunt.*

church of the virgins'.[81] On the basis of the evidence of the Martyrology of Tallaght, Elva Johnson has suggested that the *céli Dé* showed an interest in a geographical cluster of female saints located near their main centres at Finglas and Tallaght.[82] This suggestion is supported by a story in the contemporary 'Tallaght dossier', which relates how Dublitir of Finglas, accompanied by bishop Caínchomrac, entered the monastic green (*faithche*) where they encountered a poor woman seeking to sleep in the nuns' residence (*i llis caillech*). Dublitir scolded her for bothering him but Caínchomrac rebuked him for his aggressive attitude to her and insisted that he either allow her join the religious women or give her alms so that she had no need to seek their help.[83] The inference here is that a female religious community was located close to Dublitir's monastery at Finglas and, as so often described in hagiography, that these women's main function was to care for the poor and the sick. As already noted in Chapter 1, Catherine Swift has identified the functions of fostering, nurturing and protecting as key characteristics of early female monasticism in Ireland that compares well with functions associated with female religious in the east, and particularly in late antique Cappadocia.[84]

The chapter in the *Hibernensis* concerning women offers an invaluable insight into the place of women in the existing monastic tradition in Ireland which, despite its brevity, can also be compared with female monasticism elsewhere. Two kinds of veiled women (*palliata*) were recognized as being attached to the church.[85] The first were virgins who imitated Mary in their physical appearance and dress, the second were penitents, possibly widows, who imitated Anna, the mother of Mary. All lived under the constant guidance of a spiritual counsellor, a spiritual director, an *anmcharae*. Girls could be veiled from the age of twelve and once professed as nuns wore the dress of virginity and were separated from the sight of men, to 'live a cloistered life under the rule of a presbyter until death' (*sub manu prespiteri usque ad mortem clausæ uiuitæ*).[86] The latter exhortation quotes from the synod of Arles, mirroring Caesarius of Arles' Rule for Nuns.[87] The veiling of women who were dedicating their lives to a state of virginity out of the sight of men included a consecration rite of veiling and dressing that was conducted by a bishop.[88] This liturgical ceremony, the *velatio*, existed in the church from at least the fifth century. The liturgy survives in a

81 Stokes, *Félire Óengusso*, pp 222–3 (8 October). 82 Johnson, 'Locating female saints', p. 32. 83 Gwynn and Purton, 'The monastery of Tallaght', p. 130 §7. 84 Swift, 'Soul sisters', pp 52–5. 85 Flechner, *Hibernensis*, 1, p. 355: §44.12; 2, pp 739–40. On the interpretation of veils and women, see Máirín Ní Dhonnchadha, '*Caillech* and other terms for veiled women in medieval Irish texts', *Éigse* 28 (1995), 71–96. 86 Flechner, *Hibernensis*, 1, pp 355–6 §§44.14, 44.16; 2, p. 740. 87 Roger Haight, Alfred Pach and Amanda Avile Kaminski (eds), *Western monastic spirituality. Cassian, Caesarius of Arles, and Benedict. Past light on present life* (New York, 2022), pp 47–90. 88 Eliana Magnani, 'Female house ascetics from the fourth to the twelfth century' in *CHMM*, pp 213–231, at pp 220–6.

tenth-century manuscript in an Irish hand.[89] A short but accurate description of the *velatio* is found in Cogitosus' seventh-century life of Brigit of Kildare.[90] Bishop Mac Caille ('son of the veil') recognized Brigit's desire to devote herself as a chaste virgin to God and so he placed 'the white veil and white garment over her venerable head' (*pallium album et vestem condidam super ipsius venerabile caput imposuit*). Brigit knelt humbly before God and the bishop at the altar and offered her virginal crown to almighty God. Further details are added in the *Vita Prima Sanctae Brigitae*:[91]

> Then he [Mac Caille] ushered them into the bishop's presence, and while bishop Mel was intently gazing at them, a column of fire suddenly appeared rising from Brigit's head up to the very top of the church in which she dwelt.
>
> Then the holy bishop Mel placed the veil on St Brigit's head and when the prayers had been read Brigit bowed her head and seized the wooden foot of the altar in her hand and since that moment the altar foot has permanently remained fresh without any decay or blemish.

Leaving Brigit's miracle aside, this episode suggests that the ritual of veiling and dressing by a bishop was known in Ireland, and that in Kildare life in a community directed by a bishop may have been an option for women, at least during the monastery's early history. Yet, neither the *Vita Prima* nor Cogitosus's life of Brigit give any sense of an abbess and community living according to the strictures of the nuns at Arles. Unlike the latter who appear to have been enclosed and strictly controlled by their abbess and bishop, Brigit is portrayed as constantly travelling with a household of nuns as she provides for the poor and the sick. If there is any similarity with her continental sisters, it relates to episcopal direction. No abbot appears in Brigit's lives. She attends episcopal synods, she entertains bishops and seeks their advice, and they seek hers. Apart from occasional references to celebrating the major feast days of the liturgical year and an emphasis on the vow of poverty, Brigit's lived religious life is not highly regulated, although all the necessary monastic ideals – love and fear of God, charity, chastity, poverty – are expressed through her miracles and her interaction with the laity. Significantly, for Brigit the laity ranged from kings to those shunned by society, normally depicted as lepers.

Control of widows in the church was of greater concern to the compilers of the *Hibernensis* than that of virgins, who appear to be regarded as relatively easy

89 Warren, *Liturgy of Celtic church*, pp 23–4 [*De virgine investienda*]: *Accipe, puella, pallium candidum quod perferas ante tribunal Domini*; Harrington, *Women in a Celtic church*, pp 141–3. 90 Connolly and Picard, 'Cogitosus's *Life of St Brigit*, p. 14 §2.1. Original, John Colgan, *Triadis*, p. 519 Cap. III. 91 Seán Connolly, 'Vita Prima Sanctae Brigitae: background and historical value', *Journal of the Royal Society of Antiquaries of Ireland* 119 (1989), 5–49, at p. 18

to discipline. Women professing chastity and subject to a blessing by a priest might be classified as female house ascetics, a common phenomenon in the early church. Some were widows (*ordo uiduarum*) but many were married women who with or without their husbands' consent withdrew from the world.[92] Their husbands could have also withdrawn from the world and both may have become permanent penitents (*ordo poenitentium*).[93] The most acceptable widow according to the *Hibernensis* was the sixty-year-old of one husband who although she depended on alms from the church returned the favour by her prayers and their merits.[94] But even the most chaste might cause clerics or monks to stray in their imaginations, so their houses were to be avoided. Hence the *Hibernensis*' pithy remonstration 'For a gaze is polluted by a gaze' (*Conspectus enim a conspectu polluitur*).[95] A Middle Irish tale 'Rícenn and Cairech Dercáin' goes as close as texts of the period do to provide a religious woman's perspective on staving off the attention of a powerful man.[96] As noted by Máirín Ní Dhonnchadha, this tale also encapsulates the different states of virginity, marriage and holy widowhood open to pious women, although not always free from worldly dangers. Crimthann mac Lugdach, king of Uí Maine of Connacht handed his daughter Rícenn over to the cleric Mac Raith after her baptism in atonement for murdering a woman. When the girl was seven Mac Raith fostered her to Cairech Dercáin, a virgin avowed to the female community of Cluain Bairenn (Cloonburren, Co. Roscommon). Cairech Dercáin and Rícenn were beautiful women, but while her tutor used to be out among her people, Rícenn was never seen as she spent her time attending to her handiwork and studies (*fri feidm a léiginn 7 a grésa*). Tipraite mac Foramáin, king of Túadmuman, was told that there was a young nun (*maccaillech*) in Cluain Bairenn who would make a fitting consort for a king. He sent his official to take stock of the virgin Cairech's appearance. Looking through the keyhole of the locked church in which Cairech was singing the psalms, he reported back to the king that she was the most beautiful woman the world had ever seen. Tipraite sent a fleet up the Shannon to fetch Cairech but she was ready for the king's troop and locked herself into the church again. Given a respite of three days, Cairech made an agreement with Rícenn that the latter would go to the king in her place, arguing with the girl that she herself had dedicated her virginity to the Lord (*ar ro-chindes-sa m'óighe din Coimde*), while Rícenn had not yet done so. Rícenn agreed to go to the king but

§20.2. **92** Magnani, 'Female house ascetics'. **93** Follett, *Céli Dé in Ireland*, p. 77. Follet (p. 193) notes that one of the responsibilities of an *anmcharae* 'soul friend' was to provide alms to widows among others. **94** Flechner, *Hibernensis*, 1, p. 353 §44.7; 2, p. 738. **95** Ibid., 1, p. 354 §44.9; 2, p. 739. **96** Kuno Meyer (ed.), 'A medley of Irish texts: VI. The adventures of Ricinn, daughter of Crimthann mac Lugdach', *Archiv für celtische Lexicographie* 3 (1907), 308–9; Máirín Ní Dhonnchadha (trans.), 'Rícenn and Cairech Dercáin' in Angela Bourke et al. (eds), *The Field Day anthology of Irish writing vol. IV: Irish women's writing and traditions* (Cork, 2002), pp 129–30. See also Ó Riain, *DIS*, pp 535–6 on St Ríceall/Ríceann.

only if he slept with her in her own territory in Connacht. By various miraculous means she was granted her wish and as a result two churches were founded by Tipraite at Máenmag (Moyne, near Killaloe, Co. Clare). The northern church at Máenmag was founded around 'Rícenn's Stone' (*Lec Ricinde*), while the southern church was Cluain Ceneoil Dúngaile, named after Dúngal, their son. The tale ends with Rícenn becoming a pious widow dedicated to God (*fedb irisech di Dia*) who gave the threefold territory (*tríchait in tredual*) to Ciarán of Clonmacnoise, God and Cairech Dercáin of Cloonburren. In a sense this tale reflects the clear direction of the *Hibernensis* regarding marriage and virginity; when quoting Jerome, the canon states: 'Unless matrimony had existed, virginity would not have existed; the earth is populated by matrimony, but Heaven by virginity'.[97]

The rights of the kin were particularly powerful in the case of women, who were accorded very little legal status on their own except in rare cases such as the abbess of Kildare. While under the authority of a bishop, she occupied an office that was of national significance, and in that capacity dealt with local and regional kings, and with senior clerics. Another aspect of her office was the protection of churches dedicated to female founding saints. Numerous early churches in Ireland were dedicated to female saints. The vast majority of these small foundations did not develop into monastic communities, and probably reverted back to the founder saint's kin when she died. They then became proprietary churches or were annexed by larger monasteries. By this means, the monastery of Kildare brought many churches in the east and midlands into its fold. No doubt this enhanced the monastery's coffers but it also secured its position as an all-embracing female foundation. A remarkably long list of early churches subject to St Brigit is preserved among the genealogies of Irish saints included in the twelfth-century Book of Leinster.[98] Over a hundred churches dedicated to women are listed as subject to Brigit (*Brigitae sanctae subiectae erant omnes hae uirgines sanctae quarum loca et nonima enumerabimus*), the typical individual entries naming one woman (*Cainer ingen Chruthechain i Cill Chulind i Cairpre* 'Cainer daughter of Cruthnechán in Cell Chuilind in Cairpre (Old Kilcullen, Co. Kildare)'), sisters (*Lassar 7 Cummain dí ingin Cholmain mc Fhiachnai i Cluain Cain* 'Lassar and Cummain two daughters of Colmán son of Fiachnae in Cluain Caín (?Clonkeen, Co. Limerick)'), and a family of brother and sister(s) (*Finán 7 a dí shiair ic Tig Airthir* 'Finán and his two sisters at Tech Airthir').[99] This text is a testimony to the accommodation between a kin-based society and the church in its early centuries of Christianity in Ireland, and to the

97 Flechner, *Hibernensis*, 1, p. 357 §45.1; 2, p. 741. Original: *De laude matrimonii. Hironimus ait: Nisi matrimonium fuisset, uirginitas non esset; ex matrimonio terra repletur, ex uiginitate uero caelum.* 98 Ó Riain, *CGSH*, pp 112–18 §670. 99 Ó Riain, *CGSH*, §670.1, 83, 54. *Tech Airthir* is unidentified but may have been located in or near the baronies of Narragh and Reban, Co. Kildare (cf. *CGSH* p. 333).

participation of women in very small communities devoted to a regulated Christian life similar to those known to have existed elsewhere in late antiquity. These communities rarely lasted beyond the first generation, and perhaps they were not meant to, but their legacy was left in the dedications of many churches throughout Ireland that survive to the present.

IRISH VERNACULAR REGULATORY MAXIMS: *APGITIR CHRÁBAID* AND *REGULA CHOLUIMB CHILLE*

A suite of texts classified by their authors or later copyists and revisers under the title *ríagail* (< Lat. *regula*) are associated with the great monastic founders, Ailbe of Emly, Columba of Iona, Comgall of Bangor and Ciarán of Clonmacnoise. A further suite of regulations are linked to the *céli Dé* ascetic movement.[100] These texts date primarily to the eighth and ninth centuries but it is likely that they continued to circulate for a long time afterwards, and were occasionally revised or extracts from them were re-worked. The manuscript tradition that preserved them lasted until the seventeenth century, with a notable increase in compiling and copying of texts during the fifteenth century.[101] This late medieval literary activity formed part of the highly productive network of the Mac Aodhagáin family of Lower Ormond (north Co. Tipperary and its environs), who were lawyers and keepers of many older manuscripts. One source must have been the scattered remnants of the library of the former *céli Dé* house of Terryglass, Co. Tipperary. A direct witness of what was available in Terryglass exists in the twelfth-century Book of Leinster, compiled by, among others, Áed mac Crimthainn, the last abbot of Terryglass (d. *c.*1201). The Martyrology of Tallaght was, for example, copied into the Book of Leinster.[102] Two later compiler-scribes working in the region, Tadhg Ó Rígbardáin and Uilliam Mac an Leagha, specialized in copying devotional and other religious texts, some perhaps in manuscripts for use by their patrons, others copied simply as part of a long-standing tradition of preserving old texts.[103]

While these regulatory texts might be regarded as proto-customaries in that they deal with detailed practices of individual monasteries, monastic leaders and networks, as in the case of the writings of the *céli Dé*, others deal with good governance in the church in general and offer spiritual guidance on the fundamentals of clerical and monastic religious life. Notably, no version of *RB* survives in manuscripts of Irish origin prior to the late thirteenth century,[104]

100 O'Dwyer, *Céli Dé*, pp 60–121; Follett, *Céli Dé in Ireland*, pp 100–70, 220–34. **101** Ó Corráin, *CLH* ii, pp 809–12. **102** https://www.dib.ie/biography/mac-crimthainn-aed-a5024. Follett, *Céli Dé in Ireland*, pp 128–30, 139. **103** Follett, *Céli Dé in Ireland*, pp 103–4; Raymond Gillespie, 'Scribes and manuscripts in Gaelic Ireland, 1400–1700', *Studia Hibernica* 40 (2014), 9–34, at p. 20. **104** Ó Clabaigh, 'Community, commemoration and

unlike the manuscript versions of *RB* from England and the Continent that survive from earlier centuries.[105] It cannot be concluded, however, that monastic rules originating from elsewhere, including *RB*, were completely unknown in Ireland. An essential element of this present study is to identify similarities between the monastic regulatory traditions of western Christendom, and even beyond, and those of the Irish tradition. And, as Albrecht Diem and Philip Rousseau have argued, Benedict of Aniane's notion of a regularized monasticism was in reality a skilfully crafted construct of what it meant to 'follow' *RB*.[106] The imposition of one normative rule throughout the Carolingian and Anglo-Saxon worlds was not as easy as often depicted and ultimately depended on how individual monasteries produced their own customs or interpreted *RB*. From the beginning of monastic rule formation there existed what Diem and Rousseau describe as a 'a playground of regulating' that allowed for a diversity of formats to convey the content of a rule. These regulatory texts could adopt various formats: questions and answers; words of wisdom spoken by venerable fathers; vociferous admonitions; straightforward paragraphs with or without biblical grounding or theological rationales; florilegia of older monastic rules; rephrased versions of older texts. The addressees could be singular or plural and the tone could vary, even within the same text.[107]

This approach to monastic regulatory texts brings the vernacular Irish 'rules' into the frame. Their contents and ideology are similar to regulatory texts produced elsewhere but they differ mainly in language and structure, if compared to the 'standard' text of *RB*. The *Apgitir Chrábaid* 'Alphabet of Devotion', a very polished vernacular text is, as described by John Carey, 'a collection of precepts and maxims, arranged in sequences of varying length, which reflect a keen perception of the ethics and psychology of the contemplative life'.[108] Attributed to Colmán mac Beógnai, founder of Lann Elo (Lynally, Co. Offaly) (d. 611), scholars have differed about the reliability of this attribution, with some accepting a seventh-century date and others placing it in the early eighth century.[109] Many of the precepts listed in the text are applicable to a Christian community in general, but certain parts are more relevant to those following a monastic life and echo the directions of Cassian and Gregory the Great. It also resembles the early Irish vernacular version of the *speculum principum*, advice given to rulers following the format of a list of short maxims. One section of the *Apgitir Chrábaid* actually deals with truth (*fírinne*), a core

confraternity', p. 247. **105** James G. Clark, 'The rule of Saint Benedict' in Krijn Pansters (ed.), *A companion to medieval rules and customaries* (Leiden, 2020), pp 37–76. **106** Diem and Rousseau, 'Monastic rules'. **107** Ibid., p. 175. **108** John Carey, *King of mysteries. Early Irish religious writings* (Dublin, 2000), p. 231. **109** Vernam Hull (ed. and trans.), 'Apgitir chrábaid: the alphabet of piety', *Celtica* 8 (1968), 44–89; Pádraig Ó Néill, 'The date and authorship of *Apgitir Chrábaid*: some internal evidence' in Próinséas Ní Chatháin and Michael Richter (eds), *Irland und die Christenheit: Bibelstudien und Mission. Ireland and Christendom: the Bible and the*

element of princely rule, claiming that while many yearn for truth, only 'a few holy folk' can attain 'moderation and wisdom and true holiness' (*indmus 7 ecnae 7 fír-etlae*).[110] If monastic in its ideals, the text is directed at a coenobitic community. Reference is often made to charity, chastity, humility, fasting, silence and obedience. The fundamental tenets of monasticism – *amor et timor Dei* – are to the fore:[111]

> Love of the living God
> washes the soul,
> contents the mind,
> magnifies rewards,
> casts out vices, renders the earth hateful,
> washes and binds the thoughts …
> Fear is an obstacle to the sins which are ahead;
> Repentance dissolves the sins which have gone before.

And a man should learn – as with all monks:

> Constancy in holiness,
> shortness of words,
> gentle brotherliness,
> smoothness in giving,
> fulfilling the rule without urging,
> rising early before dawn, walking in obedience to God …

The format of questions and answers used in some sections of the text is a simplified version of a format known from other monastic texts, such as the Rule of the Master, except that the master asks the questions and also answers them:[112]

> What should a man learn? Not hard to answer.
>
> What should be avoided by a holy person? Not hard to answer.
>
> When a person converts his own soul to life, how many souls could he convert? The people of the whole world …

missions (Stuttgart, 1987), pp 203–15; Etchingham, *Church organisation*, pp 312–13, 327. **110** Hull, 'Apgitir chrábaid', pp 66–7 §16. Carey, *King of mysteries*, pp 238–9. **111** Hull, 'Apgitir chrábaid', pp 60–1 §6, 63 §9 Carey, *King of mysteries*, pp 234–5. Original (§6): *Serc Dé bí fo-nig anmuin; sásaith menmuin; do-formaig fochraicci; in-árben analchi; ar-corbi talmain; fo-nig, con-rig coiclea … Int omun fris-íada inda pecthu ara-biat. Ind athrige do-lega inna pecthu remi-thíagat.* Original (§9): *Foss oc etlai, ambatae mbríathar, bráithirse n-ailgen, ascaid la rédi, ríagol do chomalnad cen érchoíltiu, érge la cét-rair, céim n-erlatad ar Día …* **112** Hull, 'Apgitir Chrábaid', 62–3 §§9–10, 69 § 18; Carey, *King of mysteries*, pp 235–6, 240. Original (§9–10): *Ced as fogailsi do duiniu? Ní anse … Cid as imgabthai do duine etail? Ní anse.* (§18):*Duine do-soí a anmuin fadéisne do betha, ce mét anman do-roafath? Doíne in domain uili …*

This is a text that was didactic and easy to memorize as is clear from one section that classifies truths into threes and fours, triads being a favourite genre of the Irish literary class:[113]

> Three things that drive out the spirit of instability, and make the mind steadfast: vigil, and prayer, and labour …
>
> The four guarantees of the sons of life: decay of desires, fear of punishments, love of hardships, belief in rewards.

Whether it be in the seventh or eighth century, here is a master instructing his pupils, sons of life (*maicc bethad*), in his own vernacular, and in a very accomplished manner, what masters of the time from east to west were teaching their monastic disciples in classical Greek, Latin, Syriac and other vernacular languages. The Irish master was part of that greater monastic culture.

The *Regula Choluimb Chille* is attributed to St Columba but given that its language belongs to the eighth or ninth century and that this title occurs in two late manuscripts, it is unlikely that it was composed by Columba himself but it may have been produced in a Columban foundation during that later period.[114] Scholars have viewed it in a similar vein to other vernacular monastic texts as 'in no sense a monastic rule, it contains sententious statements on personal sanctification for … very likely a senior cleric (or a small group of such persons) in retirement from high office'[115] or 'it is more exhortative than regulatory and offers few specifics about religious life'.[116] These comments do not give due regard either to the format or the content of this short text. As with other such Irish texts it follows the style of the *Apophthegmata Patrum* ('Sayings of the Desert Fathers'),[117] short sentences on spiritual guidance and practices codified thematically. Some texts adopt the format of conversations between monastic elders, or elders and their pupils. This text addresses the singular *you* in the form of an exhortation, possibly uttered as the wise counsel of the venerable founder Columba. The person being addressed appears to be living alone but near a large ecclesiastical settlement (*prímchathair*) and is classified as a *cráibdech* which in its adjectival form simply means 'pious'. Use of *cráibdech* as a noun 'a pious person', common in such texts, suggests a person – male or female, although in this instance likely to be male – who is living a committed religious life.[118] The

113 Hull, 'Apgitir chrábaid', pp 70–1 §20, 72–3 §22; Carey, *King of mysteries*, pp 241–2; Original (§20): *Tréide in-árben spirit forlúamna 7 do-gníat mens fossad .i. frithaire 7 ernaigthe 7 lebair.* (§22) *Cethoir trebairi inda mac mbethad .i. credbud inda tol, omun inda pían, serc inna fochaide, cretem inda fochraice.* 114 Meyer (ed.), '*Regula Choluimb Chille*' *Zeitschrift für celtische Philologie* 3 (1901), 28–30; Uinseann Ó Maidín (trans.), *The Celtic monk. Rules and writings of early Irish monks.* Cistercian Studies Series 162 (Kalamazoo, 1996), pp 37–41. 115 *CLH* ii, p. 819 §634. 116 Follett, *Céli Dé in Ireland*, p. 144. 117 Benedicta Ward, *The sayings of the Desert Fathers. The alphabetical collection* (Kalamazoo, 1975). 118 *DIL sv.*

physical aspects of this committed religious life consist of standard eremitical stipulations: any possessions – residence, clothing, food and drink – are provided by 'the senior' whose office is not specified but could have been either an abbot of a coenobitic community or the latter's *cellarius*, or even a lay abbot who administered a monastery and its estates. The *cráibdech* is enclosed in a dwelling that is not conducive to allowing the outside world to enter: 'a stout dwelling enclosing you, with its one door' (§4 *locc umdaingen umut cona óendorus*). Although living in seclusion, he is not in complete isolation. He is permitted to employ a *mog*, who is discrete, dutiful and pious and who attends continually to him (§7). In this context *mog* could mean either a lay servant, an oblate or another monk, most likely a lay monk. This suggests that the *cráibdech* was of sufficiently high status or seniority in the monastic community to have a servant. It may also reflect the social superiority of the *cráibdech* either as defined in lay society or in the division between clerical and lay religious. He converses with a select community of pious people (*úathad cráibdech*), who visit on days of solemnity to strengthen him in the testament of God and the scriptures (§5 *a timnaib Dé 7 a sgélaib sgrebtræ*). The *cráibdech* is expected to participate in specific monastic activities: 'three useful works during the day: prayer, work and reading' (§16 *trí torba isind ló .i. érnaigthi 7 lubair 7 légund*). Useful work was not undertaken solely in the *cráibdech*'s own enclosed residence. He was expected to take on a share of his brethren's work and beyond that to help his neighbours. §17 suggests that he supported his *coimnesam* 'neighbour' – probably his community including novices or oblates – by teaching (*forcetal*), writing (*scríbend*) and sewing garments (*úaim n-étaig*).[119] Whatever about the task of sewing, which would be an act of humility if the *cráibdech* was a learned senior, the profile being described in *Regula Choluimb Chille* fits with the numerous annalistic obits of important religious figures who often were pious teachers and scribes.[120]

Few specific details are provided about the liturgy of the Divine Office followed by the *cráibdech*, except for a reference that he must show fervour in singing the office of the dead (§13 *léire gabála écnairci*) and that hymns for the souls (§14 *imna anma*) should be sung standing. This requirement reflects the role played by those committed to a monastic life in seeking intercession for the souls of the dead. The physical life followed by this solitary person demanded strict eating and sleeping habits, almsgiving and restricted contact with others. As in so many monastic exhortations, too much interaction with the world outside could lead to idle words and the intrusion of worldly affairs, and those murmurers who might cause distress, or worse, were not to be admitted near him.[121] The most important aspect of living this life was an inner spiritual life

119 This third task is mentioned only in the Brussels MS 5100–4. **120** One such person, for example, might have been Flaithbertach Mac Luim Laene, lector and anchorite of God (*in fer légind 7 anchara Dé*) who died in Lismore in 1076 (AI). **121** For admonition regarding gossip see *RB* Chap. 6.

and while not expansive, the text does include some notable details. The exhortation 'be always naked in imitation of Christ, and the gospels' (§2 *Imnochta do sechim dogréss ar Críst 7 ar na soiscéla*) echoes the popular formula *nudus nudum Christum sequi*, that one should imitate Christ, naked in poverty, as does the exhortation to give any surplus food or clothing to the brethren or to the poor (§22).[122] The well-known dictum relating to red, white and green martyrdom also appears insofar as the *cráibdech*'s mind (§§9–10) should be prepared for red martyrdom – death – and white martyrdom – exile. This exhortation might be regarded as particularly Irish and yet viewed in its entirety, the text's physical and spiritual provisions do not diverge from the stipulations of much longer texts such as *Regula solitariorum* ('Rule for solitaries') compiled by Grimlaicus, possibly a priest from Metz who lived a solitary life within a monastic community at the beginning of the tenth century.[123] None of the many 'tools for good works' listed by Grimlaicus would have been unfamiliar to an Irish hermit living close to a monastic community.[124] The difference is that the Irish author used a short exhortatory text rather than a lengthy treatise, and his text was in the vernacular and not in Latin. This difference in style and language, and not necessarily the basic content, between the Irish regulatory texts and those from elsewhere is often used as the basis for regarding the two traditions as separate and the Irish as unusual. Both had their distinct characteristics but one was not aberrant and the other conventional.

KALENDARS AND MARTYROLOGIES

Memorialization of saints, the power of prayer and forgiveness from God through the intercession of the holy dead has been a staple of Christianity since the early centuries of its existence.[125] The relationship between the living and the dead was in constant flux and varied depending on time, place and often the influence of an individual, such as St Augustine, whose own life experience and cultural environment impinged upon his attitude towards this vital relationship.[126] Texts such as liturgical kalendars and martyrologies, along with

122 Giles Constable, '*Nudus nudum Christi sequi* and parallel formulas in the twelfth century. A supplementary dossier' in Frank Forrester Church and Timothy George (eds), *Continuity and discontinuity in church history. Essays presented to George Huntston Williams on the occasion of his 65th birthday* (Leiden, 1979), pp 83–91. **123** Andrew Thornton (trans.), *Grimlaicus: rule for solitaries* (Collegeville, 2011), *Project MUSE* muse.jhu.edu/book/46747 accessed 30 March 2020; Paulette L'Hermite-Leclerq, 'Reclusion in the Middle Ages' in *CHMM*, pp 747–65, at p. 751. **124** Thornton, *Grimlaicus*, pp 79–82 §25. For a clear and readable survey of various forms of eremitical religious life see Louis Gougaud, *Ermites et reclus. Études sur d'anciennes formes de vie religieuse*. Moines et monastères 5 (Ligugé, 1928). **125** Robert Bartlett, *Why can the dead do such great things? Saints and worshippers from the martyrs to the reformation* (Princeton, 2013). **126** Peter Brown, *The ransom of the soul. Afterlife and wealth*

computistics, formed part of the church's apparatus of proceeding through the liturgical year (divided between the feast days of the *sanctorale* (the celebration of specific saints' feast days) and the *temporale* (the major festivals of the liturgical year)). The commemoration of renowned holy people, primarily apostles, martyrs, virgins (male and female) and distinguished bishops, was a universal Christian tradition. Allocated specific feast days – either the date of their death or some other event such as the translation of their relics – saints were invoked during the Mass and the Divine Office. Hence kalendars and martyrologies became essential reference tools for priests and other religious officiating at or participating in the liturgy. A number of complete and fragmentary texts from Ireland itself and from Irish milieux in Britain and on the Continent survive that have at their core, standard continental exemplars such as the *Martyrologium Hieronymianum*, the Martyrology of Usuard (d. 877) and the Martyrology of Ado of Vienne (d. 874).[127] These include *Félire Óenguso* and the Martyrology of Tallaght, variously dated to the late eighth/early-to-mid ninth century, and the twelfth-century Martyrology of Gormán.[128] Their use in a specifically monastic context is considered by Westley Follett as part of his study of the *céli Dé* and their liturgical practices.[129] In his estimation, the *céli Dé* were deeply concerned with matters of liturgy and private devotion.[130] Aside from celebrating the three Lents – Great/Spring Lent, Summer Lent and Winter Lent – the *céli Dé* mainly conformed to the Roman *temporale*. As to the *sanctorale*, there is a question as to how many saints between the saints of the Roman calendar and the large number of Irish saints included in these martyrologies, were remembered on a particular day. It is noticeable from the lists in the Stowe Missal, a small portable missal associated with the *céli Dé* dating probably to the early ninth century,[131] that only senior Irish saints – Patrick and early monastic founders – were commemorated in litanies of the Mass. Exceptions include Máel Ruain himself and the virgins Samthann, Monenna, Scethe (from Ardskeagh, Co. Cork) – whose relics were in Tallaght – and Sínech (from Crohane, Co. Tipperary).[132] Other more extensive litanies in the vernacular also exist, some of which mention many local early saints, both

in early western Christianity (Cambridge, MA, and London, 2015), pp 38–82. **127** Pádraig Ó Riain, *Feastdays of the saints. A history of Irish martyrologies*. Subsidia hagiographica 86, Société des Bollandistes (Bruxelles, 2006). **128** Stokes, *Félire Húi Gormáin;* Stokes, *Félire Óengusso Céli Dé*; Best and Lawlor, *The martyrology of Tallaght;* John Hennig, 'Studies in the Latin texts of the Martyrology of Tallaght, of *Félire Oengusso* and *Félire húi Gormáin*', *Proceedings of the Royal Irish Academy* 69C (1970), 45–112; Pádraig Ó Riain, 'The Tallaght martyrologies, redated', *Cambridge Medieval Celtic Studies* 20 (Winter, 1990), 21–38; David N. Dumville, '*Félire Óengusso*: problems of dating a monument of Old Irish', *Éigse* 33 (2002), 19–48; Follett, *Céli Dé in Ireland*, passim. **129** Follett, *Céli Dé in Ireland*, pp 199–202. **130** Ibid., p. 199. **131** O'Dwyer, *Céli Dé*, pp 151–9; Follett, *Céli Dé in Ireland*, pp 132–6; Lars B. Nooij, 'The Irish material in the Stowe Missal revisited', *Peritia* 29 (2018), 101–9. **132** Warner, *The Stowe Missal*, vol. 2, pp 14–16; Ó Riain, *DIS*, pp 550–1, 563.

male and female.[133] As to recollection of saints as part of a monastic Divine Office, some indications can be gleaned from various sources, especially from texts of the 'Tallaght dossier'. Follett draws attention to the passage in 'The teaching of Máel Ruain', a regulatory text, that emanated originally from a *céli Dé* milieu:[134]

> Their practice at Tallaght, when the feast of a saint came round, was to recite the psalms in the refectory immediately after supper, and to say the office appointed for that feast afterwards in the church, lest the feast should interfere with the office of the evening on which it fell.

Follett interprets this provision as suggesting that saints' feast days were not celebrated every day and that saints without a special office were simply mentioned during the devotions of the day. He quotes the custom associated with the *céli Dé* confessor Máel Díthruib who sang between every second psalm of the psalter, '*Sancte Michael, ora pro nobis, Sancta Maria, ora pro nobis*, adding the saint whose feast falls on the day'.[135]

The Prologue and Epilogue of *Félire Óenguso*, a vernacular metrical martyrology, are instructive as to the context and purpose of its composition. The author signals a number of times that compilation of the martyrology was intended to impose order on the celebration of feast days and that his audience was to understand its purpose and comply with its liturgical sequence:[136]

> You will follow the days in your pious handbooks; you will follow line by line carefully according to the feast days.
>
> If you do not understand thus the order that is followed by our verses, I declare in the presence of assemblies, it is more dull-witted for men.

He also enumerates – almost defensively – his sources, how the martyrology was constructed, and that it was approved by others:[137]

133 Plummer, *Irish litanies*, pp 54–9 (Litany of Irish saints I), 60–77 (Litany of Irish saints II), 92–5 (Litany of the virgins); O'Dwyer, *Céli Dé*, pp 113–16, 173–6; Johnson, 'Locating female saints'. 134 Gwynn, 'The teaching of Mael Ruain', 44–5 §78; Follett, *Céli Dé in Ireland*, pp 201–2. Original: *As é gnathugadh do bhí aca a tTamhlacht an tan tigeadh feusda naoim cuca, do ghabhdis na psailm san proinntigh d'eis proinne gan mhoill, 7 do nidís oific don fheusda san eaglais da eisi sin, d'eagla go ccuirfeadh an feusda toirmeasg ar oifig na hoidche 'na ttiocfadh se …* 135 Follett, *Céli Dé in Ireland*, p. 202. 136 Stokes, *Félire*, p. 30: lines 309–16. Translation updated. Original: *Lilisiu do laithib / it lebránaib lérib / lilisiu iar línib / col-léir donaib félib. Mani tuicce samlid / ord fil for ar lóidib, / nod-dlomaim fiad dálaib / is dallchéilliu dóinib.* Translation updated. 137 Stokes, *Félire*, pp 268–71: lines 93–6, 101–12, 137–44. Original: *Cáinshenad domm-ánic / im-midchuairt mo thige / dia chocertad fiaduib / fo ríaguil ríg nime … In t-ord inna caiptel / ma beth nech fod-fhúasna, / atbiur fiad in línsa / is díthár don tshlúagsa … Félire ro scrútus / i céin ocus acus, / la dúthracht dorignius, / do nóebaib doratus.* Translation updated.

> A fair synod came to me in the midcourt of my house, to correct it before you, according to the rule of the king of Heaven …
>
> The order of the chapters [of the martyrology], if there be anyone who disturbs it, I declare it before this number, it is a destructive slaughter of this host … I have searched out martyrologies far and near; with devotion I have created [it], to the saints I have given.

He then lists his sources: the extensive writings of Ambrose, the Sensus of Hilary, the Antigraph of Jerome, the Martyrology of Eusebius, and the martyrologies of the men of the Goídel ('the Irish'). The question arises as to the actual use of a metrical text such as *Félire Óenguso* in a monastic setting. That it, and indeed the Martyrology of Tallaght, continued in use until the twelfth century is implied in the preface to the Martyrology of Gormán. In his preface to this later martyrology Máel Muire Ua Gormáin, abbot of the Augustinian foundation of Cnoc na n-Apstol (Knock, Co. Louth) in the late twelfth century,[138] declares that his purpose was to revise the Irish version of the martyrology of saints because Óengus had omitted many Irish and international saints. Máel Muire also comments that 'a great number of those whom he brought in were not arranged on the days on which the Church celebrates their festivals.' These omissions had occurred because Óengus had used the Martyrology of Tallaght as the basis of his own text.[139] Apart from confirming that these were his sources and that his task was to update them, Máel Muire exhorts his readers in sentiments similar to Óengus in his Prologue and Epilogue:[140]

> For the sake of Almighty God and for the sake of the saints for whom this work of art was made, let honour be paid to it, and let it be transcribed. Let the old recite it from books and let them induce the young to commit it to memory.
>
> If errors and defects are found therein, let the erudite correct them and add [what may be needed]; but let them not spoil the course of the poem.

What can be deduced from these comments is that the martyrology was recited and that a metrical form was suitable for teaching the feast days of the saints and church festivals to novices and oblates. Whether it was read aloud as part of the

138 https://www.dib.ie/biography/ua-gormain-mael-muire-a8739. **139** Stokes, *Martyrology of Gorman*, pp 4–5. Original: *acus mórán dia tuc díbh leis nach isna laithibh chelebras in ecclas a féle ros-córaigsium. Ocus iss edh fodera dósom sin co deimhin (amhail rodherbsamar) ara fagbail amhlaidhsin im-martiroloig Thamhlachta Mháelrúain asin-derna a fhélere.* **140** Stokes, *Martyrology of Gorman*, pp 4–5. Original: *Ar Dhia uilichumhachtach ocus ar na naemhaibh dia ndernadh in grés tabar onóir dó, ocus scríbthar. Gabhat na sin hé fri lebhraibh, ocus gresset na hóccu mo mebrugud. Día fagbaiter dno mill ocus esbadha ann certaighet eolaigh iat ocus tuillet, acht na millet reim in dana.*

Chapter – as, for example, set out in the *Regularis Concordia*[141] – or the reading of the colloquy at supper is not clear, although the use of the relatively simple *rinnard* metre would suggest that it was not difficult to memorize a four-line verse on a daily basis. Nevertheless, while customs relating to where texts were read aloud remained diverse everywhere until the thirteenth century, reading of martyrologies at the Chapter (prime) was known, but not necessarily widespread.[142] The existence of Irish martyrologies dating from the ninth century along with references in saints' lives and other texts to monks following the canonical hours, gathering together – the terms *tinól* and *comthinól* are often used to describe such gatherings – suggest that the public recitation of saints' feast days from martyrologies was a standard practice in Irish monastic communities.

The provisions of two rules associated with the *céli Dé*, 'The teaching of Máel Ruain' and 'The rule of the *céli Dé*' in relation to readings in the refectory are illustrative of the books kept in their monasteries, and most likely in monasteries outside their network. 'The teaching of Máel Ruain' directs that the gospel of St John and the Acts of the Apostles were to be read each night alternating between one week and another while both texts prescribe that in the refectory the rules and miracles of the saints and the gospels, one gospel for each quarter of the year, were read along with a series of prayers in Latin. 'The rule of the Céli Dé' adds that there was a pedagogical function to these readings as well in that the audience would be questioned about the subject matter on the following day to ensure that their minds had been set on God, and not on the meal.[143] This provision was probably directed at novices and oblates.

AN ISLAND HERMIT AND A PILGRIM IN STONE

Adomnán's life of Columba is an island-based narrative that aligns very well with the ecclesiastical archaeology of the west of Ireland and the islands of Scotland. Many of these islands were inhabited permanently or seasonally by individuals and communities to perform penitential rites or in more extreme cases to withdraw completely from the world with the intention of coming closer to Heaven. Their small churches, habitations, cross-slabs and burial grounds can

141 Thomas Symons (ed.), *Regularis Concordia Anglicae nationis monachorum sanctimonialiumque. The monastic agreement of the monks and nuns of the English nation* (London, 1953), p. 17 §21. **142** Teresa Webber, 'Reading in the refectory: monastic practice in England, *c.*1000–*c.*1300', London University Annual John Coffin Memorial Palaeography Lecture 18 February 2010 (revised text, 2013), p. 8: https://www.academia.edu/9489001/Reading_in_the_Refectory_Monastic_Practice_in_England_c._1000-c.1300 accessed 17 April 2020; Colmán Ó Clabaigh, 'Community, commemoration and confraternity'. **143** Gwynn, 'The teaching of Mael Ruain'; pp 12–13 §17; 'The rule of the Céli Dé', pp 72–3 §31.

be seen or have been recovered spectacularly by archaeologists on islands such as Skellig Michael and Illaunloughan, Co. Kerry, the Aran Islands and High Island, Co. Galway, the Inishkea Islands, Co. Mayo, and Inishmurray, Co. Sligo. While these sites are well known, others have barely left any trace or the evidence for eremitical communities appears in ephemeral monuments and objects. Teampall Bhreacáin or Díseart Bhreacáin on the island of Inishmore (Árann Mór), the largest of the Aran Islands, is one of the myriad of church sites on the island. Its architectural and archaeological remains are extensive and they appear to range in date from the eighth to the sixteenth centuries.[144] In 1822, George Petrie related how on a visit to Aran a monument known as *Leaba Bhreacáin* 'Brecan's bed' at Teampall Bhreacáin in the graveyard of the church was opened, and[145]

> On digging to the depth of about six feet, they came to a large flag, of a square form, about ten feet in diameter, but no inscription was looked for, or noticed on it. On raising this flag a deep grave was found, filled with rounded stones from eight to ten inches in diameter, which had been brought from the adjacent strand; and, on throwing them out of the grave, one was found containing an inscription in the Irish character.

When he joined the great visitation of scholars to Aran in 1857, Petrie added that[146]

> The grave of St Brecan was opened about sixty years ago, and was subsequently reopened in the presence of the parish priest, and of Mr O'Flaherty, the magistrate, for the inspection of Dr Petrie, who found in it a well-shaped skull, which he believed to have been that of the saint, and which was immediately and carefully restored to its resting-place, and also the cross, or headstone of St Brecan, which was afterwards taken away by some person not now known.

A larger broken cross-inscribed slab with the inscription S[AN]C[T]I BRE[CA]NI was also said to have been dug out of *Leaba Bhreacáin* in the early nineteenth century.[147] (Fig. 5) It is not clear if this was the same monument as

144 John Waddell, 'An archæological survey of Temple Brecan, Aran', *Journal of the Galway Archæological and Historical Society* 33 (1972–3), 5–27; Conleth Manning, 'Teampall Bhreacáin, Aran, its five phases and obscured doorway' in Niamh NicGhabhann and Danielle O'Donovan (eds), *Mapping new territories in art and architectural histories: essays in honour of Roger Stalley* (Turnhout, 2021), pp 115–28. **145** George Petrie, *Christian inscriptions in the Irish language* ed. Margaret Stokes vol. 2 (Dublin, 1878), p. 20 (plate XII, figs 25–6). **146** Martin Haverty, *The Aran Isles; or, A report of the excursion of the ethnological section of the British Association from Dublin to the western islands of Aran, in September 1857* (Dublin, 1859), pp 15–16. **147** Waddell, 'Survey of Temple Brecan', p. 17.

the 'headstone' of St Brecán mentioned by Petrie in his description. Eight cross-slabs are associated with *Leaba Bhreacáin*.[148] Lionard and Henry included the inscribed slab among their Group VI (Expansional crosses) some of which, including the Teampall Bhreacáin slab, they suggested dated to the eighth century.[149] The small oval mudstone nodule, possibly a lamp, discovered in the grave in 1822 carried the inscription +OR AR BRAN NAILITHER 'A prayer for Bran, the pilgrim'.[150] How might this archaeological assemblage be interpreted? Taken altogether, it is reasonable to assume that this was the focal grave at Temple Brecan and was regarded in the eighth century as the founder's grave. A possible parallel is an object found in *Clochán Leo* on Inis Airc, a small island monastery on the Connemara coast. Subject to recent excavations, the evidence from Inis Airc has added an interesting dimension to the profile of such small monasteries.[151] *Clochán Leo* is a complex enclosed by a curvilinear stone enclosure surrounding a ruined circular stone structure with a corbelled stone roof, a pavement strewn with quartz pebbles and two platforms popularly known as *leachta*. The *leachta* overlay rectangular chambers which although filled with beach gravel and shells did not contain any skeletal remains. As with most *leachta*, these were cenotaphs possibly commemorating saints buried elsewhere or even recalling the empty tomb of Christ.[152] A small cross-inscribed granite pebble was discovered on the pavement and this has been interpreted by the excavators as a possible early medieval cursing stone used for oath-swearing, blessings or maledictions.[153] Such stones, many of them much larger and inscribed with crosses, survive at other sites, most notably on Inishmurray, Co. Sligo.[154] If anything can be deduced from the Inis Airc and Inishmurray stones, then the *Bran n-ailither* stone may have been an ex-voto gift dedicated by Bran to his community's founder through which he sought forgiveness or a blessing. While *ailithir* is usually interpreted to mean a lay pilgrim, an *ailithir* or *peregrinus* in the context of these monastic islands and of the Temple Brecan grave is more likely to have been a life-long pilgrim dedicated to a committed religious life. As noted by Thomas Charles-Edwards, this category of pilgrim is the *deorad Dé*, 'exile of God' who has a particularly high legal status[155]. Two annalistic entries support this interpretation, those recording the deaths of Ailithir, abbot of Clonmacnoise (AU 599) and Móengal *ailithir*, abbot of Bangor (AU 871).

148 SMR nos GA1 10-023013–GA1 10-023015, GA1 10-023017–GA1 10-023020. **149** Pádraig Lionard and Françoise Henry, 'Early Irish grave-slabs', *Proceedings of the Royal Irish Academy* 61 (1960–1), 95–169, at pp 128–31. **150** Waddell, 'Survey of Temple Brecan', p. 23. **151** Ryan Lash et al., '"Differing in status, but one in spirit": sacred space and social diversity at island monasteries in Connemara, Ireland', *Antiquity* 92 (2018), 437–55. **152** Tomás Ó Carragáin, 'Altars, graves and cenotaphs: *leachta* as foci for ritual in early medieval Ireland' in Nic Ghabhann and O'Donovan (eds), *Mapping new territories*, pp 129–46. **153** Lash et al., 'Differing in status', 450 (fig. 10). **154** Jerry O'Sullivan and Tomás Ó Carragáin, *Inishmurray. Monks and pilgrims in an Atlantic landscape* (Cork, 2008), pp 103–11, 335–41. **155** Charles-Edwards, 'The social background', p. 53.

Another tiny island, Inishderry (townland of Derrynameel), in Broadhaven Bay, Co. Mayo, produced a stone figure carved from local laminated shale of a monk or cleric holding a book, presumably a gospel book or a psalter.[156] (Fig. 6) The figure, which is relatively small (H 22.7cm, W 10.1cm, T 2.9cm), was discovered in a shell midden and is likely to date to the eighth century. It is similar in motif to the later Romanesque figure from Lismore, Co. Waterford (Book cover). The letters DN[I] representing *Domini* are carved above one eye. The soft brown shale and the manner in which it is carved almost imitates wood and the figure's place in a church or in the niche of a stone cell is easily imagined. The figure evokes the sentiments of the *céli Dé* text, 'The monastery of Tallaght' on the psalter:[157]

> A 'son of life' should always recite his psalms by the psalter. This is what he [Máel Ruain] used to say of this: There are three adversaries busy attacking me, my eye, my tongue, and my thoughts: the psalter restrains them all.

Having a visual image of a psalter or gospel book held by a monk in front of him/her might have assisted a hermit or lifelong pilgrim's meditation on the psalms and the scriptures, especially on a tiny island where church furnishings cannot have been too lavish.

Texts, objects and monuments resonate with the essence of the monastic tradition in Ireland from its foundational period during the sixth century. The Irish, no less than many other people from the Middle East, north Africa and Atlantic coastal regions, absorbed the monastic committed life with enthusiasm, possibly even too ardently, if early sources from all these regions are to be believed. The fundamental ideals of Christian monasticism took root in Ireland and were included in regulatory texts such as the Irish canon and vernacular laws, penitentials, and exhortations. While the fundamentals were in line with those followed elsewhere, the differences were determined by the structures of Irish society, the Irish penchant for making their own of Latin terminology, the early use of the vernacular in the written tradition, even in relation to church matters, and an early attraction to relatively extreme asceticism that left such a clear imprint on the Irish landscape, especially along the west coast. These differences, however, were not so great as to generate a separate monastic

156 Joseph Raftery, 'A stone figure from Co. Mayo', *Journal of the Royal Society of Antiquaries of Ireland* 14 (1944), 87–90; Maeve Sikora, 'Steinfigur eines Geistlichen' in Christoph Stiegemann, Martin Kroker and Wolfgang Walter (eds), *Credo. Christianisierung Europas im Mittelalter. Band II: Katalog* (Petersberg, 2013), pp 236–7, no. 198. 157 Gwynn and Purton, 'The monastery of Tallaght', p. 142 para. 39. Original: *Fri saltair do géss nogebad mac bethad a salmu. Issed asberedsom desuidiu atat tri foglaide oc mo fogail mo suil 7 mo tengæ 7 mo menme dosnaircelæ hule int saltair.*

tradition, a 'Celtic' monasticism, that diverged from an 'orthodox' monasticism prevalent elsewhere. The constant close connections between the Irish, Gaulish, Anglo-Saxon, Frankish, Germanic and Lombardic church, and of course, Rome, meant that the Irish tradition was but one of many flourishing in eastern and western Christendom. If any distinction existed between the Irish and the rest, its adherence to elements of the original Middle Eastern and north African monastic traditions, especially as regards more severe asceticism, later than elsewhere, might be singled out. This tendency would cause tension at a later stage for some Irish monks who settled on the Continent.

CHAPTER 3

Reading the primary sources for Irish monasticism: Part II: post-900 sources

From the late eighth century, Ireland became part of a vast Viking trading network, along with regions all over Europe as far east as modern Russia and into the Middle East. As an island that had not received any great influx of newcomers since the Iron Age, these new arrivals had a marked effect on Irish society and its economy.[1] They integrated gradually with the native population, and by the tenth century they had established coastal towns, the most important being Dublin, Wexford, Waterford, Cork and Limerick. The rich and varied archaeology of these towns is testament to their connection with a trading empire, and their wealth, in turn, quickly attracted the attention of the Irish aristocracy. During this period, native society also changed, partially as a result of internal political and social transformations and partially due to Norse influence. Royal authority became more centralized and clearly structured with new dynasties emerging to seize power from well-established ones. Similarly, ecclesiastical authority was in the hands of fewer and increasingly more powerful and wealthier monasteries ruled by hereditary families who were often in charge of very extensive estates. This did not necessarily lead to a sharp decline in standards, as often portrayed, as these monasteries also housed bishops, priests, monastic communities, anchorites, scribes, and many had eremitical outliers to which these religious could withdraw in contemplation. The Norse contribution to monasticism in Ireland was most evident in the coastal towns. Their conversion probably began in earnest in the mid-tenth century and once towns such as Dublin saw the need to establish an ecclesiastical structure, their kings, Norse and Irish, looked for templates elsewhere. Rome attracted many of Ireland's elite who travelled there on pilgrimage, and as a result of their travels, they became increasingly aware of the gradual changes being implemented in western Christendom.[2] Hence, the first bishop of Dublin, Dúnán (alias Donatus), who probably took up office *c.*1030, was trained in Cologne and the foundational relics of its cathedral Christ Church were brought from Cologne.[3]

1 Howard B. Clarke, Máire Ní Mhaonaigh and Raghnall Ó Floinn (eds), *Ireland and Scandinavia in the early Viking age* (Dublin, 1998). 2 Edel Bhreathnach, 'The nature of pre-"reform" Irish monasticism' in Bhreathnach, Krasnodębska and Smith, *Monastic Europe*, pp 21–43, at pp 28–30. 3 Raghnall Ó Floinn, 'The foundation relics of Christ Church cathedral

The English church, headed by Canterbury, also began to take an interest in Ireland and to consider it as a region in need of moral and structural reform, often at the instigation of Irish bishops and kings.[4] Despite these developments, apparent from the sources presented in this chapter, while aware of these changes and subject to many new influences, the Irish church maintained many of its distinctive features and the Irish monastic tradition was sufficiently vibrant to adapt to new ideas within its own cultural framework. As in Chapter 2, the sources discussed here are but a select few that are intended to demonstrate these changes and the varying strands in Irish monasticism post-900.

SAINTS' LIVES AND HOMILIES: *BETHA CHOLUIM CHILLE* AND THE LIFE OF COLMÁN MAC LUACHÁIN

The corpus of Irish saints' lives is extensive. They narrate the lives of early saints only, the exceptions being Bernard of Clairvaux's life of Malachy of Armagh and the life of Lorcán Ua Tuathail (Laurence O'Toole) compiled in the monastery of Eu in Normandy, where he died in 1180.[5] Both lives were used as dossiers for their respective canonizations in 1190 (Malachy) and 1226 (Lorcán). Both, of course, shed some light on the state of monasticism in Ireland in the twelfth century but need to be treated with caution as their authors' main objective was to promote Malachy and Lorcán as reformers of the Irish church.[6] A number of other lives can be fairly reasonably dated to the eleventh or twelfth century. They include the life of St Flannán of Killaloe, Conchubranus's life of St Monenna and the vernacular life of Colum Cille.[7] Many of the lives are best treated like the stratigraphy of an archaeological excavation. Some contain very early material which is embedded in twelfth- and thirteenth-century versions when codification of the lives into large collections, both in Latin and the vernacular, gained momentum and continued to the seventeenth century.[8] Indicators of a

and the origins of the diocese of Dublin' in Seán Duffy (ed.), *Medieval Dublin VII* (Dublin, 2006), pp 89–102. 4 Flanagan, *Transformation*, pp 39–41. 5 J. Leclercq and H.-M. Rochais (eds), *Vita Malachiae* in *Sancti Bernardi opera* (8 vols; Rome, 1957–77), iii, pp 297–378. For translations of the life see Hugh Jackson Lawlor (trans.), *St Bernard of Clairvaux's life of St Malachy of Armagh* (London and New York, 1920); Robert T. Meyer (trans.), *Bernard of Clairvaux. The life and death of Saint Malachy the Irishman* (Kalamazoo, 1978). I use Meyer's translation throughout; Plummer, 'Vie et miracles de S. Laurent'. 6 For a somewhat overly critical view of Bernard's life of Malachy see Ó Corráin, *The Irish church*, pp 45–7, 89. 7 Flanagan, *Transformation*, pp 14–16; Paulus Grosjean (transcription), 'Catalogus codicum hagiographicorum latinorum bibliothecarum Dubliniensium: vita sancti Flannani', *Analecta Bollandiana* 46 (1928), 81–148, at pp 124–41; Heist, *VSH Salm.*, 280–301; Ulster Society for Medieval Latin Studies (eds), 'The life of St Monenna by Conchubranus [part 1]', *Seanchas Ard Mhacha* 9 (1978–9), 250–73; [parts 2 and 3] 10 (1980–2), 117–41, 426–54; Herbert, *Iona, Kells, and Derry*, pp 218–88. 8 Sharpe, *Medieval Irish saints' lives*, pp 3–90.

revision to a life include allusions to hereditary families who are known from annalistic records to have dominated a particular monastery or church at a given time and rivalries between churches or attitudes to particular dynasties that can be independently dated.[9] Temporal matters, specifically ownership of estates and lands, were often a primary motive for the composition or revision of a saint's life. The spiritual concerns and lives of a religious community that formed part of a monastery are sometimes difficult to single out in hagiographical texts beyond mundane references and commonplace terminology. It would be a mistake to dismiss this large corpus, however, as irrelevant. A saint's life can contribute much, especially if the context of its composition can be established fairly reliably. One notable example is the Irish life of Colum Cille (hereafter *BCC*), a vernacular text, that was written probably in the mid- to late twelfth century during the abbacy of Flaithbertach Ua Brolcháin of Derry (d. 1175).[10] Flaithbertach also ruled all the other Columban foundations in Ireland during his abbacy. Máire Herbert has argued that *BCC* 'represents a synthesis of old and new, its content combining the venerable testimony of the *Vita Columbae* with a contemporary message', that of changes taking place in the Irish church, and specifically in the Columban *familia*.[11] Flaithbertach Ua Brolcháin himself straddled the old and new, on one hand being a member of a hereditary ecclesiastical family while also participating on a national stage in implementing changes to the Irish church during his career. Apart from extolling Colum Cille and re-telling his life and miracles, *BCC* is also a clear assertion of his successors' rights over Columban monasteries throughout Ireland, and, of course, the income due from them.

BCC follows a conventional biographical structure – homiletic introduction, the saint's life, homiletic *peroratio* at the end[12] – and was designed for use on Colum Cille's feast day on 9 June. The homiletic introduction in both Latin and Irish deals with the various categories and grades of pilgrimage (*dul i n-ailithri*), defined as leaving one's fatherland (*atharda*), within the biblical narrative of Abraham and the Israelites leaving their native land 'to set out on pilgrimage to the Promised Land' (*tidecht dia oilithre i tír thairngeri*).[13] This was not a pilgrimage undertaken readily by the laity but by men of faith who left their country, land, wealth and worldly gratification for the sake of the Lord. This was a perfect pilgrimage (*foirbthe*), a *vocatio*.[14] That the introduction was primarily directed towards a religious community is understood from the section that declares: 'then there are three forms of vocation' (*Tres autem sunt modi*

9 Mac Shamhráin, *Church and polity in pre-Norman Ireland*; Charles Doherty, 'The transmission of the cult of St Máedhóg' in Próinséas Ní Chatháin and Michael Richter (eds), *Ireland and Europe in the early Middle Ages: texts and transmission/Irland und Europa im früheren mittelalter: texte und überlieferung* (Dublin, 2002), pp 268–83. 10 Herbert, *Iona, Kells, and Derry*, pp 218–86. 11 Ibid., pp 204–5. 12 Ibid., pp 181–2. 13 Ibid., pp 218, 248 §2.15. 14 Ibid., pp 218–19, 248–9 §§3–4.

vocationum).[15] The first, *primus ex deo*, consisted of people impelled by divine grace to serve the Lord, such as Paul and Antony and other devout monks (*manaig*) who served God in Egypt. The second, *secundus per hominem*, were people persuaded by holy preachers (*trésna proceptorib noemu*) who imitated the apostle Paul when he preached to the gentiles. The third, *tertius ex necessitate*, were people like the Israelites who found themselves in danger and suffering at the hands of foreigners and who turned away from adoration of idols and images and prayed to the Lord for deliverance. These were chosen people whose pilgrimage on earth would bring them salvation. In her study of the eschatological and spiritual elements of *BCC*, specifically in a monastic context, Katja Ritari argues that the ideal of pilgrimage is salient for the understanding of medieval monastic ideology. Leaving one's home for God's sake 'acquires even weightier significance in the context of early Irish society, in which one's rights and protection were dependent on extended family, and movement outside one's own territory (or *túath*) was a perilous affair'.[16] The centrality to monastic ideology of pursuing life's pilgrimage *primus ex deo* in voluntary exile from the world is epitomized by the *deorad Dé* 'exile of God', a figure, as previously discussed in the context of early Irish law, who is regarded as committed to a religious life and highly regarded in society. Indeed *BCC*'s homily elaborates on what this type of exile meant:[17]

> In yet another instance, a person leaves his fatherland (*a atharda*) entirely, in body and mind, as did the apostles and those of perfect pilgrimage (*lucht na hailithri forpthi*), to whom the great and good Lord prophesied in the gospel, when he said: *Vos qui derelinquistis omnia propter me, patrem et matrem, uxorem, filios et filias, agrum et omnia quae habere potuistis, centuplum accipietis in hoc saeculo, et vitam eternam in futuro.* 'Be assured of this', says Jesus, 'that the small band (of you) (*uathad sochaide*) who have forsaken your country and kindred (*bar tir 7 bar coibnes collaide*), your possessions and your worldly enjoyment for my sake will receive a hundredfold of good from me here in this life and eternal life thereafter, after the Last Judgement.' *Hi sunt veri peregrini qui cum psalmista possunt dicere.* These people, truly, are the perfect pilgrims (*lucht na hoilithri comláni*), in whose person the prophet spoke in exultation and thanks to God: *Advena sum apud te, domine, et peregrinus sicut omnes patres mei.* 'I thank you, God,' says the prophet, 'because I am a pilgrim and an exile in the world, like the elders who have gone before (*is ailithri 7 is deoraidecht dam isin tshaegul iar n-inntshamail na sruthi remtechtach*).'

15 Ibid., pp 219, 249 §4. 16 Katja Ritari, *Pilgrimage to Heaven. Eschatology and monastic spirituality in early medieval Ireland* (Turnhout, 2016), p. 22. 17 Herbert, *Iona, Kells, and Derry*, pp 221–2, 250 §9.

A fundamental issue for monks since the early days, which is alluded to both in *BCC*'s homily (§4) and in the life itself (§53), concerned the monk's involvement with the world beyond his community. Within the community, as has been seen from the circumstances of the *Regula Choluimb Chille*, there could be degrees of detachment, but *BCC* suggests that some were more active than others among the laity. One could follow the example of Paul the apostle and preach the Gospel, a vocation more likely to be undertaken by those ordained to priesthood. Colum Cille was counted among these and he is specifically described as 'the holy priest Columba, namely, the noble priest of the island of Ireland' (*sanctus presbyter Columba .i. uasalshacart innse Goedel*).[18] The saint went on a preaching circuit (*cuairt procepta*) and encountered Áed mac Brénainn, king of Tethba, who granted him the site to found the monastery of Durrow.[19] When he decided to leave Ireland, his mission was 'to teach the word of God to Scots and Britons and Saxons', clearly an intention to live actively among these people. In a crucial insight into the structure of a monastic community the saint divided his community on Iona between those who were to pursue a contemplative monastic life (*ri teoir i mmanchaine*) and those who were in active ministry (*fri hactáil*).[20]

BCC may not be typical of many Irish saints' lives. It probably introduces us more faithfully to a monastic ideology that prevailed in Ireland during the eleventh and twelfth centuries than most other sources. While much would be similar to monastic ideology elsewhere, perhaps the most atypical aspect related to the survival of the monastic *familia* of Colum Cille, a network of churches bound together through a common founder, a sixth-century saint. It is also noteworthy that *BCC* never mentions any of the other great monastic fathers (Benedict, Augustine, Columbanus) apart from the desert fathers, Paul and Antony. Clearly, the life was directed at three audiences, all defined as pilgrims: monks, preachers and the laity seeking salvation.

In contrast to *BCC* the vernacular life of Colmán mac Luacháin was written during the twelfth century for the midland monastery of Lann Luacháin (Lynn, Co. Westmeath) with a different purpose in mind. Here, its hereditary patron families were trying to hold onto their lands while being squeezed between much more powerful monasteries in the region – Kells, Duleek, Clonard and Clonmacnoise – as they competed to become episcopal sees.[21] According to his life, the otherwise little-known saint Colmán mac Luacháin spent his life negotiating with other saints and local and provincial kings to gain authority over churches and lands, and to free his church from royal and ecclesiastical tributes. He also gave authority to certain families to be hereditary guardians of his

18 Ibid., pp 222, 251 §10.104–5. 19 Ibid., pp 231, 257 §37.295–7. It is worth noting the use of various terms in *BCC* to describe Colum Cille's foundations: *reclésa*, *cella*, *congbála*. 20 Herbert, *Iona, Kells, and Derry*, pp 237, 261 §53.420–1. 21 Kuno Meyer (ed.), *Betha Colmáin maic Lúacháin. Life of Colmán son of Lúachan*. Todd Lecture Series XVII (Dublin, 1911).

churches, lands and relics.[22] The service rendered by them is described as *mainchaine*, a term for the service granted by *manaig*, in the sense of church tenants:[23]

> So then they made their union in Heaven and on earth, namely, the three Colmáns[24] and bishop Etchén and Mochua son of Nemann, and thereupon they went to their own churches. And the three Colmáns had taken orders at the same time as Mochua. So that henceforth Lann and Clonfad and Tech Mochua are one church, that is, Lann is the west of the church, and the centre of the church is Clonfad and the east of the church is Tech Mochua. Then many monastic tenants (*manaig*) came to Colmán mac Luacháin and prostrated themselves before him; and they offered him the service of their families and kindred until the Day of Judgement.

Relics play a significant part in this life. They included bells, croziers, the graves of holy men and women, and Colmán's own reliquary. The re-discovery of his reliquary in 1122 may have occasioned the compilation of his life.[25] The reliquary is referred to in the text:[26]

> Now weakness came to Colmán mac Luacháin, and when the end of his life was appointed for him, his monks (*maic eclaise*) and his monastic tenants (*manaig*) came to him and wept bitterly in his presence, and begged

22 For a detailed analysis of this life see Gavin David Dillon, 'Betha Cholmáin maic Luacháin: an ecclesiastical microcosm of the twelfth-century Irish midlands' (PhD, University College Cork, 2013). Copyright Gavin Dillon https://cora.ucc.ie/bitstream/handle/10468/1253/Full%20Text%20E-thesis.pdf?sequence=5 Accessed 6 April 2020. **23** Meyer, *Betha Colmáin*, pp 34–5 §35. Original: *Dorōnsat īarum a n-œntaid ann-sin .i. na trī Colmāin 7 epscop Etc[h]ēn 7 Mochúa mac Nemaind in-nem 7 a talmain 7 lotar īarsin dia cellaib dílsib 7 a n-œnfecht rogabsat na trī Colmāin grādha 7 Mochúa. Conid œnc[h]ell ósin ille Land 7 Clūain Fota 7 Tech Mochúa .i. īarthar cille Lann 7 medón cille Clúain Fotta 7 œrthar cille Tech Mochúa. Tāncatar tra manaig imda co Colmán mac Lūachāin 7 slēchtsat dó 7 aidbret manchine a clann 7 a cinēl co brāth dó.* Translation updated. **24** These were three midland saints whose personal name was Colmán ('little dove'), a very common name for saints of the conversion period. The three Colmáns were Colmán mac Luacháin, Colmán Elo (Lynally, Co. Offaly) and Colmán Comraire (Conry, Co. Westmeath). **25** AU, AFM, ALC. AU 1122: *Scrín Cholmáin m Luacháin d'fhoghbháil i n-ailaidh Lainne ferchubat i talmhain dia Cetaín in Braith* ('The shrine of Colmán son of Luachán was found in the burial place in Lann, a man's cubit in earth, on Spy Wednesday'). In his thesis (p. 198) Gavin Dillon suggests that the saint's relics may have been hidden away in the ninth century to protect them from theft or destruction by the Vikings. The region in which Lann is located was subject to considerable Viking activity at the time. **26** Meyer, *Betha Colmáin*, pp 96–7 §96. Original: *Tāinigc tra faindi do Cholmān mac Lūachāin 7 ōrba cindti forba a bethad dó tāngcatar cugci a maic eclaise 7 a manaig 7 rochísit cáoi serb ina fīadnaisi 7 rochuincsett fair cetugud dōib fūaslucud an talman for a taisib nœma 7 a mbith i scrīn cumdachta eturru amail cech ardnœm 7 cach n-ardapstal arc[h]ena fo Ērinn. Rodeōnaig tra Colmān sin coma[d] comdīdnad torsi dōib-sium 7 comad chādus ar cach ngúasacht acside 7*

> him to allow them to open the earth on his holy relics (*a taisib náema*), that they might be kept among them in a protecting shrine (*i scrín cumdachta*) like those of every other great saint and chief apostle throughout Ireland. Then Colmán granted that, so that it might be a comfort of grief to them, and that his relics might be an amulet (*cádus*) against every visible and invisible danger.

The community of Lann clearly needed to heighten the memorialization of their lesser-known saint by following the example of other churches by adorning his relics in a suitably decorated reliquary, an object probably similar to the Breac Máedóc created for the church of Drumlane, Co. Cavan or St Manchán's Shrine made for Lemanaghan, Co. Offaly [Figs 7 and 8].[27]

Does the life of Colmán mac Luacháin suggest that a monastic community, apart from monastic tenants and hereditary ecclesiastical families existed at Lann, as *BCC* suggests for the *familia* of Colum Cille? There is a sense that the author(s)/compiler(s) understood the tenets of a religious life but that Lann was not a church – unlike Derry or Kells – in which committed monasticism was especially vibrant. The brief introductory homily was preached on the saint's feast day in the presence of his reliquary.[28] It could have been preached by a priest serving at Lann, not necessarily a member of a monastic community, as a monastic ideal is not particularly evident in the text. Its theme is based on a line in Psalm 30 (35) *Viriliter agite, et confortetur cor vestrum, omnes qui speratis in Domino* ('Be courageous, and your heart will be comforted, all those who hope in the Lord'). This phrase was commonly used to encourage both religious and laity to maintain their faith, knowing that God was with them,[29] and frequently, as in this text, applied to saints 'fighting manfully and stoutly for God'.

In his life, Colmán was ordained a priest by Bishop Etchén,[30] having spent the formative years of his religious life in Lismore, a church with particularly strong monastic traditions.[31] His ascetic practices are not praised specifically. He went to *Úaim Cholmáin* 'Colmán's Cave' which was located in a rock behind the king's fortress at *Dún Léime ind Eich* – somewhere near the river Boyne – for the three periods of Lent.[32] Reference is made in a somewhat formulaic manner to his devotional rule (*ríagol a chrábuid*). By the twelfth century, as attested by the life itself and by a note added to it in the manuscript, there were three important office holders in Lann:[33] the *airchinnech*, the hereditary successor of Colmán who administered the affairs of the church and its lands and who was married,[34] the

nemaicsidi hé. Translation updated. **27** Griffin Murray and Kevin O'Dwyer, *Saint Manchan's shrine. Art and devotion in twelfth-century Ireland* (Tullamore, 2022). **28** Meyer, *Betha Colmáin*, pp 4–5 §2. **29** Christopher Fletcher, '«Sire, uns hom sui». Transgression et inversion par rapport à quelle(s) norme(s) dans l'histoire des masculinités médiévales?', *Micrologus Library* 78 (2017), 23–50, at p. 30. **30** Meyer, *Betha Colmáin*, pp 30–1 §§31–2. **31** Ibid., pp 20–3 §§20–3. **32** Ibid., pp 43–5 §45. **33** Ibid., p. vi. **34** Ibid., pp 96–7 §98

priest (*sacart*), and the craftsman (*sáer*). It would seem, therefore, that the *manaig* of Lann were its tenants, those who worked its land or performed other manual services. Churches such as Lann were to be found all over Ireland: they were local, their allegiances were local, their priests provided pastoral care for their tenants and the local powerful families, some of whom held hereditary ecclesiastical offices. On the whole, their founder saints were revered locally, some with more extensive cults scattered regionally, and very occasionally nationally, often due to the merging of cults of similarly named saints.[35] At such churches, monasticism may have been practised during the first centuries of their existence but by the tenth century it no longer existed. What filtered through was the terminology of monasticism, especially the ubiquitous term *manaig*.

MONASTIC BOOKS AND COMMENTARIES

Instructions such as those outlined in 'The teaching of Máel Ruain' and 'The rule of the *céli Dé*' along with the routine of following the canonical hours and celebrating the Eucharist introduces another set of sources that cast light on Irish monasticism. While not surviving in great numbers, nonetheless, some Irish missals, gospel books and psalters dating to between the tenth and twelfth centuries exist in sufficient numbers to allow us to gain some idea of the books kept by various communities and what sources they had at hand.[36] The Gospel Book BL Harley 1802 is unusual in that it can be dated from the colophons inserted by its sole compiler, Máel Brigte Ua Máel Uanaig who at the age of twenty-eight was writing in Armagh in 1138.[37] He seeks a prayer for his tutor (*oite*) Máel Ísu son of the priest of Tynan, Co. Armagh,[38] possibly Máel Ísu mac Máil Choluim, chief keeper of the calendar (*prím-challadóir*) in Armagh and

refers to his wife as the *banairchindech* of Lann. 35 While this occurred occasionally, I do not agree with Pádraig Ó Riain's serial amalgamation of saints' cults in Ireland and Scotland. It is probably the case that one prominent saint caused others to adopt their name, as with Columba, but this does not mean that local cults were all to that saint and that no local historic saint actually existed. See, for example, Pádraig Ó Riain, 'Cainnech alias Columcille, patron of Ossory' in Pádraig de Brún, Seán Ó Coileáin, and Pádraig Ó Riain (eds), *Folia Gadelica. Essays presented by former students to R.A. Breatnach on the occasion of his retirement from the professorship of Irish language and literature at University College, Cork* (Cork, 1983), pp 20–35. 36 Françoise Henry and G.L. Marsh-Micheli, 'A century of Irish illumination (1070–1170)', *Proceedings of the Royal Irish Academy* 62C (1961–3), 101–66 + 44 plates; *CLH* ii, pp 823–39 §§638–53. 37 Henry and Marsh-Micheli, 'A century of Irish illumination', 148–52; *CLH*, ii, pp 833–5 §648: the texts of his colophons are transcribed and translated here. 38 William Reeves and Eugene O'Curry, 'On an Irish MS of the Four Gospels in the British Museum', *Proceedings of the Royal Irish Academy* 1st series 5 (1850–3), 45–67, at p. 58: folio 13 lower margin reads on two lines: *.i. Mac in tacairt Tuignetha* (son of the priest of Tynan') presumably glossing the name Máel Ísu of the following line which reads *Line moite hí tus ind lethinnig sea.*

its chief antiquary and librarian (*prím-chríochaire*[39] *7 leabhar-choimédaigh*) (d. 1136).[40] This is a rare encounter with a genuine connection between teacher and pupil, one of the essential relationships of the ecclesiastical educational system for monks and priests. The manuscript is a small book, measuring 16.5cm x 11.4cm. Its decoration [Fig. 9] is a complicated mix of traditional Irish decoration with Hiberno-Scandinavian and Romanesque ornamentation that appears in other eleventh- and twelfth-century Irish manuscripts.[41] While finely illuminated, Máel Brigte's book was primarily a handbook for gospel commentaries and Irish metrical texts on topics relating in particular to the apostles and Christ's disciples. It is tightly packed with interlinear and marginal texts in tiny miniscule, a feature of contemporary Irish books such as the Psalter of Caimín (MS UCD-OFM A1).[42] Máel Brigte was so eager to include commentaries that he added small slips of vellum to the main manuscript to complete his task. Studies of these commentaries and texts, especially of Matthew's gospel,[43] an exegetical text on the four evangelists,[44] and the gospel history that complemented Matthew's gospel regarding the names and callings of the apostles[45] indicate that his main sources included Jerome and Bede's commentaries on the gospels along with well-established Hiberno-Latin compilations including the *Liber questionum in evangelium* and the so-called 'Irish Reference Bible', which drew ultimately on seventh-century Irish exegesis. In concluding her study of the text on the four evangelists, Jennifer O'Reilly captures the significance of Máel Brigte's gospel book for the Irish monastic tradition:[46]

Rob cennais Dia for anmain Maelissa. Pater. ('The writing/line of my tutor at the beginning of this page. May God be gentle to the soul of Maelissa. Pater'). **39** *DIL sv.* Literally 'definer of boundaries or territories' which implies that Máel Ísu wrote tracts, possibly legal, on the lands of certain dynasties or kingdoms, an occupation that required historical skills. **40** AFM. An alternative to Máel Ísu Mac Máil Choluim is Máel Ísu Ua Coinne *saoi Gaoidheal i sencus 7 i m-breitheamhnas, 7 i n-Urd Páttraicc* ('learned of the Irish in history, in legal judgements and in the order of Patrick') (AU, AFM). **41** Henry and Marsh-Micheli, 'A century of Irish illumination', 148–52. **42** Ó Néill, 'Glosses to the psalter of St Caimín'. **43** Jean Ritmueller, 'The gospel commentary of Máel Brigte ua Máeluanaig and its Hiberno-Latin background', *Peritia* 2 (1983), 185–214; Ritmueller, 'Matthew 10:1–4: the calling of the Twelve Apostles: the commentary and glosses of Máel Brigte úa Máeluanaigh (Armagh 1138) (London, British Library, Harley 1802, fol. 25^{v}–26^{v}). Introduction, edition, translation' in Guy Guldentops, Christian Laes and Gert Partoens (eds), *Felici curiositate. Studies in Latin literature and textual criticism from antiquity to the twentieth century. In honour of Rita Beyers* (Turnhout, 2017), pp 55–69. **44** Jennifer O'Reilly, 'The Hiberno-Latin tradition of the evangelists and the gospels of Mael Brigte', *Peritia* 9 (1995), 290–309. **45** Martin McNamara, 'The "*Leabhar Breac* gospel history" against its Hiberno-Latin background' in Guldentops et al., *Felici curiositate*, pp 23–53. See also Martin McNamara, 'End of an era in early Irish biblical exegesis: Caimin Psalter fragments (11th–twelfth century) and the gospels of Máel Brigte (1138 AD)', *Proceedings of the Irish Biblical Association* 33–4 (2010–11), 76–121. **46** O'Reilly, 'The gospels of Máel Brigte', 304.

> The Gospels of Máel Brigte provides an eloquent part of the evidence for assessing the degree to which ancient Irish monastic culture was a still living tradition in Armagh in the year following St Malachy's resignation of the see and immediately before his introduction of the international Cistercian order.

That Máel Brigte lived in a religious milieu is clear from his erudition, even if that training was traditional and not obviously influenced by contemporary commentaries on the gospels. Martin McNamara regards Máel Brigte's Gospel as 'intended for instruction in the monastic or clerical school of Armagh'.[47] We cannot be certain that Máel Brigte was a monk but his life was not detached from the events of the secular world, a circumstance that would be near nigh impossible in Armagh given that it was at the centre of a struggle for dominance between the existing status quo and others such as St Malachy who were intent on wresting power from them. Máel Brigte laments (folio 60r *is mór in gním*) the killing of Cormac Mac Cárthaig, king of Desmumu, by his rival Toirdelbach Ua Briain in 1138, although he makes no reference to the death of Malachy's brother, Gilla Críst (Christianus) Ua Morgair, bishop of Clogher (Airgialla) in the same year. Gilla Críst was buried in the church of SS Peter and Paul in Armagh where Malachy had received his early education from his devout master, Ímar Ua hÁedacáin. Given that Máel Brigte appears to have been active as a compiler, scribe and glossator, it is surprising that he did not comment on this event – and others – which were important in the ecclesiastical world of mid-twelfth-century Armagh.

This complex situation in which a well-established tradition, reflected by Máel Brigte's commentaries and by Máel Muire Ua Gormáin's dependence on *Félire Óenguso* and the Martyrology of Tallaght – although later saints such as Dunstan (19 May) and Bernard (22 August) are added – existed in parallel to the gradual introduction of new practices into the Irish church is evident from other contemporary manuscripts. For example, the Corpus Christi Gospel Book (BodL. MS CCC 122), probably dating to the twelfth century, is a finely illustrated manuscript that contains the Eusebian canon tables and gospels written in a regular and compact Irish minuscule script. Commenting on the hand, Françoise Henry and G.L. Marsh-Micheli estimated that its clear and regular lay-out 'is quite obviously trying to give the illusion of continental or English script of the twelfth century'.[48] The manuscript also includes a striking illustration of the board game known as the *Alea Evangelii* ('Game of the Gospels') which an introductory note declares was brought to Ireland by Dub Innse, bishop of Bangor (d. 953) from the court of the English king Æthelstan

47 McNamara, 'End of an era', 115. 48 Henry and Marsh-Micheli, 'A century of Irish illumination', 152.

(d. 939) (Fig. 10). This game is a Christian allegory based on the gospels that was superimposed on pre-existing games such as Irish *fidchell* and Viking *tafl* games.[49] Archaeological evidence confirms the use of board games in ecclesiastical settlements: a double-sided slate *hnefatafl* board was discovered at Cathedral Hill in Downpatrick and a small gaming piece from Skellig may be a *hnefatafl* piece or a stylized chess piece. The Corpus Gospel Book may have originated from the monastery of Bangor after it had been re-founded by Malachy in 1124, although this connection depends on the reference to Dub Innse. The manuscript combines old and new, with traditional decoration, Irish minuscule script and the tenth-century board game with its instructions in Irish and Latin at the same time as using the decoration and lay-out of canon tables which Henry and Marsh-Micheli noted are closely related to the tables found in the fourth volume of the great Bible of Cîteaux dating to *c.*1109.[50]

The same blend of old and new can also be seen in the Corpus Christi Missal (BodL. MS CCC 282) in which the missal's text, probably copied from an earlier exemplar without any updating, is largely old while the lavish illumination includes Scandinavian-style ornament that also appears on twelfth-century Irish metalwork objects such as Cross of Cong and St Manchán's Shrine.[51] As noted by Timothy O'Neill, this is the most complete book to survive from the early Irish church, 'a Roman missal written for a male religious community'.[52] Its origins are unknown although links with Armagh, Munster and Tuam have been suggested, while in a detailed discussion of the missal's contents, Aubrey Gwynn argued that it was a twelfth-century copy of an earlier book.[53] Among the many perceptive observations offered by Gwynn,[54] was that the bidding prayer for the

49 https://excavations.ie/report/1986/Down/0000648/; https://www.ancientgames.org/hnefatafl-brandubh/ (image); https://excavations.ie/report/1986/Down/0000648/; Edward Bourke, Alan R. Hayden and Ann Lynch, *Skellig Michael, Co. Kerry: the monastery and the South Peak. Archaeological stratigraphic report: excavations 1986–2010* (Dublin, 2011), p. 356. Available online only at https://www.worldheritageireland.ie/fileadmin/user_upload/documents/SkelligMichaelExcavations_07Feb.pdf. For a history of the various forms of *tafl* games and their complexity see Eddie Duggan, 'A game on the edge: an attempt to unravel the Gordian Knot of *tafl* games', *Board Game Studies Journal* 15 (2020), 99–132. **50** Henry and Marsh-Micheli, 'A century of Irish illumination', 153–4. There is also a strong possibility that the Corpus manuscript may have come from Armagh or Down. **51** Henry and Marsh-Micheli, 'A century of Irish illumination', 137–8. **52** Timothy O'Neill, *The Irish hand. Scribes and their manuscripts from the earliest times* (Cork, 2014 (reprint)), p. 94. **53** Aubrey Gwynn, *The Irish church*, pp 29–33. Martin Holland argued for a date in the earlier part of the eleventh century for the Corpus Missal but this date does not fit as closely with the manuscript's illumination which belongs to the late eleventh-/early twelfth-century as explained by Henry and Marsh-Micheli, 'A century of Irish illumination', 137–40; Martin Holland, 'On the dating of the Corpus Irish missal', *Peritia* 15 (2001), 280–301; John A. Claffey, 'A very puzzling Irish missal', *Journal of the Galway Archaeological and Historical Society* 55 (2003), 1–12, with corr. vol. 56, 245. **54** He acknowledges Derek Howard Turner of the British Museum and British Library for the suggestion, Gwynn, *The Irish church*, p. 29.

king of the Irish and his army, which occurs in the litany of saints for Easter Saturday,[55] resembles a litany preserved in the so-called Winchester Troper (BodL MS 775, ff. 18v-19r) in which there is a supplication for Æthelred, king of England (reigned 978–1016) and his army.[56] That the Corpus missal was a monastic book is suggested by the inclusion of prayers for masses commemorating an abbot, 'for the brethren of our community' (*pro fratribus nostrae congregationis*) and for benefactors, the latter two texts similar to those used, for example, in the so-called missal of St Augustine's Abbey, Canterbury that can be dated fairly precisely to 1093 (Corpus Christi College, Cambridge MS 270).[57] Interestingly, prayers for the souls of deceased monks in the Corpus Missal are directed to the Virgin Mary and to St Michael the Archangel whereas those at the St Augustine's missal only mention the Virgin. Warren argued in his edition of the missal that it was a monastic missal and Gwynn agreed that this was plain from many of its instructions.[58] Of particular relevance is the votive mass *Pro custodia monasterii et habitatorum eius* ('for the protection of the monastery and its inhabitants').[59] It might be argued that the Corpus missal reflects a monastic tradition in transition, fluid in its contents and not rigidly conservative. Its contents place its liturgical and monastic tradition on a par with changes being introduced in monastic life elsewhere albeit perhaps at a slower pace and with less turbulence in Ireland. For example, the community of St Augustine's Canterbury was dispersed in 1089 and replaced with monks from Christ Church Canterbury who were more in tune with Lanfranc's *Constitutions*.[60] This was a period of adaptation and transition subject to influences from many sources but one in which existing traditions were sufficiently confident to continue to produce liturgical books that were grounded in a long-standing monastic culture while gradually absorbing new practices and texts.

This situation is supported by annalistic records but what is also apparent from these records is that there was a fundamental change in the late twelfth century. By then, monasticism was dominated by the new continental orders and their monastic traditions, and this altered the profile of personnel associated with learning in long-established monastic communities. The obit of Flann Ua

55 Frederick Edward Warren (ed.), *The manuscript Irish missal belonging to the President and Fellows of Corpus Christi College, Oxford* (London, 1879), p. 133: f. 111a. Original: *Peccatores te rogamus audi nos … ut regem hibernensium et exercitum eius conseruare digneris te rogamus.* 56 https://digital.bodleian.ox.ac.uk/objects/13e60bcb-5415-4e3d-90bd-195ead1225ee/surfaces/4747d1b6-07ab-483c-b5ec-7149de83583b/#. Accessed 5 May 2023. 57 Warren, *Irish missal*, pp 76–7: f. 31b; Martin Rule (ed.), *The missal of St Augustine's Abbey Canterbury* (Cambridge, 1896; repr. 2017), pp 151, 154; Richard Pfaff, *The liturgy in medieval England. A history* (Cambridge, 2009), pp 113–17. 58 Warren, *Irish missal*, p. 50; Aubrey Gwynn, 'Tomaltach Ua Conchobair coarb of Patrick (1181–1201): his life and times', *Seanchas Ard Mhacha* 8:2 (1977), 231–74, at p. 266. 59 Warren, *Irish missal*, p. 67. 60 Pfaff, *The liturgy in medieval England*, p. 114.

Gormáin of Armagh – likely to be a kinsman of Máel Muire, author of the Martyrology of Gormán – in 1174 reflects this change quite starkly:[61]

> Flann Ua Gormáin, chief scholar of Ard-Macha and of all Ireland, a man learned, observant in divine and human wisdom, after having been a year and twenty learning amongst the Franks and Saxons and twenty years directing the schools of Ireland, died peacefully on the 13th of the Kalends of April [March 20], the Wednesday before Easter, in the 70th year of his age.

Flann's career in England and France is noteworthy as it was during a period when collegiate schools and universities were beginning to emerge in Paris, Bologna and Salamanca among other cities, and contentious debates enlivened intellectual life throughout Europe.[62] Whether Martain Ua Brolaigh who died in 1188, described as 'chief sage of all the Goeidhil and chief scholar of Ard-Macha' (*ard-ecnaidh Goeidhel uile 7 ard-fher leiginn Aird Macha*),[63] belonged to Flann's scholastic tradition or to the more traditional learning of Máel Brigte Ua Máel Uanaig is unclear but Martain is the last individual in Armagh to be accorded the title *fer léiginn*, and indeed that same title peters out altogether by the early thirteenth century.

VERNACULAR DIDACTIC POEMS AND EXEMPLA

Vernacular texts in Middle Irish in metre and prose abound and the evidence suggests that most of these texts emanated from an ecclesiastical milieu. They include apocrypha, eschatological texts, homilies, prophecies and vernacular resumés of the bible and world history.[64] A comparable corpus of Christian texts exists in Old English, with a proliferation from the ninth century onwards.[65] From the early stages of literacy and Christianity, the Irish produced their origin-legend in the framework of biblical history.[66] The annals attest plainly to

61 AU. Original: *Flann hUa Gorma[i]n, ardfherleighinn Aird Macha 7 Erenn uile, fer eolach, comarthamail i n-ecna diadha 7 domunda, iar m-beith bliadhain ar fichit i Francaibh 7 i Saxanaibh ic foghlaim 7 fiche bliadhain ic follamhnughadh scol n-Erenn, atbath co sithamhail i tredecim Kallann Aprilis, Dia Cetain ria Caisc, septuagesimo aetatis su[a]e anno.* **62** James G. Clark, 'Monks and the universities, *c.*1200–1500' in *CHMM*, pp 1074–92, at pp 1074–80. **63** AU. **64** See, for example, *CLH* i, pp 137–225 §§103–91. **65** Elaine Treharne and Phillip Pulsiano, 'An introduction to the corpus of Anglo-Saxon vernacular literature' in Phillip Pulsiano and Elaine Treharne (eds), *A companion to Anglo-Saxon literature* (Oxford and Malden, MA, 2001), pp 1–10. **66** John Carey, *The Irish national origin-legend: synthetic pseudohistory*. Quiggin Pamphlets on the Sources of Mediaeval Gaelic History 1 (Cambridge, 1994); John Carey, *Lebor Gabala Erenn. Textual history and pseudohistory*. Irish Texts Society subsidiary series 20 (Dublin, 2009).

this integration of native vernacular knowledge with Christian and Latin learning in that those skilled in both often resided in monasteries as did poets and custodians of traditional historical lore (*senchas*) and law. Among the most renowned of such residents were Eochaid Ua Flannacáin (d. 1004: Armagh and Cluain Fiachna (Clonfeacle, Co. Tyrone)), Flann Mainistrech (d. 1056: Monasterboice) and Muirchertach Ua Cairill (d. 1083: Downpatrick).[67] Others ended their lives in monasteries, among them the eminent poets Urard mac Coisse (d. 909: Clonmacnoise)[68] and Flaithem mac Maíl Gaimrid (d. 1058: Ardfert, Co. Kerry).[69] There were scholars and poets who concentrated on ecclesiastical and devotional subjects alone, and in some cases it is most likely that they were members of a monastic community who produced works for multiple audiences. Monastic schools educated monks and priests serving the laity, and to an unknown extent probably taught privileged members of the laity. The works of some teachers survive: the most eminent of these is Airbertach mac Coisse Dobráin of Ros Ailithir (Rosscarbery, Co. Cork) (d. 1016).[70] A number of vernacular didactic poems are attributed to him and although they may not have all been composed by him, they may have originated from his school.[71] *Rochuala crecha is tír thair* ('I have heard of plundering expeditions in the east') narrates the conquest of the Midianites by the Israelites.[72] *Fichi ríg – cia rím as ferr?* ('Twenty kings, according to the best reckoning') lists the kings of Judah who ruled Jerusalem from Saul to the destruction of the city.[73] *A Dé dúlig, adat-teoch* ('O God, the creator, I implore you') interprets the Psalter[74] and *Ro fessa i cuirp domuin dúir* ('In the body of the firm world is known [five equal zones]') is a didactic poem on the geography of the world.[75] Some scholars credit Airbertach as author of the lengthy and masterly *Saltair na Rann* ('The psalter of verses'), the history of the world from creation to the Crucifixion written in one hundred and fifty short cantos following the structure of the psalms, although this conclusion has been disputed.[76] Airbertach's poem on the psalter narrates in verse the history and interpretation of the psalms, their author – reputed to be

67 AU; https://www.dib.ie/biography/flann-mainistrech-a3272. **68** AClon [983.1–5]; ATig; https://www.dib.ie/biography/erard-iorard-urard-a2938. For a full consideration of this subject see Elva Johnston, *Literacy and identity in early medieval Ireland* (Woodbridge, 2013). **69** AI. **70** https://www.dib.ie/biography/airbertach-a0079. **71** Aideen O'Leary, 'The identities of the poet(s) Mac Coisi: a reinvestigation', *Cambrian Medieval Celtic Studies* 38 (Winter, 1999), 53–71, at p. 69 (Appendix); https://www.dib.ie/biography/airbertach-a0079 accessed 26 July 2022. **72** Kuno Meyer (ed.), 'Mitteilungen aus irischen Handschriften: Die Midianiterschlacht', *Zeitschrift für celtische Philologie* 3 (1901), 23–4. **73** Gearóid S. Mac Eoin (ed. and trans.), 'A poem by Airbertach Mac Cosse', *Ériu* 20 (1966), 112–39. **74** Pádraig Ó Néill (ed. and trans.), 'Airbertach mac Cosse's poem on the Psalter', *Éigse* 17 (1977–9), 19–46. **75** Thomas Olden (ed. and trans.), 'On the geography of Ros Ailithir', *Proceedings of the Royal Irish Academy* 2nd ser. 2 (1879–88), 219–52. **76** *CLH* i, pp 137–40 §103. See Gearóid Mac Eoin, 'The date and authorship of *Saltair na Rann*', *Zeitschrift für celtische Philologie* 28 (1960–1), 51–67.

King David alone – and an explanation of the *titulus* preceding each psalm. His primary source was an eighth-century Old Irish text, the so-called 'Old-Irish treatise on the Psalter' [*OIT*] the contents of which he summarized, only occasionally deviating from it.[77] The poem is a further example of an exegetical tradition that was subject to constant renewal with Airbertach's poem representing 'a new type of receptacle for that tradition some two centuries later [than the *OIT*]'.[78] From a monastic perspective the psalter was the essential book of monastic and clerical life, used in the Divine Office and as a fundamental tool for monastic education.[79] Probably the earliest Irish evidence for psalm writing, dating to *c.*AD 600, are the Springmount wax tablets, six yew tablets filled with wax, on which parts of Psalms 30 and 31 were written with a pointed stylus in precise Irish majuscule script.[80] In his metrical history of the psalms, Airbertach extols their unrivalled heavenly sound: 'in a single choir praising God. What music on earth could be better?'[81] Psalms were to be performed as much as to be interpreted. They provided key directions towards salvation:[82]

> Whoever sings them sincerely will reach the unity of the Seraphim. He shall not be a man doomed to perdition after any judgement: he shall be in your company, o God the Creator.

The constant recitation of the psalms exemplified a monk's life, as they were at the heart of his daily prayer routine, his capacity to reflect on his life and his place in creation. This also applied to nuns or vowesses who celebrated the canonical hours. Adomnán, for example, tells of the holy virgin Maugain, daughter of Daiméne of Clogher who stumbled and broke her hip when returning to her cell from the church having celebrated the night office.[83] A monk's close relationship[84] with his psalter is rather movingly expressed in a

77 Kuno Meyer (ed.), *Hibernica minora, being a fragment of an Old-Irish treatise on the Psalter with translation, notes and a glossary and an appendix containing extracts hitherto unpublished from MS. Rawlinson, B512 in the Bodleian Library*. Anecdota Oxonienesia. Mediaeval and Modern Irish Series 8 (Oxford, 1894); Pádraig P. Ó Néill, 'Old wine in new bottles: the reprise of early Irish psalter exegesis in Airbertach Mac Cosse's poem on the psalter' in Elizabeth Boyle and Deborah Hayden (eds), *Authorities and adaptations. The reworking and transmission of textual sources in medieval Ireland* (Dublin, 2014), pp 121–40. 78 Ó Néill, 'Old wine in new bottles', p. 139. 79 George H. Brown, 'The psalms as the foundation of Anglo-Saxon learning' in Nancy van Deusen (ed.), *The place of the psalms in the intellectual culture of the Middle Ages* (New York, 1999), pp 1–24. 80 https://100objects.ie/springmount-wax-tablets/. Accessed 29 July 2023. See also a detailed study of the tablets in Gifford Charles-Edwards, 'The Springmount Bog tablets: their implications for insular epigraphy and palaeography', *Studia Celtica* 36 (2002), 27–45. 81 Ó Néill, 'Poem on the Psalter', p. 31 §8c–d. Original: *fond óenchlais ic molad Dé/ cia ceól bad ferr for bith ché?* 82 Ó Néill, 'Poem on the Psalter', p. 37 §36. *Cipé nos-gaba íar fir/ ricfaid óentaid Hiruphín./ Ní ba mac báis íar nach mbreith./biaid it gnáis, a Dé dúlig.* 83 Anderson and Anderson, *Life of Columba*, pp 100–3 [ii.5]; Sharpe, *Adomnán of Iona*, pp 158–9 [II 5]. 84 It is assumed that this poem was

poem, possibly composed in the eleventh century, in which the book is likened to a woman whom the poet has loved all his life:[85]

> Crínóc, lady of measured melody, not young, but with modest maiden mind, together once in Niall's northern land we slept, we two, as man and womankind …
>
> Your counsel is ever there to hand, we choose it, following you in everything; love of your word is the best of loves, our gentle conversation with the King …
>
> Again I offer you a faultless love, a love unfettered for which surely we will not be punished in the depths of Hell but together walk in piety.

Undoubtedly, Airbertach would have understood the sentiments of this poem, which evokes a spiritual, and yet particularly sensual, relationship between a man and his psalter, a love poem to a cherished book.

Vernacular literature of the Middle Irish period includes a strand of texts that are aptly described by Elizabeth Boyle as encompassing 'humorous entertainment, ironic parody, moral puzzle and biting social commentary'.[86] They are directed at all aspects of religious life and institutions, including monasticism. Of course, this was a tradition that was not confined to Ireland as anti-clerical and anti-monastic satire became a genre throughout Europe from the eleventh century.[87] Three texts dating to the late eleventh and twelfth centuries are well known for their commentaries on the state of the Irish church, *Aislinge Meic Con Glinne* ('The vision of Mac Conglinne'), *Caithréim Cellaig* ('The triumphal career of Cellach') and *Visio Tnugdali* composed by Marcus of Regensburg in 1149, although the latter text is more an eschatological than a political text, its main concern being a topography of the afterlife.[88] Other shorter anecdotes single out particular vices, often humorously, as a way of

composed by a monk but there is every possibility that the author was a cleric other than a monk. **85** James Carney (ed.), 'A Chrínóc, cubaid do cheól', *Éigse* 4 (1945), 280–4; James Carney (ed.), 'A Chrínóc, cubaid do cheól. To an old psalm-book', *Medieval Irish lyrics* (Dublin, 1967), pp 74–9 §§1, 4, 7. Original: *A Chrínóc, cubaid do cheól; / cen co bat firóc, at fial; / romósam túaid i tír Néill/ tan dorónsam feiss réid ríam … Erlam do chomairle chóir, / dóig nostogamne i cech tír, / is ferr rográd dot gáeis géir, / ar comrád réid frisin ríg … At inmain lem-sa cen locht, / rotbía mo chen-sa cen cacht, / ní léicfe ar mbádud i péin, / fogabam crábud léir lat …* **86** Elizabeth Boyle, 'Lay morality, clerical immorality, and pilgrimage in tenth-century Ireland: *Cethrur macclérech* and *Epscop do Gáedelaib*', *Studia Hibernica* 39 (2013), 9–48, at p. 41. **87** Sita Steckel, 'Satirical depictions of monastic life' in *CHMM*, pp 1154–70. **88** Kuno Meyer, *Aislinge Meic Conglinne. The vision of MacConglinne, a Middle-Irish wonder tale* (London, 1892); Kenneth Hurlstone Jackson, *Aislinge Meic Con Glinne* (Dublin, 1990); Albrecht Wagner (ed.), *Visio Tnugdali*. Lateinisch und Altdeutsch (Erlangen, 1882; repr. Hildesheim and New York, 1989); Eileen Gardiner, 'The *Vision of Tnugdal*' in Richard Matthew Pollard (ed.), *Imagining the medieval afterlife* (Cambridge, 2020), pp 247–63.

highlighting immoral practices. This is often done with subtlety as if only a specific audience known to an author understood the full import of the story. Such is the tale of the salvation of Máel Suthain Ua Cerbaill (d. 1010).[89] Máel Suthain is described as being of the Eóganacht Locha Léin dynasty (around Lough Leane, Killarney, Co. Kerry), 'chief scholar of Ireland' (*ardsuí na hÉrend*) who died in the church of Aghadoe, above Lough Leane.[90] His obit in the Annals of the Four Masters is the most effusive, and although the source is late it chimes with the two Middle Irish texts which mention him:[91]

> Maol Suthain ua Cerbhaill of the community of Inisfallen [an island monastery on Lough Leane], chief sage of the western world during his lifetime and lord of Eóganachta Locha Léin, died after a good life.

A poem attributed to Máel Suthain on the grades of the church and of the nobility is somewhat pedestrian but if genuine indicates that he may have been teaching his pupils metrical summaries of secular law tracts. The clerical grades are listed as are individuals, such as the cook and the guest-master, essential to a monastery's daily life:[92]

> [Psalm singer?], pupil, student, historian, not insignificant,
> teacher, scholar of scripture, a chief scholar great in knowledge.
> bishop, priest and deacon, subdeacon, noble music,
> lector, doorkeeper, powerful exorcist, brilliant, distinguished, holy.
> Superior, his successor, vice-abbot, cook, proper and right,
> counsellor, guest-master, sub-prior on a journey.
> Wisdom, understanding, counsel, fortitude, knowledge, pious zeal
> fear of the Lord in this world: God's seven divine gifts to us [the seven gifts of the Holy Spirit]

Máel Suthain's list is comprehensive and is a satisfactory reflection of legal definitions but it is noticeable that the eremitical monastic community – anchorites, hermits and *céli Dé* – and nuns are not mentioned. The latter are

89 Joseph Vendryes (ed. and trans.), 'L'aventure de Maelsuthain', *Revue celtique* 35 (1914), 203–11; Carey, *King of mysteries*, pp 49–50. **90** AI. AU s.v. accords him the title *rí Eóganachta Locha Léin*. He is not the Máel Suthain who was Brian Bórama's secretary and *anmcharae* who inscribed his name in the Book of Armagh. He died in 1031. **91** AFM 1009. Original: *Maolsuthain Ua Cearbhaill do mhuinntir Insi Faithleand, prime saoi iarthair domhain ina aimsir, 7 tighearna Eoghanachta Locha Léin, décc iar ndeighbheathaidh*. **92** Kuno Meyer (ed.), 'Mitteilungen aus irischen Handschriften: Siebenteilung aller geistlichen und weltlichen Rangstufen', *Zeitschrift für celtische Philologie* 5 (1905), 498–9 §§1–4. Original: *Cóictach, descipul, foglaintid, starige, nách dis, / forcetlaid, súi canóne, prīmsúi co mēt fis. Epscop, sacart sceo deochain, subdeochain, seōl sær, / liachtōir, dorsaid, glantaid dían, is níam nóethech nōem. Airchinnech, a thānaise, secnap, coic, cōir cert, / athc[h]omarcthid, ferdaigis, frithshecnap for fecht.*

likely to have been omitted as they did not belong to the clerical grades, whatever about offering practical services including cooking and caring for guests.

The Middle Irish story of his salvation suggests that Máel Suthain did not live a life of pure piety and that whoever wrote the tale meant not alone to convey a few moral messages but also intended to mock Máel Suthain.[93] It is also indicative of the fascination with the fate of the soul that characterizes much of eleventh- and twelfth-century theology.[94] The anecdote relates how three students all named Domnall came from Connor, Co. Antrim, to Máel Suthain. At the end of three years learning, the students informed Máel Suthain that they wished to go on pilgrimage to Jerusalem 'so that our feet may walk every road on which our Saviour travelled the earth'.[95] Máel Suthain would not allow them to go on their pilgrimage until he was paid for his teaching. As they had nothing to give him, he foretold that they would die in Jerusalem and he insisted on them promising solemnly that they would visit him from the next world to tell him how long he had to live, and his fate in the next life. Just as Máel Suthain had foretold, his pupils died and were buried in Jerusalem. In Heaven, Máel Suthain's future was imparted to them by St Michael the Archangel. He was destined for Hell for three reasons: on account of his tampering with the Scriptures, his adultery with other men's wives, and for despising the hymn *Altus Prosator*. As to the *Altus*, Máel Suthain had not recited it for seven years: his son had died despite his reciting the hymn seven times to save the child. According to a preface to the early hymn, the *Altus* had many virtues including that it guarded against every death save death on a pillow.[96] When Máel Suthain was informed of his fate and that he had three years to live, he quoted Ezekiel 33;12 'The impiety of the impious, in whatever hour he changes his life, will do him no harm'. And so he corrected his evil habits, desisting from putting his own interpretation on the Scriptures and following the holy books, no longer going with other men's wives, and reciting the *Altus* seven times a night for the rest of his life. His students returned on the day of his death and he went with them to his appointed place in Heaven. The anecdote's conclusion is fittingly sardonic: 'Then he gathered many priests around him, and received the last anointing; and his pupils did not part from him until they had gone to Heaven. And that good man's writings are still in the church in Inisfallen'.[97] Ironically, and probably

Ecna, intliuct, comarle, nert, fis, gaire gúr, / omon Fíadat for bith ché sect ndāna Dé dún. See Breatnach, *Uraicecht na Ríar*, pp 84–5. 93 Donnchadh Ó Corráin's description (*CLH* iii, p. 1508 §1132) is apt: 'Sardonic moral teaching for shady clerics, packaged as a tale of the hereafter'. I follow his summary in the above resumé. 94 Elizabeth Boyle, 'The afterlife in the medieval Celtic-speaking world' in Pollard, *Imagining the medieval afterlife*, pp 62–78. 95 Carey, *King of mysteries*, p. 49; Vendryes, 'L'aventure de Maelsuthain', 204. Original: *coro imthidsit ar cosa cech conair roimtig in slánicid i talmain.* 96 Carey, *King of mysteries*, p. 32. 97 Ibid., p. 50; Vendryes, 'L'aventure de Maelsuthain', 206. Original: *Iss annsin rothinóilit sacairt 7 clérig imda cuice; 7 rohongadh hé 7 nírscarsat a daltada fris nó condeachatar a cethrar dochum nime. Issé a screbtra in fir maith sin atá [in] Inis Faithlinn isin eclais fős …* Slightly deliberately, the term used to describe Máel Suthain's writings is *screbtra* 'scriptures'.[98]

Many issues are addressed in this satirical anecdote. In quoting Ezekiel 33:12 it would appear that the author's essential moral message is that no matter how much one has sinned and how late the repentance, it is still possible to enter Heaven. His method of imparting this message is through satire. The reference to the students going on pilgrimage and dying in Jerusalem appears to be somewhat critical of going on pilgrimages abroad, a common theme in other similar texts.[99] Máel Suthain was not a member of a religious community. He was a lay teacher and a noble of Eóganacht Locha Léin, variously described as an *ecnaid* ('wise man'), *prímshuí* ('chief scholar') and one who excelled in 'reckoning the sevens' (*ní turmi sechtu nach suí bas certu atá cóe*),[100] perhaps a reference to knowledge of the seven hierarchical grades in the laws. Yet he was associated with the two main churches in the region of Loch Léin, the island of Inisfallen and Aghadoe overlooking the lake. His dynasty, the Uí Cherbaill, are recorded in the annals as being involved in a series of dynastic struggles with other dynasties in the region during the eleventh and twelfth centuries.[101] The list of his sins is eclectic. Pursuing men's wives was not unusual and as he had a son, he probably had not committed himself to permanent chastity. Nonetheless, that he is admonished for adultery suggests that the author wished to warn against the evil of such indecent activities to an audience, both ecclesiastical and secular. But what of Máel Suthain's other sins, refusing to recite the *Altus Prosator* and offering his own interpretations of the Scriptures? As the *Altus Prosator* was a protective prayer, the author is either confirming its virtues and arguing that it should be recited correctly, or is doing quite the opposite, and mocking the superstitions surrounding what was probably regarded as a revered prayer. Whichever his view, Máel Suthain's disrespect for the prayer is subjected to censure. The final sin is the most telling, what John Carey terms as 'wilful or idiosyncratic interpretation of the Bible'.[102] This is the voice of a scriptural scholar, an individual similar to Máel Brigte Ua Máel Uanaig of Armagh, warning the untrained scholar not to dabble in biblical interpretation and commentary. The division between two grades is clear in Máel Suthain's own poem, 'a scriptural scholar, a chief scholar with great knowledge' (*súi canóne, prímsúi co mét fis*). If Máel Suthain was not versed in interpretations of the holy books, he was to follow proper guidance and not seek to offer his own interpretations. The anecdote's final sentence referring to his writings still being in Inisfallen is either a barb at that church or is a first-hand account but one from the perspective of a changed Inisfallen where by 1197 its own annals could

standardized. **98** Vendryes, 'L'aventure de Maelsuthain', p. 206. **99** Boyle, 'Lay morality, clerical immorality'. **100** Meyer, 'Siebenteilung', 409 §10. **101** AI 1046, 1061, 1064, 1108, 1128. **102** Carey, *King of mysteries*, p. 50 n. 20.

reverently and contemporaneously record the death of Gilla Pátraic Ua hÍmair:[103]

> a celibate and noble priest, archdeacon and successor (*comarbae*) of Faithlenn, head of a community (*cenn comthinóil*), chief in piety (*cenn crábaid*), charity (*déirc*) and wisdom (*ecna*), and founder and assembler (*tinóltaid*) of every church property, including a clerical commuity (*comthinól clérech*), books, and liturgical vessels (*admi*).

By the end of the twelfth century it would appear that the interpretation of the Scriptures was orthodox in Inisfallen.

LAND TRANSACTIONS

Records of church foundations, land grants and disputes in early medieval Ireland do not follow the legal tradition of charter-writing practised elsewhere in Europe.[104] The Irish tradition, according to Máire Herbert in her survey of pre-Norman property records:[105]

> … appears to be pluralist toleration of a range of modes of property documentation at least up to the period of establishment of Anglo-Norman influence towards the end of the twelfth century. From the seventh century onwards, Irish ecclesiastical communities had incorporated property records in hagiographical texts, and emphasis on property and property rights is particularly notable in vernacular Lives throughout the twelfth century. Yet hagiography could be used in conjunction with other modes of property documentation.

Thus, apart from being embedded in saints' lives, for example, land transactions occasionally form the background to an annalistic record such as that quoted by Herbert for 1176:[106]

103 AI. **104** Richard Sharpe, 'Dispute settlement in medieval Ireland: a preliminary enquiry' in Wendy Davies and Paul Fouracre (eds), *The settlement of disputes in early medieval Europe* (Cambridge, 1986), pp 169–89. **105** Máire Herbert, 'Before charters? Property records in pre-Anglo-Norman Ireland' in Marie Therese Flanagan and Judith A. Greene (eds), *Charters and charter scholarship in Britain and Ireland* (Basingstoke, 2005), pp 107–19, at p. 115. **106** Herbert, 'Before charters?', p. 115. Original (AFM 1176): *Baile biataigh do iodhbairt la Ruaidhri ua Concobhair Ri Ereann don Coimdhedh 7 do naoimh Bearach go brath .i. Baile Tuama Achadh. Itiad slana na hogh-dhilsi go brath. Cadhla ua Dubhthaigh airdepscop Tuama, Aireachtach Ua Roduibh, Flann ua Fionnachta, Aodh uá Floinn, Ruarc ua Maoilbreanainn, Ignaidhe uá Mannachain, Giollu an Coimdhedh mac an Leastair, Ua hAinlighi, 7 Concobhar mac Diarmada, a ccoraigheacht an baile sin do beith ag Dia 7 ag Bearach go brath ó*

> A ballybetagh (*baile biataigh*) was granted in perpetuity by Ruaidrí Ua Conchobair, king of Ireland, namely, the townland of Toomaghy (*Tuaim Achadh*) to God and St Berach. The following were the sureties of that perpetual gift: Cadhla Ua Dubthaigh, archbishop of Tuam, Aireachtach Ua Roduibh, Flann Ua Fionnachta, Aodh Ua Floinn, Ruairc Ua Maoil Bréanainn, Ignaidhe Ua Mannacháin, Giolla an Choimhdhe Mac an Leastair, Ua hAinlighi and Conchobar Mac Diarmada, who were to guarantee that this townland was to remain for ever the property of God and St Berach, from Ua Conchobair and his representative.

This entry is particularly valuable as it lists the guarantors to the transaction and suggests that the original document behind it was similar to the memoranda added to old, revered manuscripts such as the Book of Kells, the Book of Durrow and the Book of Deer.[107] The Kells memoranda, dated to between 1030 and 1161, are instructive in providing some idea of the various communities co-existing in that monastery, among them an ascetic community of *deorada* or *cráibdig Dé* ('pilgrims' or 'pious ones of God') whose upkeep was the responsibility of both ecclesiastical and royal authorities.[108] Sometime during the period 1073 to 1087, those who needed support because they had dedicated their lives to God and were pious (*co ro chinne a bethaid do Dia ocus corop cráidbech*) were granted immunity (*díles*) and privileges (*saíre*) by the successor (*comarbae*) of Colum Cille, Domnall mac Robartaig (d. 1098) and the king of Tara, Máel Sechlainn mac Conchobair (d. 1087), with their respective households.[109] These patrons granted all this to those in the *dísert* of Colum Cille in Kells, probably an enclosed settlement with a herb garden with medicinal plants (*lubgortán*). The term *dísert* meant a hermitage or a place of retreat, part of what Richard Morris in his work on ecclesiastical landscapes evocatively describes as 'a stylized wilderness' imitating the desert in a settlement structured 'so as to provide zones of greater and lesser privacy'.[110] The *dísert*, understood from the term itself (borrowed from Latin *desertum*), undoubtedly evoked the origins of monasticism in the desert. Further information can be gleaned from other Kells memoranda.

ua cConchobhair 7 o fhior a ionaid. I have updated the translation from the original O'Donovan text and put necessary personal and place-names in capitals. **107** Gearóid Mac Niocaill (ed.), *Notitiæ as Leabhar Cheanannais 1033–1161* (Baile Átha Cliath, 1961); Máire Herbert, 'Charter material from Kells' in Felicity O'Mahony (ed.), *The Book of Kells. Proceedings of a conference at Trinity College Dublin, 6–9 September 1992* (Aldershot, 1994), pp 60–77; R.I. Best, 'An early monastic grant in the Book of Durrow', *Ériu* 10 (1926–8), 135–42; Edel Bhreathnach, 'Observations on the Book of Durrow memorandum' in John Carey, Kevin Murray and Caitríona Ó Dochartaigh (eds), *Sacred histories. A festschrift for Máire Herbert* (Dublin, 2015), pp 14–21; Katherine Forsyth (ed.), *Studies on the Book of Deer* (Dublin, 2008). **108** Bairbre Nic Aongusa, 'The monastic hierarchy in twelfth century Ireland: the case of Kells', *Ríocht na Midhe* 8:3 (1990–1), 3–20. **109** Mac Niocaill (ed.), *Notitiæ*, pp 12–16 (II). **110** Richard Morris, *Churches in the landscape* (London, 1989), pp 118–19.

Óengus Ua Domnalláin was an *anmcharae* 'confessor, spiritual director', presumably to the leading officials of the settlement and the lay nobility of the region. He was the head (*comarbae*) of the *dísert* of Colum Cille.[111] Mac Maras, the same individual who sought a prayer for himself and who recorded the grant of immunity to the *dísert* of Colum Cille referred to above, or possibly a different person named Mac Maras, appears in a later memorandum as *cend ind recléssa* 'head of the community'.[112] This text is particularly interesting as it involved Colmán Ua Breslein (d. 1153), priest of Kells and a member of a Kells ecclesiastical family, purchasing land on behalf of his three sons from the *céli Dé* of the *dísert*. This land had been given originally as a bequest by the larger monastic community in Kells to the *dísert* from its own resources during the great mortality of livestock in 1133.[113] The bequest had been witnessed by none other than St Malachy as successor of Patrick, a confirmation that he was active in the affairs of existing monasteries beyond Armagh, Bangor or Down. The overall sense gained from the Kells memoranda is that following the difficulties of 1133 the *dísert* was in decline given that its community had to be bailed out by the wider community in Kells.[114] Herbert interprets the bequest as probably 'motivated, in some degree at least, by its [the greater community's] need in crisis to ensure the prayers of the pious, and to restate a commitment to matters spiritual'. She concludes that this transaction was a measure of the secularization of Kells and that 'the grants reveal the abbot and his officials designating the *dísert* as the locus of religious life, while they themselves act as its patrons much as worldly lords'. As to the later purchase of the *dísert*'s land by the priest Colmán Ua Breslein for his sons, Herbert views this as one example of Kells officials increasing their private holdings by further purchases,[115] although Ua Breslein may also have had a familial interest in the *dísert* as one of his sons is described as Cellach *deorad* 'the pious exile'.[116] The Uí Breslein were deeply embedded in the Kells hierarchy, both amassing material wealth while possibly investing in the salvation of their souls. Conveyed in vernacular memoranda written into a precious book, these Kells texts offer a unique template for understanding the complexities of large Irish monasteries, and the difficulty in disentangling the spiritual from the temporal.

As to understanding the landscape of the *dísert* of Coluim Cille and its community, the texts offer few details. It had its *lubgortán* and also a recently consecrated church (*tempall*) known as *Int Eidnén* 'the ivy-clad one'.[117] Other monasteries seem to have had satellite or associated churches called *Int Eidnén*,

111 Mac Niocaill, *Notitiæ*, p. 18 (III) (dated 1087x1094). 112 Ibid., p. 32 (XI) (dated 1134x1136). 113 This loss is recorded in AFM 1133 as *bó-dhíth mór* 'a great loss of cows'. ALC and CS also record it with CS adding that it led to the loss of almost all the pigs in Ireland. 114 Mac Niocaill, *Notitiæ*, p. 28 (IX). 115 Herbert, 'Charter material from Kells', pp 68–9. 116 Mac Niocaill, *Notitiæ*, p. 32 (XI). 117 Ibid., p. 24 (VII); Herbert, 'Charter material from Kells', p. 69.

among them Killeshin,[118] Clonmacnoise[119] and Clonard. One of Clonard's most distinguished clerics, Suairlech, abbot, bishop and anchorite is commemorated as *Suairlech Int Eidnéin* in his obit in 870.[120] *Int Eidnén* survives as the place-name Inan, 8 km north of Clonard. The existence of places called Ivychurch in England may be a parallel. For example, the Augustinian Priory of St Mary's, Ivychurch, in Wiltshire was a twelfth-century royal foundation which although not particularly wealthy was decorated with fine Romanesque doorway reliefs of SS Peter and Paul.[121] It may be no coincidence that Trinity Church at Glendalough was also known as 'The Ivy Church'.[122] Rather than interpreting these churches or hermitages as ivy-clad, and therefore ancient, the name may have evoked the symbolism of ivy in Christianity as evergreen and identified with immortality, everlasting life and friendship.[123] In the Kells memorandum, *Int Eidnén* was endowed by Tigernán Ua Ruairc, king of Bréifne and contender for the high-kingship of Ireland and the church was consecrated by Máel Ciarán mac Megáin whose obit in 1148 describes him as 'noble priest of the church of *Suidhe Choluim Chille* at Ceanannus'.[124] From an architectural and archaeological perspective, Tomás Ó Carragáin has argued that double-vaulted churches built during the eleventh and twelfth centuries, an example being St Columba's House in Kells, functioned as shrines and as residences for hermits or recluses.[125] Specifically in relation to St Columba's House he wonders if it was possible that it was 'at the centre of a small complex for ascetics, and that the complex also incorporated a herb garden and domestic buildings' with a domestic and reliquary function in the greater ecclesiastical settlement.[126] The term *reiclés* is often used to describe these chapels or the space in which such a community lived. Similar functions are suggested for the twelfth-century church at St Doulagh's, Co. Dublin, Temple Ciarán at Clonmacnoise, St Kevin's Church at Glendalough and St Mochta's House at Louth. While anchorites and hermits are associated with curating saints' relics, such relics were in the possession of the *comarbai* 'successors' of the saints whose authority was often linked to their power to use relics for oath-taking, negotiating alliances and peace, and gaining an income for their churches.[127] Given, however, that the *deorada Dé* or *cráibdig* often did more than withdrawing from the world or that there were degrees of seclusion, they were unlikely to have been confined to such a small area in the

118 Best, 'An early monastic grant', 138–40. **119** AFM 1024. **120** AU, CS 870, AFM 868. **121** www.british-history.ac.uk/vch/wilts/vol3/pp289-295 (Priory of Ivychurch) accessed 13 May 2020; Paul Williamson, 'Acquisitions of sculpture at the Victoria and Albert Museum 1986–1991: supplement', *The Burlington Magazine* 133 (1991), 876–80, at p. 876 (figs I and II). **122** See www.logainm.ie (Trinity Church, Glendalough) accessed 25 April 2022. **123** https://churchmonumentssociety.org/resources/symbolism-on-monuments#i (ivy). Accessed 23 July 2023. **124** AFM. **125** Ó Carragáin, *Churches in early medieval Ireland*, pp 263–82. **126** Ibid., p. 264. **127** The annals testify to the exercise of such powers. See ATig 1029, 1088; AFM 1013, 1034, 1157, 1162, 1170. For the role of the *deoràdh/dewar* as a relic-keeper in Scotland, Gilbert Márkus, 'Dewars and relics in Scotland: some clarifications and questions',

larger settlement, least of all inhabiting the loft of a small stone church. If they did spend time residing in these chapels, it would have been intermittent, at special times such as a saint's feast day. The determination to equate a regulated community with solitary ascetics has diverted scholars from considering that they were active and engaged inhabitants of ecclesiastical settlements who practised isolation but not necessarily total reclusion. One could be holy in the midst of the crowd and one could take time away from the crowd. Their physical world or landscape depended on their choice of lifestyle at a given time, and as a result they were probably far more mobile than normally perceived.

A VISUAL EXPRESSION OF MONASTIC POWER AND SPIRITUALITY

One of the most imposing stone monuments among the corpus of Irish high crosses is Muiredach's Cross located in the graveyard of Monasterboice, Co. Louth. This exquisitely carved cross is thus named from the inscription on the west face of its shaft that seems to read 'A prayer for Muiredach who caused this cross to be made'.[128] [Fig. 11] The most likely candidate for this request is Muiredach mac Domnaill (d. 924) who appears to have commissioned the cross. If he did, he was exactly the type of powerful patron who could call upon a master craftsman to execute such a magnificent monument.[129] His obit in AU speaks to his status:[130]

> Muiredach son of Domnall, vice-abbot (*tánaise abad*) of Armagh, and chief steward of the southern Uí Néill, and successor of Buite son of Brónach, chief counsellor of the men of all Brega, both laymen and clerics, departed this life on the fifth day before the Kalends of December [27 Nov.]

Muiredach directed the collection of Armagh's tribute from the Fews mountains, important uplands south of Armagh City and from there south as far as the river Boyne,[131] and also protected the interests of the southern Uí Néill kings who during this period alternated the kingship of Tara with northern Uí Néill kings. His role as chief counsellor (*cenn adcomairc*) suggests that it was to Muiredach that both ecclesiastical and secular disputes were referred for arbitration and that

The Innes Review 60:2 (2009), 95–144. **128** The original inscription in Irish is not fully legible but appears to read OR DO MUIREDACH LAS DERNAD IN CRO[SSA]. **129** For a comprehensive study of what he calls the 'Muiredach Master' see Roger Stalley, *Early Irish sculpture and the art of the high crosses* (New Haven and London, 2020). **130** AU 924. Original: *Muiredach m. Domnaill, tanuse abad Aird Macha 7 ardmaer Oa Neill in Deiscirt 7 comurba Buiti m. Bronaigh, cenn adcomairc fer mBreg n-uile ocaibh cleirchibh, quinto die Kalendarum Decimbrium uita descessit.* See Seán Mac Airt and Nollaig Ó Muraíle, 'Ecclesiastical affairs in Armagh in the ninth and tenth centuries', *Seanchas Ard Mhacha* 25 (2015), 225–38, at p. 235. **131** AFM.

as such, he held a senior legal office.[132] But he was also the successor (*abb*, *comarbae*) of Buite, founder of Monasterboice. The sources are not explicit as to Muiredach's religious status, whether he was a layman – the equivalent of a lay advocate elsewhere – or a member of a monastic community either in Armagh or Monasterboice. Muiredach is likely to have been related to the kings of Ind Airthir, the Uí Bresail Macha, in whose territory Armagh was located and who often held the office of *tánaise ab(ad)* or *secnap* of Armagh, the functionary grade of vice-abbot.[133] He was part of a network of hereditary ecclesiastical families who held offices in churches south of Armagh: Druim Inasclainn (Dromiskin, Co. Louth), Lugbad (Louth, Co. Louth), Lann Léire (Dunleer, Co. Louth) and Monasterboice (Co. Louth). Muiredach's predecessor as chief steward of Patrick as far as the Boyne was Cernach mac Flainn (d. 922) whose family were firmly embedded in Lann Léire.[134] He was succeeded by Tuathal mac Óenacáin, bishop and scribe of Dam Liac (Duleek, Co. Meath) and Lusca (Lusk, Co. Dublin), also a member of a hereditary ecclesiastical family.[135] During the early tenth century Armagh was under constant threat from the Norse of Dublin, the Uí Néill and other northern dynasties, all caught up in endlessly shifting alliances. Muiredach was probably elevated to his offices by the powerful Máel Brigte mac Tornáin (d. 927), who was abbot of Armagh and of the Columban *familia* in Iona and Kells.[136] Like Muiredach, Máel Brigte may have commissioned high crosses, and specifically the Tower Cross in Kells.[137] An insight is gained as to Máel Brigte's learning and his external contacts from the metrical Latin and Anglo-Saxon inscription in display capitals entered into the so-called Mac Durnan Gospels (London, Lambeth Palace Library 1370, folio 3v) during the tenth century. The manuscript is a pocket gospel-book, which was probably made in the late ninth century, and is understood from the inscription to have belonged to Máel Brigte. It reads:[138]

132 Breatnach, *Córus Bésgnai*, pp 148–51 §§28–9, 201 n. §28.5. **133** For Muiredach's possible pedigree see Nollaig Ó Muraíle (ed. and trans.), *Leabhar Mór na nGenealach. The great book of Irish genealogies compiled (1645–66) by Dubhaltach Mac Fhirbhisigh* vol. 2 (Dublin, 2003), pp 12–13 §§ 306.1–2: The kings of Ind Airthir during the tenth century were descended from Gairbíth mac Flaithecáin. However, Flaithecán had another son Domnall who may have been Muiredach's father. If so, Muiredach's first cousin Máel Dúin (d. 945) held the same office in Armagh. **134** Gormgal mac Muiredaig, bishop and anchorite (d. 845), Ferchar mac Muiredaig, *princeps* (d. 850), Flann mac Ferchair, *princeps* and steward of Ard Macha (d. 869), Cernach mac Flainn, *princeps* and steward of Ard Macha (d. 922), Óengus mac Flainn (a different Flann), *airchinnech* (d. 1017). All references are from AU. **135** His father was Óenacán mac Ruaidrí, *princeps* of Lusk (d. 881). **136** https://www.dib.ie/biography/mael-brigte-a5309. The Mac Durnan Gospels (London, Lambeth Palace, MS 1370 was used by Máel Brigte and given to Christ Church, Canterbury by King Æthelstan (d. 939). See Claire Breay and Joanna Story (eds), *Anglo-Saxon kingdoms. Art, word, war* (London, 2018), pp 206–7. **137** Tomás Ó Fiaich, 'The church of Armagh under lay control', *Seanchas Ard Mhacha* 5:1 (1969), 75–127, at p. 84; Stalley, *Early Irish sculpture*, p. 60. **138** Simon Keynes, 'King Athelstan's books' in Michael Lapidge and Helmut Gneuss (eds), *Learning and*

> Máel Brigte mac Tornáin propounds this gospel-book throughout the world, in a manner worthy of God; but Aethelstan, king and ruler of the Anglo-Saxons, gives it forever to the metropolitan see of Canterbury.

Simon Keynes has suggested that the verse was added to the gospel-book by Cenwald, the king's royal chaplain and bishop of Worcester (d. 958). This is one of a cluster of references that link Irish ecclesiastics with King Æthelstan's court. One was Dub Innse, bishop of Bangor (d. 953) who reputedly brought the board game *Alea Evangelii* back from the king's court. Dunstan, abbot of Glastonbury and bishop of Worcester, London and Canterbury successively (d. 988) who was instrumental in attempting to normalize monastic rules in England also had connections with the Irish. It is related that during his early life, he encountered the Irish *peregrini* who flocked to Glastonbury to venerate St Patrick, whose relics were supposedly preserved there. These *peregrini* brought books with them which, according to the early version of his life, Dunstan studied.[139] On the basis that Dunstan was born *c.*909 this would date Irish contacts with Glastonbury to the first half of the tenth century,[140] a period during which Máel Brigte Mac Tornáin or Dub Innse could have been in Glastonbury or Abingdon. Æthelstan lived at Culham which was one of the royal estates connected to Abingdon.[141] The question, as ever, is, to what extent did the ideas of Æthelstan's highly literate and connected court filter back to Ireland?

The other key question is how do the careers of Máel Brigte and Muiredach, and more importantly, the purpose and iconography of their high crosses extend our understanding of the existing Irish monastic tradition in late ninth and early tenth-century Ireland? In summary, they define the complexity of ecclesiastical life in Irish society at that time. Both men were associated with churches that were politically powerful with authority over kings and ecclesiastics alike, that owned extensive estates and collected tributes, that forged alliances, were burdened by endless internal conspiracies among officials, their families and their allies, and during this particular period were subject to intense pressure from the Norse of Dublin. And yet in the midst of this maelstrom, monastic communities thrived and influenced the spiritual life of those around them.

literature in Anglo-Saxon England. Studies presented to Peter Clemoes on the occasion of his sixty-fifth birthday (Cambridge, 1985), pp 143–201, at pp 153, 156. The original reads: *Mæielbriðus MacDurnani/ istum textum per triquadrum/ Deo digne dogmatizat/ ast / Æthelstanus Angloscæxna/ rex et rector Doruernensi/ metropoli dat per æuum.* For more comments on this inscription, see Bethell, 'English monks and Irish reform', p. 132. **139** Michael Winterbottom and Michael Lapidge (ed. and trans.), *The early lives of St Dunstan* (Oxford, 2011), pp 18–21 §5. **140** Michael Lapidge, 'The cult of St Indract at Glastonbury' in Whitelock, McKitterick and Dumville (eds), *Ireland in early mediaeval Europe*, pp 179–212, at p. 182. **141** Alan T. Thacker, 'Æthelwold and Abingdon' in Barbara Yorke (ed.), *Bishop Æthelwold. His career and influence* (Woodbridge, 1988; repr. 1997), pp 43–64, at pp 45–9.

Muiredach's Cross exemplifies this alliance of the spiritual and the temporal. In her discussion of the power of intercessory prayer and monasticism during the Carolingian period, Renie S. Choy comments in relation to Benedict of Aniane, 'in him, we can begin to resolve the imposing problem of the distinction between monasticism as a pure ascetic spiritual discipline, and eighth- and ninth-century Carolingian monasticism as a public institution standing at the centre of a medieval topography of power in which prayer featured as economic currency'.[142] This observation is as relevant to Muiredach's Cross as it is to Carolingian architecture, reforms and Benedict of Aniane.

Reading the iconography of high crosses has always been difficult and subject to dispute but the contributions in recent decades of scholars of eschatology have confirmed the sheer depth of learning that informed their creation.[143] In his study of the depiction of Christ in the tomb, 'the mysterious moment of resurrection', on the Cross of the Scriptures at Clonmacnoise, the High Cross at Durrow, the Tall Cross at Monasterboice and the Market Cross at Kells, Éamonn Ó Carragáin observes the lively intellectual process involved:[144]

> This brief examination of the different contexts given to a single panel, 'the mysterious moment of resurrection', shows us four designers thinking in a variety of ways about this single theme. They do not receive the images and ideas of the tradition passively; instead, using elements from a variety of visual, patristic and liturgical traditions, they create original, and at times remarkable meditations on history as they understood it. On these crosses, using the resources of scripture, hagiography and liturgical practice, and showing remarkable iconographic activity, history is made and remade.

The crucial elements of the history that is made and remade are Christ's crucifixion, his resurrection and his second coming on which man's salvation and redemption depends. Episodes and individuals from the Old Testament were chosen as prefigurations of the New Testament. Sophisticated iconographic programmes come as no surprise given that a monastic way of life must have been at the heart of their production. Hence here one is viewing at once Choy's 'topography of power' and a reflection of the monastic ideal. Advocating a just and ideal kingship to a royal audience is part of the topography of power set out in these iconographic programmes. The east face of the Tall Cross at

142 Renie S. Choy, *Intercessory prayer and the monastic ideal in the time of the Carolingian reforms* (Oxford, 2016), p. 8. **143** The essential reference work in this field is Peter Harbison's *The high crosses of Ireland. An iconographical and photographic survey*. 3 vols (Bonn, 1992). **144** Éamonn Ó Carragáin, 'Recapitulating history: contexts for the mysterious moment of resurrection on Irish high crosses' in Jane Hawkes (ed.), *Making histories. Proceedings of the sixth international conference on insular art, York 2011* (Donington, 2013),

Monasterboice, for example, consists of a series of Old Testament scenes which appear to touch on kingship, one scene depicting Samuel anointing David.[145] It has been suggested that the Old Testament episodes in 1 Samuel relating the destruction of Saul and the rise of David and the role of the prophet Samuel in seeking to rule the Israelites influenced the early Irish tale *Togail Bruidne Da Derga*.[146] This tale narrates the rise of the young Conaire Mór to the kingship of Tara and his downfall as he breaks taboos laid down by otherworldly beings, some of them prohibitions specifically linked to the Tara kingship and not belonging to a Christian tradition.

In addition to the scriptures and the psalms – enhanced by commentaries on these texts – the crosses include the universal scene of SS Antony and Paul breaking bread in the desert, symbolic of the Eucharist, and images of the same iconic monks – or even the lone monk – being tempted by devils, fierce beasts and other unwanted beings.[147] These saints also linked Irish monks to their Egyptian antecedents through the literature of the desert. Inclusion of such 'monastic' iconography must speak to the involvement of *fír-manaig* 'true monks' in their design. Is it possible to suggest who might have created these iconographic programmes and how monastic communities might have used such monumental crosses? The inscription on the Cross of the Scriptures at Clonmacnoise, if the reading is correct, provides a clue as to the type of person involved. The inscription appears to commemorate the creation of the cross by Flann Sinna, king of Ireland (d. 916) and Colmán, abbot of Clonmacnoise (d. 926), a contemporary of Muiredach mac Domnaill. Colmán mac Ailella or Colmán Conaillech (from the kingdom of Conaille Muirthemne on the east coast, vaguely approximating to parts of Co. Louth) is described in the annals as abbot of Clonmacnoise and Clonard who along with Flann Sinna built the stone church (*damliac*) of Clonmacnoise.[148] AU describes him as *princeps*, *scriba* and *episcopus*, suggesting that he combined the offices of administrator, scribe/teacher and bishop. Many such powerful and learned individuals were based in the larger monasteries,[149] most of them with credentials that give the impression that their lifestyle was monastic. Among the most obvious of the time were:

pp 246–61, at p. 261. **145** Éamonn Ó Carragáin, 'High crosses, the sun's course, and local theologies at Kells and Monasterboice' in Colum Hourihane (ed.), *Insular and Anglo-Saxon art and thought in the early medieval period* (Princeton, 2011), pp 149–73, at p. 165. **146** Ralph O'Connor, *The destruction of Da Derga's hostel. Kingship and narrative artistry in a mediaeval Irish saga* (Oxford, 2013), pp 250–86. The intellectual dialogue on kingship encapsulated in Latin and vernacular texts and in the iconography of the high crosses remains a subject worthy of much greater consideration than can be undertaken in this volume. **147** Colleen M. Thomas, 'Missing models: visual narrative in the insular Paul and Antony panels' in Hawkes (ed.), *Making histories*, pp 77–89. **148** AClon [901, 921], AFM [904], CS. Conleth Manning, 'References to church buildings in the annals' in Alfred P. Smyth (ed.), *Seanchas. Studies in early and medieval Irish archaeology, history and literature in honour of Francis J. Byrne* (Dublin, 2000), pp 37–52, at 38, 50. **149** Johnston, *Literacy and identity*, pp 178–96.

Suairlech of *Int Eidnén* (d. 870), bishop, anchorite and abbot of Clonard, *optimus doctor totius Hibernię*; Gnia (d. 872), *princeps* of Duleek, anchorite, bishop and *scriba optimus*; Féthgna (d. 874), bishop and successor of Patrick, *caput relegionis totius Hibernię*; Máel Pátraic (d. 888), scribe and excellent scholar (*sapiens*), *princeps* of Treóit (Trevet, Co. Meath) and steward of the community of Patrick; Mochta (d. 893), pupil (*dalta*) of Féthgna, bishop, anchorite and *scriba optimus* of Armagh; Móenach mac Siadail (d. 921), successor (*comarbae*) of Comgall of Bangor, chief master of ecclesiastical learning of the island of Ireland, *cenn ecna innse Érenn*; Cú Chongalt (d. 923), priest of Lann Léire and paragon of Ireland in voice and figure and learning, *tetra Érenn eter guth 7 cruth 7 soas*; Céle (d. 929), successor of Comgall, scribe and anchorite, *apostolicus doctor totius Hibernię* who died on pilgrimage in Rome; Ioseph (d. 936), *princeps* of Armagh, bishop, scholar (*sapiens*) and anchorite.[150] That so many of these individuals were bishops implies that they were well versed in the psalms as the Rule of Patrick required a bishop or *suí/sapiens* – a scholar learned in scriptures – to examine students in their knowledge of the psalms as part of their progression towards the priesthood.[151] Although many of them were anchorites according to the annals, this does not imply that they existed alone in desert places. They lived in large monasteries but through periods of isolation within the settlement or in places designated as hermitages – such as the churches called *Int Eidnén* – and following rigorous practices, they were regarded like the *deorada Dé* as being distinguished and devout. Muiredach mac Domnaill was likely to have called on one or more such individuals when designing his great cross at Monasterboice.

If a monastic community existed at Monasterboice, and the evidence for such a community from the annals is slight, what role did the two high crosses play in that community's life? The same question can be asked of the crosses erected elsewhere that are likely to date to the early tenth century, among them Arboe (Co. Tyrone), Castledermot (Co. Kildare), Clonmacnoise, Duleek, Durrow, Kells and Moone. Was the construction of so many sculptured high crosses at this time prompted by a renewal of the monastic ideal or a reaction to the realpolitik of political ecclesiastical affairs, the rise of powerful kings or attacks by the Norse? In the case of Monasterboice, Muiredach may have erected his cross in 919 which would have been the four hundredth anniversary of the reputed death in 519 of St Buite, the founder of Monasterboice. It may also have been venerated during the liturgical year by the greater monastic communities of Armagh and Kells. Veneration of the cross was an intrinsic element of devotion in the early

150 I have confined my references to AU as it covers the Armagh sphere of influence in greater detail. **151** Gwynn, 'The rule of the Céli De', pp 82–3 §62. **152** Gerard Murphy (ed. and trans.), *Early Irish lyrics. Eighth to twelfth century* (Oxford, 1956), pp 32–5, at 34–5 §§6, 10 (with minor changes). Original text: *Cros Chríst sair frim einech/ Cros Chríst síar fri fuined/ Tes, túaid cen nach n-anad/ Cros Chríst cen nach fuirech … Cros Chríst tar mo muintir/ Cros Chríst tar mo thempal/ Cros Chríst isin altar/ Cros Chríst isin chentar.* **153** Kate H.

Irish church, as it was elsewhere. The *lorica* attributed to Mugrón, successor of Colum Cille (d. 980), is imbued with an intensity that is a fair expression of this deep devotion:[152]

> Christ's cross eastwards facing me.
> Christ's cross back towards the sunset.
> In the north, in the south unceasingly
> May Christ's cross without delay be ....
>
> Christ's cross over my community.
> Christ's cross over my church.
> Christ's cross in the next world.
> Christ's cross in this world.

Prayers addressed to the cross were an essential part of Christian veneration articulated in Latin and in vernaculars such as Old English and Irish. Adoration of the cross through bowing, kneeling, prostration and making the sign of the cross was an element of the daily monastic routine and stational liturgies.[153] The location of the dedicatory inscription at the base of Muiredach's Cross may be an indicator for prostration if Muiredach was to be remembered in the prayers of those venerating the cross. Marking an area with crosses formed part of consecrating churches and cemeteries.[154] This may explain the drawing in the late eighth-century Book of Moling (TCD MS 60) of four paired crosses named after prophets and evangelists placed inside and outside two circular enclosures that possibly represent a monastic cemetery.[155] A number of early Irish texts that list the fundamentals of monastic life mention processions around a cross. The guide on how to be a good cleric '*Cidh as dech do cléiriuch?*' includes the phrase 'divine office/going around crosses' (*Ord n-ecalsa/Timchill cros*).[156] The Rule of Ailbe, potentially compiled by an author familiar with *céli Dé* observances,[157] stipulates that the community follows the abbot to the cross 'with gentle choirings, with vehement streams of tears from righteous haggard cheeks'.[158] No doubt, as elsewhere, these were normal daily routines that occurred inside a church, and may equally have been undertaken around highly decorated

Thomas, *Late Anglo-Saxon prayer in practice. Before the Books of Hours* (Berlin and Boston, 2020), pp 129–76. **154** I am grateful to Comán Ó Clabaigh for allowing me to include this reference in my volume prior to including it in his own publication on popular religion in late medieval Ireland. The marking of consecration crosses on interior walls was part of the ceremony of consecrating cemeteries and churches in Anglo-Saxon England from the tenth century as described in various pontificals. See Helen Gittos, *Liturgy, architecture, and sacred places in Anglo-Saxon England* (Oxford, 2013), pp 40–6. **155** https://www.tcd.ie/library/early-irish-mss/the-famous-mulling-drawing-2/. **156** Paul Grosjean, 'Two religious pieces', *Zeitschrift für celtische Philologie* 18 (1930), 299–303, at p. 301. **157** O'Dwyer, *Céli Dé*, pp 134–6; Follett, *Céli Dé in Ireland*, pp 147–8. **158** O Neill, 'Rule of Ailbe', pp 100–1 §25(c). Original: *I ndegaid in chinn manach/ do chross co classaib cóimaib,/ co srothaib dianaib dérae/ do*

monumental stone crosses outside. Given the iconographical programme of these same crosses, their monumentality, and outdoor location, however, the likelihood is that they were the focus of particular veneration at certain times of the liturgical calendar. The obvious liturgical cycle would have been the triduum of Holy Week which incorporated the *Adoratio Crucis* ('Veneration of the Cross') on Good Friday and the Vigil of the Resurrection of Easter Saturday. Although the evidence for liturgical practices in Ireland is very fragmentary and often depends on continental manuscripts and fragments,[159] primarily associated with the Columbanian tradition, enough can be inferred from these liturgical fragments, from illuminated manuscripts and from the stone crosses themselves to understand what might have occurred at Monasterboice and elsewhere during the triduum. For example, in his reconstruction of the Irish tradition of the Divine Office, Peter Jeffery speculates that the reference in the Rule of Ailbe to the community following the abbot to the cross may be a reflex of the procession to Golgotha, which formed part of the Resurrection Vigil in fourth-century Jerusalem.[160] While it may be far-fetched to link the procession of a fourth-century office with a tenth-century cross, the power of the image, especially for those whose lives revolved around the scriptures and the psalter, must have been, as expressed by Jennifer O'Reilly in the context of the Southampton Psalter, 'a meditative focus for the reader who prays the psalms and shares with Christ in the daily spiritual battle'.[161] The inclusion of *Páis hImaigine Críst*, a universal narrative on the passion of an image of Christ that was reputedly destroyed in Beirut (*passio imaginis*), included in the Leabhar Breac, suggests a belief in the power of images for religious and laity alike.[162] This text possibly dates to the twelfth century, although it survives in a fifteenth-century manuscript, but was known in eleventh-century England, and the full-sized image of Christ described in the narrative, the Volto Santo, appears on crosses in Ireland. This image appears on Irish monumental crosses of the period on the Rock of Cashel, Co. Tipperary, in Dysert O'Dea and Kilfenora, Co. Clare, and Teampall Bhreacáin on Inishmore (Aran Islands, Co. Galway). All of an image's potency, be it in a text, a manuscript, a painting or in stone, is marvellously expressed in *In Tenga Bithnua* ('The ever-new tongue'), an early Irish text cast in the form of a homily, that was probably performed as part of the Easter Vigil:[163]

grúadaib córib cóilaib. **159** Yitzhak Hen, 'The nature and character of the early Irish liturgy' in *L'irlanda e gli irlandesi nell'alto medioevo: Spoleto, 16–21 aprile 2009* (Spoleto, 2010), pp 353–78. **160** Peter Jeffery, 'Eastern and western elements in the Irish monastic prayer of the hours' in Margot E. Fassler and Rebecca A. Baltzer (eds), *The Divine Office in the Latin Middle Ages. Methodology and source studies, regional developments, hagiography* (Oxford, 2000), pp 99–143, at p. 124. **161** Jennifer O'Reilly, 'Seeing the crucified Christ: image and meaning in early manuscript art' in Mullins et al., *Envisioning Christ on the cross*, pp 52–82, at p. 71. **162** Atkinson, *Passions and homilies*, pp 277–86; Juliet Mullins, 'Preaching the Passion: *imitatio Christi* and the passions and homilies of the *Leabhar Breac*' in Mullins et al., *Envisioning Christ on the cross*, pp 195–213, at pp 209–10. **163** Carey, *King of mysteries*, pp 75–96, at pp 94–5.

> Such is the beauty and radiance of his face that if all the souls in Hell were to gaze upon the radiance of this face, they would not notice the suffering and punishment and torture of Hell.
>
> Such is the sanctity of his form, that whoever gazed upon his face would be unable to commit a sin thereafter.
>
> Such is the radiance and splendour and brilliance of his face that when the nine heavenly orders shine forth, and every angel in them is seven times brighter than the sun; and when the souls of the saints shine forth with the same semblance; and when the sun is seven times brighter than it is now – the radiance of the face of the great King who made every created thing will [still] outshine them all, so that the brightness of the Lord will surpass the angels and the stars of Heaven and the souls of the saints just as the sun's brightness and radiance surpass the other stars.

This vibrant and highly emotional description of Christ's face is the work of a master word-smith but the words can only have been inspired by a visual image imagined or actually seen by the author.

The iconographic programme of Muiredach's Cross is based on knowledge of the scriptures, psalms, apocrypha, hagiography and other sources. Its superb sculpture is a spectacular testament of living monastic landscapes in early tenth-century Ireland, built at the heart of a monastery, in its *sanctissimus*. While the laity, especially the aristocracy, and ordinary workaday clerics would have been given access to the monument, particularly for certain religious feast days or seasons, the complex interpretation that could be read into its iconography can only have been fully comprehended by very few. And it is these few that are the subject of this volume.

Once the primary sources are understood and placed in context, the next step is to strip away the layers of secondary interpretation in order to allow the accumulated mass of medieval Irish sources to create the narrative. Although different in format and language from more widely known monastic sources, they nevertheless cast much light on many aspects of the tradition in Ireland, revealing similarities with elsewhere that may not have been acknowledged to date by scholars. Without doubt there are some marked differences but these have been exaggerated by their not being easily accessible through modern editions and translations of the rich volume of sources.

CHAPTER 4

The *sámud* and the *cráibdig*: diverse monastic communities and offices

A constant issue with the study of monasticism in any culture relates to terminology and what terms are used to describe the individuals – female and male – in a community, the collective words for a community, their activities, their landscapes. In her survey of female house ascetics in late antique and early medieval western societies, Eliana Magnani calls for a large-scale study of the terminology relating to women devoted to God that would reflect the 'nuances and semantic networks in which these terms are embedded'.[1] This certainly applies to the terminology of monasticism in medieval Ireland. One difficulty with terminology is the insertion of later and contemporary terminology into the vocabulary of monasticism or the assumption that there is an equivalence between the medieval and later meanings of words. In the Irish context, Etchingham's argument that the term *manach* in early Irish texts was not confined to meaning a monk living a committed religious life but was extended, and was probably more commonly used, to mean a lay tenant of a large land-holding monastery, is an important illustration.[2] This changed in the late medieval period when *manach* was restricted to members of certain orders, especially the Cistercians (*na manaigh liatha* 'the grey monks'). Nor should the influence of seventeenth-century historians on subsequent studies of medieval Irish monasticism be dismissed. For example, the term *bean riaghalta* 'a woman bound by a rule' to describe a nun appears in late medieval texts and particularly in seventeenth-century Franciscan texts and in the works of Geoffrey Keating.[3] This became the standard term from then on due to the influence, circulated especially among Catholic clergy and orders, of texts such as Geoffrey Keating's *Trí bior-ghaoithe an bháis* (1631) and the Franciscan catechism *Parrthas an Anma* (1645), and their translations of the rules of St Francis (1641) and St Clare (1636).[4] The impact of seventeenth-century Counter-Reformation catholicism on later generations of scholars and on popular religion created a gulf between original early medieval sources and modern monastic studies in Ireland, especially in relation to understanding the centuries between the formation of the *céli Dé* movement in the late eighth century and the arrival of the continental

1 Magnani, 'Female house ascetics', p. 223. 2 Etchingham, *Church organisation*, pp 363–4. 3 *DIL riaghalta* s.v. 4 Royal Irish Academy *Corpas: riaghalta* s.v.

orders during the late eleventh and twelfth centuries. This chapter interrogates the Irish and Latin terminology of Irish monasticism of that period in the hope that a clearer impression of the various communities and individuals and their roles in a monastery might emerge from the sources.

THE *SÁMUD*: THE POWERFUL MONASTIC HOUSEHOLD

In her perceptive essay on the monastic hierarchy of Kells based on the witness lists of the Book of Kells memoranda, discussed previously,[5] Bairbre Nic Aongusa identified 'a clear division of labour between spiritual and non-spiritual posts'.[6] Máire Herbert described the division as between 'the worldly monastic settlement, whose officials were concerned with power and property' and who delegated religious duties to the brethren of the *dísert*, 'thereby ensuring that both God and Mammon were duly served within its boundaries'.[7] The spiritual offices in Kells included the priest (*sacart*), the cantor or head of liturgy (*toísech celebarta*), the head of the monastic community (*cenn in reiclésa*), and the head of the hermitage or eremitical community (*cenn in dísirt*). The offices dealing with more worldly affairs included the deputy *airchinnech* (*fosairchinnech*), the doorkeeper/bell-ringer (*aistire*) and the master of the guesthouse (*airchinnech in taige oíged*). In addition, those in charge of learning were the master of the school (*fer léiginn*) and the master of the novices or students (*toísech na macc léiginn*). This profile fits well with the annalistic evidence for the larger monasteries at least. It is also the structure described in an eleventh-century poem in praise of the Armagh bishop, Áed Ua Forréid (d. 1056), which lists him as bishop of Ireland (*úasalelscop Érenn*) who was ordained (*ro-grádaig Día*). Around him were Amalgaid, Ireland's abbot (*abb Érenn*), Echnartach who although his office is not specified, was in charge of provisions, Dubthach, the anchorite (*ancharae*), Cummascach, head of the 'poor' meaning the religious community provided for by Herbert's 'worldly monastic settlement' (*cenn deich cét bocht*), Ua Bileóice, the *fer léiginn* knowledgeable in scripture, Duiligén, the priest, Mac Gilla Chiaráin, master of the guesthouse and Ua Rúadrach, the cantor (*beóil i mbí séis aifrinn úais* 'he whose lips make the music of noble mass').[8] Áed is depicted as supporting a *sámud slán* 'a perfect community'. In Máire Herbert's estimation, this poem is an episcopal eulogy, composed in the 1040s, possibly on the occasion of an Easter feast. Áed is a preacher and teacher in charge of a school and part of a clerical community, some of whom may have followed a monastic lifestyle.[9] The

5 For introduction to the Kells memoranda, see Chapter 3. 6 Nic Aongusa, 'Monastic hierarchy', p. 7. 7 Herbert, *Iona, Kells, and Derry*, p. 103. 8 Gerard Murphy (ed.), 'A poem in praise of Aodh Úa Foirréidh, bishop of Armagh (1032–1056)' in Sylvester O'Brien (ed.), *Measgra i gcuimhne Mhichíl Uí Chléirigh. Miscellany of historical and linguistic studies in honour of Brother Michael Ó Cléirigh O.F.M., chief of the Four Masters, 1643–1943* (Dublin, 1944), pp 140–64. 9 Máire Herbert, 'A praise-poem from eleventh-century Armagh' in Caoimhín

comarbae Choluim Chille, head of Kells, Máel Muire Ua Uchtáin (d. 1040) is described in one of the Kells memoranda as being accompanied by his *sámud* with their relics, while another *comarbae* Domnall mac Robartaig (d. 1098) came with all the seniors of Kells (*co n-ulib sruithib Cenannsa*) and a third, Ferdomnach Ua Clucáin (d. 1114) was also accompanied by his *sámud*.[10] The term *sámud* is a collective noun, meaning 'congregation, assembly', a large monastery's ruling elite, who were not necessarily all celibate or in full orders. Like the term *comarbae*, the *sámud* was identified with the founder, hence references to *sámud Pátraic*, *sámud Brigte*, *sámud Choluim Chille* and *sámud Chiaráin*. It was the public face of the *familia monastica*. Most references to the *sámud* relate to larger monasteries and the power of the *sámud*, which would have been considerable, was often felt beyond the monastic enclosure. There are instances of the community of Clonmacnoise, *sámud Chiaráin*, for example, fasting against kings. In 1043, they fasted against a local king, Áed ua Confiacla of Tethbae, and Ciarán's bell, the relic known as *Bernán Ciaráin* ('Ciarán's gapped bell') was rung against him. Áed turned his back on the *sámud* and by the end of the month, he was dead, a brutal warning to any king who dared to cross them. In 1108, the same *sámud* fasted against their overking, Muiredach Ua Máel Sechlainn, seeking to free the church of Cell Mór Maige Aoinfhir (Kilmore, Co. Meath) from royal exactions.[11] A particularly dramatic scene involving *sámud Pátraic* was the funerary ceremony of Brian Bórama, his son Murchad and other allies, killed at the battle of Clontarf in 1014, as described by AU:[12]

> Máel Muire son of Eochaid, successor of Patrick, with his venerable clerics and relics (*co sruithibh 7 co minnaibh*), came moreover to Sord Coluim Chille, and brought away the body of Brian, king of Ireland, and the body of his son Murchad, and the head of Conaing and the head of Mothla, and buried them in Ard Macha in a new tomb. For twelve nights the community of Patrick (*sámhadh Pátraicc*) waked the bodies in honour of the dead king.

This was a very public ceremony led by Máel Muire and although the churches of Munster – Brian's home territory – may not have been pleased that he was buried at Armagh, nonetheless during his lifetime he had been its royal patron.[13] As the most eminent king in Ireland, it was appropriate that *sámud Pátraic* led

Breatnach, Méibhín Ní Urdail and Gordon Ó Riain (eds), *Lorg na leabhar. A festschrift for Pádraig A. Breatnach* (Dublin, 2019), pp 139–48. **10** Mac Niocaill, *Notitiae*, I, 10; II, 12, 14; III, 18. **11** ATig, CS 1043, 1108. **12** AU original: *Luidh tra Mael Muire [mc. Eochadha], comarba Patraicc, co sruithibh 7 co minnaibh co nnice Sord Coluim Cille co tuc as corp Briain righ Erenn, 7 corp Murchada a mc., 7 cenn Conaing 7 cenn Mothlai coro adhnacht i nArd Macha i n-ailaidh nui. Di aidhci dhec immorro do samhadh Patraicc ic are na corp propter honorem regis possiti.* **13** Seán Duffy, *Brian Boru and the battle of Clontarf* (Dublin, 2013), pp 138–43.

by its *comarbae*, the pre-eminent religious community in Ireland, should accompany his body to Armagh, watch over and pray for his soul for twelve nights, and bury him in a new tomb.

THE RANGE OF OFFICES IN IRISH MONASTERIES

Monastic rulers

TABLE 1: Officials in charge of monasteries

Title	Responsibility
abb/airchinnech *princeps/principatus*	abbot of a monastic community OR lay abbot in charge of monastery's temporal affairs
comarbae	head of a monastery, the founder's successor who might be a cleric, monk or layman
espoc/episcopus	bishop
sacart/sacerdos	priest
manach/monachos	monk following a committed religious life OR a lay tenant working on monastic land
fer léiginn	master of a monastic school, a lector who might be a cleric, monk or layman
anmcharae	confessor, spiritual director
ancharae	anchorite
céli Dé, deorada Dé, cráibdig	members of an eremitical community: 'clients of God', 'exiles of God', 'pious ones'
suí ecna	master of religious learning
senchaid, suí senchais	historian, master of traditional history
toísech celebarta	head of liturgy, precentor

Vernacular Irish monastic vocabulary drew on both Latin monastic and native legal terminology and was not confined in its use to coenobitic and eremitical communities. Terms such as Irish *abb*, *airchinnech*, *comarbae* and Latin *princeps* and *principatus*, could denote leadership of a monastic community or of the wider Christian population. Wendy Davies, in her commentary on the Irish clergy's appropriation of the vocabulary of royal power to themselves, notes that the terms *princeps* and *principatus* referred specifically to rulers of monasteries and their 'principates', the territories and peoples over which they ruled. Elements of this particular use also occur in some early eastern monastic materials.[14] Jean-Michel Picard's study of the use of *princeps* and *principatus* in

14 Davies, 'Clerics as rulers', pp 83–4.

the annals and other sources is of particular merit as it chronicles not only the meaning of these terms but also their replacement by vernacular terms such as *airchinnech* and *comarbae* to designate various forms of ecclesiastical leadership.[15] From the mid-tenth century, the term *princeps* was replaced by *airchinnech*. This trend, which begins during the ninth century continues into the twelfth century, after which *airchinnech* – and the anglicized version 'erenagh' – refers primarily until the seventeenth century to hereditary keepers of relics and administrators of church lands.[16] Picard argues that the function and status of the *princeps/airchinnech* was given 'a prominent role in Irish affairs in comparison to those of the bishop or the abbot'.[17] Not unlike Davies's argument, he perceives the difference as based on the extent to which the *princeps/airchinnech* was regarded as equivalent in his temporal power to a king, in his capacity to rule church lands and tenants, forge alliances with kings and dynasties, and interfere in society beyond the ecclesiastical settlement.[18] Two other terms for church leadership are used, *abb* (borrowed from Latin *abbas*) and *comarbae* 'heir', a term used in legal texts to refer to an heir in general. It is noticeable that *abb* is far less frequently used in AU after 900 and that it is replaced mainly by *comarbae* to denote the head of a monastery and the founder's successor.[19] AI, on the other hand, continues to use *abb* more frequently until the early eleventh century, when *airchinnech* and *comarbae* (anglicized 'coarb') replace it. In both annals, *abb* reappears in the twelfth century when the title becomes common with the arrival of the international orders. It must be noted, however, that there are many instances of the designation of the same individuals as either *abb*, *comarbae* or *airchinnech*, depending on the source. A study of all these titles used to describe the leaders of the most important monasteries during the period under consideration indicates that they were interchangeable and simply denoted that the person holding any one of these titles was in charge.[20] The deaths of eminent

15 Picard, '*Princeps* and *principatus*'. **16** The use of such titles in the late medieval period is not at all clear and constantly changes. For a useful narrative on the situation in Ulster, see Katharine Simms, *Gaelic Ulster in the Middle Ages. History, culture and society* (Dublin, 2020), pp 268–90. See also Henry Jefferies, 'Erenaghs in pre-plantation Ulster: an early seventeenth-century account', *Archivium Hibernicum* 53 (1999), 16–19; Ciaran O'Scea, 'Erenachs, erenachships and church landholding in Gaelic Fermanagh, 1207–1609', *Proceedings of the Royal Irish Academy* 112C (2012), 271–300. **17** Picard, '*Princeps* and *principatus*', p. 156. **18** One might note that in *DIL* there is an inference that the word *airchenn* 'certain, fixed, definite' can also mean 'chaste', albeit rarely. **19** Of a total of 471 instances of *abb* in AU, 435 date to pre-900. **20** A comparative survey by the author noted all the monastic officials recorded in AU, AI, ATig and AFM between 900 and 1250 for Armagh, Bangor, Castledermot, Clonard, Clonbroney, Clonfert, Clonmacnoise, Cong, Cork, Derry, Devenish, Durrow, Emly, Ferns, Glendalough, Iona, Kells, Kildare, Killaloe, Lismore, Lorrha, Mayo, Monasterboice, Roscrea, Tallaght, Terryglass, Tuam. In addition, account has been taken of detailed studies of *Armagh*: Ó Fiaich, 'The church of Armagh under lay control'; Hérold Pettiau, 'The officials of the church of Armagh in the early and central Middle Ages, to AD 1200' in Art J.

churchmen and kings 'in a great mortality of the men of Ireland' (*mortlaith mór for feraib hÉrend*) in 1095 recorded in detail in AI and AFM is an example of this varied use of titles. AI's entry lists the churchmen and their titles as follows:

> Mael Pátraic, **episcopus** Aird Macha (Armagh); Dubthach H. Sochaind, **suíshacard** na Ferta i nArd Macha (learned priest of In Fherta in Armagh); Mael Brigte H. Brolcain .i. Mc. Mail Issu (Kildare); Donnigus Hua Aingliu, **episcopus** Atha Cliath (Dublin); 7 in t-**epscop** H. Cethernaig, **abb** Ferno Moire (Ferns); 7 in t-**epscop** Mail Chuarain; 7 Hua Manchain do muintir Glinne do Lacha (Glendalough); 7 Hua Rinnanag, **fer léginn** Lethglinne (Leighlin); Scanlán Hua Cnamsige, **anchorita**; 7 Donnchad .H. Ferchair, **secnap** Lis Moir (Lismore); Moel Muaid mc. meic Clothnai, **abb** Cluana Huma (Cloyne); 7 Hua Maíl Mune, **abb** Inse Cathaig (Scattery Island); 7 **in sacard** .H. Gerruidir; 7 Gilla na Nóem .H. Ennae do muntir Cille Da Lua (Killaloe); 7 Hua Ábartaig, **abb** Maige hEo (Mayo); Eogan, **cend manach na Gaedel** hi Roim (head of the Irish monks in Rome).

The equivalent entry in AFM, which is a much later source, but extracting from earlier material reads:

> Donnghus, **epscop** Atha Cliath (Dublin), hUa Mancháin .i. **an bretheamh, comharba** Caoimhghin (Glendalough), Macc Maras Ua Caomháin, **comhorba** Oenai (Aran), do Dhelbhna Bhicc a chenél, Cairpre .i. an t-**espocc** Ua Ceithearnaigh, **comharba** Maedhócc (Ferns), Ua Rinnánaigh, **fear léighinn** Leithghlinne (Leighlin), Eochaidh Ua Coisi, **secnab** Achadh Bó (Aghaboe), Scannlán Ua Cnáimhsighe, **anmchara** Lis Mhóir (Lismore), Buadhach Ua Cearruidhir, **sacart** Cille Dálua (Killaloe), Dubhshlatach Ua Muireadhaigh, Aodh Mac Maoiliosa Uí Brolcháin, **áirdfhearleighind**, 7 Augustin Ua Cuinn, **áirdbreitheamh Laighean**.

Not alone does this entry offer a glimpse of the range of ecclesiastical dignitaries in late eleventh-century Ireland – and abroad – it also perhaps hints at a shift in terminology on the part of the compiler(s) of AI from the hereditary and

Hughes and William Nolan (eds), *Armagh history and society. Interdisciplinary essays on the history of an Irish county* (Dublin, 2001), pp 121–86; *Clonard*: Paul Byrne, 'The community of Clonard from the sixth to the twelfth centuries', *Peritia* 4 (1985), 157–73; *Clonmacnoise*: Kehnel, *Clonmacnois*; *Glendalough*: Ailbhe S. Mac Shamhráin, '*Prosopgraphica Glindelachensis*: the monastic church of Glendalough and its community sixth to thirteenth centuries', *Journal of the Royal Society of Antiquaries of Ireland* 119 (1989), 79–97; Mac Shamhráin, *Church and polity in pre-Norman Ireland*; *Kells*: Nic Aongusa, 'Monastic hierarchy'.

probably less monastic *airchinnech* and *comarbae* to *abb*. Clearly, AFM, or its source, adheres to *comarbae* instead of *abb*. AU begins to use *abb* again in the late twelfth century as a designation for the abbots of the Cistercian houses at Newry (1160), Baltinglass (1163) and Boyle (1174), and the community of the *reiclés* of Peter and Paul at Armagh (1174). Most significantly, the designation of Éogan, head of the Irish community in Rome as *cenn manach na Gaedel hi Róim* ('head of the monks of the Irish in Rome') singles him out as different from the monastic terminology used in relation to Ireland. One earlier reference in 1042 also seems to view an Irish community abroad as distinct. Ailill Mucnama (of Muckno, Co. Monaghan), head of the Irish community in Cologne, possibly following the Rule of St Benedict, is described as *cenn manach* (AI) and *cenn mhanach na n-Goeidhel in Colonia* (AU). In both instances the sources seem to acknowledge that these men and their communities were somehow following the Rule of St Benedict, a lifestyle that was different from the monasticism of monks at home.

While the terminology of monastic leadership began to change during the twelfth century, it did not happen immediately.

> Gnim mór aínfial do dhenum don **manach**, .i., do Amlaímh, **mac comarba Finnéin Muighi-bile** 7 do Maghnus Mac Duinnsleibhe, do righ Uladh, co toisighibh Uladh 7 co n-Ultaibh archena, cenmotha Mael-Isu, **espuc** 7 Gilla-Domanghairt Mac Cormaic, **comarba Comgaill** 7 Mael-Martain, **comarba Finnéin co n-a muinnteraibh**: .i., **Coimtinol Canonach Riagulla co n-a n-abaidh**, ro ordaigh Mael-Moedoic hUa Morgair, **Leghait Comarba Petair**, i Saball Patraic, do innarba[dh] asin **Mainistir** rocumdaigsetar féin 7 do arcain co leir, eter libru 7 aidhmí, bu 7 dainiu, eochu 7 cairchiu 7 na h-uile rotinólat ann o aímsir in Legait remraiti conice séin, cenmothat na ínair 7 na capai robatar ímpu isind uair sein, tria format 7 baidh collaidhe 7 saint onóiri dó féin. Uair rodíchuirsetar **manaigh** Drochait-atha é **asan abdaine**, tria chuisibh dlightechaibh.
>
> A great unbecoming deed was done by the monk, namely by Amlaím, son of the successor [*comarbae*] of Finnian of Movilla, and by Magnus Mac Duinn Sléibhe, king of Ulaid, along with the lords [*toísig*] of Ulaid and with the men of Ulaid as well, excepting the bishop, Máel Ísu and Gilla Domangairt Mac Cormaic, successor of Comgall [of Bangor], and Máel Martain, successor of Finnian [of Movilla], with their communities; that is, the congregation [*comtinól*] of canons regular, with their abbot, whom Máel Máedóc Ua Morgair, legate of the successor of Peter, instituted in Saul of Patrick, were expelled out of the monastery they themselves built and were despoiled completely, both of books and furniture, cows and persons, horses and sheep and all things they had collected therein from

> the time of the aforesaid legate until then, excepting only the tunics and the capes which they were wearing at that time. It was through jealousy and lustful love and greed of honour for himself [that he did this]. For the monks of Droichat Átha [Drogheda[21]] deposed him from the abbacy [of Saball?] for lawful causes.

This is AU's entry recording a violent incident that occurred in Downpatrick in 1170. Amlaím, son of the *comarbae* of St Finnian of Movilla (Co. Down), supported by the local nobility, expelled the canons regular from their house in Saul (northeast of Downpatrick). This incident is indicative of a church in flux as indeed are the titles accorded the various participants. The perpetrator Amlaím is described both as a *manach* and the son of a *comarbae*, implying that he had unsuccessfully experienced the new form of monastic life, possibly in Drogheda or Mellifont, and had then returned to the politics of a hereditary family. Amlaím's opponents, Gilla Domangoirt, abbot of Bangor and Máel Martain, abbot of Movilla, were probably reformed abbots of houses of Augustinian canons established a generation earlier by St Malachy (Malachy I) when he was bishop of Down.[22] Both maintained the title *comarbae*, as successors of their founder saints, Comgall and Finnén, while Amlaím is described as *mac comarba Finnéin Muighi Bile* ('son of the *comarbae* of Finnian of Movilla'), the title due to him as a member of a hereditary family. While the head of the Augustinian canons at Saul is described as an *abb*, Malachy is *legáit comarba Petair* 'legate of the successor of St Peter', thus transferring Irish usage to the papal title. And furthermore, Gilla Domangoirt and Máel Martain were accompanied by their *muinter*, used in both ecclesiastical and royal contexts to denote a dignitary's household and also as a translation of *familia*. The Augustinian abbot of Saul was part of a *comthinól* of canons regular. *Comthinól* is a native term used to describe an assembly that in this instance was used to refer to a community of canons.

During the twelfth century, many hereditary families took advantage of changes, and retained their titles while at the same time gaining new ones. AFM 1158 records the death of *an breitheamh Ua Dúileandáin, airchindeach Eassa dara, ollamh feineachais, 7 taoiseach a thuaithe* ('the judge Ua Dúilennáin, *airchinnech* of Ballysadare, master of native Irish law and his people's lord'). This man was both a lawyer and a secular leader while at the same time exercising ecclesiastical authority as *airchinnech* of a church. His kinsman, possibly a son, Gilla in Coimded Ua Dúilennáin died in 1230 and is accorded the titles of *comharba*

21 It is not clear if Mellifont is the monastery referred to here or an early foundation of canons regular in Drogheda. **22** Marie Therese Flanagan, 'John de Courcy, the first Ulster plantation and Irish church men' in Brendan Smith (ed.), *Britain and Ireland, 900–1300. Insular responses to medieval European change* (Cambridge, 1999), pp 154–78, at pp 161–2. I follow Flanagan's translation on p. 161.

Feichín and *abb reicclésa cananach Eassadara* ('the *comarbae* of Feichín of Cong (Co. Mayo) and abbot of the community of canons of Ballysadare (Co. Sligo)'). Gilla in Coimded was probably an Augustinian canon but he also was successor to Feichín, reputed founder saint of both Cong and Ballysadare. This is a further instance of the fluctuations in the Irish church at a time when two monastic systems overlapped and individuals and families sought to navigate between the two to their own advantage.

In his assessment of church organization in early Ireland, Sharpe describes the term *comarbae* 'heir' of a patron saint as a word that 'is neutral in its ecclesiastical significance and provides a convenient label for the controller of the church's temporalities. The coarb's powers could be combined, as at Armagh in the seventh century, with the pastoral jurisdiction of a bishop and the paternal authority of an abbot, or, as happened at Armagh in the tenth and eleventh century, they could be exercised by laymen; here, as often elsewhere, the coarbial office became hereditary in a group of families, in the same way as the royal office'.[23] Both Sharpe and Picard's views on the structure and culture of Irish monasteries require a degree of refining. Fundamental to any new assessment is the need to acknowledge the diverse nature of an early Irish monastery and to finally move away – particularly in relation to the centuries under consideration – from the view that Irish monasteries under lay control were politically and spiritually corrupt. More than four decades ago, Kathleen Hughes and Ann Hamlin made the following astute comment:[24]

> A monastery must be seen as an estate, directed to a religious purpose, but on which only some people, at times comparatively few, led an ascetic life. Even the abbot might be married, and if so his descendants often held the abbacy after him. Thus the question 'Why did people go into monasteries?' needs to be re-phrased. We should rather ask 'What were monasteries for?'

Like many modern monasteries, which run schools, third-level institutions, farms, health-care and social-care institutions with the assistance of government and community support, early Irish monasteries operated on a similar basis. Not only did they own large estates, the larger monasteries had guesthouses, hospices and libraries and were centres of ecclesiastical and vernacular learning. Most large and middle-sized foundations housed coenobitic communities who followed an ascetic lifestyle based on universal monastic precepts, and on occasion either individuals or groups of monks lived more eremitical lives in specially designated hermitages, some close to their monasteries, others quite a distance away.

The common profile of the monasteries surveyed show that they were all led by an *abb*, *airchinnech* or *comarbae*, these titles used interchangeably. Beyond this

23 Sharpe, 'The organization of the church in early medieval Ireland', 264. **24** Hughes and

leading office, most are regularly recorded as housing bishops, priests, and *fir léiginn*, scholars of various disciplines, teachers and heads of monastic schools. These latter offices were dedicated to the monasteries' educational and spiritual activities both in organizing the church's pastoral role among the laity (*cura animarum*) and in caring for and directing their own coenobitic and eremitical communities. Other offices were associated with specific activities outlined in the following table:

TABLE 2: Specific offices in Irish monasteries

Title	Responsibilities
tánaise abbad	possibly an office similar to the office prior or a potential successor to an abbot
secnap/secundus abbas	possibly similar to the office of prior
fosairchinnech	either second-in-command or an heir apparent
máer	a steward in charge of collecting tributes and on occasion the care of relics
cenn adchomairc	chief counsellor, arbiter
ferthigis/equonimus	steward in charge of the household, guesthouse, hospice, *cellerarius*
airchinnech tigi/lis n-óigid	head of the guesthouse
aistire	doorkeeper

The first five offices in the above table were either administrative roles to do with representing or substituting an abbot or were specific to a monastery's administration such as dealing with kings and nobles, collecting tithes and tributes, organizing agricultural production and ruling church tenants. As there are so many references to kings, nobles and eminent ecclesiastics dying and being buried in large monasteries, they must have been cared for in guesthouses and hospices, specifically founded to care for people at the end of their lives. The spiritual aspects of such care, however, were probably carried out by bishops, priests and other members of the community, most often accorded the title *anmcharae* 'soul-friend, confessor, spiritual director'. In the sphere of learning and literacy, apart from the *fer léiginn*, there are many references to scribes, many of whom were bishops, and individuals with specific titles such as *suí ecna* ('a scholar of religious learning'), *toísech mic léiginn* ('head of the novices or students') and *brethem* ('judge'). Máel Ísu mac Maíl Cholaim held the titles of Armagh's *prímh-challadóir* ('chief keeper of the calendar'), *prímh-críochaire* ('chief keeper of the boundaries') and *leabhar-coimédaigh* ('keeper of books').[25]

Hamlin, *Celtic monasticism*, p. 7. **25** AFM 1136.

In essence, the larger monasteries were governed by an abbot, often a member of a hereditary family and regarded as the founder's successor. These were lay people, some in minor orders, although not exclusively so, supported by a coterie of officers (the *sámud*), whose main interests focused on the temporal aspects of their monasteries but they did not necessarily neglect their foundations' spiritual and educational activities. The latter responsibilities were in the hands of bishops, priests and religious scholars, many of whom belonged to monastic and eremitical communities and who were learned in scripture, canon law, computistics, and history, both biblical and native.

Liturgical and spiritual offices

A variety of other titles suggests that the liturgical, monastic and spiritual life of some monasteries was regulated and vibrant. There are many references to anchorites (*anchorita*, *ancharae*) but also a few to very particular offices. The offices of *cenn ríagla* and *cenn coiméta ríagla* literally, 'head of the rule' are recorded in Glendalough and Clonmacnoise. Donnchadh Ó Corráin interpreted the entry relating to Dúnchad mac Dúnadaich (d. 1006), who is described as *fear léighind Cluana Mic Nóis, 7 a hangcoire iarsin, ceand a riaghla, 7 a seancais* ('lector of Clonmacnoise, and its anchorite thereafter, head of its rule and its history'),[26] as meaning that Dúnchad, a member of the most important hereditary family in Clonmacnoise and not a celibate, withdrew not to become a simple hermit but 'the head or *protos* of a community of stricter observance within Clonmacnoise'. Ó Corráin likens this community to that of a Greek *lavra* – 'a cluster of cells with a church and sometimes a refectory and kitchen, inhabited by monks who largely lived alone, practised celibacy, poverty, austerity, and silence, and assembled only for divine service and some common needs'.[27] This is a fair description of the communities already encountered in the *Regula Choluimb Chille* and in the Kells memoranda. Dub Scuile ua Mancháin (d. 967) probably held a similar position as *anchoiri 7 cend riaghla Glinne Dá Locha* ('anchorite and head of the rule of Glendalough') in his monastery.[28] As regards Céleachair mac Cormaic Uí Chuinn na mBocht (d. 1134), a later member of Clonmacnoise's leading hereditary family, his fulsome obit describes him as *sruith sheanóir, ceann comhairle, 7 tobar eccna seanchusa, ceand einigh 7 coimheda riaghla Cluana mic Nóis* ('learned senior, head of counsel, fount of wisdom and history, paragon of honour and custodian of the rule of Clonmacnoise').[29] In this instance Ó Corráin interprets *cenn coiméta ríagla* as custodian of canon law,[30] but given that his family provided sustenance for the committed monastic community at Clonmacnoise, although were not necessarily members themselves, it is likely that Célechair held a position of authority over that community. Further

26 AFM 1005. **27** Ó Corráin, 'Máel Muire, the scribe', pp 10–11. **28** AFM 965. **29** AFM 1134. **30** Ó Corráin, 'Máel Muire', p. 18.

evidence for the Clonmacnoise community is gleaned from the obit of Uaréirghe Ua Neachtain described as *ceand chéledh nde Cluana mic Nois, 7 a sruith sheanóir* ('head of the *céli Dé* of Clonmacnoise and its learned senior').[31] That his son Máel Mórda (d. 1170) and grandson Úaréirge (d. 1200)[32] also held the office of head of the *céli Dé* of Clonmacnoise suggests either that this family took over the office from the Meic Cuinn na mBocht as their power declined, or that there was a division in the duties of the office. A difficulty also lies in the definition of *céli Dé* by the late twelfth century.[33]

Mention of offices dedicated to liturgy rarely occurs in the sources. According to AFM, Dub Innse (d. 1032) was the *líachtaire* of Clonmacnoise. A *líacht(re)óir*, borrowed from Latin *lector*, seems to mean from its few attestations a lector who arranges the order of service, especially at Christmas and Easter.[34] A further indication that Clonmacnoise had such an office is understood from the obit of Connmhach ua Tomrair (d. 1012), described as *sacart, 7 toiseach ceileabhartha Cluana mic Nóis* ('priest and chief cantor/liturgist of Clonmacnoise'), possibly a rare reference to chant in the Irish sources.[35] Finally, it is worth noting the obit in 1126 of Máel Ísu Ua Coinne of Armagh, *sui Goeidhil i senchus 7 i mbrithemhnacht 7 i n-urd Pátraic* ('eminent among the Irish in history and secular law and the rule of Patrick').[36] This was an office that held a national writ, at least in the eyes of the clergy of Armagh, dedicated to implementing the Rule of Patrick, regulations aimed at normalizing the education of clerics in Ireland. Máel Ísu combined knowledge of history, native law and canon law. Given that he was a contemporary of Cellach, the reforming archbishop of Armagh (d. 1129) and of St Malachy's tutor and founder of the church of SS Peter and Paul at Armagh, Ímar Ua hÁedacáin (d. 1134), Máel Ísu's obit may be somewhat understated in that his possible role in implementing the Rule of Patrick on a national level was a key position in the twelfth-century transformation of the Irish church.

A further group of individuals were in charge of specific chapels – the term *reiclés* is often used – usually dedicated to a monastery's founder saint but also to other saints. These offices are most prevalent in Armagh where reference is made to the custodians – the term *airchinnech* is regularly used – of *reiclés Choluim Chille*,[37] *reiclés Brigte*,[38] and *reiclés Petair ocus Póil*.[39] The *Eclais Beg* 'small church' in Clonmacnoise,[40] the *dísert* and *Dubreiclés* 'black chapel' in Derry,[41] and *Cró Chóemgin*, *Cró Chiaráin* and *reiclés in dá Sinchell* in Glendalough were also served by a community or individuals.[42] *Reiclés Petair ocus Póil* in Armagh, built under the direction of Ímar Ua hÁedacáin, was consecrated by Cellach,

31 AFM 1132. 32 AFM. 33 See p. 366. 34 DIL s.v. 35 AFM 1011. 36 AU 1126. 37 AFM 1011, 1152. 38 AU, AFM 1085. 39 AU 1126; AFM 1134; AFM, ATig, AU 1174; AFM, AU 1175; AFM 1203; AFM 1255. 40 Kehnel, *Clonmacnois*, pp 41–3, 289–90. AFM 893 (r. 898), 921 (r. 923), 947 (r. 949), 977 (r. 978), 986 (r. 987), 1037, 1060, 1097; AClon 1092. 41 AU, AFM 1122 (*dísert*), AU, ATig, AFM 1173, AU 1175. 42 AFM 1125, 1163.

successor of Patrick in 1126.[43] Ímar died in 1134 while on pilgrimage in Rome.[44] Later references to the head of Ímar's foundation bear the titles *abb mainistrech Petair ocus Póil* ('abbot of the monastery of Peter and Paul')[45] and *abb reiclésa Petair ocus Póil* ('abbot of the chapel/community of Peter and Paul').[46] While the *reiclés* became a house of Augustinian canons later on, there is no clear evidence that it had adopted the Augustinian rule in the early twelfth century.[47] Nevertheless, it is understood from Bernard's life of Malachy that Ímar was Malachy's spiritual mentor in ascetic discipline and humility and that he had submitted himself to following his teacher's committed religious life.[48] This would suggest that Ímar had created a community around the chapel of SS Peter and Paul in Armagh, possibly as an embryonic collegiate church. Ímar may have died in the Irish foundation of the Holy Trinity in Rome, although there is no evidence to that effect.[49] The officials of the *Eclais Bec* at Clonmacnoise and *Cró Chóemgin* at Glendalough were probably keepers of the founders' tombs. The *Eclais Bec* may have been a mortuary chapel that contained St Ciarán's grave (*imdaid* literally means 'bed'),[50] apparently a place where eminent religious and nobles were brought in their final hours or were laid out after death. Among them were Agda mac Duibcinn, king of the local kingdom of Tethbae (d. 980),[51] Tigernach ua Braein, *comarbae* of Ciarán and Commán (Clonmacnoise and Roscommon) and compiler of the Annals of Tigernach (d. 1088),[52] and as previously noted, Céilechair mac Cormaic, son of Conn na mBocht and his brother Máel Ciaráin, a priest, both of whom died in 1134.[53] Although it cannot have housed the founder's tomb, as Columba was buried in Iona, the *Dubreiclés* at Derry had a similar function. There is no reference to a custodian but three very eminent ecclesiastics died there, Muiredach Ua Cobthaig, styled bishop of Cenél Eógain and all of the northern half of Ireland (d. 1173),[54] Gilla Meic Liac (Gelasius), abbot of Derry and Malachy's chosen successor as archbishop of Armagh (d. 1174),[55] and Flaithbertach Ua Brolcháin, abbot of Derry and head of all Columban churches in Ireland.[56] The reference to Máel Tréna, the custodian of *Cró Chóemgin*, *Cró Chiaráin* and *reiclés in dá Sinchell* in Glendalough in 1125 is of particular interest. Máel Tréna was a priest, senior elder of *Cró Chóemgin*, and, most significantly, the pupil of Máel Muire Ua Dúnáin, the main episcopal protagonist for the reorganization of the Irish church in the early twelfth century. The existence of a building dedicated to

43 AFM, AU 1126. 44 ALC, AFM. 45 AFM, ATig, AU 1174. 46 AFM, AU 1175; AFM 1203; AFM 1255. 47 *MRHI*, 157; Flanagan, *Transformation*, p. 136. 48 Meyer, *St Malachy the Irishman*, pp 19–20 §II.4; Flanagan, *Transformation*, p. 118. 49 For the intriguing and slight surviving evidence regarding this foundation, see André Wilmart, 'La Trinité des Scots à Rome et les notes du *Vat. Lat. 378*', *Revue Bénédictine* 41 (1929), 218–30. 50 Kehnel, *Clonmacnois*, pp 41–3. 51 AFM 979. 52 AFM. 53 AFM. 54 AFM, ATig, AU. 55 AFM 1173; AI, ATig, AU. 56 AFM, ALC, AU; Herbert, *Iona, Kells, and Derry*, pp 115–23; Flanagan, *Transformation*, pp 166–8.

JACOBUS USSERIUS ARCHIEPISCOPUS ARMACHANUS
TOTIUS HIBERNIÆ PRIMAS
Antiquitatis primævæ peritissimus, orthodoxæ Religionis vindex
errorum malleus, in concionando frequens, facundus, præpotens
Vitæ inculpatæ exemplar spectabile.
Rob: Pinck Vicecancellarius Oxoniensis posuit:
Joh: Stafford excudit.
W.M. sculpsit

1 James Ussher, archbishop of Armagh (d. 1656), engraved by William Marshall sometime between 1611 and 1649 © National Library of Ireland.

2 Gougane Barra lake with the hermitage of St Finbar by George Petrie, *c.*1831

3 Pilgrims praying around a high cross at Clonmacnoise, engraved by Henry Griffiths *c.*1842 based on an image by William Henry Bartlett © National Library of Ireland.

4 Details of doorway at Clone, Co. Wexford, by George Victor du Noyer, 1862

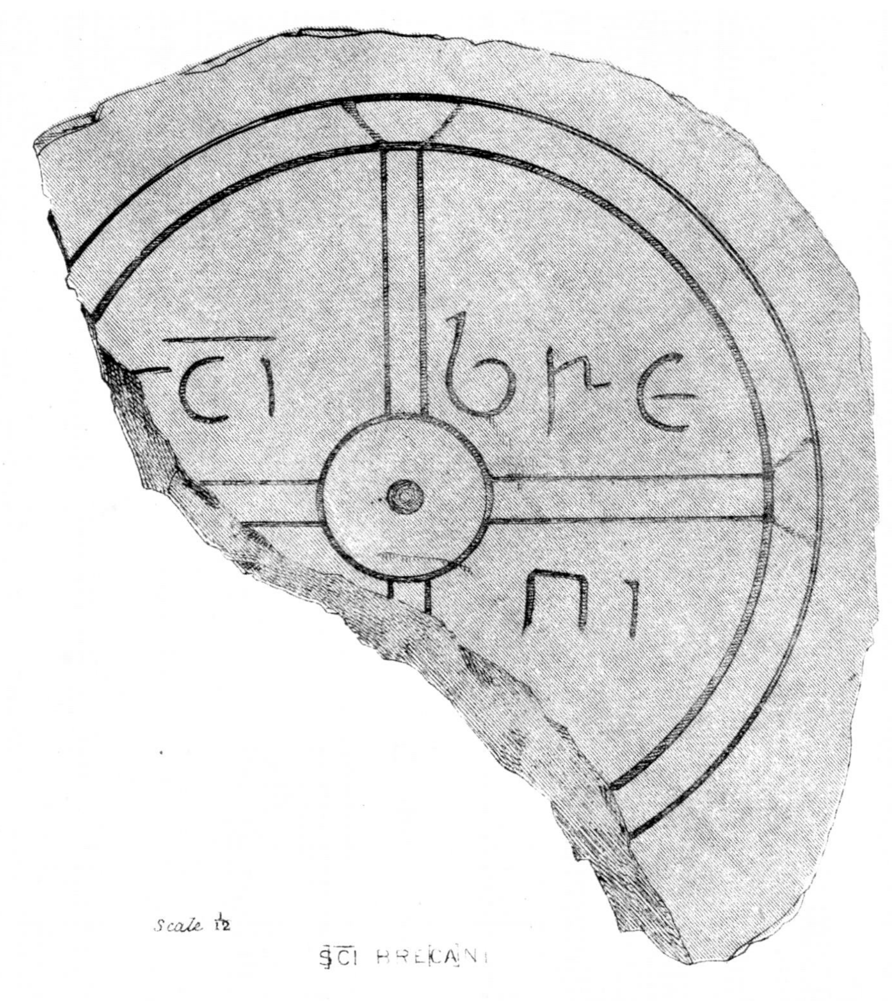

5 Fragmentary cross-slab inscribed S[AN]C[T]I BRE[CA]NI, Teampall Bhreacáin, Aran, Co. Galway. Drawing from George Petrie (ed. Margaret Stokes), *Christian inscriptions in the Irish language*, vol. 2 (Dublin, 1878), Pl. XII, fig. 24.

6 Stone figure from Inishderry (townland of Derrynameel), in Broadhaven Bay, Co. Mayo © Yvonne McDermott.

7 Figures from the Breac Máedóc made for the church of Drumlane, Co. Cavan
© Yvonne McDermott.

8 Figures from St Manchán's Shrine made for the church of Lemanaghan, Co. Offaly © Yvonne McDermott.

9 Gospel Book BL Harley 1802 compiled by Máel Brigte Ua Máel Uanaig of Armagh *c.*1138

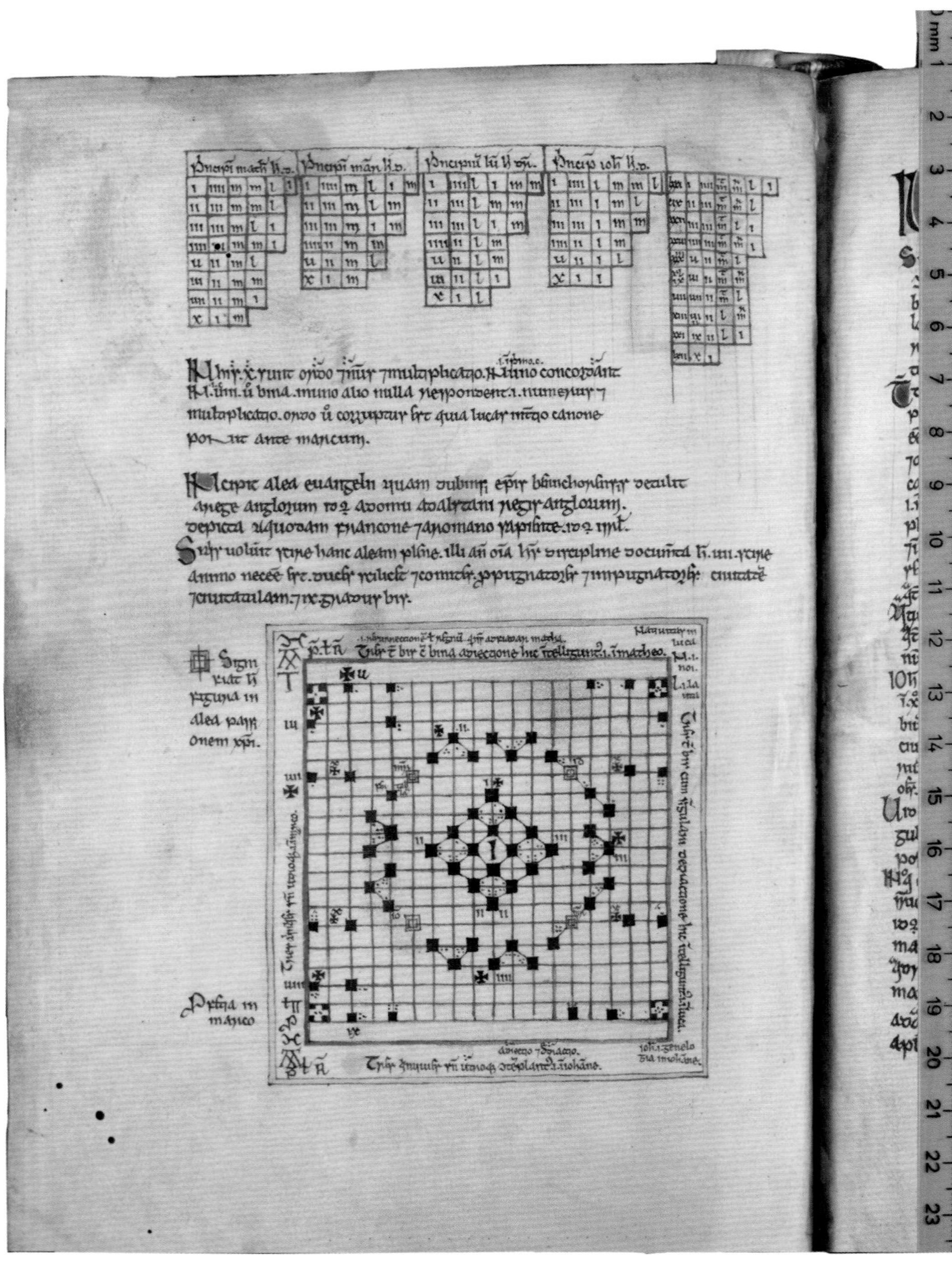

10 The board game known as the *Alea Evangelii* ('Game of the Gospels') in Corpus Christi College Oxford MS 122 f. 5v © Corpus Christi College, Oxford.

11 Muiredach's Cross, Monasterboice, Robert John Welch (d. 1936) photographed *c.*1910

12 Tuam cathedral restoration, progress of the works, August 1865, lithograph by R. Clay and Son, and Taylor *c.*1866 © National Library of Ireland.

13 Doorway of church at Inchagoill, Co. Galway, 1857 by George Victor du Noyer

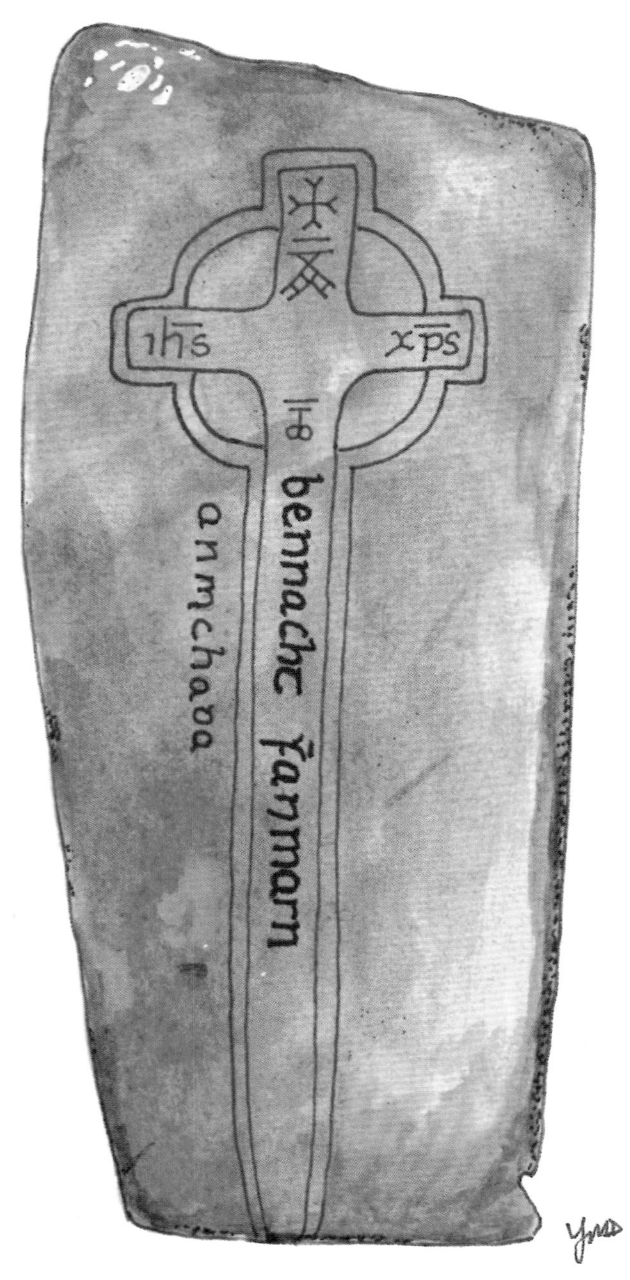

14 Grave slab commemorating Anmchad Ua Dúnchada (d. 1058) on Inis Uasail (Church Island, Lough Currane, Co. Kerry) © Yvonne McDermott.

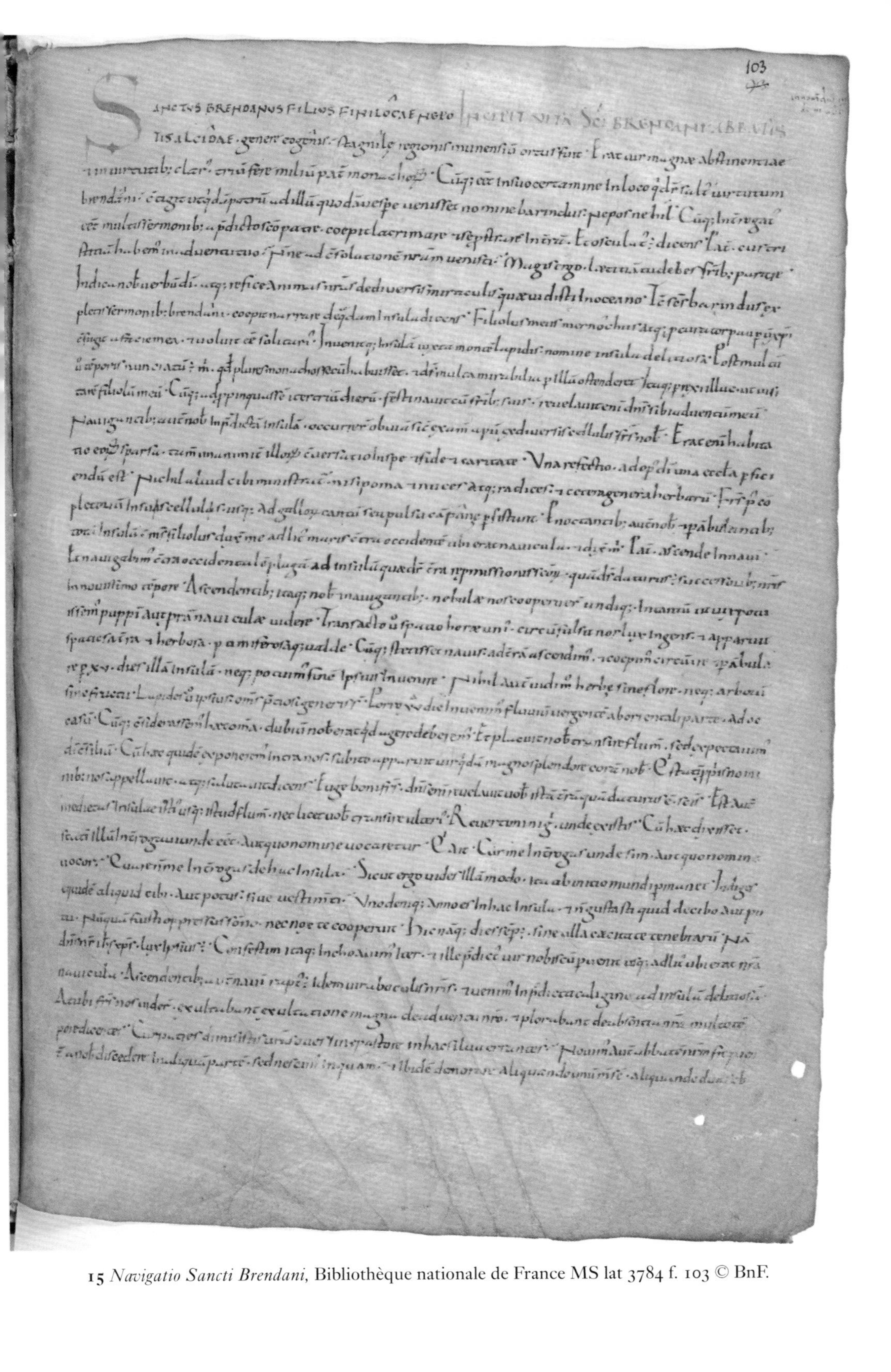

15 *Navigatio Sancti Brendani*, Bibliothèque nationale de France MS lat 3784 f. 103 © BnF.

16 The upper church Temple-na-Skellig, Glendalough, by Thomas Westropp (d. 1922), RIA 3A 46/112 © Royal Irish Academy.

Ciarán in Glendalough probably reflects the close relations between Glendalough and Clonmacnoise during the tenth and eleventh centuries.[57] As noted in Chapter 3, Tomás Ó Carragáin has argued in favour of identifying *Cró Chóemgin* 'Cóemgen's enclosure' with St Kevin's Church in Glendalough, a double-vaulted stone church with a round tower-like belfry possibly dating to the early twelfth century and similar to St Flannan's Church at Killaloe and St Columba's House at Kells.[58] He views its primary function as housing St Kevin's relics and as a shrine-chapel with its dark upper chambers accommodating recluses in a monastery that fostered an eremitical tradition from its foundation. The reference to Máel Tréna as the senior elder of *Cró Chóemgin* implies that rather than being a solitary recluse in charge of the shrine-chapel that he was in charge of a community dedicated to the upkeep of St Kevin's relics and tasked with celebration of a community's daily liturgy. Like the *Eclais Bec* at Clonmacnoise and the *Dubreiclés* at Derry, the bodies of eminent individuals, especially clerics and religious, may have rested in these chapels for overnight vigils prior to burial. Ó Carragáin has suggested that the large grave-slabs in and around St Kevin's Church 'could well have marked the graves of twelfth-century bishops'.[59] It is unclear if the *airchinnig* of these chapels were priests, but many held other senior offices. Fergal Ua Ferchubais (d. 1152), *airchinnech* of *reiclés Choluim Chille* in Armagh, was the monastery's *fer léiginn* for a while and also a member of an ecclesiastical family, another of whom, Máel Cainnig, was also *fer léiginn* of Derry (d. 1189).[60] Óenacán mac Ecertaig (d. 949) is the only one of the *airchinnig* of the *Eclais Bec* at Clonmacnoise who was ordained. AFM accord him the title of bishop and virgin. Otherwise, one, Áed Ua Congaile, appears to have been the guest master of Clonmacnoise (d. 1092/3),[61] and a member of a family who held that office to the late twelfth century.[62]

ABBESSES, NUNS AND PATRONS

What about the structure and vocabulary of female monasticism? The term *mainches* 'a nun' is not widely attested and when it occurs it seems to mean a woman who made a religious profession and was likely to be under the direction of an abbot or bishop.[63] There is also an element of servitude in the meaning of

57 Ailbhe S. Mac Shamhráin, 'The "unity" of Cóemgen and Ciarán: a covenant between Glendalough and Clonmacnois in the tenth to eleventh centuries' in Ken Hannigan and William Nolan (eds), *Wicklow, history and society. Interdisciplinary essays on the history of an Irish county* (Dublin, 1994), pp 139–50. 58 Tomás Ó Carragáin, 'Recluses, relics and corpses: interpreting St Kevin's House' in Doherty, Doran and Kelly, *Glendalough. City of God*, pp 64–79. 59 Ó Carragáin, 'Recluses, relics and corpses', p. 75. 60 AFM 1152, 1189. 61 AClon 1092; AFM 1093. 62 See Ceinnéittigh Ua Conghaile (AFM 1128), Céilechair Ua Conghaile (AFM 1166). 63 DIL sv. 1 *mainches*.

this term as the masculine noun *mainches* relates to the service due to the head of a monastic community and also monastic profession.[64] In the lives of Patrick, Mathona, sister of Benén, Patrick's disciple, was given the veil (*tenuit pallium*) by Patrick and the priest Rodán and she then served them (*robo manchess dóib = monacha fuit illis*). Similarly, the holy Comgella was described by bishop Cethiach's monks as being a nun to the bishop (*quia Cethiachi monachi dicunt monacham esse Comgella<m> Cethiacho*) with whom he stayed on the second day of Easter.[65] The evidence for female leadership is very incomplete and most of it relates to Kildare. That monastery's profile is unique in that its abbesses (*banabb Cille Dara*, *comarbae Brigti*, *ban-airchinnech*) are recorded relatively consistently from the sixth to the twelfth centuries – the last reference is to Sadb daughter of Glún Iarn Mac Murchada (d. 1171) – many of whom belonged to prominent Leinster dynasties.[66] If the obits of Brigit's successors reflect a genuine record, these women either ruled their monastery for lengthy periods, some successors were not recorded, or there were periods when Kildare had no abbess. But this may reflect a deficit in Kildare's surviving records as the lists of all monastic officials have similar lacunae, the office of bishop being the most numerous.[67] Priests and *fir léiginn* are also recorded, one of whom, Ferdomnach Dall ('the blind'), is described as a master of harping (*suí cruitirechta*).[68] As Brigit's early lives imply that her foundation was not only female but was primarily episcopal, this model of episcopal primacy combined with female abbatial authority probably lasted until the twelfth century. The symbolic, and potentially political status of Kildare's abbess might be deduced from an episode recounted in the Fragmentary Annals of Ireland, admittedly in its final form a seventeenth-century source.[69] In 908, the abbess Muirenn ingen Suairt, 'along with a large group of clergy and many relics' (*7 slúagh mór cleireach uimpe 7 mionda iomdha*), escorted the defeated joint king of Munster and abbot of Inis Cathaig, Flaithbertach mac Inmainéin, to the boundary of Leinster and Munster where he was handed over to representatives of his own province. This procession resembles the processions of the abbots of Armagh as they travelled the country to collect their tribute or to make peace between provincial kings.

64 *DIL* sv. 2 *mainches*. **65** Whitley Stokes, *The tripartite life of Patrick*. Part I (London, 1887), pp 98–9, 104–5; Bieler, *Patrician texts* (Tírechán), §24 (2), §27(4). **66** For the period under consideration, the deaths of abbesses of Kildare are recorded in 916 (AU, AFM 916), 918 (AU, AFM 916), 962 (AFM), 964 (AI), 979 (AU, AFM 977), 1016 (AU, AFM 1015), 1047 (AU, AI, AFM), 1072 (AU, AI), 1112 (AU, AI, ATig, AFM), 1171 (AU). **67** Abbots: 905 (AFM 903), 922 (AFM 920), 955 (AFM 953), 965 (AFM). Bishops: 931 (AFM 929), 950 (AU), 981 (ATig, AFM 980), 1030 (AFM), 1041 (AFM), 1085 (AFM), 1097 (AU, ATig, AI), 1100 (ATig, AFM), 1101 (AU, ATig, AFM), 1108 (AFM), 1160 (AU, ATig, AFM), 1175 (ATig). Priests: 929 (AFM 927), 931 (AFM 929), 1046 (AFM), 1069 (AU, AI, AFM), 1103 (AFM). *Fir léiginn*: 964 (AFM 962), 967 (AFM 965), 991 (AFM), 1038 (AFM), 1050 (AFM), 1063 (AFM), 1110 (AU, AFM), 1126 (AFM). It is notable that in many instances AFM is the only source of Kildare obits. **68** AU 1110. **69** Radner, *FAIre*, pp 158–9.

No parallel excursions are recorded for an abbot of Kildare. The annalistic records for the few other female foundations, Cloonburren (Cluain Boirenn), Co. Roscommon, Clonbroney (Cluain Brónaig), Co. Longford, Killevy (Cill Sléibe), Co. Armagh, and Killeedy (Cill Íte), Co. Limerick, are scant for this period. Four abbesses of Clonbroney are recorded between 933 and 1163.[70] Anlaith (d. 933) was abbess of Clonbroney and Cloonburren, while Cocrích (d. 1109) and Caillech Domnaill (d. 1163) belonged to the same family, the Uí Nóennenaig. The existence of two male *airchinnig* of Cloonburren, Macrodaide mac Dúnchada (d. 921) and Fiachra Ua Riacáin (d. 1066)[71] would suggest that they acted as agents in collecting tributes or in dealing with tenants for the monastery. An inscribed slab in Cloonburren commemorates Máel Moichéirge, the *oeconomus* of Clonmacnoise who died in 929.[72] Given that Cloonburren is not very far from Clonmacnoise, on the opposite side of the river Shannon and linked by the Slige Mór ancient routeway and a bridge over the river near Clonmacnoise, the community at Cloonburren must have been served by the greater monastery's spiritual and temporal officials. In effect, it belonged to the hinterland of Clonmacnoise.[73] The life of St Monenna of Killevy offers possible corroboration as to why the women of Cloonburren might have needed *airchinnig*, even if Monenna is portrayed as well able to carry out such tasks herself. The author comments that[74]

> Daily the number of virgins of Christ grew, and not only from nearby but also from distant districts alms in plenty were sent daily in the form of cattle and sheep or an abundance of foodstuffs and clothes according to the custom of those lands. All of which the holy virgin spent on the needs of the poor and pilgrims, the widows and orphans, scarcely leaving enough to comfort the sick, both the very young and the very old.

The emphasis on caring for the poor rhymes well with similar works of charity that appear so frequently in the lives of Brigit. Of course, care for the poor and the sick was not the sole preserve of female saints and their foundations. The death of Dublitir of Killevy, priest of Armagh, at the hands of the Vikings in 923 confirms a relationship similar to the Clonmacnoise–Cloonburren association

70 AFM 931, 933,1108 (AU 1109), 1163. 71 AFM 919, 1066. 72 AFM [927]. 73 Linda Doran, 'Medieval communication routes through Longford and Roscommon and their associated settlements', *Proceedings of the Royal Irish Academy* 104C (2004), 57–80, at p. 59 (fig. 1). 74 Ulster Society for Medieval Latin Studies, 'The life of Saint Monenna by Conchubranus: Part III', *Seanchas Ard Mhacha* 10:2 (1982), 426–54, at pp 430–1. Original: *Cotidie crescebat numerus uirginum Christi et non solum de propinquis sed et de longinquis regionibus elemosine multe cotidie mittebantur siue in iumentis et pecoribus siue in ciborum et uestimentorum habundantia iuxta illarum terrarum consuetudinem. Que omnia expendebat sancta uirgo in pauperum et peregrinorum uiduarum et pupillorum necessitates uix relinquens que infirmis prime et*

whereby female foundations were served by larger churches with which they had connections, and links between Armagh and Killevy would not have been unusual, given their relative geographical proximity. Nothing could be more striking as evidence for this relationship than the record of the death in 1077 of Ailbe, daughter of Amalgaid, abbot of Armagh, wife of the local king of Ind Airthir, and *comarbae Moninne*.[75] The life of St Monenna also illustrates how spiritual guidance was imparted to women when describing how the saint was instructed in the psalms. St Patrick entrusted her to a pious priest 'to teach her first of all the psalms and always to nurture her in divine studies'.[76] In the *Vita Prima* of St Brigit, Patrick also plays the role of instructing the saint on a number of occasions, and in one episode he ordains her charioteer, Natfroích, as a priest, declaring to Brigit that as she could never travel without a priest, her charioteer always had to be a priest.[77]

The virtual absence of women holding offices other than that of abbess in the records is usually interpreted as reflecting the lesser role of women in the early medieval church. It could be argued, however, that this reflects the sources that survive, as much as the absence of women who were scribes, were literate or were involved in the liturgy. A reference to the grand-daughter of Tadg Ua Cellaig Maine as a *caillech léiginn* ('a learned woman/nun') in a Middle Irish anecdote might just be a fleeting witness to women's literacy that never made it into the sources.[78] Aristocratic women through their marriages could often play a central part in dynastic and ecclesiastical alliances and networks. Lann, daughter of the king of Osraige (d. 890) and wife of two kings of Tara, is depicted as supervising the building of a church dedicated to St Brigit at Kildare for which she had many carpenters chopping down and shaping trees.[79]

The *Banshenchas* ('The lore of women'), compiled during the twelfth-century, depicts how senior ecclesiastical officials were members of the secular elite through their mothers. Cumascach mac Ailella, *secnap* of Armagh (d. 909),[80] was the son of Gormlaith *rebach* ('skilled, lively'), daughter of Muiredach mac Echach, king of Ulaid (d. 838). More significantly, she was also mother of Domnall mac Áeda Finnléith (d. 915), king of Ailech (northwest of Ireland), whose father, Áed Finnliath (d. 879) had held the kingship of Ireland.[81] Sadb daughter of Máel Mórda ua Domnaill , king of Uí Chennselaig in Leinster

extreme etatis solatio forent. **75** AU, AFM 1077. There may be confusion in this record as AU records the death in 1078 of Dub Esa daughter of Amalgaid and also wife of the king of Ind Airthir. Perhaps Ailbe was not married to the king. **76** 'The life of Saint Monenna by Conchubranus: Part 1', *Seanchas Ard Mhacha* 9:2 (1979), 250–73, at pp 256–7. Original: *ut eam imprimis salmos doceret et in diuinis studiis semper nutriret.* **77** Connolly, '*Vita Prima*', p. 24 §40.6. **78** Brian Ó Cuív, *Catalogue of Irish language manuscripts in the Bodleian Library at Oxford and Oxford college libraries. Part I: descriptions* (Dublin, 2001), p. 251: MS Rawl. B.512, f. 141va5–17. **79** FAIre 866. **80** AU, AFM [904]. **81** Margaret Dobbs (ed.), 'The Banshenchus [part 2]', *Revue celtique* 48 (1931), 163–234, at pp 186–7.

(d. 1024), was mother of Gilla Comgaill Ua Tuathail (d. 1127), *comarbae Cóemgin* of Glendalough, and also of the three sons of Tadc mac Briain, king of Munster.[82] The daughters of ecclesiastical officials were also regarded as sufficiently prestigious to become royal consorts, as in the case of Caintigern daughter of Guaire Ua Lachtnáin (d. 1054), *fer léiginn* of Clonmacnoise and a member of the local dynasty of Tethbae, who was the mother of Murchad mac Flainn Ua Máel Sechlainn (d. 1076) and his brother Domnall (d. 1094).[83] The Uí Máel Sechlainn were kings of the midlands and hence the kings of Tethbae were subject to them. They were also generous patrons of Clonmacnoise. As will be discussed in Chapter 9, the Uí Máel Sechlainn became patrons of the new orders during the twelfth century. Caintigern, for example, was the great-grandmother of Derbforgaill Ua Máel Sechlainn (d. 1193), patron of Mellifont, the first Cistercian foundation in Ireland.

MONASTIC OFFICES ON THE THRESHOLD OF CHANGE

It is not surprising to find the full complement of officers, lay and religious, consistently in the largest monasteries. It is useful to trace offices in a range of different monasteries with a view to gaining a clearer sense of changes occurring in monastic life during the eleventh and twelfth centuries. Emly, the primary church in Munster and a centre of record keeping, gradually lost its primacy to other churches, especially Killaloe, Cashel, Cork and Lismore, from the end of the eleventh century onwards. This was due mainly to changes in the patronage of monasteries by the Uí Briain kings – descendants of Brian Bóruma – and the Meic Cárthaig, their rivals for the kingship of Munster. The offices of *airchinnech* or *comarbae* and bishop existed in Emly during the period under consideration, the former office being occasionally subject to external political interference by the Uí Briain. The most explicit instance of this seizure of power was the imposition of Marcán (d. 1010), Brian Bóruma's brother, as abbot of Emly in 990. He also took control of Killaloe, Inis Cealtra and Terryglass.[84] Occasionally, one individual held both offices of *airchinnech* or *comarbae* and bishop of Emly: Tipraite mac Maíl Finn (d. 913: *princeps*, *epscop*, *abb*),[85] possibly Fáelán mac Cóellaide (d. 980: *espoc*, *abbad*)[86] and Diarmait Ua Flainnchua (d. 1114), who is hailed as the successor (*comarbae*) of Ailbe of Emly, 'a noble bishop and lector, a bestower of goods and food, of honour and alms' (*huasalespoc 7 fer leighinn ernedach seoit 7 biidh einigh 7 deirce*).[87] Diarmait was related to Máel Ísu Ua Flainnchua, *airchinnech* of Emly (d. 1058)[88] and Ragnall Ua Flainnchua (d. 1197)

82 Ibid., 195. 83 Ibid., 190. 84 Donncha Ó Corráin, 'Dál Cais – church and dynasty', *Ériu* 24 (1973), 52–63, at p. 53 n. 4. 85 AU, AI, AFM (908). 86 AI, ATig, AFM (979). 87 AU. 88 AU, AI, AFM.

who is described as bishop and abbot (*abbas*) of Emly.[89] The only other office recorded for Emly was that of *fer léiginn* (1024, 1052, 1081, 1089, 1114, 1147),[90] not surprising as whoever held that office is likely to have maintained its records. Emly's profile is replicated elsewhere, for example, in Cork, where those whose deaths were recorded included the *airchinnig* or *comarbai* and bishops with a few references to *fir léiginn* and anchorites. The two anchorites recorded were probably exceptional individuals, most especially Cellach Ua Selbaig, *comarbae* of Barre, Cork's founder saint (d. 1036), a member of an ecclesiastical family, described as 'one who had made a pilgrimage to Rome, and chief anchorite of Ireland' (*ailithir Róma 7 primanchara Herend*).[91] Priests are not mentioned in Emly or Cork, and the role is likely to have been maintained by the bishop. Anchorites appear at intervals in some churches. Three anchorites are recorded in Clonfert between 954 and 1044, the most distinguished of them being Cináed in Durthaige 'of the oakwood church/oratory' (d. 973) who was the 'anchorite of Ireland' (*anchara Herend*).[92] Although a very small number, the association in literature between Clonfert's founder, Brendan, and traditional monastic ideals could have fostered a coenobitic and eremitical community there and it is noticeable that bishops are regularly recorded as residing at Clonfert from the tenth century onwards. In 1068, the elders of Clonfert (*a sruithe*) left and went to Iarmumu (west Munster), possibly to St Brendan's other reputed foundation, Ardfert, Co. Kerry. Given that the annalistic record for Ardfert is relatively late,[93] the foundation may have flourished from the middle decades of the eleventh century, a period that seems to coincide with the building of its original *damliac* ('stone church'). Evidence for this *damliac* was discovered during excavations of the cathedral at Ardfert although it is not clear which phase the archaeology reflected given that the *damliac* was destroyed in 1046 and 1089.[94]

Clonard was consistently a centre of learning and of a monastic community which included an eremitical tradition. The abbot of Clonard who died in 763 was named Bec Laitne 'Bec of the Latin', presumably a learned monastic given name.[95] Suairlech of *Int Eidnén* (d. 870), the monastery's hermitage, was abbot, bishop and anchorite and is praised for his religious learning and piety.[96] The first three tenth-century abbots (*princeps*, *airchinnech*) were scribes and they included Colmán, abbot of Clonmacnoise and Clonard (d. 926) and Máel Mochta, abbot of Clonard (d. 942), described as 'the head of the piety and wisdom of Ireland' (*ceann crábhaidh, egna Ereann esidhe*).[97] A particular indication of the strength of a monastery's spiritual life was its capacity to attract eminent religious individuals to end their lives there. The phrase *ina ailithre* 'as a pilgrim' or 'on a pilgrimage' does not signify undertaking a pilgrimage in the

89 AI. **90** AI 1024, 1052, 1081, 1089; AI, AU, AFM 1114; AFM 1147. **91** AI. **92** AI, AFM (971). **93** AI 1032. **94** AI 1046, AFM 1089. See also https://excavations.ie/report/1991/Kerry/0001121/ accessed 9 November 2020. **95** AU. **96** AU, AI, AFM (868), CS. **97** AFM 940.

popular sense but rather to end life's pilgrimage in a suitably holy place where pilgrims' spiritual needs were looked after, often as they approached death. Most of the population in early Irish society was bound by legal restrictions on movement and travel which militated against the kind of popular pilgrimages evident from the later medieval period. The aristocracy was also afforded such a facility although it is likely that this involved a mutual agreement of patronage in return for supplication for their souls. Clonard was one such place. Among the notables to end their days in Clonard were Cormac Mainistrech, bishop and elder of Monasterboice (d. 1092)[98] and Máel Muire Ua Dúnáin (d. 1117), the eminent reforming bishop and ally of the king of Ireland, Muirchertach Ua Briain.[99]

One of the most popular end of life destinations for prominent religious individuals and nobles during the eleventh and early twelfth centuries was Lismore, Co. Waterford. The monastery's offices reflect this vibrant community. Apart from the standard *abb/airchinnech/comarbae/princeps*, priest and bishop, the annals record the offices of *secnap*, *cenn crábuid* ('head of religious life'), *ancharae* ('anchorite'), *cenn cléirig* ('head of the clergy'), *fer léiginn* and *anmcharae* ('spiritual director, confessor'). Lismore's spiritual vitality is reflected in the obits of individuals such as Corcrán Clérech (d. 1040) 'head of religious life of Ireland' (*cenn crabuid na Herend*)[100] and Cétfaid (d. 1056), bishop, anchorite and 'head of the clerics of Munster' (*cenn cleirech Muman*).[101] Its reputation attracted senior religious to Lismore, especially from Armagh, among them, Máel Ísu Ua Brolcháin (d. 1086), Óengus Ua Gormáin (d. 1123), abbot of Bangor, and most eminent of all Cellach, successor of Patrick and archbishop of Armagh who died in Ardpatrick, Co. Limerick, while on visitation to Munster in 1129. At his own request his body was brought to Lismore where an elaborate funeral was conducted. He was 'waked with psalms and hymns and canticles' (*ro frithairedh co salmaibh 7 ymnaibh 7 canntaicibh*).[102] and was buried 'in the burial-ground of the bishops' (*i n-ailaidh na n-espoc*).[103] Cellach's funeral took place during a period when Lismore was the focus of ecclesiastical renewal in Ireland when Malachy of Armagh resided there as well as the Winchester-trained Benedictine Máel Ísu Ua hAinmire, first bishop of Waterford. At the same time, the hereditary family, the Uí Rebacháin, held the title of *comarbae*, a title that they had intermittently assumed since 1041. They probably descended from Rebachán mac Mothlai (d. 934), compromise king of Dál Cais and head (*abb*) of Tuamgraney, Co. Clare. It is likely that his descendants were compensated for their loss of the kingship to the Uí Thairdelbaig – to whom Brian Bóruma belonged – and of the church at Tuamgraney (Co. Clare) by gaining a foothold in other churches in Munster, namely Lismore and Mungret, Co. Limerick.[104]

98 AI, AClon [1090], AFM. 99 ATig, CS. 100 AI. 101 AU. Cétfaid's obit is also recorded without this title in AI. 102 AU. 103 AU. 104 Ó Corráin, 'Dál Cais – church and dynasty', 55. AI 934, 1041, 1090, 1106, 1129 (2); AU 1090, 1129; AFM 994, 1142.

Ironically, Gilla Mo-Chutu Ua Rebacháin and Máel Brénainn Ua Rebacháin also died in Lismore in 1129, the same year as Cellach, bishop of Armagh died, but there is no evidence that their funeral rites were as elaborate as those of Cellach of Armagh.

Derry, although it claimed to be Colum Cille's first foundation, was overshadowed first by Iona and later Kells, and only really began to appear frequently in the annals from the death of Cináed mac Domnaill as *princeps* (d. 921).[105] Derry's hierarchy was dominated by the office of *airchinnech* or *comarbae*. So much so that Bé Bhinn daughter of Mac Con Chaille (d. 1134) is described in AFM as *ban-airchindeach Doire* 'female *airchinnech* of Derry'. This may simply be a late source's representation of a member of a leading ecclesiastical family, as her brother Congalach mac meic Con Chaille died as *airchinnech* of Derry in 1112.[106] The title *ban-airchinnech* occurs, as previously noted, in the life of Colmán mac Luacháin, where it is related that every *airchinnech*'s wife (*ban-airchinnech*) had to prepare a special meal for the clergy of Lann on Easter Monday.[107] It may be that Bé Bhinn's role was domestic – perhaps dealing with supplies and domestic servants – for her brother and his successor, much as was expected of a queen in a royal household. Derry's profile changed under the leadership of the ascetic Gilla Meic Liac (Gelasius) who held its abbacy between 1121 and 1137, at which point Malachy left Armagh and installed Gilla Meic Liac to succeed him as archbishop. Gilla Meic Liac is credited with particular sanctity by Giraldus Cambrensis – not a person who praised anyone readily – who relates how the archbishop despite his physical infirmity and advanced years came to Dublin in 1171/2 to meet Henry II: 'The common people thought of him as a saint. Wherever he went he took with him a white cow, and lived only on its milk'.[108] In his seventeenth-century life of Gilla Meic Liac, mainly based on the annals and Bernard's life of Malachy, John Colgan speculated about Gilla Meic Liac's monastic affiliation, noting that it remained controversial as to whether he was an Augustinian canon regular or a Benedictine.[109] Whatever his affiliation, he belonged to that circle around Malachy who were active in transforming the Irish church, and, as noted by Flanagan, like others among them, he adopted the Latin name Gelasius probably intending 'to highlight a direct link with the papacy in his role as primate of the Irish church and to recall Pope Gelasius' [(492–6)] particular attribute of emphasizing the independence of the church from secular interference'.[110] There is plenty of evidence that Gilla Meic Liac followed this principle during his long career as he challenged Irish kings when they interfered in church matters.

105 AU. **106** AU, AFM. **107** Meyer, *Betha Colmáin meic Lúacháin*, pp 26–9 §28. **108** A.B. Scott and F.X. Martin (ed. and trans.), *Expugnatio Hibernica. The conquest of Ireland by Giraldus Cambrensis* (Dublin, 1978), pp 100–1 §35: lines 59–61. Original: *vulgi opinione vir sacer, vaccam candidam, cuius solum lacte vescebatur, secum quocunque venerat circumducens.* **109** Colgan, *Acta SS*, p. 772. **110** Flanagan, *Transformation*, pp 110–11.

During the twelfth century Derry assumed the headship of the *familia* of Colum Cille in Ireland from Kells, and did not flinch from meddling in the affairs of Iona.[111] As a result, the *comarbae* of Derry became particularly powerful, and especially in the person of Flaithbertach Ua Brolcháin (1150–75), a member of the prominent northern ecclesiastical family, and possibly even son of Máel Coluim Ua Brolcháin, styled a bishop of Armagh who died in the *dísert* of Derry in 1122.[112] Flaithbertach was supported by Gilla Meic Liac and also by the powerful northern king Muirchertach Mac Lochlainn. Of particular relevance was his status as a monastic abbot of the most important monastic *familia* in Ireland. This question was addressed at the synod of Brí Mhic Thaidc (possibly Bray Mount, b. Lower Moyfenrath, Co. Meath)[113] in 1158 convened by Gilla Meic Liac and the papal legate Gilla Críst Ua Conairche and attended by twenty-five bishops. They agreed to appoint 'a chair for the successor of Colum Cille, that is, for Flaithbertach Ua Brolcháin, the same as [for] every bishop and the arch-abbacy in general of the churches of Colum Cille throughout all Ireland'.[114] It may be no coincidence that Robert, abbot of St Albans was also authorized by papal grant in 1156 to use pontifical regalia (crozier, mitre, pectoral cross) which, according to Richard Pfaff might be interpreted as granting St Alban's 'liturgical equality with any cathedral', even Canterbury.[115] Flanagan has come to a similar conclusion about Flaithbertach's elevation, that on ceremonial occasions, he would have been regarded as of equal or nearly equal status to other bishops. She also explains that from a practical perspective Flaithbertach may have been exempted from episcopal jurisdiction or that he was permitted by the bishops to collect revenues from Columban churches in their dioceses.[116] After a very active career, courting bishops and kings to maintain the honour of the *familia* of Colum Cille, Flaithbertach died in the *Dubreiclés* of Colum Cille in Derry.[117] What the significance of the term *dubreiclés* 'black chapel' was for Flaithbertach, and indeed Derry's overall spiritual life, is worth contemplating. As noted earlier, two other prominent Derry religious died in 1173 in the *Dubreiclés*, Muiredach Ua Cobthaig, 'bishop of Cenél nEógain and all of the north of Ireland' (*espoc Ceneoil Eogain 7 Tuaisceirt Erenn uile*),[118] who had attended the Synod of Kells in 1152, and his relative – perhaps even his son – Ainmire Ua Cobthaig, described in AU as *ab reiclesa Daire* ('the abbot of the *reiclés* of Derry') in 1214.[119] The *Dubreiclés* may

111 Herbert, *Iona, Kells, and Derry*, pp 107–23. 112 Ibid., p. 115. 113 Pádraig Ó Riain, Diarmuid Ó Murchadha and Kevin Murray (eds), *Historical dictionary of Gaelic placenames. Foclóir stairiúil áitainmneacha na Gaeilge* fasc. 2 (Names in B–) (London, 2005), p. 198. 114 AU original: *Is don chur-sin ro ordaighset cleirigh Erenn, im chomarba Patraic 7 im in Leghait, cathair do comarba Coluim Cille, .i., do Fhlaithbertach h-Ua Brolchan, amal gach n-epscop 7 ard-abdaine cell Coluim Cille fo Erinn uile co coitcenn.* 115 Pfaff, *Liturgy in medieval England*, pp 195–6. 116 Flanagan, *Transformation*, pp 166–7. 117 AU, AFM. 118 AU's entry. His death there is also recorded in AFM. 119 AU. Amlaím Ua Cobthaig, Muiredach's son, is

have been part of a complex, similar to that of Ó Corráin's *lavra* in Clonmacnoise,[120] in which a community resided. In 1192, for example, the door for the *Dubreiclés*'s refectory was erected under the patronage of Ua Catháin of Fir Craíbe and his wife.[121] Taking all these annalistic entries together, it could be surmised that this complex consisted at least of a church, a hospice and a refectory. The abbey of SS Peter and Paul at Armagh may have housed a similar community, and although not necessarily following the rule of the canons' regular, the *vita apostolica* may have been a model which these communities were beginning to emulate.[122] Flanagan sees the vernacular *Betha Choluim Chille* – probably composed during the abbacy of Flaithbertach Ua Brolcháin, as previously discussed – as affording some evidence 'for the monastic ethos within the Columban milieu'. She cites the text's reformist tendencies, consisting of a clear commitment to religious values, with an emphasis on the saint's chastity, wisdom and pilgrimage, as an indication of this prevailing ethos.[123] Yet, as Herbert concluded in her study of twelfth-century Derry, with the passing of Gilla Meic Liac and Flaithbertach Ua Brolcháin, 'the last links which connected the traditional Irish monastic organization with the reformed diocesan church were severed'.[124] What survived in Derry until the mid-thirteenth century was an institution in the grip of hereditary families – the Uí Daigri, Uí Fercomais, Uí Brénáin, Uí Muiredaig, Uí Brolcháin – who persisted in holding the traditional offices of *airchinnech* or *comarbae* and *fer léiginn*. They had one final fierce dispute over these offices in 1220 which was settled by the successor of Patrick, unnamed in annals, but possibly Donat Ua Fidubhra (d. 1237). From the mid-thirteenth century, bishops were in charge of Derry, a number of them belonging to international orders,[125] and a monastic community, which became Augustinian, limped on until the 1570s.[126]

A final example is that of Tuam, which was declared an archbishopric at the Synod of Kells in 1152,[127] and which had developed rather differently. (Fig. 12) Etchingham in his study of Tuam's progress towards a prominent status details how this church was promoted by ambitious kings, Muirchertach Ua Briain (d. 1119) and his protegée Toirdelbach Ua Conchobair (d. 1156). He notes that prior to the eleventh century, Tuam is only sporadically mentioned in the annals.[128] The majority of officers mentioned between the eleventh and thirteenth centuries were bishops, and in most instances, they were archbishops

recorded as dying in 1185 in Dún Cruithni (Duncrun, Co. Derry). He was buried in Derry at his father's feet beside the *Tempall Bec* 'small church'. **120** See pp 138–9. **121** AU. See Chapter 9, pp 366–9 for the later history of the *Dubreiclés* as the *Cella Nigra*. **122** It is worth noting that Echmarcach Ua Catháin died in the abbey of SS Peter and Paul in Armagh in 1195. **123** Flanagan, *Transformation*, p. 167. **124** Herbert, *Iona, Kells, and Derry*, p. 123. **125** *NHI*, vol. ix, pp 278–80: these included Dominicans, Cistercians, Franciscans and one Benedictine. **126** *MRHI*, pp 168–9. **127** Colmán Etchingham, 'Episcopal hierarchy in Connacht and Tairdelbach Ua Conchobair', *Journal of the Galway Archaeological and Historical Society* 52 (2000), 13–29. **128** Etchingham, 'Episcopal hierarchy in Connacht', 19.

of Tuam or the province of Connacht, under the control of hereditary families, especially the powerful Uí Dubthaig.[129] The titles *comarbae Iarlaithe* – the reputed founder of the church at Tuam –,[130] *airchinnech Tuama Dá Ghualann*,[131] and *fer léiginn* occur infrequently.[132] There are hints of a monastic culture in Tuam, both before or after its elevation to an archbishopric. Muirgius Ua Nioc, an *airchinnech*, died in Inis an Ghaill (Inchagoill, Co. Galway) an island on Lough Corrib in 1128.[133] (Fig. 13) This is the only reference to this island in the annals although it contains a very rich archaeological landscape including two churches, Teampall na Naomh and a subsidiary church dedicated to St Patrick, and a collection of pre-Norman cross slabs. The nave of St Patrick's is pre-Romanesque while its chancel and Teampall na Naomh are Romanesque.[134] Inchagoill is closer to Cong than it is to Tuam, and it may have functioned as a hermitage for individuals from both places. The connection between Cong, Roscommon and Tuam is evident from the deaths in Cong of Muiredach Ua Dubthaig, styled 'archbishop of Connacht and Ireland'(*aird-espoc Connacht 7 Érenn in Cristó quieuit*)[135] in 1150, Flannacán Ua Dubthaig 'bishop of the Tuatha (Síl-Muiredaigh) [Elphin], the master of wisdom and history in all the west of Ireland' (*suí ecnai 7 senchais Iarthair Érenn uile*)[136] in 1168, and Cadla (Catholicus) Ua Dubthaig, archbishop of Connacht in 1201.[137] AFM notes that not only did Flannacán die in Cong but that he expired in Muiredach's bed having retired there to end his days. It is possible that Muiredach was regarded as particularly holy, thus leading to his kinsman choosing to die in his bed. Tuam itself was subject to development as an episcopal town. In 1127, Toirdelbach Ua Conchobair granted land to the church and planned the settlement with its *comarbae*, presumably Muirguis Ua Nioc who died in the following year.[138] Much later, in 1172, Toirdelbach's son Ruaidrí Ua Conchobair, along with Cadla Ua Dubthaig, held a synod in Tuam during which three churches (*trí tempuill*) were consecrated.[139] What the functions of these churches were or who was in charge of them is not specified but by the thirteenth century Tuam's monastic profile had followed the model of many other Irish episcopal centres as it embraced new continental orders, Holy Trinity Abbey, a Premonstratensian house,[140] and the Augustinian foundation of St John the Evangelist, which appears in the 1302–6 calendar of ecclesiastical taxation as existing in the suburbs.[141] Not that the local hereditary families stood aside completely. For example, the abbot of Holy

129 Ibid., 28. **130** AI, AFM 1032; AFM 1085; ATig 1127; AU, AFM 1128; ATig 1134. **131** AU 949; AFM (947). **132** AFM 1097. **133** AU, AFM. **134** Ó Carragáin, *Churches in early medieval Ireland*, p. 309. **135** ATig. It is interesting that AClon 1135 records that Clonmacnoise was burnt on Easter Sunday 'with the churchyard of Muireadhach Ó Dubhthaigh and the place called Lios an Aba', the latter presumably the abbot's residence. **136** AU. **137** ALC, AI. **138** ATig. **139** ATig, AFM. **140** Miriam Clyne, 'The founders and patrons of the Premonstratensian houses in Ireland' in Burton and Stöber, *The regular canons*, pp 145–72, at pp 155–7. **141** *CDI 1302–7*, p. 226; *MRHI*, p. 197.

Trinity, Ua Giollaráin, who died in 1256,[142] must have belonged to an ecclesiastical family as in 1229 Diarmait mac Fiaich, abbot of the chapel of Gilla Molaise Ua Gillaráin in Tuam (‘*abb reiglesa Gilla Molaisi h-Uí Gillurán i Tuaim*’), died in Ardcarne, Co. Roscommon.[143] This is yet another example of the continuing hold by families on some form of power in the church, be it within the new orders, managing church lands or guarding saints’ relics, all a legacy of the culture of early monasticism.

THE *CRÁIBDIG* OF IRELAND: A LEARNED MONASTIC ELITE?

In 1101, Muirchertach Ua Briain, king of Munster and contender for the kingship of Ireland, held an assembly of ecclesiastics and laity at Cashel (Co. Tipperary), a site that since at least the seventh century was regarded as the royal capital of Munster. This assembly, commonly known as the Synod of Cashel, was one in a series of synods held by Irish kings to implement changes in the Irish church at a time when similar initiatives were being taken elsewhere in western Christendom.[144] One of the spectacular outcomes of this synod was Muirchertach Ua Briain’s handing of Cashel itself over to the church, and specifically, according to AFM, a witness which, of course, can be challenged as a source due to its lateness, ‘to religious, without any claim of layman or clergyman upon it, but the religious of Ireland in general’ (*do eadhbairt do chráibhdheachaibh cen orlaimh laoich ná cleirich fair acht craibhdich Ereann co coitcheand*). Who were these *cráibdig* and is it correct to translate the term as ‘the religious’? Assuming that the AFM record is reliable, I have argued elsewhere that this may be a reference to the transfer of Cashel to a metropolitan bishop, and specifically, to Máel Ísu Ua hAinmere (d. 1135) and his household, which like himself may have followed the Rule of St Benedict.[145] Máel Ísu was trained in Winchester and during his lifetime corresponded with Anselm of Bec and Canterbury.[146] As noted previously, the evidence of the Kells memoranda is explicit in associating the *deorada cráibdecha* with the *dísert* of Colum Cille in Kells, hence apparently identifying a particular group as distinct among the community of eleventh-century Kells. While the word *cráibdech* is usually understood to be an adjective generally meaning ‘pious, devout, faithful’,[147] use of the term as a singular and plural noun (*cráibdech*, *cráibdig*), as with the noun *deorad*(*a*), seems to have had the more specific meaning of a person dedicated to

142 AC, AFM. 143 AU. 144 Damian Bracken and Dagmar Ó Riain-Raedel (eds), *Ireland and Europe in the twelfth century. Reform and renewal* (Dublin, 2006). 145 Edel Bhreathnach, ‘Benedictine influence in Ireland in the late eleventh and early twelfth centuries: a reflection’, *The Journal of Medieval Monastic Studies* 1 (2012), 63–91. 146 Dónal O’Connor, ‘Did bishop Malchus of Waterford resign because of the Synod of Raithbreasail?’, *Decies* 68 (2012), 1–16. 147 *DIL* s.v.

a committed monastic life. Just as Armagh and Clonmacnoise were to the fore along with the *céli Dé* in attempts to promote an infrastructure of clerical education, as suggested by the contents of *Ríagail Pátraic* ('Rule of Patrick'), the *cráibdig* of Ireland may have formed a national network of eminent men who are likely to have held some form of supervisory position over committed religious life in Ireland. This is most evident in annalistic records from the early eleventh century onwards. Individuals, lay and religious, are often singled out as having led a pious life, with specific reference to their generosity towards the poor, as in the notable case of Mac Raith mac Con Duib, *ardtoísech* (lord) *Clainne Scandláin*, a branch of the Dál Cais, a penitent (*athláech* 'former layman') who died in Mungret (Co. Limerick) in 1067. He is praised for his piety and alms-giving, 'the best "ex-layman" since Nár son of Guaire, for piety and bestowing of food to poor people' (*in t-athlaech as fherr tánic dar héis Náir mac Gúare i crabud 7 i tidnacul bíd do bochtaib*).[148] Many ecclesiastics are described as being *suí ind ecnai ocus crábuid*, possibly best translated as 'a scholar of religious learning and religious life', interpreting *crábud* as an attribute associated with individuals who lived an intentional religious life. The influential *cráibdig* whose deaths are recorded in the annals are characterized as holding high office with use of the words *cenn* 'head', *prím* 'chief', *ard* 'high, chief', and *tuir* 'upholder, paragon' attributed to them.

TABLE 3: Eminent *cráibdig* tenth to twelfth centuries

Name	Obit	Monastery	Offices	Additional attributes	Translation
Máel Mochta	942 AU, AFM (s.a. 940)	Clonard	abbot *airchinnech* scribe	*cenn crábhaidh, egna Éreann* (AFM)	head of piety/ religious life, learned religious scholar of Ireland
Áed Treoiti Áed 'of Trevet'	1005 AU	Trevet, Co. Meath Armagh		*suí ind ecnai ocus crábaid*	scholar of religious learning and religious life
Máel Muire mac Eochadha	1020 AU, CS	Armagh	*comarbae Pátraic*	*cenn cléirech iartair tuaiscirt Eorpa uile* (AU) *cenn clérech Érenn* (CS)	head of the clerics of all northwest Europe head of the clerics of Ireland

148 Mac Niocaill, *Annals of Inisfallen*, pp 222–5 (1067.3). Muirchertach Nár mac Guaire (d. 668) was a possible heir to his father Guaire Aidne's kingdom of Uí Fiachraich Aidni (a territory in south Co. Galway). His sobriquet *nár* 'generous' links him with Mac Raith, although his father Guaire is more renowned for his generosity and appears in early Irish sagas as such.

TABLE 3: Eminent *cráibdig* tenth to twelfth centuries *(continued)*

Name	Obit	Monastery	Offices	Additional attributes	Translation
Conaing Ua Cerbaill	1031 AFM	Glendalough	*airchinnech*	*ceann crábhaidh 7 déirce na n-Gaoidhel*	head of religious life and almsgiving of the Irish
Corcrán Cléirech Corcrán 'the cleric'	1040 AU, AI	Lismore		*cenn Eorpa im crábad 7 im ecna* (AU) *cenn crábuid na h-Érend* (AI)	head of religious life and religious learning in Europe head of religious life of Ireland
Áed Scelic Áed 'of Skellig'	1044 AI	Skellig	priest	*in macc óge 7 cenn crábuid na n-Goedel*	the virgin and the head of religious life of the Irish
Cléirchen Ua Muineóc	1050 AU, AFM	Leighlin	bishop	*tuir crábuid na h-Érenn* (AU) *ceann crábhaidh Osraighe* (AFM)	paragon of religious life of Ireland head of religious life of Osraige
Cétfaid	1056 ATig, AI, AFM	Lismore	bishop anchorite	*cend crábhaidh Muman* (ATig)	head of religious life of Munster
Domnall Déisech Domnall 'of the Déise'	1060 AI, AU	Taghmon	confessor	*cenn crábuid 7 déirce na n-Goedel* (AI) *prím-anmchara Érenn* (AU)	head of religious life and almsgiving of the Irish chief confessor of Ireland
Céle mac Donnacáin	1076 AI, AU, AFM (1050)	Glendalough		*cenn crábaid Érenn*	head of religious life of Ireland
Coibdenach Ultach Coibdenach 'of Ulster'	1078 AI, AFM	Emly	confessor	*in sruithsenóir 7 in cráibdech as dech* (AI) *anmchara Imleacha Iubhair … cenn crábhaidh Éreann* (AFM)	the venerable senior and the best religious man [in Ireland] the confessor of Emly … head of religious life of Ireland
Máel Ísu Ua Brolcháin	1086 AU, ATig, AI, AFM	Armagh Lismore		*suí in ecna 7 in crábaid 7 i filidecht i mbérlai cechtardai; in sruithshenóir 7 in t-ardshuí na hÉrend; co n-derna fén liubra 7 eladhna*	scholar in religious learning and piety and poetry in both languages the venerable senior and chief scholar of Ireland …who made books and treatises …

Name	Obit	Monastery	Offices	Additional attributes	Translation
Cormac Mainistrech Cormac 'of Monasterboice'	1092 AI, AFM	Monasterboice Clonard	bishop abbot	*in sruithsenóir h-Érenn* (AI) *cend eccna 7 crábhaidh na n-Gaoidhel* (AFM)	the venerable senior of Ireland head of religious learning and religious life of the Irish
Senóir mac Maíl Molua	1095 AI, AU	Downpatrick	anchorite	*prímanchara h-Érend* (AI) *ard-senóir Érenn* (AU)	chief anchorite of Ireland chief senior of Ireland
Domnall Ua hÉnna	1098 AI, ATig, AU, AFM	Killaloe	bishop of Munster confessor canon lawyer native jurist	*ardsuí ecnai 7 ardepscop h-Érenn* (AI) *aird-espoc Érenn 7 cenn crábaidh 7 egna 7 dérci fer n-Érenn* (ATig) *uasal-espoc iarthair Eorpa 7 tobur condercli in domain, suí in uird cechtardha .i. Roman & na n-Goeidhel* (AU; AFM)	chief religious scholar and eminent bishop of Ireland eminent bishop of Ireland & head of religious life and religious learning & almsgiving of the men of Ireland noble bishop of western Europe & fountain of all charity of the world, a scholar of both orders [laws], Roman and Irish
Cathasach Ua Ledai	1111 AI, AU	Armagh		*cend crábuid Érend* (AI) *uasal-senóir Érenn* (AU)	head of religious life of Ireland noble senior of Ireland
Máel Muire Ua Dúnáin	1117 AU, CS, ATig, AI, AFM	Clonard	bishop of the Irish/ of Ireland	*suí espoic Goidhel 7 cenn cléirech n-Érenn 7 muire dérce in domain* (AU) *airdepscop Érenn, cenn ecna et crádbaidh iartuir domain* (CS) AI and AFM similar	scholar-bishop of the Irish & head of the clerics of Ireland & steward of almsgiving of the world eminent bishop of Ireland and head of religious learning and religious life of the western world
Máel Coluim Ua Connacáin	1124 AFM	St Patrick's Island, Skerries	priest	*saoi eccna 7 crábhaidh airthir Éreann*	scholar of religious learning and religious life of the east of Ireland

TABLE 3: Eminent *cráibdig* tenth to twelfth centuries (*continued*)

Name	Obit	Monastery	Offices	Additional attributes	Translation
Máel Brigte Ua Brolcháin	1139 AFM	Armagh	bishop	*cend crábaidh tuaisceirt Éreann*	*head of religious life of the north of Ireland*
Máel Brénainn Ua Rónáin	1161 AI, ATig	Ardfert	bishop	*ardepscop iarthar h-Érend, in mac óg, c(e)nn crábaid [7] dérci iarthair - hEr(end)*	eminent bishop of the west of Ireland, the virgin, head of religious life and almsgiving of the west of Ireland
Áed Ua hOisséin	1161 AU, ATig, AI, AFM	Tuam	archbishop of Connacht (Tuam)	*cenn crábhaidh 7 genmnaighechta Leithe Chuinn* (AFM) *ard-epscop Connacht* (AU, ATig, AI)	head of religious life and chastity of Leth Cuinn eminent bishop of Connacht
Máel Ísu Ua Corcráin	1163 AU	Bangor	*comarbae Comgaill*	*cenn crábaid Uladh uile*	head of religious life of all Ulaid
Gilla Áeda Ua Maigín	1172 AI, ATig, AU, AFM	Cork	bishop	*tuir chrábuidh 7 egna 7 óighe na h-Érenn*	upholder of religious life and religious learning and virginity of Ireland

The annals suggest that religious communities in Ireland during the eleventh century, and perhaps at an earlier stage, recognized certain individuals as holding an elevated position among those following a committed religious life. Given the tendency of the annals, especially AFM, to exaggerate, this evidence needs to be viewed cautiously, but nevertheless is worth considering. AU 874 records the obit of bishop Féthgna, 'successor of Patrick and head of religion in all Ireland' (*episcopus, heres Patricii 7 caput relegionis totius Hibernie*). Féthgna was a distinguished cleric, who participated in a royal assembly in 851 at Armagh between Máel Sechlainn mac Maíl Ruanaid, king of Tara (d. 862), and Matudán mac Muiredaig, king of the northeast kingdom of Ulaid (d. 857). Féthgna and Diarmait ua Tigernáin, both in charge of Armagh at the time, attended with *sámud Pátraic*, as did Suairlech (d. 870), head of *Int Eidnén* at Clonard with the clerics of Mide (*co cleirchibh Midhe*).[149] Mochta, Féthgna's pupil or fosterling

149 AU, AFM (849), CS.

(*dalta*), died in 893 and is described in AU as 'bishop, anchorite, and excellent scribe of Ard Macha' (*episcopus, ancorita, 7 scriba optimus Aird Macha*). In 915, Máel Ciaráin mac Eochucáin, head (*princeps*) of Clones and Muckno, and bishop of Armagh died.[150] AFM (912) adds that Máel Ciaráin was also one of Féthgna's pupils. There is even further evidence of Féthgna's importance and legacy in two references to the head of Tech Féthgna 'Féthgna's house'. AFM (936) records the obit of Conaingen, 'head of Tech Féthgna, and chief priest of Armagh' (*abb Tíghe Fethgna, 7 prímhsagart Arda Macha*) and AU 953 notes the death of Máel Muire 'superior of Tech Féthgna' (*airchinnech Taighi Fethgnai*).[151] Was Tech Féthgna a school or a building where the *cráibdig* and learned of Armagh congregated? In 1116, Máel Ísu Ua Brolcháin's oakwood house (*dairtech*) in Lismore was burned.[152] While a *tech* 'house, chapel' was usually dedicated to early saints – and perhaps Féthgna and Máel Ísu were actually revered in Armagh and Lismore –, there are instances of houses dedicated to specific officials or groups or even functions. In 996, parts of Armagh were set on fire by lightning and, according to AI, this did not leave unburnt 'a steeple (?) therein nor a house, nor the house of a senior inside the enclosure' (*conna fargaib bennchobbor i nArd Macha ná tech na tech srotha for lár na rátha cen loscud*).

The description of Féthgna as *caput relegionis totius Hibernie* became a common designation from the mid-eleventh century represented in the vernacular as *cenn crábuid Érenn* or variations on this title. It might be argued that the descriptions of these individuals simply praise their renowned personal piety and that the term *cenn crábuid* is no more than recognition of their sanctity. However, there are enough common features in these entries to suggest that the annalistic descriptions signify more than exaggerated tributes. As might be expected, Armagh, Clonard and Lismore housed a number of these senior religious, with other major monasteries – Glendalough, Leighlin, Emly, Monasterboice, Downpatrick, Killaloe, Ardfert, Tuam, Bangor and Cork – occurring at least once. They appear primarily between 1020 and 1172 at an average interval of ten to fifteen years.[153] There are sufficient time lapses between the entries, especially during the eleventh century, to contend that they are not just general descriptions used for holy men, but represent distinguished offices with either national (*cenn crábuid Érenn/na nGaedil*) or regional (Osraige, Muman, Ulaid, Leth Cuinn, Tuaisceirt Érenn, Airthir Érenn) authority. Nor are all these supervisory offices confined to the title *cenn cráibdig*. Máel Muire, successor of Patrick (d. 1020) is described as 'head of the clerics of all of the north-west of Europe' (*cenn cléirech iartair tuaiscirt Eorpa uile*)[154] which is in line with Armagh's ambition to be in charge of educating priests, not only in Ireland but also in parts of Scotland and in the Isle of Man. Most of them were recognized scholars of religious learning (*suí ecna*), either scriptural, didactic,

150 AU. **151** Also recorded in AFM (951). **152** AU, AFM, ALC. **153** For example, it occurs in AU 1207 and AFM 1306. **154** AU.

canon law or other branches of religious knowledge. A number were scribes, spiritual counsellors (*anmchairde*), anchorites and priests. As noted in Table 3, Cléirchén Ua Muineóc of Leighlin (d. 1050), Cétfaid of Lismore (d. 1056), Cormac Mainistrech of Monasterboice (d. 1092), Senóir mac Maíl Molua (d. 1095), Domnall Ua hÉnna (d. 1098), Máel Muire Ua Dúnáin (d. 1117), Máel Brigte Ua Brolcháin of Armagh (d. 1139), Máel Brénainn Ua Rónáin of Ardfert (d. 1161), Áed Ua hOisséin of Tuam (d. 1161) and Gilla Áeda Ua Maigín of Cork (d. 1172) were all bishops or archbishops. Some were in charge of a monastery, as in the case of Conaing Ua Cerbaill, *airchinnech* of Glendalough (d. 1031). It is noticeable that only a few are given the title *airchinnech* or *comarbae*, suggesting that these individuals were primarily directing scriptural, spiritual, liturgical and regulatory aspects of religious communities and clerical education. The increasing division between clerical and lay officials became more pronounced during the twelfth century as development of a new diocesan structure gathered pace and international orders competed with the existing monastic system. If these eminent clerics were involved with the laity, their main role was as confessors (*anmchairde*), primarily to the aristocracy, although the description *cenn déirce na nGóedel* 'head of almsgiving of the Irish' attributed to Conaing Ua Cerbaill of Glendalough (d. 1031), Domnall Déisech of Taghmon (d. 1060), Domnall Ua hÉnna of Killaloe (d. 1098), Máel Muire Ua Dúnáin (d. 1117) and Máel Brénainn Ua Rónáin (d. 1161) may not be hyperbole, but an indication of the existence of a system of almsgiving operating among Irish religious. In the life of Lorcán Ua Tuathail, as abbot of Glendalough he directed the distribution of alms to those affected by war and poverty,[155] not an unusual motif in saints' lives, but known to have been a genuine responsibility expected of monastic communities. That a person holding the title *cenn cráibdig Érenn* was held in high esteem probably explains Céle mac Donnacáin's (d. 1076) role, who along with Donnchad mac Briain, king of Munster, convened an assembly in Killaloe at a time of crisis in 1050, at which law and peace were restored:[156]

> Much inclement weather happened in the land of Ireland, which carried away corn, milk, fruit, and fish, from the people, so that there grew up dishonesty among all, that no protection was extended to church or fortress, or gossipred or mutual oath, until the clergy and laity of Munster assembled, with their chieftains, under Donnchadh, son of Brian, i.e. the son of the King of Ireland and under Céle mac Donnacáin, under the head

155 Plummer, 'Vie et miracles de S. Laurent', 133 (VI). 156 AI and AFM record the assembly at Killaloe, the more detailed description being in AFM. Original: *Doineand mhór do thiachtain hi ttír Ereann, co rucc ith, 7 bliocht, 7 mess, 7 iascc ó dhaoinibh, co ro fhás eisionnracus hi cach, co ná hainceadh ceall na dún na cairdes Críost na comluighe, go ro tionólsat cléirigh Mumhan, 7 a laoich, 7 a rioghraidh im Donnchadh mac Briain .i. mac righ Ereann, 7 im Céle mac Donnacáin, im ceann crabhaidh Ereann co Cill Dalua, co ro ordaighsiot cáin 7 coscc gach indlighidh*

> of religious life of Ireland, at Cill Dalua, where they enacted a law and a restraint upon every injustice, from small to great. God gave peace and favourable weather in consequence of this law.

Single occurrences of eminent individuals of particular monasteries may reflect an individual's renown or that the particular church at the time housed a vibrant religious community. This might have been the case in relation to Cleirchén Ua Muineóc, bishop of Leighlin, who is described in AFM (1050) as 'head of the religious of Osraige' (*ceand crábhaidh Osraighe*). As for Cormac of Monasterboice (1092), he must have had links with the community in Clonard where he died *ina ailithre* 'on his final journey'. The single reference in 1124 to Máel Coluim Ua Connacáin is unusual.[157] He was a priest and scholar of religious learning and religious life of the east of Ireland (*saoi eccna 7 crábhaidh airthir Ereann*), who died on St Patrick's Island (Church Island) off the coast of Skerries, Co. Dublin. An eminent scholar dying on such a small island in the middle of winter must signal intense asceticism, although it should be noted that in 1148 St Malachy convened an important synod on the same island, a decision that also remains somewhat puzzling.[158] It is possible that St Patrick's Island acted as a hermitage for the religious of the Norse city of Dublin. Máel Coluim's life on an island fits in with an elite group of individuals who are associated with the more extreme form of life as *milites Christi*, and appear to have been held in esteem nationally or provincially, and who died in places that enabled them to follow more reclusive lives. They are likely to have been affiliated to larger monasteries during their lives. Among the more renowned among them were Gormgal of High Island, Co. Galway, 'chief spiritual confessor of Ireland' (*prímanmcharae Érenn*) (d. 1018), Gormgal *prímanmcharae Innsi Dar Cairgrenn* (Ram's Island, Co. Antrim) (d. 1056),[159] Áed Scelic, 'the noble priest, the virgin, and the chief of the Gaedil in piety' (*in t-huasalshacart 7 in macc óge 7 cend crábuid na nGoedel*) (d. 1044),[160] and Anmchad Ua Dúnchada, 'anchorite of God' (*ancharae Dé*), died in 1058 on Inis Uasail (Church Island, Lough Currane, Co. Kerry).[161] One of the most elaborate cross-inscribed slabs at Church Island, a long-established monastery dating back to the sixth/seventh century, invokes a blessing for Anmchad and features rare examples of alpha and omega symbols (Fig. 14).[162]

o bhiucc co mór. Tucc Dia síth 7 soineann for sliocht na cána sin. **157** AFM 1124. **158** St Patrick's Island may have contained an early tomb-shrine that given the place's association with St Patrick may have been significant. See Michael Ryan, Kevin Mooney, Frank Prendergast and Barry Masterson, 'Church Island: a description' in Ailbhe MacShamhráin (ed.), *The island of St Patrick. Church and ruling dynasties in Fingal and Meath, 400–1148* (Dublin, 2004), pp 106–24, at pp 116–17; Martin Holland, 'The twelfth-century reform and Inis Pátraic' in MacShamhráin, *The island of St Patrick*, pp 159–78, at p. 175. **159** AU. **160** AI. **161** AI. **162** John Sheehan, 'Early medieval Iveragh, AD 400–1200' in John Crowley and John Sheehan (eds), *The Iveragh Peninsula. A cultural atlas of the Ring of Kerry* (Cork, 2009), pp 113–21, at p. 120 (fig. 9).

The careers of bishops Domnall Ua hÉnna (d. 1098), Máel Muire Ua Dúnáin (d. 1117) and Áed Ua hOisséin (d. 1161) as participants in the transformation of the Irish church have been covered frequently by scholars over many years.[163] All three were members of ecclesiastical hereditary families, but there is no indication as to their monastic credentials, or indeed if they had any. As Ó Corráin points out in relation to Máel Muire Ua Dúnáin, annalistic entries and references in other sources are florid, and probably not accurate.[164] It is possible that Máel Muire retreated to Clonard's community of *Int Eidnén*, if that was still in existence. Domnall Ua hÉnna, as a correspondent with Lanfranc on theological matters such as the administration of the Eucharist to infants, and as the senior among Irish bishops corresponding with Anselm on the appointment of Máel Ísu Ua hAinmere, a monk of Winchester, to the see of Waterford, must have been aware of, if not following, monastic practices prevalent not only in England, but in Dublin, where the bishop's household was probably following the Rule of St Benedict. As regards Áed Ua hOisséin, archbishop of Tuam, he was not only the 'head of religious life of the northern half of Ireland' (*ceann crábhuidh Leithe Cuinn*) in AFM (1161) but also 'head of virginity'(*ceann geanmnaighechta*) of the same region. This information could again be construed as an exaggeration by a late source, except that Áed is described in ATig 1134 as the *comarbae* of Iarlaith of Tuam and a *mac óigi* 'a celibate, virgin'. And similar to others holding the title of *cenn cráibdig*, Áed appears to have had distinguished pupils as the annals known as Mac Cárthaigh's Book (Misc. Ir. Annals, 1159) note that Gilla Áeda Ua Maigín, bishop of Cork (d. 1172), also eminent in *crábud* ('piety'), *ecna* ('religious learning') and *óige* ('virginity'), adopted the name Gilla Áeda 'servant of Áed' as a mark of respect for Áed Ua hOisséin.[165]

The requirement of *stabilitas*, interpreted as being attached to one monastery, did not necessarily apply to these eminent *cráibdig*. Coibdenach Ultach, who from his sobriquet probably came from the northeast, resided in Emly in the southwest. Máel Ísu Ua Brolcháin moved from Armagh to Lismore, a monastery that during the eleventh and twelfth centuries attracted men and women, clerics and laity alike for apparently penitential and spiritual renewal, and for death and burial. The traditional narrative, often based on twelfth-century texts, that members of hereditary ecclesiastical families and indeed dynastic families had little interest in monasticism in its strict sense and needed reformers such as

163 Aubrey Gwynn and Dermot F. Gleeson, *A history of the diocese of Killaloe*. Part 1 (Gwynn) (Dublin, 1962), pp 105–9; Ó Corráin, 'Dál Cais – church and dynasty', pp 57–8; Donnchadh Ó Corráin, 'Mael Muire Ua Dúnáin (1040–1117), reformer' in de Brún, Ó Coileáin and Ó Riain, *Folia Gadelica*, pp 47–53. See also Ó Carragáin, *Churches in early medieval Ireland*, pp 258–63 where he argues that Máel Muire Ua Dúnáin had a hand in the building of St Flannan's church in Killaloe and counts it among twelfth-century churches dedicated to *reclusi*. **164** Ó Corráin, 'Mael Muire Ua Dúnáin'. **165** Séamus Ó hInnse (ed. and trans.), *Miscellaneous Irish annals (AD 1114–1437)* (Dublin, 1947), pp 42–3.

Malachy, supported by Bernard, to sweep them out of the church is in essence discredited by these annalistic entries. Máel Ísu Ua Brolcháin belonged to a powerful family who held offices in Armagh, Kildare and Derry.[166] Cathalán Ua Forréid was probably the son or nephew of Áed Ua Forréid (d. 1056), the eminent bishop of Armagh for whom the praise poem mentioned earlier was composed during his lifetime.[167] In addition, Mac Raith Ua Forréid, no doubt closely related to Cathalán, died in 1137 and is described in AFM as a learned historian (*saoi seanchaidh*) and confessor (*anmcharae*). Notably, Cathalán died in Emly where he also functioned as an *anmcharae*.

The Irish sources from the tenth century onwards are sufficiently detailed to reconstruct the organization of at least the large monasteries. Their communities and households, not surprisingly, were divided between those who governed the spiritual and temporal life of a foundation. Most supported a relatively small monastic community in the midst of their busy settlements. These communities were under the authority of either abbots committed to religious life or quite often bishops who were also scribes and versed in various disciplines of religious learning. Monastic abbots and bishops might be in charge of the monastery's powerful *sámud* 'household' or join forces with those governing the temporal activities in a *sámud*. During the eleventh century, a national and regional move towards normalization of the formation of clerics and monks developed, and the use of titles such as *cenn cráibdig* and *cenn cléirech Érenn/na nGóedel* is testimony to this reorganization. An increasing emphasis was placed on liturgy and the virtues of chastity and virginity, although deviation from a celibate life only gradually became an obstacle to holding a spiritual office. Many foundations depended on the zeal of individuals at various times to sustain or re-establish a monastic presence. By the first quarter of the twelfth century there is a sense that long-standing traditions were being replaced by new religious lifestyles that were being endowed by Irish kings and promoted by Irish bishops and abbots. The power of some monasteries contracted, among them Emly and Kells, while others succeeded in transforming themselves and thrived at least into the thirteenth century, among them Louth, Clones and Ferns. The early Irish monastic model did not stand still after the seventh century, and as elsewhere, in Britain and on the Continent, it adapted to change and from the tenth century onwards was receptive to external influence and internal transformation. Until the late twelfth century, the Irish monastic tradition continued to be swathed in the native culture, and was one of the many 'monasticisms' in the Latin west, and indeed in the wider monastic world.[168] And even with the acceptance of 'normal' monastic rules and structures introduced by international orders, elements of the earlier tradition survived to the dissolution.

166 AU 1097, 1107, 1155; Muireann Ní Bhrolcháin (eag.), *Maol Íosa Ó Brolcháin* (Maigh Nuad, 1986); Muireann Ní Bhrolcháin, 'Maol Íosa Ó Brolcháin: an assessment', *Seanchas Ard Mhacha* 12:1 (1986), 43–67. **167** See p. 129; Murphy, 'A poem to Aodh Ua Forreidh, bishop of Armagh'. Herbert, 'A praise-poem'. **168** Vanderputten, *Medieval monasticisms*.

CHAPTER 5

The *Vita Communis*: creating a spiritual community

Early Irish monasteries were multi-purpose institutions that to varying degrees, depending on their interests and size, were active in political, economic, social, educational and spiritual pursuits. One of the most challenging tasks in attempting to understand early monasticism in Ireland pertains to its communal, liturgical and spiritual way of life. The creation of a monastic community, no matter the type, size or geographical location, involves human relationships, personal networks and charismatic individuals. Monastic communities and individuals following a more solitary lifestyle often reflect the cultural and social norms of a given society, even if they operate as a counter-culture striving towards perfection based on an intense spiritual relationship with the divine. And, of course, brotherhoods and sisterhoods, familial bonds that are formed outside blood relations, fellowships and friendships other than monastic existed in many societies, and were even transformed into Christian communities, monastic and otherwise. In his seminal work *Friendship and community. The monastic experience, 350–1250*, Brian Patrick McGuire explored in depth the principles of friendship that formed the basis for monastic communities and individual relationships, some of which, such as the aristocratic Roman concept of *amicitia* 'close friendship', were already in existence.[1] More significant, however, was the scriptural basis for living together either in a monastic community or somehow attached to a coenobitic foundation. Psalm 133[132]:1 'How good and pleasant it is when brothers live together in unity'[2] offered a clear direction as did Christ's words to the apostles: 'Amen, I say to you, there is no one who has given up house or wife or brothers or parents or children for the sake of the kingdom of God who will not receive [back] an overabundant return in this present age and eternal life in the age to come' (Luke 18:29–30).[3] Hence the urge to follow Christ through a *vita apostolica* or *vita communis* emerged in which new bonds were created on the basis of becoming friends of Christ – *cor unum et anima una* ('one heart and one soul': Acts 4:32). Monasticism was based

1 Brian Patrick McGuire, *Friendship and community. The monastic experience, 350–1250* (Michigan, 1988; repr. Ithaca, 2010), p. xv passim. 2 Psalm 133[132]:1 *Ecce quam bonum et quam iucundum habitare fratres in unum.* 3 Luke 18:29–30: *qui dixit eis amen dico vobis nemo est qui reliquit domum aut parentes aut fratres aut uxorem aut filios propter regnum Dei et non recipiat multo plura in hoc tempore et in saeculo venturo vitam aeternam.*

on following the example of Christ and his disciples, the 'apostolic college', a community under the direction of one head and with one purpose. Even though the fundamental precepts, based on the scriptures, were the same, cultural differences manifested themselves in the types of committed religious life that emerged throughout Christendom during late antiquity.[4] Monasticism in Egypt, for example, involved a partial retreat from city and village life and what that entailed in leaving behind blood kinship, marriage and economic production.[5] In her study of the Byzantine ritual associated with 'brother-making' *adelphopoiesis*, the origins of which she regards as based in small-group Eastern monasticism of late antiquity, Claudia Rapp makes many observations that are fundamental to understanding the ideals and structures of Irish monasticism – and in reality, monasticism universally – none more so than her comment that:[6]

> ... it is important to acknowledge the simultaneous existence of a large variety of monastic models, depending on the size of the group and its distance from society, a distance that is determined largely by the economic activity that provided the support and livelihood for these monks. The fluidity between monastic lifestyles is played out in the lives of individual ascetics.

Rapp's examination of the terminology used in the monastic environment, be it kinship terminology, concepts of discipleship, friendship and paired monasticism, points to a potentially productive exercise in elucidating concepts of monastic community and relationships in an Irish context:[7]

> ... relationships were conceptualized in kinship terms: 'father', 'son' and 'brother'. These terms were crucial in establishing one's place in the alternative world of monasticism, where they denote one's ancestry and membership in a particular kinship group that was achieved not through bonds of blood and marriage, but through a shared purpose and acquisition of knowledge and skills. The shared purpose was the quest for spiritual perfection ...

4 Peter Brown has covered much ground in regard to Christianity in Late Antiquity. Among his volumes that have given me a deep insight into the mindsets of that period are *The body and society. Men, women, and sexual renunciation in early Christianity* (New York, 1988; repr. 2008) and Brown, *The ransom of the soul.* 5 Helvétius et al., 'Re-reading monastic traditions, p. 51. 6 Claudia Rapp, *Brother-making in late antiquity and Byzantium. Monks, laymen, and Christian ritual* (Oxford, 2016), pp 91–2. This point is also at the heart of Vanderputten's study *Medieval monasticisms.* 7 Rapp, *Brother-making*, p. 101.

BONDS OF BLOOD AND KINSHIP IN EARLY IRISH SOCIETY

There is no doubt that bonds of blood and kinship were fundamental to early Irish society and were enshrined in its laws,[8] but other bonds also existed. The relationship between a king and his clients and the people of his kingdom was of particular consequence.[9] Early Irish sagas such as the epic *Táin Bó Cúailnge* depict a form of brotherhood or fellowship that developed between young warriors that lasted throughout their lives, no matter if they became rivals or remained friends. The most poignant episode of such a fellowship is that of the foster brothers Cú Chulainn and Fer Diad who are forced to face one another in a single combat which leads to Fer Diad's death. Scholars have long debated the etymology of the name Fer Diad, with various suggestions that it means 'one of two', 'man of the two' or 'the two-footed one'.[10] Whatever the origins of the personal name, the tale is a fine example of the tragic end to a heroic brotherly relationship and their fellowship is beautifully expressed in a poem in the saga:[11]

> You are my heart's companion
> You are my kin, you are my family,
> Never has there been found a dearer treasure,
> Alas your destruction.

Similarly, the late twelfth-/early thirteenth-century text *Acallam na Senórach* ('The colloquy of the elders'), which narrates the lengthy encounter between St Patrick and the *fiana*, the most famous warrior band in medieval Irish tales, encapsulates their brotherhood in the following oft-quoted extract:[12]

> 'What has kept you warriors alive for all these years?' asked Patrick. Caílte replied, 'The truth of our hearts, the strength of our arms, and the constancy of our tongues.'

8 Charles-Edwards, *Early Irish and Welsh kinship*. **9** T.M Charles-Edwards, 'A contract between king and people in early medieval Ireland? *Críth Gablach* on kingship', *Peritia* 8 (1994), 107–19. **10** Eric P. Hamp, 'Varia VII.1. *Fer Diad*', *Ériu* 33 (1982), 178; David Greene, 'Varia I', *Ériu* 33 (1986), 161–4; Joseph Falaky Nagy, *Conversing with angels and ancients. Literary myths of ancient Ireland* (Dublin, 1997), p. 218; Mícheál Ó Flaithearta, 'The etymologies of (Fer) Diad' in Brian Ó Catháin and Ruairí Ó hUiginn (eds), *Ulidia 2. Proceedings of the second international conference on the Ulster Cycle of tales, National University of Ireland, Maynooth, 24–27 June 2005* (Maynooth, 2009), pp 218–25. **11** Cecile O'Rahilly (ed.), *Táin Bó Cúailnge Recension 1* (Dublin, 1976), p. 93: lines 3062–5. Original: *Tú mo choicli cridi/ tú m-acme tú m-fine/ní fúar ríam ba dile/ ba dirsan do díth.* **12** Ann Dooley and Harry Roe (trans.), *Tales of the elders of Ireland. A new translation of Acallam na Senórach* (Oxford, 1999), p.6. Original: Whitley Stokes (ed.), 'Acallamh na Senórach' in Ernst Windisch and Whitley Stokes (eds), *Irische Texte* 4 (Leipzig, 1900), pp1–438, at p. 4: lines 118–20: *'Cia ro chomét sibhsi mar sin,' ar Pátraic, 'in bar mbeathaidh?' Ocus ro frecair Caílte .i. 'Fírinde inár*

This text is likely to express a later Christian ideal of the institution of *fénnidecht* or being a *fénnid* 'a brigand, hunter, warrior' which is also portrayed in earlier texts as malevolent *díbergaig* 'brigands, raiders' operating on the margins of society either cursed outright by saints or converted to a good Christian life.[13] It is likely that tales of these benign or malevolent bands recall a long-established institution that allowed young aristocratic men to be in a temporary state, described by Joseph Falaky Nagy as 'a prelude to the assumption of full adult status, responsibility, inheritance, and marriage'.[14] There is evidence, however, that many *díbergaig* devoted their lives to violence. Although admittedly slim evidence, an annalistic record hints at genuine mayhem caused by a roaming band, which by the mid-ninth century was likened to the behaviour of Vikings:[15]

> Máel Sechnaill destroyed the island of Loch Muinremor, overcoming there a large band of wicked men of Luigni and Gailenga, who had been plundering the territories in the manner of the heathens.

Notably, the phrase used to describe this large band of wicked men in both annals is *fianlach már di maccaibh báis* 'a large band of the sons of death'. In a monastic context of brotherhood, this is significant as monks and religious are sometimes described as *meic bethad* 'sons of life'. 'The teaching of Máel Ruain' for example, notes that Muirchertach mac Ólchoboir, *airchinnech* of Clonfert (d. 802),[16] learned the practice of saying the Magnificat after the Beati from a *mac bethad*.[17] The Irish life of St Berach contrasts the characteristics of the two, the *mac bethad* is mild, gentle, obedient and humble, while the *mac báis* is very dark and threatening.[18] In this particular life, the *mac bethad* refers to a monk, while elsewhere in the literature it would appear that the *mac bethad* and *mac eclaise* simply meant a cleric or ecclesiastic of any type.

The most obvious parallel with a coenobitic community adhering to rules and customs in early Irish society is that of the professional classes, the most prestigious of which were the lawyers and poets. Indeed, Liam Breatnach has repeatedly demonstrated that poetic grades were derived from or at least defined by clerical grades.[19] The term *clíar* could refer either to the clergy or the

croidhedhaibh 7 nertt inár lámhaibh, 7 comall inár tengthaibh.' 13 Richard Sharpe, 'Hiberno-Latin *laicus*, Irish *láech* and the devil's men', *Ériu* 30 (1979), 75–92; Kim McCone, 'Werewolves, cyclopes, *díberga* and *fianna*: juvenile delinquency in early Ireland', *Cambridge Medieval Celtic Studies* 12 (Winter, 1986), 1–22; Nagy, *Conversing with angels and ancients*, pp 293–300; Máire West, 'Aspects of *díberg* in the tale *Togail Bruidne Da Derga*', *Zeitschrift für celtische Philologie* 49–50 (1997), 950–64. 14 Nagy, *Conversing with angels and ancients*, p. 295. 15 AU 847; AFM (845). AU original: *Toghal Innsi Locha Muinnremair la Mael Sechnaill for fianlach mar di maccaibh bais Luigne 7 Galeng ro batar oc indriudh na tuath more gentilium.* 16 AU, AI (refers to him as Ólchobar only), AFM (797). 17 Gwynn, 'The teaching of Mael Ruain', pp 22–3 §37. Original: *O mac beathadh fuair se an gnathugadh sin .i. Magnificad do radh ar deireadh gach biaide.* 18 Plummer, *BNnÉ*, i, p. 42 (88). 19 Breatnach, *Uraicecht na Ríar*,

professional lawyers and poets. Members of the professions, high or low, were deemed to need particular qualifications to practise. The composite text known as the 'Triads of Ireland' lists the three qualifications each for the comb-maker, carpenter, physician, blacksmith, artificer, harper and poet.[20] Given that the professional classes, especially lawyers and poets, had to follow a specific curriculum to reach the highest grade of their craft and were expected to belong to a hierarchical order depending on their ability, lifestyle and belonging to a professional family, conceptually the idea of privileged or distinct communities operating in society was a fundamental premise of medieval Irish society. The crossover between the clerical profession and lawyers and poets is well recognized and members of these professions lived in monasteries. Muirchertach Ua Cairill, *airchinnech* of Downpatrick, is described in 1083 as eminent in law and history (*suí brethemnachta 7 seanchais*), while Eochaid Ua Flannacáin (d. 1004) was a master of poetry and historical lore (*suí fhilidechta 7 senchusa*) and guest master associated with Armagh.[21] And, of course, as is clear throughout this volume, professional hereditary families dominated monastic offices from abbots to heads of monastic schools and guest masters.

The challenge to determine the nature of Irish monastic communities as a distinct social group can be tackled by using various yardsticks.[22] Is there a continuing influence of earlier monastic rules or handbooks such as John Cassian's *Conferences* or *Institutes*, St Augustine's *Praecepta* or *Ordo Monasterii*, the Rule of St Benedict, the works of Pope Gregory the Great, or native rules that are reflected in the works of Columbanus? Are monastic communities constructed around the Augustinian *vita apostolica* or Benedictine *vita communis* and *ordo disciplinae*, Gregory the Great's balancing of the *vita activa* and *vita contemplativa*, or does an echo of all of these run through the Irish monastic experience? Do commonplace monastic ideals guide Irish coenobitic and eremitical communities, ideals covered by expressions such as *fraternitas, societas, unitas, cor unum et anima una, habitus, puritas cordis, amor et timor Dei, imitatio Christi, opus Dei, obedientia, humilitas, propria uoluntas, caritas, amicitia*? Can changes be detected between tenth-century native monasticism and its manifestation in the twelfth century, and how does the arrival of the new orders change the existing monastic communities? And finally, what is the relationship

pp. 85–7. **20** Kuno Meyer (ed.), *The triads of Ireland*. RIA Todd Lecture Series 13 (London, 1906), pp 16–17 §§117–23; see also John Carey, 'The three things required of a poet', *Ériu* 48 (1997), 41–58, at p. 43. **21** AU. **22** This chapter has been informed by the research of many current monastic scholars but most especially by the following works: Christina Lutter, '*Vita communis* in Central European monastic landscapes' in Eirik Hovden, Christina Lutter and Walter Pohl (eds), *Meanings of community across medieval Eurasia. Comparative approaches* (Leiden, 2016), pp 362–87; Albrecht Diem, 'The limitations of asceticism' in Walter Pohl André Gingrich (eds), *Medieval worlds. Comparative and interdisciplinary studies. Monasteries and sacred landscapes and Byzantine connections* (Vienna, 2019), pp 112–38.

between coenobitic and eremitical communities and individuals and their extensive ecclesiastical settlements, and beyond that, with society as a whole? Christina Lutter's comments on the relationship between large Augustinian and Cistercian monasteries in Central Europe – such as Admont and Klosterneuburg – and the society in which they were embedded is apt also in the Irish context: 'kinship, property, and gender cannot be separated from either the political or spiritual practices constitutive for these institutions – or from the visions of the people who made them into communities'.[23]

There are numerous means by which the above questions could be answered but the most profitable approach calls for a detailed analysis of saints' lives and the 'rules' associated with Irish saints. Comparison with rules that were emerging elsewhere and with earlier rules and customs could establish how much the Irish clung to an existing monastic tradition and how much change was occurring prior to the arrival of the international orders during the eleventh and twelfth centuries. While saints' lives are often full of fantastical miracle tales and occasional historic details, some present a fair reflection of monastic ideals and customs, often depending on the strength of the monastic tradition of a particular saint and his/her *familia*. Hence this chapter relies on the evidence of Irish saints' lives and concentrates on the literature around SS Brendan, Monenna, Flannán, Malachy and Lorcán Ua Tuathail.

THE SAINTS' LIVES AS MIRRORS OF MONASTIC COMMUNITIES

The great monastic founders in Ireland belonged primarily to the extended age of conversion in Ireland during the sixth and early seventh centuries. This was the age of zealous Christian leaders, many of whom reputedly founded Ireland's monasteries and lesser churches. Between that period and the twelfth century, few new monasteries were founded or new saints' cults emerged, the most significant being the foundations of the late eighth/early ninth-century established by the leaders of the *céli Dé* movement. Efforts were made to promote royal cults, especially in Munster where Feidlimid mac Crimthainn (d. 847), Cormac mac Cuilennáin (d. 908) and Brian Bórama (d. 1014) are portrayed in literature as saintly. Their cults did not take root and did not gain popular support. The lives of *céli Dé* founders were not compiled, either deliberately – thus breaking with existing tradition – or they were overshadowed by the earlier great saints. Their sanctity was transmitted through their teachings and regulatory texts.

The medieval lives of Irish saints are best approached like archaeological excavation: even in their final redactions, many probably compiled during the eleventh and twelfth centuries and even later, they retain layers of earlier

23 Lutter, '*Vita communis*', pp 379–80.

material. This reflects a general tendency among the Irish literary class to preserve older material while at the same time adding a contemporary stratum and revising the old to fit in with a new narrative or style. The aims of authors or compilers of saints' lives also varied considerably: some sought to bolster the interests of royal dynasties and hereditary families, some to confirm land-ownership as charters did elsewhere, others to boost their saint's cult in order to gain an income from pilgrims, and finally, a small number genuinely reflect an interest in their founder's monastic life. Adomnán's seventh-century *Vita S. Columbae*, modelled on Gregory of Tours' life of St Martin and on Gregory the Great's *Dialogues* Book 2, which contained the life and miracles of St Benedict, and also informed by genuine memories of Columba, might be regarded as a work that is seriously interested in the monastic lifestyle and tradition of a great founder. This can also be said of the literature around St Brendan of Clonfert, be it the Latin lives, the Irish lives or the *Navigatio Sancti Brendani*. Similarly, Bernard's life of Malachy is very much concerned with the purity of monasticism in Ireland and Malachy's efforts, from Bernard's perspective, to bring Irish monasteries into line with his own views on monasticism. Then there is the great corpus of Irish saints' lives that on the whole follow a given template of a combination of heroic biographies of the great founders, their miracles, the churches and lands owned by them, and their dynastic affiliations. Among the classics of this template are the lives of Cóemgen of Glendalough and Ciarán of Clonmacnoise. Finally, some deviate from the standard template to varying degrees, among them the lives of Monenna of Killevy, Flannán of Killaloe and Cellach of Killala.

Key to the construction of a monastic community and of envisioning the type of lifestyle of that community was the *érlam*, the historic founder and spiritual patron of the monastery whose memory was kept alive through the upkeep and veneration of his/her grave or relics, constant memorialization of their life, use of the office title *comarbae* 'successor of', and, occasionally, the existence of their 'rule'. Personal names that consisted of the elements *Máel* -, *Gilla* -, *Caillech* - – all in this usage denoting 'devotee of' – followed by a saint's name was a further recognition of devotion to a founder.[24] Hence the characteristics attributed to a founder, some holier than others, shaped a tradition and that of the churches associated with them.

24 As regards such personal names, during the period under consideration, the most common names following this formula are those who are devotees of the Lord (Gilla Críst, Gilla in Choimded, Gilla Ísu, Máel Ísu, Caillech Dé, Céile Críst, Céile Ísu), the Blessed Virgin (Máel Muire), universal saints (Máel Martain, Máel Eóin, Máel Póil, Máel Petair, Céile Petair), national saints (Gilla Pátraic, Máel Pátraic, Máel Brigte, Máel Coluim (especially in Scotland)), other Irish saints (Gilla Molaisi, Gilla Mo-Chutu, Gilla Ciaráin, Máel Ciaráin, Máel Máedóc, Máel Mochta, Máel Finnéin, Máel Brénainn, Caillech Finnéin, Caillech Cóemgin) and the generic Gilla na Náem and Caillech na Náem, the male and female version of 'devotee of the saints'.

The Brendan cycle: ideal monasticism and monastic regulation

One of the most popular medieval texts that circulated and was translated throughout Europe was the Brendan legend, the *Navigatio Sancti Brendani* (*NSB*).[25] (Fig. 15) Probably composed in Ireland or at least by an Irishman on the Continent during the late eighth or early ninth century, the *NSB* aimed at portraying the ideal monastic life. Later texts around Brendan of Clonfert, Irish and Latin lives and homilies, are either conflated with the *NSB* or record separate traditions that do not depend on it. The relationship between *NSB* and the lives is complex and has been subjected to much debate.[26] The following list of the sources quoted in this section is included here to assist the reader:

TABLE 4: Summary of the Latin and Irish lives of St Brendan and their use of *NSB*

Title	**Possible date**
Navigatio Sancti Brendani	late eighth/ninth century
Latin lives Versions exist in the following collections: *Codex Salmanticensis*: thirteenth/fourteenth-century Brussels MS 7672–4 contains two *vitae*, one not conflated with *NSB* *Codex Insulensis*: fourteenth-century MSS Bod. Lib. Rawl. B 485 and 505. Conflated with *NSB* *Codex Kilkenniensis*: fifteenth-century Dublin Marsh's Library MS Z3.1.5. A copy also in fifteenth-century TCD MS 175. Conflated with *NSB*	partially contemporary or earlier than *NSB*, but as these versions are included in late medieval MSS they must include later material or at least later interpretation of *NSB* episodes and traditions about St Brendan
Valle Crucis Latin life: late twelfth-century Bod. Lib. MS 3496 related to an Anglo-Norman poem on St Brendan	early thirteenth century
First Irish life: in late fifteenth-century MS, the Book of Lismore and other MSS. Influenced by *NSB*	late twelfth century
Second Irish life: in one seventeenth-century MS Brussels 4190–4200. Incorporates Irish translation of *NSB*	late twelfth century

25 There is a vast literature available on this subject. See Carl Selmer (ed.), *Navigatio Sancti Brendani abbatis from early Latin manuscripts* (Notre Dame, 1959; repr. Dublin, 1989); John J. O'Meara (trans.), *The voyage of Saint Brendan. Journey to the Promised Land* (Dublin and New Jersey, 1976–8); Glyn S. Burgess and Clara Strijbosch (eds), *The Brendan legend. Texts and versions*. The Northern World vol. 24 (Leiden and Boston, 2006); Ó Corráin, *CLH* i, pp 290–305 §231; David Stifter, 'Brendaniana, etc.', *Keltische Forschungen* 1 (2006), 191–214; Rossana E. Guglielmetti and Giovanni Orlandi (eds and trans), *La navigazione di San Brendano. Navigatio sancti Brendani* (Firenze, 2018) (Kindle digital edition). **26** Plummer, *VSH*, i, pp xxxvi–xliii; Kenny, *Sources*, 412–14 §202; Sharpe, *Medieval Irish saints' lives*, pp 390–1;

The Brendan legend – taken as the entire corpus – is particularly valuable, as the role of an abbot and the construction of an ideal monastic community can be traced in texts dating from approximately the late eighth century to the late twelfth century. This offers an opportunity to track any changes in terminology or in approach, and although the full complexity and enormity of such an exercise cannot be covered here, nonetheless evidence of continuity or change is worth pursuing. The role of Brendan as abbot and spiritual counsellor to his community, the ideal communities of the abbots Mernóc and Ailbe, and Brendan's dialogue with other saints enable us to gain an insight into an evolving tradition. The *NSB* portrays Brendan as his community's spiritual guide but one who is willing to seek their advice, who comforts them and even on occasion is very human and falls out with them. Before they embark on their voyage, he shuts himself in an oratory with his fourteen companions and asks their opinion on his resolution to seek the Promised Land, an action that, as Selmer and Ó Clabaigh have pointed out, is in line with Chapter 3 of *RB* where an abbot summons the brothers for counsel whenever an important decision needs to be taken.[27] The response from Brendan's monks is telling:[28]

> 'Abbot, your will is ours. Have we not left our parents behind? Have we not spurned our inheritance and given our bodies into your hands? So we are prepared to go along with you to death or life. Only one thing let us ask for, the will of God.'

When in difficulty or in need of direction, Brendan constantly reminds his brothers that God's will should be followed and that he will provide:[29]

> 'Brothers, do not fear. God is our helper, sailor, and helmsman, and rudder. Ship all the oars and the rudder. Just leave the sail spread and God will do as he wishes with his servants and their ship.'

A detail worth noting in relation to this part of the text are the terms that the various versions of Brendan's life use to describe the choosing of a temporary successor to Brendan while he is seeking the Land of Promise:

Séamus Mac Mathúna, '*The Irish life of Saint Brendan*: textual history, structure and date' in Burgess and Strijbosch, *The Brendan legend*, pp 117–58; *DIS*, pp 115–17; *CLH*, i, pp 290–306 nos 231–2. **27** Selmer, *Navigatio*, p. 84, n. 15. **28** Ibid., pp 9–10 Cap. [2]; O'Meara, *Voyage of Saint Brendan*, p. 7; Guglielmetti and Orlandi, *La navigazione*, digital folder 1326 [II]; Original: '*Abba, voluntas tua ipsa est et nostra. Nonne parentes nostros dimisimus? Nonne hereditatem nostram despeximus et corpora nostra tradidimus in manus tuas? Itaque parati sumus sive ad mortem sive ad vitam tecum ire. Unam tantum queramus Dei uoluntatem*'; Ó Clabaigh, 'Beneticines in medieval and early modern Ireland', pp 81–2. **29** Selmer, *Navigatio*, p. 12 §6; O'Meara, *Voyage of Saint Brendan*, p. 10; Guglielmetti and Orlandi, *La navigazione*, digital folder 1371 [VI]. Original: '*Fratres, nolite formidare: Deus enim noster adiutor est et nautor et*

NSB: … *commendatisque (omnibus)* ***preposito monasterii sui****, qui fuit postea suus successor in eodem loco* … [30]

Latin life (*Codex Insulensis*): … *atque* ***preposito monasterii*** *recommendatis, qui postea fuit successor suus in eodem loco* …[31]

Valle Crucis life (Bodleian MS 3496): … *et eos* ***priori tanquam pastori*** *tradidit, et eius sicut suis subministrare iussit preceptis* …[32]

Second Irish life: *Éirghis Brenainn cona muinntir iar sin, 7 faccbaitt bennacht ag* ***prepoist na mainistreach*** *adubhramar romhainn .i. neoch do báoi i nionad Brenainn ag na braitribh da éis.*[33]

Apart from the *Valle Crucis* life the later versions follow *NSB* by using the term *prepositus*, presumably understood to mean the *secnap/secundus abbas* of Brendan's monastery and an office also provided for in *RB*.[34] In all the Latin versions, Brendan decides on his successor and this is also implied in the Irish version.

Brendan's conversation with Paul the Hermit – described in the *NSB* as a *miles Christi* living in a cave – is particularly enlightening. Paul, the celebrated desert hermit, greets Brendan with a line from Psalm 133[132]:[35]

Ecce quam bonum et quam iucundum habitare fratres in unum

How good and joyful it is that brothers live in one

This recalls the universal monastic ideal of *cor unum et anima una* as a fundamental basis for a successful community. Paul, the ideal hermit, addresses Brendan as the model abbot of a monastic community in response to Brendan's desire to be *spiritalis perfectus*:[36]

gubernator atque guberna. Mittite intus omnes remiges et gubernam; tantum dimittite vela extensa, et faciat Deus sicut vult de servis suis et de sua navi.' **30** Selmer, *Navigatio*, p. 3 §3; Guglielmetti and Orlandi, *La navigazione*, digital folder 1337 [III]. **31** Plummer, *VSH*, i, p. 107 §xiv. **32** Ibid., ii, p. 272 §iv. **33** Plummer, *BNnÉ*, i, p. 52 §xiv; ii, p. 51 §xiv. **34** *RB* 65. **35** Selmer, *Navigatio*, p. 72 §26; O'Meara, *Voyage of Saint Brendan*, p. 62. **36** Selmer, *Navigatio*, pp 72–3 §26; O'Meara, *Voyage of Saint Brendan*, pp 62–3; Guglielmetti and Orlandi, *La navigazione*, digital folder 2114 [XXVI]. Various sources, including the *Vita Pauli*, *Vita Onuphrii* and the *Vitae Patrum*, have been cited as influencing this *NSB* episode. See Anna Maria Fagnoni, 'Oriental eremitical motifs in the *Navigatio Sancti Brendani*' in Burgess and Strijbosch, *The Brendan legend*, pp 53–79, at pp 68, 76–8. Original (Guglielmetti and Orlandi, *La navigazione*, digital folder 2127 [XXVI]. Original: '*Vae mihi, qui porto habitum monachicum, et sub me constituti sunt multi sub nomine illius ordinis, cum video modo in angelico statu hominem in carne adhuc sedentem illaesum a vitiis corporis.*' *Cui ait vir Dei: 'O venerabilis pater, quanta et qualia mirabilia Deus ostendit tibi quae nulli sanctorum patrum manifestavit! Et tu dicis in corde tuo non esse te dignum monachicum portare habitum, et tu cum sis maior quam monachus! Monachus vero labore manuum suarum utitur et vestitur. Deus autem de suis secretis per septem annos pascit te cum tua familia et induit; ego vero miser sedeo sicut avis in ista petra, nudus excepto meos pilos.*'

> Brendan: 'Alas for me who wears a monk's habit and has many owing allegiance to me by virtue of being monks: here I see sitting before me a man already in the angelic state, untouched by the vices of the body, although he is still in human flesh.'
>
> The man of God said to him: 'O venerable father, how great and marvellous are the wonders that God has shown you that he did not show to any of the holy fathers! You say in your heart that you are not worthy to carry the habit of a monk. But you are greater than a monk! A monk uses the labour of his hands with which to feed and clothe himself. But God from his own secret supplies feeds and clothes both you and your companions for seven years. And I, unhappy, sit here like a bird on this rock, naked but for my hair.'

This single passage reveals the recurrent crux of monastic life which is a theme that permeates the entire the Brendan cycle.[37] Which is the best path to follow, a *vita activa* or *vita contemplativa*, or both, if a monk occasionally withdraws from the world? If following a *vita contemplativa*, how extreme should it be? In *NSB*, Paul the Hermit, despite his extreme asceticism, does not recommend it, but on the contrary, praises Brendan for his adventures. Extremism can become destructive and this is not necessarily the path of a monastic life.[38] In addition, this passage is replete with monastic language: *miles Christi*, *habitus monachicum*, *in corde tuo*, *labore*, *Deus*, *familia tua*, *ego miser*. How does this passage translate into the later texts? The Latin lives (*Codex Insulensis* and *Codex Salmanticensis*[1]) retain the *NSB* text with minor changes.[39] The *Valle Crucis* life omits the conversation while *Codex Salmanticensis*[2] changes the narrative altogether.[40] Paul the Hermit, not named in the latter text, welcomes the visitors to his island with joy as their arrival heralds his release to the real Paradise. He prays with them and feeds them, and then dies. Brendan expresses a wish to stay on his island but this cannot happen. The main monastic element in this version relates to the canonical hours and prayer: *Hora vero tercia, sonante simbalo, laudes dicunt divinas, fixis in Deum mentibus.* The *Second Irish life* also retains the passage using the common terms of *manach*, *aibítt mhanaigh imum* ('wearing a monk's habit') and a few lines later *do hoiledh meisi i mainistir Pattraicc* ('I was formed in Patrick's monastery').[41] Paul the Hermit had been a monk in the 'monastery of Saint Patrick' where he had looked after the cemetery of the brothers and where

37 For a discussion of the audiences the various texts might have had in mind, see Jude S. Mackley, *The legend of St Brendan. A comparative study of the Latin and Anglo-Norman versions* (Leiden, 2008), pp 17–20. 38 For further thoughts on the meaning of Greek ἀσκητὴς, Latin *askētēs* 'practitioner, athlete' which in scholarly language was transformed in ascetic(ism), see Diem, 'The limitations of asceticism'. 39 Plummer, *VSH*, i, p.131 §lxi; Heist, *VSH Salm.*, p. 75 §47. 40 Plummer, ii, pp 289–90 §§xlix–li; Heist, *VSH Salm.*, pp 328–9 §§11–12. 41 Plummer, *BNnÉ*, i, pp 68–9; ii, p. 67 §§110–12.

he encountered Patrick who instructed him to embark on a sea voyage. Tending to the monks' cemetery or even doing circuits of the cemetery is a theme that occurs occasionally in saints' lives. When Molua of Clonfert was going around the monastery's cemetery (*circumiens leuicianum*), he came upon four brothers behind the shrine (*sanctuarium*) that was located there, who were planning a pilgrimage. Teaching them the lesson of stability, he told them that no matter how far they went, they would be buried in that cemetery, and thus they remained in their monastery (*stabiles in suo monasterio postea permanserunt*).[42]

Two further passages from the *NSB* are worth examining in the context of monastic life as perceived by its author/compiler(s). The first episode comes at the beginning of the text when Brendan is visited by Barrind (of Kilbarron, Co. Donegal) who tells him about Mernóc's monastery on an island near Slieve League, Co. Donegal. Mernóc had wished to live a solitary life but was followed onto his island by others. The description of Mernóc's community as they run to greet the visitors corresponds with other depictions of the layout of Irish monasteries:[43]

> As we were crossing in a boat to the island the brothers came, like bees swarming, from their various cells to meet us. Their housing was indeed scattered but they lived together as one in faith, hope and charity. They ate together and they all joined together for the divine office in one church. They are given nothing to eat but fruit, nuts, roots and other greens. But after compline each remained in his own cell until the cocks crowed or the bell was struck.

Despite their separate living quarters and their isolation on an island, this was a community whose world revolved around *opus Dei* – the liturgy of the Divine Office – and following all the fundamental prerequisites for a successful monastic community, best expressed in the terms *fraternitas*, *unitas*, *cor unum et anima una* and *caritas*. The reference to compline (*post completorium*) may echo knowledge of the Benedictine *cursus*, although it does not necessarily reflect an Irish custom.[44] The tension between coenobitic life and a more reclusive life also appears in the Barrind episode. Barrind and Mernóc set off to seek the Promised

42 Plummer, *VSH*, ii, p. 219 §xxxvii. Regarding the physical evidence for pathways in monastic cemeteries, see Roberta Gilchrist and Barney Sloane, *Requiem. The medieval monastic cemetery in Britain* (London, 2005), pp 36–40. 43 Selmer, *Navigatio*, pp 4–5 §1; O'Meara, *Voyage of Saint Brendan*, p. 3 §1. Original (Guglielmetti and Orlandi, *La navigazione*, digital folder 1265 [I]). Original: *Navigantibus nobis in praedictam insulam occurrerunt obviam sicut examen apum ex diversis cellulis fratres. Erat enim habitatio eorum sparsa; tamen unanimiter illorum conversatio in spe et fide et caritate, una refectio, ad opus Dei una ecclesia perficiendum. Nihil aliud cibi ministratur nisi poma et nuces atque radices et cetera generes herbarum. Fratres post completorium in suas singulas cellulas usque ad gallorum cantus seu pulsum campanae [permanserunt].* 44 Ó Clabaigh, 'Beneticines in medieval and early modern Ireland', pp 81–2.

Land of the Saints and when they returned Mernóc's monks rebuked them for leaving them alone:[45]

> Why, fathers, have you left your sheep wandering in this wood without a shepherd? We knew of our abbot going away from us frequently somewhere or other – but we did not know where – and staying sometimes there for a month, sometimes for a fortnight or a week or more or less.

This might also be a rebuke directed at an abbot who for reasons other than following periods of a *vita contemplativa* is far too busy following a *vita activa*. Once more, there is an echo in the text of *RB* on the qualities of an abbot in which the metaphor of the shepherd and his flock occurs consistently.[46] The *Codex Insulensis* life's description of Mernóc's island monastery tallies with *NSB*,[47] although Mernóc's monastery is called a *heremitorium*, a relatively rare word for a hermitage.[48] The *Second Irish life* similarly follows *NSB* while maintaining its own narrative style:[49]

> And when we reached the island, the brethren came to us out of their cells, like a swarm of bees; and though their dwellings were divided from one another, there was no division in their converse, or counsel, or affection. And their only victuals were apples and nuts, and roots of such kinds of herbs as they found. And the brethren used to go to their separate cells from compline till cock-crow.

The second passage in *NSB* that pertains particularly to monastic practices is the description of the community of the abbot Ailbe. Brendan and his companions land on an island and are met by an elder (*senex*) who 'prostrated himself three times on the ground before embracing the man of God' (*qui tribus*

45 Selmer, *Navigatio*, p. 7 §1; O'Meara, *Voyage of Saint Brendan*, p. 5 §1. Original (Guglielmetti and Orlandi, *La navigazione*, digital folder 1294 [I]. Original: *Cur, patres, dimisistis vestras oues sine pastore in ista silva errantes? Novimus autem abbatem nostram frequenter a nobis discedere in aliquam partem, sed nescimus in quam, et ibidem demorari aliquando unum mensem, aliquando duas ebdomadas seu unam ebdomadam vel plus minusve.* **46** *RB*: Chap. 2.7–9: 'The abbot must, therefore, be aware that the shepherd will bear the blame wherever the father of the household finds that the sheep have yielded no profit. Still, if he has faithfully shepherded a restive and disobedient flock, always striving to cure their unhealthy ways, it will be otherwise: the shepherd will be acquitted at the Lord's judgement'. **47** Plummer, *VSH*, i, p. 105 §xiii. **48** Du Cange, *Gloss.*, sub *Eremitae* http://ducange.enc.sorbonne.fr/EREMITAE accessed 13 January 2021. **49** Plummer, *BNnÉ*, i, p. 49; ii, p. 49 §30. Original: *Ocus 'ar ndol dochum an oilein duinn, tangattar na braithre chuccainn asa selladhaibh amach, amail saithe bech; 7 ger sccáilte ind aittrebh sin, do ba nemh-sccaoilte a cconuersaid, 7 a ccoccús, 7 a ngradh. Ocus ni raibhe do bhethaid aca acht ubhla, 7 cna, 7 fremha cecha cenéoil luibhe da b-aghdais. Ocus no theiccdis na braitre dochum a selladh féin ó chompleitt go gairm an choiligh.*

vicibus se ad terram prostravit antequam oscularetur virum Dei).[50] Silence was part of the island community's rule (*decretum loci*) as was ceremonial ritual: they were met by eleven brothers with reliquaries, crosses and hymns, 'chanting the versicle: "Rise, saints of God, from your dwellings and go to meet truth. Sanctify the place, bless the people, and graciously keep us your servants in peace".' This antiphon is sung when processing with relics particularly during the ceremony of consecrating or dedicating a church.[51] Further bodily gestures convey without words that Brendan and his companions were welcome: the father of the monastery (*pater monasterii*) embraced Brendan and the community embraced his companions. Then, significantly:[52]

> When they had exchanged the kiss of peace, they led them to the monastery as the custom is in western parts to conduct brothers in this way with prayers. Afterwards the abbot of the monastery with his monks washed the feet of the guests and chanted: 'A new commandment.' When this was done the abbot led them in great silence to the refectory. A signal was sounded, hands were washed, and then the abbot made them sit down.

From the outset, gesture and the use of the body became integral to monastic communication and prayer.[53] Prostration could be a sign of deference, humility, honour, penance and silent prayer while embracing or exchanging a kiss of peace, a sign of fraternity. As noted by Selmer there are echoes of *RB*, especially on the reception of guests (Chapter 53), in this episode,[54] and in the context of Irish monasticism by the eighth century, Follett's observations on the *NSB* are judicious:[55]

> In this immensely popular work, cenobitical, anchoritical, and eremitical monks engage in ascetic pursuits entirely consistent with our earlier

50 Selmer, *Navigatio*, p. 29 §12; O'Meara, *Voyage of Saint Brendan*, p. 26 §12; Guglielmetti and Orlandi, *La navigazione*, digital folder 1605 [XII]. Original: (Guglielmetti and Orlandi, *La navigazione*, digital folder 1619 [XII]). Original: *cum capsis et crucibus et ymnis dicentes istud capitulum: 'Surgite, sancti Dei, de mansionibus vestris et proficiscimini obviam veritati. Locum sanctificate, plebem benedicite, et nos famulos vestros in pace custodire dignemini.'* 51 *Pontificale Romanorum: de ecclesia dedicatione seu consecratione* http://www.liturgialatina.org/pontificale/041.htm accessed 15 January 2021. 52 Selmer, *Navigatio*, p. 31 §12; O'Meara, *Voyage of Saint Brendan*, p. 27 §12. Original (Guglielmetti and Orlandi, *La navigazione*, digital folder 1633 [XII]). Original: *Data pace vicissim, duxerunt illos in monasterium, sicut mos est in occidentalibus partibus ducere fratres, per orationes. Post haec abbas monasterii cum monachis coeperunt lavare pedes hospitum et cantare: 'Mandatum novum.' His finitis, cum magno silentio excepit illos ad refectorium. Pulsato signo lavatisque manibus fecit omnes residere.* 53 Columba Stewart, 'The practices of monastic prayer: origins, evolution, and tensions' in Philip Sellew (ed.), *Living for eternity. The White Monastery and its neighbourhood. Proceedings of a symposium at the University of Minnesota, Minneapolis, March 6–9, 2003* (Minneapolis, 2009 internet version), pp 97–108 http://egypt.cla.umn.edu/eventsr.html accessed 16 January 2021. 54 Selmer, *Navigatio*, p. 87, n. 44. 55 Follett, *Céli Dé in Ireland*, pp 86–7.

sources against the backdrop of a detailed monastic office that shows the influence of the Benedictine Rule. However fantastic the story, the monasticism of the *Navigatio* reflects an ideal that was very much alive.

When it comes to the other versions of Brendan's life, did this ideal monasticism survive simply as a literary trope left unchanged even though monastic institutions and practices had changed? The *Codex Insulensis* and *Codex Salmanticensis* (*Vita 1*) lives adhere fairly closely to the *NSB* text relating the episode with the community of Ailbe,[56] as does the *Second Irish life*, although it is abridged and merged with the Paradise of Birds episode.[57] One nod towards a later type of monasticism occurs when describing those inhabiting the monastery in the middle of the island as *ord arsaidh eladhanta cunnail craibhtech innte* ('a venerable wise decorous and devout order in it'). While the term *ord* (borrowed from Latin *ordo*) 'order, sequence, degree, rank, rule' is attested in texts from the early Irish glosses onwards, its attestation meaning 'a religious order or community' is rare and does not occur until the late medieval period.[58] The version of this episode recorded in the *Valle Crucis* life, which probably dates to an early thirteenth-century Cistercian milieu, is peculiar to this manuscript and probably reflects Anglo-Norman or Welsh twelfth-century material culture.[59] The original depiction of the monks meeting Brendan and his companions with reliquaries, crosses and hymns is transformed into a sumptuous account that flies in the face of the simple ascetic life of the community of Ailbe. The *Valle Crucis* life emanates from a very different and florid written tradition:[60]

> The abbot orders the relics to be conveyed to the church, namely, crosses, shrines, valuable woven fabrics glittering with gold and gems, with thuribles sparkling with gold and precious stones. Indeed their vestments glittered with gold, which Arabia could not match. These were decorated with large carnelian stones, topaz and jasper; brighter jaspers do not exist. All the monks wearing white leave with the abbot …

In contrast to the spiritual abbot who can have such a painful conversation with Paul the Hermit about his monastic calling, the later lives – if the interpolated texts of *NSB* are excluded – are much closer to the forceful saints

56 Plummer, *VSH*, i, pp 116–19 §§xxx–xxxv; Heist, *VSH Salm.*, pp 60–2 §§15–18. **57** Plummer, *BNnÉ*, i, pp 57–9; ii, pp 56–8 §§67–73. **58** *DIL* sv. **59** Bodleian *Summary Catalogue*, vol. 2 part 2, p. 657 https://medieval.bodleian.ox.ac.uk/images/ms/aaq/aaq0016.gif accessed 17 January 2021. **60** Plummer, *VSH*, ii, p. 278 §xxvi. *Abbas ecclesie reliquias iubet exportare, cruces 'silicet', scrinia, texta simul preciosa auro et gemmis fulgentia, cum turribulis auro et lapidibus preciosis nitentibus. Vestimenta quidem eorum auro micabant, quo melius Arabia non habebat. Sardinibus quidam magnis decorantur, et topaziis et iaspidibus; clariores uero iaspides non habent. Monachi omnes indutis albis cum abbate exeunt …*

whose heroic biographies follow a particular template: born to nobility, recognized as exceptional from birth and fostered to a bishop who prepared him for a career in the church. This is best illustrated by looking at two themes, Brendan formulating a rule, and his relations with other saints. Once the saint had learned the scriptures, he 'wished to write out and learn the rule of the saints of Ireland' (*dob ail leis riaghail naomh Erenn do sscriobhadh 7 d'foglaim*).[61] His master Bishop Erc advised him to learn the rules and to bring them back, at which point Erc would ordain him. He visited his foster-mother Íte of Killeedy who advised him not to learn from women or virgins lest it cause scandal. He then visited Iarlaith, a devout man (*fer cráibdech*) in Connacht where he increased his knowledge of the rules. At Mag nAí, a territory around Rathcroghan, Co. Roscommon, an angel met him on the road. The Irish and Latin lives differ in their style in relating this episode:

> *Second Irish life*:[62]
> Leaving Iarlaithe there, Brendan proceeded to Magh nAí. An angel met him on the road, and said to him: 'Write down,' said he, 'from my mouth the words of devotion.' Brendan wrote from the mouth of the angel all the rules (*ríacchla*) of the holy Church, and all these rules are still extant.
>
> *Codex Insulensis life*:[63]
> Afterwards Brendan, like an assiduous bee, gathering flowers from a variety of precedents of the mighty works of saints, in his heart, as if pouring honey into a hive, he concealed in his memory the honey of charity and the wax of humility. Leaving the holy bishop Iarlaith behind, he reached Mag nAí, where an angel of God appearing to him said: 'Take this charter (*sume cartam*),[64] and write the rule (*scribe normam*) for your way of life according to God's will.' Thereupon Brendan wrote, with the angel dictating, an ecclesiastical rule (*scripsit Brandanus … regulam ecclesiasticam*) essential to maintain a religious life, which till today remains in some places.

The *NSB* does not refer to an existing common monastic rule. On the island of the community of Ailbe, the rule of silence is called a *decretum loci* and the

61 Plummer, *BNnÉ*, i, p. 47; ii, p. 47 §18. **62** Ibid., i, p. 48; ii, p. 48 §23. Original: *Iar ffccbháil Iarlaithe annsin, gabhais Brenainn roimhe fo Magh nÁi. Teccmaidh immorro aingiol dó forsan sliccidh, 7 isedh atbert friss: 'Scriobh', ar se, 'briathra in chrabaidh uaim si'. Scriobais Brenainn a gion an aingil ina huile ríacchla na noemh-eccalsa, 7 maraid fós na riaghla sin huile.* **63** Plummer, *VSH*, i, p. 103 §x. *Post hec sanctus Brandanus, uelut apis argumentosa, ex diuersis sanctorum exemplis uirtutum colligens flores, in corde suo, tanquam in alueari quodam mellifluo, mel caritatis et ceram humiltatis recondebat. Recedens quoque a sancto pontifice Iarlatheo, peruenit ad campum Ae, vbi angelus Domini ei apparens dixit: 'Sume cartam, et scribe tibi vivendi secundum uoluntatem Dei normam.' Scripsit ibi Brandanus, angelo dictante, regulam ecclesiasticam ad custodiam uite religiose necessariam, usque hodie in nonnullis locis manet.* **64** The term *carta*

community leading Brendan and his followers to the monastery do so *sicut mos est in occidentalibus partibus*.[65] The liturgical calendar and the Divine Office are to the forefront in *NSB*, a message expressed clearly by one of the birds on the Paradise of Birds:[66]

> God has ordained for you four places for four periods of the year until seven years of your pilgrimage are over, namely: Maunday Thursday with your stewart who is present every year; you will celebrate Easter on the back of a beast; and with us from the paschal feast to the octave of Pentecost; you will celebrate Christmas with the community of Ailbe, Pentecost.

The use of the terms *ríagal*, *regula*, *carta* and *norma* speak to a period later than *NSB*, as does the idea of Brendan drawing up a rule essential to maintain religious life. Leaving aside the angelic intervention, the idea that this rule was devised by Brendan consulting all the saints of Ireland appears to echo vaguely the great exercises of Benedict of Aniane or of the tenth-century English *Regularis Concordia* agreed at the Council of Winchester in 970. Although details of Brendan's rule are not provided, if it ever existed, nevertheless it could be argued fairly that the compilers of final versions of the Irish and Latin lives, probably writing sometime during the late twelfth century,[67] reflect contemporary monastic norms. If compiled in Clonfert – although it has to be admitted that Clonfert does not feature very prominently – a possible context might be the episcopacy of Petrus Ua Mórda, bishop of Clonfert and abbot of the Cistercian house at Boyle (Co. Roscommon) who drowned in the Shannon in 1171. The audience of such a milieu would understand the full significance of their founder codifying various rules into one standard rule that was conveyed to him by an angel. It would also be familiar with the florid language comparing Brendan with a bee whose mind learned 'the honey of charity and wax of humility' (*mel caritatis et ceram humiltatis*) evoking the language of Bernard of Clairvaux's tract on the Passion of the Lord and the mystic vine in which he includes many metaphors about bees, flowers, honey and wax with among other concepts, charity and humility.[68]

could mean 'charter, constitution, letter' in this context. **65** Selmer, *Navigatio*, pp 30–1 §12; Guglielmetti and Orlandi, *La navigazione*, digital folder 1633 [XII]). **66** Selmer, *Navigatio*, pp 42–3 §15; O'Meara, *Voyage of Saint Brendan*, p. 38 §15; Guglielmetti and Orlandi, *La navigazione*, digital folder 1784 [XV]. Original: *Deus proposuit vobis quatuor loca per quatuor tempora usque dum finiantur septem anni peregrinationis vestrae, idest: in coena Domini cum vestro procuratore, qui praesens est omni anno; in doro beluae Pascha celebrabitis; nobiscum festa paschalia usque in octavas Pentencosten; apud familiam Ailbei navitatem Domini celebrabitis.* **67** Mac Mathúna, '*Irish life of Saint Brendan*', pp 155–8. **68** For example, see Bernard's Sermon 8 on the Song of Songs where he compares the Holy Spirit to 'the bee carrying its burden of wax and honey' (*qui instar apis ceram portantis et me*) (The Matheson Trust for the Study of

As seen from Brendan's approach to his spiritual foster-mother Íte regarding the codification of rules, where she made it clear that it should not involve virgins or women, he occasionally sought the advice of holy women throughout his life and while this motif occurs in other lives, Brendan is shown as being particularly close to Íte. She does not feature in *NSB*, a text that is devoid of women. In the *Codex Insulensis* life in a crisis of conscience having carelessly caused the drowning of a young man, Brendan sought advice from all the saints of Ireland and of Íte who instructed him to go to Britain to instruct the souls of men there. Hence he went to consult with Gildas to repent for his perceived sin.[69] Almost as significant as Íte's instructions to Brendan is his encounter with Brigit who like Íte seems to admonish him for his lack of *stabilitas*. Brendan came across two flying monsters involved in a combat, one of which in a human voice beseeched the other to let it be 'in the name of St Brigit'. Taken aback that the monster did not seek his assistance, Brendan went to Brigit to ask her why this had happened. The Irish and Latin lives differ slightly in how this is expressed and the differences are worth noting as they reflect the divergence in style between the two traditions, the Latin more formal than the florid vernacular:[70]

> *Latin:*
> And she responded: 'I will tell you, father, the true cause of this matter. From the very day that I first put myself into my Christ's hand, I never bowed my mind to worldly business. You, however, have placed yourself frequently in temptation, and the world goes after you.'
>
> *Irish:*
> 'What more good do you do for God than I, when the monsters entreat you, though absent, and me, though present, they left uninvoked.' Brigit said to Brendan: 'Make your confession.' 'I declare,' said he, 'that I never crossed seven furrows without turning my mind to God. Make your confession,' said Brendan. 'I confess,' said Brigit, 'that since I first fixed my mind on God, I have never taken it off, and never will, till doom. You, however,' said she, 'are so constantly incurring great danger by sea and land, that you must give your attention to it, and it is not because you forget God that your mind is fixed on Him only at every third furrow.'

Comparative Literatures, St Bernard of the Song of Songs (Latin text: Sermo VIII), p. 11 para. 6 https://www.themathesontrust.org/library/st-bernard-on-the-song. Accessed 1 October 2023. **69** Plummer, *VSH*, i, pp 140–1 §§lxxxi–iii; *BNnÉ*, i, pp 82–3, ii, 80–1 §liv–lv; Heist, *VSH Salm.*, p. 329 §13. **70** Plummer, *VSH*, i, p. 143 §lxxxvi; *BNnÉ*, i, pp 85–6; ii, 83 §lvi. Original Latin: *Et respondit illa: 'Tibi, pater, veram causam huius rei indicabo. Ex illo enim die quo semel dedi me in manus Christi mei, mentem meam nunquam in res mundanas flexi. Tu autem in temptationibus frequenter positus es, et mundus post te uadit.'* Original Irish: *'Cidh do maith', ol sé, 'doghní si do Dia seochamsa, an tan rod guidhet in bleidhmil tú, 7 tusa ecnairc, 7 meisi frecnairc, 7 rom fáccaibh cen atach.' Atbert Brigit fri Brénainn: 'Tabair do chubhais.' 'Atberim', or*

Even though Brigit is a national saint, a slight step above Brendan, this admonishment is somewhat unexpected, especially for lives that were compiled or revised during the twelfth century although echoing an episode in the life of Brigit.[71] This, along with Íte's various reprimands, gives a female voice to matters relating to monasticism, in this instance, monastic stability and mental detachment from the world and its affairs. Finally, Brendan visits another woman, his saintly sister Bríg at Enach Dúin (Annaghdown, Co. Galway) where he dies. Prior to his death, the siblings converse.[72] Brendan makes it clear to Bríg that his body is to be buried in his own monastery at Clonfert: '*Locus iste virorum est, non mulierum*' ('That place is for men, not women'). This episode may relate to a general situation regarding the burial places of female and male religious, although as the founder of Clonfert Brendan's grave would hardly have been elsewhere. It might also allude to some contemporary issue between Annaghdown and Clonfert in the late twelfth century, as both churches were dedicated to St Brendan.[73]

The Brendan cycle, consisting of the *NSB* and the *vitae*, contains much material that can be dismissed as fanciful and fictional or, more correctly, as an allegory depending largely on classical and Christian sources.[74] Yet it also contains much substantial material that is likely to reflect both the ideal and lived experience of Irish monks and nuns over many centuries. The great difficulty with these texts, and particularly *NSB*, is how to extract genuine lived monastic experience in Ireland from potential external influences or lived monastic experiences observed elsewhere.

From Darerca to Modwenna: the dossier of a female community

The dossier of St Darerca or Monenna of Killevy, Co. Armagh, matches the Brendan cycle to a certain degree in that both span a period from perhaps the eighth to the twelfth century. Yet they also offer a different perspective: the Monenna texts are all written in fairly scholarly Latin, two of them cover traditions gathered from Ireland, England and Scotland, and their subject is a woman and her life as a *virgo venerabilis* ('a venerable virgin').[75] In addition, three

sé,' 'nach dechadhus tar secht niommaire riamh, gan mo mhenmain i nDia. Tabair si do chubas', ar Brenainn. 'Dobheirim', or Brigitt, 'ó dorattus mo mhenmain i nDía, nach tardas ass, 7 nach tibher go brath. Tusa immorro', or sí, 'atá dia mheince fogheibe gábadh mor mara 7 tire, ní fhétta gana thabairt dot úidh; 7 ni haire go ndermaittea do Dhia beith do mhenma gacha tres iomaire ann …'.
71 Mac Mathúna, '*Irish life of Saint Brendan*', p. 158. **72** Heist, *VSH Salm.*, p. 331 §17. **73** See pp 378–9. **74** Emanuel Grosu, '*Navigatio Sancti Brendani abbatis*: allegory of the characters', *Philobiblon. Transylvanian Journal of Multidisciplinary Research in the Humanities* 22:1 (2017), 7–18. **75** Mario Esposito (ed.), 'Conchubrani vita sanctae Monennae', *Proceedings of the Royal Irish Academy* 28C (1910), 202–51; Heist, *VSH Salm.*, pp 83–95; Ulster Society for Latin Medieval Studies, 'The life of Saint Monenna by Conchubranus Parts I–III', *Seanchas Ard Mhacha* 9:2 (1979), 250–73; 10:1 (1980–1), 117–41; 10:2 (1982), 426–54; Ingred Sperber (ed.), 'The life of St Monenna or Darerca of Killevy' in Hughes and Nolan, *Armagh history and society*, pp 63–97; Robert Bartlett (ed. and trans.), *Geoffrey of Burton. Life and miracles of St Modwenna*. Oxford Medieval Texts (Oxford, 2002); Harrington,

Latin hymns in her honour survive.[76] A poem in Irish *Moninne caid arcanam* ('Holy Moninne, we sing [to you]') is included in early saints' genealogies.[77] These texts cast some light on the ideal and institutional attributes of female monasticism in early Ireland and their approach to virginity, the capacity of women to be educated in the liturgy, on the dangers to a community of women, and on their sanctity, toughness and virility.

Chastity, virginity and the dangers of consorting with men surface occasionally in the lives of Monenna. The life preserved in the *Codex Salmanticensis* is the shortest and probably earliest surviving version, possibly dating to the eighth or ninth century.[78] Although Monenna is described as a *virgo venerabilis*, *virgo Christi*, *famula Dei* throughout the text and is known by tradition to have looked at no man (*ut certissime fertur, nullum fuit intuita virum*),[79] the theme of chastity and virginity does not dominate this text. Unlike the early lives of Brigit, the *Salmanticensis* text concentrates on Monenna's constant wish to withdraw further and further from the world, in the first instance from her parental home and later from her noisy neighbours in Fochart (Faughart, Co. Louth) to the mountainside at Killevy.[80] It was said of Monenna that it was 'the habit of the bride of Christ to travel at night rather than in daytime, so that the sight of worldly things would not corrupt [her] dovelike appearance' (*moris enim erat sponse Christi de nocte plus quam de die ambulare, ne columbinos aspectus rerum humanarum species corumperet*).[81] If she needed to visit the sick or to free prisoners from captivity, she travelled by night and if she met anyone on her way she covered her face with a veil (*velata facie alloqui solebat*).[82] Like Brigit, she was inclined to reduce herself and her companions to poverty by giving everything to the poor, indeed on a number of occasions incurring the wrath of the same Brigit by her extreme rejection of worldly materials. Monenna's relations with Brigit are instructive of the period when the *Salmanticensis* version was written, and possibly of the source(s) on which it drew.[83] Given that Killevy was within

Women in a Celtic church, pp 82–3, 217–20. **76** David Howlett (ed.), 'Three poems about Monenna', *Peritia* 19 (2005), 1–19. **77** Ó Riain, *CGSH*, pp 166–7 §718.1. **78** Mario Esposito argued that this version dated to the early seventh century, see Mario Esposito, 'The sources of Conchubranus' life of St Monenna', *English Historical Review* 35 (1920), 71–8, at p. 76. This date was challenged by Alexander Boyle who argued for a date *c*.822, see Alexander Boyle, 'The list of abbesses in Conchubranus' life of St Monenna', *Ulster Journal of Archaeology* 34 (1971), 84–6. Sperber decided on a date in the late eighth or early ninth century, see Sperber, 'Life of St Monenna', p. 68. Elva Johnston, 'Transforming women in Irish hagiography', *Peritia* 9 (1995), 197–220, at p. 211 suggested that it dates to the late seventh/early eighth century when Gnáthat was abbess of Kildare and of Killevy and that this is reflected in the relationship between Brigit and Monenna. **79** Heist, *VSH Salm.*, p. 87 §14; Sperber, 'Life of St Monenna', p. 72 §14. **80** Heist, *VSH Salm.*, p. 84 §3; Sperber, 'Life of St Monenna', p. 69 §3; Heist, *VSH Salm.*, pp 88–9 §18; Sperber, 'Life of St Monenna', p. 73 §18. **81** Heist, *VSH Salm.*, p. 88 §16; Sperber, 'Life of St Monenna', pp 72–3 §16. **82** Heist, *VSH Salm.*, p. 87 §14; Sperber, 'Life of St Monenna', pp 72 §14. **83** If Elva Johnston is correct ('Transforming women', p. 211) some of these sources could date to as

the ambit of Armagh, it is not surprising that Monenna was reputedly baptized by St Patrick, who arranged for a pious priest to instruct her. Spending some time in Kildare, at Brigit's request, she became the gate-keeper of the guest-house (*fit portaria hospitalis*) and such was her humility that 'she was thought to be second only to Brigit in holiness of life, honesty of character, and grace of virtues' (*ut etiam post Brigidam vite sanctitate et morum honestate et virtutum gratia secunda putaretur*).[84] She also performed the classic miracles wrought by many Irish saints such as saving a calf from wolves, causing food and beer to appear in time to feed guests, and correctly guessing a sin committed by one of her companions that was causing difficulties in her community.

The portrayal of Monenna's monastic lifestyle differs from that of Brigit, the head of a powerful monastery. As noted earlier, Monenna's inclination was towards seclusion, and although she was surrounded by a community, at times she was so detached that she neglected them and on one occasion they were in danger of starvation during a famine.[85] She is compared to the early hermits (*ita namque priorum heremitarum vestigia secuta fuit*) in her battles with demons and her manual labour which, following an existing patristic topos, meant that 'she had a man's soul in a woman's body' (*virilem enim animum in femineo gerebat corpore*).[86] Her relics venerated after her death were her hoe, spade, leather garment and sheepskin, possessions that occur in the more extensive list of belongings left by a *manach* – a monk or possibly a monastic tenant – after his death.[87] The sheepskin has echoes of St Antony of Egypt's sheepskin cloaks, one of which he bequeathed to St Athanasius, the other to St Serapion. It could be argued that Monenna's virility is best depicted in her dealings with those in authority, not unlike Brigit, where despite their apparent subservient status, they often interacted determinedly with bishops and kings. Seeking instruction and an episcopal protector, she and her companions followed Bishop Íbar from the western seaboard to Becc Ériu (Begerin, Co. Wexford), a relationship that ended not altogether peacefully as Íbar landed Monenna with a local noble girl to be reared 'in monastic discipline' (*monasterialibus nutriendum disciplinis*). As

early as the seventh century. **84** Heist, *VSH Salm.*, p. 84 §§4–5; Sperber, 'Life of St Monenna', p. 69 §§4–5. **85** Heist, *VSH Salm.*, p. 89 §21; Sperber, 'Life of St Monenna', p. 74 §21. **86** Heist, *VSH Salm.*, p. 89 §19; Sperber, 'Life of St Monenna', p. 74 §19; Johnston, 'Transforming women'; Dorothy Ann Bray, 'The manly spirit of St Monenna' in Ronald Black, William Gillies and Roibeard Ó Maolalaigh (eds), *Celtic connections. Proceedings of the 10th international congress of Celtic studies* (East Linton, 1999), pp 171–81. **87** Kuno Meyer, 'Mitteilungen aus irischen Handschriften: Hinterlassenschaft eines Mönches', *Zeitschrift für keltische philologie* 6 (1908), 271; Etchingham, *Church organisation*, pp 441–2. A monk's belongings are listed in this text as a cloak (*bratt*), tunic (*léine*), *a chaindten foirpe* (?), a pillow of down (*cerchaill clúimhe*), a seat of hide for choir (*geimhin claisi*), *a chris cuipre* (a … belt), sandals (*a dá ass*), two keys (*a di eochra*), gloves (*a dí lámann*), a staff (*fidbocc*), a spade (*fec*), a shovel (*slúasat*), a basket (*cummain*), a dish (*mías*), a drinking-vessel (*ardán*), a yearling bullock (*colpach fhirenn*), a pack-animal (*iuman*), bacon fat (*saillméth*), hundred loaves of half a bushel

predicted by the saint, this girl caused friction between her community and the girl's kin to such an extent that Monenna moved back to the north.[88] She also withstood demands of the aristocracy. As she was approaching death, the kings and nobility of Muirthemne, Cuailnge and Coba pleaded with her to live for a further year, offering her whatever she requested. She responded that this was not possible as God had already sent SS Peter and Paul as venerable guests to bring her soul with them and she exhorted them not to venture across borders to destroy other regions. Contrary to her own exhortation, she also promised them that if they carried her relics into battle against enemies who came to devastate their lands that victory would be theirs, echoing similar protection guaranteed by Brigit to the Leinstermen and Colum Cille to the Uí Néill.[89]

What form of female monasticism does the *Salmanticensis* life of Monenna present? While taking account of the many stereotypical motifs and miracle tales in the life, a few interesting and to some extent surprising details relating to female monasticism emerge from the text. Monenna began her monastic life at home with her parents but she withdrew from her kin as she feared that interaction with them would weaken her resolve. Hence her first step was to become a 'house ascetic' – elsewhere described as a *puella Dei* or *religiosa puella* –,[90] a decision the text puts down to the fact that there were no nunneries among her newly converted kin (*sed in sua gente, licet ad fidem conversa, nullas monialium mansiones aspiciens*).[91] This may be a retrospective assumption but not necessarily incorrect. Once she gathered a community around her it was small and surprisingly mobile, moving around Ireland, and settling in various places before finally retreating to their hermitage in her home territory in Killevy. While mainly described as virgins, she attracted a wider section of the female population, characterized by the description of her stay at *Árd Conais* (a site possibly in Co. Wexford) where Bishop Íbar lived. This is likely to be a fairly accurate reflection of an early female community:[92]

> After this, she returned to the aforementioned bishop and lived under his protection in Árd Conais, and, as their instructress in rectitude, she showed to the very many virgins and widows who were assembled in that place, and likewise to the queens and noble matrons who were joining her, the rule of a good life, in words as well as in examples.

(*cétbairgen lethmech*), twelve black vessels of ale (*dá dublestur déc*). **88** Heist, *VSH Salm.*, p. 86 §10; Sperber, 'Life of St Monenna', p. 71 §10. **89** Heist, *VSH Salm.*, pp 93–4 §§29–31; Sperber, 'Life of St Monenna', pp 77–9 §§29–31; Pádraig Ó Riain (ed.), *Cath Almaine*. Mediaeval and Modern Irish series 25 (Dublin, 1978), pp 6–7 §10: *As-bert co n-accas Brigit ós cinn Laigen: at-ches dno Colum Cille ós cinn Úa Néill.* **90** Magnani, 'Female house ascetics' in *CHMM*, p. 217. **91** Heist, *VSH Salm.*, p. 84 §3; Sperber, 'Life of St Monenna', p. 69 §3. **92** Sperber, 'Life of St Monenna', p. 70 §8; Heist, *VSH Salm.*, p. 85 §8. Original: *Post hec, prefatum episcopum adiens, sub eius tutela in Ard Conays habitavit, virginibus et viduis*

Another unexpected feature, which is much expanded in the other lives, is the value Monenna placed on learning. Not only was she instructed by Patrick and a priest chosen by him, she herself sent one of her companions Brignat to Britain 'to learn the monastic rules at the monastery of Rosnat' ([Brignat] *eam in Brittanium insulam, de Rosnatensi monasterio conversationis monastice regulas accepturum, misisse perhibetur*). Whether Rosnat was Whithorn or not,[93] the significant point is that the author, at least, recognized that women could be educated in reading scriptures, liturgy and monastic rules, which is not the case in the lives of Brigit or Samthann of Clonbroney.

Conchubranus's life of Monenna, while containing much of what is found in the *Salmanticensis* life, belongs to a different milieu. Like the life of Patrick known as the *Vita Tripartita*, Conchubranus divided his narrative into three books and introduced homiletic material worked around lines from the scriptures and psalms, and also around themes such as virginity, the apostolic life and poverty. Stock miracles are included but often with additional moral observations. And of course, unlike the *Salmanticensis* life, Conchubranus incorporates an extensive section on Monenna and her companions' journeys to England and Scotland, and their foundations in these parts. To date, neither Conchubranus nor his origins have been identified, although scholars have tended to date his work to the eleventh or twelfth centuries.[94] There are hints in the text, however, that point towards the origin of Conchubranus's sources and possible connections other than with Killevy and its mother church at Armagh. In his introduction to his twelfth-century life of St Modwenna, the alter ego of Monenna, Geoffrey of Burton-on-Trent relates that in the process of gathering material he sent letters to a bishop in Ireland (*misi literas ad quendam episcopum in Hiberniam*).[95] As a result of his Irish contacts a codex was sent to him that Geoffrey at once praises and condemns: its contents were 'a hidden treasure containing priceless riches' (*thesaurum absconditum continentem diuicias inestimabiles*) but its style was displeasing and 'a disorderly jumble' (*inordinata confusio*). With great toil he drew material 'from the barbarous language of the book and the treasure chests of the Irish, as if from hidden and obscure places' (*ex hoc codice et scriniis Hibernorum … de lingua barbara uelut de obstrusis et abditis*).[96] Who the Irish bishop was who received letters from Geoffrey and where the Irish codex came from is unknown. It might be speculated that as Geoffrey was prior of Winchester cathedral priory between 1107 and 1111 and a Benedictine, it is possible that he may have known Máel Ísu Ua hAinmere (d. 1135) who had been chosen by Walkelin, bishop of Winchester, as bishop of

quampluribus inibi congregatis, nec non et reginis ac nobilibus matronis ad eam undique confluentibus, totius probitatis magistra tam verbis quam excemplis bene vivendi <normam> monastravit. **93** Heist, *VSH Salm.*, p. 91 §25; Charles Thomas, 'Topographical notes: III. *Rosnat*, *Rostat*, and the early Irish church', *Ériu* 22 (1971), 100–6. **94** Esposito, 'Conchubrani vita sanctae Monennae'. **95** Bartlett, *Life and miracles of St Modwenna*, pp 2–3. **96** Ibid.

Waterford in 1096. As noted previously, Máel Ísu was also a Benedictine in Winchester and during his episcopacy corresponded with Anselm of Bec and Canterbury.[97] It is also possible that Geoffrey was acquainted with Samuel Ua hAingliu, bishop of Dublin (d. 1121), originally a monk in St Albans who was also sent back to Ireland by Anselm.[98] A further line of transmission between Geoffrey and Ireland, and especially Dublin, was possibly through Chester where there was a Hiberno-Norse settlement involved in trade across the Irish Sea.[99] Geoffrey's monastery at Burton-on-Trent was located within the bishopric of Chester during most of the twelfth century.[100] Conchubranus's text includes two salient references to a connection with Norse Dublin. Monenna's mother was Coman, daughter of King Dalbranaith who ruled the lands from Dublin to *Regumlech*.[101] Coman is not mentioned in the earlier life. Conchubranus mentions Swords, Co. Dublin twice, once in a strange tale about Cóemgen of Glendalough where Monenna and Cóemgen met to resolve a dispute between them. Included in a list of Monenna's foundations is Swords, located north of Dublin, which was very much within the ambit of the Norse kingdom of Dublin.[102] For example, Gruffudd ap Cynan, king of Gwynedd (d. 1157) spent his childhood there with his Norse mother, Ragnhildr daughter of Amlaíb son of Sitric Silkenbeard and his foster-mother. Given such links, it is not implausible that a copy of Conchubranus's text was sent to Geoffrey through the good offices of the bishop of Dublin, and possibly the Benedictine, Samuel Ua hAingliu. There is a specific reference in Conchubranus's Book 3 to St Benedict in the context of one of Monenna's miracles which puts her on a par with the great abbot:[103]

> For he who once worked through the mighty prophet Elisha also did like things through one Benedict, a monk whose life and virtues were described by Pope Gregory. Now He does not disdain to act also through His handmaiden Monenna, though she dwells at the furthest boundary of the world, so that from the rising sun to its setting His excellent name should be magnified. For in Christ there is neither male nor female, but Christ is all things in all.

97 Bhreathnach, 'Benedictine influence in Ireland'. **98** Martin Rule (ed.), *Eadmeri historia novorum in Anglia* Rolls Series 81 (London, 1884; repr. Cambridge, 2012), pp 73–4. **99** Marie Therese Flanagan, *Irish society, Anglo-Norman settlers, Angevin kingship. Interactions in Ireland in the late twelfth century* (Oxford, 1989), p. 75. **100** Bartlett, *Life and miracles*, p. xxx. **101** Ulster Society, 'Life of St Monenna', I, pp 254–5 §2. **102** Ibid., pp 432–3 §3. **103** Ibid., III, pp 430–3 §2.Original: *Qui enim in Heliseo quondam propheta maximo operatus est per Benedictum quendam monachum similia fecit cuius uita et uirtutes a sancto Gregorio Papa describuntur. Nunc etiam per suam famulam Monennam licet in extremis terrarum finibus sitam facere non dedignatur ut a solis ortu usque ad occasum suum laudabile nomen magnificetur. In Christo enim neque masculus neque femina sed omnia in omnibus Christus* (Gal. 3.28).

Of particular significance with reference to Conchubranus's cultural world is the insertion of English and Scottish material into his *vita*. This is not in the *Salmanticensis* text but the gist of it is succinctly described in a short Latin poem preserved in the BL MS Cleopatra A.II, which also contains Conchubranus's work:[104]

> To Modwenna Ireland gives birth [lit 'rise'], Scotland an end,
> England gives a tomb, God gives the heights of the pole.
> The first land gave life but the second death,
> and the third land gave [her] earth to the earth.
> Longfortin takes away whom the land of Conaille brings forth;
> happy Burton holds the bones of the virgin.

English and Scottish foundations are listed in detail. In Scotland, Conchubranus associates her with St Michael's church 'on the summit of a mountain which is now called Edinburgh' (possibly one and the same as St Margaret's church in Edinburgh Castle), Chilnecase in Galloway (possibly Kilcais in Ayrshire), Dundevenal (Dundonald), Dunbreten (Dumbarton), the fortress at Stirling which had a chapel dedicated to St Michael in its complex, Dunpeleder (Traprain Law), Alyth, Longfortin (?Luncarty), and Eccles near Stirling. In England, Monenna is associated with Andresey on the river Trent (an island near Burton-on-Trent), the wood of Arderne (possibly the Forest of Arden) and Mount Calvus (Scalpcliff on the bank of the Trent opposite Burton).[105] Among the English female saints mentioned in Conchubranus's text, although not particularly clearly, are Os(g)yth and Eadgyth, referred to as Osid and Ede.[106] Scholars have debated at length the transmission of these English female saints' lives and the links between them and Monenna, especially when she restored Osid to life after she had been submerged for three days in a swollen river, the earliest version of which is narrated by Conchubranus.[107] In comparison to Geoffrey of Burton's life of Modwenna, Conchubranus's understanding of the extraneous material is really quite jumbled. He may have been asked to incorporate this extraneous material to reflect an increasing interest in new

104 Howlett, 'Poems about Monenna', p. 19. Original: *Ortum Moduenne dat Hibernia Scotia finem/ Anglia dat tumulum dat Deus alta poli/ Prima dedit uitam sed mortem terra secunda/ Et terram terre tertia terra dedit/ Auffert Lanfortin quam terra Conallea profert/ Felix Burtonia uirginis ossa tenet.* **105** Ulster Society, 'Life of St Monenna', III, pp 440–1 §8. **106** Ibid., II, pp 130–1 §9. **107** Among the articles dealing with this matter see Denis Bethell, 'The lives of St. Osyth of Essex and St. Osyth of Aylesbury', *Analecta Bollandiana* 88:1–2 (1970), 75–127; Jane Zatta, 'The "Vie Seinte Osith": hagiography and politics in Anglo-Norman England', *Studies in Philology* 96:4 (1999), 367–93; Andrew Sargent, 'A misplaced miracle: the origins of St Modwynn of Burton and St Eadgyth of Polesworth', *Midland History* 41:1 (2016), 1–19 https://core.ac.uk/download/pdf/43762774.pdf accessed 5 January 2021. Robert Bartlett discusses the matter in his edition, *Life and miracles of St Modwenna*, pp xviii–xix.

ecclesiastical connections with England and Scotland from the eleventh century onwards. If Conchubranus's life of Monenna was written in this milieu – incorporating Benedictine and English influence – can that be detected in his portrayal of female monasticism and the changes that were occurring in the lives of holy women during the eleventh and twelfth centuries? Is there an element of preaching to a community of women in the text? This is possible given Conchubranus's final comments in seeking support from his 'sisters' (*sororum mearum*):[108]

> … those commands of God which I cannot, because of the hindrance of the adversary, accomplish as I ought by my own strength, I may be able to perform before my own death through the intercession of my sisters' merits …

Not unlike the *vitae* of Anglo-Saxon female saints written during the eleventh century, among them the *vitae* of the saints of Ely, some of which were compiled by Goscelin of Saint-Bertin in the late eleventh century,[109] Conchubranus opens Book 1 with scriptural quotations and stresses the importance of Monenna's virginity. Although stylistically not as elaborate as Goscelin or Geoffrey of Burton's prose, he moves away from the normal template of Irish saints' lives – progeny, miraculous birth, rejection of a forced marriage, childhood miracles – by beginning with a homiletic introduction:[110]

> For virginity is first of all a sign of virtue, nearer to God, like to the angels, source of life, friend of healing, mistress of joy, guide of virtue, foundation and crown of faith, buttress of hope and sustainer of charity.

The virginity signalled by Conchubranus here has echoes of the early Christian virgin, Thecla, 'the imagined inviolate virgin'.[111] Virginity and obedience in their most extreme manifestation are attained by one of Monenna's companions, Órbile, a double of the saint herself.[112] The text tells how Monenna decided to leave their settlement in Fochart and to retreat to Killevy in mountainous territory, having been disturbed by the raucous celebration of a marriage feast closeby. Monenna asked Órbile, 'a king's daughter of good sense

108 Ulster Society, 'Life of St Monenna', III, pp 448–9 §14. Original: *ut quod impediente aduersario uiribus meis inplere de Dei preceptis non ualeo ut debet sororum mearum meritis pro me intercedentibus ante mortem meam perficere possim …* **109** Rosalind C. Love (ed.), *Goscelin of Saint-Bertin. The hagiography of the female saints of Ely*. Oxford medieval texts (Oxford, 2004). **110** Ulster Society, 'Life of St Monenna', I, pp 254–7 §3. Original: *Virginitas enim prima est uirtutis indicio, Deo proximior, similis angelis, parens uite, amica sanitatis, domina gaudii, dux uirtutis, fundamentum et corona fidei, spei amminiculum et caritatis subsidium.* **111** Brown, *Body and society*, pp 157–9. **112** Ulster Society, 'Life of St Monenna', I, pp 258–61 §7.

and distinction' (*prudentisssima filia regis et nobilissima*) to remain in Fochart to guard the place. Órbile refused as her physical beauty would likely attract the attention of young men. Monenna breathed on her and put her belt around her body causing her to become an old woman – an action, as discussed by Johnston, that is opposite to that of the sovereignty goddess in early Irish literature who turns from hag to beautiful young woman.[113] Órbile was from then on named *Servile* (Latin) or Sá(i)rbile, Monenna's original name.[114] Once this transformation had taken place, Sáirbile gave thanks to her abbess and agreed with all her heart to guard Fochart ('*Intento corde uolo locum custodire*'). Monenna's retreat from the world with her companions frames the opening of Book 3 in which Conchubranus highlights the inflictions she meted out to herself and her fortitude in withstanding her harsh life as a *miles Christi*:[115]

> How much indeed she inflicted on herself bodily in incessant watching and praying and amid many hardships; how much with frequent fasting and devoted attention to reading meanwhile she refined and mortified her flesh; in what spiritual battles she sweated against demons …

Monenna, like so many of her male counterparts, led two lives: one as abbess directing her community, often sternly, the other as hermit, treating herself harshly. Interestingly, Conchubranus occasionally includes remarks that seem to reflect topical issues in the monastic world. When Monenna refused a cooked piglet offered to the community on the basis that they did not eat animal flesh other than that of the wild beast of the desert, the swineherd brought them instead a stag, which they accepted. Conchubranus follows with the lengthy observation:[116]

> But some holy men and particularly monastics among those peoples who have a great and thriving abundance of cattle are accustomed not to eat the flesh of all animals in case they might seem to conform with worldly people

113 Johnston, 'Transforming women'. 114 Ó Riain, *CGSH*, p. 166 §718.1: *Sarbili ainm Moninni prius o tustidib. Darerca o baithiss. Moninne ond fhilid* [Ninníne Éices]. 115 Ulster Society, 'Life of St Monenna', III, pp 428–9 §1. Original: *Quantum uero se in uigiliis et orationibus incessabiliter cum multis etiam laboribus corpusculum afflixerat, quantum ieiuniis creberrimis et lectionis interrea adsiduitate nimia carnem adtenuans macerauit, qualibus spiritalibus preliis contra demones desudauerat …* 116 Ulster Society, 'Life of St Monenna', I, pp 262–5 §9. Original: *Sed solent nonnulli sancti et maxime monasteriales inter illas gentes homines cum quibus magna peccorum habundantia uiget omnium animalium non uesci carnibus, ne secularibus uideantur adsimilati, quibus semper in hoc pendit omnis cura, ne aliquod desit in mensa. Ceruis uero et apris siue capreis uescuntur eo quod rarescentius adprehenduntur, et ne putentur licita dampnare, illorum carnes, quando Dominus transmittit, cum gratiarum actione percipiunt. Sed illorum consimiles personas si omnibus carnibus quibus utuntur Christiani uiuant non refutant recte intelligentes quod scriptum est: 'Qui manducat, Domino manducat, et gratias agit Deo,' et 'qui non manducat, manducantem non spernet' et reliqua, scientes per omnia locum et personam esse seruanda.*

> whose whole concern at all times is that nothing should be missing from the table. Indeed they do eat stags and boars or roe deer because they are caught less frequently and they say grace as they receive the flesh of these animals whenever the Lord sends it so as to avoid being thought to condemn what is lawful. But at the same time they do not oppose people who live on all kinds of flesh consumed by Christians, rightly understanding what is written: 'He who eats eats to the honour of the Lord and gives thanks to God' [Romans 14:6] and 'he who does not eat will not scorn the one who eats' etc., [Romans 14:3] knowing that in every thing place, time and person are to be observed.

Geoffrey of Burton omits this observation from his life of Modwenna.[117] Monks eating stags, roe deer and boar runs contrary to the general view expressed in Irish hagiography where these animals are protected and even adopted by saints. Ciarán of Saigir's first follower was a wild boar who gathered the materials for the saint's first church.[118] Archaeological evidence, however, supports Conchubranus's comments as deer bone is quite prevalent on church sites, discovered, for example, at Armagh, Clonfad, Clonmacnoise, Inis Cealtra, Inishkea and Nendrum.[119] Conchubranus's observation also appears to be in line with *céli Dé* practices. 'The rule of the *céli Dé*' states that the relaxation at Easter permitted the consumption of eggs, lard and the flesh of wild deer and wild swine.[120] 'The teaching of Máel Ruain' goes further:[121]

> Also no bit of flesh meat was ever eaten at Tallaght in Máel Ruain's lifetime, except when the flesh of deer or wild swine was set before guests, such of them as desired flesh meat.

Comparing Conchubranus's text to that of Geoffrey of Burton in the context of the depiction of female monasticism, Robert Bartlett observes that in revising the Irishman's text Geoffrey imposes 'a historicizing Benedictine mentality characteristic of twelfth-century England' on it.[122] He also argues that Geoffrey places a much greater emphasis on regular monastic life – the *militia regularis* as opposed to the *disciplina divina* – although that has as much to do with his amplification of the original as with his own Benedictine mindset. Monenna and

117 Bartlett, *Life and miracles of St Modwenna*, pp 39–43. **118** Plummer, *BNnÉ*, i, p. 113 §iii; ii, p. 100 §iii. **119** Lorcan Harney, 'Fasting and feasting on Irish church sites: the archaeological and historical evidence', *Ulster Journal of Archaeology* 73 (2015–16), 182–97, at pp 192–3. **120** Gwynn, 'The rule of the Céli Dé', pp 66–7 §6. Original: *is e in tuaslocud ar Cháisc .i. oga 7 blonaca 7 feoil oss n-allaid 7 mucc n-allaid*; O'Dwyer, *Céli Dé*, pp 68–81. **121** Gwynn, 'The teaching of Mael Ruain', pp 24–5 §40. Original: *Nir hitheadh fos mír feola a tTamhlachta riamh re beo Maoile Ruain, acht feoil fhiadha 7 muic allta do beirthi dona haoidheadhaibh, an chuid diobh ler bh'ail feoil.* **122** Bartlett, *Life and miracles of St Modwenna*,

her alter ego Modwenna operate in the same way: in summary, they are peripatetic, ruling over a network of churches in Ireland, England and Scotland, journeying to Rome, and occasionally withdrawing from the world, to Killevy or to Burton-on-Trent respectively. They are not cloistered, and although they come under the authority of Bishop Íbar for a while, they seem to follow an independent semi-eremitical religious life. As in the *Salmanticensis* text Monenna/Modwenna is praised for her assiduous learning and her wish to impart that learning to her community. One episode in all three versions alludes to the rule of silence which the sisters had broken just two days after Monenna's death. She appeared to Taunat, one of the sisters to whom she expressed her displeasure. Monenna's words differ between the three versions, although Geoffrey's text diverges from the others to a greater extent:

> *Codex Salmanticensis*: 'Turn back to the dormitory and bid the sisters take pains to observe the rule of silence with assiduous care in times like these and not to let their voices be heard outside the dormitory. Why have they overstepped the rule whose limits are not to be transgressed? O my daughters, you should not disregard the lesser things, lest afterwards you neglect also the greater things in like manner.'[123]

> *Conchubranus*: 'You will go into the house and tell all the sisters to keep holy silence more at a time like this and not let their conversation be heard abroad outside the house. Why do they so quickly forget the fixed rule, the limits of which may not in any degree be crossed? You should not, my daughters, neglect even minor things in case more important things also are likewise neglected.'[124]

> *Geoffrey of Burton*: 'This is what your mother commands to you: do not, my daughters, consider that I am dead, for I truly live with our Lord Jesus Christ, and I have heard some of you speaking together at times when it is not permitted, not maintaining holy silence as you should. Have you forgotten the testimony of the prophet, "The effect of righteousness shall be quietness"? [Isa. 32:17] My body still lies unburied among you and have you forgotten so quickly the teachings of God and of monastic observance,

p. xxi. **123** Heist, *VSH Salm.*, p. 94 §32; Sperber, 'Life of St Monenna', p. 79 §32. Original: *'Dormitorium repeda et sororibus manda quatenus in tali tempore silencii legem diligenti studio custodire laborent, nec suas voces extra dormitorium audiri permittant. Cur enim transgresse sunt regulam, cuius terminos nullatenus transgredi liceat? O mee filie, non debetis necgligere modica, ne[c] postmodum simili modo necgligatis et maiora.'* **124** Ulster Society, 'Life of St Monenna', III, 444–5 §10. Original: *'Introiens domum ad cunctas dices sorores ut magis in tali tempore habeant sanctum silentium et ne earum sermones sonare audiantur foras extra domum. Quid tam cito obliuiscuntur statute regule cuius terminos non licet ullatenus transgredi? Non debetis, filie mee, negligere etiam modica ne similiter neglegantur et maiora.'*

> whose boundaries it is not right for you to transgress in the least? Do not, my daughters, do not despise these small things, lest perhaps by offending in your neglect of small things you fall – God forbid – into greater [transgressions].'[125]

While Geoffrey of Burton probably understood Monenna/Modwenna's *regula observantia* to refer to *RB*, there may also be a hint of a similar understanding in Conchubranus's use of the phrase *regula statuta* – in other words it was a given rule rather than a vague custom.

The manuscript in which Conchubranus's text is preserved – BL Cleopatra A II – also contains two Latin hymns (both are given the title *ymnus*) dedicated to St Monenna, one *Audite sancta studia* precedes Conchubranus's text, the other *Audite facta sine ullo crimine* follows it.[126] Both are alphabetical poems, the first paraphrasing Monenna's life, the second concentrating on all her mystical virtues, and especially her chastity. David Howlett has argued that both hymns belong to a Hiberno-Latin canon of hymnody dating as far back as the late sixth or early seventh centuries, beginning with *Audite omnes amantes Deum*, reputedly composed by bishop Secundinus in honour of St Patrick.[127] While an early date might seem acceptable, Howlett suggests on orthographical grounds that the Monenna hymns may have been composed by Conchubranus himself or by 'someone who thoroughly understood his work and shared his habits of thoughts and composition'.[128] Whatever about the date of composition, their importance lies in their inclusion in the manuscript along with the list of Monenna's early successors at Killevy and of a tale about a stone 'bed' (*lectus*) that lay at the entry to a monastery in Ireland founded by Monenna – presumably Killevy – that was used to test the virginity of novices.[129] This collection is a superb example of a commemorative dossier that celebrates the distinctiveness of an Irish female community around the life of their founder. The hymns in praise of Monenna might be compared to new music for hymns and offices composed during the eleventh century which according to Susan Boynton was 'an effective means of commemorating a monastery's identity'. Such works include the Winchester Troper celebrating St Swithun, which formed part of a special commemoration by the monastic community of the cathedral priory at Winchester.[130] The

125 Bartlett, *Life and miracles of St Modwenna*, pp 165–6 §39. *'Hec mandat uobis mater uestra: Nolite, filie, putare me mortuam, uiuo enim uere cum Domino Christo Iesu, et audiui ex uobis aliquas loquentes ad inuicem in incompetentibus horis, nec tenentes sanctum silentium sicut oportuit. An excidit uobis quod attestificatur propheta, cultus iusticie silentium est? Adhuc corpus meum inter uos inhumatum iacet et uos tam cito obliuiscimini doctrine Dei ac regularis obseruantie, cuius terminos non uobis expedit aliquatenus transgrediendo preterire? Nolite, filiole, nolite contempnere minima, ne forte paulatim per minorum negligentiam offendentes, decidatis – quod absit – in maiora.'* **126** Howlett, 'Three poems about Monenna'. **127** Ibid., 14–16. **128** Ibid., 18. **129** Esposito, 'Conchubrani vita Sanctae Monennae', 244–6. **130** Susan Boyton, 'Monastic liturgy, 1100–1500: continuity and performance' in *CHMM* pp 958–74, at p. 967.

Monenna hymns are an invocation by virgins of their chaste founder, as the second stanza of *Audite sancta studia* declares:[131]

> Hear the holy zealous activities, sane, lofty, salutary, very many thousands of virgins of Christ of holy Monenna, whom, with the grace of Christ granting, industry advanced, whom You, Christ, have placed together [with Yourself] in perpetual glory.
>
> *Audite sancta studia / uirginum Xpisti milia / sancte Monenne plurima / sana summa salubria / quam porrexit industria / donante Xpisti gratia /* ***quam tu Xpiste perpetua / collocasti in gloria***

The highlighted lines are the final lines of all but one of the stanzas, repetition that possibly signifies a sung response at the end of each stanza. Medieval symbolism of chastity and fidelity abound in this hymn: Monenna is likened to a turtle dove who is a worthy spouse for Christ (*kasta electa columba / perfecta matri unita / turtur atque castissima* 'chaste chosen dove, perfected, united to the mother, and a most chaste turtle-dove').[132] She is 'the prudent chosen daughter [who] goes over to the joys of the Spouse' (*prudens edocta filia / Sponsi transit ad gaudia*).[133] The final stanza alludes to Monenna's relic, a miraculous belt, which was probably placed on the altar on her feast day while the community proclaimed this hymn:[134]

> With the firmest girdle of Christ she has girded round [her] holy viscera, which, laid down, perfected, vested with a linen stole among throngs of holy ones for ages of ages whom You, Christ, have placed together [with Yourself] in perpetual glory.
>
> *Zona Xpisti durissima / percinxit sancta uiscera / qua perfecta deposita / uestita stola bissina / inter sanctorum agmina / seculorum in secula /* ***quam tu Xpiste perpetua / collocasti in gloria***

Monenna's girdle reputedly confirmed or otherwise an individual's virginity. A similar miraculous girdle (*cingulum*, *zona*) belonging to St Colmán mac Duach of Kilmacduagh was in the possession of the Ó Seachnasaigh family who were patrons of his church in the late medieval period.[135]

In the final lines of the second hymn *Audite facta sine ullo crimine* the importance of memorialization is alluded to:[136]

131 Howlett, 'Three poems about Monenna', 2, 8. 132 Ibid., 4, 9. On the complex symbolism of the turtle dove see Lasse Hodne, 'The turtledove: a symbol of chastity and sacrifice', *IKON: Journal of Iconographic Studies* 2 (2009), 159–66. 133 Howlett, 'Three poems about Monenna', 6, 10. 134 Ibid., 7, 10. 135 Colgan, *Acta sanctorum*, p. 246 (XIII) (3 February). I owe this reference to Colmán Ó Clabaigh OSB. 136 Howlett, 'Three poems

A hymn of Christ rising up to all ears, the memory of which remains with praises.

Ymnus exoriens Xpisti cunctis auribus/cuius memoria permanet cum laudibus

In that memory and exaltation of Monenna, her community and other supplicants sought her intercession to 'wipe away our sins and delicts through penitence' (*ut peccata atque delicta nostra per penitentiam deleamus*)[137] and in turn, the author, possibly Conchubranus, sought through the merits of her community to cross over to the company of the saints in Heaven. In the lives of Monenna and through her alter egos (Darerca, Órbile, Sáirbile and Modwenna), a complex tapestry of female monasticism has been woven in which so many facets of the tradition appear and which, like the lives of St Brendan, crosses chronological, genre and geographical boundaries. This copious dossier underscores the importance of Irish lives for the study of medieval monasticism and the need to understand the milieu in which the various texts were composed.

ABBOT-BISHOPS: THE LIVES OF FLANNÁN, MALACHY AND LORCÁN UA TUATHAIL

The three Latin lives discussed in this section diverge somewhat from the corpus of Irish saints' lives in that two of them – those of Malachy and Lorcán Ua Tuathail – were written by authors from elsewhere – St Bernard of Clairvaux in the case of Malachy and a canon regular of the abbey of Eu in Normandy for Lorcán – and mainly for reasons other than the usual glorification of a monastery's founder. Bernard wrote his life of Malachy ostensibly at the request of Congan, abbot of *Surium* (Inishlounaght, Co. Tipperary) but clearly also because of his own close relationship with him and his admiration for his life's mission.[138] The life of Lorcán Ua Tuathail was written in Eu, where he died in 1180, as part of the campaign for his canonization, which ended successfully in 1225 with the agreement of Pope Honorius III.[139] The life of the third saint, Flannán of Killaloe, an early saint of dubious historical origin, was composed by an Irishman who had been trained on the Continent, possibly in one of the Irish foundations in imperial Germany.[140] Despite this continental background, all three lives represent what Donnchadh Ó Corráin coined as 'a compromise in which … elements of the old and the new, the native and the foreign, are

about Monenna', 12–13. **137** Ibid., 7, 11. **138** Lawlor, *Life of Malachy of Armagh*, p. 4; Meyer, *St Malachy the Irishman*, p. 13 (preface). **139** Plummer, 'Vie et miracles', p. 126. **140** Heist, *VSH Salm.*, pp 280–301. A relatively inaccurate translation exists in Sylvester Malone, *Life of Flannan, patron of Killaloe diocese* (Dublin, 1902). For a discussion of the context, see Donnchadh Ó Corráin, 'Foreign connections and domestic politics: Killaloe and the Uí Briain in twelfth-century hagiography' in Whitelock, McKitterick and Dumville,

mingled',[141] although not consciously on the part of Bernard of Clairvaux or the canon of Eu. These three lives concern the careers of abbot-bishops who are portrayed as being involved – Flannán retrospectively – in church and royal politics, and in introducing changes to the Irish church that were in line with the wishes of the papacy and other external agents. The power of bishops to transform the spiritual life of the church and the laity is embedded in all three lives, while the lives of Malachy and Lorcán also concentrate on the re-organization of monastic life in Ireland.[142] The early monastic careers of all three follow the pattern of most Irish saints' lives whereby the saintly boys are sent to study the scriptures under the direction of scholarly, holy men, although Malachy veered away from the traditional route at an early stage. Flannán was sent by his father Toirdelbach (Theodricus) to St Blathmac who taught him sacred learning (*puer in sacris litteris erat eruditus*).[143] He then came under the direction of Molua, founder of Killaloe (Cell Dá Lua), and more senior than Blathmac. Flannán showed such sanctity and miraculous powers that Molua decided to hand his episcopacy over to the young man, much to the reluctance of the latter. The description of Molua calling an assembly to announce his resignation evokes the atmosphere of an imperial scene:[144]

> As a result [of Flannán's sanctity and miracles] the said senior Molua, called the prelates of the churches and the territories in the presence of King Theodricus, with the majority of people standing around in a circle, seated on high on his episcopal seat, he said: 'Most clement king, most Christian king, and true worshippers of the faith, the time approaches and it is now, as foretold by the holy father Brendan and as the angel of the Lord warned me in my sleep, that I should retire and cede my place, to that holy one, whom God has chosen, whom God has exalted with clear signs.'

If the canon of Eu and his Irish sources are to be believed, Lorcán's early life was marred by Diarmait Mac Murchada, king of Leinster, although they later became allies. In a dispute with Lorcán's father the boy was taken hostage by the king and mistreated: the similarity between the description of Diarmait as a cruel and inhumane man in the text and that provided by Giraldus Cambrensis in his *Expugnatio Hibernica* is striking.[145] When released, Diarmait sent the boy

Ireland in early mediaeval Europe, pp 213–31. **141** Ó Corráin, 'Foreign connections and domestic politics', p. 230. **142** Flanagan, *Transformation*, pp 118–68. **143** Heist, *VSH Salm.*, p. 282 §3. **144** Ibid., p. 284 §7. *Quapropter senior factus antefatus Molua, convocatis ecclesiarum ac terrarum prelatis in presentia regis Teodricii, maioris populi circumstante corona, trono sic orsus ab alto, ait: 'Regum clementissime, regum christianissime, ac vere fidei cultores populi, tempus iminet et nunc est quod, iuxta sancti patris Brandani vaticinium et quod etiam angelicus Domini spiritus in sompnis michi precepit, huic sancto, quem Deus elegit, quem Deus per manifesta signa exaltavit, cedere locum ac discedere debeam'.* **145** *Plummer*, 'Vie et miracles', pp 129–30;

to the bishop of Glendalough asking him to act as an intermediary to have a troop of his soldiers released by Muirchertach, Lorcán's father. While waiting for this transaction to be completed, the bishop of Glendalough entrusted the boy to the care of his chaplain (*capellano suo*) who, realizing that Lorcán was illiterate in spiritual matters, began to educate him. At Lorcán's request his father agreed that he stay in Glendalough and gave him 'to God and to St Kevin the patron of the cathedral church of that region' (*eumdem Deo obtulit et sancto Coemghenio, ecclesie cathedralis illius regionis patrono*).[146] And thus he continued to be trained into the priesthood and was elected abbot at the age of twenty-five. Among the many virtues of Lorcán, according to the life, were those essential for an abbot – at least seen through the lens of a canon of Eu – humility, honesty, chastity, sobriety, erudition and almsgiving.[147] The author also comments on Glendalough's administrative structure during the mid-twelfth century, a structure reflected in the monastery's annalistic obits:[148]

> In fact in that church there was the office of bishop and abbot; but the abbot as far as temporal possessions [were concerned] , which it seems is rare, was by far the wealthier; from ancient times the people elected bishops [who were] not only nobles but men [who could] offer most protection throughout the whole region.

While Malachy was educated in the church as a child, the great influence on him in the early stages of his spiritual life was Ímar Ua hÁedacáin, founder of the *reiclés* of SS Peter and Paul at Armagh. Described by Bernard as 'a holy man and of great austerity of life, a pitiless castigator of his body', Ímar introduced Malachy to a religious life. Thus Malachy did not follow the traditional route and, although possibly exaggerating the situation, Bernard suggests that by subjecting himself to the severe discipline of Ímar, he caused a stir in Armagh 'all the more because it was unusual in a rude people'.[149] It would seem that opposition to Ímar's religious way of life strengthened because other students followed Malachy's example, thus probably attracting pupils from other masters. But Malachy was on a different trajectory and under the tutelage of Cellach, bishop of Armagh, and Ímar, he was ordained a priest before he reached thirty. In 1121, he went to Lismore for further instruction in the divine offices and the veneration of the sacraments from Máel Ísu Ua hAinmere, bishop of Lismore and Waterford. There is no indication that Malachy became a Benedictine in

Scott and Martin, *Expugnatio Hibernica*, pp 40–1 §6. **146** *Plummer*, 'Vie et miracles', p. 131: lines 11–13. **147** Ibid., p. 132: lines 19–27. **148** Ibid., p.132: lines 15–19. Original: *In hac siquidem ecclesia et episcopatus erat et abbatia; <sed abbatia> quoad temporales diuicias, quod raro uidetur, longe ditior erat; in episcopos non nisi nobiles maxime uiros in tocius <regionis> presidium ab antiquo populus eligebat.* **149** Meyer, *St Malachy the Irishman*, p. 19 §II.4 (Leclercq and

Lismore but it is clear that he built up a network of useful connections there, among them Cormac Mac Cárthaig, king of Munster, who was to support Malachy's later endeavours in transforming the hierarchy of Armagh.[150]

Each of these lives reflects the changes occurring in the Irish church during the twelfth century far more than other saints' lives acknowledge. Marie Therese Flanagan has alluded to the many reformist elements in the life of Flannán including his role as the ideal bishop making visitations, seeking to make peace between kings, living an apostolic life with few possessions, no outward signs of high office and willing to do manual labour.[151] Monasticism does not play a prominent part in the text with the exception of the portrayal of the retirement of Flannán's royal father, Theodricus to Lismore. Theodricus decided to live a *vita contemplativa*, donning a monastic habit and following a certain Colmán of Lismore's asceticism.[152] The life acknowledges that Lismore attracted individuals from all parts of Ireland to lead religious lives, a detail that is supported by annalistic obits.[153] The language used to describe Colmán's community (*congregatio*) and its mission is contemporary:[154]

> From this community of Colmán's many leaders of the churches in the remote regions of Ireland were chosen.

And of the nobles who joined his community they were 'naked following the naked Christ' (*nudi nudum sequentes Christum*), an ideal already encountered in the *Regula Choluimb Chille* and, of course, central to the later mission of St Francis.[155]

Theodricus as a *pauper Christi* put aside all worldly possessions, took on hard labour and was employed cutting a road through the rough terrain around Lismore. When he returned to Killaloe to save his kingdom, he would not put aside his poor garments or mount a horse or vehicle and when Flannán offered him fine foods and a luxurious bath he responded that as he would not be treated with such luxuries in Lismore, he would not accept them in Killaloe.[156] The final scene involving Flannán pleading with his father not to return to Lismore, mainly because he wished to have the holy king buried in his own church and not in Lismore, pitches the saint against the pilgrim, which is in a sense a metaphor for the conflict between the *vita activa* and the *vita contemplativa*. In fact, the section following Theodricus's death concentrates on Flannán's own life of poverty and service, as if rebalancing his life more towards asceticism: he

Rochais, *Sancti Bernardi opera*, iii, pp 316–19). **150** https://www.dib.ie/biography/mac-carthaig-cormac-a5005. **151** Flanagan, *Transformation*, pp 95–6, 205, 222–3. **152** For the little-known Colmán of Lismore see Ó Riain, *DIS*, p. 195. **153** Heist, *VSH Salm.*, pp 287–8 §14. **154** Ibid., p. 288 §14. Original: *De cuius Colmani congregatione multi rectores ecclesiarum in semotis finibus Hybernie eligebantur.* **155** Michael Robson, *St Francis of Assisi. The legend and the life* (London and New York, 1997), pp 35–6. **156** Heist, *VSH Salm.*, pp 290–1 §20.

did not wear silk garments, enjoy dogs or hunting; he employed himself in hard labour and distributed the episcopal revenues to pilgrims and the sick (*immo, cuncta que ad episcopalem cathedram vel mensam pertineba<n>t peregrinis et hospitibus, claudis, infirmis atque debilibus propria manu distribuebat*).[157]

Like Malachy and his training under Ímar and Malchus, Lorcán Ua Tuathail's encounter with developments in monasticism may have begun in Glendalough itself. Given the monastery's connections with Dublin and the likelihood that influences were coming into the city from the Continent and Britain from at least the early eleventh century, Glendalough must have been the recipient of such contacts. Indeed, in its own right it had been open to welcoming scholars from elsewhere, as evidenced by the possibility that Sulien of Llanbadarn Fawr in Wales (d. 1091) spent time there and by fragments of mathematical and philosophical tracts surviving in early twelfth-century manuscripts.[158] And yet, if the account of the canon of Eu can be trusted, once Lorcán became abbot he had to face hostility from within his monastery's wider community. This may have been caused by tension with the Uí Chathail, a local hereditary ecclesiastical family that had supplied four abbots from the early eleventh century. They were denied the abbacy by Lorcán's own grandfather Gilla Comgaill Ua Tuathail who was slain by subject people (*fortúatha*) of north Leinster in 1127.[159] Given Lorcán's own familial connections, his ascent to the abbacy at a young age would not have been universally welcomed, and from a monastic perspective, the life implies that his own ascetic way of life may not have been well received by some. The canon of Eu, however, stresses that Lorcán dealt with the hostile brethren compassionately. In any case, he had far more pressing matters to deal with, as famine and a resulting instability was rife in the territory around Glendalough.[160] Apart from organizing relief for the general populace, he sought divine intercession through prayer and fasting (*et ecclesiam ingressus cum clericis suis incessanter Dominum deprecabatur*).[161] According to his life, on becoming archbishop of Dublin in 1162, Lorcán re-organized the secular canons in Christ Church cathedral into the Arrouaisian community of the Holy Trinity. His life, although written in apostolic terms, suggests that he was particularly concerned to correct liturgical performance by the canons: 'he established regular singers around the altar so that they praised the holy name of the Lord' (*fecitque regulares cantores circa altare, ut laudarent nomen sanctum Domini*).[162] He followed the Arrouaisian rule himself, dining with the community,

157 Ibid., p. 292 §23. 158 Pádraig P. Ó Néill, 'An Irishman at Chartres in the twelfth century: the evidence of Oxford, Bodleian Library, MS Auct.F.III.15', *Ériu* 48 (1997), 1–35; Mary Kelly, 'Twelfth-century ways of learning: from Worcester or Cologne to Glendalough', *Journal of the Royal Society of Antiquaries of Ireland* 141 (2011), 47–65; Charles Doherty, 'Was Sulien at Glendalough?', in Doherty, Doran and Kelly, *Glendalough. City of God*, pp 261–77. 159 Mac Shamhráin, 'Prosopographica Glindelachensis, pp 85–6. 160 Plummer, 'Vie et miracles', pp 132–4. 161 Ibid., p. 134: lines 19–20. 162 Ibid., p. 138: lines 15–16.

remaining silent, celebrating the Divine Office in the cathedral, fasting and praying, and wearing the simple habit of a regular canon. As a canon, it would also appear that his pastoral mission in the archdiocese of Dublin was fortified by his monastic ideology and he zealously confronted any opposition.[163] But every Lent, Lorcán imitated his patron Cóemgen and retreated to Glendalough, to the cave, now known popularly as St Kevin's Bed located in the cliff above the Upper Lake in Glendalough, which is described in detail in the life.[164] (Fig. 16) There Lorcán contemplated and prayed, subsisting on bread and water and some vegetables sent up to him from the monastery. If he needed to leave the cave and set aside his retreat – usually to tend to diocesan affairs – there was a ladder attached to the cliff and hanging down into the water to facilitate his departure (*Erat accessus ad ipsum per scalam, cuius yma pars in aqua figebatur, superior tenebatur ad rupem*).[165] Retreating to the cave that was reputedly carved out of the rock by his *érlam*, Cóemgen, whose successor (*comarbae*) Lorcán was for a time, demonstrates that the reforming archbishop and regular canon had not eschewed all aspects of Glendalough's monastic traditions. Even more significantly he acted out his highest form of monastic practice during Lent away from his *sedes episcopalis* and the Holy Trinity community in Dublin and went to what he considered to be the desert (*in miranda solitudine*) and presumably the *fons* of his own monastic commitment.

Monasticism was at the heart of Malachy's spiritual life, and as observed by Marie Therese Flanagan, his interest in more than one continental monastic observance reflected a general twelfth-century engagement with different interpretations of monastic life.[166] During his career Malachy experienced the evolution of normalized Augustinian, Benedictine and Cistercian monastic rules as well as being formed in existing monastic tradition in Ireland. As evident from so much of his life, Malachy was strategic in his involvement with these orders. One phase in his early monastic career has been somewhat overlooked, that of the time spent in Armagh under the direction of Ímar Ua hÁedacáin and Cellach, abbot-bishop of Armagh, in Lismore under Máel Ísu Ua hAinmire, and in Bangor once more under Ímar. If the sources can be trusted, Malachy was included in an existing network of religious, at least some of whom had external connections, and whose common link was Lismore. Ímar may have been related to Niall mac meic Áeducáin, bishop of Lismore who died in 1113 and for whom the Lismore Crozier was made.[167] Óengus Ua Gormáin, successor of Comgall

163 Ibid., p. 142: lines 20–5: *Ibatque uir sanctus per arma iusticie a dextris et a sinistris, detruncans cruentas uiciorum acies, predicans assidue uerbum Dei, et opus faciens euangeliste, instans oportune <importune> , arguens, obsecrans, increpans in omni patiencia et doctrina, ne de manu sua requireretur sanguis commissi sibi populi pereuntis.* **164** Ibid., p. 141; Conleth Manning, 'Rock shelters and caves associated with Irish saints' in Tom Condit and Christiaan Corlett (eds), *Above and beyond. Essays in memory of Leo Swan* (Bray, 2005), pp 109–20, at pp 110–13. **165** Plummer, 'Vie et miracles', p. 142. **166** Flanagan, *Transformation*, p. 118. **167** AI 1113;

of Bangor,[168] also accorded the title *in epscup Ultach* 'the Ulidian bishop',[169] died in Lismore in 1123, possibly during Malachy's sojourn there. Was Malachy prompted to return to Bangor to re-establish a monastic community there, not only in accordance with Ímar and Cellach's wishes, but even more so at the behest of Óengus Ua Gormáin? And if, as Bernard states, the Lord prepared him in Lismore to pursue his spiritual life, did he bring with him the Benedictine monastic ideology of Máel Ísu Ua hAinmire? Bernard does not provide answers but hints at the existence of a community led by Malachy and guided by Ímar:[170]

> Malachy was in charge for a while, by the appointment of Father Imar being both rector and rule for the brethren. They used to read in his life how they should be converted and he walked before them in justice and holiness in God's presence.

Two other factors were to the fore in Malachy's use of emerging monastic traditions, the regularization of episcopal elections and cathedral communities, and improving the standard of liturgy and learning.[171] When he became bishop of Down in 1136 he established a community of 'regular clerics', not necessarily following the Arrouaisian rule,[172] but living by 'the humility of holy poverty, the rigour of monastic discipline, the quietness of contemplation, continuance of prayer', all basic precepts of religious life. As in Bangor, here Malachy led by example, and like Lorcán Ua Tuathail, was at the same time diverted from the contemplative life by the active life of a bishop 'arranging and judging on ecclesiastical matters with complete authority like one of the Apostles'.[173] Flanagan has argued that Malachy's keen interest in the Cistercians was not necessarily their institutional structure, which was only evolving during his lifetime, but the in-house monastic routine at Clairvaux and their liturgical rites.[174] Running throughout Bernard's life of Malachy is the Irishman's interest in chant and music, once more reminiscent of Lorcán Ua Tuathail's concern with the musical aspects of the liturgy. Malachy is said to have learnt singing in his youth and to have introduced chanting and psalmody to Armagh, and even, if the text is understood correctly, to Ímar's foundation of SS Peter and Paul.[175] He appreciated fine singing to the end of his life as Bernard remarks in his first

Raghnall Ó Floinn, 'Bishops, liturgy and reform: some archaeological and art historical evidence' in Bracken and Ó Riain-Raedel, *Ireland and Europe*, pp 218–38. **168** AU, AFM. **169** AI. **170** Meyer, *St Malachy the Irishman*, p. 32 §VI.14 (Leclercq and Rochais, *Sancti Bernardi opera*, iii, p. 323). **171** Flanagan, *Transformation*, p. 141. **172** He did not visit Arrouaise until 1139/40. Cf. Flanagan, *Transformation*, p. 139. **173** Meyer, *St Malachy the Irishman*, p. 48 §XIV.32. **174** Marie Therese Flanagan, 'Saint Malachy and the introduction of Cistercian monasticism to the Irish church: some suggestive evidence from Newry Abbey', *Seanchas Ard Mhacha* 22:2 (2009), 8–24, at pp 19–20; Flanagan, 'St Malachy, St Bernard of Clairvaux, and the Cistercian order', *Archivium Hibernicum* 68 (2015), 294–311. **175** Meyer, *St Malachy the Irishman*, p. 22 §III.7 (Leclercq and Rochais, *Sancti Bernardi opera*, iii, p. 316).

sermon on November 2, the day of Malachy's death, that the Irishman had complimented the monks of Clairvaux on their psalmody during a ceremony of re-burial of monks' bones in a new monastic cemetery.[176] Bernard describes Malachy as in constant conflict with the established hereditary families whom he regarded as malevolent and endlessly trying to harm him. That this was not necessarily accurate and that Malachy followed traditions and interacted with established monastic communities is revealed very occasionally in the sources. Following in the steps of his predecessors, once Malachy attained the see of Armagh, he made a visitation of Munster, possibly twice, in 1134 and 1136.[177] The first visit was probably linked to the consecration of Cormac's chapel at Cashel in 1134 with his royal ally Cormac Mac Cárthaig (d. 1138). (Fig. 17) He may have also visited the monastery of *Ibracense*, which Bernard intimates was jointly founded by Malachy and Cormac.[178] Nevertheless, his visitation to Munster was a symbolic gesture that confirmed a long-standing tradition of Armagh's primacy. A clearer indication that he was involved with the affairs of old foundations is his appearance as a witness in one of the Kells memoranda, mentioned in a transaction relating to *céli Dé* lands.[179] Malachy may have witnessed the endowment to the *céli Dé* of Kells in his role not alone as the successor of Patrick (*comarbae Pátraic*) but also as an advocate for committed religious communities, which he sought to renew, as he attempted to do in Bangor. By the end of the twelfth century, creating a monastic community in Ireland had changed and the brotherhood and sisterhood was beginning to be based on normalized rules which had their origins in long-standing monastic precepts. That the existing monastic tradition was also based on the same fundamental ideology may have facilitated the proliferation of new Augustinian and Cistercian foundations in Ireland.

The creation of a monastic community in early medieval Irish society did not depend on apostolic principles based on the scriptures alone. The bonds of kinship, so strong in Irish society, played a fundamental role in the establishment of communities as did other existing ties such as brotherhoods of aristocratic warriors, and companies of the professional classes. Early Irish saints' lives, including the *Navigatio Sancti Brendani abbatis* and the lives of St Monenna, while swathed in an Irish cultural milieu, nevertheless incorporate universal components of monasticism such as *cor unum et anima una* and *fraternitas*. A strong eremitical strand is evident in these lives as is an emphasis on liturgy (*opus Dei*), and in the case of Monenna on learning in female communities. Later versions of the lives of Brendan and Monenna place a greater emphasis on common rules, authority, virginity and poverty. The lives of Flannán, Malachy and Lorcán Ua Tuathail really belong to a different hagiographical tradition, the

176 Meyer, *St Malachy the Irishman*, p. 98 §2. 177 These visitations are recorded in AFM only and may be a doublet. 178 Flanagan, *Royal charters*, pp 185–9. 179 Mac Niocaill, *Notitiae*, p. 32 (XI).

latter two written very shortly after their subjects' deaths. Authority is vested in active abbot-bishops who have constant interaction with both kings and ordinary people. In addition, Malachy and Lorcán Ua Tuathail are portrayed as campaigners intent on overhauling the Irish church including its monastic life. Yet, despite their prominence during their lives in the twelfth century and their early canonizations – Malachy in 1190, Lorcán in 1226 – their cults did not flourish in medieval Ireland. It may be that Malachy was appropriated by the Cistercians while Lorcán Ua Tuathail's was promoted by Anglo-Norman archbishops of Dublin, particularly by John Cumin (d. 1212).[180] The earlier saints' cults thrived outside the cloisters of the new orders – who introduced their own suite of saints to Ireland – and their lives were revised and collated in large hagiographical collections during the twelfth and thirteenth centuries.

180 https://www.dib.ie/biography/cumin-comyn-john-a2290. Accessed 7 July 2023.

CHAPTER 6

Ríagla: exhortations, precepts, rules and customs

From its origins, following a monastic life has required a pledge to observe precepts that separate an individual from the norms of their wider community and signal that they have decided to live according to a particular form of life. This does not necessarily mean that they cut off all ties with society but it does mean that their interaction with society is atypical and, at least in principle, is supposed to create material and spiritual spaces between the monastic person or community and the multitudes surrounding them. Their lives are dedicated to the salvation of their souls, fearing and loving God, and avoiding the temptations of the devil 'to give up your own will, once and for all, and armed with the strong and noble weapons of obedience to do battle for the true king, Christ the Lord'.[1] The separation from worldly activities is clearly expressed in the sixth-century Rule of the Master when laying out how a monastery's domain should be managed. The Master advises against spiritual men working the estates as 'they do not entangle themselves in worldly affairs' and 'should not occupy our thoughts with things which remain in the world after we depart from this life and which cannot follow our soul after death, but always desiring what is on high and setting all our hope on the future we should let it be seen that we are still waiting for the life of happiness rather than enjoying it already'. Hence the lands should be rented out to someone outside the community 'a man who does not know how to be concerned exclusively about his soul and whose interests are limited to love of this world'. This worldly man is left to work in the fields, care for the estate, deal with the clamours of tenants and quarrels with neighbours, all of whom due to their lack of fear of eternal punishment, bring nothing but their sins with them when they die.[2]

To prepare a path for the novice and to keep monastic communities on their path to God, all strands of the tradition produced texts on the principles (rules) and practices (customs) governing the ideals and conduct of monastic life,[3] influenced, of course, by the cultures in which they were written. The world of the Middle East, Egypt, Palestine and Syria provides the contexts of the earliest

1 *RB*: Prologue (3). 2 *RM*: LXXXVI.1–13. 3 The terminology to describe these texts is the subject of a huge scholarly literature but I have tended to follow the most recent studies. See Krijn Pansters, 'Medieval rules and customaries reconsidered' in Krijn Pansters (ed.), *A companion to medieval rules and customaries* (Leiden, 2020), pp 1–36.

texts, among them the *Apophthegmata Patrum* ('Sayings of the Desert Fathers')[4] and John Cassian's *Institutes* and *Conferences*.[5] The greater Roman world of late antiquity is the background to works such as Augustine's precepts (the *Praeceptum*, *Regula recepta*, *Ordo monasterii*),[6] the Rule of Benedict,[7] Isidore of Seville's rule,[8] the Rule of the Jura Fathers[9], and of course, the works of Pope Gregory the Great.[10] Rules for women religious were compiled by Caesarius of Arles (d. 542), Donatus of Besançon (d. post–658) and possibly Jonas of Bobbio (d. 659).[11] These 'monasticisms', and many others besides, were, as defined by Diem and Rousseau, 'an almost infinite variety of forms – more-or-less communal, more-or-less ascetic – [that] played very different roles in a rapidly changing and geographically diverse society [in late antiquity]'.[12] As there were many 'monasticisms', so too were the many genres in which monastic ideals, theology and disciplines were expressed, listed by Diem and Rousseau as including ascetic treatises, narrative texts, letters and sermons, while the formats used to convey the parameters of a monastic life were also diverse: questions and answers, words of wisdom spoken by venerable fathers at monastic gatherings, vociferous admonitions, florilegia of older monastic rules and revised texts of older rules.[13] An understanding of the diversity of regulatory monastic texts is vital to understanding the vernacular Irish texts that seem to have been produced mainly during the eighth and ninth centuries, followed by other assorted regulatory texts that continued to be compiled into the twelfth century, often based on earlier material. These were not 'rules' in the sense that *RB* gradually became a normative text regulating monastic life, but as with all such texts, the fundamental precepts of monasticism formed their core ideals.

4 Ward, *The sayings of the Desert Fathers*. 5 Boniface Ramsey (trans.), *John Cassian. The conferences* (New York, 1997); Ramsey, *John Cassian. The institutes*; Stewart, *Cassian the monk*. 6 Luc Verheijen (ed.), *Nouvelle approche de la Règle de Saint Augustin* 2 vols (Bégrolles en Mauges, 1980; Louvain, 1988). 7 Timothy Fry (trans.), *The Rule of St Benedict in English* (Collegeville, 1981; repr. 2018). 8 Aaron W. Godfrey, 'The rule of Isidore', *Monastic Studies* 18 (1998), 7–29. 9 Tim Vivian et al., *The lives of the Jura fathers. The life and rule of the holy fathers Romanus, Lupicinus, Eugendus, abbots of the monasteries in the Jura mountains* (Kalamazoo, 1999). 10 Leyser, *Authority and asceticism*. 11 Adalbert de Vogüé and Joël Courreau (eds), *Rule for nuns. Sources Chrétiennes*, vol. 345 (Paris, 1988), pp 170–272; Victoria Zimmerl-Panagl (ed.), *Monastica 1: Donati Regula, Pseudo-Columbani Regula Monialium (frg.)*. Corpus scriptorum ecclesiasticorum Latinorum 98 (Berlin, Munich and Boston, 2015); Haight et al., *Western monastic spirituality*. 12 Diem and Rousseau, 'Monastic rules' in *CHMM*, p. 164. 13 Ibid., pp 165–6, 175.

THE PURPOSE AND AUDIENCE OF IRISH 'RULES'

The Irish texts that warrant detailed consideration in the context of this study are mainly in the vernacular and, as far as they can be dated – mainly on linguistic grounds –, were probably compiled in the eighth or ninth centuries, although some may belong to a later date.[14] Most of them are metrical texts and such is the nature of the metre and style that like so much of the corpus of late Old and Middle Irish didactic poetry they are mnemonic and could be added to easily or even created from stray verses on related topics. Preference for a metrical format probably reflects the teaching methods of monastic schools – and other schools of learning – in early Ireland. That these texts survive in late medieval and early modern manuscripts only adds to questions as to the authenticity of the formats in which they survive. Three manuscripts, RIA MSS 23 N 10 (late sixteenth century), 23 P 3 (Fragment A, fifteenth century) and KBR Brussels MS 5100–4 (seventeenth century), contain most of these vernacular rules. Some may have been genuinely composed as single texts during the early Irish period, some may reflect texts that were added to over the centuries, and others were simply constructed from stray verses or summarized by late medieval and early modern scribes. For example, Liam Breatnach has demonstrated that the text entitled *Ríagail na Manach Líath* ('The Rule of the Grey Monks') is a late fabrication, 'a collection of heterogeneous verses', many of them in early Irish, but put together into one text and supplied with a title by the fifteenth-century learned scribe, Uilliam Mac an Leagha.[15] Other texts, among them the so-called 'Monastery of Tallaght' or 'Tallaght dossier', went through the hands of the seventeenth-century Irish Franciscans, who although mostly loyal to their exemplars, sometimes approached these early texts with an Observant Franciscan mentalité.

The texts that represent an insight into the culture of early Irish monasticism include those listed below. The title *ríagail* (from Latin *regula*) attributed to a saint is usually one that is provided in the later manuscripts: these could be genuine and copied from earlier manuscripts associated with the particular saint's monastery or, more likely, added at a later date. Nonetheless, whatever about their authenticity, the idea that various saints imposed their own regulations on their communities is a recurring topos in Irish hagiography, and is clear from the texts of the *céli Dé*.

14 Louis Gougaud attempted to assemble what he defined as *des règles monastiques irlandaises* but this inventory is not reliable although it contains some valuable insights. See Gougaud, 'Inventaire des règles monastiques irlandaises'. For a popular anthology of this material, see Ó Maidín, *The Celtic monk*. 15 Liam Breatnach, '*Ríagail na Manach Líath* "The Rule of the Grey Monks": a late medieval fabrication', *Celtica* 32 (2020), 77–100.

TABLE 5: A summary of Irish 'rules'

Title	Content and Format	Possible date[16]	Edition/*CLH* reference[17]
Regula Choluimb Chille	A list of exhortations ascribed to St Columba advising an anchorite	eighth/ninth century	Kuno Meyer, '*Regula Choluimb Chille*', *Zeitschrift für celtische Philologie* 3 (1901), 28–30; Ó Maidín, *Celtic monk*, pp 37–41; *CLH* §634
Ríagail Chormaic maic Cuilennáin	A personal poem listing the basic precepts of a monastic life ascribed to the bishop-king of Munster, Cormac mac Cuilennáin (d. 908)	Late eighth/early ninth century	John Strachan (ed. & trans.), 'Cormac's rule', *Ériu* 2 (1905), 62–8; Ó Maidín, *Celtic monk*, pp 53–4; *CLH* §637
Ríagail in Choimded/ Ríagail Comgaill Bendchair	A poem of advice likely addressed to a priest involved in pastoral care	?eighth century	John Strachan (ed. & trans.), 'An Old-Irish metrical rule', *Ériu* 1 (1904), 191–208; 'Addenda to *Ériu* 1, 191 *sq.*', *Ériu* 2 (1905), 58–9; Ó Maidín, *Celtic monk*, pp 29–36; *CLH* §633
Ríagail Ailbi Imlecha	A composite poem on monastic precepts and customs ascribed to St Ailbe of Emly	?eighth/ninth century with later additions	Joseph O Neill (ed. & trans.), 'The rule of Ailbe of Emly', *Ériu* 3 (1907), 92–115; Ó Maidín, *Celtic monk*, pp 17–27; *CLH* §632
Comad Mainchín Léith; Anmchairdes Mancháin Léith	Two poems, one on the ideal monastery, the other on the most appropriate life for a monk ascribed to Manchán Liath, founder of Lemanaghan, Co. Offaly (d. 665)	?tenth century	Kuno Meyer (ed. & trans.), 'Comad Manchín Léith', *Ériu* 1 (1904), 38–40; Kuno Meyer, '*Anmchairdes Mancháin Léith so*' *Zeitschrift für celtische Philologie* 7 (1910), 310–12; *CLH* §867a

16 These dates are subject to serious caveats given the nature of the texts, their language and manuscript transmission. 17 Many of these texts were transcribed by Kuno Meyer without a proper edition or translation in his series 'Mitteilungen aus Irischen Handschriften' that was published in the journal *Zeitschrift für celtische philologie*. I list the most accurate and accessible editions that are available. More extensive lists are provided in *CLH*. Peter O'Dwyer summarizes some of the rules, *Céli Dé*, pp 122–39. He argued that the literature of the *céli Dé*, in his view the output of a reform movement, 'in time found its way into many of the important monasteries of the country' (p. 122).

TABLE 5: A summary of Irish 'rules' (*continued*)

Title	Content and Format	Possible date	Edition/*CLH* reference
Ríagail Chiaráin	An admonitory poem directed at a monk who may be a priest or an abbot	?eighth/ ninth century	John Strachan, 'Two monastic rules', *Ériu* 2 (1905), 227–9, at pp 227–8; Ó Maidín, *Celtic monk*, pp 43–7; *CLH* §635
Regula Mochutu Raithni	A metrical tract on prescriptions for bishops, abbots, priests, confessors, monks, *céli Dé*, kings and others. Ascribed to Mochutu of Rahan and also to Fothud na Canóine of Fahan, Co. Donegal (d. 819). It also includes a text on the customs of the refectory and on fasting. Ó Corráin ascribes the tract to Dochutu, bishop & anchorite of Slane (d. 839) *CLH* §630. Likely to be a composite text.	ninth century and later	Kuno Meyer (ed. & trans.), 'Anecdota from Irish MSS XV: Regula Mochutu Rathin', *Gaelic Journal* 5/12 (1895), 187–8; Meyer, 'Duties of a husbandman', *Ériu* 2 (1905), 172; Meyer, 'Incipit Regula Mucuta Raithni', *Archiv für celtische Lexikographie* 3/4 (1907), 312–20; Meyer, 'Ord prainni 7 prainntighi inn so sís', *Zeitschrift für celtische Philologie* 13 (1921), 27–30; Ó Maidín, *Celtic monk*, pp 59–73; *CLH* §630
The 'Tallaght dossier': 'The monastery of Tallaght', 'The teaching of Máel Ruain'	The teachings of the leading figures of the *céli Dé* movement relating particularly to liturgy, penance, food and fasting, and encounters with the wider world	eighth century and later	E.J. Gwynn & W.J. Purton (eds & trans.), 'The monastery of Tallaght', *PRIA* 29C (1911–12), 115–79; E.J. Gwynn (ed. & trans.), 'The rule of Tallaght', *Hermathena* 44 (1927), 2nd supp. vol., 1–63; Ó Maidín, *Celtic monk*, pp 97–130; Follett, *Céli Dé in Ireland*, pp 101–14, 220–1; *CLH* §628
The 'Tallaght dossier': 'The rule of the *Céli Dé*'	A composite text of *céli Dé* customs probably including material of different dates	ninth century and later	E.J. Gwynn (ed. & trans.), 'The rule of Tallaght', *Hermathena* 44 (1927), 2nd supp. vol., 64–87; Ó Maidín, *Celtic monk*, pp 81–96; Follett, *Céli Dé in Ireland*, pp 114–17; *CLH* §629
A Rule on clerical life '*Cidh as dech do cleiriuch*'	A list of the basic principles of clerical life, not necessarily monastic	?eighth/ ninth century	Paul Grosjean (ed.), 'Two religious pieces', *Zeitschrift für celtische Philologie* 18 (1930), 299–303; Ó Maidín, *Celtic monk*, pp 75–9

Title	Content and Format	Possible date	Edition/ *CLH* reference
A chuirp, not chaith fri crábud	A poem on rescuing the soul and mortifying the body by following a regulated life. Appears to be addressed to ecclesiastics who are living a comfortable life	?eighth century	Kuno Meyer, 'MIH: Ermahnung den Leib zu kasteien', *Zeitschrift für celtische Philologie* 6 (1908), 264–6
Cinnus atá do thinnrem	Advice to a student on how to live a good life and to avoid losing his soul. It may be addressed to a clerical student or to a monastic novice	eleventh century	Liam Breatnach (ed.), '*Cinnus atá do thinnrem.* A poem to Máel Brigte on his coming of age', *Ériu* 58 (2008), 1–35
Ocht n-airich go ngolgaige	How the eight canonical hours can fight the eight deadly sins. Reference is made to the evil clerics who do not follow the correct rule	?eighth/ninth century	Kuno Meyer, 'MIH: Die acht Horen zur Bekämpfung der Todsünden', *Zeitschrift für celtische Philologie* 6 (1908), 271
The *Leabhar Breac* tractate on the canonical hours	A text explaining the various canonical hours and their scriptural basis	eleventh/ twelfth century	R.I. Best (ed.), 'The Lebar Brecc tractate on the canonical hours' in Osborne J. Bergin & Carl Marstrander (eds), *Miscellany presented to Kuno Meyer* (Halle, 1912), pp 142–66

Why compose regulatory texts in the vernacular? Who were they addressed to? When Æthelwold of Winchester translated *RB* into Old English in the late tenth century, he explained why he had done so in the text known as 'King Edgar's establishment of monasteries'.[18] In the first instance, the king had asked him to translate the rule as it provided for 'the practice of a just life and an honourable will'. A translation was not needed by 'keen and wise men' who understood the temporal and spiritual wisdom of *RB* in its original form. But for nuns and unlearned laymen, knowledge of this holy rule in their own language was

18 Jacob Riyeff (trans.), *The Old English rule of Saint Benedict with related Old English texts* (Collegeville, 2017), pp 151–9, at pp 157–8.

necessary 'that they may serve God the more eagerly and have no defense [sic] that they were compelled by ignorance to misbehave'.[19] He also addressed his successors, presumably abbatial and episcopal, and abbesses in particular, to observe the rule and not to stray from it, as had happened in England before to the detriment of God's patrimony in landed estates or in any other property: 'lest through poverty and indigence the surging flame of holy observance grow lukewarm and then completely cool'.[20] Æthelwold's reasons for translating *RB* not only for use by monastic communities but more so among the laity as a protection of the church's property is unexpected. Yet it touches on a key element of the Irish vernacular regulatory texts, that of the existence of a wider audience than a monastic community subject to rules and customs. These texts, or parts of them at least, speak to three audiences: monastic communities of men and women, and especially novices, clergy active in pastoral care, and lay penitents. For example, some verses of *Ríagail in Choimded* ('The Rule of the Lord'), otherwise called *Ríagail Comgaill Bendchair* ('The Rule of Comgall of Bangor'), probably like so many of these texts, are addressed to a priest working among the laity:[21]

> If you are a shepherd to church-tenants, it is fitting that you have compassion for [them] and love them, hold them in a cherishing embrace.

The 'Rule of Mochutu of Rahan / Fothud na Canóine'

The metrical tract attributed variously to Mochutu of Rahan, Fothud na Canóine and Dochutu of Slane addresses all those who have a position in the church or influence church affairs: bishops, *céli Dé*, kings, priests, confessors, novices and lay tenants.[22] Bishops are dealt with in two passages. In one passage, they are described as straddling between church and worldly matters – not that these are easily separated. They make peace between great kingdoms (*mórthúatha*), rein in great kings, regulate hospitality and teaching, and are knowledgeable in holy scripture. In the second passage, if the bishop is a good leader (*taísech ecalsa*), he will take care of offerings made to churches of all sizes and in preaching to all, practise what he preaches.[23] No more than with Æthelwold, the author shows concern for the church's possessions. The *céli Dé* live in a monastic environment following the canonical hours, praying, kneeling and prostrating, performing vigils, reading, living obediently in silence and with fervour, in serenity without complaining or rivalry.[24] Kings should be truthful and avoid violence, otherwise they will bring famine and plague on their people, a topos known from the earliest Irish texts on kingship.[25] The primary function of priests is to administer

19 Riyeff, *Old English rule*, pp 157–8. **20** Ibid., p. 158. **21** Strachan, 'An Old-Irish metrical rule', 202: line 28a. Original: *Masa tuse aedhaire/ do mhanchaibh, is techta/ ar do cese, noscara,/ nosgabha gabail gerta*. **22** Meyer, 'Regula Mucuta Raithni'. **23** Ibid., 313 §§9–17; 316–18 §§45–64. **24** Ibid., 313–14 §§18–29. **25** Ibid., 314–15 §§30–7; Fergus Kelly (ed.), *Audacht*

the sacraments, especially confession and communion, to ensure the salvation of all.[26] The confessor (*anmcharae*) is addressed in a rather reproving tone in which he is reminded to care for the penitent honestly and diligently, and not to profit from his position. If he receives offerings from penitents he is to disperse them among widows, the poor and the elderly. Among his duties are following the canonical hours, offering Mass on Sundays and Thursdays, offering requiem or intercessory prayers without profit. He is not to be vain or niggardly nor does he eat or sleep in the houses of the laity.[27] One senses that these practices were not being adhered to by confessors and that it was deemed necessary to improve the standard of spiritual guidance (*anmchairdes*). As to the unfortunate novices (*maccléirig*), they are burdened with a long list of prohibitions and recommendations, most of which reappear in the eleventh-century poem addressed to a student, *Cinnus atá do thinnrem*,[28] although the evil temptations of women are of greater concern to the latter. Prescriptions for lay tenants are also included in one recension of the rule, its main messages advising generosity to guests, paying tithes and first-fruits (*ba dechmadach prímedach*) and performing their penance and prayers for God and not man.[29] This message fits in with another Middle Irish poem from the metrical insertions in the vernacular life of Mochutu.[30] Mochutu promised that every lay tenant (*manach*) who made his due offerings to the church and fulfilled his manual labour obligations would have his own herd of cattle on church lands until his old age. On the other hand, the fields and labour of church tenants who did not fulfil their obligations would not be fruitful.

Clearly, the so-called Rule of Mochutu is not just a monastic rule but like so many of these early Irish texts is a *vademecum* aimed at all levels of ecclesiastics from bishops to the laity, described by Ó Corráin as 'a clericist prescription for the good ordering of christian society'.[31] Follett has argued that it is a *céli Dé* text on the basis of its similarity to the 'Tallaght dossier' texts, and also stylistically that the *céli Dé* section is in the first person plural ('we') while the rest is in the second person singular ('you'), and hence reminders by the *céli Dé* to others about their duties and responsibilities.[32] If so, it is plausible that Fothud na Canóine (d. 819), or less so, Dochutu of Slane (d. 838), was the author, at least of certain sanctions of the text. Fothud was an eminent cleric who in 804 gained a concession from Áed Oirdnide, king of Tara, for the clerics of Ireland that they were not obliged to attend military expeditions or hostings.[33] It is also noticeable that the tone of the *céli Dé* section is far less severe than that addressed, for

Morainn (Dublin, 1976; repr. 2010). **26** Meyer, 'Regula Mucuta Raithni', 316 §§38–44. **27** Ibid., 318–19 §§65–86. **28** Breatnach, '*Cinnus atá do thinnrem*'. **29** Kuno Meyer, 'The duties of a husbandman', *Ériu* 2 (1905), 172. **30** Kuno Meyer, 'Mitteilungen aus irischen Handschriften: Mochutta cc.', *Zeitschrift für celtische Philologie* 10 (1915), 43–4; Plummer, *BNnÉ*, i, p. 309; ii, p. 300. **31** *CLH* pp 812–13 §630. **32** Follett, *Céli Dé in Ireland*, pp 121–4. O'Dwyer also came to a similar conclusion, *Céli Dé*, pp 123–31. **33** AU, AFM (799).

example, to the *anmcharae*. The text's significance lies in its compiler's attempt to provide a basic normative guide in the vernacular for ecclesiastical officials and church tenants that remained applicable to the twelfth century to judge from the similar sentiments of the poem in the vernacular life of Mochutu. A detailed text on the appropriate etiquette in the refectory and on periods of fasting entitled '*Ord prainni ocus prainntighi*'[34] is included with the Rule of Mochutu in three manuscripts (RIA MSS 23 N 10 and 23 P 16 (*Leabhar Breac*), TCD MS 1318 (The Yellow Book of Lecan)). It appears to be mainly addressed to a community eating together but the sections on fasting would have been relevant to the laity, especially during Lent.[35] As its provisions mirror details in the 'Tallaght dossier', it is also likely to have emanated from a *céli Dé* milieu. Hence it could be argued that the Rule of Mochutu, as it survives in these late medieval manuscripts, is an amalgam of earlier prescriptions and regulatory texts that were gathered together by later scribes, as demonstrated by Breatnach regarding *Ríagail na Manach Líath*.

The Rule of Ailbe

The same can be said of the so-called Rule of Ailbe, which its editor Joseph O Neill argued consisted of a variety of metres that in general corresponded to general maxims and practical regulations, the latter interpolated into the original exhortatory text.[36] It is addressed to Éogan mac Saráin, otherwise unknown, but somehow linked to the church of Cluain Cóeláin, which may explain the association with Ailbe of Emly. Although the only surviving place-name Cluain Cóeláin is Clonkeelan, Co. Monaghan, St Cóelán (Mod. Ir. Caolán) is associated with Youghalarra (b. Owney and Arra, Co. Tipperary), a parish that also has traditional links with Ailbe of Emly.[37] The metrical tract opens with an exhortation *Apair dam fri mac Saráin* 'Bear witness to the son of Sarán on my behalf'[38] and closes with an interesting insight into how such texts were imparted:[39]

> You shall recite it, you shall write it in Cluain Cóeláin, let you not conceal it, o son (pupil), for the sake of dutifulness, you will declare them to Éogan.

Ailbe is called upon in one verse, which may be an interpolation and may have caused the later scribes to associate him with the text, although it may also reflect the connection between Cóelán and Ailbe:[40]

34 Kuno Meyer, 'Ord prainni 7 prainnthighi inn so sís', *Zeitschrift für celtische Philologie* 13 (1921), 27–30. 35 For detailed discussion of this text, see pp 246, 249–50. 36 O Neill, 'Rule of Ailbe', 94–5. 37 Ó Riain, *DIS*, pp 135–4; National Folklore Collection UCD, The Schools' Collection, volume 0538, pp 57–9: the local rendition of the saint's name is St Conlan or Coulan. 38 O Neill, 'Rule of Ailbe', 96–7 §1. 39 Ibid., 108–9 §56. Original: *Aralėga, nascríba, i Clúain Cóiláin ní chela, / a maicc, fobithin goire fri hEogan atabera.* 40 Ibid., 106–7

> A command to you from Ailbe, do not desert your monastery, let it be for the good of the soul what you do, not for the good of your body.

The first twenty verses of the Rule of Ailbe could apply to a priest with a pastoral mission. Not only is it addressed in the third person singular, it consists of a list of worthy exhortations:[41]

> [Let him be] without weeping, without wailing after prosperity, he must never go without sandals, without a fringe of red Parthian leather, without blue, without red, without finery.
>
> ... Let him be gentle, close, and zealous; let him be modest, generous, and gracious; against the torrent of the world let him be watchful; against the brood (?people: *ál*) of the world let him be warlike/generous (*cathmar/caithmech*).

He is to administer the sacraments, give alms, follow the canonical hours and practice silence. But midway through the text, it addresses a community headed by an abbot (*ríaglóir*, *cenn manaig*) and vice-abbot (*secnap*) with particular advice to an *airchinnech*, understood as the head of a *cathair* (*civitas*). The *airchinnech* is in charge of church tenants[42] – although the verse dealing with *manaig* as church tenants may be an accretion to the original – but the crux of his leadership relates to a committed religious community:[43]

> If the *airchinnech* be wise, his rule will not be harsh; as the rations of food shall be, so will the rule be.
>
> Let it not be too strict, let it not be lax, let it not be a rule without knowledge; that each may be able to take his yoke, that he may not leave his enclosure.

These are fundamental prescriptions of the coenobium. *RB* entreats the abbot to rule according to varying circumstances:[44]

> This means that he must vary with circumstances, threatening and coaxing by turns, stern as a taskmaster, devoted and tender as only a father can be.

§48. Original: *Timarnad duit-siu ó Ailbiu, nephdéirge do phuirt, / bad less do anmae dogné, ná bad less do chuirp.* **41** Ibid., 96–7 §5. Original: *Cen choí, cen chessacht lessa, ní té dogrés cen assu, cen chorthair partaing russi, cen gorm, cen derg, cen maissi*; §8. Original: *Bad timm, bad docht, bad bruthmar, bad nár, bad fhial, bad rathmar / fri sráb ndomuin bad fhethmech, fri hál ndomuin bad chathmar / chaithmech.* **42** Ibid., 106–7: line 41a: *fodlad día manchaib co cert, ní rucca as a richt* ('let him distribute justly to his church tenants, let him not take them beyond his power'). **43** Ibid., 103–5 §§32–3. Original: *Mad ecnaid int aircinnech a riágol níb borb, / amal bies int acnamad bid samlaid int ord. / / Ná bad rothend, ná bad lax, níp ríagol cen fhiss, / ara rucca cách a mám, ná farcba a liss.* **44** *RB*: Chap. 2.24–5.

> With the undisciplined and restless, he will use firm arguments; with the obedient and docile and patient, he will appeal for greater virtue; but as for the negligent and disdainful, we charge him to use reproof and rebuke.

The metaphor of a monastic life as serving under the burden of a yoke of obedience is commonplace as is confinement within the monastic enclosure, most lucidly expressed by John Cassian in the *Conferences* when condemning wandering anchorites:[45]

> There is in fact a fourth kind [of monk] as well, which we see has appeared recently among those who fancy themselves in the style and likeness of anchorites and who seem, when they are starting out, to long for the perfection of the coenobium with a sort of short-lived fervor [sic]. But all at once they grow lukewarm, contending the curtailment of their earlier behavior [sic] and vices, not content with bearing the yoke of humility and patience any longer and disdaining to place themselves under the rule of the elders ... This form of life – or rather lukewarmness – does not permit those whom it has once infected ever to attain to perfection.

A constant theme, presumably addressed to the keeper of the rule – the *ríaglóir* or *airchinnech* – in the Rule of Ailbe is the necessity to be wary of encroachment by the world beyond the enclosure: the rule of a religious life, including praying in a chapel (*reiclés*) is not subject to lay judgment.[46] Travelling on the roads for business or begging is frowned upon,[47] and the inevitable prohibition against warriors and women entering the monastery also appears (although this may be an interpolation).[48] Yet a monastery's guest master (*ferthigis*) should be ready to receive guests by having a fire of appropriate size ready, offering the correct ceremony of washing guests' feet and ensuring good bedding is available.[49] These were the very comforts that Mac Con Glinne was deprived of when he stayed overnight in the monastery guest house in Cork in the twelfth-century satire *Aislinge Meic Con Glinne* ('The Vision of Mac Con Glinne').[50] Finally, the most worthy form of religious life was that of the *mugada Dé* 'the servants of God' who according to a Middle Irish addition deserved a

45 Ramsey, *Conferences*, p. 642 (VIII.I). **46** O Neill, 'Rule of Ailbe', 108–9 §49. Original: *Dlúthad ríaglae cléirchide, dogrés bad a lúath, / it recles oc ernaigdi, cen etarcert túath.* **47** Ibid., 108–9 §52 Original: *Timarnad duit nád dechis for taired na sét / fri caingin ná athchuingid as do liss cot' écc* ('A command to you that you do not go on the way of/along the roads for business or begging outside your monastic enclosure until your death'). **48** Ibid., 104–5: line 37a. Original: *Ní raib fénid ná banscál 'sind loccán i mbíat* ('there should not be a warrior or a woman in the place where they live'). **49** Ibid., 104–5: line 41a. Original: *Tech glan donaib óigedaib ocus tene mór, / ossaic is indlat doib la dergad cen brón* ('A clean house for the guests and a big fire, washing and bathing of their feet for them with bedding without sorrow'). **50** Meyer, *Aislinge Meic Conglinne*, pp 10–12l; Jackson, *Aislinge Meic Con Glinne*, pp 4–5.

visit, as nothing could be better than to follow them.[51] The term *mug Dé* 'servant of God' is yet another phrase, such as *deorad Dé*, *céle Dé*, applied to ascetics following the purest religious life.

The 'Tallaght dossier'

In dealing with the so-called 'Tallaght dossier' and its associated texts,[52] it is necessary to be conscious of the manuscript tradition of its various texts. This matter has been discussed in great detail by Westley Follett in his volume on the *céli Dé* in Ireland, but for the purposes of this present discussion the late date of the manuscripts in which these texts are preserved – fifteenth century and later – and the form in which they are preserved are significant. These are composite texts and parts of them are a jumble of prescriptions for various audiences. The fifteenth-century *Leabhar Breac*, for example, combines 'The rule of the *céli Dé*', a later derivation of the original 'Tallaght dossier', with the *Regula Choluimb Chille* and the *Ríagail Pátraic*, which deals with the formation of priests and is primarily addressed to bishops.[53] As an aside, this may also reflect the contemporary purpose of the *Leabhar Breac* itself, in that it may have been prepared as a compilation for the training of late medieval priests.[54] One version of 'The monastery of Tallaght' – otherwise labelled by its editor as 'The teaching of Máel Ruain' – survives as a modern Irish paraphrase in a seventeenth-century Franciscan manuscript that introduces the contemporary vocabulary of Franciscan customs into the text.[55] Despite surviving in late sources, their language, context and deviation from later medieval monastic rules testify to their composition in the early medieval period. By analysing the potential audiences for the regulation in 'The monastery of Tallaght', 'The teaching of Máel Ruain' and 'The rule of the *céli Dé*', different groups can be identified: monastic communities, lay penitents, bishops and priests involved in pastoral care, confessors (*anmchairde*), and possibly female religious. The context for the regulations addressed to the *céli Dé* in particular presupposes conversations – a less complex version of the *Apophthegmata Patrum* ('Sayings of the Desert Fathers') and Cassian's *Conferences* – among the leaders of the movement about certain situations. Some involved fairly sharp exchanges, the following instance reflecting the tone of exchanges between Máel Ruain and Máel Díthruib:[56]

51 O Neill, 'Rule of Ailbe', 104–5: line 39[a]. Original: *Nech dothéi do chélidiu co mugada Dé/ ní bes dech adcethar bad ed ón foglé.* 52 Follett, *Céli Dé in Ireland*, pp 220–34. 53 *Leabhar Breac*, RIA MS 23 P 16, folios 9–12. 54 I owe this suggestion to Colmán Ó Clabaigh. 55 UCD-OFM MS A 31 folio 10. I follow Follett's titles of these texts for ease of reference. 56 Gwynn and Purton, 'The monastery of Tallaght', 135–6 §24. Translation updated. Original: *Ceth Máolruoin nipo calad arnadafuimed asended. Nírbo mór accubar laisim ceth airitu Maoilidíthraib. Is ed asbertom didiu ind raibi athcomarc lat iar do chúl ria tudechd húc. Tó ol Máoldithruib Ceth ind táos dánae ol Máolrúin in gobuid ind tsáoir 7 reliqui ní maith lá cách díob a fer muindtiri do daul connech hailé. Fotroich lethsú ol Máoldithruib Tuccusæ lictiguth 7*

> As for Máel Ruain he was not severe in refusing to receive them [holy persons] in the end. He had no great desire even to receive Máel Díthruib. This is what he said: 'Did you seek permission from those whom you left before coming here?' 'Yes', said Máel Díthruib. 'Even craftsmen', said Máel Ruain, 'the smiths, the wrights, and the rest, none of them likes a man of his household to go to anyone else.' 'What you say has been looked into', said Máel Díthruib; 'I obtained authorization and permission.'

The conversations also signal that varying customs were followed in *céli Dé* foundations, especially with regard to liturgy, food and fasting, and penance, but that the customs of Máel Ruain and his foundation at Tallaght were generally viewed as superior among other *céli Dé* leaders. Viewing the *céli Dé* as a reform movement led by particularly charismatic clerics, O'Dwyer characterized them as an anchorite movement whose rule concentrated on charity, self-denial, useful occupation and perseverance. Their means to salvation was through prayer, attending Mass, receiving the sacraments and performing penance and mortification. They were particularly active in advocating improved standards in devotion and liturgy, and being very literate produced influential texts that continued to circulate during the following centuries.[57] Pursuing a very different explanation, Craig Haggart has argued that the phenomenon of the *céli Dé* as 'a recognizable historical entity' did not emerge until the tenth century, and that the communities designated as *céli Dé* from that period onwards were concerned 'with provision for the sick and the poor'.[58] Prior to that, according to Haggart's assessment, the term *céle Dé* was one of several vernacular renditions of the term *miles Christi* 'soldier of Christ', among the others being *míl Críst* (borrowed from Latin *miles*), *céle Críst* 'client of Christ', *céle maic Maire* 'client of Mary's son' and *mac bethad* 'son of life'.[59] To a certain extent, this matches with Brian Lambkin's view of the *céli Dé* in their original guise as 'fundamentally aristocratic' and aspiring to a higher status, in order 'to prepare for this higher status and to earn it, the *céle Dé* set himself apart from his fellow men'.[60] The practice of assigning different appellations to members of eremitical monastic communities continued after the ninth century, as in the use of *deorad Dé*, *mug Dé* as well as *céle Dé*, but Haggart's observation regarding the importance of the concept of *miles Christi* to the eighth-century leaders, and in particular to Máel Ruain, is germane to understanding their spiritual life. That Máel Ruain chose St Michael the Archangel as the founding patron of Tallaght must be seen as an expression of a Christian and masculine militant mind, and if, as Follett argues,[61] the hymn *Archangelum mirum magnum* was genuinely composed by Máel Ruain,

comarleccud. **57** O'Dwyer, *Céli Dé*, pp 192–201. **58** Haggart, 'The *céli Dé* reassessment', 61–2. **59** Ibid., 39, 44. **60** Brian Lambkin, 'Blathmac and the céili Dé: a reappraisal', *Celtica* 23 (1999), 132–54. **61** Westley Follett, 'The veneration of St Michael at Tallaght: the evidence of *Archangelum mirum magnum*', *Cambrian Medieval Celtic Studies* 66 (Winter, 2013),

its depiction of the saint concentrates particularly on him as the great heavenly warrior:[62]

> In the army of Heaven, in the troop of the virtuous, does not wonderful Michael blaze with the most beautiful flame? …
>
> God made Michael general to the many thousands of the officers and legions of Heaven.

How much of and for how long this mentality survived as a legacy of the eighth-century *céli Dé* leaders among monastic communities needs to be addressed. St Michael remained a favourite intercessor: a hymn to him is attributed to Máel Ísu Ua Brolcháin, although it is notably less militant than Máel Ruain's.[63] As to the relevance of the 'Tallaght dossier' to monastic communities in Ireland after the eighth/ninth century, the probability, understood from the many stray Middle Irish texts dealing with aspects of monastic legislation, is that it became an authoritative source. That 'The rule of the *céli Dé*', which was compiled later than 'The monastery of Tallaght' and the 'The teaching of Máel Ruain',[64] moved away from the 'sayings'/conversation format to a regulatory format citing prescriptions as those of the *céli Dé* as a collective group or referring to them on one occasion as *muintir Maíle Ruain* 'the family of Máel Ruain' hints at its progress towards a normative text. As to the audiences envisaged in the 'Tallaght dossier', the texts suggest that they were aimed at those with different levels of literacy or were read in communal settings. 'The monastery of Tallaght' stipulates that the four Gospels were to be read at mealtimes starting with Matthew in the springtime.[65] 'The rule of the *céli Dé*' goes further in its direction on readings at mealtime:[66]

> It is the practice of the *céli Dé* that while they are at dinner one of them reads aloud the Gospels and the Rule and miracles of saints, to the end that their minds may be set on God, not on the meal: and the man who preaches at that time has his dinner in the afternoon, and in the course of the next day they are questioned severally about the subject of the sermon, to see whether their minds were occupied with it on the previous night or not.

37–56. **62** Follett, 'The veneration of St Michael at Tallaght', 54: lines 17–18, 23–4; Follett, '*Archangelum mirum magnum*: an Hiberno-Latin hymn attributed to Máel Rúain of Tallaght', *The Journal of Medieval Latin* 19 (2009), 106–29, at p. 128 §§9, 12. Original: *In exercitu caelorum, in virtutum agmine, Nonne fulget Michel mirus pulcherrimo ardore? … Magistratibus caelorum atque legionibus Deus dedit Michaelem ducem multis milibus.* **63** Kuno Meyer (ed.), 'Maelisu's hymn to the archangel Michael', *The Gaelic Journal. Irisleabhar na Gaedhilge* 4:36 (1890), 56–7. Ní Bhrolcháin, *Maol Íosa*, pp 42–3. **64** Follett, *Céli Dé in Ireland*, pp 114–17. **65** Gwynn and Purton, 'The monastery of Tallaght', 138 §29. **66** Gwynn, 'The rule of the Céli Dé', 72–3 §31. Original: *Is ed fosgni lasna Celiuda De .i. fer oc airrlegend tsoscela 7 riagla 7*

This provision may be a unique reference to readings in the refectory as such detail does not appear in *RB* or indeed in monastic customaries elsewhere until the eleventh century.[67] An indication of the capacity of monks and penitents to know all the psalms and what to do if they were not fully versed in them is related with respect to Muirchertach mac Olchobair, abbot of Clonfert (d. 802) who laid down that his vigil involved saying the *Beati* twelve times in place of the hundred-and-fifty psalms 'because he knew that there were more of the monks or penitents (*dona manchaibh, nó don aos peannaide*) who knew the *Beati* by heart than knew the psalms'.[68] Of course, Muirchertach's requirement may have applied to *manaig* as 'church tenants' and to lay penitents, none of whom would have been expected to know the psalms in Latin by heart.

This brief survey of some Irish vernacular 'rules' presents an overview of how they were compiled, both in their original forms and in later compilations, who their authors intended to address, both inside and outside the monastery. The next section deals with the extent to which these texts reflect the core ideals of a committed monastic life.

IRISH 'RULES' EXPRESSING THE CORE IDEALS OF MONASTICISM

All Christian monastic traditions profess core ideals and the Irish tradition is no exception. Hence in their regulatory texts, no matter what type of format or language, the usual monastic precepts are expressed: love and fear of God (*amor et timor Dei*), purity of heart (*puritas cordis*), obedience and humility, discipleship of Christ (*imitatio Christi*), poverty, spiritual love and communal fraternity lived out under the eyes of God.[69] The main activity for monks was progressing their spiritual life through the liturgy, prayer, penance, meditation and reading, the all-encompassing *opus Dei* ('the work of God'), and through the centuries there was much debate everywhere about the degree to which monks were to be involved in manual labour (*opus manuum*), other than certain prescribed occupations such as teaching and writing. No more than a desire to have possessions, idleness in a monastery was viewed as dangerous, clearly declared

fertai noem cen bit oc praind, dáig na beth a menma isin praind sed hin Deo, 7 praindid o nóin in fer pritchas and, et in die singuli 7 rogantur de quod predicatum est, dus in and bis a menma in nocte an ann. **67** Webber, 'Reading in the refectory'. **68** Gwynn, 'The teaching of Mael Ruain', 22–3 §37. **69** The literature on this subject is extensive. The following articles reference many of the essential works and in their own content deal with these core ideals from diverse perspectives: Albrecht Diem, 'Disimpassioned monks and flying nuns. Emotion management in early medieval rules' in Christina Lutter (ed.), *Funktionsräume, Warhnehmungsräume, Gefühlsräume. Mittlealterliche Lebensformen zwischen Kloster und Hof* (Vienna and Munich, 2011), pp 17–40; Diem and Rousseau, 'Monastic rules'; Clark, 'The rule of Saint Benedict'. See also the extensive bibliography of monastic literature http://www.earlymedieval monasticism.org/bibliographymonasticism.htm.

in *RB*: 'Idleness is the enemy of the soul'.[70] Monks read, prayed or served their neighbour, whereas anchorites lived in solitude or in small groups surviving by the labour of their own hands or were provided regularly with provisions to sustain themselves. On the whole, manual labour was for *manaig* 'lay tenants' or illiterate monks while coenobitic communities confined themselves to reading the scriptures, following the Divine Office, teaching and engaging in labour such as preparing manuscripts and writing materials and even sewing clothes. Clearly, laws and regulations reflect ideal behaviour – be it in the wider society or the church – and the reality was far more complicated. Saints' lives, although so often operating in the realms of the fabulous, are more likely to depict daily practices, or at least a more realistic image of life. The life of Fintan of Taghmon, which may date to sometime between the eighth and tenth centuries,[71] tells how Fintan spent some time on Devenish Island in Lough Erne under the rule of a strict abbot reading the scriptures. So strict was the rule that the monks were not allowed to sift the meal, but had to mix it with its husks and water with heated stones in a shallow bowl. That was their daily ration.[72] Of course, God occasionally intervened to provide for a holy man. In Fintan's life, when he resided in Aird Crema on the southeast coast,[73] God gave him the abundant fruits of the sea and of the land, 'which neither before nor afterwards existed in that place'.[74] When Máel Díthruib sought Máel Ruain's advice on the requirement to sing the whole psalter when he was teaching, Máel Ruain retorted rather sarcastically that if the man who worked with sickle and flail, used the mallet or made a ditch – unlikely, therefore, to be a *fír-manach* 'true monk' – could recite one hundred-and-fifty psalms despite his burden, 'you consider what is right for yourself to do, who are a monk'.[75] Nevertheless, out of necessity, some monks (*fír-manaig*) must have undertaken manual work. Colmán of Lann Elo (Lynally, Co. Offaly) chose a site for his church that had no water source and his brethren 'with great labour and danger' went about diverting water from a mountainside through a valley to the site. Colmán took pity on them and broke the stone blocking the water with his staff and water flowed from it, thus providing for his monastery from then on.[76] While this action is reminiscent of Moses and his staff, archaeological evidence confirms that large-scale

70 *RB*: Chap. 48.1. 71 Sharpe, *Medieval Irish saints' lives*, pp 297–339; Etchingham, *Church organisation*, p. 9. 72 Heist, *VSH Salm.*, p. 199 §6. 73 Identified as in the townland of Hooks, parish of Kilcowan, barony of Bargy, Co. Wexford, in Pádraig Ó Riain, Diarmuid Ó Murchadha and Kevin Murray (eds), *Historical dictionary of Gaelic placenames. Foclóir stairiúil áitainmneacha na Gaeilge fasc. 1 (Names in A -)*. Irish Texts Society (Dublin, 2002), p. 37. 74 Heist, *VSH Salm.*, p. 202 §15. 75 Gwynn, 'The teaching of Mael Ruain', pp 38–9 §65: *feuch-sa creud as coir duit fein, ata ad mhanach, do dheunamh.* 76 Heist, *VSH Salm.*, p. 211 §4. Original: *In loco autem illo aqua not erat, sed fratres cum magno labore et periculo per diversa montis latera aquam suis humeris de ymis convallibus deferebant. Tunc sanctus Colmanus, misertus illis, baculo suo pinxit petram, et fluxerunt aque, que usque hodie illius loci proficiunt monasterio.*

undertakings such as diverting water from mountain sides and down valleys were carried out in Irish monasteries.[77]

A monastic life was defined practically by stability, regulation of conversations and silence, dress, possessions, learning, mealtimes and types of permitted food, fasting and penance, punishment, sleeping hours, moving within the confines of the enclosure, relationships within the community and with the outside world, degrees of withdrawal from the world, sexuality and travelling. The monastic day was regulated by the liturgy and the canonical hours. Again the Irish texts deal with all the requirements of such regulated lives, albeit in somewhat unconventional formats and often not in great detail. The essentials of the Irish monastic life are condensed in the short Old Irish text, *Teist Chóemáin Cluana meic Treóin for scoil Óc-Sinchill Chille Ached* 'The testimony of Cóemán of Cluain mac Treoin as to the school of Sinchell the Younger of Killeigh (Co. Offaly)':[78]

> These are the arrangements and customs that were at Sinchell the Younger's school. Devotion without weariness. Obedience without murmuring. Dressing without excess. Fasting without violation. Exile without returning. Constancy (?) against idleness. Blessing the meal. Dining without leavings. Perseverance in learning. Observance of the canonical hours. Constant cultivation of Heaven. Strengthening every weak one. Not caring for the world. Desiring Mass. Listening to elders. Adoration of chastity. Standing by the weak. Frequent confession. Contempt of the body. Respect for the soul. Humanity in need. Attending the sick. Cross-vigil in silence. Compassion for sickness. Contemplating the scriptures. Proclaiming the gospels. Honour to the old. Keeping festival days holy. Brevity in chanting. Maintaining (spiritual?) friendship. Seriously avoiding women. Dread of their stories. Great hatred of their talk. Not reaching for their excess chatting. Not to be alone with one of them(?) in one house. Without eagerness to converse with them. Purity in these men, the better for their souls. Humility to their master. Their master, their servant. Finit.

77 See the UCD School of Archaeology Glendalough Project https://www.ucd.ie/archaeology/research/glendalough/ accessed 26 April 2022 in which potential monumental mill races have been discovered in the monastic precinct. 78 Meyer, *Hibernica minora*, pp 41–2 (Appendix). Minor amendments to translation. Original: *Teist Choemain Cluana meic Treoin for scoil Oc-Sinchill Chille Ached inso. Iss iat so cinte 7 gnathaighthe buí oc scoil Oíc-Sinchill. Crabath cen scís. Umla cen fodord. Eitiud cen forcraid. Aíne cen elniud. Ailithre cen tintudh. Bidecht fri hespaib. Beannachadh prainde. Praind cen fuidell. Fedli fri foglaim. Frithailim tratha. Sírfrecar nime. Nertath cech faind. Nemsnim don tsaegal. Sanntugadh oifrinn. Eistecht fri sruitheib. Adrath do genus. Gabail ic fannaib. Faisidiud menic. Michata cuirp. Catu do anmain. Doennacht fri hecin. Torrama gallrach. Croisfigeall hi toi. Troige do deidnius. Scrutach sgreptra. Adscela do faisneis. Onair do senaib. Saire do sollamnaib. Cumbri canta. Coimed cairdesa. Mna do*

This text is mnemonic and was used probably to drill the fundamentals of monasticism into novices. Although not consistent throughout the text, alliteration and repetition of phrases and word endings occur frequently, presumably to as a way of prompting a student's memory:[79]

> … Áine cen el**niud**. / Ailithre cen tin**túdh**. / **Bi**decht fri hespaib. / **B**eannachadh ***p**rainde*. / ***P**raind* cen **f**uidell. / **F**edli fri **f**oglaim …

This text then contained the basic level of knowledge needed for a monastic life, more rudimentary and less polished than the *Apgitir Chrábaid*. A comparison between 'The monastery of Tallaght', 'The teaching of Máel Ruain', 'The rule of the *céli Dé*', 'The rule of Ailbe', a fragmentary customary in Latin in MS Codex Augiense CCXXIII,[80] the poems of Máel Ísu Ua Brolcháin, the eleventh-century poem *Cinnus atá do thinnrem*,[81] the eighth-century continental customary known as the *Memoriale qualiter*,[82] and the English *Regularis Concordia* on core monastic precepts and the lifestyle is worth pursuing to contextualize the Irish regulatory texts within the wider world of monasticism. This survey, by referring to some texts dating to pre-900, attempts to establish changes that might suggest more cohesion – or indeed less, as Bernard and Malachy would have argued – between early Irish monasticism and monastic cultures being lived elsewhere. A further essential element in this discussion has to be the Irish reliance on foundational texts such as John Cassian's *Institutes* and *Conferences* and Gregory the Great's *Moralia in Job*.

'Amor et timor Dei', 'puritas cordis': obedience, humility and spiritual love

Fundamental to monasticism is the fear and love of God and the manner in which a purity of heart leads the monk, and indeed all Christians, away from evil, and towards a final goal of salvation. John Cassian's works are instilled with these concepts, the doctrine of *puritas cordis* based on Cassian's 'biblical anchor' of the Beatitudes 'blessed are the pure in heart, for they shall see God' (Matthew 5:8).[83] In his *Institutes*, Cassian's forceful declarations offer a clear path in life to monks:[84]

> Hear, then, in a few words the method by which you will be able to ascend to the highest perfection without any effort or difficulty.

mórimgabail. Athuath dia n-érscelaib. Romiscais dia raidsecbaib. Nem-rochtain a rocomraid. Cen oentaig an oentige. Cen escus dia n-acallaim. Idna isna feraib se, ferrdi dia n-anmaib. Inisli dia maigistir. A maigistir amodh [mog]. Finid. 79 Meyer, *Hibernica minora*, p. 41. 80 Gearóid Mac Niocaill (ed.), 'Fragments d'un coutumier monastique irlandais du viiie-ixe siècle', *Scriptorium* 15:2 (1961), 228–33. 81 Breathnach, '*Cinnus atá do thinnrem*'. 82 Matthew Mattingly (ed.), 'The *Memoriale Qualiter*: an eighth century monastic customary', *The American Benedictine Review* 60:1 (2009), 62–75. 83 Stewart, *Cassian the monk*, p. 43. 84 Ramsey, *Institutes*, pp 102–3 (Book IV, Chapter XLIII).

> According to the Scriptures, 'the beginning' of our salvation and 'of wisdom is the fear of the Lord.' From the fear of the Lord is born a salutary compunction. From compunction of heart there proceeds renunciation – that is, the being deprived of and the contempt of all possessions. From this deprivation humility is begotten. From humility is generated the dying of desire. When desire has died all the vices are uprooted and wither away. Once the vices have been expelled the virtues bear fruit and grow. When virtue abounds purity of heart is acquired. With purity of heart the perfection of apostolic love is possessed.

Gregory the Great, whose works like Cassian's were known in Ireland,[85] elucidated further on these ideals in his *Moralia in Job*:[86]

> But holy men, in proportion as they contemplate the mysteries of heavenly truths with more perfect purity of heart, pant after them with daily increased ardour of affection. They long to be henceforth filled to the full at that fountain head, whence they as yet taste but a little drop with the mouth of contemplation. They long entirely to subdue the promptings of the flesh, no longer to be subject to any thing unlawful in the imaginations of the heart springing from the corruption thereof.

Hence purity of heart and fear and love of God lead to tears of repentance, humility, renunciation of possessions, mortification of desires, apostolic love and purity of body. Unceasing prayer is necessary as purity of heart is 'a fragile state in this life' and fear of failure is a constant anguish, as expressed by Columba Stewart in his analysis of Cassian's treatment of induced tears: 'The monk progresses from fear to love and then to a "more sublime fear" lest the God who has loved and forgiven so much should be disappointed (*Conf.* 11.13)'.[87]

What are the echoes of these fundamental monastic ideals in the Irish regulatory literature and associated texts? Jennifer O'Reilly argues that in his life of Columba, Adomnán, aware of *timor Dei* in monastic literature, 'shows Columba to have been so filled with the wisdom which is the perfect fear of the Lord that all temporal preoccupations were driven out; he was already, therefore, living the heavenly life and mediating Christ's pattern of perfection to others'.[88] In a sequence of episodes, lessons in fearing God as steps towards attaining

85 Brian Ó Cuív, 'St Gregory and St Dunstan in a Middle-Irish poem on the origins of liturgical chant' in Nigel Ramsay, Margaret Sparks and Tim W. T. Tatton-Brown (eds), *St Dunstan: his life, times and cult* (Woodbridge, 1992), pp 273–97. 86 *Morals on the Book of Job*, p. 263 (Book VIII, para. 40) http://www.lectionarycentral.com/GregoryMoraliaIndex.html Accessed 25 September 2023. 87 Stewart, *Cassian the monk*, p. 129. 88 Jennifer O'Reilly, 'The wisdom of the scribe and the fear of the Lord in the Life of Columba' in Dauvit Broun and Thomas Owen Clancy (eds), *Spes Scotorum. Hope of the Scots* (Edinburgh, 1999),

perfect wisdom and becoming a vessel of the Holy Spirit were taught by Columba to his monks Fergnae, Colcu and Berchán. Each monk demonstrated varying degrees of advancement towards perfection, Fergnae being the most advanced in his wisdom.[89] As demonstrated by O'Reilly, Adomnán, albeit through a hagiographical work, was fully aware of universal monastic ideals and of the need to transmit them to generations of novices as fundamentals of their vocation. Success in transmitting the fundamental ideals of monasticism is evident in the Irish vernacular 'rules'.

The Rule of Cormac Mac Cuilennáin, which reads like an elegant metrical résumé of monastic principles, uses all the mnemonic features of its metre to prompt the memory, as it proclaims:[90]

> **Ní** heress nolc, **ní** báegul:
> Serc Dé dliges a úaman:
> **C**éim **c**en **c**hlóenúaill ó Díabul,
> Nebbuith óenúair i núabur …
>
> It is no evil heresy, it is no mistake: **God's love demands His fear**. A step without wicked pride away from the Devil; not to be one hour in arrogance …

> D*í*n **a**nma, **a**scnam nime,
> **Br***í*g **a**mra, **a**ltrom glaine,
> **B***í*ad **b***í*s iar nd*í*bdud toile,
> **C**orp **C**r*í*st la fuil **M**aic **M**aire.
>
> A protection of the soul, an approach to Heaven, a wonderful power, **a fostering of purity, is the food which is after the extinction of desire**, Christ's body with the blood of Mary's Son.

The eleventh-century monastic poet Máel Ísu Ua Brolcháin in his treatment of the eight vices and the remedies for them equally conveys the need for the fear of the Lord as part of overcoming the world's challenges:[91]

> Hence this is what is permitted, fear of noble Christ, his hope in the Creator and listening with humility.
>
> His humble, blessed mind from the heart, fair the appearance, his truly evident humility in action and in speech …

pp 159–211, at p. 203. **89** Anderson and Anderson, *Life of Columba*, pp 208–11 [iii. 19]; Sharpe, *Adomnán of Iona*, pp 220–3 [III 19–21]. **90** Strachan, 'Cormac's rule', 64, 66 §§7, 12. A slightly amended translation. **91** Ní Bhrolcháin, *Maol Íosa Ó Brolcháin*, pp 70–1 §§44–5. Original: *Is ed dlegar deside / omun Ísu uais, / a fhrescisiu in Dúileman / a umla co cluais. / / A menma bec bennachtach / ó chride, coín cruth, / a inísle fhírfhollus / i ngním is i nguth* … My own

God's revenge on those who do not fear him and his capacity to protect those intent on a religious life – be it monastic or clerical – is also a recurrent motif. The master who gives advice in the eleventh-century poem *Cinnus atá do thinnrem* warns his pupil:[92]

> Let your thoughts be fixed, o dear boy, on the noble King of holy Heaven;
> it is he who is capable of protecting you, crowning you, destroying you.

Humility, obedience, compassion (*caritas*) and spiritual love constitute the essence of a community in the eyes of the compiler of the Rule of Ailbe, sentiments that in their brevity correspond to many similar ideals expressed throughout monastic literature:[93]

> Their father is noble God, their mother is Holy Church;
> let it not be humility in word, let each have compassion on his brother.
>
> If they meet the obligation of obedience together with work,
> rigorous that command, 'o brother, let it be I who does it.'
>
> Let them be holy, let them be pure in heart, in [times of] infidelity let them be true,
> In their exchange of words (?), in aiding their deeds.

Likely to be inspired by similar sources, the above[94] section of the vernacular Irish rule finds an echo in *RB* on the good zeal which monks ought to have:[95]

> … earnestly competing in obedience to one another. No one is to pursue what he judges better for himself, but instead what he judges better for someone else. To their fellow monks to show the pure love of brothers; to God, loving fear; to their abbot unfeigned and humble love …

The Rule of Ailbe requires leniency towards those who transgress, a sentiment not particularly prevalent in monastic literature, although the solution is common:[96]

English translation. **92** Breatnach, '*Cinnus atá do thinnrem*', 8–9 §4. Original: *Bíd do menma, a meic cride, / re Ruirig náir naímnime; / is é con-ic do shnádud, / do rígad, do robádud.* **93** O Neill, 'Rule of Ailbe', 102–3: §§27[a–c]. Original: *Is Dia úasal a n-athair, is ecclais noíb a máthair, / níp umaldóit for bréthir, airchised cách a bráthair. / Dia tíasat fri haurlataid d'obair immalle / trummae int ord sin, a bráthair, bad messe do-d-gné. / Bad noíb, bad glan a cride, i n-amairse bat fhíra, / i n-immairim a mbríathar, i fortachtain a ngnímae.* **94** O Neill, 'Rule of Ailbe', 106, 47b. Original: *fo mám aurlatad.* **95** *RB*: 72:6–10. **96** O Neill, 'Rule of Ailbe', 104–5 §§36–7. Original: *Iar ngrád ocus aurlataid bad shamlaid fodáilter, / cia beith nech bess anumal, tacair ní rochráiter. / Nech nád daim a chúrsachad ocus nád ataim cairi / dlomaid dó in t-anmcharae dochum nach loccáin aili.*

> According to rank and obedience let it [food] be thus shared out,
> Though there should be one who is naturally disobedient, it is fitting that he should not be tormented.
>
> A person who does not endure reproof, and who confesses not his blame,
> The confessor should warn him off towards some other place.

Constancy, perseverance and stability under the yoke of obedience – staples of the monastic ideal – are to the fore in the Rule of Ailbe, more explicitly conveyed than in the 'Tallaght dossier', and 'The rule of the *céli Dé*', both of which largely contain prescriptions on food, punishment and liturgy. The rule is to be intelligible and fair so that monks will not leave their monastery.[97] The community ruled by a just abbot (*airchinnech*) living fraternally in obedience and humility is successful:[98]

> He [the abbot/*airchinnech*] should not be too great, he should not be scant, he should not utter any evil,
> Let him proclaim to everyone his transgression, his monastery should not be idle …
>
> A community humble, obedient, which says not 'I will not go'; a gentle, compassionate abbot (*airchinnech*) without private possession of goods.

There is a clear message addressed in this tract to *airchinnig*: if you are to be the head of a monastic community, you may have tenants, but you must treat them well, not amass wealth and rule your community following the fundamental ideals of monasticism.

Curbing the eight deadly sins

The 'Tallaght dossier' and 'The rule of the *céli Dé*' are not addressed solely to monastic communities. Transgressions and punishment of the laity and clerics, many of whom were not monks, dominate these texts which also include advice to confessors on how to handle all the church community in general. Indeed, 'The rule of the *céli Dé*' specifically mentions that some prescriptions are *céli Dé* practices (*lasna céliuda Dé*) and one prescription is specifically practised by Máel Ruain's community (*la muintir Moelruain uli*).[99] Putting the strictures addressed to the laity and non-monastic clerics aside, specific directions, punishments and remedies are prescribed for monks and nuns for various transgressions as well as dealing with the practicalities of encountering normal human issues while

97 Ibid., 104–5 (§33), 106–7 (§48), 108–9 (§52). **98** Ibid., 106–7 §§41[b], 45. Original: *Ní rop romór, ní rop terc, ní epre na olc, / fúacrad do chách a chlóini, níp espach a phort … Munter umal, aurlaithe, nád epir ní reg, / airchinnech ciúin, condircel, cen sain-techtad feb.* **99** Gwynn, 'The

living a spiritual life with all its obligations. Provision is made in 'The rule of the *céli Dé*', for example, for nuns when menstruating:[100]

> During the monthly sickness of daughters of the church they are excused from vigils, morning and evening, so long as it lasts, and gruel is to be made for them at terce, at whatever time this happens, because it is right that this sickness should have attention. They do not attend communion in such cases, for they are unclean at these times.

Although the view that women were unclean during menstruation and after childbirth was commonplace, this more caring attitude towards menstruating nuns reflects a less severe approach than the oft-expressed medieval ambivalence about menstruation and other natural bodily functions. Caroline Walker Bynum points to the debate among medieval theologians as to whether the Virgin Mary menstruated and the degree to which consistent fasting suppressed menstruation.[101] It was also one of the issues Heloise raised with Abelard when discussing how the Rule of Benedict 'was written for men alone'.[102] Relieving them from austerity and feeding them with extra gruel runs contrary to other harsher practices.

Central to the monastic life was suppression of the eight deadly sins which were the greatest obstacles to perfection: gluttony, impurity, covetousness, anger, dejection, accidia (dissatisfaction/boredom), vainglory, and pride. Cassian concentrates on these vices in his works and on remedies that might lead to perfection:[103]

> Thus, penetrating the dark shadows of our vices with the most pure eyes of our soul, we shall be able to expose them and bring them into the light, and we shall be in a position to disclose their causes and natures both to those who are free of them and to those who are still under their sway. In this way, according to the prophet, we shall pass through the fire of the vices that burn our minds most terribly and immediately to pass unharmed as well through the waters of the virtues that extinguish them, and, bedewed with spiritual remedies, we shall deserve, thanks to our purity of heart, to be led to a place of refreshment and perfection.

rule of the Céli Dé', 72–3 §36. **100** Ibid., 78–9 §50. Original: *Galar mistai bís for ingenaib eclaise, saire a figle doib oiret bis foraib, maiten 7 fescor, 7 brochán do denam doib am theirt, secip aimser, fobith dlegar airmitiu in galair sin. Nis tiagat dino do laim ind quia [immundae] sunt in illo tempore.* **101** Caroline Walker Bynum, 'Fast, feast, and flesh: the religious significance of food to medieval women', *Representations* 11 (1985), 1–25, at p. 11. **102** Betty Radice (trans.) (revised by M.T. Clanchy), *The letters of Abelard and Heloise* (London, 2003 (revised ed.)), p. 94. I owe this reference to Colmán Ó Clabaigh. **103** Ramsey, *Institutes*, p. 116 (Book V, Chapter II).

As in most of western Christendom, and monastic traditions, the concept of the seven or eight deadly sins was embedded in the Irish tradition, as evidenced from the *Homily on the deadly sins* – possibly a *céli Dé* text derived from earlier penitentials –[104] and Máel Ísu Ua Brolcháin's poem *Ocht n-éric na ndualach* 'The eight payments of the vices'.[105] Suppression of these vices involved not just individual and communal prayer and meditation, education in recognizing and challenging them, but when all else failed punishing them spiritually – through confession and repentance – and materially by fasting. A considerable amount of the *céli Dé* legislation, including the fragment, unusually in Latin, of a customary preserved in MS Codex Augiense CCXXIII, is taken up with diet and fasting as a means of penance. Some punishments were absurd. A combination of pride and vainglory on the part of Máel Díthrub once led to a comical episode, not unlike the account in the twelfth-century *Aislinge Meic Con Glinne*:[106]

> It is not the practice of the *céli Dé* to do anything whatever after vespers on Saturday. Once it happened to me that I chanced to stay in the bath for a while after vespers on Saturday. He [Máel Ruain] told me to go without condiments of bacon or butter on the Saturday evening and the Sunday following.

If true, it is a personal account that testifies – similar to the stories in 'The Sayings of the Desert Fathers' – to the degrees of severity followed by different 'masters' and the fear they might have instilled in others. Anger and lust were countered by fasting and abstinence, the belief being that less food – and indeed sleep deprivation – subdued these earthly emotions and bodily desires.[107] The 'Tallaght dossier' was in step with these common curative beliefs:[108]

> Those whose desires are excited, it may be through hearing confessions, or merely with meditating, or through youth, need strict abstinence to subdue them, because it is excess of blood in their body that is the cause. Afterwards, when the blood subsides, then lust and desire subside.

104 Kuno Meyer (ed.), 'Mitteilungen aus irischen Handschriften:II Aus Rawlinson B. 512. Von den Todsünden', *Zeitschrift für celtische Philologie* 3 (1901), 24–8; Follett, *Céli Dé in Ireland*, p. 225. See also E.J. Gwynn (ed.), 'An Irish penitential', *Ériu* 7 (1914), 121–95. **105** Ní Bhrolcháin, *Maol Íosa*, pp 60–77. **106** Gwynn and Purton, 'The monastery of Tallaght', 144 §45. Original: *Ni fogní lasna celiu dé ni di nach ret do denam iar nespartain domnaich. Fecht robúi damsæ domchaomnacuir airisem hi fothrucud sel bec iar nespartain domnaich. Asrubartsom buith cen anland de saill na him aidchi ndomnaig 7 dia domnaig tara heis.* **107** Gwynn and Purton, 'The monastery of Tallaght', 141 §36, 148–9 §§58–9; Mary W. Helms, 'Before the dawn. Monks and the night in late antiquity and early medieval Europe', *Anthropos* 99:1 (2004), 177–91. **108** Gwynn and Purton, 'The monastery of Tallaght', 149 §59. Original: *Aos duanat foibdi a tolæ bes la coibsenugud no imradad tantum no la oitid. Aibstinit*

As is obvious throughout the ages, these beliefs could lead to cruel and destructive outcomes, an illustration of which is told from the rather extreme – and not necessarily typical – ascetic's perspective in 'The monastery of Tallaght'. Molaise of Daiminis's sister Copar was weighed down by sexual desire, 'for it is a third part as strong in women as in men', and to counter this quite normal human yearning her saintly brother decided to ration her food.[109] After a year, she came to him while he was sewing and to measure her desire, he thrust a needle into her palm. Three streams of blood issued from her hand, an indication to Molaise that her meals needed to be reduced further. This happened a second year and her food was further reduced until her third visit to him when no blood issued from her palm, at which point Molaise advised that she should maintain these rations until her death. While in no way historical, this story underlines the commonplace convictions that women were more lustful than men and that desire could be quenched physically by subduing the blood through fasting. Of course, this had to be complemented by spiritual exercises and good works. In Máel Ísu Ua Brolcháin's pithy words:[110]

> *Lubair, aíne, airnigde,*
> *inísle co mór,*
> *léigenn díthrom, dímicin,*
> *is é a leiges lór.*
>
> Work, fasting, praying, great humility, serious study, despising [the world], that is its ample cure.

At variance with the portrayal of women as weak and hostages of their fiery desires and closer to Máel Ísu Ua Brolcháin's image of how to counter evil ways was St Samthann of Clonbroney who is praised in the following terms:[111]

> She was full of the grace of good works, decked with the display of all virtues, and in her life fully endowed with good examples, a pious teacher of the lowly, but a most humble servant in the maintenance of the body … Thus she spent the course of this present life in holiness and justice in the sight of her spouse, Christ.

'The teaching of Máel Ruain' and 'The rule of the *céli Dé*' deal less with such penances and prescriptions. There is a possibility that this has to do with the structure of both texts, especially 'The rule of the *céli Dé*' which is closer to being a customary – a reflection of a monastery's daily routine – than a

dedirn doa troathad fobithin is roimmad fola inda cuirp ised adrali. Andand fofeiscren iarum ind fuil is and fofeiscren ind tol 7 an accobar. **109** Gwynn and Purton, 'The monastery of Tallaght', 149 §60. **110** Ní Bhrolcháin, *Maol Íosa*, pp 64–5 §20. **111** Africa, 'Life of the holy virgin

penitential, as it deals in sections with matters such as adhering to correct liturgical practices, diets consumed during the liturgical year, administering the sacraments, sleep, hygiene and so forth. In the case of deviating from a chaste life, both texts concentrate on the outcome for bishops and priests rather than on the consequences for monks. According to 'The rule of the *céli Dé*', falling into sin while in holy orders was one of the four sins for which no penance could be done in the land of Ireland.[112] Máel Ruain is credited with ruling that any priest who was unchaste could not become a bishop even if he did penance.[113] On vices such as anger, idleness or backbiting, both texts are somewhat lenient towards monks in that such faults were to be confessed immediately and not left until the Sunday reckoning.[114] The intense dislike of murmuring expressed in *RB*, for example, is absent and there is no great concentration on resolving internal disputes.[115] Compassion for one's brother is stressed in the Rule of Ailbe.[116] Of course, *RB* being a more practical rule reflected a reality of human conflict that every community had to face, rather than the ideal expressed in some of the Irish regulatory texts. As for the administration of physical punishment, the term *fiach aibne* 'flagellation' (*abann* borrowed from Latin *habena* 'strap, whip'[117]) occurs as a form of punishment in all the *céli Dé* texts, just as corporal punishment was meted out in *RB*, particularly to the obdurate monk who refused to show humility and repentance.[118] Such harsh punishment was administered, however, at certain times including between Epiphany and Easter, and on Saturday rather than on Sunday evening. The explanation for the latter practice, as narrated in the 'The teaching of Máel Ruain', suggests a consciousness on the part of these ascetics that their lifestyle was monitored by the mainstream church, described by them as *áes na sen chell* 'the people of the old churches':[119]

> The reason for administering it [punishment] on Saturday was this: Máel Díthruib asked Máel Ruain whether he would allow the Sunday evening's castigation to be inflicted on Saturday, 'for' said he, 'if the folk of these large old churches all round us hear that we administer castigation on Sunday, there is no kind of work that they will not do on Sunday.' So Máel Ruain allowed castigation to be administered on Saturday for this reason.

Samthann', pp 108–9 para. 25. **112** Gwynn, 'The rule of the Céli Dé', 74–5 §38. The other unpardonable sins were to lie with a dead woman, to transgress with a kinswoman (daughter and sister) and to divulge a confession. **113** Gwynn, 'The teaching of Mael Ruain', 40–1 §69. **114** Gwynn, 'The rule of the Céli Dé', 68–9 §16; Gwynn, 'The teaching of Mael Ruain', 13–15 §20. **115** *RB*: Chap. 6.7–8. **116** O Neill, 'Rule of Ailbe', 102–3 §27a. **117** Joseph Vendryes, 'Étymologies. II. – GALLOIS *afwyn* et *afn*; BRETON *aven*', *Études celtiques* 4:2 (1948), 327–34, at pp 329–33. **118** *RB*: Chap. 2.28; Chap. 23.5; Chap. 71.9. **119** Gwynn, 'The teaching of Mael Ruain', 48–9 §82. Original: *as uime do buailtí é san satharn .i. Maol dithraib do fhiafraigh do Maol Ruaín an bhudh cead leis an fiach aibhni na haidhchi luaín*

Of course, this passage could also be read as condemnation of the 'old churches' for their laxity in regard to Sunday observance, a subject of concern to the church and reflected in texts such as the ninth-century *Cáin Domnaig* 'The law of Sunday' and *Epistil Ísu* 'The epistle of Jesus'.[120]

How often flagellation was administered is difficult to estimate but its practice distinguished those following an ascetic life from the rest of the population living in a monastery and from the rest of the laity. The text *Anmchairdes Mancháin Léith* justifies the practice in the following terms:[121]

> *.. fiach inna haibne*
> *doberar cid díchra,*
> *annsa ferg maic Muiri*
> *cona chlaidem díghla.*
>
> .. the debt of the strap (i.e. flagellation) is administered although strict, dearer the wrath of the son of Mary with his sword of punishment.

Didactic poems and prose treatises on the eight vices and remedies to counter them were part of the common culture of monasticism. Aldhelm of Malmesbury (d. 709), abbot and poet, added the verses *De octo vitiis principatibus* to his *Carmen de virginitate*.[122] Hermann of Reichenau (d. 1054) composed a lengthy Latin poetic dialogue on the eight vices. The dialogue takes place between Hermann, a female muse and the sisters (*sorores*), who may represent a female monastic community.[123] Hermann details the vices in vivid descriptions of horror and evil. Even at the end when the *sorores* beg the muse for the remedies, they are not forthcoming. The theme of the eight vices and, unlike Hermann of Reichenau, remedies to counter them crops up in the poetry of Máel Ísu Ua Brolcháin. In her assessment of the latter's poems, Muireann Ní Bhrolcháin contrasts them with earlier Irish so-called 'nature poetry' popularly ascribed to the *céli Dé*,[124] 'only the stricter constituents of the culdee's teaching emerges;

do bhualadh de sathair[n], 'oir,' ar se, 'ma chluinid áos na sean-cheall mor-sa do gach leith dinn go mbuailmid-ne fiach aibhne dia domhnaigh, ni fhuil obair ar bith nac[h] diongna siad dia domhnaig', 7 do cheaduigh Maol Ruain an fiach aibhne do bhualadh día sathairn ar an adhbar sin. **120** For a detailed discussion of these texts see Elizabeth Boyle, 'Eschatology and reform in early Irish law: the evidence of Sunday legislation' in Matthew Gabriele and James T. Palmer (eds), *Apocalypse and reform from late antiquity to the Middle Ages* (Abingdon, 2018), pp 121–38. http://thecelticist.ie/wp-content/uploads/2020/02/Cain-Domnaig.pdf Accessed 11 August 2023. **121** Meyer, '*Anmchairdes Mancháin Léith so*', 312 §22. **122** Michael Lapidge and James L. Rosier (eds), *Aldhelm. The poetic works* (Cambridge, 1985). **123** Hannah Williams, 'Authority and pedagogy in Hermann of Reichenau's *De Octo Vitiis Principalibus*' (PhD, University of Manchester, 2006). British Library EThOS online dissertation no. 693454 (https://ethos.bl.uk/) accessed 8 September 2020. **124** This popular ascription has been questioned by scholars. See Donnchadh Ó Corráin, 'Early Irish hermit poetry?' in Donnchadh Ó Corráin, Liam Breatnach and Kim R. McCone (eds), *Sages, saints and*

continuous emphasis on celibacy, abstinence, purity and self-criticism are recommended as a means of penance and retribution for sin'.[125] Máel Ísu composed invocations, prayers and hymns mainly in the vernacular, although it would appear from the AU obit that he was also versed in Latin.[126] The central theme of his compositions revolves around his pleading with God for protection against evil and especially the eight vices:[127]

The Holy Spirit living
in our bodies and souls;
readily protect us
from danger, from disease,

from devils, from sins,
from Hell with its every evil,
O Jesus! may your Spirit
bless and save us.

In a didactic poem *Ocht n-éric na ndúalach* 'Eight remedies of the vices', Máel Ísu describes the eight vices and the remedies applicable to each one, concentrating on chastity, poverty, abstinence, prayer and reading. Of greed he says:[128]

Greed what it does is
to force miserliness upon you;
a craving for all things,
pillage, plunder, and robbery.

Those weeds should be cleared
from the soul and from the body;
according to the dictates of the apostle –
it is the root of all evil.

The sole cure is
contempt for the dark world,
being in continual poverty
without acquiring wealth.

storytellers. Celtic studies in honour of Professor James Carney (Maynooth, 1989), pp 251–67. **125** Ní Bhrolcháin, 'Maol Íosa Ó Brolcháin: his work and family', 50. **126** Original: *Mael Isu H. Brolcan sui in ecna 7 in crabaid 7 i filidhecht i m-berlai cechtardhai suam spiritum emisit.* **127** Ní Bhrolcháin, 'Maol Íosa Ó Brolcháin: his work and family', 50. Ní Bhrolcháin, *Maol Íosa Ó Brolcháin*, p. 58 §§2–3. Original: *In Spirut Naem d'aitreb / ar cuirp is ar n-anma, / diar snádud co solma / ar gábud, ar galra. / / ar demnaib, ar phecdaib, / ar iffern co n-iliuc; / A Ísu ron-naema, / ron-saera do Spirut.* **128** Ní Bhrolcháin, 'Maol Íosa Ó Brolcháin', 53. Original: Ní

On the greatest sin, lust, Máel Ísu defines it and prescribes a remedy:[129]

> Toil, abstinence, prayer
> and great humility,
> weighty study, contempt for this world,
> that is its entire remedy.

Despite the disparity between Máel Ísu and Hermann of Reichenau's poems, a common tradition is evident, as may be appreciated from a few lines from Hermann's tract on the subject of greed and the material pleasures of the world:[130]

> This dread creature then seems
> to herself most just and pious,
> if she does not snatch away things belonging to others,
> and piles up her own things around herself,
> not realizing that, to Christ,
> he is guilty of pillage, the cruel man who
> piles up things around himself,
> holding on to riches which ought to be given in gift to the pauper.
> For the greater number of things
> God gave to one man, he hardly gave to him alone,
> but so that everything superfluous to him
> he should give to the man in need.

In her consideration of Hermann's poem and of its place in the intellectual and educational shifts in German monastic culture of the time, Hannah Williams argues that 'the marriage of the arts and specifically poetry with the ideals of the moral life' is evident in *De octo vitiis* in which Hermann, the teacher, attempts to preserve a sense of his continued presence as a master of the moral life, thus providing an important insight into the educational ideals of the eleventh-century cloister.[131] Given that there was a strong tradition of composing didactic poetry in Irish monasteries, it would seem that these educational ideals also

Bhrolcháin, *Maol Íosa Ó Brolcháin*, p. 64 §§§21–3: *Saint is ed do-gní-side / gainne d'asluch ort, / accobar cech aenréta, / slat, brat, airchell olc. / / Is dibdide is lusar-sa / ó anime ó chorp, / iar forgell in ardapstail / is frém do cech olc. / / Is é so a haenleiges / dínsem domain duib, / beith di neuch a sírbochtai, / cen tinól nach cruid.* **129** Ní Bhrolcháin, 'Maol Íosa Ó Brolcháin', 54. Original: Ní Bhrolcháin, *Maol Íosa Ó Brolcháin*, p. 64 §20: *Lubair, aíne, airnigde, / inísle co mór, / léigenn díthrom, dímicin, / is é a leiges lór.* **130** Williams, 'Authority and pedagogy', pp 201–2. Original: *Haec dira tunc iustissima / sibi uidetur ac pia, / aliena si non auferat / sua atque se cum congerat, / non cogitans, Christo reus / quod sit rapinae, qui ferus / donanda lucra pauperi / tenenda congregat sibi. / Nam plura cui Deus dedit, / soli tenenda haud tradidit, / sed indigenti ut omnia / donet sibi superflua.* **131** Williams, 'Authority and pedagogy', p. 18.

prevailed among its monastic teachers, and that although ATig's praise of Máel Ísu's learning – 'so great was it that he himself made books and treatises replete with acuteness and intellect'[132] – initially appears far-fetched, perhaps it reflects a truth that cannot be supported due to the loss of his original works.

Degrees of withdrawal from the world

The image of the anchorite or hermit existing alone in the desert – be it the actual desert, a cave or a rocky island – facing his demons is a common motif in popular literature about early monasticism – and not just in 'Celtic' monasticism. But this was not necessarily the norm. The coenbitic life was preferred and stricter asceticism was for the more experienced monk, and often only for short periods. As noted previously, this was the view of the *Hibernensis*. The annals suggest that on the whole anchorites lived either within monastic settlements or in separate quarters within easy reach of the main settlement. The sentiments expressed in the so-called hermit poetry are often wishful thinking on the part of clerics or monks, or even other lay church officials, weighed down by the burdens of their duties.[133] The well-known poem *Comad Manchín Léith* 'The prayer of Manchín Liath' touches on accidia – one of the eight vices which describes a state of spiritual listlessness – as it draws a picture of the ideal monastic life sought by the poet. This idyll consists of a community of twelve monks, a church with a linen altar cloth and a single candle and a concealed hut as living quarters, good food (fragrant leek, hens, salmon, trout and honey). This, his *díthrub* 'hermitage', would be located in an ideal wilderness in a wood, with a clear pool and a southern aspect. A desirable desert for anyone, at least for a period! But the origin of this wishful thinking is revealed subtly in the poem. Describing the men Manchín wishes to have in his community, he says:[134] 'A few men of sense – we will tell their number – humble and obedient, to pray to the King'. And it would be a community 'for the care of the body, without buffoonery, without indulgence, without thought of evil'.[135] Perhaps these undesirable features describe the community among whom the poet lived and sought to leave behind for the pleasant wooded desert. Leaving a community to follow a stricter life was not necessarily approved of and in 'The monastery of Tallaght' and 'The teaching of Máel Ruain', Máel Ruain is rather scathing about two particular anchorites. Cornán, the anchorite piper of south Leinster, to whom Máel Ruain used to send gifts, wished to play a tune to the founder of Tallaght. Máel Ruain would have none of it as his ears only listened to the music

132 Original: *Mael-Issu Húa Brolchan, sruith-senóir Erenn 7 ardshai na hecna, conidh e a med co nderna fen liubra 7 eladhna lanmora do amaíndse 7 do índleacht, 7 fuair bass a ngradsaib De.* 133 Ó Corráin, 'Early Irish hermit poetry?'. 134 Meyer, 'Comad Manchín Léith', 39–40 §5. Original: *Húathad óclaoch innide, innisem al-lín, / it é umle irlataidh d'urguidi ind Rígh.* 135 Ibid., 39–40 §9. Original: *Óenteg[d]ais do aithigid fri deit[h]ide cuirp, cen drúid[e], cen indláduth, cen imrádud uilc.*

of Heaven.[136] An even harsher judgement is pronounced by Máel Ruain about the anchorite who was variously associated with Cluain ua Dubáin (?Cloonoan, parish Kilkeedy, Co. Clare) or Clonard:[137]

> ('The monastery of Tallaght' version): There was a great anchorite at Cluain ua Dubáin. Great was his labour: two hundred genuflections he used to perform at matins and a hundred every canonical hour, a hundred at nocturns – seven hundred in all. This was told to Máel Ruain. 'By my word,' says Máel Ruain, 'a time will come to him before his death when he shall not perform a single genuflection.' This came to pass: his feet were seized so that he could not perform a vigil for a long time before his death, on account of the excessive amount he had performed in other days.

It was not without reason that the Rule of Ailbe advised against monks leaving the monastic enclosure, in line with many other monastic rules of all traditions, as the lone individual could stray in either of two directions. He could fall prey to the temptations of the world or to unsustainable and extreme ascetic practices. Máel Ruain's advice to the anchorite Colcu of Slane, who refused to eat supplies being sent to him from his own monastery 'as he was much given to austerities and strict abstinence', was that he was not fit to join his community as he would not be strong enough to undertake his proper share of work. The anchorite's objection to the 'fruit of the patron's land' (*torad na n-érlam*) because it was impure was also overridden by Máel Ruain who maintained that he should eat enough to sustain himself and give the rest away to the poor.[138] 'The rule of the *céli Dé*' lays out a practical guide to how those who wished to practise dietary abstinence should proceed, namely, reduce one's intake by one eighth over six months and continue at that rate up to a total reduction of five eighths. If done gradually according to this prescription, a substantial reduction in food or sleep could be achieved but again the text cautions against severe discipline which could lead to sickness or disease.[139] One of the shorter Old Irish rules – named The Rule of Comgall in one late manuscript and not necessarily solely directed at monks – sums up the need for guidance in pursuing a religious life:[140]

136 Gwynn and Purton, 'The monastery of Tallaght', 131 §10; Gwynn, 'The teaching of Mael Ruain', 30–1 §50. **137** Gwynn and Purton, 'The monastery of Tallaght', 141 §34; Gwynn, 'The teaching of Mael Ruain', 60–1 §103. Original (Gwynn and Purton): *Búi alaile anchore i cluain úa duban hé. Mór iarum a sáothar. da cet slechtain matin ised dognid 7 cét cacha tratha 7 cet im ermergi secht cet ule. Adfes do maolrúaoin indní. Asbir mo bríathar ol maólrúaoin. Beith ré dosom ríanecaib 7 ni dognéa cid oenslechtain. Doronad ón rogabtha a cossæ cona dernæ figild rée mór ria necaib lasind forcrid dorigni día naild.* **138** Gwynn and Purton, 'The monastery of Tallaght', 159–60 §77. **139** Gwynn, 'The rule of the Céli Dé', 76–7 §46. **140** Strachan, 'A Old-Irish metrical rule', p. 197 §15. Translation updated. Original: *Ecnaid cráibthech dot airli / is maith d'imgabáil péne / cid mór latsu do dúre, ní bé dot réir fodéne.*

> A devout scholar to guide you, it is good to avoid punishment. Though you deem great your rigour, be not under your own guidance.

Poverty and almsgiving

When a monk or a nun is on a life journey of fearing and loving God and hoping for salvation by concentrating on purity, humility and divine love, then the world of ordinary human beings can only be regarded as a place full of distractions and temptations ready to divert the servants of God from their chosen pilgrimage. Eadmer's description of St Oswald's distress while living among the wealthy canons of Winchester captures the inner conflict faced by many religious during their lives. When Oswald realized that he could not alter the canons' lifestyle of wealth and pomp, and that he might be drawn away from his vocation, he consulted his uncle Bishop Oda:[141]

> When he spoke with the bishop in heartfelt discussion and wept over the miseries of this mortal life, and they had considered in the conversation which ensued between them how difficult it is for a man advancing amidst the attractions of the world not to be ensnared by those allurements, Oswald, the soldier of Christ, said that it had now dawned upon him that he wished henceforth to follow Christ, to be stripped of every worldly thing, and truly to become a monk.

Oswald was sent to Fleury for his formation as a Benedictine monk where he was 'given by the abbot a withdrawn location in the church in which he might attend more closely to God according to the manner of his religious life'.[142] He was challenged by the Devil through various tricks but triumphed through his own zeal and faith. Of course, Irish saints had similar experiences and they also prevailed. But what were the great temptations of the world and how did they undermine the monastic pilgrim's intentions? The allure of material possessions, sexual desire and idle talk could all lead to scandal and downfall. Owning land, gathering tributes and having subject tenants were the basis of wealth and power, both ecclesiastical and secular. Attempting to live separately from, or devolving the responsibility for, the administration of these economic and social activities characterized the aspirations of a monastic community drawn towards an ascetic life. This was difficult, if not impossible, to achieve and, therefore, the emphasis

141 Andrew J. Turner and Bernard J. Muir (eds), *Eadmer of Canterbury: Lives and miracles of Saints Oda, Dunstan, and Oswald*. Oxford Medieval Texts (Oxford, 2006), pp 226–7. Original: *Vbi miserias uitae mortalis cum pontifice loquens pia consideratione defleuit, ubi quam difficile sit hominem inter mundi illecebras gradientem ipsis illecebris non irretiri utrinque sermo procedens appendit, infert Christi miles Oswaldus sibi iam cecidisse in mentem se nudum saecularibus cunctis uelle amodo Christum sequi, et uere monachum fieri.* **142** Turner and Muir, *Eadmer of Canterbury*, pp 228–9. Original: *Hic idem Domini seruus secretum in aecclesia locum ab abbate acceperat, in quo pro modo conuersationis suae Deo familiarius adhaereret.*

had to be on avoiding wealth accumulation and what ensued from that. The 'Tallaght dossier' and 'The rule of the *céli Dé*' do not explicitly mention greed and possessions but regulate how tithes (*dechmad*, borrowed from Latin *decima*) were collected. 'The teaching of Máel Ruain' is the most specific in this regard:[143]

> The *decimnóir* (that is the name of the vessel which they had to take the tithe) was kept for the purpose of receiving the tithe of fish and curds (?*grúisle*) … Every slice of fish that they ate and every curd (?) used to be put first into the *decimnóir* to measure it. They used to keep nine slices and nine curds (?) for themselves, and gave the tenth slice and the tenth of curds (?) to the poor. They kept the *decimnóir* for the purpose of weighing their portions accurately, lest they should eat anything whatever in excess, and so fail to pay the poor their tithe.

While this system of tithing could be relevant to all churches, and is dealt with in the laws,[144] the emphasis of sharing with the poor is particularly prevalent in the 'Tallaght dossier'. Food in a house of someone who had died, no matter how holy they were, was to be blessed and distributed among the poor,[145] while food brought to one of the *céli Dé* on a Sunday was not to be eaten but could be given to the poor.[146]

What became of those who fell foul of the temptations of comfort and possessions? The poem *A chuirp, not chaith fri crábud* 'O body, apply yourself to sanctity!', the sentiments of which are directed against those who renege on their pious lives and chose material comfort instead, warns:[147]

> They will meet with the plagues of sinners for they are full of faults
> their black souls in captivity, they prefer luxury for their bodies.

Among the luxuries of their indulgent lives were resting on a mattress (*cach æn fo bí coim colcaidh*), sexual activity, sleeping and pleasure.[148] What is worth commenting on in the context of the twelfth-century 'reform' is that the

143 Gwynn, 'The teaching of Máel Ruain', 18–19 §31. Original: *Decimnoir .i. ainm don tshoidheach do bhiodh aca ag gabhail na deachmhuidhe, as chuigi do bhiodh se aca dochom deachmuidhe eisg 7 gruisle do ghabhail … Gach orda eisg dá n-ithdis 7 gach gruisle do chuirdis da thomhas san decimnoir e ar tus. Do chongmhadis naoi n-oirdni 7 naoi ngruisle dhoibh fein, 7 do beirdis an deachmhadh ordu 7 an deachmhadh gruisle dona bochtaibh. As uime do bhiodh an decimnoir aca do chom a ccoda do thomhas go cothrom d'eagla go n-iosdaois ní ar bith d'iomurcaigh gan a deachmhaidh do dhiol ris na bochtaibh.* 144 Breatnach, *Córus Bésgnai*, pp 162–5. 145 Gwynn, 'The rule of the Céli Dé', 74–5 §43. 146 Ibid., 78–9 §51. 147 Meyer, 'Ermahnung den Leib zu kasteien', 265 §24. Original: *Fogebat plágha pecthaig, ar it lána do lochtaib/ a n-anman duba i ndaíre, ferr leo cæime dia corpaibh.* 148 Ibid., 265 §§16, 26. Original: *Léic úait do lothrad lúarda! Léic do chodlad is do chæmda* 'Let go of your uncouth

question of who in the church, monastic or not, could or should possess material wealth, was a constant conflict. An idea of how this dilemma was resolved in Ireland is provided, quite reprovingly, by St Bernard in his life of Malachy when describing the latter's refoundation of the monastery at Bangor:[149]

> The holdings of Bangor were extensive, but Malachy was content with the holy place alone and he yielded all its possessions and lands to another. Certainly from the time of the destruction of the monastery [by the Vikings] there was always someone who held it with its possessions. Men were duly elected and even bore the title of abbot, preserving in name, but not in fact, that which had once been. When many urged him not to alienate the possessions, but to keep everything for himself, this lover of poverty did not give in, but enjoined election upon another to hold them as was customary. But the place was held in trust for Malachy and his monks as we said above. As it later turned out, he might better have kept it all, but he was regarding humility rather than peace.

While Bernard portrays Malachy as following his vow of poverty by alienating Bangor's possessions to another 'abbot' as proof of his sanctity, it is apparent from the evidence of the Irish sources that his decision probably reflects an existing practice in many of the larger monasteries where spiritual and temporal affairs were separated. Authority in the church was divided between bishops and priests, abbots heading monastic communities, and lay administrators, most of whom were members of hereditary families.

Chastity, sex and virginity

The other great temptation of the human condition was to succumb to natural bodily desires, the most obvious and most discussed being sexual desire. The complexity of this subject is often misconstrued and needs to be seen through the lens of many cultural and chronological perspectives, as demonstrated so vividly by Peter Brown in his study on celibacy and virginity in the late antique period.[150] In a monastic context, *RB* associates curbing one's will and renouncing human desire with the fundamental monastic vow of humility:[151]

> The second step of humility is that a man loves not his own will nor takes pleasure in the satisfaction of his desires; rather he shall imitate by his actions that saying of the Lord: *I have come not to do my own will, but the will of him who sent me*. Similarly we read, 'Consent merits punishment; constraint wins a crown.'

?wenching, let go of your sleeping and your pleasure!'. **149** Meyer, *St Malachy the Irishman*, p. 31 §VI.13 (Leclercq and Rochais, *Sancti Bernardi opera*, iii, p. 323). **150** Brown, *The body and society* (repr. 2008). **151** *RB*: Chap. 7.31–3.

And as Brown explains, virginity and celibacy in a given context, in this case a monastic community, did not necessarily mean the denial of sex, but were as much linked to mortification of the body in the hope of renewal, and ultimately life beyond human death. For early Christians, 'if they appeared to neglect these bodies, it was because they had more urgent things to think about – martyrdom and the imminent return of Christ. It was not because their bodies had caused them disquiet'.[152] An immediate concern for Irish monastic communities as regards the safety of their bodies had nothing to do with sexual or spiritual issues but with the constant endemic violence, perpetuated both by Irish and Vikings, directed towards ecclesiastical settlements. This was acknowledged forcefully in the *Lex Innocentium* 'Law of the Innocents' or *Cáin Adomnáin*, promulgated by Adomnán, ninth abbot of Iona in 697, which attempted to protect clerics, children and women from the ravages of war and participation in battle.[153] This law was renewed in 727,[154] and it is understood from the later introduction to the law, possibly dating to the tenth century, that such violence had not abated. Annalistic evidence supplemented by archaeology such as savage mutilation and trauma evident from skeletal remains confirms the violence that permeated throughout Irish society often ignored the ecclesiastical enclosure with disastrous results.[155]

The Irish sources, and in particular the penitentials, deal with sexual activity and the penances incurred as a result. They are directed variously at the laity, priests and monks. Virginity and degrees of chastity are inevitably mentioned in monastic rules, canon laws and penitentials of the pre-tenth century period. The subject is covered by the *Hibernensis* in particular in the chapter concerning women.[156] While quoting Jerome on the blessed qualities of virginity, there are warnings about the dangers of pride among those who practised chastity. Hence the canon declares that not all men understand virginity, 'except for those to whom it has been granted by my father', but in a contrary sentiment, quoting the Council of Agde (AD 506), the canon states that 'if someone despises marriage and detests a faithful or religious woman sleeping with her husband or deems her blameworthy, as though she cannot enter the kingdom of God, let him/her be anathema'.[157] Monks were to be punished severely if they fathered children,[158] but of far greater concern to the *Hibernensis* was the wandering monk not subject to abbatial authority. Monastic chastity is, of course, mentioned elsewhere, especially in the penitentials and in the 'Tallaght dossier', but, as

152 Brown, *Body and society*, pp xxx–xxxi. 153 Thomas O'Loughlin (ed.), *Adomnán at Birr, AD 697. Essays in commemoration of the Law of Innocents* (Dublin, 2001). 154 AU. 155 Elizabeth O'Brien, *Mapping death. Burial in late Iron Age and early medieval Ireland* (Dublin, 2020), pp 136–46. 156 Flechner, *Hibernensis*, 1, pp 350–7 §44; ibid., 2, pp 736–41 §44. 157 Ibid., 1, §44.1–2. Original: *Si quis uituperat nuptias, dormientem cum uiro suo fidelem aut relegiosam detestatur aut culpabilem estimat, uelut que in regnum Dei introire non possit, anathema sit.* 158 Ibid., 1, p. 297 §38.14.; 2, p. 694 §38.14.

noted by Follett, the *céli Dé* seem not to have been any stricter except in expecting celibacy in all clerical orders whether monastic or otherwise.[159] This is consistent with their apparent preoccupation with improving the conduct, education and spirituality of clerical orders in general.

Nevertheless, the fear that men and women meeting could lead to temptation and transgression is not ignored. Women, whose blood and nature were so inclined, were viewed as more sexually inflamed and hence more likely to act as temptresses luring monks into sexual liaisons. Of course, it should be stressed that the role of women as temptresses causing the downfall of eminent men in society in general is a common universal theme, including in early Irish sagas. *Fingal Rónáin* 'The kin-slaying of Rónán', dating to the ninth/tenth century, tells of the attempts of an elderly king's young wife to seduce his son and the tragic consequences of her actions.[160] This moral tale has many aspects to it including warning kings about their choice of wife and about internal family disputes. For a monk, leaving his monastery could lead to sexual encounters, as narrated in 'The monastery of Tallaght':[161]

> Once a certain monk went on a journey to Findio mac Fiatach [St Finian of Movilla]. A woman happened to meet him on the journey, and she demanded sexual intercourse with him. She laid her hands on him at last and sexual intercourse happened between them.

The monk was immediately remorseful – the woman disappeared altogether from the tale – and sought Findio's advice as to a suitable penance which the saint gave quite leniently, directing him to go to confess his sin and to fast. But the Devil goaded him to ignore Findio's advice and to approach Comgall and Columba respectively for their advice. Columba punished him severely with fifteen years' penance, not only for his sexual sin but for the contempt he showed Findio. The import is that the woman – like Eve – not only instigated the sexual intercourse but led to the monk's encounters with the Devil and to disobedience. And hence, as monks were so often reminded, encounters with women outside the enclosure – or indeed within – were dangerous and punishable. 'The teaching of Máel Ruain' deals with this possibility, in a lenient ruling not unlike Findio's above:[162]

159 Follett, *Céli Dé in Ireland*, pp 181–2. **160** David Greene (ed.), *Fingal Rónáin and other stories*, Medieval and Modern Irish series 16 (Dublin 1955; repr. 1993). **161** Gwynn and Purton, 'The monastery of Tallaght', 153–4 §66. Original: *Fecht robai luid araile manoch do findio mac uiatach for sétt. Tecmoncuir banscal immaildi fris arsin teit 7 postulauit ilda concubitum eius. Foceirtt lamae fair fadeoig commaranic caradrad irse.* **162** Gwynn, 'The teaching of Mael Ruain', 36–7 §59. Original: *Antí da n-eirgheadh dortadh sil 'na dhusgadh (.i. gan beith 'na chodladh) ab tre feuc[h]ain ar mhnaoí do thaiteonadh ris no tre smuaintigthibh salcha 'na chroidhe, no tre briathraibh neamhghlana, seachdmhuin do ordaigheadh Maol Ruain do chor do pheannaid*

> If it happened to a man to pollute his body in his waking hours, (that is, not in his sleep), either through looking at a woman who might please him, or through filthy thoughts in his heart, or through impure words, Máel Ruain ordered a week's penance to be imposed on him.

This forgiving and tolerant approach to what is a natural human physical and emotional longing is also the approach taken in relation to monks encountering young nuns with the additional need to protect them from unwanted male attention:[163]

> Devout young nuns (*maccaildecha cráibdecha*) he [Máel Ruain] thinks it right to go and converse with and to confirm their faith, but without looking on their faces, and taking an elder (*senóir*) in your company: and it is right to converse with them standing on the grave slab/penitential station by the cross in front of the enclosure or in the hermitage where they live (*for aulaid oc cros ind dorus lis no isin dísirt i mbíatt*). And the elder who goes with you, and the senior nun (*senóir caildidi*) who lives in the company of the young nuns, should be present and not far from you, where they are. When ill desires or ill thoughts overtake you, through seeing women or conversing with them, if the mind forbids that one should indulge it even as an idle thought (?), then he considers that such desire is no great matter: it is meritorious, however, if a man gets clear of it. When the thoughts are constantly straying towards ill meditations, they must be checked and recalled as far as possible; and he should resort to reading or to examining himself against it, and keep his mind fixed on prayer …

As in the life of Monenna, this is one of the rare allusions in Irish sources to the existence of organised female religious communities in Ireland, and also to the long-established practice of how monks and priests should behave when among nuns. They were to be accompanied by a brother and the nuns, especially the young ones, were supervised by the abbess or another senior nun.[164] Of particular interest is the detail that the man should stand: 'on the grave slab/penitential station (*ailad*) by the cross in front of the enclosure or the *dísert*'.

air. **163** Gwynn and Purton, 'The monastery of Tallaght', 151 §62. Original: *Maccaildecha craibdecha id serc lais daul doa hacaldaim 7 do nertud irsi doib 7 i nemfecsiu inda gnuis 7 senoir it coimitecht 7 anacaldaim iarum for aulaid oc cros ind dorus lis no isind disirt imbíatt 7 ind senoir dano teiti latsa 7 senoir caildidi bis a comaitecht na maccaildidi do bith hi farrad 7 ni cian huaib imbíat. Andand donetarrat míaccobar nó míimradad tre faicsin no ac acaldaim mbanscál ma atrocuil am menme nad cometesta dó ceith folam deit ni fil bríg laisiom hisind accobar sin. IS fochric immurgu ma gabthair tairis andand mbis a foindel inda menmain commór fri mimradud a timtasad for caúlæ feib dorrontar 7 tuidecht légind nó a scrutain fris 7 menme isind aurnaigti.* **164** Alison I. Beach and Andra Juganaru, 'The double monastery as a historiographical problem (fourth to twelfth century)' in *CHMM*, pp 561–78, at pp 572–8.

The existence of slabs at Killevy and Ballyvourney – traditionally regarded as the graves of Monenna and Gobnait respectively[165] – might be genuine physical evidence of such a practice. Given the vulnerability of young women in early Irish society, devout young nuns were more likely to experience actual sexual assault than young monks were from predatory women, although the vernacular laws do punish a woman who 'tempts a hostage of God or of man with the offer of her body' (*ben adguid aitiri Dé nó duine i formatu a cuirp*).[166] Episodes relating to the seduction of young nuns appear in the lives of Monenna and Samthann. In the latter, the abbess's retribution is cruel although it would seem that the young nun may have been complicit in the sexual adventure, probably not an uncommon escapade:[167]

> Once a lustful cleric came into the sisters' community and took a fancy to a young girl who caught his eye there. She in turn paid out love to the lover. So, he undertook to go off to the woods nearby, and the girl was to follow him. He first addressed himself to Samthann, seeking her prayer that his journey be unobstructed. When she asked him where he was going, he replied, 'I wish to go to Connacht.' Then the holy virgin said to him, 'Wherever you may go, do not trouble my sisters with sweet talk or misdeeds.' 'Far be that from me, mistress,' he responded, and with this remark, he left. He reached the river and began to cross it. The water had risen as high as his belt when a huge eel encircled his loins and clinched tightly around him. After this happened, he was so deeply terrified that he returned to the virgin of God, fell to his knees, and sought her pardon. After she had given it, the eel immediately fell away from his limbs. He took heed of his fright, and swore that he would never come again to a female community.

165 Ann Elizabeth Hamlin (Thomas R. Kerr (ed.)), *The archaeology of early Christianity in the north of Ireland*. BAR British Series 460 (Oxford, 2008), p. 240 (iv); NMS Historic Viewer CO058-034004 (Glebe tl., Ballyvourney par., Co. Cork) www.archaeology.ie accessed 29 April 2021. **166** *AL* v, pp 274–5; *CIH* i, 42.17. **167** Plummer, *VSH*, ii, p. 256 (xi); Dorothy Africa, 'Life of the holy virgin Samthann' in Head, *Medieval hagiography*, p. 105 (11). Original: *Quidam clericus lasciuus monasterium sororum eius ingressus, quandam inibi pulcram intuens puellam, eam adamauit, et amanti uicem amoris ipsa impendit. Cumque ille ad siluam vicinam se preire promitteret, et puella sequi eum deberet, ad sanctam Samtannam prius ipse se conuertens, orationem ab ea pro itinere expediendo peciit. Cui interroganti quo ire uellet, 'In Connacciam,' inquit, 'uolo ire.' Tunc sancta uirgo ad eum ait: 'Quocumque ieris noli sorores meas uerbis illecebrosis aut factis malis uexare.' Et respondit ille: 'Absit hoc a me, domina.' Et hoc dicto, egressus est. Cumque riuum quendam transire inciperet, excrescens aqua, usque ad cingulum sibi peruenit; ac tunc mire magnitudinis ang[u]illa, lumbos eius mordens, eum fortiter circumcingit. Quo facto uehementer ille perterritus, ad uirginem Dei reuersus, genua flexit, ueniamque peciit. Qua data, de lumbis eius anguilla statim cecidit. Itaque uexacio dans sibi intellectum, ad monasterium uirginum se nunquam iterum uenturum cum iuramento promisit.*

Although no mention is made of the errant sister's fate, the message is clear: men were not to seduce sisters, and young women were not to succumb to the amorous overtures of men, in this case a cleric.

The relatively low priority given to chastity in the vernacular rules is in contrast with the tortured human emotion or fierce condemnation evident in vernacular literature. The Rule of Ailbe simply states that neither warrior (*fénid*) nor woman (*banscál*) should be in the place in which monks dwell,[168] while the Rule of Ciarán advises that when in the company of nuns, as read in other rules (*legtur i ríaghlaib aili*), one's heart should be pure.[169] Máel Ísu Ua Brolcháin's prayer, *A Choimdiu nom-chomét* ('O Lord take care of me') offers some insight into the real human emotion surrounding chastity:[170]

Protect my male organ
in pure chastity;
may lust not conquer me,
never come to me, never be near me.

The poem *Cinnus atá do thinnrem* 'What is your course of action', dated by its editor to the eleventh century,[171] offers his master's advice to Máel Brigte, a star student, who has to decide on his future path. From the poem's context, Máel Brigte is deciding to become either a priest or a monk, and far from being sparing or lenient towards his pupil, the author offers harsh directions accompanied by lurid images. He should not be arrogant, envious, violent, loquacious and should avoid the company of half-lay students who from the description enjoyed a dissolute life:[172]

> If the half-lay students are your friends and companions – then that will be a foolish and ignorant decision – you will be neither a layman nor a cleric.
>
> Their gowns over their heels; their occupations, their trysts are evil; tainted, uncouth, like demons; their hair red and overlong.

This depiction is reminiscent of similar sentiments expressed by Anselm of Bec and William of Malmesbury who at various times warned their students, canons and royal courtiers against wearing long hair and brightly coloured clothing, not only for being extravagant but also effeminate and consorting with prostitutes.[173]

168 O Neill, 'Rule of Ailbe', pp 104–5 §37a. 169 Strachan, 'Two monastic rules', 228. 170 Ní Bhrolcháin, 'Maol Íosa Ó Brolcháin: an assessment', 53; Murphy, *Early Irish lyrics*, pp 56–7 §11: *Coimét mo ball ferda / im genus co nglaine: / étrad ní rom-báide, / ním-tháirle, ním-thaire.* 171 Breatnach, '*Cinnus atá do thinnrem*', 2, 6. 172 Ibid., 10–11 §§9–10. Original: *Mád íat t'áes comtha is cúarta / na meic léiginn lethtúatta / – is dé bas báeth borb in breth – / níba láech, níba cléirech. // A scuirde tara sála; / olc a cuirde, a comdála; / lochtaig lúarda mar demna; / a fuilt rúada rolebra.* 173 Jennifer D. Thibodeaux, *The manly priest. Clerical*

The master's greatest opprobrium was directed at women, and again this fierce vitriol fits well into the clamour for clerical celibacy that became intense during the eleventh and twelfth centuries. In her study of clerical celibacy in England and Normandy from the eleventh to fourteenth century, Jennifer Thibodeaux argues that chastity was promoted as an ultimate form of virility. Monastic authors such as Orderic Vitalis and William of Malmesbury, among many, narrated stories of monks who threw off their habits and died in the arms of whores. If the male body was impenetrable when in a state of chaste perfection, rejection of that state, led it to become penetrable and disorderly.[174] That is also the strong message of *Cinnus atá do thinnrem* emanating from some scholarly ecclesiastic in eleventh-century Ireland, a much more forceful message than relayed in exhortations of an earlier period. The Irish author's negative view of women concurs rather stridently with this thinking:[175]

> Avoid married women, know you; avoid the women of comrades and friends; avoid from afar, for the sake of Christ, the evil, shameless women.
> … He who pollutes his (sacred) wisdom with evil impure women, has cast his wine on the ground; he will obtain contempt and disgrace.

If his student was unable to maintain constant celibacy, he should sleep with 'his own dear wife on lawful, regulated nights' (*cotail ret mnaí ndílis ndil i n-aidchib dírgib dligid*).[176] Unable to leave it at that, the master quotes greater authorities with a final dire, misogynistic warning:[177]

> We have heard from sages that to acquire knowledge of the groin of a woman who has deluded you is [like] putting one's head into a pit; it is not usual that prosperity accompanies it.

Indeed Giraldus Cambrensis expressed parallel views in his commentary *Gemma ecclesiastica* 'The jewel of the church':[178]

> For they [women] rob you of your money and property, and you spend on them what should be used to adorn the churches and help the poor … To lose Heaven because of this shameful part of the body and over a

celibacy, masculinity, and reform in England and Normandy, 1066–1300 (Philadelphia, 2015), pp 27–30. **174** Ibid., pp 25–6 (quoting an anonymous monastic writer from Bec). **175** Breatnach, '*Cinnus atá do thinnrem*', 12–13 §§15, 19. Original: *Imgab mná fer, finnta lat; / imgab mná cáem is carat; / imgab ar Chríst i cíana / na mná olca ainfíala. / / In tí elna a ecna / re mnáib olca anetla, / tuc a chuit fína fo lár; / fo-géba dígna is dígrád.* **176** Ibid., 12–13 §21. **177** Ibid., 12–13 §23. Original: *Ro-chúalammar la sruithe / is tabairt chinn i cuithe / foglaimm i mbléoin mná rot mert; / ní gnáth rath 'comaitecht.* **178** John J. Hagen (trans.), *The jewel of the church. A translation of* Gemma ecclesiastica *by Giraldus Cambrensis* (Leiden, 1979), pp

> relationship which you possess neither by personal right nor as yours forever …

That the most prominent Irish churchmen during the eleventh to thirteenth centuries are praised for their chastity and were monks or canons was not accidental, given the rise of this 'new' apparently chaste masculinity in the universal church. However, there is a need to be cautious in regarding this view of women as commonly held. The comments of the Irish master and of Giraldus Cambrensis had as much to do with the church's concern that clerical families were a drain on its resources – manpower and material – as they were to do with dislike of women. Yes, women could tempt and defile bishops, priests and monks, but there were many pious, lay and religious women who had no intention of acting as jezebels. The annals record numerous noble women endowing churches and ending their days in penitence in monasteries.[179] Visual evidence for a woman acting as a patron, with her husband, can be seen on the elaborate Romanesque doorway at St Lachtain's church, Freshford, Co. Kilkenny, where Niam daughter of Corc and Mathgamain Ua Ciarmeic are commemorated as causing the church to be built.[180] If the references to the *céli Dé* of the tenth century onwards are an indicator of their particular role in caring for the poor and the sick, highlighted by Haggart,[181] they would have also ministered to both the physical and spiritual needs of lay and religious individuals dying among them. This phenomenon increased from the eleventh century onwards when women retired to larger monasteries such Armagh, Clonmacnoise, Glendalough and Lismore, only like their menfolk to turn to the new orders' foundations from the late twelfth century onwards.

In her study of brother-making in late antiquity and Byzantium, Claudia Rapp surveys the question of male-male relations, homosociability and homosexuality in early societies as approached by various eminent twentieth-century scholars, Michel Foucault, James Boswell and James Davidson.[182] The answer to the possibility of sexual relations occurring between men or women living together in close quarters as a community in Rapp's view 'depends on the definition and interpretation of male-male relations, whether spiritual, emotional, or physical'.[183] The likelihood is that, as in any society, monks and nuns were attracted to their own sex but the danger with modern interpretations of earlier texts is that there is an assumption of greater same-gender sexual

137–8, 144; Thibodeaux, *The manly priest*, p. 1. **179** AU 917, 948, 1063, 1073, 1077, 1080, 1186, 1188, 1193; *AI* 1028, 1058, 1076, 1126, 1253; ATig 1077, 1098, 1167; AFM *s.v.* 921, 926, 946, 1063, 1073, 1077, 1098, 1137 (2), 1151, 1167, 1168, 1188, 1193, 1226, 1229, 1231, 1247, 1253; ALC 1186, 1188, 1193, 1226, 1230, 1231, 1247, 1253, [1269, 1296, 1315]; AC 1226, 1229, 1231, 1239, 1247, 1253, 1269; *CS* 928. **180** R.A.S. Macalister, *Corpus inscriptionum Insularum Celticarum*. 2 vols (Dublin, 1945–9), ii, p. 24. **181** Haggart, 'The *Céli Dé* reassessment', 20–3. **182** Rapp, *Brother-making*, pp 40–7. **183** Ibid., p. 40.

activity occurring in a monastic or eremitical community. Boswell constructed three archetypes of 'gay love' in monastic communities, one analogous to family love apparent in the use of kinship terms (father, brother, sister), another fostered by the formation of novices, namely, the master-pupil relationship, and finally, 'romantic love', which may or may have been consummated physically.[184] All three archetypes can be tested against the sense of brotherhood and sisterhood evident in the Irish sources. As to the possibility that male-male and female-female relations happened in Irish monastic communities, the regulatory texts appear silent on the matter, either satisfied with regarding women as most likely to arouse a monk or priest or wishing to ignore same sex relationships. Early Irish penitentials acknowledge, if only to condemn, the existence of relations between men, including monks, although, as noted by Bitel, the penalties for homosexual acts were not particularly onerous.[185] Nor were the punishments confined to those following a religious life but were addressed to the laity as well.[186] The family analogy can be compared with the use in Irish sources of *muinter* and *familia* to refer to a monastic community. The intensity of the master-pupil relationship is evident in the term *bron-daltae* 'bosom fosterling/pupil' but despite its use in the annals and in hagiography, there is no indication that it had a sexual connotation. Reading 'romantic love' and sexual longing into a medieval text can be rather precarious when the author and his audience's reception bears no relation to a modern interpretation. A tale in the commentaries added to *Félire Óenguso* exemplifies this problem. It explains why Cianán of Duleek's body was lying incorrupt in his tomb, normally a sign of sanctity. Another local saint, Cairnech of Dulane (Co. Meath), came to Duleek and proceeded to give Cianán a bath. Cianán complained that the tub had no bottom to it but Cairnech insisted that water be poured into the tub and the washing be done. Miraculously, not a drop of water leaked out and Cianán told Cairnech to get into the tub. And so the conversation continued:[187]

> 'Let us go together,' says Cairnech. They go.
> 'Beautiful is the body, o cleric,' says Cairnech.
> 'As it is now, indeed,' says Cianán.
> 'I beseech God,' then says Cairnech, 'that it may remain as it is forever without corrupting, without dissolving, until Christ shall come to the great assembly of judgement.' And that is fulfilled.

184 James Boswell, *Rediscovering gay history. Archetypes of gay love in Christian history* (London, 1982), pp 18–21. **185** Lisa Bitel, 'Sex, sin, and celibacy in early Christian Ireland', *Proceedings of the Harvard Celtic Colloquium* 7 (1987), 65–95, at p. 77. **186** Gwynn, 'An Irish penitential', 143–6. **187** Stokes, *Félire Oengusso*, pp 244–5. Original: *Tiagam araen, ar Cairnech. Tiagait. Is alaind in corp, a clerig, ar Cairnech. Amal ata dna, ar Cianán. Ailimsi dano Dia, ar Cairnech, amal ta corab amlaid bes tre bithu cen lobad cen legad, co tora Críst do mordáil*

Erotic as the modern reader might find this conversation, the author's message relates to the prized relic of Duleek's founder saint and of his perfect body that could not become corrupt. Finally, the 'Tallaght dossier' regards nocturnal emissions as a minor transgression, as long as not brought on by a dream, worthy of singing four psalms and a good wash because 'this is an evil recollection of the spirit, accompanying a discharge of some of the excess of liquid that is in the body'.[188] This attitude conforms with Cassian's rebuttal of Augustine's strict notion of concupiscence in which he echoed the desert fathers sense, that sexual temptations were caused by much greater human failings – anger, greed, pride – and that sexual fantasies and temptations warned the monk that 'these drives still lingered, unconsciously, within his soul'.[189]

Finally, the noise from the busy world of men could easily divert an ascetic community's attention from their concentration on the divine. *RB* warns brothers sent on a journey 'not to relate to anyone else what he saw or heard outside the monastery, because that causes the greatest harm'. If they did so, they would be subject to punishment.[190] Máel Ruain advised Máel Díthrub not to meddle in worldly affairs, nor to accompany anyone to a law-court or an assembly (*airecht*).[191] Furthermore, not unlike Benedict, Máel Ruain:[192]

> bade them not to ask the people who came to visit them for news, or to talk to them, but only to transact the business that they came about: because great is the harm that is done and the disturbance that is caused by such news to the mind of him to whom it is told.

The dangers of gossiping were ever-present, whether in Tallaght, or in monasteries in the Egyptian desert or on the Italian citadel of Monte Cassino.

A GLIMPSE OF LIFE INSIDE THE MONASTERY

No more than *RB* and other monastic legislation, the Irish vernacular texts do not go into great detail about the normal daily lives of monastic communities, except for the regulations regarding diet, fasting and the etiquette of the refectory, all of which seems to have been a particular concern of legislators. There are passing references to manual labour, clothing and hygiene. Some of these details, especially with regard to clothing, can be supplemented by

bratha. Ocus is ed ón comalltar. **188** Gwynn and Purton, 'The monastery of Tallaght', 164 §88. Original: *acht is míchumne spiride fri télach neich din imacraid lenda bís isind churp.* **189** Brown, *Body and society*, pp 420–3. **190** *RB*: Chap. 67.5–7. **191** Gwynn, 'The teaching of Mael Ruain', 8–11 §12. **192** Ibid., 20–1 §33b. Original: *Do ordaigh dhoibh gan sgeula d'fhiafraighe don mhuinntir thigeadh ar cuairt chuca no do chaint riu , acht na gnothaighi fa ttangadar amhain do dheunamh, do bhrigh gurb mor an urchóid do nid 7 an toirmeasg chuirid ar*

examining the vocabulary of monastic dress, while archaeological evidence offers an insight into food production and its consumption. When discussing life inside the monastery, the issue of definition of 'monastery' recurs once more: are these provisions and restrictions confined to a committed monastic community and individuals following an eremitical lifestyle, or do they extend to others within the monastic settlement and to the laity, most specifically to lay penitents? As always, the answer is complicated.

Diet, fasting and etiquette in the refectory

A restricted diet, constant fasting and privation of the human body might lead to drastic physical changes that 'after years of ascetic discipline, registered with satisfying precision the essential, preliminary stages of the long return of the human person, body and soul together, to an original, natural and uncorrupted state'.[193] Echoes of this reasoning reverberate through the Irish material, the only pure food after the extinction of desire, according to 'Cormac's Rule', is Christ's body and blood.[194] The Rule of Ailbe advises that bread and watercress, not mead or princely malt, should be the fitting food for elders: the word *idan* is used to describe this grim diet, a term which also means 'pure' and 'chaste'.[195] 'The monastery of Tallaght' and 'The rule of the *céli Dé*' comment that a small pittance is safer and better for the soul than a rich diet, 'for the small light diet is better to sustain a man and make him healthy, and it excites human nature to ill desires less than a large diet of coarse food'.[196] Máel Ruain claimed that the monks who heeded his rule would reach Heaven without judgement 'because they will be clean already', while Máel Díthrub's monks, who were allowed to drink while on earth, would have to experience some of the fire of doomsday to be cleansed.[197]

The customs on diet and fasting in *céli Dé* texts have been discussed in detail by Follett,[198] and rather than rehearse them here again, the focus will be on the order of daily meals, the actual food consumed and on refectory etiquette, as understood from 'The rule of the *céli Dé*' and the text on refectory etiquette '*Ord prainni ocus prainntighi*', a text added to the Rule of Mochutu.[199] A comparison with other rules, specifically *RB* and the *Regularis Concordia*, places the Irish legislation in a wider context. Of course, it is necessary to be mindful of the difficulty with 'standard' customs. Isabelle Cochelin rightly questions the idea of such 'standard' customs, arguing that prior to the late eleventh century,

mheanmain antí da n-aisneidhtear na sgeula sin. **193** Brown, *The body and society*, p. 223. **194** Strachan, 'Cormac's rule', 66 §12. **195** O Neill, 'Rule of Ailbe', 104–5 §35; *DIL sv* (*idan*). **196** Gwynn, 'The rule of the Céli Dé', 74–5 §39; Gwynn and Purton, 'The monastery of Tallaght', 152 §63. Original: *is ferr lais 7 is inildiu do anmin neich ind fit bec mín quam ind fit mór de tuari anmín. Fobithin is ferr do fulang duine 7 da blath ambecc mín 7 is lugai dodúsci ind daonacht fri miaccobar quam ammór den gantuarai.* **197** Gwynn, 'The teaching of Mael Ruain', 24–5 §40. **198** Follett, *Céli Dé in Ireland*, pp 184–8. **199** Meyer, 'Ord prainni 7

customs that guided the daily life of a monastery emerged from traditions created and kept by a community of monks or nuns over generations, not by statutes imposed by a superior or a text.[200] The change came when customaries began to be written down to cope with the influx of adult novices into monasteries, unlike previously when the monasteries depended on oblates as the new arrivals. These oblates became accustomed to a monastery's customs by assimilation.[201] The Irish vernacular texts may be an exception to this trend if they were written down, as seems likely, prior to the late eleventh century. According to the Irish texts, different customs existed between communities, especially with regard to diet and fasting, the matter of consuming meat being foremost in divergences. As to oblates, archaeological evidence suggests that boys lived in monastic communities, although the rules – apart from the Rule of Patrick which deals primarily with the recruitment of boys to the priesthood – barely mention them.[202] '*Ord prainni ocus prainntighi*' mentions that young people who were weak and unable to eat their rations were to be treated with compassion, possibly an indication of a pattern recognized elsewhere, that some boys with health issues were handed over to monastic communities as oblates by their own families.[203]

The same text offers the clearest indication of the regulations followed by the *maicc eclaisi* 'sons of the church', understood to be those following a religious life, when dining, as opposed to other *céli Dé* texts which concentrate on diet and fasting. For example, it provides details on mealtimes at different times of the year:[204]

> But the sons of the church, it is normal for them, every period of time for them is Lent, is a fast.
>
> This is the praiseworthy, moderate fast with glory, from none to none, an utterance without falsehood, as long as he fulfils it …
>
> From the feast of John's nativity to Easter, sweet the melody, from vespers to vespers it is permitted to go for a meal.
>
> Then from Easter to the feast of St John, it is from none to none, they are entitled to a meal on alternate days at vesper-time.

prainntighi'. **200** Isabelle Cochelin, 'Monastic daily life (*c*.750–1100): a tight community shielded by an outer court' in *CHMM*, pp 542–60, at p. 544. **201** Cochelin, 'Monastic daily life', p. 543. **202** Gwynn and Purton, 'The monastery of Tallaght', p. 145 §48. Allowances were permitted in Lismore to the infirm and youth (*gille, macóclaích*) regarding more rigorous fasting practices. See Follett, *Céli Dé in Ireland*, p. 98. **203** Meyer, 'Ord prainni 7 prainntighi', p. 28 §4. Original: *Airchisecht for ócdóenaib co laghat a neirt, meni thormalat a cuit asind fodail cheirt.* See Cochelin, 'Monastic daily life', pp 551–2. **204** Meyer, '*Ord prainni 7 prainntighi*', 29 §§16–20. Original: *Air inna maic eclaisi bíit ina coir, sech is corgus is áine cech óentremsi dóib. // Is í ind óene molbthaide mesraigthe co llí ó nóin co nóin, núall cenn gói, céinmár nodusgní … Ó fhéil comperta Iohain co cáisc, caín int shéis, is ó fhescor co fescor dlegar dul do méis. // Ó cháisc íarom co féil Iohain is ó nóin co nóin / is i fescur cachlacein delgar dídnad dóib.*

If this was a common custom in Ireland, it was more rigorous than *RB* and the similar provision in *RC*. What was eaten, where did the food come from, and who cooked it? The Rule of Ailbe includes a generous and hospitable cook among a monastery's important personnel: '... whether his repast be salt meat or flesh, whether it be ale, curds, or fresh milk'.[205] Yet both 'The teaching of Máel Ruain' and 'The rule of the *céli Dé*' imply that the cook was among the servants, probably lay people, who were subject to punishment for their carelessness:[206]

> He [Máel Ruain] used to inflict additional punishment on the cooks and dairy-maids and scullions because they used to waste much of the produce, both milk and corn.

Diet varied according to the seasons, essential fasting periods, and liturgical festivals. The staple diet included bread, cabbage (*braisech*), milk, fish, cheese, hard-boiled eggs, apples, leeks (*lus*), curds (*gruth*) and whey-water (*medcuisce*).[207] The Rule of Ailbe, or at least an additional verse to the text, measures out a monk's daily loaf as weighing thirty ounces and twelve inches in diameter.[208] On certain feast-days and the Sundays of great Lent, the meal was supplemented variously with milk, beer and *selann*, a delicacy which seems usually to have consisted of butter with added flavours, and sometimes honey or salted meat.[209] At Easter, eggs, lard and the flesh of deer and wild pig are unequivocally permitted in 'The rule of the *céli Dé*',[210] while 'The teaching of Máel Ruain' notes that no flesh was eaten in Tallaght during Máel Ruain's lifetime, 'except when the flesh of deer or wild pig was set before guests, such of them as desired flesh'.[211] A relaxation of the regulations on eating meat was allowed when food was scarce and the choice was between consumption of an undesirable foodstuff such as meat and death from hunger. This relaxation was allowed particularly at Easter to guard against scarcity or hunger in the following year. That different houses followed their own customs is understood from a particular custom followed at Terryglass:[212]

205 O Neill, 'Rule of Ailbe', 104–5 §34, 106–7 §42. Original: *céne mbess coic fial, findbalc, cid saill, cid feoil a airbert, cid coirm, cid croith, cid lemlacht.* **206** Gwynn, 'The teaching of Mael Ruain', pp 8–9 §10[b] (slight update of translation). Original: *Do ghnathuigheadh se iomarcaidh feich aibhne do bhual[adh] ar na cocairibh 7 ban-airghibh 7 ar na cuchtroraibh do bhrigh go ndoirtidis an toradh go mór idir bhainne 7 arbhar.* **207** Gwynn, 'The rule of the Céli Dé', 64–7 §§4–6; Fergus Kelly, *Early Irish farming* (Dublin, 1997), pp 254–6, 327–31. **208** O Neill, 'Rule of Ailbe', 102–3 §31[a]; Kelly, *Early Irish farming*, p. 330. *Original: Bargen trichat ungae mes ar dá ordlach déc is cóir.* **209** Kelly, *Early Irish farming*, p. 345. See also Gwynn, 'The teaching of Mael Ruain', 28–9 §45. **210** Gwynn, 'The rule of the Céli Dé', 66–7 §6. **211** Gwynn, 'The teaching of Mael Ruain', 24–5 §40. **212** Gwynn and Purton, 'The monastery of Tallaght', 132 §12; Gwynn, 'The teaching of Mael Ruain', 36–7 §61. Original (Gwynn and Purton): *asenad uli amail notreigtis addurtaig medón láoi dia caisc dochum na chuchdiri dóib fochetoir co ndenad cách díob and pars de feoil fri foimtin terci no bochde in ando ar*

> … the whole community, when they left the oratory at noon on Easter day, used to go straight to the kitchen that each of them might take a particle of flesh there, as a precaution against scarcity or poverty during the year; for unless a man relaxes at Easter, it would not be easy for them to do so afterwards until the next Easter a year later.

As to particular fasts, beyond fasting during the two Lents, 'The rule of the *céli Dé*' specifies that the community of Máel Ruain at Tallaght fasted once a month on half-rations of bread and whey-water, while the *céli Dé* were not given an increase in bread even on festivals.[213] The food consumed by these monastic communities, at least according to their texts, was similar to that available to wider society.[214] As might be expected, the secular laws specify that meat – beef, mutton and pork/bacon – was prominent in the diet of the aristocracy and it may be that the shunning of meat, apart from 'cleaner' wild meat, in the monastic regulations was a deliberately constructed contrast. *Milites Christi*, the warrior aristocracy of the church, thrived on a restricted diet and moderate eating with regulated fasts, and in doing so, actually gained strength to fight their battle for purity and salvation. This mentality was well rooted in the universal monastic tradition expressed in John Cassian's *Institutes*:[215]

> For it is impossible for a full stomach to undertake the struggles of the inner man: nor is it right for someone to be made trial of by more violent battles if he can be overcome in a less important conflict.

Archaeological evidence from monastic sites suggests that in general the mixed picture gained from the texts about food consumption is fairly accurate. In his study of this topic, Lorcan Harney examined evidence from monastic and church sites for the consumption of cereals, fruit and vegetables, meat, fish and bird, and 'wild foods'.[216] An important element of Harney's analysis was his effort to distinguish between various church sites on the basis of size and location, and to identify the needs of the different communities living in ecclesiastical settlements. As might be expected, the evidence is complicated. Given that bread was a staple as were soft foods such as cereal-based gruels, it is not surprising that barley, oats and wheat occur to a greater or lesser extent, with a preponderance towards oats. Domesticated fowl and geese are found on ecclesiastical sites of all types, from the tiny island of Illaunloughan, Co. Kerry, to Clonmacnoise. This may signify the importance of eggs in what was so often a meatless diet. Fruit, herbs, pulses and vegetables were cultivated, as

mani thuaslaicea isind chaisc nipo assa doib iarum cosin caiscc naili post andum. **213** Gwynn, 'The rule of the Céli Dé', 72–3 §§3, 36. **214** Kelly, *Early Irish farming*, p. 336. **215** Ramsey, *Institutes*, p. 124 (Book V, Chapter XIII.13). **216** Harney, 'Fasting and feasting', 182–97.

demonstrated by the existence of gardens in Illaunloughan and on Skellig, and although under-represented in the archaeological record, cabbage, apples and peas have been identified on various sites. 'Wild foods', fruit, herbs, roots and seaweed are not confined to ecclesiastical sites, they occur in abundance in Dublin, for example, but Harney has suggested that these may have been particularly sought after by penitents and ascetics given their mainly vegetarian diets.[217] As a caveat to this suggestion, it is likely that society in general depended on 'wild foods' (e.g., wild berries, nuts) at certain times of the year and that they were preserved to stave off scarcity during winter months or worse during famines. There is ample evidence for the rearing, butchering and consumption of cattle, sheep and pigs. Cattle dominate in many sites but it is noticeable that in landscapes dominated by woodland, mountains and boggy land, pigs and sheep thrived. Of the 160 'countable' mammal specimens excavated at the monastery on Skellig, for example, they consisted of stock or farm animals, cattle, sheep, goats and pigs. Sheep and goats dominated, which might be expected given the difficult terrain. If following a restricted diet both species could not only be exploited for milk, cheese and meat but from the butchery evidence on the bones these animals were also exploited for their skin, wool and horns. It would appear from the small assemblage of cattle and pig bones that these were not kept on the island but were brought from the mainland for their meat.[218] Finally, Harney's study suggests differences between ecclesiastical sites mainly based on their geographical location, but also based on their ethos. Red-deer bone assemblages and wild salmon occur on larger, wealthier sites such as Armagh, Clonmacnoise and Kilkenny, while sea fish, seals, shellfish and wild sea birds are found on western coastal sites in Ireland and Scotland. This difference may reflect the need of these western communities to maximize their food supplies by developing a varied diet of domesticated animals and wild resources but also, as Harney concludes, 'it is also possible that such high incidences of wild resources reflect their monastic character, as the monks integrated a monastic preference for 'wild foods' with an attempt to be as self-sufficient as possible, given the environmental limits'.[219]

Refectories in ecclesiastical settlements, likely to have been mainly made of wood, are alluded to very occasionally in the annals. In 912, Muiredach mac Cormaic, *princeps* of Dromiskin (Co. Louth) and Gairbíth mac Máil Mórda were killed in a fire in the settlement's refectory by Congalach, Gairbíth's rival for the

217 Ibid., 186. **218** Emily Murray, 'The faunal remains: the mammal bones' in Bourke et al., *Skellig Michael, Co. Kerry*, pp 426–7, 429–30. Available online at https://www.worldheritageireland.ie/fileadmin/user_upload/ documents/SkelligMichaelExcavations_07Feb.pdf **219** Harney, 'Fasting and feasting', 188 quoting Emily Murray and Finbar McCormick, 'Environmental analysis and food supply' in Jenny White Marshall and Claire Walsh (eds), *Illaunloughan Island. An early medieval monastery in County Kerry* (Bray, 2005), pp 67–80, at 69, 78.

regional kingship of Conaille.[220] In 971, Cellach ua Nuadat, *airchinnech* of Swords (Co. Dublin), was killed by the Norse of Dublin in front of the refectory.[221] It is not clear if these refectories provided for both the religious and upper echelons of the lay communities living in these ecclesiastical settlements, although the import of '*Ord prainni ocus prainntighi*' is that its setting is in a monastic refectory. This is a place (*tegdais*) in which the labourers were given more food and the elderly and weak youths were cared for with compassion and there were special conditions for increasing or reducing portions for the rest with a reference to punishments meted out for sinfulness.[222] Fast periods were regulated throughout the liturgical calendar. There was some relaxation on Sundays in honour of Christ, on the feast days of apostles, martyrs and saints, while vigils were eased and portions increased between Christmas Eve and the Epiphany.[223] Provisions for Easter, Pentecost and other feast days are mentioned as are the three Lents, Spring (Great) Lent, Summer Lent and Winter Lent,[224] some of which applied also to the laity who were not expected to fast normally.[225] As to the *maic eclaisi* 'sons of the church', these were committed monks: 'for every period is lent and fasting for them' (*sech is corgus is áine cech óentremsi dóib*).[226] A bell was rung to call the brethren to the refectory and when they entered they chanted the *pater noster*, sought pardon and prostrated themselves three times (*canid patir, arco fuin, sléchtaid sís fo thrí*). They sat in their allocated places and the food was blessed.[227] They sat at table, blessed their ration, sang a hymn of praise, said *Benedictus* to which the elders replied '*Dia lib*!' ('God be with you'). If anyone had a grievance he was to admit it to a senior. If it was a proper grievance, help was provided, if not, a penance was imposed.[228] Once they finished their meal they went silently and without anger to their cells (*cubiculum*) to read, to pray and appeal to the Lord. They went to vespers and afterwards to bed.[229] As previously mentioned, 'The rule of the *céli Dé*' explains that while they were eating their meal the gospels, the rule and the miracles of the saints were read to them to keep their minds on God and not on food.

Clothing, personal hygiene, rest

In a note on late antique and early medieval terminology relating to the monastic habit, Adalbert De Vogüé demonstrated that the underlying philosophy for all traditions was simplicity and use of inexpensive material.[230] While the monastic

220 AU, AFM 908. **221** AU, AFM 969. **222** Meyer, 'Ord prainni 7 prainntighi', 27–8, §§3–5. **223** Ibid., 28, §§6–7. **224** They came before Easter, Pentecost and Christmas. **225** Meyer, 'Ord prainni 7 prainntighi', 28–9, §§9–15. Regarding the laity see §15: *Samchorgus nó gemchorgus isa gáinem gléss / is do thúattaib dlegar sin nad óenat (dénut) do gréss.* **226** Meyer, 'Ord prainni 7 prainntighi', 29 §16. **227** The word used for the monks' ration is *fit* 'a small quantity of food, a light collation' which according to *DIL* (*pít*) following LEIA (P-10) may be an early loan from Lat. *vita* meaning in this context 'the ration of food necessary to keep the body alive'. **228** Meyer, 'Ord prainni 7 prainntighi', 30 §§25–6. **229** Ibid. **230** Adalbert de

habit varied depending on the customs of different monastic leaders, regions and seasons, tunics, cowls, scapulars, veils, mantles, satchels and sandals were commonplace. Breeches were worn in some traditions. The Irish vernacular monastic legislation has little to say about clothing as an identifier of a member of a religious community or of an anchorite, and the terms used in the literature in general suggest that their dress was not dissimilar from the basic clothing worn by the rest of the population. Perhaps the main indicator of an ecclesiastical origin for items of clothing, and this is by no means definitive, is that many terms are early Latin borrowings from the vocabulary of monastic dress.[231] The following terms might be cited:

caille Ir. < *pallium* Lat. 'veil'
casal Ir. < *casula* Lat. 'mantle, cloak, chasuble'
cilic Ir. < *cilicium* Lat. 'sackcloth, haircloth'
cochall Ir. < *cocullus* Lat. 'cowl, hood, hooded cloak'
cuilche Ir. < *?pellica* Lat. 'an outer garment'
culpait Ir. < *culcita* Lat. 'cowl, hood'

Native words often associated, although by no means exclusively, with monastic clothing include:

assae: 'shoe, sandal'
brat 'cloak, mantle'
bréit 'head-covering'
cubal 'frock, habit'
dechelt 'cloak'

Visual representations provide the most valuable, if somewhat stylized, evidence for monastic garb. The pilgrim wearing a long tunic and holding a simple staff on an early cross-slab from Ballyvourney, Co. Cork depicts the simplest form of clothing (illustrated on back cover).[232] The figure stands in stark contrast to the richly clothed figures on the Breac Máedóc, an eleventh-century reliquary that was possibly made in Dublin. Although rather abstract, the carved figures from White Island, Co. Fermanagh, dating to the ninth/tenth century, are likely to depict the elite in Irish society, among them a master of canon law (*suí ecna*) with his book, an abbot or bishop with his crozier and bell, and possibly a *fer léiginn*, poet or teacher with his rod to instruct, the *secnap* or *airchinnech* with provisions

Vogüé, 'Aux origines de l'habit monastique (IIIe – IXe siècle)', *Studia Monastica* 43:1 (2001), 7–20. **231** Damian McManus, 'A chronology of the Latin loan-words in early Irish', *Ériu* 34 (1983), 21–71. McManus notes, for example, that the terms *caille*, *cochall* and *cuilche* belong to the earliest strand of Latin borrowings, which he dates to a terminus ante quem of approximately the mid-fifth century (at p. 49). **232** SMR CO058–013001–3. Accessed 10

for the church, a king and a jester/sheelagh-na-gig. The figures are divided into two groups distinguished by how their heads are represented: the abbot/bishop wears a cowl, the seated *suí ecna*'s head is damaged but he may be sporting a beard, the *fer léiginn* appears to have a tonsure or a hairstyle that distinguishes him from the curly locks of the *secnap/airchinnech* and the king.[233] (Fig. 18). 'The teaching of Máel Ruain' offers the most detailed description of tonsuring:[234]

> They used to tonsure (*berraid*) on the last Thursday of each month, and when it chanced that they did not do so on that Thursday, they used to tonsure on the Friday or Saturday following: or if it were left undone until the following Sunday, they did not tonsure until the time for it came round again, that is, until the end of next month. This was Máel Ruain's ruling.

No detail is provided on the shape of the tonsure during this period but the importance of any reference to tonsuring is that again it was a distinctive marker for the committed religious individual. Allusion is made to the length of hair in the satirical conversation between the saintly and erudite Cumméne Fota and Comgán, the chief fool of Ireland (*prímóinmid Érenn*) in the tale, possibly dating to the tenth century, *Mac Da Cherda and Cummíne Foda*.[235] The term used for a tonsure is *corann*, a borrowing from Latin *corona*:[236]

> Cumméne: And as to the tonsure
> if learning be not read?
> Comgán: Flowing hair is none the worse
> if there is no disgrace beneath it.

As the word *lebar* 'long, flowing' is not unlike *lebor* 'book', there is a play here on the vanity of monastic scholars who eschewed the tonsure or equally the opposite, a dislike for those who are tonsured and without learning – or both.

Hygiene in the monastery is mentioned in passing and it would appear from the few references that a regime existed for personal cleanliness and keeping a community's settlement and materials clean. There is nothing to compare, for example, with Lanfranc's lengthy guide to bath time in the monastery.[237] Máel

August 2023. **233** http://www.3dicons.ie/3d-content/sites/58-white-island-2#images. **234** Gwynn, 'The teaching of Mael Ruain', 48–9 §83. *A cionn gach miosa dardaoín do bhiodh bearradh aca, 7 an tan do theagmhadh dhiobh an dardaoín sin nach diongnadaoís e do bhearrdaois dia haoine no dia sathairn fa neasa: no da leigthi do chom an domhnaigh é ní bearrdaoís go haimsir an bhearrtha aris .i. go ceann miosa oile: Maol Ruaín do ordaigh sin.* **235** Thomas Owen Clancy, 'Saint and fool: the image and function of Cummíne Fota and Comgán Mac Da Cherda in early Irish literature' (PhD, University of Edinburgh, 1991) http://hdl.handle.net/1842/7381 accessed 31 July 2022. **236** J.G. O'Keeffe (ed.), 'Mac Dá Cherda and Cummaine Foda', *Ériu* 5 (1911), 18–44, at pp 22–3. Original: *(Cumain) Ocus dala na coirne mine legthar in súithi/ (Comgán): Nocha mesa in mong lebar mine be mebal fúithe.* **237** David Knowles and

Díthrub's lingering in the bath has been alluded to already. At terce, the monks dressed and washed their hands before going to the office.[238] No one was permitted to bathe in polluted water and persons in orders on whose head defiled water was poured were to anoint and cross themselves as a means of cleaning away the defilement.[239] Equally, privies (*fíaltech*) and urinals (*fúaltech*) housed evil spirits and the sign of the cross was to be made over such places.[240] The mark of a good monastery was its cleanliness, and most particularly its guest house, where guests would be provided with a good fire, washing and bathing facilities, and a comfortable bed.[241] Sleep was regarded as essential to enable a monk to diligently observe the canonical hours.[242] Given the layout of Irish ecclesiastical settlements and references to cells, and not dormitories,[243] as the community's sleeping quarters, the likelihood is that most individuals slept alone or in small groups, with the possible exception of oblates and novices. For example, Cell F on Skellig incorporates three cupboards in the walls and projecting stone pegs as well as upright slabs that define raised sections on three sides, which is where the monks might have slept.[244] As mentioned above, no reference is made to intimate relations in sleeping quarters, not that this did not occur if the penitentials are to be trusted. 'The teaching of Máel Ruain' specifies that it was not their custom to sleep in a tunic (*léine*) or in the garment that had been worn during the day.[245] This was a different practice to *RB* which specified that all the community slept in the same room and were clothed and girded with belts or cords.[246] In the cold and damp Irish climate, it would have been necessary to have had a fire for heat, a basin of water, sufficient under-bedding and probably a woollen blanket as the basic furniture in a cell. The evidence of the insect fauna discovered by excavation on Skellig suggests that materials such as wood, moss and other organic materials were brought onto the island for use as floor covering, bedding and toilet purposes.[247] Sleeping was not allowed in the oratory or at mealtimes and, according to 'The rule of the *céli Dé*', while praying overnight, a relay of two monks at a time remained in the oratory to recite the necessary psalms.[248]

The canon of Irish regulatory texts, different as they might seem from well-known monastic rules and customs in language and format, nonetheless covered

C.N.L. Brooke (eds), *The monastic constitutions of Lanfranc*. Oxford medieval texts (Oxford, 1951, repr. 2002), pp 15–17: Section 7. On baths. **238** O Neill, 'Rule of Ailbe', 100–1 §24. **239** Gwynn, 'The rule of the Céli Dé', 76–7 §47. **240** Ibid., 74–5 §42. **241** O Neill, 'Rule of Ailbe', 106–7 §41. **242** Gwynn and Purton, 'The monastery of Tallaght', 161 §82. **243** There is no word for a pre-Norman monastic dormitory. The words *cotailtech/cotultech, dortúr, tech leptha* are rare and occur either in a secular context or in late medieval texts. *DIL sv.* **244** Bourke et al., *Skellig Michael excavations*, p. 11. **245** Gwynn, 'The teaching of Mael Ruain', 6–7 §7. **246** *RB*: Chap. 22. **247** Eileen Reilly, 'The insect remains' in Bourke et al., *Skellig Michael excavations*, pp 399–413, at pp 402–4, 411. **248** Gwynn, 'The rule of the Céli Dé', 72–3 §30.

the same ground as to monastic ideals, restrictions and lifestyle. Many surviving texts are composite or fragmentary, due in a large part to their transmission and appearance for the first time in late medieval manuscripts. Once considered together as a single corpus, however, it can be argued that they were the equivalent to monastic florilegia or *vademecums* for those in charge of monastic communities. They functioned as short-hand guides on how to behave properly in living a committed religious life and on the consequences of straying too far into worldly affairs.

CHAPTER 7

Learning and praying on the path to Heaven

The eleventh-century poem *Deus meus adiuva me* attributed to Máel Ísu Ua Brolcháin is a fitting opening to this chapter that attempts to deal with the very substantial interrelated subjects of monastic spirituality and monastic culture. Máel Ísu's poem at first glance appears to be a pleasant and straightforward plea for God's love and the monk's pilgrimage to Heaven. Consisting of four-line quatrains, the first and last a repetition of the same Latin line, the second and third a repetition of an Irish line, the poem is an exhortation of monasticism's fundamental dictum of *amor et timor Dei* 'love and fear of God'. Máel Ísu pleads with God and Christ to grant him their love on earth and in Heaven, an earnest request in Irish for *amor Dei* and his expression of *timor Dei*:[1]

> *Deus meus, adiuva me!* 'My God, help me' (1a and d)
> *Tuc dam do sheirc, a meic dil Dé* 'Give me love of you, O son of my God' (1b and c)
>
> *In meum cor, ut sanum sit* 'Into my heart, that it may be whole' (2a and d)
> *Tuc a Rí rán, do grád co grib* 'O glorious King, swiftly bring love of you' (2b and c)
>
> *Domine, da quod peto a te* 'Lord, give what I ask of thee' (3a and d)
> *Tuc, tuc co dían, a grían glan glé* 'Give, give speedily, O bright and gleaming sun' (3b and c)
>
> *Hanc spero rem et quaero quam* 'This thing which I hope and seek' (4a and d)
> *Do sherc dam sunn, do sherc dam tall* 'Your love for me here, your love for me yonder' (4b and c)
>
> *Tuum amorem, sicut vis* 'Love of you, as you wish' (5a and d)
> *Tuc dam co trén, ad-bér da-rís* 'Give me powerfully, I will say again' (5b and c)
>
> *Quaero, pulso, peto a te* 'I seek, I beg, I plead with you' (6a and d)
> *Mo beith i nem, a meic dil Dé* 'That I be in Heaven, dear son of God' (6b and c)

1 Ní Bhrolcháin, *Maol Íosa*, pp 52–3 (poem 5); Murphy, *Early Irish lyrics*, pp 52–5 (translation

> *Domini mi, exaudi me!* 'O Lord, hear me!' (7a and d)
> *M'anam rob lán dot grád a Dé* 'May my soul be full of love for you, O God' (7b and c)

The language of the Latin lines immediately evokes the prayers of the Carolingian *libelli precum*, prayer books used for liturgical and personal use.[2] And, without doubt, Máel Ísu also used phrases from the psalms that were familiar to him, the phrase *Deus meus adiuva me* echoing the line in Psalm 109: 26 *Adiuva me Domine Deus meus.* Máel Ísu represents what Jean Leclercq in his seminal study of monastic culture *The love of learning and the desire for God* defines as among the basic tenets of monastic culture:[3]

> ... On the one hand, learning is necessary if one is to approach God and to express what is perceived of Him; on the other hand, literature must be continually transcended and elevated in the striving to attain eternal life ...
>
> ... The first, the most important, of the themes to which the monks of the Middle Ages applied literary art is what could be called devotion to Heaven ...

Despite the dearth of functional monastic liturgical books surviving from medieval Ireland, there is a wealth of other texts that provide an insight into Irish devotion to Heaven and to 'the end and beyond'.[4] These include a wide range of texts in Irish and in Latin: commentaries on the Bible, specific commentaries on the psalms, patristics, apocrypha, eschatological texts such as visions, world history wherein the Irish integrated themselves into a biblical and hence Christian schema of the past, homilies and hymns.[5] In addition, the Irish

revised). 2 Owen M. Phelan, *The formation of Christian Europe. The Carolingians, baptism, and the Imperium Christianum* (Oxford, 2014), pp 251–2. 3 Jean Leclercq, *The love of learning and the desire for God. A study of monastic culture* (trans. Catharine Misrahi, New York, 1982), p. 53. 4 I have taken this all-encompassing phrase from the two volumes *The end and beyond*, eds Carey, Nic Cárthaigh and Ó Dochartaigh. 5 There is a huge canon of primary and secondary literature on this subject, listed in detail in Ó Corráin, *CLH*, vols I–II. Essential introductory books include Martin McNamara, *The apocrypha in the Irish church* (Dublin, 1975); McNamara (ed.) *Biblical studies. The medieval Irish contribution.* Proceedings of the Irish Biblical Association I (Dublin, 1976); Máire Herbert and Martin McNamara (eds), *Irish biblical apocrypha. Selected texts in translation* (Edinburgh, 1989); Martin McNamara, *The psalms in the early Irish church* (Sheffield, 2000); Carey, *King of mysteries*; Martin McNamara, *The Bible and the apocrypha in the early Irish church (AD 600–1200). Collected essays* (Turnhout, 2015). Bernard McGinn's foreword 'Medieval visions of the end: the Irish contribution' in Carey et al., *The end and beyond*, vol. I, pp 11–36 offers an introductory insight into the Irish reception and contribution to Christian eschatological culture while the bibliography compiled by Nicole Volmering in vol. II, pp 855–912 is comprehensive. For a recent study of Irish conceptions of salvation history and the resultant influence on culture, identity and society, synthesized grammar and spirituality, reflecting Leclercq's linking of the two as essential to medieval monastic culture,[6] and produced many grammatical tracts, endless glosses, and a further corpus dealing with the computus.[7] This huge body of ecclesiastical literature raises many issues about monastic learning, devotion and spirituality in the early Irish church.

Rather than trying to reconstruct the liturgy of the Irish monastic tradition or lamenting the absence of sources the core of this chapter deals with prayer and knowledge, both concentrated on the Bible, and especially the psalms and hymns. Can universal monastic ideology be identified in the communal and personal prayers and intellectual tradition of Irish monks? Was performance part of their liturgy? What distinguished them from the mainstream church and what changed with the arrival of the new orders in the late eleventh century? Many of these questions deserve studies in their own right. This chapter is meant to illustrate how sources might be distilled to identify the monastic element of a variety of devotional texts.

PSALMS, LITERACY AND LITURGY

An important consideration, which is often overlooked, is the paucity of material surviving in early manuscripts that have a definite Irish provenance. Liturgical evidence is fragmentary in comparison to elsewhere, and whatever has survived needs to be analysed to elicit similarities with other monastic cultures, and to identify unique characteristics. One apparent difference, for example, is the existence elsewhere of a 'cathedral' or 'urban' liturgy led by a bishop with the clergy and laity, alongside communal monastic worship which as *opus Dei* 'God's work' concentrated on the continual recitation of the psalms in unceasing praise (*laus perennis*). Local practices pervaded and tensions between the two traditions broke out in various regions at different times.[8] The fairly violent tussles between canons and monks, abbots and bishops, and even abbots and communities in tenth and eleventh-century England provide witness to such tensions. Probably one of the most violent episodes occurred in Glastonbury in 1083 when the new abbot Thurstan attempted to replace the community's existing Gregorian chant with that of William of Fécamp, a plan that resulted in a physical encounter between the two factions.[9] New practices must have been introduced in Ireland from the eleventh century, once an urban cathedral staffed by a bishop and an episcopal household was set up in Christ Church cathedral, Dublin from a

see Elizabeth Boyle, *History and salvation in medieval Ireland* (Abingdon and New York, 2021). 6 Leclercq, *Love of learning*, p. 53. 7 For the extensive secondary literature on the computus and the Irish contribution, see Ó Corráin, *CLH*, pp 677–86. 8 Peter Jeffery, 'Psalmody and prayer in early monasticism' in *CHMM*, pp 112–27, at pp 113–21. 9 Pfaff, *The liturgy in medieval England*, pp 139–42.

Benedictine milieu in Cologne.[10] If Bishop Dúnan brought relics and the plan for a cathedral with him to Dublin, as argued by Ó Floinn and O'Keeffe respectively,[11] would it not follow that he also came with Ottonian Benedictine books and liturgy? Pádraig Ó Riain has argued for the transfer of a copy of the Martyrology of Ado of Vienne from Cologne to Dublin at this time, probably along with the relics.[12] A century later, Lorcán Ua Tuathail instituted the canonical rule of Arrouaise at Christ Church and among the changes made was the institution of a new liturgy and trained cantors to sing the Divine Office.[13] The archbishop may have replaced existing practices that had been introduced by his predecessors, among them Samuel Ua hAingli, who had been trained in English Benedictine schools. Bernard of Clairvaux identifies Malachy's introduction of the correct observation of 'chanting and psalm-singing at the canonical hours according to universal custom.' He adds:[14]

> There was very little of this done before that, even in the city [Armagh]. While a boy he had learned singing at a time when no one in the city or in the bishop's retinue knew how to sing or even cared. Then, too, Malachy re-instituted that most wholesome use of confession, the sacrament of confirmation and the marriage contract – something again about which they knew nothing and cared less.

This is Bernard creating a saint, but perhaps the more significant point in Bernard's comments is not that the canonical hours were hardly observed in Armagh but that a community followed the canonical hours and taught them to young novices, among them Malachy. The likelihood is that Malachy learned his singing under the tutelage of Ímar Ua hÁedacáin in Armagh. There is plenty of evidence, however, that the canonical hours were followed and that the psalms were revered in Ireland, as elsewhere, prior to the introduction of new liturgies during the eleventh and twelfth centuries. Bell ringing as part of monastic regulation, for example, is amply attested to both in the survival of many early medieval bells and references in the sources, some of which specify bells rung at prime, terce and vespers.[15] The problem facing scholars is that the essential

10 Edel Bhreathnach, 'Saints' dedications and the ecclesiastical landscape of Hiberno-Norse Dublin: Irish, Scandinavian and others' in Seán Duffy (ed.), *Medieval Dublin XVIII* (Dublin, 2020), pp 143–68, at pp 155–62. **11** Ó Floinn, 'The foundation relics of Christ Church cathedral'; O'Keeffe, *Romanesque Ireland*, p. 101. **12** Pádraig Ó Riain, 'Dublin's oldest book? A list of saints "made in Germany"' in Seán Duffy (ed.), *Medieval Dublin V* (Dublin, 2004), pp 52–72, at pp 65–72. **13** Plummer, 'Vie et miracles de S. Laurent', 138: lines 15–17. Original: *Fecitque regulares cantores circa altare, ut laudarent nomen sanctum Domini, et dedit in celebrationibus decus, et in sonos eorum dulces fecit modos.* **14** Meyer, *St Malachy the Irishman*, p. 22 §III.7 (Leclercq and Rochais, *Sancti Bernardi opera*, iii, p. 316). **15** Cormac Bourke, *The early medieval hand-bells of Ireland and Britain* (Dublin, 2020), pp 154–7.

evidence – the liturgical books – do not survive in sufficient numbers to provide a complete picture of the practices followed.

Devotional and spiritual literacy and the Beati (Psalm 118 [119])

A major issue about monastic learning and spirituality, not often alluded to by scholars, is the level of literacy and intellectual learning, especially in Latin, that existed among monks, nuns, the clergy and the laity. In a sense, authors such as Airbertach mac Coisse, *fer léiginn* of Ros Ailithir (d. 1016) or Echtgus Ua Cúanáin who composed a metrical tract on the Eucharist sometime between *c.*1050 and *c.*1150,[16] and the illustrious learned individuals who appear in the annals dominate the narrative. Equally, the many anonymous texts of the period written in Irish and Latin on an extensive range of subjects are regarded as reflecting the general levels of literacy, learning and spirituality in the Irish church including among its monastic communities. This view has merit but it overlooks the devotion to Heaven as understood by less literate, even illiterate, monks, nuns, novices, and does not consider levels of spiritual learning and literacy among the ordinary clergy and their capacity to communicate abstract religious concepts to the laity. In a monastic context, for example, Airbertach mac Coisse composed didactic poems for students – monastic novices and possibly students intending to be ordained – but it is not clear if he shared his knowledge with kings and their royal households or went further and preached among the laity. The Rule of Patrick, which appears to be an ordinance on the proper structure of the church and especially on the education of the clergy, specifically lays down what a bishop or teacher (*suí*) must teach students and their reward for carrying out their duties correctly:[17]

> Any one moreover with whom the boys study who are thus offered to God and to Patrick has a claim to reward and fee at the proper seasons, namely, a milch-cow as remuneration for [teaching] the 150 Psalms with their hymns, canticles and lections, and the rites of baptism and communion and intercession, together with the knowledge of the ritual generally, till the student be capable of receiving Orders ... But the milch-cow is made over immediately after the student has publicly proved his knowledge of the Psalms and hymns, and after the public proof of his knowledge of the ritual, the fee and habit are due.

16 Elizabeth Boyle, 'Sacrifice and salvation in Echtgus Úa Cúanáin's poetic treatise on the Eucharist' in Mullins, Ní Ghrádaigh and Hawtree, *Envisioning Christ on the cross*, pp 181–94.
17 Gwynn, 'The rule of the Céli Dé', 82–3 §62. Original: *Nach oen tra lasa legait na meic audparthar and do Dia 7 Patraic, dlegait side fochraic 7 dulchinde i n-aimseraib corib .i. loilgech i fochraicc na .III. cona n-imnaib 7 cantacib 7 liachtanaib 7 co mbathis 7 comna 7 gabail n-ecnarci 7 co n-eolas a n-ordaigthe olchena co mba tualaing airiten grad ... Acht iar taisfenad na salm 7 na n-imond focetoir dorenar in loilgech, iar taisfenad dino in ordusa dlegar in dulchinde 7 in decelt.*

'The teaching of Máel Ruain' suggests that in certain communities the proficiency of some monks was lacking, even to the point of not knowing the psalms:[18]

> The vigil which Muirchertach mac Olcobhair, *airchinnech* of Clonfert, used to keep was to say the *Beati* twelve times in place of the hundred and fifty psalms, because he knew that there were more of the monks or penitents who knew the *Beati* by heart than knew the Psalms; and he used to say the *Magnificat* after each repetition of the *Beati*.

It is possible that the text may be referring to *manaig* in the wider sense of lay tenants rather than to a religious community. The penitents (*aos pennaide*) were most likely to have been laity. In the Irish tradition, the *Beati* [Psalm 118 [119]] *Beati immaculati in via qui ambulant in lege Domini* 'Blessed are the undefiled in the way who walk in the law of the Lord' was regarded as one of the most efficacious prayers of all, as expressed in a Middle Irish *exemplum* on two clerical students and the next life:[19]

> §11. For the Beati is the ladder and chain and collar which is most powerful for bringing a person's soul from Hell …
> §12. … And so the Beati is the best prayer that there is.

This belief about the *Beati* explains, therefore, why an abbot might compensate for liturgical inadequacies in his community by reducing a reliance on the full cycle of psalms and make allowances by repetition of the prayers that everyone knew. This situation may have pertained in some small monastic communities but larger communities had the educational resources to teach novices, and in particular communities in which monks and nuns had been handed over during childhood.

The early Irish law *Uraicecht Becc* on the status of various professions distinguishes between three categories of laws practised by a jurist: the rule [*breth*: judgement] of the *Féni*, the rule of the *filid*, and the rule of the pure language of the *Beati*.[20] The *Féni* were freemen of full legal capacity, the *filid* were the poets and the last rule was *bélra bán bias*, scriptural and canon law. The

18 Gwynn, 'The teaching of Mael Ruain', 22–3 §37. Original: *As í figheall do niodh Muirceartach mac Olcobhar airchinneach Cluana Fearta, da bhiaid deug do radh ar son na tri ccaocat psalm, ar an adbar go raibhe a fhios aige gurb lia dona manchaibh, no don aos peannaide, aga mbiodh an bhiaid do mhebhair ina na psailm, 7 adeireadh se Magnificad a ndeireadh gach biaide.* 19 John Carey (ed.), 'The two clerical students and the next life' in Carey et al., *The end and beyond*, pp 139–43 §§11–12. Original: §11 *Ar is arada 7 slabra 7 muince is treisi do tabairt anma duine a iffiurn in biait*; §12 *& in biaid tra as i urnaigte is dech fil ann hi.* 20 Eoin MacNeill (trans.), 'Ancient Irish law: the law of status or franchise', *Proceedings of the Royal Irish Academy* 36C (1921–4), 265–316, at p. 277 and pp 277–8 n. 5.

significance of this provision for our purposes is the description of canon law as *breth bélra bán bias* or *biait* (derived from *Beati*) which identifies canon law with the psalms, and probably even more specifically with Psalm 118. As demonstrated by McNamara and Boyle, this psalm's popularity in Ireland is expressed throughout literature to the extent that it was regarded as a *lorica* and 'was held to possess exceptional salvific power'.[21] Boyle also comments that the psalm's language of commandments and discipline 'resonates with the regulations of monastic life'.[22] *RB* also confirms the importance of the *Beati* as part of the Divine Office and specifically of the 'small hours' (terce, sext and none), when sections of Psalm 118 were said on Sundays and Mondays.[23] The same psalm is quoted in key chapters on humility, celebration of the Divine Office and the procedure for receiving brothers.[24] The prevalence of references to the *Beati* in the vernacular devotional literature and in vernacular rules accords with Cassian's monologistic or repetitive prayer as if its commandments regarding humility, prayer, constant praise of God, the law and many other injunctions were being repeated ceaselessly in an individual's mind, be they monks, nuns or secular priests. This exercise is best illustrated in 'The monastery of Tallaght', which opens with an *athláech*, a layman who had retired into religious life, commenting to his companion, a *mac bethad* 'son of life', that he did not understand his continual singing of the *Beati* and the *Magnificat*, to which the monk responded:[25]

> 'As a man, being now at the foot of the gallows, would pour out praise and lamentation to the king, to gain his deliverance; in like manner we pour forth lamentation to the King of Heaven in the *Beati*, to gain our deliverance.'

Psalm 118 is not simply a lamentation seeking deliverance. The text is full of what Leclercq dubbed 'hook-words', a phenomenon of recollection 'whereby the verbal echoes so excite the memory that a mere allusion will spontaneously evoke whole quotations and, in turn, a scriptural phrase will suggest quite naturally allusions elsewhere in the sacred books'.[26] For the novice and the experienced monk, therefore, the *Beati* contained many 'hook-words' that were keys to unlocking the memory and reminding them of basic precepts of their committed religious way of life. Abbreviated psalters, such as those ascribed to Jerome and

21 Boyle, *History and salvation*, p. 99. See also McNamara, *The psalms*, p. 358. **22** Boyle, *History and salvation*, p. 99. **23** *RB*: Chap. 18.2–3, 7–8. **24** *RB*: Chaps 7.54, 66; 16.1–2, 4–5; 58.21. **25** Gwynn and Purton, 'The monastery of Tallaght', p. 127 §1. Original: *'Fer indorsa fri bun cruche ind molad ocus ind nemeli noferfad frisind rig immo saorad. is foion iondas sin fermaidni nemeli fri rig nime isind bíaid immo ar sáorad.'* See Boyle, *History and salvation*, pp 99, 117. **26** Leclercq, *Love of learning*, pp 73–4. Leclercq's original in French is more expressive (Leclercq, *L'amour des lettres et le désir de Dieu* (Paris, 1957; repr. 1990), p. 73: 'chaque mot fait

Bede, were a step beyond the *Beati* and often personal miscellanies of passages from the Book of Psalms. The *Orationes excerptae de psalterio*, an abridgement of the psalter, contained in the Irish *Liber Hymnorum*, amounts to an Irish version of an abbreviated psalter, and like the *Beati*, was not only recommended for its brevity but also for the efficacy of certain verses of the psalms above others.[27] Undoubtedly, this text was a useful handbook for those who were well-versed in the psalms and who only needed prompts to fulfil their canonical obligations.

Psalters for liturgical and scholarly use

At the other end of the spectrum, the psalms were a subject of much scrutiny for ecclesiastical scholars in Ireland, as elsewhere.[28] Psalters survive from the early conversion period, the most important example being the Cathach or Psalter of Columba (RIA MS 12 R 33), a late sixth-/early seventh-century copy of the Gallican psalter and the earliest example of insular majuscule script.[29] There is a sufficient number of surviving Irish psalters dating to between the tenth and twelfth centuries to gain an idea of the scholarly tradition of commenting on the psalms.[30] Many scholars have and continue to work on the multiple facets of these psalters – their layout, the sources used for commentaries and glosses, the hierarchy of scripts, the decoration – but discussion here concentrates on how these manuscripts can provide insights into liturgical use and pedagogical methods.

Two characteristics dominated the medieval Irish scholarly approach to commenting on the psalms: their interpretation was primarily literal and historical, as opposed to Christological, mystical and moral, and their exegetical method of commenting and glossing on the whole remained unchanged from the eighth to the twelfth centuries. For example, the oldest surviving Irish commentary on the psalms, the so-called *Glossa ad Psalmos* of Vatican Library Codex Pal. lat. 68, dated to the mid-eighth century, or a text closely related to it, was a major source for the tenth-century glossator of the Double Psalter of St Ouen.[31] The glosses in the Southampton Psalter, dated to the late tenth or

agrafe, pour ainsi dire: il en accroche un ou plusieurs autres …'). **27** Bernard and Atkinson, *Irish Liber Hymnorum*, i, pp 144–56; ii, pp 216–18. **28** McNamara, *The psalms*, pp 353–78. **29** See note https://www.isos.dias.ie/RIA/RIA_MS_12_R_33.html. **30** McNamara, *The psalms*, pp 19–142; McNamara, 'End of an era in early Irish biblical exegesis'. McNamara (at p. 77) briefly lists the following psalters and fragmentary psalters: BL Codex Cotton Vitellius F.XI (*c.*AD 920), the Southampton Psalter (tenth/eleventh century), MS Rouen Bib. Mun. 24 [A41] the Double Psalter of St-Ouen, Rouen (tenth century), Paris fragments BNF MS Fr. 2450 (tenth century), fragmentary psalter in the Vatican Library Codex lat. 12910 (eleventh century), Edinburgh Psalter (Edinburgh University Library MS 56 (*c.*1025), Psalter of Ricemarch TCD MS 50 (A.4.20) (*c.*1055), Psalter of Caimín (Psalm 118) UCD-OFM MS A1 (eleventh/twelfth century), BL Codex Cotton Galba A.V. (twelfth century), Coupar Angus Psalter MS Vatican Library Pal. lat. 65 (*c.*1170), Psalter of Cormac BL Add. 36929 (*c.*1150–1200). **31** McNamara, 'End of an era', 79–81. **32** Ó Néill, *Psalterium Suthantoniense*, p. lxxxvi. **33** Ó

eleventh centuries, depend almost totally on the seventh-century anonymous *Glossa Psalmorum ex traditione seniorum*, a source described by Pádraig Ó Néill as 'very much a monastic work both in origins and in its intended audience'. It was designed to make the psalms applicable to the monastic lifestyle.[32] It is not clear, however, for whom this psalter was compiled. Ó Néill argues that this de luxe scriptural text was not a scholar's psalter, despite the commentaries and glosses, while Máire Herbert has raised the possibility that it may have been 'a copy for presentation, which had to be adapted to meet an expectation that scholarly apparatus would be included'.[33] To a certain extent the fragmentary late eleventh/early twelfth-century manuscript known as the Psalter of Caimín may be another example of a heavily glossed de luxe psalter. It consists of some verses and a commentary on the *Beati*, Psalm 118.[34] (Fig. 19) But these are not exceptional in the wider world of psalters where many manuscripts such as the opulent mid-twelfth-century Eadwine Psalter (Cambridge, Trinity College MS R.17.1) linked to the monastic community of Christ Church Canterbury, is both highly illuminated and extensively glossed.[35] The production of these psalters must have been a statement of the wealth, scholarship, scribal capacity and artistic competence of Irish monasteries. Alderik Blom in his work on the glossing of psalms has made the interesting comment that the Southampton Psalter appears to include punctuation in the form of *positurae* in the principal text of the psalms that suggests an element of orality and performance and 'that the manuscript, or its exemplar, is likely to have been involved in monastic worship'. No such punctuation is used in the Double Psalter of St Ouen or the Psalter of Caimín, both regarded as 'scholarly' psalters.[36]

Blom's and Ó Néill's work demonstrates how commentaries and glosses, when analysed in detail, can yield so much regarding the actual methodology of learning in Irish monastic schools. Of the many examples available, the methods of the Southampton Psalter (*SP*) and Psalter of Caimín (*PC*) glossators and scribes are revealing. A hierarchy of scripts is evident in the commentaries and glosses of both manuscripts, from the *PC* main text (Psalm 118) written in large half-uncial insular majuscule to glosses in both texts in small insular minuscule. The dense glossing in *PC* follows a deliberate schema of separate blocks with, for example, historical interpretations of the principal text in the left margins and allegorical interpretations confined to the right margins.[37] In *SP*, two principal glossators (G1 and G2) worked on the manuscript following a

Néill, *Psalterium Suthantoniense*, pp xxxiv–v; Máire Herbert's review of Ó Néill's edition, *Études celtiques* 40 (2014), 341–2. 34 https:// www.isos.dias.ie/UCD/UCD_MS_A_1.html. 35 Breay and Story, *Anglo-Saxon kingdoms*, pp 350–1. 36 Alderik H. Blom, *Glossing the psalms. The emergence of the written vernaculars in western Europe from the seventh to the twelfth centuries* (Berlin and Boston, 2017), p. 57. 37 Blom, *Glossing the psalms*, p. 77; Ó Néill, 'Psalter of St Caimín'.

consistent strategy, at times creating a highly complicated stratigraphy of sources, textual affiliation and language.[38] This should not be surprising given the generations of scribes, who were also variously abbots, bishops, priests, anchorites and teachers, recorded in the annals. A colophon added to the Cotton Vitellius Psalter (BL Codex Cotton Vitellius F. XI), ascribed by various scholars to the early tenth century, gives an intriguing clue as to who its patron might have been. The quatrain reads:[39]

> The blessing of God on Muiredach, bright fulfilment!
> May the scholar be successful and long-lived here,
> may his time here not be short;
> may the outstanding(?) abbot without falsehood
> be a dweller in the kingdom of God.

It has been suggested by Anne O'Sullivan, following Françoise Henry's dating of the manuscript's decoration and a similarity to Muiredach's Cross at Monasterboice, that the abbot-scholar referred to in the quatrain was none other than Muiredach mac Domnaill, the likely patron of that same monumental cross.[40]

The use of sources, many of them early, through these generations could be viewed as a sign of innate conservatism and lack of receptivity or knowledge of new sources. Yet, there are hints in later psalters that this was not necessarily the case. *SP* includes readings of the Gallican psalter text that are in common with the 'Alcunian' recension.[41] There is also a divergence between its two main glossators in that, unusually, G1 preferred allegorical and mystical interpretations while G2 followed the Irish tradition of historical and literal interpretations. Their main sources also differed, G1 using the *Glossa psalmorum ex traditione seniorum*, G2 the *Glossa psalmorum* of Vatican Codex Pal. lat. 68. One wonders if this was a deliberate scribal strategy of copying from an older exemplar and does not reflect an intellectual choice on the part of the scribes, and if so, does this, along with the repeated use of the same commentaries and glosses, indicate that Irish monastic schools had limited and outdated resources, and followed a set pedagogical programme that did not encourage the introduction of contemporary interpretations? The inclusion of Old Irish glosses in *SP* is regarded as mere copying by Ó Néill given that the glossators' vernacular would have been Middle Irish, two hundred years on from the

38 Blom, *Glossing the psalms*, pp 73–5. 39 Anne O'Sullivan, 'The colophon of the Cotton Psalter (Vitellius F XI)', *Journal of the Royal Society of Antiquaries of Ireland* 96 (1966), 179–80. Original: *Bendacht dé for Muiretach comall glé!/ rop sen sutin sunn in suí/ ní rop duthain sunn ha ré/ int ap thanthemail(?) cen goeí/ rop attrabthaid flatha dé.* 40 Françoise Henry, 'Remarks on the decoration of three Irish psalters', *Proceedings of the Royal Irish Academy* 61 (1960–1), 23–40, at pp 31–2. 41 Ó Néill, *Psalterium Suthantoniense*, pp xxxviii–xxxvix; Blom, *Glossing*

original.[42] They may have been mere copyists or, as in the case of psalters such as the Eadwine psalter that includes earlier Anglo-Saxon glosses, older glosses may have added to the prestige of a de luxe psalter. As Ó Néill has demonstrated in detail,[43] although 'textually old-fashioned', the fragmentary Psalter of Caimín is carefully laid out with the main psalm text in 'monumental semi-uncial' placed centrally in each folio, with a hierarchy of miniscule scripts used for the *explanatio*, the text of the Hebraicum, the marginal glosses, and the interlinear and supralinear glosses. All this seems a far cry from the monks and others who had to depend on an abbreviated version of the psalms and the *Beati* as a *lorica* and monologistic prayer but these extremes offer a clear manifestation of the multi-faceted nature of early Irish monasticism and the use of the psalter.

Two psalters of possible Scottish origin that follow the Irish psalter tradition, the eleventh-century so-called Edinburgh Psalter (Edinburgh University Library MS 56) and the late twelfth-century Coupar-Angus Psalter (Vatican Library Pal. lat. 65) hint at the introduction of new influences.[44] Françoise Henry suggested that the Edinburgh Psalter may have been illuminated in Scotland and it has been argued that the influence of a Pictish style is evident.[45] One folio (50r) is in a distinctive blue and gold-wash that is normally associated with the 'Winchester' style. It seems to have been inserted into the psalter, and if original, suggests contacts with English illuminators. There is some doubt, however, that this might be a fourteenth-century imitation added along with a prayer attributed to Alcuin.[46] The Coupar-Angus psalter has some affinity to the Corpus Missal (Corpus Christi College MS 122), described by Françoise Henry as 'at times a sort of caricature of the style of the Corpus Christi Gospel-Book'.[47] Martin McNamara dates it to *c*.1170, although a later scribe added to the manuscript as its biblical text reflects the recension used in the University of Paris in the thirteenth century.[48] There is a possibility, although not fully substantiated, that this psalter came from St Malachy's foundation of *Viride Stagnum* (Soulseat in Scotland), and when the monastery failed that its books were moved to Coupar-Angus, a later Cistercian foundation. This psalter is written in Irish majuscule and miniscule and follows the traditional 'three-fifties' layout of Irish psalters. The text is Gallican and is accompanied with variants by Peter Lombard's *Maior* (*Magna*) *Glossatura*, completed in 1142/3. Martin McNamara speculated that the Coupar-Angus psalter represents new learning,

the psalms, p. 56. 42 Ó Néill, *Psalterium Suthantoniense*, p. lxviii. 43 Ó Néill, 'Psalter of St Caimín'. 44 Stephen Mark Holmes, 'Catalogue of liturgical books and fragments in Scotland before 1560', *The Innes Review* 62:2 (2012), 127–212, at pp 136–8 (items 11, 14); McNamara, *The psalms*, pp 74–6. 45 Françoise Henry, *Irish art during the Viking invasions (800–1020 AD)* (London, 1967), p. 106. 46 https://archives.collections.ed.ac.uk/repositories/2/archival_objects/147391 accessed 30 June 2023. 47 McNamara, *The psalms*, pp 83–4; Françoise Henry, *Irish art in the Romanesque period (1020–1170 AD)* (London, 1970), p. 69. 48 Martin McNamara, 'Five Irish psalter texts', *Proceedings of the Royal Irish Academy* 109C

the introduction of which is associated with the Cistercians.[49] Even more significantly in the context of Malachy's possible connection with the manuscript itself or its exemplar is that it provides a striking example of the fusion of an existing monastic tradition with a contemporary twelfth-century commentary. This was a monastic, and general ecclesiastical, culture in transition.

OPUS DEI: UNCEASING PRAYER IN THE MONASTIC COMMUNITY AND IN THE DESERT

Devotion to Heaven and spiritual direction

And what of spirituality, Leclercq's monastic devotion to Heaven? The Irish corpus of religious literature is replete with evidence of intellectual monastic spirituality and theology (*summa scientia*) and of the daily practice of *opus Dei*, constant prayer in the guise of the Divine Office focussing on the psalter, penance and hymns, and later in the period under consideration, the Mass and sacraments, especially the Eucharist. Unlike other monastic cultures of the eleventh and twelfth centuries, there are no known ardent Irish letter writers such as Lanfranc, Anselm, Bernard or known homilists such as Ælfric of Eynsham (d. *c.*1010). That is not to deny that Irish ecclesiastics were involved in correspondence and composing tracts on issues that were subject to fierce debates across western Christendom. Lanfranc, an expert on practical and theological details, corresponded *c.*1080/1 with Domnall Ua hÉnna, household bishop of Muirchertach Ua Briain, king of Munster, on the administration of the Eucharist to newly baptized infants.[50] Máel Ísu Ua hAinmire, bishop of Waterford, corresponded with Anselm and sought a copy of the latter's treatise on the Holy Spirit and of a sermon on the Incarnation.[51] Echtgus Ua Cúanáin's treatise on the Eucharist is significant as it is an example of an Irish author writing in the vernacular and in line with better-known writers elsewhere, in Boyle's words, 'articulating an orthodox theological position on the Eucharist for the purpose of promoting uniformity of belief throughout the church'.[52]

But what of a more intimate devotion? Personal religious experience is best measured by devotional Middle Irish poetry which unfortunately is often anonymous and hence not necessarily composed in a monastic milieu, although the likelihood is that most of it was at least influenced by monastic devotion. Máel Ísu Ua Brolcháin's eleventh-century compositions are important as they highlight subjects of concern to a monastic community. In his own words it is worth fasting and doing penance:[53]

(2009), 37-104, at p. 67. **49** McNamara, *The psalms*, p. 84. **50** Helen Clover and Margaret Gibson (eds), *The letters of Lanfranc, archbishop of Canterbury* (Oxford, 1979), pp 155–61, no. 49; Boyle, 'Echtgus Úa Cúanáin', pp 181–2. **51** Flanagan, *Transformation*, p. 50. **52** Boyle, 'Echtgus Úa Cúanáin', p. 193. **53** Ní Bhrolcháin, *Maol Íosa*, pp 56–7 §9. I include

Fil a dó
atom-agat do throscad;
tene ná díbtai usce,
aig nád lega fria loscad.

> Two things drive me to fasting: fire that water cannot quench, ice that does not melt with burning.

The sources place much store on the spiritual guidance of the *anmcharae* 'soul-friend, confessor' both to monastic communities but also to the wider clergy and the laity, or at least to the aristocracy. The Old Irish legal tract *Córus Bésgnai* demonstrates the role of the *anmcharae* in society, referencing in particular his directing male ecclesiastics (*cléirig*), probably both secular clergy and monks, and nuns (*caillecha*) in law (*co racht*) and rule (*ríagail*). The additional glosses specify that the *anmcharae* should be teaching them the gospel (law) and rules such as not consuming meat on Wednesdays and Fridays, and consuming a single meal from one none to the next.[54] Many confessors whose obits are recorded in the annals were held in high esteem and were regarded as national figures as, for example, Dubthach Albanach, *prímanmchara Érenn 7 Alban* ('chief confessor of Ireland and Alba') (d. 1065)[55] or Fothud Ua hAille, *ard-anmchara Cluana Mic Nóis 7 Leithi Cuinn* ('noble confessor of Clonmacnoise and the southern half of Ireland') (d. 1081).[56] Both probably assumed the role of spiritual directors to senior ecclesiastics and to kings and their wives, when they were penitents in larger monasteries such as Armagh, Iona, Kells and Clonmacnoise. While these men mainly followed a life in the community, monastic and lay, as previously mentioned, others withdrew from busy settlements to their own 'deserts' to spend lives of complete contemplation.

Columba Stewart commenting on Cassian's attitudes to the Bible and prayer is as true of Irish monasticism as it is of early eastern and western monasticism:[57]

> The 'professions and pursuits' of the practical life are many, embracing both monastic and lay forms of life ... The important point is perseverance in the way one has chosen (*Conf.* 14.5–6). Cassian then turns to the kinds of contemplative knowledge of the Bible. None of these is restricted to a particular way of life. Distinctions between anchorites and cenobites, indeed between monastic and lay Christians, are left behind. All who are intent on practical knowledge, that is, on attaining purity of heart, have access to contemplative knowledge of the Bible by perseverance in their chosen way of life.

the original in the main text to illustrate the poet's simple, yet skilful, artistry. **54** Breatnach, *Córus Bésgnai*, pp 134–5 §13. **55** AU, AFM. **56** AFM. **57** Stewart, *Cassian the monk*, p. 93.

Cassian and other early monastic commentators, especially Evagrius Ponticus (d. 399), characterized the monk's encounter with the fundamental medium of contemplation, the Bible and spiritual knowledge as *praktikē* and *theōrētikē*. *Praktikē* was accomplished by improvement of morals and purging of faults while *theōrētikē* consisted of contemplation of divine things and awareness of the most sacred meaning (*sensum*), that is, of the biblical text. As Stewart makes clear in his discussion based on Cassian's *Conferences*, both are essential for monastic perfection.[58] How far Irish monastic communities and individual monks knowingly understood Cassian and Evagrius's distinction between *praktikē* and *theōrētikē* is open to question and depends on the evidence of various sources. On the basis mainly of hagiography, Follett concludes that 'we may yet determine that Irish or Insular writers in general did not fully apprehend the concept of *theoria* "in the Greek or Cassianic sense".'[59] Despite this, however, the lived experience of a community inhabiting islands such as Skellig speaks to a deeper understanding than what the sources suggest if the layout of the monastery and hermitage there is read as a physical manifestation of the Cassianic sense of leaning towards Heaven and re-creating the new Jerusalem.[60]

Seeking protection through unceasing prayer

There is a delightful episode in the twelfth-/thirteenth-century late Middle Irish text *Acallam na Senórach* 'The dialogue of the ancients' that captures the spirit of the power of prayer as understood in medieval Ireland. It is not particularly surprising, as the concept is well known, the idea that the canonical hours could cancel out the vices. This fits with Irish penitential practices of virtuous actions compensating for one's sins. In the text, the warrior Caílte is on an adventure with St Colmán Elo and after observing the saint and his companions following the canonical hours asks:[61] '… what is the reason for those

58 Ibid., pp 92–3. 59 Westley Follett, 'Cassian, contemplation, and medieval Irish hagiography' in Gernot R. Wieland, Carin Ruff and Ross G. Arthur (eds), *Insignis sophiae arcator. Medieval Latin studies in honour of Michael W. Herren on his 65th birthday* (Turnhout, 2006), pp 87–105, at p. 90. 60 Edel Bhreathnach, 'Skellig Michael, Co. Kerry: a lonely island hermitage at the edge of the world?', *Journal of Medieval Monastic Studies* 11 (2022), 35–49. 61 Dooley and Roe, *Tales of the elders of Ireland*, p. 90; see also Standish Hayes O'Grady (ed. and trans.), *Silva Gadelica (I–XXXI): a collection of tales in Irish with extracts illustrating persons and places* (London, 1892), vol. 1, p. 160; vol. 2, pp 177–8. Original: *Crét adbar na [nocht trá]th úd chum anéirgenn sibse etir lá ocus adhaig. mór a nadbar ar Colmán .i. ocht caire atá ac lenmain chuirp ocus anma gach duine ocus díolait na hocht trátha sin iat. ocus adubairt Colmán: – Na hocht caire colnaide . congeiltet co grian; na hocht trátha togaide . dá ndíochur co dian/ Prímh fria craes nach coimside . tert fria feirg na fáth;/ medón lái suairc soillside . uainn re hétradh ngnáth/ Nóin i nagaid noccabair . ar brú talman teinn;/ esbarta shuairc shocamail . uainn re toirrse teinn/ Coimpléid re sníom sechmallach . óir is comroinn chóir;/ iarmeirge fhuar lethrannach . re máidhmige móir/ Maiden mheic dhé dhilgedhaig . fria ndiumas ndaor ndrocht; curomsoera a ríg bhrethaig . a Isa ar na hocht. 'Adrae buaid ocus bennachtain a Cholmáin,' ar Cáilte, 'is maith ro fhuaslaicis in cheisd sin' 'ocus cid damsa,' ar Cáilte, 'gan na hocht trátha sin do*

eight hours for which you arise both day and night?' Colmán explains: 'there are eight faults that adhere to the body and soul of each man, and the eight hours make atonement for them.'

Then Colmán recited this poem:

> The eight carnal faults that graze us to the ground,
> The eight choice hours drive them soon away.
>
> Prime against gluttony, Terce against rage,
> Pleasant, bright Sext keeps nagging lust at bay.
>
> Nones against greed, while we are on earth,
> Pleasant, cheerful Vespers save me from despair.
>
> Compline against sorrow and unworthy grief.
> Stern, cold Nocturns combat unseemly pomp.
>
> Christ's merciful Matins against hard, sullen pride.
> That you may save me, Jesus, from the body's sins.

Cáilte the warrior responds to Colmán the saint:

> 'May you have victory and blessing, Colmán Éla,' said Caílte, 'well have you answered that question. And why should I not observe those eight hours now that God has preserved me until your era?'

This is not just one of the many entertaining episodes in *Acallam na Senórach*, it links directly into the ideology in which the efficacy of prayer and the canonical hours was essential in overcoming the vices that beset monks, and indeed everyone, during their lives. The monastic connection is heightened by the existence of versions of Colmán's poem elsewhere. The *Acallam na Senórach* version omits a final verse that appears to condemn some clerics for being lax or too strict – depending on the interpretation of the texts – in their observance of the daily *horarium*:[62]

> *Is tuidecht dar [ ]ríagail, bid bithbúan a olc,*
> *a ndénat na fúathc[h]léirigh na trí tráth da hocht.*
>
> It is a transgression of [the?] rule, perpetual will be the misfortune,
> What the sham clerics do, the three canonical hours of the eight.

Máel Ísu's version reads:[63]

thathaigid ó ro fhuirig dia mhé i comaimsir friu.' **62** Meyer, 'Die acht Horen', 271 §6. **63** Ní Bhrolcháin, *Maol Íosa*, pp 76–7 §66.

Bid adbul a pianriagail,
bid bithbuan a n-olc,
a ndénat na cruaidchléirig
trí tráth dona hocht.

The punishment against them will be vehement,
Their misfortune will be forever,
What the strict clerics do
Three canonical hours of the eight.

Tensions often existed within communities about following the canonical hours, some adhering to the eight hours, others perhaps to the major hours, Matins, Lauds and Vespers, which probably explains the condemnation of the *fúathchléirig* or *cruaidchléirig* in the above verse. Patricia Rumsey argued that the liturgy as portrayed in the *Navigatio Sancti Brendani* – in her estimation an earlier monastic liturgy derived from Cassian – and the *céli Dé* texts – a liturgy of the hours lost in a clutter of subjective pious practices – reflect different perspectives on liturgy and time. The author(s) of *NSB* had a sacramental view of time, 'seeing time as sacred in itself', while the *céli Dé* were 'concerned with the best way to use time in this life in order to prepare for eternity'.[64] One wonders if Máel Ísu Ua Brolcháin had similar difficulties with his former community at Armagh, causing him to transfer to the more liturgically literate Lismore, a monastery in which he could follow a stricter committed religious life? There is an echo of a similar departure in the poem attributed to Céle Dabaill mac Scanaill, abbot of Bangor, described in the annals as *scriba 7 anchorita 7 apostolicus doctor totius Hibernie*, who died on pilgrimage in Rome in 929:[65]

Time for me to prepare to pass from the shelter of a habitation,
To journey as a pilgrim over the surface of the noble, lively sea...

Time to defy the clayey body, to reduce it to religious rule,
Time to barter the transitory things for the country of the King of Heaven...

But only a part of one year is wanting of my threescore,
To remain under holy rule in one place it is time.

64 Patricia Rumsey, 'Tensions over time: conflicting understanding of monastic prayer in late-eighth-century Armagh', *Seanchas Ard Mhacha* 25:2 (2015), 29–49, at p. 30. **65** AU, AFM [927]. The poem survives only in AFM [926]. Original: *Mithigh damh-sa tairir / do thriall o thoraibh teghlaigh, / do asccnamh imm ailither, / tar tuinn mara muaidh menmnaigh... / / Mithigh lámh corp crédbhaidhe, / costadh im chrábhaidh n-glinne, / mithigh reic na n-earchraidhe / ar thír na flatha finne... / / Acht inge di aen-bliadhain, / ní thesta dom trí fichtibh / Airisemh fo naomh-riaghail / in nách maighin ba mithigh.*

This poem, if genuinely composed by Céle Dabaill, along with Máel Ísu's poems, encapsulates the plight of a busy abbot whose desire at the end of his days is to devote himself to a committed religious life and make up for time spent dealing with temporal matters. He travelled further than Máel Ísu, dying in Rome in the end.

The belief that the canonical hours could ward off the eight vices could be considered as a form of *lorica* and it may be no coincidence that Máel Ísu's poem on the eight vices contains a *lorica*:[66]

Do chathbarr form chléithi-sa,
do chathsciath form shlis,
do lúirech dom imdedail,
do chlaidim form chris.

Your helmet on my head,
your battle-shield by my side,
your breastplate protecting me,
your sword in my belt.

And far from being a throwback to a pre-Christian formula, Máel Ísu's *lorica* and the idea that the canonical hours could protect individuals from the ever-active vices echo the psalms on God's protection, expressed, for example, in Psalm 5, 11–12:

> But let all who take refuge in you be glad; let them ever sing for joy. Spread your protection over them, that those who love your name may rejoice in you.
>
> For surely, O Lord, you bless the righteous; you surround them with your favour as with a shield.

It could be argued that this format, which is relatively straightforward, was an introduction to the discipline of prayer, not necessarily confined to monks, categorized by Cassian as 'supplication', the first step on the progress of prayer towards *excessus mentis* 'ecstasies of mind'.[67] This form of prayer was viewed by Cassian as 'prayer suitable to the *vita actualis* of eliminating faults and cultivating virtues' from which a monk gradually advanced to 'the higher, ineffable prayer'.[68]

Monologistic prayers, tears and performance

Unceasing prayer undertaken communally and individually is a distinct aspect of monasticism. *RB* is quite regulated in how *opus Dei* 'the work of God' is to be organized throughout the day and night. Quoting Psalm 118, the *Beati* beloved of the Irish, 'Seven times a day have I praised you' (Ps 118(119): 164), *RB* (Chap. 16) lists the hours of praise as Lauds, Prime, Terce, Sext, None, Vespers,

66 Ní Bhrolcháin, *Maol Íosa*, pp 74–5 §59. **67** Stewart, *Cassian the monk*, p. 108. **68** Ibid.,

Compline. But there were the other hours of the day and night when monks were not in the church praying together, but were engaged in manual work, caring for the sick, on journeys and in their cells alone. Keeping one's mind on God and devotion to Heaven, as well as keeping a pure heart was not easy even for the most ascetic monk, and hence, formulae were devised to redirect a wandering mind or an aroused body back to purity and praising the Creator. Cassian recommended 'monologistic prayer' such as the repetition of the name of Jesus or lines from the Psalms such as from Psalm 69(70): 2) *Deus in adiutorium meum intende Domine ad adiuvandum me festina* 'O God, come to my assistance; O Lord, make haste to help me'. Such formulae were what Stewart describes as 'the river of words that carries both anchorites and cenobites through day and night, coming to the surface in the interstices of other forms of prayer or in times of particular need'.[69] While not particularly edifying, this use of Cassian's formula occurs in 'The rule of the *céli Dé*':[70]

> Privies and urinals are abodes for evil spirits. The sign of the Cross should be made over these places, and a man should cross himself when he enters them, and it is not lawful to pray in them, except to repeat *Deus in adjutorium*, down to *festina*.

As a complete contrast to seeking protection while undertaking the most basic of human functions, protection and even ecstatic prayer could be achieved through another common human action: the shedding of tears. Cassian, Gregory the Great and *RB* (20: 3) specified that tears and compunction (*compunctio*) were key to the monastic tradition: they 'signify more than simply repentance and sorrow; tears, too, are marks of ecstatic prayer'.[71] A Middle Irish poem expresses rather fervently the power of tears granted by God to protect the author from the eight vices and to purify his heart. I quote both the original Irish text and translation to provide a sense of the poet's fervour:[72]

Dera damh, a Coimde, *do dicur mo cionadh;* *dib, a De, nar anar* *co rabur co hiodhan.*	Grant me tears, O Lord, to blot out my sins; may I not desist from them [the tears], O God, until I have been purified.
Loiscitir mo chride *do tene na híce;* *déra damh co ngloine* *ar Muire 's ar m'Ide.*	May my heart be burned by the fire of requital; grant me tears with purity for Mary and for Íte.

p. 108. **69** Ibid., p. 112. **70** Gwynn, 'The rule of the Céli Dé', 74–5 §42. Original: *Fial-tige dino 7 fual-tige, it adbai do demnaib indsin. Senad do neoch na tiged sin 7 a shénad fén in tan tiassair inntib, ocus ni dlegair irnaigthe inntib sin, sed 'Deus in adi[u]torium usque festina'.* **71** Stewart, *Cassian the monk*, p. 115. **72** Brian Ó Cuív (ed.), 'Some early devotional verse in Irish', *Ériu* 19 (1962), 1–24, at pp 4–6.

Ag iomradh mo cionadh
dera damh gach n-uaire,
daigh as mor a fotha
na srota tar gruaide

Contemplating my sins
grant me tears always,
for great are the claims
of tears (running) down cheeks.

Dera damh ag eirge,
dera damh ag loige,
os gach dan deit uile
dot gradh, a Meic Muire.

Grant me tears when rising,
grant me tears when resting,
beyond every gift of thine altogether
for love of thee, O Son of Mary.

Dera dam im leabaid
co ro fliucat m'adart,
do leighes na hanma
co cabra a cuid carat.

Grant me tears in bed
so that they may wet my pillow,
so that its dear ones
may help to cure the soul.

Tug dhamh congain cride
na rabar fo mela;
a Coimde, nom-ainic
ocus tabair dera.

Grant me contrition of heart
so that I may not be in disgrace;
O Lord, protect me
and grant (me) tears.

Sa coibligh do-ronus
re mnaip nach ttucc era
na srota tar suiliph,
a Duilimh, tug dera.

For the dalliance which I had
with women who rejected (me) not,
grant me tears, O Creator,
(flowing) in streams from my eyes.

Im feirg is im format
's am diumus, gniomh ngenda,
anall ina linnip
as m'innip tug dera.

For my anger and my jealousy,
and my pride, a foolish deed,
hither in pools
from my inmost parts bring tears.

Mo brega ocus m'eithech,
mo saint, trom in tredha,
da ndicur uaim uile,
a Muire, tug dera.

My falsehoods and my lying
and my greed, grievous the trio,
to banish them all from me,
O Mary, grant (me) tears.

Mo chraos is mo codladh,
mo meisge, fath méla,
nar agrat mo biodbaid,
a inmain, tug dera.

My gluttony and my excessive sleeping
and my drunkenness, reason for sorrow,
lest my enemies invoke them against me,
O dear one, grant (me) tears.

M'achmusan is m'egnach,
mo splega is mo sccela,
dib, a De, co n-anar
is co fagur déra.

My reviling and my complaining,
my boastings and my reproaches,
may I cease from them, O God,
and may I get tears.

Na himraite olca
tegait amail nella
im chroide nar anat
is ro glanat déra.

May the evil thoughts
which come like clouds
not remain in my heart,
and may tears cleanse them.

Gach gnimh riam do-ronus
nach at maith a sgéla,
deaman na-rot-maoidi,
a Coimdi, tuc déra.

Every deed which I have heretofore done
which is not a matter of good account,
lest the demon boast of it to thee,
O Lord, grant (me) tears.

Ocus leabar diapail
ar sgriobadh mo sgela,
a litri ro traigit
co mbaidit mo déra. Dera.

And the devil's book,
when my life's story has been written,
may its letters recede
until my tears drown them.

As this poem, and many other devotional poems, only survives in a seventeenth-century manuscript,[73] its original context is lost to us. The reference to St Íte might indicate a location in the southwest or a foundation associated with St Brendan such as Clonfert. The poem's significance, however, lies in its reflection of the fundamental monastic belief that tears could purify the heart, act as a protection against the eight vices and wash away the sins recorded in the Devil's book: 'may its letters recede until my tears drown them'. While the level of ecstatic prayer or contemplation that inspired such a poem is difficult to gauge, the poet realizes that human tears do not have any power unless they are produced with divine grace. The poem appears to be a personal plea on behalf of the author, composed in the first person singular, and as with so many such texts, it introduces the question of how to recognize private and public devotion. As argued by Caitríona Ó Dochartaigh in her consideration of orality, performance and transmission in medieval Irish prayer, much work has to be done to establish the contexts in which these prayers were composed, how they were performed as an act of worship and whether their circulation and transmission was aural, oral or written. One conclusion is that 'even when composed on paper, prayers rely heavily on traditional formula[e] of a marked oral nature'.[74] It may be that some prayers such as *Dera damh, a Coimde* were recited in monastic circles, while others, even if composed in a monastic environment, could have circulated among priests and the laity. For example, the poem *It ucht, a Ísu inmain* 'In your breast, o dear Jesus',[75] is replete with monastic hope for a better life in Heaven after a difficult life spent on earth. Such a short and easily memorized prayer could have become popular among the laity although the intensity of the monastic experience may have been lost on many supplicants:[76]

> As for me, my poverty is lasting here in the pitiful boundless world so that I may be rich in thy truly good kingdom after victory of devotion and bondage.
>
> This is the course of brevity: poverty I prefer to wealth so that, having expiated my hundreds of faults, my place (may be) among the angels.
>
> By thy victory, by thy death, by thy hard cross without tribute, my soul after this wayward body mayest thou see in thy breast, O Jesus.

73 KBR Brussels MS no. 20978–9, folio 54r; Ó Cuív, 'Some early devotional verse', 1. Ó Cuív (p. 19) notes that extracts from the poem survive in the thirteenth-century Book of Uí Maine (RIA D ii 1 (no. 1225) folio 77vb) and in BL MS Sloane 3567 (folio 27b). 74 Caitríona Ó Dochartaigh, 'Questions of orality, performance and transmission in relation to medieval Irish prayer' in Gisbert Hemprich (ed.), *Festgabe für Hildegard L.C. Tristram. Überreicht von Studenten, Kollegen und Freunden des ehemaligen Faches Keltologie der Albert-Ludwigs-Universität Freiburg* (Berlin, 2009), pp 69–79, at p. 76. 75 Ó Cuív, 'Some early devotional verse', 11–12 (V). 76 Ó Cuív, 'Some early devotional verse', 12 §§4–6. Original: *Mad meisi, is buan mo bochta / sunn for bith truag nach tacta / gurbam soim it flaith lanmaith / iar mbuaid*

The use of the vernacular, the complexity of the metre or otherwise, are keys to understanding transmission between author and a wider audience. While the original intention may have been confined to personal or even community devotion within a restricted group, as with prayers in any religion, certain texts were easily circulated in written form, and if committed to memory circulated beyond exclusive communities.

THE LITURGY OF THE HOURS, CHANT AND HYMNS

A community prays together: the daily cursus of the liturgy of the hours

For more than a century there has been speculation among scholars of liturgy as to the structure of monastic liturgy in Ireland, much of it determined by the regime laid down in Columbanian monasteries on the Continent and what can be gleaned from disparate sources such as the Antiphonary of Bangor and the Stowe Missal. Once more the lack of source material, including any form of notation, has greatly hampered work on this topic. Earlier scholars argued for the existence of 'Celtic' as opposed to 'Roman' rites, with Warren in his volume *The liturgy and ritual of the Celtic church* (published in Oxford in 1881), contending that this 'Celtic' church was independent of Rome and a primitive Christian church 'in these islands differing from the Anglo-Roman or Scoto-Roman Church of later days'.[77] The monastic tradition of Ireland and Britain, even to the twelfth century, had emanated from this primitive church, and was actively a missionary tradition 'having its own Liturgy, its own translation of the Bible, its own mode of chanting, its own monastic rule, its own cycle for the calculation of Easter; and presenting both internal and external evidence of a complete autonomy'. Warren acknowledged, however, that the church in Ireland gradually adopted Roman practices although not fully so until the twelfth century.[78] While popular books tend to perpetuate this belief, it has been refuted by scholars in their evaluation of the complex nature of Christian liturgy and the plurality of Christian experience, similar to diverse monastic traditions, of which Irish practices were but one of a myriad.[79] Acknowledged by Jane Stevenson in the second edition of Warren's volume as a 'somewhat unhistorical and controversialist treatment of the relationship between Rome and the early Irish church', she corrects this approach although she maintains the view that the Irish church from the tenth century onwards 'were perceived as lax, eccentric,

cravaidh is cacta. // As é tochta na cumhre, / ferr lem bocht[a] inda saidhbre / ar nglanadh mo chét cinadh / ar m'inad itir aingle. // Ar do buaidh, ar do bas-[s]a, / ar do croich cruaid cen cisae, / m'anim iarsin curp cle-su / at-ce-su it ucht, a Isu. 77 Warren, *The liturgy and ritual*, p. 35 (1st ed.). 78 Warren, *The liturgy and ritual*, p. 46 and 46 n. 1. 79 For a useful survey of previous scholarship and future directions, see Liam Tracey, 'Celtic mists: the search for a Celtic rite' in Ann Buckley (ed.), *Music, liturgy, and the veneration of saints of the medieval Irish church in a European context* (Turnhout, 2017), pp 291–304.

and worldly'.[80] Indeed, Thomas O'Loughlin demonstrates on the basis of the various forms of the Liturgy of the Hours described in the *NSB*, none of which necessarily reflect the genuine cursus of any Irish monastery, that a ninth-century Irish author knew about diversity in monastic practices, but that the moral of his tale was to stress that the Liturgy of the Hours was central to the monastic journey to Heaven. Improving and simplifying the liturgy was a worthy exercise.[81]

In his comprehensive study of the possible traditions that can be detected in early Irish forms of the Divine Office, Peter Jeffery traces parallels in the references to the office in the Rule of Ailbe with rituals known from Jerusalem, Lérins and traditions implicit from Cassian's works, and practices in Columbanian monasteries. Key to the Irish cursus was the division of the Psalter into three groups of fifty psalms, coined by Jeffery as 'The Office of the Three Fifties' and regarded as ultimately harking back to forms of ascetic exercises performed by the Desert Fathers.[82] Jeffrey also comments on parallels with the practices gleaned from the 'Tallaght dossier', a subject that Westley Follett has also addressed.[83] Follett argues that from the evidence of the 'Tallaght dossier' there was no standard form or manner of performing the so-called 'Office of the Three Fifties', but he identified two distinct versions (Version A and Version B). Version A divided the Psalter into three sections comprising one hundred psalms, thirty-seven psalms, and thirteen psalms respectively, recited in three daytime cross-vigils which seem to have followed the hours of terce, sext, and none. There were evening and night-time vigils as well, to round out the day, although their content differed from the daytime cross-vigils, since by that point the *foropair* or 'additional labour' of the *céli Dé* was complete.[84] Version B, which is not associated with any particular hours of the Divine Office, was divided into exactly three sections of fifty psalms each, and then each fifty was divided into smaller sections of twelve or thirteen psalms.[85] Whichever version was adopted by any particular *céli Dé* foundation, it was arduous and may have been subject to criticism by the church outside their circle. O'Loughlin suggests that the utterly simple liturgy encountered by Brendan and his monks on the Isle of Paradise, which consisted of a cursus of seven hours in which one verse of a psalm was chanted for an hour by birds, was 'the perfect liturgy of creatures at

80 Jane Stevenson in Warren, *The liturgy and ritual* (Woodbridge, 1987 2nd ed.), pp ix, li. 81 Thomas O'Loughlin, 'The monastic Liturgy of the Hours in the *Nauigatio sancti Brendani*: a preliminary investigation', *Irish Theological Quarterly* 71 (2006), 113–26. 82 Jeffery, 'Eastern and western elements', pp 102, 106 (Table 5.2). 83 Westley Follett, 'The Divine Office and extra-Office vigils among the culdees of Tallaght', *The Journal of Celtic Studies* 5 (2005), 81–96. https://www.academia.edu/712123/The_Divine_Office_and_Extra_Office_Vigils_among_the_Culdees_of_Tallaght accessed 18 August 2021. 84 Follett, 'The Divine Office and extra-Office vigils', pp 91, 95 (Table 1). 85 Ibid., pp 91–2, 96 (Table 2).

the perfect time'.[86] This was the simplest liturgy that could be imagined and, in fact, has echoes of Cassian's monlogistic prayer exercise.

While the structure of the daily *cursus* of Irish monastic communities may have been diverse and is difficult to establish definitively, references in a variety of sources add to our understanding of the performative and intercessory nature of the monastic *laus perennis*. The vocabulary of liturgy and liturgists, although not extensive and also applicable not just to monastic communities, nevertheless provides some indication of the range of offices that existed. Beginning with compounds of *sa(i)lm* 'psalm',[87] one finds *salmchétlach* 'a psalm-singer' (although the references are post-twelfth century), *salmchétlaid* 'a psalmist', *sailmchiallach* 'one versed in the psalms' and *sailmthech* 'a psalm-house', simply meaning a church. A comment in the early law tract *Uraicecht becc* specifies that the *salmchétlaid* of the ecclesiastical learned class (*grád n-écna*) sang his psalms in verses, lines, pauses and breaths – signifying the essentials of chanting the psalms – while the *salmchétlaid* of the church grades (*grád n-eclaisi*) simply sang the psalms in prose. It would appear that the *salmchétlaid* was the lowest grade of nine church grades, as expressed in the Old Irish litany *Scúap Chrábaid*: 'I beseech the nine orders of the church on earth, from psalm-singer to bishophood'.[88] Armagh was a house of psalms – another term for a church – according to the verse attached to the obit of the Dúnchad ua Braein, abbot of Clonmacnoise, who died in Armagh in 987:[89]

> Macha, the opulent house of which noble poets sing, is a psalm-house (*sailmthech*) of its assembly that is owned by saints. The dyke of its rampart (*múrchlad a múir*) never closed over a person like Dúnchad ua Braein.

The verbal noun *coicetal* (vb. *con-cain*) appears to refer to harmonious singing in a religious setting including a reference to the chanting of the Passion during Lent in Cashel among the prescriptions enjoined upon the king of Cashel.[90]

A Middle Irish poem *Mac at cuala is domain tair* 'A child I have heard of in the eastern world', dated by Brian Ó Cuív to the twelfth century, would appear to have been composed by someone familiar with liturgical music.[91] The poem begins with a fanciful account of the origins of liturgical chant. This is credited

86 O'Loughlin, 'The monastic Liturgy of the Hours', 117–19. 87 *DIL sv.* 88 Kuno Meyer (ed. and trans.), 'Stories and songs from Irish manuscripts: VI. Colcu ua Duinechda's Scúap Chrábaid, or Besome of Devotion', *Otia Merseiana* 2 (1900–1), 92–105, at pp 94, 100 §3. Original: *Ateoch frit nói n-gráidh na heccalsa talmanda ó shalmcétlaid co hepscopóti.* 89 AFM. Kuno Meyer (ed. and trans.), *Bruchstücke der älteren Lyrik Irlands* (Berlin, 1919), p. 63 no. 146. Original: *Macha mainbthech medrait múaid, sailmthech a slúaig selbait nóib, ní tarla múrchlad a múir dar dúil mar Dúnchad úa mBröin.* 90 Myles Dillon (ed. and trans.), 'The taboos of the kings of Ireland', *Proceedings of the Royal Irish Academy* 54C (1951–2), 1–6, 8–25, 27–36, at pp 14–15. Original: *coigital chésta Corguis hi Caissil.* 91 Ó Cuív, 'St Gregory

to a certain Gamut, one of King Herod's courtiers who heard the music (*ceóla*, *orgán*, *cantairecht*) of an angelic choir. He sang the *Gloria* and other angelic melodies to another courtier, Gregory. Wonderfully, Gregory's pupils are referred to as the personification of musical notes:[92]

> **Be**, **Mi**, **Re**, **La**, **Fa**, fair **Mi**, diligent pupils of Gregory, these forthwith fashioned correctly the chant.
>
> Clear pure **Sol** came with renown to his own tutor, to Gregory, and he added his share exactly and fittingly to the chant.
>
> **Re** and **Ut** with fair course, it is they who arranged the organum so that their share is exactly and fittingly in the chant.

As noted in his detailed introduction, Ó Cuív surmises from these verses that the poet had some knowledge of the Harmonic or Guidonian Hand, the system of pitch notation and sight-singing based on these syllables attributed to the Italian Benedictine Guido of Arezzo who died around 1050.[93] This would date the poem no earlier than the second half of the eleventh century and for various other reasons, the editor dates it more precisely to 1120/52.[94] Most of the poem concerns Gregory who not only transforms into Pope Gregory the Great, but is made out to be Irish, a legend that was in general circulation in medieval Ireland.[95] Of course, Gregory's reputation as a liturgist and proponent of a universal plainchant was part of western religious literature, and that there was an Irish version accords with many other tales that were adapted to a local audience. A metrical Latin version of Gregory's musical achievements, *Gregory presul*, was possibly composed by the Anglo-Saxon Aldhelm, or more likely by someone imitating his style.[96] Finally, in the Middle Irish poem St Dunstan appears along with Gregory and others as one who composed chants for various parts of the Mass:[97]

> Poliponus (and) clever Dunstan composed the Kyrie of the Mass; Poliponus and Dunstan composed the Kyrie splendidly …
>
> The high king of the noble English composed here, however, the Septenarius; the Septenarius by Solomon, moreover, and the Agnus [Dei] by Dunstan.

and St Dunstan'. **92** Ibid., pp 293–4 §§10–12. Original: *Be, Mi, Re, La, Fa, Mi find/ dalta da Grigair go grind,/ do cumsadar sin gu cóir,/ in cantairecht fo cédóir. // Tánic Sol glé glan co mbloid/ co oidi féin co Grigair/ gor cuir a cuitig co ceart/ go cubaidh san cantairecht. // Re ocus Ut go réim n-án,/ is iat ro glés in t-orgán/ go fuil a cuitigh go ceart/ go cubaidh sin caintairecht.* **93** https://www.oxfordmusiconline.com/grovemusic/view/10.1093/gmo/9781561592630.001.0001/omo-9781561592630-e-0000011968 accessed 21 September 2021; Anna Reisenweaver, 'Guido of Arezzo and his influence on music learning', *Cederville University: Musical Offerings* 3:1 Article 4 (2012): https://digitalcommons.cedarville.edu/musical

Both of Dunstan's biographers, Eadmer of Canterbury and William of Malmesbury, attribute great musical acumen to Dunstan, although the tangible evidence is difficult to trace.[98] Of this talent, Eadmer comments:[99]

> In addition to these things he often used to pleasantly divert not only himself but also the minds of many from the turbulent business of the world by playing musical instruments, in the science of which he was very skilled; he used to move them to meditation of celestial harmony as much by the sweetness of the words (both in his mother tongue and another language) interwoven in the musical measures, as by the harmonious music he produced through them.

William of Malmesbury adds that although Dunstan learned a lot from the Irish masters who frequented Glastonbury, he did not bother with their training in composition and correct Latin – as they were less accomplished at these subjects! – but he practised his music:[100]

> Hence Dunstan was captivated by music in particular; he took delight in playing musical instruments, and thought it agreeable when they were played by others. Whenever he had time left over from reading, he took up the harp, and in person 'struck the resounding strings with pleasant noise'. He spread through England knowledge of what the ancients call *barbiton* and we call 'organs', in which, to cause the pipe to resound through a channel with many holes, 'the anxious bellows vomit out the air they receive from blows'. Dunstan practised on this instrument not because of its enticing pleasures, but to arouse his love for God, so that to the very letter might be fulfilled the injunction of David: 'Praise the Lord with the psaltery and harp. Praise him with stringed instruments and organs.'

offerings/vol3/iss1/4 accessed 22 September 2021. **94** Ó Cuív, 'St Gregory and St Dunstan', p. 291. **95** Ibid., pp 275–89. **96** Constant J. Mews, 'Gregory the Great, the Rule of Benedict and Roman liturgy: the evolution of a legend', *Journal of Medieval History* 37:2 (2011), 125–44, at p. 137. **97** Ó Cuív, 'St Gregory and St Dunstan', pp 296–7 §§ 28, 32. Original: *Poliponus, Dunstán grind, / ro cumsat Kirie inn aiffrind; / ro cumsat Kirie go hán / Poliponus is Dunstán … Ro cum Septenair sund trá / ardríg Saxan saerdha; / Septinair fri Solam trán / ocus Agnus fri Dunstán.* **98** David Hiley, *Western plainchant. A handbook* (Oxford, 1993), p. 581. **99** Turner and Muir, *Eadmer of Canterbury*, pp 59–61 Original: *Super haec instrumentis musici generis, quorum scientia non mediocriter fultus erat, non tantum se, sed et multorum animos a turbulentis mundi negotiis sepe demulcere, et in meditationem caelestis armoniae, tam per suauitatem uerborum quae modo materna, modo alia lingua musicis modulis interserebat, quam et per concordem concentum quem per eos exprimebat, concitare solebat.* **100** Michael Winterbottom and Rodney M. Thomson (eds), *William of Malmesbury: saints' lives: lives of SS Wulfstan, Dunstan, Patrick, Benignus and Indract* (Oxford, 2002; online version, 2019), pp 178–81. Original: *Quapropter cum ceterarum tum maxime musicae dulcedine captus, instrumenta eius cum ipse libenter exercere, tum ab aliis exerceri dulce habere. Ipse citharam si quando <a>*

Ó Cuív suggests that in choosing Dunstan for special mention, the author of the Irish poem 'had in mind that Dunstan's Glastonbury background was an important element in the course of his [Dunstan's] career which brought him eventually to Canterbury'.[101] It may have been through his education at Glastonbury and his contacts with Irish teachers and visitors that Dunstan became known in Ireland. The author's knowledge of Guido of Arezzo's musical system is somewhat more unexpected but could also have been transmitted to Ireland through English contacts where his works were known. For example, BM MS Harley 3199, which dates to *c.*1100 and is of English or French origin, contains a suite of Guido's treatises on music and is one of many such manuscripts of the period.[102]

What was the purpose of this unusual Irish poem? One verse offers a clue to its use:[103]

> It is not right for anyone who does not know what chanting comes from – festivity without exception – to sing (lit. 'raise') proper chant at the altar.

It could be understood from this verse that the poem, like so many others encountered in this study, was didactic and was taught to pupils learning chant, not necessarily all monastic, in some late eleventh- or twelfth-century Irish school such as Armagh, Glendalough or Lismore. The amalgam of influences evident from the poem, Roman, continental and Anglo-Saxon, is in line with the influences that have been detected, especially in recent studies by Frank Lawrence, in sources likely to have originated from twelfth-century Irish foundations, among them, the so-called Downpatrick Gradual, the Corpus Missal, the Rosslyn Missal and the three-voice polyphonic colophon *Cormacus scripsit* in a twelfth-century Irish psalter (BL Add. MS 36929). Lawrence has argued that as with art and architecture, the Irish church of the period was particularly open to innovation and reform, and monastic and secular liturgy was not left untouched during this transformation.[104]

litteris uacaret sumere, ipse dulci strepitu resonantia fila quatere. Iam uero illud instrumentum quod antiqui barbiton, nos organa dicimus, tota diffudit Anglia, ubi ut fistula sonum componat per multiforatiles tractus 'pulsibus exceptas follis uomit anxius auras'. Hoc porro exercebatur non ad lenocinium uoluptatum sed ad diuini amoris incitamentum, ut etiam ad litteram impleretur illud Dauiticum 'Laudate Dominum in psalterio et cithara; laudate eum in chordis et organo.' **101** Ó Cuív, 'St Gregory and St Dunstan', p. 290. **102** http://www.bl.uk/catalogues/illuminated manuscripts/record.asp?MSID=7347&CollID=8&NStart=3199 accessed 22 September 2021. **103** Ó Cuív, 'St Gregory and St Dunstan', p. 296 §27. Original: *Ní dhligend cantairecht cóir/ do tóchbáil ag un altóir/ neach nach findfa, líth gan acht,/ inní dá tá in cantairecht.* **104** Frank Lawrence, 'What did they sing at Cashel in 1172?: Winchester, Sarum and Romano-Frankish chant in Ireland', *Journal of the Society for Musicology in Ireland* 3 (2007–8), 111–25: https://www.musicologyireland.com/jsmi/index.php/journal/article/view/24/37 accessed 23 September 2021.

The Liber Hymnorum: catching a glimpse of liturgical education

The Irish *Liber Hymnorum* [*LH*] is a unique treasury of liturgical materials that until recently has defied precise classification and dating.[105] It is unique in that two relatively contemporary copies exist, TCD MS 1441 [*LH*(*T*)] and UCD-OFM MS A 2 [*LH*(*F*)].[106] Kenney described the two copies of *LH* as 'antiquarian, not liturgical, compilations', a view also taken by Stevenson.[107] Timothy O'Neill, dating them to the late eleventh or early twelfth century, categorizes the quality of their Hiberno-Norse Ringerike artwork as pointing to the work of top-class scriptoria. In his estimation, LH(F) was carefully designed for study and teaching.[108] Following Susan Boynton's studies on continental hymnals, and more germanely to *LH*, on the purpose of the profuse glossing,[109] Kathryn Izzo has classified *LH* as a 'glossed hymnal'.[110] And both Boynton and Izzo plausibly suggest that these glossed hymnals, including *LH*, were used as teaching aids and offer a window into liturgical training. Boynton explains the educational function of such hymnals: they were used to train novices and oblates to memorize psalms and hymns 'probably before any systematic study of the Latin language'. She argues that the glosses 'may reflect methods used by monastic teachers, who were often both cantors and librarians, to explain these texts to their students'.[111] The existence in *LH*(*T*) of *Orationes excerptae de Psalterio,* an abridgement of the full suite of psalms, also suggests that this collection is a teacher's *vademecum*, as well, of course, as providing evidence of the use of this shortened version of the psalms in the Irish church, a practice already noted.[112] There are references, although sparse, in Irish sources to such teachers who held some form of liturgical office. Connmhach ua Tomrair, who died in 1011, is described as priest and head of liturgy (*sacart 7 toíseach ceileabhartha*) of Clonmacnoise.[113] One of the Kells memoranda mentions the directors of liturgy and of the novices (*[in] dá toísech c[e]lebarta ocus toísech na mac légind do muntir Cenannsa*) as being members of the community.[114] Ua Ruadrach of the mid-eleventh century bishop of Armagh's household may have also held such an office.[115] Máel Petair ua hAilecáin, who was killed by the men of Fernmag in 1042, was the *fer léiginn* and head of the students (*toísech meic léiginn*) in Armagh.[116]

105 Bernard and Atkinson, *The Irish Liber Hymnorum.* On the literature to date, see Ó Corráin, *CLH* i, pp 364–85. **106** Digital versions available on https://digitalcollections.tcd.ie/ and https://www.isos.dias.ie/. **107** Kenney, *Sources*, p. 716 §574; Stevenson in Warren, *The liturgy and ritual* (2nd ed.), p. lxxxiv. **108** O'Neill, *The Irish hand*, pp 36, 90. **109** Susan Boynton, 'Eleventh-century continental hymnaries'; Boynton, 'Latin glosses on the office hymns'. **110** Izzo, 'The Old Irish hymns of the Liber Hymnorum', pp 50–3. I am very grateful to Dr Izzo and Professor Catherine McKenna for granting me permission to consult this thesis. **111** Boynton, 'Eleventh-century continental hymnaries', p. 200. **112** Bernard and Atkinson, *Irish Liber Hymnorum*, i, pp 144–56. **113** AFM. **114** Mac Niocaill, *Notitiae*, p. 20 (V: lines 10–11). **115** Murphy, 'A poem in praise of Aodh Úa Foirréidh'. **116** AU, AFM. The term *mac léiginn* may refer to novices, clerical students or a

Reading *LH* as a liturgical and educational aid requires a study in its own right by experts in the field, but in the context of this volume it is worth noting a few aspects insofar as they cast light on Irish eleventh- and twelfth-century monastic liturgical practices. In the first instance, the existence of two versions of the *LH* is not alone fortuitous but rare in an Irish context. The likelihood is that versions of the *LH* were commonplace, at least in larger monastic foundations. While the surviving copies have many hymns and other texts in common, they are not exact copies.This may be due to the loss of folia or indeed to a choice made by the respective compilers, or may reflect distinct repertoires in different places. Most scholars maintain that a common hypothetical early eleventh-century original existed. The texts included in *LH* (*T* and *F*) comprise universal Latin hymns, Hiberno-Latin hymns, vernacular hymns, canticles, as well as biblical and apocryphal texts. With regard to the universal hymns, it is worth comparing the *LH* list with the Anglo-Saxon *Regularis Concordia* to gain an idea as to their use in the liturgy. The hymns common to both are basic to the Divine Office: the *Te Deum laudamus, Gloria in excelsis Deo, Magnificat, Benedictus, Quicunque vult, Cantemus Domino, Christe qui lux es*. The comments in *LH* and *RC* on their use can be compared in the knowledge that *RC* refers to a monastic context:

- *Te Deum laudamus*: In *RC* this hymn was sung at Nocturns during the Christmas vigil and was followed by the gospel read by the abbot; during the Easter vigil the abbot sang the hymn followed by the antiphon *Surrexit Dominus de sepulchro*.[117] *LH* (*F*) notes *Ymnum in die dominica*.[118]
- *Gloria in excelsis Deo*: In *RC* it was clearly sung as part of the Mass between the feast of the Innocents and the Octave of Christmas, and specifically during the Easter vigil when the lights of the church were lit, the *Gloria* was sung and all the bells were rung; at Pentecost, following the singing of litanies, a priest said the *Gloria*; Whit week was kept solemnly except that the *Gloria* was not sung on fast days.[119] *LH* (*F*) notes *ad uesperum et ad matutinam*.[120] The *LH* (*T*) version of *Gloria in excelsis Deo* has a series of glosses that although probably superfluous nevertheless emanate from a monastic milieu:[121] *laudamus .i. in anima nostra uel in teorica uita; benedicimus .i. in corpore nostro uel in actuali uita; adoramus .i. subiectione corporis et animæ .i. totis uiribus.*
- *Magnificat*: In *RC* this antiphon was sung as part of Vespers.[122] *LH*: no comment.

cross-section of students, including lay students. **117** Symons, *Regularis concordia*, pp 28, 50. **118** Bernard and Atkinson, *Irish Liber Hymnorum*, i, p. 59 (FAD *tit*.). **119** Symons, *Regularis concordia*, pp 29–30, 48, 57, 58. **120** Bernard and Atkinson, *Irish Liber Hymnorum*, i, p. 50 (FABS *tit*.). **121** Ibid., i, p. 50 gl. 3. It is worth noting the contrast between the spiritual life of the soul and the active life of the body. **122** Symons, *Regularis concordia*, p. 51.

- *Benedictus*: In *RC* this antiphon was sung as part of Matins.[123] *LH*: no comment.
- *Quicunque vult*: The Athanasian Creed, possibly the *Credo* mentioned in *RC*.[124] *LH*: no comment.
- *Cantemus Domino*: In *RC* this was a canticle sung on Holy Saturday.[125] *LH*: no comment.
- *Christe qui lux es*: In *RC* this hymn was sung in winter at Compline.[126] *LH (F)*: entitled *Hymnus Uespertinus* and the preface states that this hymn was to be sung at night (*ocus i n-aidche as dír a chantain*).[127]

From the above, it is clear that *RC* and *LH* do not have much detail in common but they agree at least on *Christe qui lux es* being a compline hymn. A similar divergence in the contents of hymnals is also plain when the Irish hymnals are compared with those of the Old Anglo-Saxon and Frankish hymnals, the *Te Deum laudamus* and *Christe qui lux es* being the only hymns in common. This divergence continued after the introduction of the so-called New Hymnal with the compilation of the *Regularis Concordia*.[128] Other universal Latin hymns in *LH* include *Hymnum dicat turba fratrum* attributed to Hilary of Poitiers – although the evidence for this attribution is slight – and *Parce domine parce populo*. While the Rule of Ailbe suggests that the *Hymnum dicat* was sung at Matins, the note in the *LH* preface states *sic nobis conuenit canere post prandium* 'thus for us it is fitting to sing [the hymn] after the noon meal'.[129] In a detailed study of the hymn *Hymnum dicat*, Helen Patterson notes that it appears in Irish manuscripts from the seventh-century Antiphonary of Bangor to the eleventh-century *Liber Hymnorum* and argues that in a monastic setting this hymn is woven around the life of Christ:[130]

> If the brothers are being 'called' they are being motivated towards an action. The action of gathering the community together gives rise to spiritual performance. The sounding of the bell brings the monks together as a band of brothers who are a worshipping community. The hymn is human utterance and animates the practice of devotion. More than a collection of rhythm and metrics, a spiritual message is conveyed in the text.

123 Ibid., p. 51. **124** Ibid., p. 51 n. 9. **125** Ibid., p. 47. **126** Ibid., p. 25. **127** Bernard and Atkinson, *Irish Liber Hymnorum*, i, p. 197. **128** For a discussion of the Old and New Hymnals, see Inge B. Milfull, *The hymns of the Anglo-Saxon church. A study and edition of the 'Durham Hymnal'* (Cambridge, 1996) including the contents of hymnals, pp 473–8. **129** O Neill, 'Rule of Ailbe', pp 100–1 §24; Bernard and Atkinson, *Irish Liber Hymnorum*, i, p. 35. **130** Helen Patterson, 'The Antiphonary of Bangor and its musical implications' (PhD, Toronto, 2013), pp 60–1. https://tspace.library.utoronto.ca/bitstream/1807/70131/3/Patterson_Helen_201311_PhD_thesis.pdf.%20%5B1.2.2%5D.pdf accessed 16 September

The efficacy of *Hymnum dicat* is also at the centre of the Middle Irish exemplum *Tríar maccléirech di fheruib Érenn* 'Three clerical students of the men of Ireland', which is part of the Brendan cycle.[131] Three students and their cat go on pilgrimage overseas and find an island on which to build a church. They divide the daily liturgy between them, one singing the full cycle of psalms (150) along with celebrating the canonical hours and the Mass, the second, 150 prayers along with the canonical hours and Mass, and the third, 150 *Hymnum dicats* along with the canonical hours and Mass. The first two die and the third is left with the burden of fulfilling all their promises so he fasts against the Lord in anger. An angel appears with a message from Heaven and explains that his choice of singing 150 *Hymnum dicats* was the most rewarding of the three as 'long life to him [who chose], and the kingdom of Heaven'.[132] One can understand the hymn's lasting attraction to those who regarded themselves as *milites Christi* 'soldiers of Christ':[133]

Majestatemque immensam
Concinemus uniter,
Ante lucem nuntiemus
Christum regem sæculo

> Let us declare in unison that boundless glory, let us proclaim before the dawn Christ the king forever!

In Izzo's estimation *Parce domine parce populo* is similar to a set of antiphons found in a twelfth-century French antiphonary: it is not a Hiberno-Latin hymn, despite it being attributed to St Mugint, an alternative name of St Ninian of Whithorn, in *LH*.[134] The additional Latin hymns in *LH* (*F*), *In laudem hymnodie*, *Hymnus in laudem trium regum* and the *Benedicite*, also belong to the universal church, and the preface to the first provides an insight into the Irish view of hymnody:[135]

2020; see also Kenney, *Sources*, p. 252. **131** Whitley Stokes (ed.), *Lives of saints from the Book of Lismore*. Anecdota Oxoniensia (Oxford, 1890), pp viii–x. Two copies of this tale exist in the Book of Leinster (folio 283a) and the Book of Lismore (folio 42b1). **132** Stokes, *Lismore Lives*, p. ix. Original: *Imnum dicat, sírshægul do saidhe 7 flaith nime.* **133** Frederick E.Warren and W. Griggs, *Antiphonary of Bangor. An early Irish manuscript in the Ambrosian Library at Milan*. 2 vols (London, 1893–5), part II, p. 5 (Latin original only). **134** Bernard and Atkinson, *Irish Liber Hymnorum*, ii, pp 112–13; Izzo, 'Old Irish hymns of LH', p. 39. **135** Bernard and Atkinson, *Irish Liber Hymnorum*, i, p. 193; ii, 89; Izzo, 'Old Irish hymns of LH', p. 113. Original: *gib e dogebud as a … imnaidi corup duan molta intoga ic Dia dogein, oir scrisaig si na huile pecud ocus glanaig si … ibrigi na colla ocus bathaig si toil in cuirp d'a aindeoin ocus minig si in truamdacht ocus … si gach uile dasacht ocus brisig si in ferg ocus luathaigig si na haingil ithfirnd ocus deluigid si na diabuil ocus scrisaig si dorchodus na hindtind ocus methaigid si in naimdacht ocus comedaig si in tslainte ocus crichnaidig si na deg-orprigi ocus lasaig si tene spirudalta isin croidi .i. grad Dé ri grad daine ocus do(ni) si sithchain etir in corp ocus in t-anum.*

> Whoever should recite the hymnody, would be making a song of praise dear to God, for it wipes out all sins, and cleanses the powers of the body and subdues involuntarily the lusts of the flesh; it lessens melancholy, and banishes all madness; it breaks down anger, it expels Hell's angels, and gets rid of the devils; it dispels the darkness of the understanding, and increases the holiness; it preserves health, and completes good works, and it lights up a spiritual fire in the heart, i.e. the love of God (in place of) the love of man, and it promotes peace between the body and the soul.

LH includes an extensive selection of Hiberno-Latin hymns on a variety of subjects, many of which are addressed to universal and Irish saints. If the authorship of these hymns is to be trusted – and many are doubtful – they were overwhelmingly composed by the ninth century, but continued in use centuries later, a practice already noted in relation to commentaries on the psalms. A few glosses added to them allude to their origin and function. While it is best to be cautious about the content of these prefaces, some of them are likely to retain nuggets of genuine information. The hymns *Celebra Iuda festa*, a hymn to the apostles, is associated with Derry, as is *Noli Pater* that seeks protection from fire from God, Christ and John the Baptist.[136] It would seem plausible that the Armagh and Columban communities had a strong tradition of hymnology: while the vernacular hymn *Sén Dé* is attributed to Colmán mac uí Clúasaig, *fer léiginn* of Cork, one gloss in *LH* (*F*) attributes some verses of this hymn to Mugrón, abbot of Iona (d. 981), who also composed the vernacular hymn *Cros Chríst tarsin n-gnúisse*.[137] And of course, Columba himself is the reputed author of *Altus Prosator*, *In te Christe* and *Noli Pater*: whether he was or not is less important than arguing for a Columban tradition for composition of these hymns.[138]

An additional value of many of *LH*'s prefaces are their comments on the metre/rhythm and style of the Latin and Hiberno-Latin hymns. These comments have not been given any detailed attention and while they do not provide great clarity in relation to the performance of liturgical chant, the formula that is used consistently, in conjunction with other annotations, speaks to practices in teaching and learning the liturgy. The standard formula notes that a hymn consists of X number of *caiptel* (Lat. *capitulum* 'short excerpt from religious text' but in this instance 'stanza'),[139] Y number of lines per stanza, Z syllables per line. If the hymn follows an abecedarian model this is also noted as in the case of *Audite omnes*: *secundum ordinem alfabeti factus est* and *ord aibgitrech fil fair, more Ebreorum, sed non per omnia*.[140] An appreciation of different metres

136 Bernard and Atkinson, *Irish Liber Hymnorum*, i, pp 18, 87. **137** Ibid., i, pp 25, 30; Thomas Owen Clancy (ed.), *The triumph tree. Scotland's earliest poetry AD 550–1350* (Edinburgh, 1999), p. 159. **138** On the date of the *Altus Prosator*, see Jane Stevenson, 'Altus Prosator', *Celtica* 23 (1999), 326–68. **139** The *capitulum* is normally the biblical excerpt read during vespers followed by a hymn. **140** Bernard and Atkinson, *Irish Liber Hymnorum*, i, pp

or rhythms in free verse (*rithim*) is evident.[141] *Hymnum dicat* is attributed to a Graeco-Latin tradition (*metrum trochaicum tetrametrum est*) to be sung (*is for binnus canair*) according to Augustine, although the preface's author is not particularly well versed in classical metres.[142] Many of the Hiberno-Latin hymns are classified simply as poems (*tré rithim dána*), referring to native metrical systems, or less flatteringly, as *oscarda* 'unprofessional, artless', possibly referring to the influence of vernacular verse.[143] The preface to *Altus Prosator*, attributed to Columba, directs how the hymn should be recited or sung:[144]

> *Rop é tra dliged gabála huius ymni co ra-gabtha 'Quis potest Deo' etir cech dá caiptil; ocus is de no-biad a rath fair, ar is amlaid rochanat prius.*
>
> This then is the proper way of reciting/singing this hymn, that *Quis potest Deo* be recited/sung between every two *capitula*; and it is from this that its grace would be upon it, for thus they first sang it.

This suggests that either the opening phrase of the antiphon at the end of the hymn *Quis potest Deo placere nouissimo in tempore*[145] or the complete antiphon (three lines) was sung at the end of each stanza. This possibility offers a fleeting glimpse of a cantor or cantors singing the hymn and the community responding at given intervals. Other fleeting indications of responsorial or communal singing is the very clear distinction in both manuscripts between the hymn and an *Alleluia* at the end of each verse.[146] Similarly, the layout of *Benedicite omnia opera* in *LH* (*F*) in which each line is broken into four parts divided by clear spaces may hint at communal singing,[147] while the hymn dedicated to SS Peter and Paul *Christi patris in dextera* is annotated with 'a' (*Alleluia*) at the end of every line of verses 1–11, with 'c' (*cantor*, *cantat*) at the end of the two lines of verse 12, 'an' (*Amen*) at the end of every line of verses 13–18, and back to 'a' (*Alleluia*) in verses 19–25.[148] (Fig. 20)

Seven Old Irish texts have been classified as hymns in most discussions of *LH*. In her detailed study of these texts, Izzo concludes that: 'Vernacular hymnody in medieval Ireland may be understood as part of a general expansion of the Irish language into areas previously occupied by Latin'.[149] She regards the seven hymns as falling into various categories:[150]

4, 6. **141** Ibid., ii, pp ix–lviii provide a detailed explanation of the metrical systems of all hymns. A further study is needed to understand the style of all *LH*'s hymns in a liturgical context. Kathryn Izzo's work has progressed our understanding of the vernacular hymns as para-liturgical texts. **142** Ibid., i, pp 35–6. **143** Ibid., i, p. 14 (Ultán's hymn to Brigit *Christus in nostra insula*). **144** Ibid., i, p. 65; ii, p. 26. **145** Ibid., i, p. 81. **146** LH (T): TCD MS 1441 f. 3a-b p. 12 (digital version) https://digitalcollections.tcd.ie/concern/works/tm70no19s?locale=en accessed 12 October 2021; UCD-AFM MS A2 pp 17–18 https://www.isos.dias.ie/12 October 2021. **147** UCD-AFM MS A2 pp 24–5 https://www.isos.dias.ie/ accessed 12 October 2021. **148** Ibid., pp 27–8 https://www.isos.dias.ie/ accessed 12 October 2021. **149** Izzo, 'Old Irish hymns of LH', p. 118. **150** Ibid., p. 115.

> *Brigit bé bithmaith* and *Admuinemmar nóeb Patraicc* are hymns of invocation and praise comparable to the Hiberno-Latin hymn *Martine te deprecor*. *Ní car Brigit* and *Génair Patraicc* are biographical hymns comparable to *Hymnum dicat*, one of the most important and renowned hymns in medieval Ireland. And as loricae, *Ateoch ríg*, *Sén Dé* and *Atomriug indiu* belong to an Irish hymn type that has always been recognized in both Latin and the vernacular.

What the vernacular texts demonstrate above all is the importance of saints, universal and native, in the Irish church for both religious and laity. The question remains open as to whether *LH* was a strictly monastic compilation or if it was relevant to the wider Christian community. The two manuscripts are the products of monastic schools of learning and, given our knowledge of learned masters and of similar compilations elsewhere, the likelihood is that many of these masters, led regulated, if not always celibate, lives. The *LH* (*F* and *T*) are the Irish equivalent, and should be recognized as such, of continental manuscripts which include a rich array of didactic and liturgical material which Boynton views as exemplifying 'the multipurpose nature of such collections and their many potential uses in monastic communities'.[151]

COMRAIR CHRÁBUID: PRAYER, GESTURE AND PERFORMANCE

Bodily gestures were an integral part of monastic prayer, and indeed remain so in Eastern Christian churches (*metanoia*).[152] In his study on the origins and evolution of monastic prayer, Columba Stewart provides the necessary outline of gestures that were also practised in the Irish monastic tradition:[153]

> The typical posture was standing, with kneeling or prostration regularly practised to emphasize humility, penance, and adoration. The typical gesture was to pray with outstretched hands, and to make frequent use of the Sign of the Cross, traced simply on forehead, lips or breast rather than in the later form of a larger cross made by touching forehead, breast, and shoulders.

151 Susan Boynton, 'Prayer as liturgical performance in eleventh- and twelfth-century monastic psalters', *Speculum* 82 (2007), 896–931, at pp 899–900. **152** For a useful guide to the different forms of prostrations (*metanias*) in the Orthodox Coptic church see https://www.stshenoudamonastery.org.au/prostrations-orthodox-church-rite/ accessed 15 October 2021. **153** Stewart, 'The practices of monastic prayer', p. 103. See also Dmitri Zakharine, 'Medieval perspectives in Europe: oral culture and bodily practices' in Cornelia Müller et al. (eds), *Body-language-communication. An international handbook on multimodality in human interaction*. Vol. 1 (Berlin and Boston, 2013), pp 343–64, at pp 348–51.

There are many vernacular terms for kneeling, prostration, making Signs of the Cross and praying involving various levels of humility and intensity, some of which were universal rituals of obedience and displaying honour. For example, one of the most common terms *sléchtaid* 'kneels, bows, prostrates oneself, submits to', while mainly used in ecclesiastical contexts, could be used in relation to submission to a higher lay authority. Use in both contexts conveys an array of signals: submission, humility, obedience, seeking forgiveness, repentance, greeting, showing honour and suggesting fear, all of which were part of monastic prayer. The Middle Irish text *Anmchairdes Mancháin Léith* 'The spiritual direction of Manchán Liath' sets out the basic forms of prayerful gestures:[154]

> Always in the morning after rising let him bow down three times, over his breast, over his face, let him make the sign of Christ's cross.

A more elaborate set of gestures is described as the *Lúirech Léiri* 'The *lorica* (or corslet) of devotion' or *Comrair Chrábaid* 'Shrine of Piety' in 'The teaching of Máel Ruain':[155]

> The 'Corslet of Devotion' was the old name formerly given by the elders to the cross-vigil. They used to make the 'Shrine of Piety' after the cross-vigil of the Pater Noster, and this was how they made it – by saying the Pater first, facing eastward, and *Deus in adjutorium* as far as *festina*, three times, with both hands raised to Heaven, clear of their vestments (only they would not perform the cross-vigil as they performed it when returning thanks): and thereafter they made the sign of the Cross with the right hand, eastward: and they did the like towards each of the four quarters, and the same with their faces bent down towards the ground, and finally the same with their faces upturned to Heaven. Their name for this ceremony was the 'Shrine of Piety'.

These bodily gestures are steeped, consciously or otherwise, in Christian – and many originally in Judaic – symbolism. Outstretched hands in the form of the cross, the *orans* position, meant praying in the posture of Christ crucified,

154 Meyer, 'Anmchairdes', 310 §2. Original: *Maiden (matan) íar n-éirge do grés/ sléchtuid fo thrí síos/ tar a broinde, tar a gnúis/ tabrad airdhe croiche Críst.* This verse is also added to the so-called Rule of Comgall, see Strachan, 'Old-Irish metrical rule', 193 §3[b]. **155** Gwynn, 'The teaching of Mael Ruain', 6–7 §6. Original: *Luireach leiri fá sean-ainm o chein don chrosadh ag na sruithibh. Comhrair chrabhaidh do nídis a ndiaidh chrois-fhighle na paidre, 7 as mar-so do nídis í .i. Paidior do radh, 7 a n-aghaidh sair ar tus, 7 Deus in adiutorium fa thri go nuigi festina, 7 a nda láimh suas go flaitheamhnas taobh amuigh da n-eudach, acht ni dhiongnadaois croisfhighill mar do nidis ag altughadh, 7 comhartha na croiche do deunamh soir lena laimh dheis da eisi sin : a letheid ceudna do dheunamh in gach en-aird dona ceithri hairdibh, 7 a letheid ceudna do dheunamh 7 a n-aighthe crom do chom an talaimh, 7 a letheid ceudna do dheunamh 7 a n-aighthi suas go.*

challenging Satan and giving direction to one's prayers.[156] (Fig. 21) Lifting one's eyes or face to Heaven recalled the words of the psalms: 'I lift up my eyes to you, to you who sits enthroned in Heaven' (Psalm 123:1). And, of course, praying *ad orientem* 'to the east' was associated with the belief that Paradise, the Garden of Eden, was located in the east. Through Christ's death on the cross and man's salvation, the supplicant prayed towards Paradise and came face to face with God, looked at the tree of life and sought forgiveness of his/her sins.[157]

That this tradition did not disappear with the passing of time or ongoing changes in the Irish church is implied in the intriguing text known as the 'Second Vision of Adomnán'. This has been dated to *c*.1096 when it was prophesied that disaster would strike the Irish on the feast of the Decollation of John the Baptist (29 August) on account of their sins and their reverting to paganism.[158] Although attributed to Adomnán, the prominence of Patrick as the arbiter between the Irish and God strongly suggests that this text was composed in Armagh, possibly during the abbacy of Domnall mac Amalgaid (d. 1105), who traversed Ireland imposing Armagh's primacy and tribute between 1092 and 1094 and who also conducted peace negotiations especially between the rival kings for the kingship of Ireland, Muirchertach Ua Briain and Domnall Ua Lochlainn during his abbacy. To save themselves from doom, Patrick imposes, among other strictures, a severe regime of fasting and prayer on the Irish – 'a three-day fast every three months', otherwise known as 'ember days', for a year. Exceptions were made in relation to the young, the infirm and the elderly but penalties were imposed on anyone who deliberately shunned the command or mocked those undertaking the fast. Of particular interest, however, is the description of intense prayer to be undertaken during this period. Given that the laity in general were unlikely to be capable of following these instructions, they seem to have been addressed to the clergy, and perhaps specifically to monastic communities. Whoever was subject to them, the text demonstrates that a similar sequence of bodily gestures continued to form part of intense prayer in the late eleventh century. It also illustrates how hymns preserved in the *Liber Hymnorum* might have been performed:[159]

flai[th]eamhnas fa dheoidh. Comhrair chrabhaidh fa hainm don tsermonias sin aca. **156** Helen M. Roe, 'The orans in Irish Christian art', *Journal of the Royal Society of Antiquaries of Ireland* 100 (1970), 212–21. **157** For a guide to all such gestures in the Christian tradition, see Gabriel Bunge (translated by Michael J. Miller), *Earthen vessels. The practice of personal prayer according to the patristic tradition* (San Francisco, 2002). **158** Nicole Volmering, 'The second vision of Adomnán' in Carey et al., *The end and beyond*, vol. 2, pp 647–81. **159** Volmering, 'The second vision of Adomnán', pp 664–5 §11. Original: *Ar ni dlegar ní eile do imradud isin amsir do-berar do Dia fri haine 7 irnaigthi, acht less anma itir precept 7 celebrad .i. cét slechtain fri Biait 7 Magnificat 7 Benedictus 7 Miserere mei Dominus, 7 crosfigell fri himmund Patraic, 7 immund na n-apstal 7 lamchomairt fri Himmnum dicat 7 imnum Míchil 7 slechtain uli fo tri hi forcend cech immuind 7 buailit a mbruinde fo tri la cech slechtain 7 at-berat uli: 'Don-fair trocaire, a De, 7 ron be flaith nime, 7 don-ringbai Dia dind cech plag 7 cech dunibad. Is iarum con-ocbat a*

> For it is not allowed to think of any other thing, in the time given to God in fasting and prayer, other than the care of the soul, by preaching and celebrating the offices; that is, a hundred prostrations at the *Beati* and *Magnificat* and *Benedictus* and *Miserere mei Dominus*, and a cross-vigil with Patrick's hymn, and the hymn of the apostles and clapping the hands together at the *Hymnum dicat* and Michael's hymn, and three prostrations by all at the end of each hymn and they beat their breast three times at every prostration and all say: 'May mercy come on us, O God, and may we have the kingdom of Heaven, and may God avert from us every plague and mortality'. After that they raise their hands to Heaven and they give blessings to God and Patrick and with the saints of Ireland, and to each soul which is in the assembly of these fasts, both individuals and groups, and every request they ask thereafter of God and Patrick is given to them, for God gives them everything they seek through fasting and prayer.

An equally striking – and contemporary – description of the use of gestures occurs in Conchubranus's life of Monenna, indicating that women were as likely to be acquainted with them as men. One of the saint's nuns, Bríg, went to Monenna's cell where she was praying intensely on a bare rock. Bríg experienced a vision of two swans flying skywards from the little house:[160]

> Watching them at first very carefully she began to wonder, and knowing that they were other than their appearance indicated, she did not dare to look at them longer, but quickly *throwing herself to the ground, she began to pray very earnestly to the Lord*, fearing that struck by the heavenly vision she might perish. Then at last she raised herself trembling from the ground and approaching the little door began to knock gently. When her knocking had been heard in the little house, she said : 'I am your handmaid whom you sent, and we have carried out what we believe to have been your command. But now shaken with fear and trembling in all my limbs I can scarce keep a hold on life'. Saint Monenna calmly replied : '*Make the sign of the Cross over your heart*; perhaps you came upon horrible beasts or devils, all of them things which tend to turn up in lonely places – and a little thing can upset a woman'.

llamu dochumm nime, 7 dos-berut benachtu for Dia 7 Patraic co noemu Erenn, 7 for cech n-anmain bis oc tinol na tre<d>an-sa, itir uathad 7 sochaide, 7 cech itge chuinchit ina degaid co Dia 7 Patraic do-berair doib, uair dos-beir Dia doib cech ni thurit tri aine 7 ernaigthi. **160** Life of Monenna, III, 436–9 §6. Original: *Quos diligentius primo intuens mirari cepit et alios esse sciens quam forma monstrabat non audebat diutius aspicere sed cito in terram corruens cepit Dominum instantius orare timens ne periret perculsa stupore uisionis angelice. Tandem ergo tremebunda leuat se de terra et appropinquans hostiolo cepit leniter pulsare. Audito in domuncula pulsantis motu dixit : 'Ego sum ancilla tua quam misisti et fecimus que nobis ut putamus iussa sunt. Sed nunc timore concussa et omnibus tremulatis membris uix spiritum cohibeo meum'. Cui sancta Monenna clementer respondit:*

While some in Armagh may have been advocating spectacular displays of contrition and fear, others during the same period were mocking these public performances, and in doing so, were possibly seeking to move away from these traditions. The satire *Aislinge Meic Con Glinne*, for example, describes Mac Con Glinne's exaggerated singing of the Divine Office in a typically sardonic tone:[161]

> He took down his book-satchel, and brought out his psalter, and began singing his psalms. What the learned and the books of Cork relate is, that the sound of the scholar's voice was heard a thousand paces beyond the city, as he sang his psalms, through spiritual mysteries, in lauds, and stories, and various kinds, in dia-psalms and syn-psalms and sets of ten, with paters and canticles and hymns at the conclusion of each fifty. Now, it seemed to every man in Cork that the sound of the voice was in the house next to himself. This came of original sin, and Mac Con Glinne's hereditary sin and his own plain-working bad luck; so that he was detained without drink, without food, without washing, until every man in Cork had gone to his bed.

Of course, the disturbance caused by Mac Con Glinne's loud chanting ran contrary to the humility of silence and a soft voice, as expressed in the Rule of Ailbe:[162] '… without converse with an arrogant person, without a loud, proud voice'.

The opening section of this chapter rehearsed the view that the apparent absence of early medieval Irish liturgical sources has prevented scholars from gaining a detailed idea of personal and communal monastic devotion. Yet, this is far too negative an approach. Seen together, the surviving sources are sufficient to open up the subject and to present a fair idea of devotional and liturgical practices followed in Ireland, and how these compared with elsewhere.

'Signa diligenter tuum cor. Forsitan bestiarum uel demonum horrorem inuenistis que omnia in desertis solent accidere et sexum femineum potest modicum commouere'. **161** Meyer, *Aislinge meic Conglinne*, pp 6, 12; Jackson, p. 5 §16. Original: *Tucc fadessin a théig libair chuca 7 benais a shaltair essi 7 fo-róbairt cantain a shalm. Iss ed at-fiadat eólaig 7 libair Chorccaige co closs míle cémend sechtair chathraig immach son a gotha in scolaige oc cétul a shalm tria rúnib spirtálta, for aillib 7 annálaib 7 ernalib, for diapsalmaib 7 sinsalmaib 7 decáidib, co paitrib 7 cantaccib 7 immnaib hi forba cacha coecait. Ba dóig imorro fria cach fer i Corccaig ba isin tig ba nessa dó no bíth son in fhoguir. Iss ed ro imfhulaing, in chomrargu bunatta 7 a pheccad bunad-gendi 7 a mí-rath follus-gnéthech fodéin, cor erfhuirged cen dig cen biad cen indlat, co ndechaid cach duine i Corccaig i n-a immdaid.* **162** O Neill, 'Rule of Ailbe', 98–9 §12: … *cen chomrád fri duine mborb, cen guth n-úabair n-ard.*

CHAPTER 8

Private and public monastic spaces

Maps and plans of renowned monasteries such as the early ninth-century Plan of St Gall or the plan of Cluny III built between 1089 and 1131–2 explain why such places were the *axis mundi* of their regions.[1] In Cluny, monastic life was spatially focused on the monastery church, monastic cloister, refectory, novitiate, dormitory, abbot's chapel and other smaller chapels, chapter house, calefactory, monks' kitchen and monastic cemetery. Monks encountered the laity to various degrees, mainly in the church, in the segregated guest houses, hospices, lay kitchen, cellars and bakery. In addition, the Plan of St Gall, that of the ideal monastery, includes a library, an abbot's house, an infirmary for monks, a school for the laity, a herb garden, servants' quarters, a brewery, granary, pens for animals and poultry houses. The layout of all these spaces, orientated around the main church and the cloister, is the plan that is most familiar to scholars of medieval western Christian monasticism. As a result, monasteries that do not conform, such as Irish monasteries, are regarded as unique and not mainstream or are often set aside due to lack of physical evidence for buildings or comprehensible plans. Ireland is regarded as being particularly outside the norm until the arrival of the new orders, and then not until well into the twelfth century, if not later. Etchingham makes a very valid assessment on the subject:[2]

> … It cannot be stressed too strongly that the Irish [textual] evidence, both Latin and vernacular, reveals no systematic distinction between monastic and non-monastic churches. The assumption, rather, is that any ecclesiastical settlement may house a monastic element, just as it may provide for the exercise of specifically clerical functions and concern itself with the administration of temporalities. The extent to which one or the

1 For an anthropological discussion on the cosmic symbolism of cloisters and monasteries see Mary W. Helms, 'Sacred landscape and the early medieval European cloister: unity, paradise and the cosmic mountain', *Anthropos* 97:2 (2002), 435–53. See also Gert Melville, 'Inside and outside. Some considerations about cloistral boundaries in the central Middle Ages' in Steven Vanderputten and Brigitte Meijns (eds), *Ecclesia in medio nationis. Reflections on the study of monasticism in the central Middle Ages* (Leuven, 2011), pp 167–82; Elizabeth Valdez del Álamo, 'The cloister, heart of monastic life' in Bhreathnach, Krasnodębska-D'Aughton and Smith, *Monastic Europe*, pp 171–94. 2 Etchingham, *Church organisation*, p. 457.

> other element predominates, even to the exclusion of others, may vary from church to church, but designations of churches are generally undifferentiated and terminology which is arguably of a distinctively 'monastic' kind is, in fact, most unusual: *monasterium* is comparatively rare and the vernacular *mainister* almost unknown in the period studied.

Ó Carragáin views this assessment as according very well with the archaeological evidence which indicates a wide spectrum of sites of varying functions that nonetheless are broadly similar in overall layout, being usually delimited by two concentric enclosures. He also argues that the architectural conservatism evident at Irish ecclesiastical complexes had significant implications for their overall layout.[3] That they were not totally static in their architecture and layout is apparent from increasing evidence that the great enclosures were backfilled and became redundant from the ninth century onwards, at some major sites at least.[4] In their re-assessment of Iona, based on the evidence of Charles Thomas's excavations there between 1956 and 1963, Ewan Campbell and Adrián Maldonado note that it is increasingly being realized 'especially in Ireland, that the indiscriminate use of the term "monastic" for all ecclesiastical settlements is not helpful. Study of the historical sources and the terminology used of their officials has shown that ecclesiastical settlements had a mixture of monastic, episcopal, pastoral, and economic functions'. A range of ecclesiastical sites existed: monastic possessions with proprietorial, hereditary and parochial churches or burial grounds, as well as hybrid sites such as the recently coined 'cemetery settlements', or more correctly familial cemeteries, which may or may not have included an ecclesiastical element.[5] There is also a long-standing pattern of over-use of the term 'monastic' in studies of the early Irish church. Foundations may have been monastic originally but by the tenth century monasticism had either not flourished in them or they had changed course.[6]

Irish place-name evidence offers an insight into this complex ecclesiastical landscape. One of the most common elements in Irish place-names is *cill* (anglicized *kil(l)*) 'church' more often than not combined with a personal name, hence 'the church of X'. These place-names are distributed throughout Ireland, although attested somewhat less commonly in the north. As far as can be ascertained either from written sources or archaeological evidence, a fair number of these names originated in the conversion period, prior to AD 700, and are therefore a solid indicator of the distribution of churches at the time. Other less

3 Ó Carragáin, *Churches in early medieval Ireland*, pp 215–17. 4 An excavated example of this phenomenon is Clonfad, Co. Westmeath. See Paul Stevens, 'For whom the bell tolls: the monastic site at Clonfad 3, Co. Westmeath' in Michael Stanley, Ed Danaher and James Eogan (eds), *Creative minds. Production, manufacturing and invention in ancient Ireland* (Dublin, 2010), pp 85–98. 5 Campbell and Maldonado, 'A new Jerusalem', p. 35. 6 For detailed regional case studies of churches between 400 and 1100 see Ó Carragáin, *Churches in the Irish*

common ecclesiastical place-name elements, some of which probably date back to the same period, include *domnach* (from Latin *dominicus*), *tech* 'house', *tempall* (from Latin *templum*) and *termonn* (from Latin *terminus*).[7] The term *mainister*, borrowed from Latin *monasterium*, occurs only in the case of Monasterboice, *Mainister Buíthe*, and is rarely used in texts, most often to describe the new foundations of the twelfth century and later or in revised saints' lives. The physical sites of early medieval churches are often marked by contemporary ruined buildings or medieval architecture incorporated into later building fabric and spaces. Stone churches along the west coast may date to the pre-Norman period, although the possibility that they were subject to constant later rebuilding cannot be precluded. In addition, many ecclesiastical sites do not contain the more common place-name elements but reflect their surrounding environment, best illustrated by place-names such as Glenn Dá Locha 'valley of the two lakes' (Glendalough) or Corcach 'a marsh' (Cork). Such is the density of churches throughout the country that their function, who served them, how they were supported and which were contemporary is unclear. They are also crucial to the continuing debate around the development of a parochial system in Ireland prior to the thirteenth century.[8] Regional studies, assisted in recent decades by an exponential increase in archaeological excavations that are yielding crucial chronological horizons, are beginning to distinguish between these diverse types of churches and their functions.[9] Many were proprietary churches serving local populations and controlled by a founder's descendants[10] – probably the most common arrangement – followed by large monasteries, episcopal churches, small eremitical monasteries and isolated hermitages.[11]

How can this fusion of functions and variations between sites be disentangled, and in the context of this volume, can the monastic components be determined? Is it feasible or even justifiable to seek to do so? A potential approach, which will be the basis of this chapter, is to look for textual, spatial and material evidence of the functions known to have been performed by contemporary monasteries

landscape. 7 See www.logainm.ie (accessed 26 November 2020). Modern place-name spelling: *domhnach*, *teach*, *teampall* and *tearmann*. 8 Colmán Etchingham, 'Pastoral provision in the first millennium: a two-tier service?' in Elizabeth FitzPatrick and Raymond Gillespie (eds), *The parish in medieval and early modern Ireland. Community, territory and building* (Dublin, 2006), pp 79–90; Tomás Ó Carragáin, 'Church building and pastoral care in early Ireland' in FitzPatrick and Gillespie, *The parish*, pp 91–123. 9 Gill Boazman, 'Hallowed by saints, coveted by kings: Christianization and land tenure in Rathdown, *c.*400–900' in Tomás Ó Carragáin and Sam Turner (eds), *Making Christian landscapes in Atlantic Europe. Conversion and consolidation in the early Middle Ages* (Cork, 2016), pp 22–53. 10 Ó Corráin, 'The early Irish churches'; Thomas Charles-Edwards, '*Érlam*: the patron- saint of an Irish church' in Alan Thacker and Richard Sharpe (eds), *Local saints and local churches in the early medieval West* (Oxford, 2002), pp 267–90. 11 Sheehan, 'Early medieval Iveragh', p. 116; Ó Carragáin, *Churches in the Irish landscape*, passim.

elsewhere, including pastoral care, caring for the poor and the sick, operating schools and guest houses, and controlling pilgrim sites. In defining private and public spaces, the conflict so often underlying religious life between the *vita activa* and the *vita contemplativa* surfaces as does the proximity of a monastic community or individual to the rest of society, what the twelfth-century text composed by a regular canon in Liège *Libellus de diversis ordinibus et professionibus qui sunt in aeclessia* aptly characterizes as the distinction between monks *qui iuxta homines habitant* ('who live close to men') and those *qui longe se ab hominibus faciunt* ('who remove themselves far from men').[12] Monastic spaces might be communal, personal, ascetic, spiritually and physically pastoral, pedagogical, economic and political, divided between the *domus interior* and the *domus exterior*. And even that clear divide was often opaque as some spaces, especially churches, schools and hospices, were spaces shared with many others outside monastic communities.

A debate on the concept of the 'monastic town' in early medieval Ireland has persisted ever since Charles Doherty proposed its existence in a series of articles during the 1980s.[13] The main arguments in favour of defining large Irish ecclesiastical complexes – Armagh, Clonmacnoise, Kildare, Kells, Glendalough – as towns have concentrated on economic activity and trade, with less emphasis on the monastic activity in these places.[14] Discussion of their religious and spiritual facets has been confined in general to their status as *civitates refugii*, places of sanctuary, the resting places of founder saints and other holy people, the theological meanings of the three enclosures that often surround these sites,[15] and the perception of them as the New Jerusalem or New Rome.[16] Even in the continuing debate on the 'monastic town', Colmán Etchingham, for example, treated the issue of monasticism in the context only of the role and jurisdiction of the various church officials and their dependents – bishops, abbots (in the guise of *ab*, *airchinnech*, *comarbae*, *princeps*) and *manaig* whom he defines in an essay on Glendalough as mainly a 'para-monastic' Christian elite who paid their dues in exchange for pastoral care. There is virtually no discussion of the place of monks following a committed religious life, who are defined briefly as living 'under a more-or-less conventional regime of self-mortification – including those withdrawing permanently or temporarily to the solitude of a hermitage – headed

12 Giles Constable and Bernard S. Smith (eds), *Libellus de diversis ordinibus et professionibus qui sunt in aeclessia (revised edition)* (Oxford, 2003), pp 16–17, 38–9. https://www.oxfordscholarlyeditions.com/view/10.1093/actrade/9780198222187.book.1 accessed online on 29 October 2021. See also Melville, 'Cloistral boundaries', 171–2. 13 Doherty, 'Exchange and trade in medieval Ireland'; Doherty, 'Some aspects of hagiography'; Doherty, 'The monastic town in early medieval Ireland'. 14 Richard Sharpe sought to address the absence of consideration of pastoral activity and religious practices in general from this discussion in his article 'The organization of the church in early medieval Ireland'. 15 Swift, 'Forts and fields'. 16 Ó Carragáin, *Churches in early medieval Ireland*, pp 57–66; Jenkins, *'Holy, holier, holiest'*; Maddox, 'Finding the City of God'.

by an abbot'.[17] His conclusion about the nature of Glendalough, the main focus of his study, is that 'Glendalough was a multi-functional ecclesiastical establishment, and not merely a monastery'. There was a monastic component but this was only part of what conferred a high status on the settlement.[18] Conleth Manning comes to a similar conclusion about Clonmacnoise, which he regards as 'a heterogeneous settlement ruled over by a layman called the "successor of Ciarán" and consisting of a bishop and other religious functionaries and a lay population involved in agriculture, fishing, services, craftwork, and probably trade. Elements of monastic life continued with the maintenance of a scriptorium and the study of religious texts and canon law'.[19] These conclusions have merit but, as always in this debate, the 'monastic component' is not recognized on its own terms, either spatially or in its way of life. In a reasoned discussion on the various arguments on the 'monastic town', Catherine Swift proposes that one potential way out of the impasse 'may be a more systematic depiction of what we envision monasticism to be, how it may have evolved, both chronologically and spatially, and whether the monks in individual settlements could also be craftsmen and farmers, family men and/or priests'.[20] This accords very well with the direction of this present volume.

In order to extract the 'monastic' from all the other activities taking place in an early Irish monastery and also to identify the 'monastic' from the 'clerical' among the hundreds of medium-sized and small churches that were dotted throughout the Irish landscape, it is worthwhile again to explore understandings based on international monastic scholarship. Of course, there is a huge literature available on this topic,[21] but two particular studies merit attention. In his review of evidence from Latin sources in the period before AD 600 in which monastic approaches to space and time were used to reinforce *fuga mundi* 'flight from the world' on both practical and theological levels, Columba Stewart draws attention to differentiations of space and time fundamental to monasticism.[22] *Functional differentiation* of material space responds to the need to pray, eat, sleep, read, work, receive guests and so on and some spaces can serve both a monastic community and others from outside. Time is apportioned according to various duties and tasks particular to day and night. Functional differentiation of monastic space and time cannot be fully understood without reference to

17 Etchingham, 'What was Glendalough?', pp 27–8. **18** Ibid., p. 53. **19** Conleth Manning, 'The decline of the settlement at Clonmacnoise' in Victoria L. McAlister and Linda Shine (eds), *Rethinking medieval Ireland and beyond. Essays in honor of T.B. Barry* (Leiden and Boston, 2023), pp 175–88, at p. 178. **20** Swift, 'Religion (as a factor in Irish town formation)', p. 84. **21** Note the bibliography attached to Michel Lauwers' chapter 'Constructing monastic space in the early and central medieval west (fifth to twelfth century)', in *CHMM*, pp 317–39, at pp 338–9. **22** Columba Stewart, 'Monastic space and time' in Hendrik W. Dey and Elizabeth Fentress (eds), *Western monasticism* ante litteram. *The spaces of monastic observance in late antiquity and the early Middle Ages* (Turnhout, 2011), pp 43–51,

ideological differentiation which has to do with certain qualities attributed to particular spaces and times. As Stewart explains:[23]

> In a religious environment, the most obvious example is the conferral of degrees of sacrality. In a monastery, the oratory, shrines and burial places are most sacred, followed by semi-sacred places such as the refectory and dormitory, where rituals take place that echo those of the oratory. There is also differentiation of space according to the status of the users, maintaining monastic separation by designating some spaces exclusively for members of the community (e.g., dormitory and other domestic spaces, often including the refectory), others as shared spaces (e.g., church, parlors, and sometimes the refectory), and finally spaces specifically for visitors (e.g., guest quarters for sleeping and eating).

Approaching the Irish evidence from this functional and ideological perspective – which is also evident in the Plan of St Gall – perhaps offers some clearer direction towards pinpointing exclusively monastic spaces as well as highlighting what changed from the eleventh century onwards. At the other end of the chronological spectrum Michel Lauwers in dealing with the mid-twelfth century inventory plan of Marmoutier describes how it represents the monastery's property within three nested spaces: at the centre of the plan the various places of worship (the abbey church, the parish church and two chapels) and a circle symbolically representing the monastic enclosure; the 'march' of Marmoutier which contained sixteen buildings, a privileged region close to the monastery where the monks held a majority of the rights over lands and persons. Lastly are the possessions furthest from the monastery.[24] Lauwers concludes that a western monastery was 'a kind of laboratory of representations and practical applications of space', that is, a spatialized complex, an organized territory, and even a microcosm of the universe.[25]

To differentiate public and private monastic spaces in the early Irish church, the evidence has to be extracted through the prism of texts, archaeology, architecture and landscapes, an exercise worthy of a much more comprehensive study than can be accomplished here. As with previous chapters, the discussion here sets the scene for that greater study and also focuses on particular texts – the saints' lives, rules and the annals – and on a small number of diverse sites and landscapes.

at pp 43–4. **23** Stewart, 'Monastic space and time', p. 44. **24** Michel Lauwers, 'Constructing monastic space', pp 335–6. **25** Ibid., p. 338.

THE COMMUNITY'S PRIVATE SPACES

One of the most important recent advances in early medieval Irish monastic landscape studies has been the detection of spatial patterns common to many complexes. This has meant that we can now see the reasoning for the location of stone buildings, mainly constructed during the eleventh and twelfth centuries, and the spatial relationships between the main components of a monastic landscape such as churches, crosses and round towers. As to the architecture associated specifically with monastic communities prior to the coming of the continental orders to Ireland, Ó Carragáin in his discussion of double-vaulted churches – St Flannan's, Killaloe; St Columba's House, Kells; St Doulagh's, Kinsealy; Temple Ciarán, Clonmacnoise; St Kevin's Church, Glendalough; Mochta's House, Louth; Cormac's Chapel, Cashel – argues that they may have housed founders' relics and also functioned as the residences of recluses.[26] He points to the situation in Britain and Europe where relics were usually entrusted to committed monks, often renowned for their asceticism, and that it was not uncommon for recluses to reside near important shrines.[27] Whether the custodians of relics in Irish monasteries were recluses is not so clearcut, as many relics were in the possession of hereditary families who were unlikely to reside permanently as committed monks in the lofts of double-vaulted churches. Nevertheless, these families may have handed over relics to monks for safe-keeping and to organize ceremonial rituals around the relics on certain days of the year. Citing references to *reiclésa* in the twelfth-century annals, Ó Carragáin notes that they make it clear that such specialized chapels rarely stood in isolation, 'rather, they were at the centre of small complexes of domestic and other buildings'.[28] In 1163, three small churches in Glendalough – *Cró Chóemgin* (St Kevin's Church), *Cró Chiaráin* and *Reiclés in dá Sinchell* – and their environs were burned.[29] Two other ascetic complexes existed near the upper lake, namely, Temple-na-Skellig[30] and Reefert Church (probably Dísert Chóemgin).[31] Trinity Church may have functioned as a hermitage if the name 'Ivy Church' associated with it is a translation of *Int Eidnén*.[32] In total, Glendalough could have had a population of up to twenty monks attached to these shrine-chapels and hermitages. These complexes probably consisted of a church or chapel, an enclosure, a cemetery, a herb garden and residential spaces for the monks, some, as argued by Ó Carragáin in relation to St Kevin's Church, inside the double-vaulted churches, others in cells or houses around the church. During excavations undertaken by Françoise Henry in the 1950s at Temple-na-Skellig,

26 Ó Carragáin, *Churches in early medieval Ireland*, pp 255–91. **27** Ibid., p. 267. **28** Ibid., p. 270. **29** AFM. **30** Note the use of the term *Scelic* in Glendalough as well on Scelic Mhichíl (Skellig Michael). **31** Ó Carragáin, *Churches in early medieval Ireland*, p. 268. **32** https://www.logainm.ie/en/113200 accessed 22 February 2023.

a sequence of four sub-rectangular house sites built with a mix of schist stone and timber was discovered. The houses were set on terraced drystone revetted platforms adjacent to the church. These were linked by paths and slabs. As at Skellig, stone crosses, recumbent slabs and a possible *lecht* existed, a space most likely used for liturgical prayers and processions. Finds included a fragment of a tile made from green porphyry – an exotic import also found at other church sites of the period such as Armagh, Dublin and High Island – a cross-inscribed disc-headed pin for an episcopal *pallium*, all suggesting that this place was frequented by senior ecclesiastics.[33]

While the annals provide fairly substantial detail about complexes including Armagh, Clonmacnoise and Derry, which will be discussed below, their references to smaller monastic settlements are less frequent, except for the occasional mention of their churches and oratories. Abbots' houses are recorded at Armagh, Dromiskin (Druim Inasclainn), Donaghpatrick (Domnach Pátraic), Emly and Trevet along with the abbess's house at Kildare.[34] These houses may have been the houses of lay officials rather than those of monastic abbots. The destruction of refectories (*proinntig*) are recorded in Dromiskin, Dunleer and Swords.[35] Whether these refectories served more than a monastic community is unclear. There were many others who needed sustenance, although at certain times of the day a monastic community may have had exclusive access to a refectory. One fairly reliable reference to a monastic refectory is that of 1192 when Ua Catháin of Fir Craíbe and his wife were patrons of a new door for the refectory of Derry's *Dubreiclés*. This door or doorway must have been sufficiently elaborate, perhaps built in stone, to have been recorded in the annals.[36] As discussed in Chapter 6, the text '*Ord prainni 7 prainntighi*', provides a fairly detailed description of the etiquette and prayer sequence at mealtimes as well as commenting on the periods of fasting to be followed during the liturgical year.[37] On the basis of the text's other provisions, it would seem that these instructions relate to a monastic community only. The meal appears to have taken place before vespers as after eating the monks retired to their individual cells or chambers (*cubucail* from Latin *cubiculum*) to read, pray or make entreaties to the King (Christ). Later on, Vespers were sung, further rest was taken and then they performed the night hours without fail or delay.[38] The mention of the monk's

33 Matt Seaver, Conor McDermott and Graeme Warren, 'A monastery among the glens', *Archaeology Ireland* 32:2 (Summer, 2018), 19–23, at pp 20–1; C.J. Lynn, 'Some fragments of exotic porphyry found in Ireland', *The Journal of Irish Archaeology* 2 (1984), 19–32; Raghnall Ó Floinn, 'Personal belief in Hiberno-Norse Dublin' in Anne Pedersen and Søren M. Sindbæk (eds), *Viking encounters. Proceedings of the eighteenth Viking Congress, Denmark, August 6–12, 2017* (Aarhus, 2020), pp 235–48, at pp 242–4. 34 AU 912, 1116, 1127, 1151 (Armagh); AU 913 (Dromiskin); AU 1123 (Emly); AU 1132 (Kildare); AFM s.a. 917 (Trevet). 35 AU 912, AFM s.a. 908 (Dromiskin); AFM s.a. 968 (Lann Léire); AU 971; AFM s.a. 969 (Swords); AU 993 (Domnach Pátraic). 36 AU; AFM. 37 Meyer, '*Ord prainni*'. 38 Ibid.,

cubucail matches the descriptions throughout Irish saints' lives and poems on ascetic ideals as well as the archaeological evidence, particularly along the western seaboard, and explains the absence of references to monastic dormitories.[39] Indeed, the vocabulary of monastic habitations is fairly sparse, as are any detailed descriptions. The terms for individual huts or stone cells include *airecal* 'chamber, oratory' (from Latin *oraculum*), *both* 'hut, bothy', *bothnait* 'small hut, a hermit's abode' and *cell*, none of which has a distinctive architectural meaning. *Carcar*, borrowed from Latin *carcer*, can mean a prison, a monk's stone or penitentiary cell, and even a strong-room for books and treasures. There is a reference in *Lebor na hUidre* to a manuscript known as the *Lebor Buide* ('The Yellow Book') which was kept in the *carcar* of Armagh, most likely some form of chained library as known from major monasteries elsewhere.[40] Compounds of the word *tech* 'house', although with very few attestations, provide some idea of buildings in the *domus interior* and *domus exterior*: *tech n-abbad* ('abbot's house'), *tech forcetail* ('school'), *tech n-immacallmae* ('meeting or reception house'), *tech n-óíged* ('guest house'), *tech péne* ('penitentiary'), and *tech screptra* (lit. 'scripture house', a library, a scriptorium).

THE *DÍSERT* 'HERMITAGE': *FUGA MUNDI* FOR THE ELECT?

The Middle Irish vernacular text *Caithréim Cellaig*, dated by Máire Herbert to between the late eleventh and early twelfth century, relates how Cellach mac Éogain Bél renounced the kingship of Connacht and handed it over to his brother Muiredach.[41] He returned to Clonmacnoise and his teacher St Ciarán ordained him bishop of Killala (*tucad gráda espoic fair 7 Ceall Alaid tucad do chathair espoic dó*).[42] Entangled in a poisonous relationship with Guaire mac Colmáin, king of Uí Fiachrach Aidne (south Galway) and tiring of his role as bishop, Cellach came upon a lake known as Clóenloch and seeing angels hovering over *Oilén Édgair* on the lake,[43] he decided to go onto the island as it had been ordained that he should become a hermit there and sanctify it ('*is indti atá a ndán dam-sa díthromacht do dénam 7 mo náemud indti*').[44] He lived on the island with four young clerics:[45]

> They were there over Lent performing their divine office and praying and it was made known throughout all Ireland that Cellach mac Éogain was

30 §§27–9. **39** There are a few early references to a *cotail-tech* or *tech-ligi* but these are the bed-chambers of kings. **40** *LU*, p. 94 line 2921. **41** Máire Herbert, '*Caithréim Cellaig*: some literary and historical considerations', *Zeitschrift für celtische Philologie* 49–50 (1997), 320–33. **42** Kathleen Mulchrone (ed.), *Caithréim Cellaig*. Mediaeval and Modern Irish Series 24 (Dublin, 1933; repr. 1971), p. 7: lines 211–12. **43** Possibly near Gort, Co. Galway or near Lough Conn, Co. Mayo. **44** Mulchrone, *Caithréim Cellaig*, p. 8: lines 265–5. **45** Ibid., p. 9:

17 Interior, Cormac's Chapel, Cashel © Yvonne McDermott.

18 Figures in White Island, Co. Fermanagh © Discovery Programme 3D Icons.

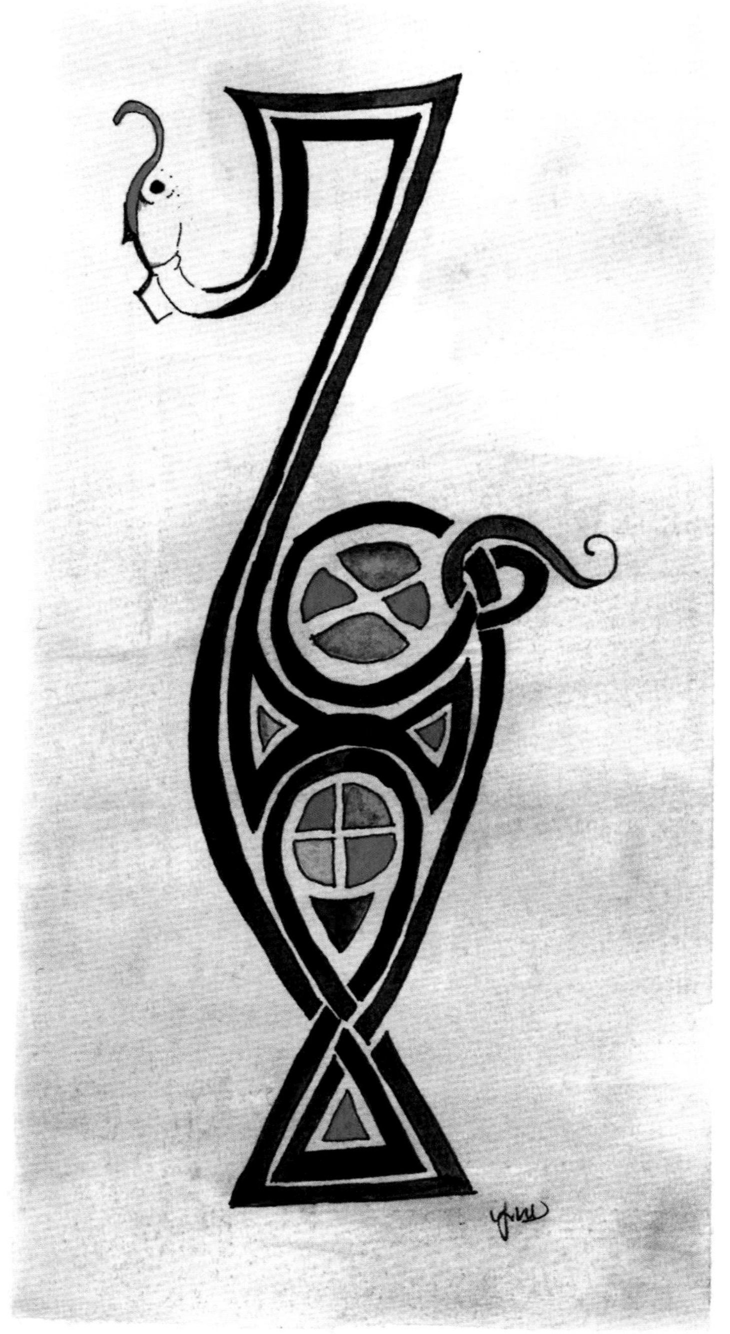

19 UCD-OFM A1 Psalter of Caimín capital © Yvonne McDermott.

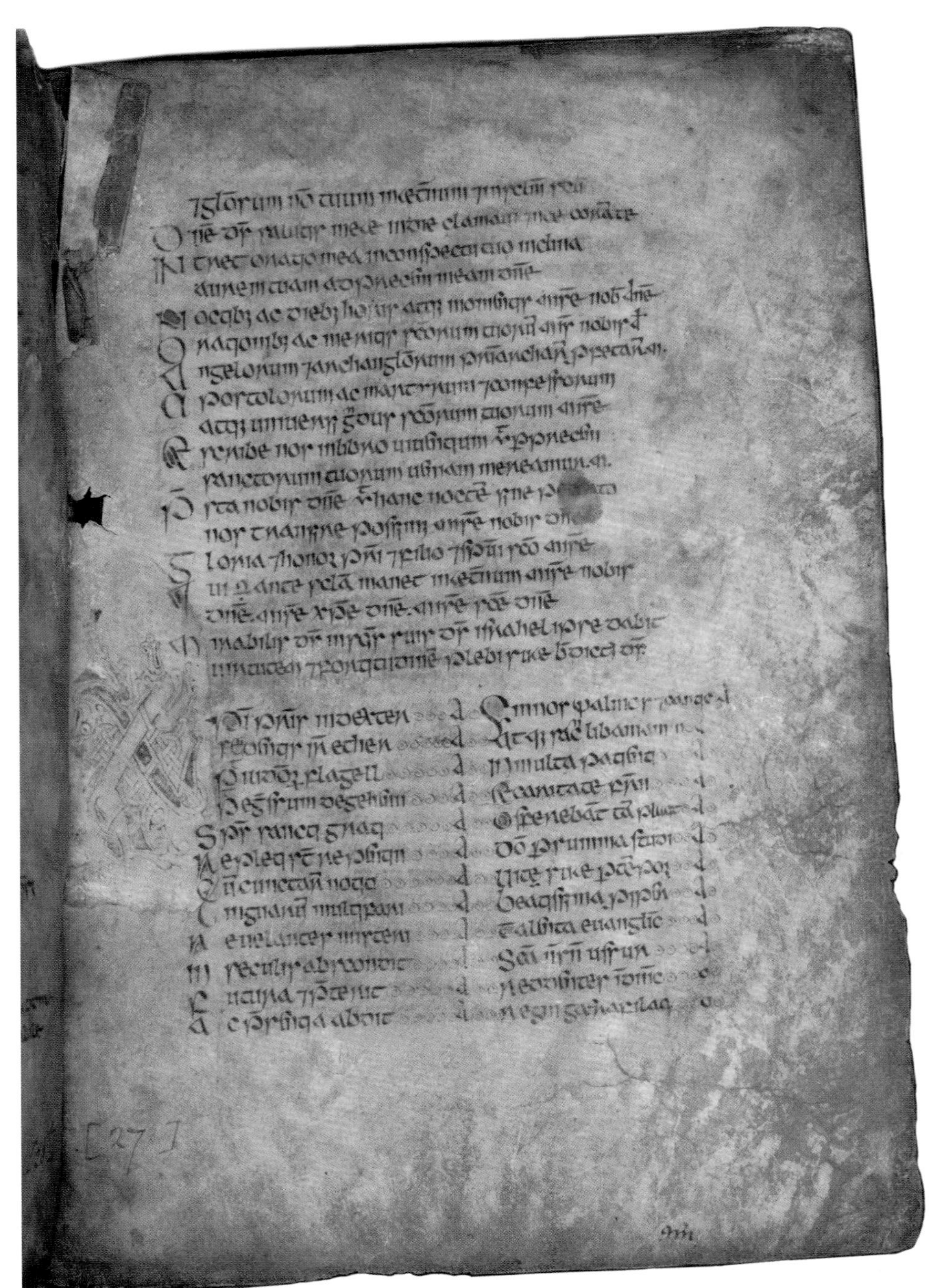

20 UCD-OFM A2 Liber Hymnorum, p. 27 © UCD-OFM Partnership/Irish Script on Screen.

21 Orans figure depicted on a slab at Gallen, Co. Offaly © Yvonne McDermott.

22 Monaincha choir arch, Co. Tipperary, engraved by James Ford (d. 1812), *c.*1804. NLI ET B243 © National Library of Ireland.

23 View of the Great Skellig, 1897, by Thomas Westropp, RIA 3A 50/53

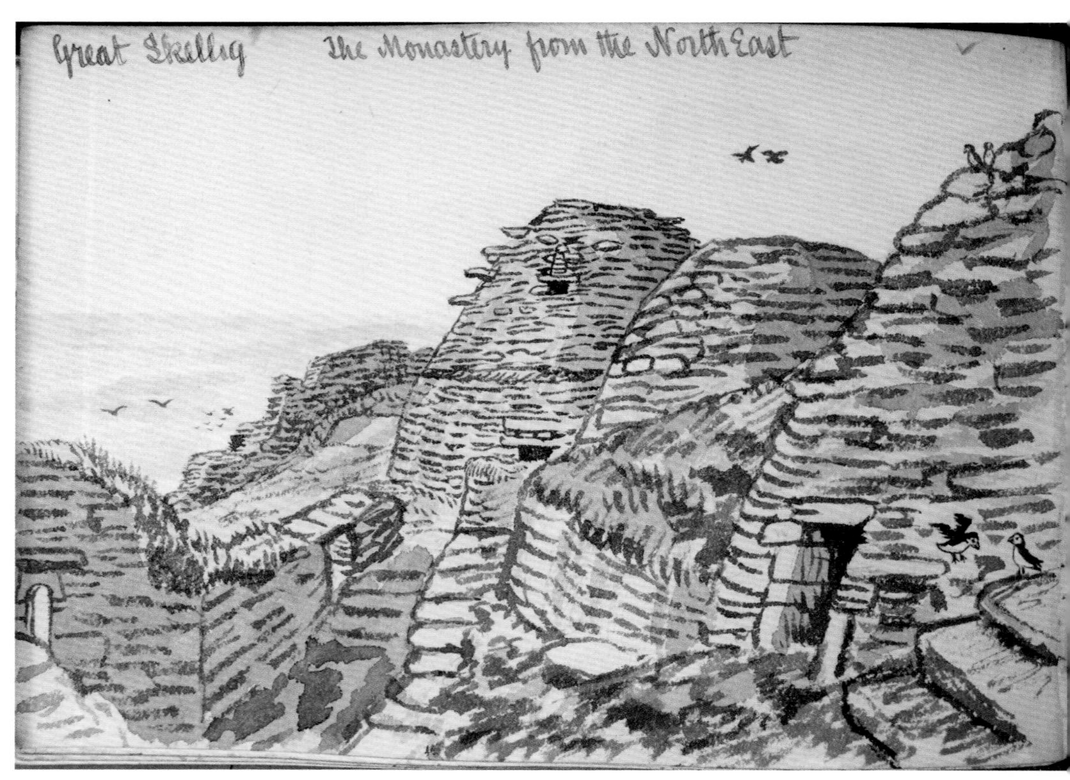

24 Great Skellig monastery from the north-east, 1897, by Thomas Westropp, RIA 3A 50/52 © Royal Irish Academy.

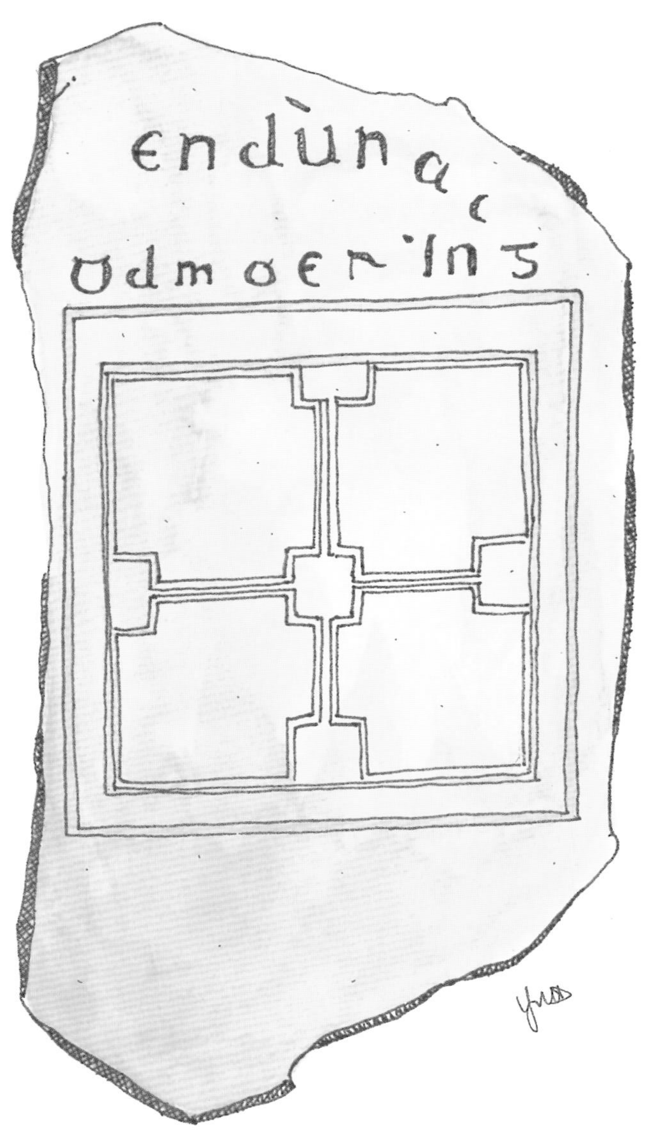

25 Inscription commemorating a woman named Admoer at Clonmacnoise based on Lionard and F. Henry, 'Early Irish grave slabs', *PRIA* 61C (1961) p. 113 fig. 10(6) © Yvonne McDermott.

26 Inscription commemorating a woman named Meind, daughter of Mac Srappan from Clonard, based on Petrie, *Christian inscriptions*, vol. 2 (Pl. xxxvi, fig. 73) © Yvonne McDermott.

27 Mellifont Abbey, Co. Louth, Gabriel Beranger (d. 1817), drawn between *c.*1770 and 1780 © National Library of Ireland.

28 Portal of Clonfert cathedral, Co. Galway © Yvonne McDermott.

29 St Saviour's, Glendalough, Co. Wicklow, Robert French (d. 1917) photographed end nineteenth century (Lawrence Collection) © National Library of Ireland.

30 Shrine of St Patrick's Bell, a chromo-lithographic drawing published 1850 to illustrate William Reeves' essay on the object (*Transactions of the Royal Irish Academy* 27) © Royal Irish Academy.

60
The Church & Tower of St Declan at Ardmore near Youghall Co. of Waterford,
1 Old Church, 2 Church now in use, 3 Tomb or Mausoleum of St Declan, 4 Glebe house,
The Tower is 100 feet high & 15 feet Diamr at the base, there is a Leaden Weather cock on the Tower which in 1777
Was in the position here represented, the workmanship of the Tower is Equal to that of the Romans,

31 The churches and round tower at Ardmore, Co. Waterford, Gabriel Beranger
© Royal Irish Academy.

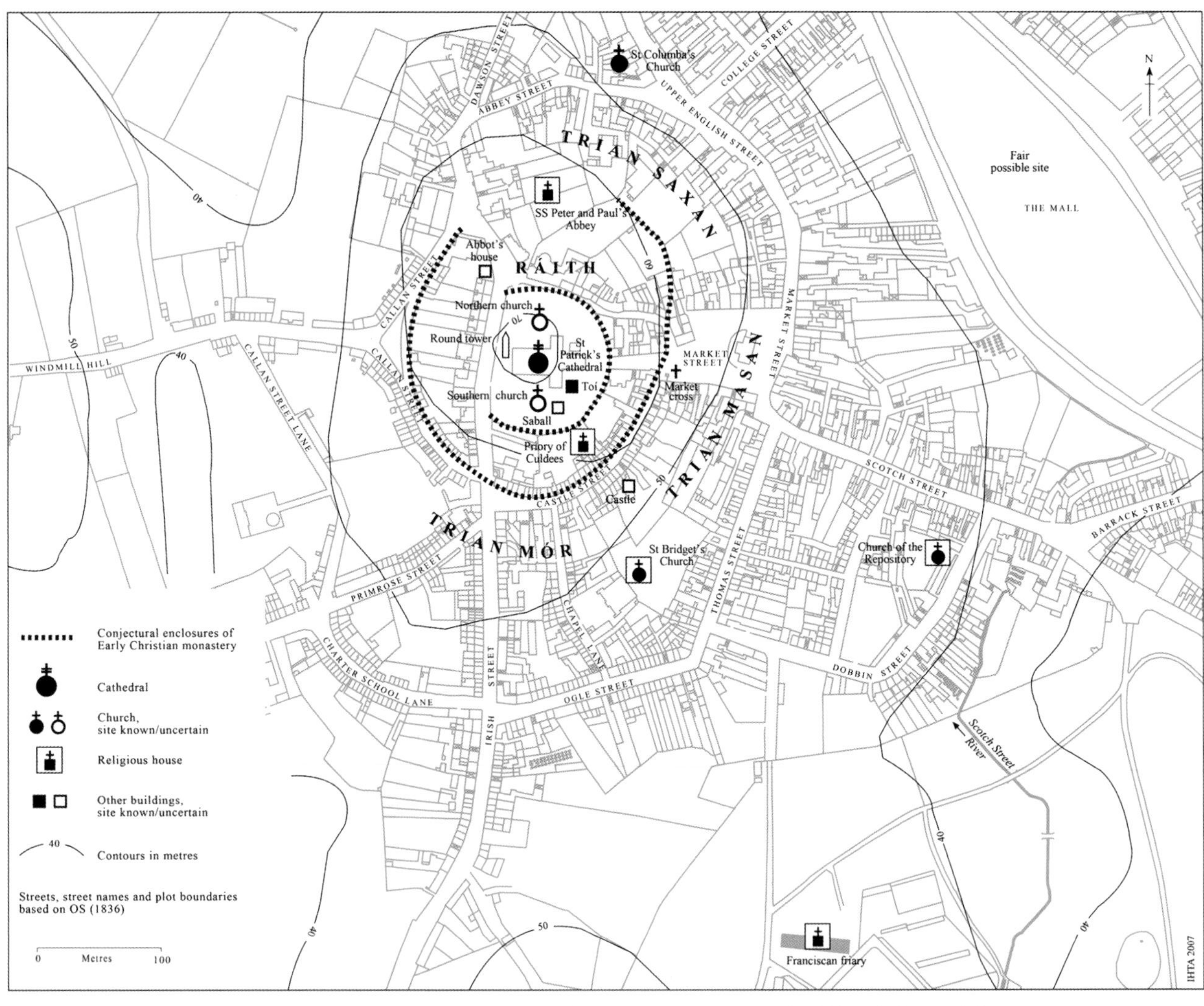

St Columba's Church
DAWSON STREET
ABBEY STREET
COLLEGE STREET
UPPER ENGLISH STREET
N
Fair possible site
THE MALL
TRIAN SAXAN
SS Peter and Paul's Abbey
Abbot's house
RÁITH
60
CALLAN STREET
Northern church
70
Round tower
St Patrick's Cathedral
Toi
Southern church
Saball
Priory of Culdees
MARKET STREET
Market cross
TRIAN MASAN
50
WINDMILL HILL
40
CALLAN STREET LANE
CASTLE STREET
Castle
TRIAN MÓR
SCOTCH STREET
BARRACK STREET
St Bridget's Church
Church of the Repository
PRIMROSE STREET
THOMAS STREET
CHAPEL LANE
DOBBIN STREET
CHARTER SCHOOL LANE
IRISH STREET
OGLE STREET
Scotch Street River
Franciscan friary
Conjectural enclosures of Early Christian monastery
Cathedral
Church, site known/uncertain
Religious house
Other buildings, site known/uncertain
Contours in metres
Streets, street names and plot boundaries based on OS (1836)
0
Metres
100
IHTA 2007

Early Christian and medieval Armagh © Royal Irish Academy Irish Historic Towns Atlas

> living as a hermit having left his episcopacy. Easter came then and Muiredach [Cellach's brother] frequently visited him and took no action except on his [Cellach's] advice.

This episode follows a common universal trope of the holy bishop or saint deciding to abandon a busy and often intense world that was distracting him from a contemplative life and withdrawing to the desert to gain peace. This text ends particularly violently as his four pupils kill Cellach after conspiring with Guaire. Of particular relevance to this volume is Herbert's argument that the text was composed in a Clonmacnoise milieu and that Cellach, and even more so Ciarán of Clonmacnoise who would prefer if Cellach had remained in his own monastery, are depicted as retreating back into traditional monasticism and away from the new diocesan system.[46]

The reasons for withdrawing and the locations regarded as deserts or wilderness varied. Many places were – and still are – called *dísert*, often followed by a personal name. Hence Dísert Chiaráin (Castlekeeran, Co. Meath), Dísert Diarmata (Castledermot, Co. Kildare), Dísert Nuadáin (Estersnow, Co. Roscommon), Dísert Maíle Tuile (Dysart, Co. Westmeath), Dísert Tóla (Dysart O'Dea, Co. Clare) and so forth. Most of these place-names indicate the original presence of genuine monastic settlements and the remains of medieval churches, enclosures, cross slabs and other monuments at some of these sites are likely to preserve the imprint of early sites. What in origin may have been a hermitage sometimes became a much more active church as in the case of Dísert Chiaráin (Castlekeeran, Co. Meath) and Dísert Diarmata (Castledermot, Co. Kildare), which were situated in the strategic passes of Belach Dúin and Belach Mugna respectively. Others such as Dísert Óengusa (Dysartenos, Co. Laois), traditionally associated with the author of *Félire Óenguso*, and Dísert Maíle Tuile (Dysart, Co. Westmeath) were situated close to royal residences, Dún Másc (Dunamase, Co. Laois) and Cró Inis on Lough Ennell respectively. The potential to flee the world in such places was negligible. On the evidence of surviving archaeology and of textual references, monastic retreats were most often located on lake and marine islands, in bogs and in woodlands. One of the most renowned of these in the period under consideration was Inis Locha Cré, also known as Inis na mBeó 'Island of the Living' (Monaincha, Co. Tipperary), an island near the larger ecclesiastical complex of Roscrea (Ros Cré). (Fig. 22) The island appears in saints' lives with a definite aura of sanctity associated with it. St Cainnech of Aghaboe crossed onto the island miraculously without a boat and without wetting his feet to spend the biblical forty days and forty nights there

lines 275–81. Original: *Do bádar ann sein car an C[h]orgais ag dénam a tráth 7 a n-urrnaigthi 7 [do] hoirdearcaigthe ar fud Érenn uili Ceallach mac Eógain do beith i ndíthrub ar fágbáil [a] easpocóide dó 7 táinig tráth na Cásc and sin 7 do bí Muireadach ag tathaigi co minic c[h]uigi 7 ní dénad áenní acht do réir a c[h]omairli.* **46** Herbert, '*Caithéim Cellaig*'.

without food or shelter. No one knew that he was on the island and following the usual motif, he encountered demons there. When it came to dying, Cainnech returned to his own monastery.[47] The life of St Crónán of Roscrea specifically states that Inis Locha Cré was always a monastery of religious monks (*in qua est monasterium monachorum semper religiosorum*),[48] a designation also attributed to Daire Eidnech – another church with 'ivy' characteristics – otherwise known as Doire na Flann (Derrynaflan, Co. Tipperary) (*in quo semper viri religiosissimi habitant*) in the life of St Rúadán of Lorrha.[49] While annalistic references to Inis Locha Cré are scant, nevertheless they provide a useful profile of its inhabitants and their status. The first mention appears in 807, an obit of Elair, anchorite and scribe of Loch Cré (*ancorita 7 scriba Locha Cré*), a combination of offices that tends to signify an individual following a committed religious life.[50] Similarly, Fergal of Inis Locha Cré was most probably following a religious life when he died there in 1119–20, as he is described as 'a reverend elder, and select soldier of God' (*senóir airmitnech milidh toghaidhe Dé*).[51] The death of Máel Pádraic Ua Druccáin in Monaincha in 1138, who was somewhat exaggeratedly described by AFM as 'paragon of the wisdom of the Irish, chief lector of Ard Macha, head of council of the west of Europe in piety and devotion' (*saoi eagna na nGaoidheal ardfhear léighinn Arda Macha, ceann athchomhairc iarthair Eorpa i ccrábhadh, 7 caondúthracht*), is an example of a senior cleric, probably a monk, ending his life in a hermitage in the hope of salvation.[52]

The case of Flaithbertach mac Inmainén, abbot of Inis Cathaig and joint king of Cashel with Cormac mac Cuilennáin, illustrates another function of these 'deserts'. Flaithbertach was accused of inciting conflict between the Uí Néill and the Leinstermen and causing the battle of Belach Mugna in 908 in which the royal bishop-scholar Cormac died. Flaithbertach was captured by the Leinstermen and held in Kildare for a year, after which he was escorted to the borders of Munster by Muirenn, successor of Brigit, along with a large group of clergy accompanied by many relics. He returned to his own monastery at Inis Cathaig where he lived piously until he assumed the kingship of Cashel again in 914.[53] His death is recorded in 944. However, Flaithbertach seems to have been subjected to further trials when in 921 he was taken by Vikings from Inis Locha Cré and conveyed to Limerick.[54] Given his previous record and his precarious position as king of Cashel, Flaithbertach may have been seeking sanctuary on the island hermitage or residing temporarily in penance there. Later, Mac Raith Ua Fídan, head (*cenn*) of Inis Locha Cré died in 1143[55] and thereafter, the nature of the monastery becomes unclear. In his description of what is taken to be Monaincha, Giraldus Cambrensis alludes to a settlement of *céli Dé*, suggesting that at least in the late twelfth century, a community clung on to the 'old'

47 Plummer, *VSH*, i, pp 167–8 §§xlii–xliii. 48 Ibid., ii, p. 26 §xvi. 49 Ibid., ii, p. 250 §xxv. 50 AU. 51 AU, AI, AFM. 52 AFM. 53 FAI, AI. 54 AFM. 55 AFM.

tradition there before being replaced by Augustinian canons, although in common with a pattern found throughout Ireland the evidence for a community of canons there is slight until the late fourteenth century.[56] Some time prior to 1173, however, a community of canons was established in Roscrea, as Conaing Ua hÁengusa, head of the canons of Roscrea (*ceann canánach Rosa Cré*) died in that year.[57] That community did not thrive and Roscrea, as part of the diocese of Killaloe, became instead a parochial centre. The fine Romanesque architecture of the churches at Roscrea and Monaincha probably belong to a period during which Roscrea contended to become a diocese in its own right during the mid-to-late twelfth century.[58] Of Monaincha, Giraldus's comments although mainly fanciful include some relevant remarks:[59]

> There is a lake in the north of Munster which contains two islands, one rather large and the other rather small. The larger one has a church from the time of the old religion (*antiquae religionis*). The smaller one has a chapel cared for most devotedly by a few celibates, called *Cœlicolas* or *Colideos*.

The smaller island inhabited by the *céli Dé* was known as 'the island of the living' (*insula viventium*) as no one living on the island, no matter how close they were to death, could die there. Once they left the island and set foot on the larger island they died. Although strange to the modern mind, this may also have been a way of keeping the world at bay, and by doing so creating the ultimate *domus interior* on an artificial island wilderness.

Without doubt, the best examples of 'deserts' in Ireland are offshore islands, particularly, although not exclusively, those off the south and west coasts that have evidence of ecclesiastical monuments. They range from small sites to large complexes as at Church Island, Co. Kerry, Inishmurray, Co. Sligo, High Island, Co. Galway, and the most spectacular of all, Skellig Michael (Sceilig Mhichíl), Co. Kerry.[60] Lake islands also account for 'desert' locations, among them

56 Bhreathnach, '*Vita apostolica*'. 57 AFM. 58 Edel Bhreathnach, 'Who controlled Roscrea in the twelfth century?' in Peter Harbison and Valerie Hall (eds), *A carnival of learning. Essays to honour George Cunningham and his 50 conferences on medieval Ireland in the Cistercian Abbey of Mount St Joseph, Roscrea, 1987–2012* (Roscrea, 2012), pp 33–40; Pádraig Ó Riain, 'The medieval story of Saint Crónán of Roscrea' in Harbison and Hall, *A carnival of learning*, pp 158–62. 59 James F. Dimock (ed.), *Giraldi Cambrensis opera*. 8 vols. Vol. 5 (London, 1867), pp 80–1 (Cap. IV); John J. O'Meara (trans.), *Gerald of Wales. The history and topography of Ireland* (London, 1982; repr. 1988), p. 60 §37 (O'Meara's translation is altered slightly here). Original: *Est lacus in Momonia boreali, duas continens insulas, unam majorem et alteram minorem. Major ecclesiam habet antiquæ religionis. Minor vero capellam, qui pauci cœlibes, quos Cœlicolas vel Colideos vocant, devote deserviunt.* 60 Tomás Ó Carragáin, 'The view from the shore: perceiving island monasteries in early medieval Ireland', *Hortus Artium Medievalium. Journal of the International Research Centre for Late Antiquity and Middle Ages*

Inchagoill, Co. Galway, and Inisfallen, both in Co. Kerry. Many similar 'deserts' occur in Scotland where a coast so replete with islands, rocks and isolated peninsulas must have attracted those seeking to live extreme eremitical existences. Among the many such sites are Eileach an Naoimh north of Jura and Eilean Mor at the head of Loch Sween.[61]

During the eleventh and twelfth centuries, the annals record the deaths of senior churchmen in these seemingly isolated places. Some were long-term inhabitants, others retreated to them to die, to complete their life's pilgrimage:

AU 1018: *Gormghal in Ardailéan,* ***prímanmchara Érenn****, in Christo quieuit* ('Gormgal of Int Ardailéan, **chief confessor of Ireland**, rested in Christ')

AI 1033: *Cond Hua Sinnaich,* ***ánchara Herend****, quieuit i nInis Celtra* ('Conn Ua Sinnaig, **anchorite of Ireland**, rested in Inis Celtra')

AI 1044: *Áed Scelic,* ***in t-huasalshacart 7 in macc óge 7 cend crábuid na nGáedel****, quieuit in Christo* ('Áed Sceilic, **the noble priest, the celibate, and the head of religious life of the Irish**, rested in Christ')

AU 1056: *Gormgal,* ***prímanmcara Innsi Darcairgrenn****, plenus dierum in penitentia pausauit* ('Gormgal, **chief confessor** of Inis Darcairgrenn, whose days were many, rested in penitence')

AI 1058: *Anmchad Hua Dúnchada,* ***ánchara Dé****, quieuit i nInis Ausail* ('Anmchad Ua Dúnchada, **anchorite of God**, rested in Inis Ausail')

AI 1075: ***Epscop Lothra*** *do eitsecht i nInis Faithlind, .i. Aicher Hua Domnalláin* ('The **bishop of Lothra**, i.e. Aicher Ua Domnalláin, died in Inis Faithlind')

AI 1092: *Connmach Hua Cairill,* ***in t-uasalepscop 7 in sruithshenóir*** *aile, quieuit in Christo i nInis dá Drumman* ('The **noble bishop** Connmach Ua Cairill, **another venerable senior**, rested in Christ in Inis dá Drumann')

AI 1111: *Cathasach,* ***cend crábuid Érend****, quieuit in Christo i nInis Celltra* ('Cathasach, **the head of religious life of Ireland**, rested in Christ in Inis Celtra')

AFM 1124: *Maolcolaim, mac Maoilmaith Uí Connaccáin,* ***uasal shaccart, 7 saoi eccna 7 crábhaidh airthir Éreann****, d'écc i nInis Páttraig an treas lá ficheat December* ('Maelcoluim, son of Maelmaith Ua Connaccáin, **noble priest, and master in learning and religious life of the east of Ireland**, died at Inis Pádraig, on the twenty-third day of December')

19 (2013), 21–33. **61** https://www.historicenvironment.scot/visit-a-place/places/eileach-an-naoimh/history/; https://www.historicenvironment.scot/visit-a-place/places/eilean-mor/ accessed 22 November 2021.

AU 1128: *Muirghius H. Nioc* ***airchinnech Tuama Dá Ghualann fri ré*** *do éc i nInis in Ghaill*. ('Muirgius ua Nioc, **superior of Tuaim dá Gualann for a time**, died in Inis in Ghaill')

AFM 1128: *Muirgheas Ua Níoc,* ***comharba Iarlaithe Tuama da ghualann fri ré****, d'écc i nInis in Ghoill* ('Muirgheas O'Nioc, **successor of Iarlaith of Tuaim dá Gualann for a time**, died on Inis an Ghoill')

While the locations of these retreats appear isolated and wild they were carefully planned and most have evidence of sturdy stone buildings, especially churches. The remains of decorated Romanesque churches and/or round towers survive on Inis Cealtra, Inis Dair Cairgrenn (Ram's Island on Lough Neagh, Co. Antrim), Inis Uasail (Church Island on Lough Currane, Co. Kerry), Inis Faithlinn (Inisfallen on Lough Leane, Co. Kerry) and Inis an Ghoill (Inchagoill on Lough Corrib, Co. Galway. Decorated cross slabs, some with inscriptions, are also common on these sites and in a few instances actually commemorate individuals recorded in the annals. Such is the case with a slab on Inis Uasail which commemorates Anmchad Ua Dúnchada (d. 1058) and more spectacularly the high cross on Inis Cealtra which commemorates Cathasach of Armagh who died there in 1111. The inscription memorializes both Cathasach and the sculptor: '*or(óit) do ardse[n]óir hErenn i(d est) do Cathas[ach]*', '*or(óit) do Thor[n]oc do rigni i(n) croiss*' ('a prayer for the chief elder of Ireland, that is, for Cathasach' and 'a prayer for Tornóc who made this cross').[62]

Regarded as one of the most isolated of all sites, the island monastery of Skellig was carefully planned and considerable resources were put into its construction.[63] (Figs 23 and 24) I have argued elsewhere that like the plans of St Gall or Marmoutier, the layout of Skellig can be best understood with reference to monastic ideology and spirituality as expressed in works such as John Cassian's *Conferences* and *Institutes*.[64] Katja Ritari makes a similar argument for Adomnán's spiritual monastic map of Iona, a theory that has been recently confirmed by Ewan Campbell and Adrián Maldonado in their reassessment of Charles Thomas's excavations at Iona.[65] At the core of reading Skellig are the monastic ideals of the monk as a *miles Christi* constantly involved in military warfare with St Michael the Archangel as his role model. The plan reflects the

62 For a detailed description of Inis Celtra and its monuments see the report produced by Solearth Architecture for Clare County Council, Inis Cealtra: Appendix 2. Detailed Support Material (authors Bernadette McCarthy, Clíodhna O'Leary and Patrick Wallace) (p. 50) https://www.clarecoco.ie/services/planning/publications/inishcealtra/inish-cealtra-appendix-2-detailed-support-material-26764.pdf accessed 18 November 2021. **63** A comprehensive study of all aspects of Skellig Michael and the Little Skellig is available in the recent publication, John Crowley and John Sheehan (eds), *The book of the Skelligs* (Cork, 2022). **64** Bhreathnach, 'Skellig Michael: a lonely hermitage at the edge of the world?'. **65** Ritari, 'Holy souls and a holy community'; Campbell and Maldonado, 'A new Jerusalem'.

layout of mainland sites with a *coenobium* inhabited by a community (the main monastery) and a hermitage (the South Peak) which by scaling dangerous pathways brought the extremely ascetic monk closer to the horizon and hence closer to God and Paradise. Only the elect could stay on this island hermitage, as leaving a monastic community to live an isolated life as an anchorite or hermit was subject to constraints, as already noted in the eighth-century Irish canons, the *Hibernensis*.[66] The background to building a monastic complex such as Skellig must be seen in the belief that monks could transition from this life to the Promised Land, the heavenly Jerusalem, by re-creating the earthly Jerusalem in their own environs. In so doing, they could contemplate the fundamentals of Christianity: death and salvation through Christ's death on the cross, looking forward to salvation and resurrection through Christ's empty tomb, aided by the intercession of the saints whose tombs were a reminder of the ultimate prize of gaining Heaven. Despite the apparent desolation of Skellig and the possibility that one could be stranded there in terrible conditions, the archaeological evidence tells us that this was a busy place, and that it was inhabited probably continuously from the eighth century to the twelfth or thirteenth century.[67]

The main components of the Skellig monastic complex consist of oratories, enclosures, cells, terraces, steps, hand/footholds, gardens, *lechta* (stone platforms, cenotaphs), shrines, a cemetery, crosses and cross slabs, water cisterns, paving stones, and the later St Michael's church, which may represent a change in the monastery's function, or at least its relations with the mainland. Many of these structures had both practical and theological functions. Enclosing walls were clearly built to protect the monks from the weather and from falling off dangerous inclines but they could also be used to define a space and mentally protect the monks from the incursions of demons. This is what Theodoret of Cyrrhus (d. 466) described as the spatial demarcation of the fortified citadel of the ascetic senses, an unassailable fortress, manifest spiritually in the monk's lifestyle and physically in his monastic stronghold.[68] Building a 'new Jerusalem' must have also involved imitating the real Jerusalem or at least an imagined version of it, one form of which is represented in the conceptual replication of Jerusalem based on Adomnán of Iona's description in *De Locis Sanctis*.[69] This can be seen on Skellig in the areas in which an oratory, a *lecht* and a cross-slab were built and substantial paving was laid. Three areas are of particular note:

66 Flechner, *The Hibernensis*, vol. 2, pp 688–9 §38.3. Original: Flechner, *The Hibernensis*, vol. 1 pp 289–90. **67** Bourke, Hayden and Lynch, *Skellig Michael, Co. Kerry*; Tomás Ó Carragáin and John Sheehan, 'The early medieval archaeology of Skellig Michael' in Crowley and Sheehan, *The book of the Skelligs*, pp 99–114. **68** Lynda L. Coon, 'The architecture of the ascetic body' in Kaczynski, *Oxford handbook of Christian monasticism*, pp 51–65, at p. 53. **69** Jenkins, *'Holy, holier, holiest'* pp 104–46; for a recent discussion of this topic in the context of Iona see Campbell and Maldonado, 'A new Jerusalem', 376.

(a) the small oratory space in the main monastery:[70]
(b) the oratory terrace on the South Peak;[71]
(c) the large oratory terrace[72]

Although the *lechta* are often interpreted as pilgrim stations – which they may have become in the late medieval period or even later – this was not their primary function. Indeed, as Ó Carragáin has demonstrated, monuments that have been labelled as *lechta* probably had a myriad of functions including the sites of burial plots, cenotaphs, altars and pilgrim stations.[73] For example, the excavated *lechta* on Skellig did not contain burials but consisted of rectangular drystone constructions erected on large paving slabs. They probably date to the main building phase on the island, between the eighth and ninth centuries. Just east of the *lecht* on the South Peak was a setting that probably held the fine ninth-century cross-inscribed slab found close by in the 1980s. These areas were laid out quite schematically. It is likely that they were meant to represent Jerusalem: the *lecht*, as the empty tomb of the Holy Sepulchre, the South Peak cross as Golgotha, the paving stones were possibly replicating in a stylized manner either the Via Dolorosa or the paving stones of the Constantinian basilica in Jerusalem. What all three excavators noted about these areas was the careful layout that allowed for circumambulation, spaces that were necessary for processing and prostration, both activities integral to monastic liturgy. The other significant elements in these areas were the possible slab shrine on the South Peak, the small collection of human bones discovered under a rectangular stone to the south southwest of the small oratory, and the two burials placed south of the *lecht* close to the large oratory. It may be that these individuals were buried close to the empty tomb to await their own resurrection and at the end of time meet with the resurrected Christ on Skellig. As for the possible slab shrine on the South Peak, it appears to resemble similar shrines found along this coastline and on the mainland.[74] Although it produced no evidence for burial, it may have been a founder's shrine or simply another reminder to the monastic inhabitants of their temporary transition from this world to the heavenly next world, if they succeeded in their battles as soldiers of Christ. And to give them hope, the extensive view offered them a glimpse towards the heavenly Jerusalem beyond the ocean's horizon, as the Desert Fathers sought to view it in the desert stretching away into their sandy horizon.

As noted previously, those seeking a reclusive life did not have to retreat very far from the coenobium or ecclesiastical complex. A *dísert* could exist within a

70 Bourke, Hayden and Lynch, *Skellig Michael excavations 1986–2010*, pp 37–60. **71** Ibid., pp 309–12. **72** Ibid., pp 61–80. **73** Ó Carragáin, 'Altars, graves and cenotaphs' in NicGhabhann and O'Donovan, *Mapping new territories*, pp 129–46. **74** Bourke, Hayden and Lynch, *Skellig Michael excavations 1986–2010*, pp 284–7.

busy settlement or not far from it. The churches containing the element *eidnén* 'ivy' were not very far from larger churches. On islands such as Inis Cealtra, ecclesiastical grandees such as Cathasach of Armagh, followed a committed religious life while probably encountering the local or provincial aristocracy. After all, some of the latter were buried there: in 1076, for example, Gormlaith, daughter of Ua Fócarta, wife of Toirdelbach Ua Briain, died in Killaloe and was buried in Inis Cealtra.[75] The most popular places that were destinations for final pilgrimages, in the monastic sense, were Rome, Armagh, Clonard, Derry, Lismore and from the mid-twelfth century, Cong, Co. Mayo and Derry's *dísert* or *Dubréicles* Choluim Cille.

Rome attracted Irish ecclesiastics from early days and during these later centuries many important individuals including aristocrats went there on pilgrimage. The Irish monastery, the *Sancta Trinitatis Scotorum*, was located at an intersection between the Palatine, Caelian and Aventine hills (the *clivus Scauri*) from at least the eleventh century. André Wilmart demonstrated that this foundation had close relations with the Benedictines of *Sancta Maria in Palladio,* which was a house under the supervision of Monte Cassino.[76] He published two lists that he argued recorded the names of members of the community, one possibly pre-eleventh century, the other late eleventh or early twelfth century.[77] Further corroboration for this house is the existence of an eleventh-century *libellus precum* which contains prayers of various origins – native Irish, Carolingian and Roman reform – a number of which are strictly monastic in function including offices for specific feast days, prayers for the monastery's dead, hymns, prayers and psalms for the various canonical hours.[78] It is not known when *Sancta Trinitatis* was founded or by whom but, like the dozens of such small houses in Rome, it probably acted as a guest house for the Irish ecclesiastics and kings who visited the city during the eleventh and twelfth centuries. As noted earlier one was the distinguished Céle Dabaill, abbot of Bangor, bishop and preacher, *scriba et anchorita*, *apostolicus doctor totius Hiberniae* who left Ireland in 928 and died in Rome in 929.[79] He may have attended the processing of Columbanus's relics from Bobbio to a council in Pavia in 929.[80] Fergil, abbot of Terryglass, possibly influenced by Céle, went on a pilgrimage to

75 AI. 76 Wilmart, 'La Trinité des Scots à Rome'. 77 Ibid., 229–30; André Wilmart, 'Finian parmi les moines romains de la Trinité des Scots', *Revue Bénédictine* 44 (1932), 359–61. List I: Columbanus (*abbas*), Mauricius (*sacerdos*), Felix, Maurinus, Donatus. List II: Nicolaus (*abbas*), Malchus (*prepositus*), Andreas (*prepositus*), Fortunatus, Germanus (monk), Donatus, Donatus, Petrus, Finianus (*monachi omnes*), Dominatus, Adam, Iohannes, Martinus, Grigorius, Antonius, Grigorius. 78 Pierre Salmon, 'La composition d'un *Libellus precum* à l'époque de la réforme grégorienne', *Benedictina* 26 (1979), 285–322, at pp 311–13. 79 AU 928–9; AFM 926–7. 80 For the context of this event, see Alexander O'Hara and Faye Taylor, 'Aristocratic and monastic conflict in tenth-century Italy: the case of Bobbio and *Miracula*

Rome and also died there in 929.[81] Fachtna, the *fer léiginn* and priest of Clonmacnoise, *airchinnech* of *Int Eidnén*, who died in Rome in 1024, is styled 'abbot of the Irish' (*abb na nGaoidheal*).[82] This suggests that *Sancta Trinitatis* existed by then and may even have hosted Sitric, king of Dublin, and his entourage – possibly among them Dúnán, future bishop of Dublin and a Benedictine – in Rome in 1028. It should also be noted that Donnchad mac Briain Bóraime, king of Munster and contender for the kingship of Ireland and his brother-in-law Echmarcach mac Ragnaill, who had intermittently ruled Dublin and other Norse territories around the Irish Sea, reputedly died and were buried in 1064 in the monastery of Santo Stefano Rotondo (St Stephen the Protomartyr) on the Caelian Hill.[83] The only other direct reference to an abbot of the Irish in Rome, apart from Fachtna of Clonmacnoise, is that of Éogan who died in 1095.[84] He may be one and the same as the *Iohannnes* mentioned in Wilmart's List II of purported members of the community. Among the other notables who died in Rome were Ímar Ua hÁedacáin, founder of the church of SS Peter and Paul at Armagh and St Malachy's teacher and spiritual director who died there in 1134, while Cellach Ua Selbaig *comarbae* of Barre (Cork) and 'chief anchorite of Ireland' returned to Ireland from Rome and died in 1036.[85] And unlike the ninth-century Irish poem on the futility of going to Rome without Christ on the journey with the pilgrim,[86] the annals regard the pilgrimage to Rome as a fulfilment of a life's journey by these religious, a journey that is also lauded in Irish hagiography as an essential episode in a saint's life. But, given the location of *Sancta Trinitatis Scotorum* in Rome, a place teeming with monks of Monte Cassino, Cluny, Gorze, among them individuals who became particularly influential in the eleventh-century 'Gregorian reform',[87] it is plausible that those who returned to Ireland came with new ideas on monasticism. The constant difficulty is to pinpoint the changes that may have flowed from these contacts.

THE LEARNED 'DÍSERT': LIVING AMONG SCHOLARS

Seeking spiritual solace especially at the end of one's life in a busy monastery might not be regarded as the equivalent of living the ascetic life of those on Skellig. However, senior scholars and *anmchairde* 'confessors' could have formed a religious community in an existing monastery, serviced by a library, a hospice

sancti Columbani', *Viator* 44:3 (2013), 43–62. **81** AFM [927]. **82** AFM. **83** I owe this information to Colmán Ó Clabaigh who with his expert knowledge of Rome suggested the connection. See also Seán Duffy, 'See Rome and die: the burial-place of Donnchad mac Briain', *History Ireland* 22:2 (2014), 6–7. **84** AI. **85** AI. **86** Whitley Stokes and John Strachan (eds), *Thesaurus paleohibernicus. A collection of Old-Irish glosses, scholia, prose, and verse*. 2 vols (Cambridge, 1901–3; repr. Dublin, 1975 and 1987), ii, p. 296. **87** Salmon,

and a *dísert* building *in situ*. This arrangement could have been an ideal place to end one's pilgrimage on earth. This was not a unique Irish phenomenon especially during the eleventh and twelfth centuries with the rise of 'new hermitism' in Britain and on the Continent, and consequent on this greater eremitical activity, the development of many important monasteries from hermit cells. Selby in Yorkshire and Melrose in the Scottish borders are prime examples of this movement.[88] What is unique in Ireland is that communities and individuals sought reclusion in existing foundations. No new monasteries grew out of hermits' cells. Hence, Máel Giricc, described as 'the head of the house of elders of Clonmacnoise' (*abb Tighe Sruithe Cluana mic Nóis*) in his obit in 927, may have been in charge of a residence inhabited by scholars and anchorites.[89] Dúnchad ua Braein, successor of Ciarán of Clonmacnoise, *optimus scriba 7 relegiosissimus* went to Armagh in 974 and died there in 989, as did Áed Treoiti (Trevet, Co. Meath), a bishop lauded as a biblical and monastic scholar (*suí ind ecnai 7 i crábad*) (d. 1005).[90] The very senior Dubthach Albanach (d. 1065), a scholar from Scotland who had studied in Armagh, returned to Scotland, but came back to Armagh at the end of his life where he was an *anmcharae* in bishop Áed Ua Forréid's household.[91]

Lismore's significance as a *caput* of learning and reform during the eleventh and twelfth centuries has been mentioned already. It attracted important individuals such as Corcrán Clérech (d. 1040), Máel Ísu Ua Brolcháin (d. 1086), Óengus Ua Gormáin, abbot of Bangor and first bishop of Ulaid (d. 1123),[92] Cellach, archbishop of Armagh who was buried there in 1129, and much later Ua Cerbaill, bishop of Ross (d. 1168) and Laurence Ua Súillebáin, bishop of Cloyne (d. 1205). Why Lismore became such a vibrant centre of learning and reform open to external influences is unclear. It had been a centre of learning and liturgy in earlier centuries.[93] Peter O'Dwyer put forward the hypothesis, based on the evidence of the number of eminent early ascetics associated with Lismore and Dairinis, a hermitage on the river Blackwater (Molana, Co. Waterford), that the *céli Dé* movement originated in this region. While not generally accepted as a theory, it is notable that Lismore included a strong eremitical tradition from the seventh century onwards.[94] At a later stage, the Norse town of Waterford may have been one source of external influence and certainly the appointment of Máel Ísu Ua hAinmire, a Benedictine monk of

'*Libellus precum*', 320–1. **88** Kathryn Jasper and John Howe, 'Hermitism in the eleventh and twelfth centuries' in *CHMM*, pp 684–96. **89** AFM [927]. **90** AU, AFM 1004. **91** AU, AFM 1065; Murphy, 'A poem in praise of Aodh Úa Foirréidh', pp 152,159 §25; Benjamin T. Hudson, *Prophecy of Berchán. Irish and Scottish high-kings of the early Middle Ages* (Westport, CT, and London, 1996), pp 120–1. **92** Flanagan, 'John de Courcy', pp 157–8. **93** Constant J. Mews, 'The flight of Carthach (Mochuda) from Rahan to Lismore: lineage and identity in early medieval Ireland', *Early Medieval Europe* 21:1 (2013), 1–26. **94** O'Dwyer, *Céli Dé*, pp 46, 49, 55–7, 193. O'Dwyer also includes Daire Eidnech/Daire na Flann (Derrynaflan, Co. Tipperary)

Winchester, as the first bishop of Waterford in 1096 was significant as it would appear that he resided in Lismore.[95] There was also a continental influence possibly through the Schottenklöster network in the Ottonian Empire, especially Regensburg. The fanciful twelfth-century life of Albart (Ailbe), styled archbishop of Cashel, was said to have conducted St Erhard of Regensburg to Lismore for an assembly of bishops and nobles at which Albart was moved to greater sanctity by the bishop of Lismore's sermon.[96] This may be an allusion to the consecration of a new church at Lismore by Gilla Críst Ua Conairche (Christianus), bishop of Lismore and papal legate, in 1166, at which twelve bishops attended as well as Gregorius, abbot of Regensburg. A synod was also held on that occasion.[97] Since the mid-tenth century, Lismore had assumed a political significance for the leading dynasties of Munster, the Uí Briain and Meic Cárthaig. In 1093, for example, Diarmait Ua Briain submitted to his brother Muirchertach and they agreed the peace terms in Cashel and Lismore 'with the relics of Ireland, including the Staff of Jesus, as pledges, and in the presence of Ua hÉnna [their bishop] and the nobles of Mumu'.[98] In 1116, Diarmait violated the agreement and Muirchertach retired from his kingship to Lismore, dying there of illness in 1119. He was buried in the Ua Briain *eigenkirche* in Killaloe. Similarly, Cormac Mac Cárthaig, king of Munster, fled to Lismore in 1127 when he came under pressure from Toirdelbach Ua Conchobair, king of Connacht.[99] From within Ireland, therefore, royal patronage of a monastery and its intellectual vibrancy, as elsewhere, lent it a higher profile and attracted novices from influential families. It would appear, for example, that Mathgamain (d. 1129) and Domnall (d. 1135), two sons of Muirchertach Ua Briain, king of Munster and Leth Cuinn, were members of Lismore's community.[100] Domnall died as a religious cleric (*i cuincc cléircechta*). That he took the habit in Lismore is no surprise given his father's attachment to the place. He may even have become a Benedictine under the tutelage of the bishop of Waterford, Máel Ísu Ua hAinmere. This lifestyle choice stood in direct contrast to the uncomfortable life lived on an island or in a fastness. It was the life of an intellectual monastic community grappling with issues that pertained

among the monasteries in which the *céli Dé* movement originated. **95** O'Connor, 'Did bishop Malchus of Waterford resign?'; Bhreathnach, 'Benedictine influence in Ireland'. **96** Wilhelm Levison (ed.), 'Vita Albarti archiepiscopi Cassellensis' in Bruno Krusch and Wilhelm Levison (eds), *Passiones vitaeque sanctorum aevi Merovingici* VI (Hannover and Leipzig, 1913), pp 21–3, at p. 22: lines 15–16. Original: *conventum facerent in civitate cui nomen Lesmor*. https://www.dmgh.de/mgh_ss_rer_merov_6/index.htm#page/22/mode/1up accessed 22 November 2021; Dagmar Ó Riain-Raedel, 'The question of the "pre-Patrician" saints of Munster' in Michael A. Monk and John Sheehan (eds), *Early medieval Munster. Archaeology, history and society* (Cork, 1998), pp 17–22. **97** Flanagan, *Transformation*, p. 116. **98** AI. Original: *Diarmait m. Tairdelbaig Huí Bríain do thíchtain i tech Muirchertaig, .i. a bráthar, 7 co ndersat síth 7 chomluge i Cassiul 7 i lLis Mór fo minnaib Hérenn im Bachaill Ísu i fiadnaisi Huí Énnai 7 mathi Muman.* **99** AFM. **100** AI1129; AFM1135.

throughout the church such as the Real Presence of Christ, which Malachy discussed with Máel Ísu Ua hAinmire while residing in Lismore.[101] The memory of these eminent men was imprinted on the surrounding ecclesiastical landscape. Máel Ísu Ua Brolcháin's oratory (*dairthech*) at Lismore was burned in 1116 and the annalistic entry on the death of Cellach of Armagh mentions that he was buried in the bishops' cemetery (*i n-ailaidh na n-espoc*) in Lismore.[102] The Latin life of St Carthach/Mochutu of Lismore, possibly compiled in its current versions during the twelfth or thirteenth centuries,[103] articulates clearly that this was a wonderful and holy *civitas* crowded with cells and saintly monasteries (*set plenum est cellis et monasteriis sanctis*). Many holy men – women were not allowed to enter this monastic part of the *civitas* although the life implies that a nunnery existed nearby – not only from all parts of Ireland but from England and Britain (*ex Anglia et Britannia*) resided there wishing to migrate there to Christ (*uolentes ibi migrare ad Christum*).[104] This account seems to be a fairly accurate description of the monastery when read against other sources.

Clonard seems to have attracted senior clerics, especially from Clonmacnoise with which it often shared an abbacy, to end their life's pilgrimage there. Echtigern Ua hEgráin, *comarbae* of Ciarán and Commán (Roscommon) died there in 1052 as did Aillil Ua hAirretuich, *ard-chomarbae Chiaráin*, in 1070.[105] Of course, as *comarbai*, neither of them was necessarily a monk, although they may have taken vows in Clonard. In contrast, Cormac Mainistrech, of Monasterboice, who died in Clonard in 1092, was most likely a monk as he is described as 'the noble bishop and wise senior [scholar] of Ireland' (*in t-uasalepscobb 7 in sruithshenóir Herenn*).[106] Cormac's renown as a scholar hints at another reason why Clonard and Lismore were appealing: their learned teachers created learned networks throughout Ireland. This phenomenon can be traced through annalistic references in the use of the term *daltae* which can cover a range of meanings 'a fosterling, nursling, pupil, disciple'. Its use, and especially of the compound *bronn-daltae* 'bosom-fosterling, pupil', in these references suggests that the relationship was that of master and pupil in a monastic school.[107] Of particular relevance are the pupils of Máel Ísu Ua Brolcháin and Máel Muire Ua Dúnáin, all of whom on the basis of their profiles lived committed religious lives:

101 Flanagan, *Transformation*, p. 107 (Leclercq and Rochais, *Sancti Bernardi opera*, iii, p. 316). **102** AU, AFM, LC. **103** Sharp (*Medieval Irish saints' lives* p. 385) comments that the life of St Mochutu shows signs of an eighth-century origin. **104** Plummer, *VSH*, i, p. 197 §lxv. **105** AFM. **106** AI. Also recorded in AFM, CS. **107** Examples include the following: AFM [912]: Máelciarain, son of Eochagán, Abbot of Cluain-Eois and Mucnamh, died. He was the foster-son (*daltae*) of the archbishop Fethghna [bishop and abbot of Armagh d. 874. A house/school at Armagh was known as Tech Fethgna]; AFM [915]: Feidhlimidh, foster-son (*daltae*) of Máelmaedhóg, abbot of Gleann-Uisean, the sage of Leinster [Máelmáedóc in his obit following the battle of Cenn Fuait in 917 'a scholar and bishop of Laigin' (AU),

AI 1091: *Cainchomrac Húa Cel( ) do Cheneul Eoga(in), in macc óge 7 in t-huasalshacart 7* ***bruinndalta Muíl Ísu Huí Brolacháin****, quieuit in Christo hi Cluain Findglaissi hi Múscrugu Breogain* (Caínchomrac Ua Cel … from Cenél Eógain … a celibate, a noble priest, and **favourite disciple of Máel Ísu Ua Brolcháin**, rested in Christ in Cluain Finnglaise in Múscraige Breogain (Cloonfinglass, Co. Tipperary))

AFM 1125: *Maoltréna uasal shagart, 7 sruith sheanóir Chraoi Caoimhghin,* ***brondalta toghaidhe hUí Dhúnáin*** *uasal sheanórach Éreann, décc co heglastacda, iar ndeighbheathaidh* (Máel Tréna, a noble priest and learned senior of Cró Caeimhghin, **the bosom fosterling of Ua Dúnain**, noble senior of Ireland, died piously, after a good life)

AFM 1168: *Macraith Ua Móráin .i. epscop Fear mBreifne,* ***mac dalta Uí Dhúnáin*** *décc i nArdachadh Epscoip Mél isin treas bhliadhain ochtmoghat a aoisi* (Macraith Ua Móráin, i.e. bishop of the men of Breifne, **Ua Dúnáin's fosterson,** died at Ard Achadh of Bishop Mel (Ardagh, Co. Longford), in the eighty-third year of his age)

Máel Muire Ua Dúnáin's role in the early twelfth-century transformation of the Irish church, participating as he did in the Synod of Ráith Bresail in 1111, is well known but his influence as a teacher who perpetuated that transformation through his pupils has rarely been acknowledged.[108] A similar role can be attributed to Ímar Ua hÁedacáin as Malachy's first teacher in Armagh. The impression gained from these distinguished masters and pupils, and also from the gathering of eminent individuals in monasteries such as Armagh and Lismore, is that an elite, learned monastic network existed in eleventh- and twelfth-century Ireland, some of whom were to the forefront of transforming the Irish church, while others were occupied with intellectual activities. All of them probably existed in religious communities within the great monastic settlement, in deserts within the walls.

CONVERSING WITH THE WORLD BEYOND THE ENCLOSURE

Adomnán as abbot of Iona and aristocrat, like Columba before him, was in no sense detached from the affairs of the world beyond the monastery. Adomnán

'a distinguished scribe, anchorite, and an adept in the Latin learning and the Irish language' (*scribhnidh tocchaidhe, ancoire, 7 saoi isin eccna Laitiondae, 7 isin mbérla Scoiteacdha*) (AFM 915). Nothing of Máelmáedóc's work survives but one Middle Irish poem on the prowess of the Laigin is ascribed to his son, Flann Mac Máelmáedóc (d. 979)]; AFM 971 and 981: Dúnchadh, the foster-son of Diarmaid, distinguished bishop and chief poet of Osraighe, died. Ailill, the foster-son of Dunchadh, died. **108** Ó Corráin, 'Mael Muire Ua Dúnáin', p. 50

was the instigator of the *Lex Innocentium* promulgated in 697 to protect women, children, clerics and other non-combatants in times of conflict, a truly innovative piece of legislation for its time.[109] Adomnán portrays Columba in his own guise, which was not unlikely given Columba's own noble affiliations, blessing and cursing kings in Ireland, Dál Riata and Pictland. One of the rare occasions on which the saint contested a command from Heaven relates to the ordination of Áedán mac Gabráin (d. 606/9) as king of Dál Riata.[110] He received a glass book of the ordination of kings, which an angel bade him to read. In it there was a command that he should ordain Áedán but Columba refused as he held the king's brother in higher regard. The angel struck him with a whip leaving a scar with him for the rest of his life. Following three threatening visits from the angel, Columba obeyed and ordained Áedán but not without a vengeful warning that should the king or any of his successors commit treachery against him or his successor abbots or kindred in Ireland 'the scourge that I have endured from an angel on your account will be turned by the hand of God to a great disgrace upon them'.[111] During the early medieval period abbots and bishops are known to have intervened in dynastic and ecclesiastic politics and on some occasions died as a result, although not as frequently as might be expected. During the eighth and ninth centuries, abbots and bishops were active in promulgating and reviving ecclesiastical laws (*cánai*), the laws of Adomnán and Patrick being the most frequently imposed by the senior churchmen of Armagh and Iona respectively, usually in collaboration with the king of Tara or with provincial kings.[112] Abbots increasingly assumed the role of peace-makers between warring kings, at times invoking *cánai* as penalties against the culprits and their kingdoms. In 893, for example, Máel Brigte mac Tornáin, abbot of Armagh and Iona, intervened between the northern dynasties Cenél nÉogain and the Ulaid when a brawl broke out in Armagh itself, and as a result received compensation from all the provinces of Ireland for the dishonour done to himself and to St Patrick.[113] Special enforcement officers known as *muiri* were appointed to enforce ecclesiastical laws and tributes, many of whom were abbots, bishops, anchorites and scribes. In 814, Feidlimid, abbot of Cell Moinne (Kilmoon, Co. Meath) and *muire/máer* of Patrick 'a distinguished anchorite and excellent scribe' (*ancorita*

mentions this aspect of his life briefly in relation to the two obits mentioned above. **109** For a study of the significance of this law see James W. Houlihan, *Adomnán's Lex Innocentium and the laws of war* (Dublin, 2020). **110** https://www.dib.ie/biography/aedan-a0051. **111** Anderson and Anderson, *Life of Columba*, pp 190–1 [iii.5]; *Sharpe, Adomnán of Iona*, pp 208–9 [III 5]. Original: '… *flagillum quod causa tui ab angelo sustenui per manum dei super eos in magnum flagitium uertetur* …'. **112** T.M. Charles-Edwards, *The early mediaeval Gaelic lawyer*. E.C. Quiggin Memorial Lectures 4 (Cambridge, 1999), pp 25–30. **113** CS 893, AFM 889. Original (CS): *Cumusc cengigis a nÁrd Macha etir Cinel nEógain 7 Ulltu dú a ttorchair sochaidhe .i. eidir Aidéid mac Laigne 7 Flaithbertach mac Murchadha cor sgar Mael Brígde. Ríar Maoilbrigde iar sin et enigh Padraicc ó cuigedaibh hErend la gabail a naitire tricha secht ccumal et cethrar hi crocaib ó Ulltaibh cenmothád cealla et manchu.*

precipuus scribaque optimus) died.[114] Similarly, Máel Pátraic, *princeps* of Treóit (Trevet, Co. Meath) (d. 883), who enforced Patrick's law south of the Fews (Co. Armagh), was a learned scribe and scholar (*scriba et sapiens optimus*) as was Tuathal mac Óenacáin, scribe and bishop of Duleek and Lusk (d. 929).[115] Cáenchomrac mac Maíl Uidir, abbot and bishop of Derry (d. 929) was the protector of the *Lex Innocentium*, and possibly the individual who revived the law in the early tenth century, although his death is only recorded in AFM. The legal position and expertise of anchorites, bishops and scribes, already noted in relation to the *deorad Dé*, and further supported in the later discussion on *cráibdig*, meant that while they were likely to be following a committed religious life they were often part of the ruling and learned elite. This tradition was firmly established by the great founders of monasticism in Ireland during the sixth century.

Monastic rulers in Ireland, as elsewhere, were primarily drawn from the aristocracy and their social status and education not only prepared them for leadership roles, but also enabled them to impose order on an ecclesiastical community, just as their kinsmen were doing the same over the general populace. As always with privileged elites, their familial origins inculcated a sense of entitlement to the office, whether or not one was capable of exercising it. One such person, for example, was Máel Póil mac Ailella, who according to AU (922) was 'master of learning and bishop of Síl nÁeda Sláine' (*suí 7 epscop Síl nAedha Sláne*). AFM (920) adds that he was abbot of *Int Eidnén* (*epscop, anchoire, 7 scríbhnidh Leithe Chuinn, 7 abb Ind Edhnén*), the eremitical community associated with Clonard. His remit as bishop may have extended across the over-kingdom of Brega and it is possible that his brother was none other than Colmán mac Aillela, abbot of Clonmacnoise and Clonard (d. 926), and patron with Flann Sinna (d. 916), king of Ireland, of the Cross of the Scriptures at Clonmacnoise. If that was the case, then one brother was in charge of the economic and political aspects of Clonard while the other ruled the spiritual necessities of an extensive territory and a monastic community located at *Int Eidnén*.[116] Although only surviving in the seventeenth-century Annals of the Four Masters – as with so many such quatrains – the following verse pithily captures the standing of these individuals in society. It could be argued that the verse is satirical, feigned praise directed at Máel Póil and his influential relatives:[117]

> Máel Póil, who was in great dignity,
> a bishop who took the road of a king,
> a learned master who enforced the law upon all,
> a man who dispensed peace all round.

114 AU, AFM. 115 AU, AFM. 116 For an assessment of Máel Póil's episcopal remit, see Etchingham, *Church organisation*, pp 180, 184, 188. 117 AFM 920. Original: *Maelpóil baoí fo orddun mór / epscop gaibheadh ramat rígh, / suí no neartadh recht for cach / fear foceirdedh*

Yet it encapsulates his life as an aristocratic bishop, a canon lawyer who participated in his society, inside and outside the monastery, and withdrew as an anchorite to his hermitage in *Int Eidnén*.

Some monastic leaders, however, warned against interacting with the world outside. 'The teaching of Máel Ruain' includes a specific warning about conversing with visitors:[118]

> He bade them not to ask the people who came to visit them for news, or to talk to them, but only to transact the business that they came about: because great is the harm that is done and the disturbance that is caused by such news to the mind of him to whom it is told.

Yet monastic communities had to interact with the world intruding from beyond the enclosure. Some communities, such as those existing on inaccessible islands, could evade the attention of the general populace and even their own brethren but what of other monastic communities who lived in or close to large ecclesiastical complexes or even close to royal residences, roads or other communication routes? Saints' lives are full of instances in which saints seek to flee from daily demands but are unable to do so. The life of St Crónán has the saint conflicted between the *vita activa* and *vita contemplativa*, where he chose the former and founded his monastery at Roscrea:[119] 'I will not live in an isolated place where guests or the poor cannot find me easily; but I will remain on this public road, where they can find me.' Crónán's interaction with the laity finds a mirror image in the Plan of St Gall as well as in Irish hagiography from Adomnán's life of Columba onwards: the *domus exterior* consisted of a church, guest house, hospice, school, cemetery, places where the materially poor could find support and the poor in spirit and sinners, forgiveness and peace of mind.

A key question is whether the task of pastoral care (*cura animarum*) of the laity was in the hands of monks, bishops, priests or a combination of all of them. Who preached to the laity and to what extent was the general populace cared for pastorally? After all, Etchingham has argued that the primary recipients of *cura animarum* were the *manaig* 'lay tenants' of the church, whom he regards as a para-monastic Christian elite.[120] In his detailed study of structures of pastoral care and the wide spectrum of church sites in Ireland, Ó Carragáin suggests that

sechtair sídh. **118** Gwynn, 'The teaching of Mael Ruain', pp 20–1 §33(b). Original: *Do ordaigh dhoibh gan sgeula d'fhiafraighe don mhuinntir thigeadh ar cuairt chuca no do chaint riu, acht na gnothaighi fa ttangadar amhain do dheunamh, do bhrigh gurb mor an urchóid do nid 7 an toirmeasg chuirid ar mheanmain antí da n-aisneidhtear na sgeula sin.* **119** Plummer, *VSH*, ii, p. 27 §xvii. Original: '*In locum desertum, ubi non possunt hospites et pauperes me facile inuenere, non ero; set hic in uia publica manebo, ubi ipsi poterunt inuenire me.*' This echoes the foundation legend of Kilmacduagh in which St Colmán mac Duach is coaxed out of an eremitical life in the wilderness by the local king Guaire Aidne to establish the greater monastery (Colgan, *Acta*, p. 245). **120** Etchingham, *Church organisation*, pp 363–454.

many churches established by kin-groups close to their settlements were, to a greater or lesser extent, monastic in ethos.[121] This deduction implies that hundreds of the lesser churches dotted throughout the country supported single individuals or communities who followed a committed monastic life. This lifestyle might offer a context for the text *Cidh as dech do cléiriuch?* 'What is best for a cleric?' edited by Paul Grosjean.[122] While reference is made to the monastery being close by and to fraternal love (*searc bratardai*), the cleric's responsibilities, apart from following a chaste, regulated and modest life (*lám fri bannscálaib, nemfrichnam édaigh … forcoimét riagla* 'hand against women, no regard for clothes … observing a rule'), include intelligible preaching of scripture (*réidh precept canóne, scélugud sgreptra*), practising instruction (*gnás forcetail*), dispensing alms (*tabairtt n-almsan*), acting as confessor (*tabairt coibhsen*), continuous learning (*léighenn grésach*). That the priest was not necessarily a member of a monastic community might explain the responsibility of donating alms to *caraid cráibthecha* 'pious friends', perhaps those living in a *dísert* nearby? A parallel system has been proposed by Wendy Davies for northern Iberia where a single priest and small groups of committed religious persons worked and lived together. Describing them as 'small rural monasteries', Davies differentiates them from medium and great monasteries in which a community lived a regulated day with a formalized commitment to following a rule.[123] This system prevailed until the eleventh century when different kinds of church relationships and institutions developed, offering a further parallel for Ireland.

I have argued elsewhere that the eighth-century text – possibly revised in the tenth century – *Ríagail Phátraic* reflects an attempt by Armagh to create an infrastructure of pastoral care in Ireland and that the one priest serving a *túath* was at the heart of this proposed organization.[124] These priests were educated as boys in 'the Psalms with their hymns, canticles and lections, and the rites of baptism and communion and intercession, together with the knowledge of the ritual generally'.[125] The stipend due to a priest was a house, a garden, a bed, a robe every year, a sack of seed with its yield and a cow in milk every quarter.[126] His responsibilities included conducting baptisms, distributing communion, praying for the living and the dead, saying Mass every Sunday, on every chief high-day and every chief festival (*cech prím-shollaman 7 cech prím-fhéli*). In addition, he had to celebrate all the canonical hours, chanting the 150 psalms

121 Ó Carragáin, *Churches in the Irish landscape*, p. 152. 122 Grosjean, 'Two religious pieces'. 123 Wendy Davies, 'Local priests in northern Iberia' in Steffen Patzold and Carine van Rhijn (eds), *Men in the middle. Local priests in early medieval Europe* (Berlin and Boston, 2016), pp 125–44. I wish to thank Professor Davies for bringing her article to my attention. 124 Bhreathnach, '*Vita Apostolica*', pp 6–10. 125 Gwynn, 'The rule of Céli Dé', pp 82–3 §62. Original: *na .III. cona n-imnaib 7 cantacib 7 liachtanaib 7 co mbathis 7 comma 7 gabail n-ecnarci 7 co n-eolas a n-ordaigthe olchena …* 126 Gwynn, 'The rule of Céli Dé', pp 80–1 §58; Catherine Swift, 'Early Irish priests within their own localities' in Fiona Edmonds and Paul Russell (eds), *Tome. Studies in medieval Celtic history and law in honour of Thomas Charles-*

daily, and make sure that the church was properly furnished with liturgical vessels (*aidme*), a task often associated in later times with regular canons.[127]

The appropriate education of priests was placed in the hands of bishops who played a pivotal role in the Rule of Patrick. Not all bishops were monks or celibate but during the period under consideration, some bishops, especially in Armagh, are recorded variously as also being anchorites, scribes and in charge of monastic schools.[128] It would seem, however, that the *fir léiginn* 'heads of schools', some of whom were monks but many others who belonged to hereditary learned families, were the educators of monastic novices, lay clerics and scholars of *senchas*, the 'history' of the Irish.[129] Johnston reads the rise of references to *fir léiginn* from the tenth century onwards as signalling a concentration of the control of high-level literacy in a few centres such as Armagh and Clonmacnoise to the detriment of the smaller schools of earlier centuries presided over by a single master. While there was an increasing use of the vernacular, she argues that *fir léiginn* must have also maintained professional standards of Latin literacy in the monastic *schola*. Indeed this interaction between the two cultures led to the production of vernacular poems based on the Bible such as *Saltair na Rann*, *Sex Aetates Mundi*, and the many vernacular apocryphal texts of the period.[130] To what extent the laity, apart from children handed over to the church as oblates, attended monastic schools is unclear. Ó Corráin in his consideration of the education of the twelfth-century king of Leinster, Diarmait Mac Murchada (d. 1171) forcefully countered the assumption of earlier historians that he had been educated in the monastery of Terryglass, Co. Tipperary, arguing instead that as was the custom among the aristocracy he was placed in fosterage and that the only training that he is likely to have received 'was in the normal warlike skills of the twelfth-century Irish aristocracy'.[131] He cites the law on fosterage *Cáin Iarraith*, and more specifically the associated glosses, which mentions skills – depending on the status and gender of the fostered child – such as herding, kiln-drying, wood-cutting, swimming, horsemanship and chess-playing for boys, kneading and sieving, sewing and embroidering for girls.[132] Provisions regarding compensation and fines for sons handed over to the church are listed in *Córus Bésgnai*, although no detail as to their programme of education is specified.[133]

Edwards (Woodbridge, 2011), pp 29–40. **127** Gwynn, 'The rule of Céli Dé', pp 78–81 §§57–8. Most of these requirements are listed in the law-tract *Córus Bésgnai* (Breatnach, pp 34–5 §38). **128** Armagh: 903, 929 (AU) 936 (AU, AI), 948 (AFM), 1005 (AU, AFM s.a. 1004), 1006 (AU, AFM), 1056 (AU, AFM). **129** On the concept of *senchas* see Francis John Byrne, '*Senchas*: the nature of Gaelic historical tradition' in J.G. Barry (ed.), *Historical Studies* IX (Belfast, 1974), 137–59; Edel Bhreathnach, 'The *seanchas* tradition in late medieval Ireland' in Bernadette Cunningham and Edel Bhreathnach (eds), *Writing Irish history. The Four Masters and their world* (Dublin, 2007), pp 17–23. **130** Johnston, *Literacy and identity*, pp 127–30. **131** Donnchadh Ó Corráin, 'The education of Diarmait Mac Murchada', *Ériu* 28 (1977), 71–81, at p. 76. **132** Kelly, *Guide to early Irish law*, p. 87. **133** Breatnach, *Córus*

The student master at Kells (*toísech na mac légind*, *toísech na scolóc*), Óengus Ua Gamna, whose name is not attested elsewhere, is mentioned in four of the Book of Kells memoranda dating between 1114 and 1154.[134] His office is separate from that of the *fer léiginn* of Kells, Guaire Ua Clucáin, who is also mentioned and who belonged to the most prominent family in Kells at the time.[135] His Uí Clucáin relatives, Ferdomnach (d. 1114) and Muiredach (d. 1154) were *comarbai* of Kells who also participated in the transactions recorded in the memoranda.[136] A survey of obits recorded in the annals between 900 and 1250 is instructive. During the tenth and eleventh centuries many churches are recorded – often only once – as having a *fer léiginn*,[137] but as the eleventh century progressed, the office was mainly confined to Armagh, Clonmacnoise, Clonard, Derry, Emly, Glendalough, Iona and Kells, with Armagh becoming increasingly prominent. By 1162, when the synod of Clane decreed that 'no one should be a *fer léiginn* in a church in Ireland, except an alumnus (*dalta*) of Ard Macha',[138] the office had virtually disappeared. What Armagh had set out to do throughout the centuries, to centralize ecclesiastical education, was for a period, at least, accomplished at that point. And, if the following damning Middle Irish verses echo the sentiments of those outside the privileged learned classes of both Irish and Latin, there were some who had little regard for their erudition:[139]

> I worry that the learned class
> Will go to painful Hell,
> And the person who does not read wisdom
> Will go to bright paradise.
>
> What is best for a senior (scholar)
> Is to rise very early in the morning,
> Chant the psalms commending himself [to God],
> Intercede on behalf of the dead …
>
> Learning philosophy is futile,
> Irish scholarship and commentary,
> Diligent literature and metrics,
> Little their power in the house above [i.e., Heaven].

Bésgnai, pp 242–5 §§79–80. **134** Mac Niocaill, *Notitiae*, VI, 9; X, 10, 28. **135** Ibid., V, 9; VI, 5; IX, 9; X, 8; XI, 16. **136** Ibid., III, 20; VIII, 10; IX, 7; X, 1, 25; XI, 16. **137** These include Agha, Aghmacart, Ardbraccan, Ardfert, Clonfert, Cloyne, Connor, Cork, Devenish, Dísert Diarmata, Downpartick, Durrow, Ferns, Fore, Inchcleraun, Killaloe, Killeigh, Killeshin, Kilmallock, Leighlin, Lismore, Louth, Monasterboice, Roscrea, Rosscarbery, Roscommon, Slane, Swords, Tallaght, Timahoe, Tomfinlough, Tory, Trevet, Tuam, Tuamgraney. **138** AU. Original: *Ocus is don cur-sin ro cinnset cleirich Erenn gradha ardespuic Erenn do chomarba Patraic, amail ro boi riam 7 na badh fer leighind i cill i n-Erinn nech acht dalta Aird Macha.* **139** Kuno Meyer (ed.), 'Ein Gedicht aus Additional 30,512, fol. 34b2 [*Is saoth lem in t-aos léigind*]', *Zeitschrift für Celtische Philologie* 9 (1913), p. 470. https:// celt.ucc.ie/published/G206005/

When the office of *fer léiginn* had declined it must have had an effect on the contents of monastic libraries and who gained possession of their books. That such collections existed is understood from a few rare annalistic entries. Derry with its books (*cona lebraibh*) was burned in 1095 and the same happened at Monasterboice in 1097 when its round tower (*cloicthech*) was burned with its books and many relics (*cona lebraibh 7 taiscedhaibh imdhaibh*).[140] In 1020, many of Armagh's buildings were destroyed except for its *tech screptra* (literally, the 'scripture house' understood to mean the library or perhaps scriptorium).[141] They also lost the books in the students' houses (*a liubhair i t-taighibh na mac leighinn*).[142] Inisfallen's books and church furnishings were saved in 1180 from the depredations of Máel Dúin mac Domnaill Ua Donnchada who took its gold and silver, mantles and cloaks.[143] Notably, the same fate befell the books and furniture of the Cistercian foundation at Newry in 1162, not long after its foundation in 1157.

SAVING THE SOULS OF THE ARISTOCRACY AND THEIR SUBJECTS

If a hierarchical ranking was in place among the religious inside the enclosure, as it was in society in general, that extended to dealing with the laity as well. As previously noted, the cleric in the text *Cidh as dech do cléiriuch?* had particular obligations towards the laity.[144] Furthermore, there is a distinction between those who served kings and the aristocracy and those who were more likely to serve the wider populace. The bishop, for example, was of the highest noble grade – as exemplified in the laws – and made peace and prevented conflicts between great kingdoms (*mórthúatha*). Senior bishops and abbots, the latter mostly laymen, did indeed carry out these duties, especially the officials of Armagh. Domnall mac Amalgaid, abbot of Armagh tried to mediate in the conflict between Muirchertach Ua Briain and Domnall Ua Lochlainn in 1097, 1099, 1102 and 1105, when he finally died in Duleek on his way from Dublin to Armagh. Cellach, archbishop of Armagh, attempted to make peace between the same two in 1107, 1109 and 1113, and between the men of Connacht and Munster in 1128. As might be expected, a bishop was to be versed in the holy scripture when ordained as no one was a successor of Christ unless knowledgeable in his law (*don Choimdi[d] ní comharba nech ná léga a recht*).[145] In his hands was placed the

index.html accessed 5 December 2021. Original: *Is saoth lem in t-aos léigind / do dul ind-ifern píanach, / is indtí nát lég ecna / do dul hi parrthus ngríanach. // Is ed is dech do senóir, / érge romoch ón dedóil, / cétul na salm dia eráil, / éccnairc na marb do gabáil. // Érlam grind is manach mín, / eccluiss dalta co nglanbríg, / combrugaid is deorad Dé, / úadaib dlegar apdaine. // Fogluim feallsamnachta is fás, / léigend Gáideilge 7 glúas, / litirdacht léir 7 rím, / is becc a mbríg is tig thúas.* See also Liam Breatnach, 'A verse on succession to ecclesiastical office' in Breatnach et al., *Lobháin*, pp 32–41, at p. 39. **140** AU, AFM. **141** ATig, AFM. **142** AFM. **143** AI. **144** Meyer, 'Regula Mucuta Raithni'. **145** Ibid., p. 313 §14.

spiritual healing of all, teaching young people to ensure that the devil would not lead them to a foul death and of course, preaching, dispensing of the sacraments and celebration of Mass.[146] The priest was expected to be hard-working, celebrating Mass, hearing the confessions of the dying and giving them communion and he was to be well informed in the church's rules and laws.[147] The *céli Dé* were to spend their time in the church at all hours, humbly observing rules regarding chanting, gestures, vigils, reading, prayer, Mass and the canonical hours.[148] Less distant from the laity, or at least penitent nobles, were the *anmchairde* and 'the Rule of Mochutu' concentrates on the potential for avarice among confessors given that they were likely to receive gifts for their service. They were also warned against eating and staying with the laity. Gifts were to be dispersed among the poor, elderly, widows and guests.[149] This concern about the dangers of being a confessor is also implied in 'The teaching of Máel Ruain'. Their penance might be ignored, the incorrect punishment meted out, and people might seek out more than one confessor to receive a lighter punishment.[150] Máel Ruain was strict also regarding receiving gifts from the laity (*áes tuaithe*) and insisted on handing them over to the poor. His reasoning for this reluctance to retain gifts is insightful in the context of monastic life and the power of confessors:[151]

> He did not find it easy to accept any presents from the laity. Some accept them in order to give them to the poor, because the laity would not give them to the poor. Laymen fancy that in order to get to Heaven it is enough for them to give something to their confessors, and that their confessors will thenceforth be at their command. However, for those whose aim is to be perfect it is better [not to accept such gifts].

The question arises as to who these *anmchairde* were and to whom they dispensed their spiritual guidance (*anmchairdes*), such that they were tempted to avarice. The annals may not include names of ordinary confessors, most likely local priests, who strove to improve the spiritual lives of the general populace, but there are plenty of obits of important confessors residing in major churches who served the ecclesiastical and lay elite alike. The relationship between king and *anmcharae* could be close, but as illustrated by the saga-like narrative entry in

146 Ibid., p. 317 §§49, 57. **147** Ibid., p. 316 §§38–9, 41–2. **148** Ibid., 313–14. **149** Ibid., 318–19. **150** Gwynn, 'The teaching of Mael Ruain', 42–3 §74; 'The rule of Céli Dé', 68–9 §17; 70–1 §28; 74–5 §37. **151** Gwynn, 'The teaching of Mael Ruain', 60–1 §105. Original: *Ni hurusa leis tiodhlaicthe ar bith do ghabhail on aos tuaithe: gabaid drong oile íad do chom a ttabhairthe dona bochtaibh, do brigh nach tiobhradaois aos na tuaithe dona bochtaibh íad. Dar lasna tuatadhaibh as lór doibh do chom dola go flaitheas Dé ní do thabhairt da n-anmchairdibh, 7 go mbid na hanmchairde aca ar a ttoil fein o shoin amach . Gidheadh as fearr don mhuinntir chuirios rompa beith foirbthe [a neamhghabháil].*

AFM describing the death of Niall Glúndub, king of the northern half of Ireland, at the hands of the Vikings of Dublin in 919 (AFM [917]), an *anmcharae*'s advice was sometime neither spiritual nor wise:[152]

> Céle Dabhaill, son of Scannall, successor of Comhghall, and confessor of Niall Glúndubh, was he who had requested of Niall to come to this battle; and it was he that gave the viaticum to Niall, after having refused to give him a horse to carry him from the battle.

This is the same illustrious Céle Dabaill, abbot of Bangor, who went to Rome in 928 and died there in 929. Perhaps the regret expressed in the poem attributed to him, quoted previously,[153] and his wish to end his years following a religious life was related to such unfortunate events while he was abbot of Bangor.

Other prominent royal confessors were Máel Suthain *anmcharae* to Brian Bórama (d. 1031) and more importantly, Domnall Ua hÉnna, bishop of Killaloe and spiritual and political adviser to Uí Briain kings, who corresponded with Lanfranc and Anselm on issues of church reform.[154] The death of Fingart, *anmcharae* of Corcu Modruad, a kingdom roughly equivalent to the Burren in mid- and north Clare, in 1128, suggests that lesser kings or their households also retained a confessor.[155] Most recorded *anmchairde* lived in larger monasteries such as Armagh, Clonmacnoise, Kells, Inis Cealtra, Glendalough, Emly, Lismore and Inisfallen, although the absence of obits from other monasteries may reflect a bias of the sources towards these prominent foundations. As discussed earlier, some were associated with specific churches in these complexes, some living as anchorites within their monasteries. In 1106, for example, Eochaid son of the *fer léiginn* Ua Fothadáin, a priest and noble senior and *anmcharae* of Dísert Chóemgin in Glendalough died. Not all were celibate. Tigernach Bairrcech, *comarbae* of Finnéin of Movilla (Co. Down), although described as an anchorite and chief *anmcharae* of Ireland, had a son Flaithbertach who succeeded his father in the same office (d. 1098).[156] This was the same Tigernach who sent the eleventh-century monk and anchorite (*inclusus*), Marianus Scotus, into exile as a *peregrinus* on the Continent.[157]

Eminent *anmchairde* were valuable for churches as they probably attracted kings and nobles to spend their final days in their midst, and to grant endowments for care given to them and for the redemption of their souls and those of their families. Certain dynasties show a predictable affiliation to

152 AFM [917]. Original: *Céledabhaill, mac Scandail, comharba Comhgaill, 7 anmchara Néill Glundubh, as é ro aslaigh for Niall tuidhecht don chathsa, 7 as é do rat a chuit fochraicce do Niall ar claomhclodh ech do thabhairt dhó dia bhreith féin as in ccath.* **153** AFM [926]. See pp 270–1. **154** *DIB* https://www.dib.ie/biography/ua-henna-domnall-a8744 accessed 7 December 2021. **155** AFM. **156** AU, AFM. **157** Peter Verbist, 'Reconstructing the past: the chronicle of Marianus Scotus', *Peritia* 16 (2002), 228–334.

particular churches. Domnall ua Néill (d. 980) died in Armagh as did Ardgar mac Lochlainn, king of Ailech (d. 1064). According to AU, Ardgar was buried in the cemetery of the kings (*in mausolio regum*) there. An additional note to AU 935 records the burial of an earlier member of the same dynasty, Conchobar mac Domnaill, *in cimiterio regum* in Armagh. The most spectacular description of a king's burial in Armagh is that of Brian Bórama, his son Murchad and the heads of two allies 'in a new tomb' (*i n-ailaidh nui*) after the battle of Clontarf in 1014.[158] Northern kings sought refuge and burial in Derry during the twelfth century with one of the most powerful of them, Domnall Ua Lochlainn dying there in 1121. Local affiliations also counted. In 979, Agda mac Duibcinn, king of Tethbae, died in Clonmacnoise in *Imdaid Chiaráin* 'Ciarán's bed', probably the church known today as Temple Ciarán, the reputed burial-place of the saint.[159] Lying on the saint's deathbed or grave was a privilege and what suffering or comfort one experienced during this ordeal depended on the saint's reaction and on the supplicant's spiritual state. Chosen to succeed Máedóc of Ferns, St Moling decided to sleep on Máedóc's bed – probably his grave – despite warnings not to do so, defiantly saying 'Whoever is bishop in his place, may fitly and rightly sleep in his bed'. But once he lay on the bed, he was seized with a dreadful disease and was only cured after pleading with Máedóc to relieve him. Once restored, he declared 'It is true … no man in the world in these days, however great his excellence and sanctity, is worthy to sleep or rest in the bed of Máedóc of great devotion'. The author deduces from this episode that this was a sign of God conferring great honour and dignity on Máedóc's relics on earth.[160] It was also a sign that the right to lie on a saint's deathbed – and hence grave – was an exclusive privilege. A monastery could become popular with the aristocracy as in the case of Lismore during the late eleventh and twelfth centuries, where the attraction was as much for spiritual reasons as it was material comfort.

Noble women were also attracted to these places and may have spent their final years as vowesses and nuns under the spiritual guidance of an *anmcharae*. Sadb, daughter of Ua Conchobair Cíarraige, from the southwest of Ireland, died in Lismore in 1126[161] while Derbforgaill, daughter of Tadc mac Gilla Pátraic, king of Osraige, and mother of Muirchertach Ua Briain and his brother Tadc, died in Glendalough in 1098.[162] As Tomás Ó Carragáin has demonstrated, Muirchertach was involved in the re-configuration of Glendalough between

158 AU. **159** AFM. Conleth Manning, *Clonmacnoise, Co. Offaly* (Dublin, 1998 2nd ed.). The Latin Life of Ciarán mentions Ciarán's stone pillow which was venerated by all (Plummer, *VSH*, i, p. 215 (xxxii)). **160** Plummer, *BNnÉ*, i, pp 275–6; ii, p. 267. Original: *Do raidh Moling: 'Gibe 'na' easpucc ina ionad, fhédadh sein doréir cora 7 ceirt codladh ina leabaidh' … 'As fir', ar sé, 'nach diongmála do dhuine ar domhan isin aimsir si, d'iomatt a mhaithesa nó a mhór-naomhthachta, codladh no cumhsanadh i lleabaidh Maodhóg mór-craibhtigh'.* **161** AI. **162** AFM.

*c.*1096 and 1111.[163] It may be no coincidence that his mother was buried there during that period. In the life of Monenna, reference is made to queens laying aside 'their royal rank, [who] came daily to her in supplication, prostrating themselves on the ground, and prayed that they might, if it were possible, by her command be enriched even by conversing with her'.[164] On their deaths, there were probably cemeteries set aside for virgins, widows and other saintly women. In 1082, *Reilic na Caillech* ('the cemetery of the veiled women') at Clonmacnoise along with its stone church and the eastern section of the whole complex were destroyed (*do losccadh*).[165] Two very rare inscribed grave slabs, one from Clonard, the other from Clonmacnoise, commemorate women (Figs 25 and 26). And, of course, the proximity between women and their confessors was often a source of concern. A colourful Middle Irish *exemplum* relates how a noble woman tried to seduce her handsome confessor who responded that he had lived since childhood in a monk's bed in God's service and had never known 'the sin with a woman' (*cin ó banscáil*). Undaunted, the woman threatened an unruly scene and the monk appeared to acquiesce by leading her to a tryst in the monastic garden (*lubgort*). Miraculously, the *lubgort* was crowded with all the local nobles, including her husband, and forcing her into greater embarrassment, the monk insisted that they make love in the midst of the crowd, but she refused. Teaching her a further lesson, the monk exclaimed that this crowd was as nothing in comparison with the hosts of Heaven, at which point Christ and the Blessed Virgin, and all the heavenly orders appeared in the sky. Needless to say, the woman threw herself to the ground and repented dramatically. He sent her off to her husband swearing that he would never have contact with a woman again.[166] Was this tale related to monastic novices or even monks as a warning about the potential perils of hearing noble ladies' confessions, or was it directed at wayward women who cast their eyes on attractive monks? The former seems more likely.

While seeking refuge or seeing out their years in monasteries, where did these noble individuals stay? They may have had their own lodgings or have stayed in the abbot's or *comarbae*'s house or they may have joined the monastic community in their *dísert*. For temporary visits, as with monasteries elsewhere, guest houses were part of the *domus exterior*. The *Tech/Lis Oíged* 'guest residence/house' at Armagh and Clonmacnoise is mentioned a number of times in the annals.[167] It appears to have been under the stewardship of hereditary families, such as the

163 Ó Carragáin, 'Rebuilding the "city of angels"'. **164** Life of St Monenna, III, pp 430–1 §1. Original: *Nobilissime etiam regine audita sancta Monenna deposito regali fastigio ad illam cotidie ueniebant suppliciter in terram prostrate et deprecabantur ut eius iussu si esset possibile uel etiam colloquio ditarentur.* **165** AFM. **166** Joseph Vendryes, 'Trois historiettes irlandaises du manuscrits de Paris', *Revue celtique* 31 (1910), 300–11, at pp 302–6. **167** AU: 1004, 1016.

Uí Flannacáin in the case of Armagh. Eochaid Ua Flannacáin (d. 1004), the eminent poet and scholar of *senchas*, was superior of the *Lis Oíged* of Armagh and of its dependent church of Cluain Fiachna (Clonfeacle, Co. Armagh).[168] The Uí Congaile and the Meic Cuinn na mBocht held the same office in Clonmacnoise. That the building of a guest house could be as a result of royal patronage is implied when Toirdelbach Ua Conchobair and the successor of Íarlaithe planned the episcopal seat at Tuam in 1127:[169]

> Toirdhealbhach Ó Conchobhair, overking of Ireland, and the successor of St Iarlaithe surround the (common) of Tuam from the southern end of Clad in Renda to Fidmag. Then the king gave an offering of land from himself to the church in perpetuity from Áth mBó to Caill Clumain, that is, the south-western half of the western part of Cluain, to every good cleric of the Síol Muireadhaigh who should dwell in Tuam, and the other half of it, at the guesthouse (*teach n-aighedh)* of Tuam, into the hands of the prior (*in t-secnabadh*).

Occasionally, an *anmcharae* or monastic scholar must have encountered the poor whose needs were immediate and not in the realm of spiritual guidance sought by the aristocracy. Obviously, there are many references to almsgiving but these often follow universal motifs and are devoid of emotion. One exception is the poignant Middle Irish tale about Dúnchad ua Braein, the abbot of Clonmacnoise who moved to Armagh and died there in 989.[170] He is described in AU as *optimus scriba et relegiosissimus*. In this tale, Dúnchad is credited with the last instance in Ireland of bringing someone back from the dead. A woman was at the door of the *reiclés* in Armagh with a baby boy in her arms (*bannscál baí i ndorus an reigleisa a nArd Macha 7 mac bec ana hucht*). She left the child's corpse on Dúnchad's doorstep – he was renowned for his miracles – and hid. Once Dúnchad saw the baby he realized that he had been placed there in the hope that he would be revived and presumably baptized, which is what happened as a result of Dúnchad's prayers. The woman reappeared thanking God and Dúnchad for the miracle. Much as a monastic community or individual might wish to be enclosed or dealing only with certain sections of society, the greater populace, poor and rich alike, were drawn to such places for a myriad of reasons, seeking physical assistance and spiritual comfort. They also often appeared with

AFM: 1003, 1031, 1093, 1106, 1116, 1128, 1155, 1166. **168** AU, CS, AI (1005), AFM (1003). **169** ATig 1127. Original: *Tairrdelbach Húa Conchobair, airdrí Erenn, 7 comurba Íarlaithe timchill coitchend Tuama da gualand ota cend descertach Cluidh in renda co Finnmagh. Tuc didiu in rí idhbairt ferainn uadha fen don eclais doghres ota Ath mbó co Caill Clumaín .i. in leath descertach íartharac[h] d' iarthar Cluana do cach cleireach maith do biadh do Sil Muiredaigh a Tuaím, 7 an leath aile di ac teach n-aighedh Tuama il-laim in tsecnabadh.* **170** Paul Grosjean, 'Textes hagiographiques irlandais', *Études celtiques* 2:4 (1937), 269–303, at pp 296–300.

violent intent as attested by the numerous annalistic references to raids on monasteries and the ensuing loss of life and destruction of buildings and property.

The impression given by the 'Tallaght dossier' is that the laity were to be kept at arm's length because they were irreligious and sinful. 'The monastery of Tallaght' warns that[171]

> A garment that is brought from the laity a demon accompanies it until it has been washed; and it is no protection to shake or beat it, but only to wash it.

The same text makes one of the few references to preaching to the laity, a task viewed as confined to those who were under spiritual direction.[172] Homilies and sermons rarely feature in this literature. 'The teaching of Máel Ruain' refers to two sermons (*seanmóir*)[173] being preached to penitents (*aos peannaide*) – who probably included lay penitents as well as monastics – one at midday on Maundy Thursday on Christ and the apostles eating the paschal lamb, the other in the evening on Christ's washing the apostles' feet. Two versions of the sermon on the last supper exist, one in MS Vatican Codex Reginensis 49 (ff 17–18v), possibly dating to the eighth or ninth century, the other in the early fifteenth-century *Leabhar Breac* [*LB*] (RIA MS 23 P 16 ff 48b-52b).[174] The *LB* version, an extensive retelling of Matthew 26.17–29 in Irish and Latin, occasionally hints at a context in which the homily is being preached to educate the laity, albeit probably a select cohort, as well as to a clerical and monastic audience.[175]

The saints' lives suggest that monastic communities following a regulated life, whose numbers were small and who may have considered themselves an elite, were not devoted to ministering and preaching among the general populace, whatever about among the extended ecclesiastical and lay elite. Few are ascribed preaching skills and the references are solely in AFM: Céle Dabaill, abbot of Bangor (d. 929), Gilla Críst Ua Morgair, bishop of Clogher (d. 1138) and St Malachy (d. 1148). An episode in the Irish life of Cóemgen might be an

171 Gwynn and Purton, 'The monastery of Tallaght', pp 154–5 § 67. Original: *Étach berar do áos tuati cotaot demun coronaoenastar 7 nídnanaid a crothad nach a flescad acht a nidi.* 172 Gwynn and Purton, 'The monastery of Tallaght', pp 156–7 §71. 173 Gwynn, 'The teaching of Mael Ruain', pp 60–1 §25. It is necessary to be cautious about the terminology used in this text as it has gone through the filter of a seventeenth-century Franciscan historian. *Seanmóir* 'sermon' is a term more of the early modern period than the early medieval. 174 Jean Ritmueller, 'The Hiberno-Latin background of the Leabhar Breac homily "In Cena Domini"', *Proceedings of the Harvard Celtic Colloquium* 2 (1982), 1–10. 175 For example, Robert Atkinson, *The passions and the homilies from Leabhar Breac. Text, translation, and glossary.* Todd lecture series vol. 2 (Dublin, 1887), p. 186, lines 5196–5202. A particular difficulty with the LB texts, apart from Atkinson's decision to separate the Irish from the Latin texts, lies with their dating and how many of them include pre-twelfth century material.

expression of frustration among others in the church about their resistance to undertaking pastoral care:[176]

> Seven years was Cóemgen without food but nettles and sorrel; and for a long period of years he never saw a single human being; and he would stand up to his waist in the lake saying his hours.
>
> One time when Cóemgen was reciting his hours, he dropped his psalter into the lake; and great grief and vexation seized him. And the angel said to him: 'Do not grieve,' said he. Afterwards an otter came to Cóemgen bringing the psalter with him from the bottom of the lake, and not a line or letter was blotted (lit. drowned).
>
> The angel told Cóemgen to go to teach and preach the word of God to the peoples, and not to hide himself any longer.

Later the angel pleaded with Cóemgen to leave his *cró* 'hermitage' which the saint would only agree to if he obtained a series of promises from God, among them that anyone buried on Saturday in Glendalough would receive remission of his soul.[177] And hence kings and nobles of Ireland and of Britain chose to be buried there for love of God and Cóemgen.[178] This vignette exemplified the various functions of a church like Glendalough, the eremitical and the material, a combination that must have led to tensions and opposing interests.

The complex, and as yet not fully resolved, nature of preaching in early medieval Ireland makes it difficult to distinguish material that was solely preached to a monastic community or to the extended ecclesiastical community – including Etchingham's *manaig* 'church tenants' – the lay aristocracy and the wider populace.[179] While no *homilarium* or *libelli* of homilies survive, texts that may in themselves have been homilies or were materials towards homilies and sermons do exist. Among them are the passions and homilies in *LB*, partly in the vernacular and partly in Latin,[180] some hagiographical texts such as the life

176 Plummer, *BNnÉ*, i, pp 126–7 §§13–15; ii, pp 122–3 §§13–15. Original: *Seacht mbliadhna ro báoi Caoimhghin gan biadh acht nenntocc 7 samhadh. Do bi Caoimhghin fada do bliadhnaibh nach faca sé aon duine; 7 do bíodh goa crios isin loch ag radh a trath. Fecht náon dia raibhe Cáoimhgin ag gabail a trath ro thuit a psaltair uadh isin loch. Ro gabh sniomh 7 toirrsi mor-adbal é. Ocus do raidh an taingel fris: 'nár bhad brónach', ar sé. Tainic an dobhrán iaramh go Caoimhgin, 7 tucc an tsaltair leis as iochtar an locha gan báthad líne no litre. Asbert an taingel fri Caoimhgin dul do proicept 7 do shenmóir breithre Dé dona poiplibh, 7 gan a bheith aga cleith ní búdh sía.* 177 This 'indulgence' has echoes of the so-called Sabbatine Privilege associated with the Carmelite Order and issued in a fourteenth-century papal bull, whereby through the intercession of the Virgin Mary souls could be released from Purgatory on the first Saturday after death. 178 Plummer, *BNnÉ*, i, pp 127–8 §20; ii, pp 123–4 §20. 179 On the tradition of preaching in early medieval Ireland at this time, see Brian Murdoch, 'Preaching in medieval Ireland: the Irish tradition' in Alan J. Fletcher and Raymond Gillespie (eds), *Irish preaching 700–1700* (Dublin, 2001), pp 40–55. 180 Atkinson, *Passions and homilies*.

of Patrick known as the *Vita Tripartita*,[181] and many apocryphal texts. Comparisons of Heaven and Hell and of Doomsday are particularly prevalent in the Irish homiletic tradition.[182] The themes covered in *LB* texts are standard and fit well with topics covered elsewhere, although dating *LB* texts is problematic, and it has yet to be established how much material pre-dates the twelfth century. Nevertheless, in comparing *LB* with Ælfric's homilies,[183] for example, the two include texts on the passions of John the Baptist, Stephen, Peter and Paul, Bartholomew and Andrew; the Epiphany, Christ's circumcision, Palm Sunday/Christ's entry into Jerusalem, Easter Sunday/the Resurrection, Pentecost; on St Michael and on the Lord's prayer. The main difference is that Ælfric's book is a *homilarium* and it follows the liturgical year, which is not the case with *LB*, which deals with themes such as almsgiving, fasting, temptation, charity, penitence as well as the image of the Cross and the *Sermo ad Reges* 'A sermon for kings'.[184] The texts on almsgiving, fasting and temptation appear to form a compendium that could have been used in a monastic setting, given the importance of these themes to a community, but they could also have been directed at the laity.[185] In her discussion of eschatological themes in the twelfth-century codex *Lebor na hUidre* (*LU*), in which she concentrates on three 'eschatological homilies' *Fís Adamnáin* ('The Vision of Adamnán'), *Scéla Laí Brátha* ('Account of Judgement Day') and *Scéla na Esérgi* ('Account of the Resurrection'), Elizabeth Boyle argues that such texts had different functions: versions of them could have been used as homilies, but of the *LU* versions she believes that 'they are not conceived of as serving a homiletic function, but rather are appropriate for private consultation … public reading in a non-liturgical setting, perhaps by an ecclesiastical *file* ('poet') or some other similarly qualified individual'.[186] Though homiletic in origin, they have been reshaped for a new purpose, 'which explicate themes of great importance for the rest of *LU*, including the body, judgement, and the end of salvation history'.[187] That the audience of the text on Judgement Day, *Scéla Laí Brátha*, may have been

181 Stokes, *The tripartite life of Patrick*; Kathleen Mulchrone (ed.), *Bethu Phátraic. The tripartite life of Patrick* [I. Texts and sources] (Dublin, 1939). **182** Carey et al., *The end and beyond*; Caitríona Ó Dochartaigh, 'Homiletic texts and the transmission of eschatological apocrypha in a medieval Irish context', *Apocrypha: International Journal of Apocryphal Literatures* 23 (2012), 141–53. **183** Benjamin Thorpe (ed.), *The homilies of the Anglo-Saxon church. The Sermones Catholici or homilies of Ælfric*. Vol I (London, 1844), pp xii–xiii. **184** Mullins, 'Preaching the Passion'; Brent Miles, 'The *Sermo ad reges* from the Leabhar Breac and Hiberno-Latin tradition' in Boyle and Hayden, *Authorities and adaptations*, pp 141–58. **185** Róisín McLaughlin (ed.), 'A Latin-Irish text on fasting in the *Leabhar Breac*', *Ériu* 60 (2010), 37–80; 'A text on almsgiving in RIA MS 3 B 23 and the *Leabhar Breac*', *Ériu* 62 (2012), 113–83. **186** Elizabeth Boyle, 'Eschatological themes in Lebor na hUidre' in Ruairí Ó hUiginn (ed.), *Lebor na hUidre. Codices Hibernenses Eximii 1* (Dublin, 2015), pp 115–30, at p. 128. **187** Boyle, 'Eschatological themes', p. 130.

monastic – as opposed to monks preaching it – might be discerned from the section in which the inhabitants of Hell are described as a perverted monastic community, ruled by the Devil as abbot, and the sinners his *manaig*:[188]

> There will be there, moreover, sorrow and groaning, weeping and wailing, sighs and screaming, from every single mouth. And ceaseless malediction from the sinners on their abbot, i.e., on the Devil, for what makes them suffer is everything they did at his instigation; and a malediction, moreover, from him on his monks around him, i.e. on the sinners, because his own pain is greater for every evil that they did through his persuasion, on account of him inducing every evil.

This is a mild version of what awaited the sinful religious in *Visio Tnugdali* and even Mac Con Glinne's condemnation of the communities in Kells and Cork, possibly indicating that this was one approach taken by those wishing to 'reform' Irish monasticism during the eleventh and twelfth centuries.[189] It would match St Bernard's claim about the Irish church that 'in the churches there was heard neither the preacher's voice nor singer's chant', leading to St Malachy's mission to follow St Paul in preaching the Gospel.[190]

In sum, that all those leading a committed monastic life were totally detached from the laity is an exaggeration. An exhortation on how to pray attributed to a certain Fergal, an anchorite, serves as an example of the other modes of instruction that were in circulation:[191]

188 Ibid., pp 119–20. This extract follows Elizabeth Boyle's translation. Original: *Bíaid dano and sin mairg 7 íachtad. gol 7 egmech. cnet 7 grechach. cach óenbeoil. 7 mallacht cen chumsanad ona pecthachaib fora n-apaid .i. for Díabul. ar iss ed dosbeirsium ic fulang phéne cach olc dorónsat triana aslachsom. Ocus mallacht dano úadsom fora manchaib imme .i. forsna pecdachaib ar is moti a píansom féin cach olc doronsatsom triana aslom forro oc aslach cach uilc* (LU 2434–40). 189 Brigitte Pfeil, *Die 'Vision des Tnugdalus' Albers von Windberg* (Frankfurt am Main, 1999): https://celt.ucc.ie/published/L207009/index.html accessed 15 December 2021, pp 27–30 (*De pena sub habitu religionis et ordine fornicantium. vel quacumque conditione se inmoderate coinquinantium*). Meyer, *Aislinge Meic Coinglinne*, pp 10–11, 114, 148; Jackson, *Aislinge Meic Con Glinne*, p. 9 §24. 190 Meyer, *St Malachy the Irishman*, p. 34 §VIII.16; p. 58 §XIX.44. 191 Grosjean, 'Textes hagiographiques irlandais. VI – Les prières de l'anchorète Fergal', *Études celtiques* 2:4 (1937), 269–303, at pp 282–4. Grosjean suggests that this text might date to the twelfth century. Original: *Ac so na seacht paidrecha tuc Feargul angcaire do nímh do slanugadh a dherbseathar 7 tsil Adhaímh uile, 7 gebe neach dogiabhadh iad do bedh a <a>num ar nímh. An ced pater dibh fo aithní an tsaeghail co hímshlan 7 fona cur ar neifní 7 fona mealladh 7 fona sarugadh arna aithne. An dara pader fo gradh Isu Crist 7 Muire bantigera os cínn gacha gradha a nímh 7 a talmhuin. An triomhadh paider fo oiburtibh na trocaire do coimlínadh co hímslan. An ceathramhadh paider fod mathar hEclaisi do reir gan íngnamh gan índeochadh. An cuigeadh paider fo lobugadh na n-uile pecadh dorínnis 7 fo dhibert na pecad a fuile do deoín co toileamhail 7 fod dhín arna pecaibh nach taíníc 7 nach dearnais fos 7 fod thshlanugadh arna cuig ard-gonaibh bais. An .vi. paider gan fhaicsin can tadhall an clochaín at- a n-ifernn sleamhuin. An .uii. paider a n-aigidh na seacht peaccadh marbtha 7 a n aigidh ficha 7 feirgi an Tigerna 7 reliqua.*

> Here are the seven Paters that Fergal the anchorite brought from Heaven for the salvation of his sister's soul and all Adam's descendants, and whoever recites it, his soul will go to Heaven. The first of these Paters, to recognize the whole world and regard it as nothing, having known it to disappoint him and to conquer him. The second Pater to love Christ and Mary queen over every grade in Heaven and on earth. The third Pater to accomplish works of mercy perfectly. The fourth Pater to be obedient to Mother Church without recourse to arms without vengeance. The fifth Pater for the remission of all the sins that you have committed and for the expulsion of sins that you committed willingly and voluntarily, and to protect you from the sins that have not arrived and that you have not committed yet and to save you from the great five wounds of death. The sixth Pater not to see, not to touch the small stone that is in slippery Hell. The seventh Pater against the seven mortal sins and against the anger and fury of our Lord. Finit. Amen.

This instruction may have been part of a general medieval devotion that placed a particularly strong emphasis on the Pater Noster, probably the prayer most widely known in societies everywhere, the primary prayer of Christianity. Repetition of the Pater Noster was often part of a penitential rite, and as noted by Eric Leland Saak in his edition of Jordan of Quedlinburg's fourteenth-century 'Exposition of the Lord's Prayer', 'the words themselves of the prayer took on magical powers, serving as a textual amulet as, among other things, protection against the devil and functioning as a demarcation of sacred space'.[192] This potential magical efficacy of anchorites' actions and prayers was a phenomenon in medieval – and early modern – society and hence, perhaps, the attribution of the prayer to Fergal 'the anchorite'.[193]

GIFTS AND OFFERINGS: THE ECONOMIC LANDSCAPE OF MONASTICISM

If the complex structure that Irish monasteries embodied is to be disentangled, understanding the structure of their economic organization is a necessary step. Tomás Ó Carragáin has made a significant contribution to the subject in his study of the various categories of pre-1100 churches that have physically survived or are known to have existed based on a detailed analysis of the

Finid. Amen. **192** Eric Leland Saak (ed.), *Catechesis in the later Middle Ages I.* The exposition of the Lord's Prayer *of Jordan of Quedlinburg, OESA (d. 1380). Introduction, text, and translation* (Leiden and Boston, 2015), pp 2–3. **193** Tom Licence, 'Anchorites, wise folk and magical practitioners in twelfth-century England', *History. The Journal of the Historical Association* (December, 2021). Online at https://doi.org/10.1111/1468-229X.13227 accessed

kingdoms of southern Uí Fáeláin, Mag Réta, Fir Maige and Corcu Duibne.[194] His model distinguishes between large ecclesiastical estates, often consisting of widely dispersed landholdings and mostly owned by large or medium-sized monasteries – the term *civitates* is used – and lesser churches, small ascetic monasteries, churches with or without a resident priest, family and royal churches (*túath* churches). The spatial relationships between churches and their landholdings and other churches, their positioning in royal and assembly landscapes is analysed as is the long-standing model of the 'monastic town' and its economic structure. The breadth of churches included in the study presents us for the first time with a comprehensive account of the physical reality of early Irish Christianity in all its complexity. Combining this study with other textual evidence has allowed for a clearer picture to emerge about the economy of monastic communities, whether they were living in large complexes or existing as separate ascetic monastic communities elsewhere. Among Ó Carragáin's conclusions for the period 800–1100 based on archaeology, landscape and textual evidence is that 'monasticism declined, or ceased altogether, at a significant number of substantial *civitates* but continued, or was revived, at others, facilitated it seems by the fact that they often managed to retain the bulk of their landholdings'.[195] This deduction accords well with the thesis of the present study that regulated, ascetic monastic communities were not as numerous as widely believed and that Ó Carragáin's 'middle-tier' churches were more often than not served by individual priests and rarely by monastic or even clerical communities. Where a monastic community existed, the likelihood is that it was rarely numerous even in more extensive ecclesiastical complexes such as Armagh, Clonmacnoise or Glendalough. If such was the case, then the economic needs of actual monastic communities can begin to be assessed and the sources of their subsistence identified.

What did a monastic community need to sustain themselves? Apart from the obvious resources such as food and clothing, it depended on their activities. If involved in teaching, the production of books and texts or maintaining a library, for example, it required dedicated buildings and a supply of vellum, tools, pigments, wax and source material.[196] The upkeep of shrines and relics could also be costly especially if it involved the enshrinement of relics in elaborate metal reliquaries, a trend that appears to have escalated during the eleventh and twelfth centuries. However, this cost was most likely borne by patrons, kings, aristocrats and senior ecclesiastics.[197] The economic needs of even a small community living in relative or complete isolation, those on High Island or Skellig Michael being the most renowned examples, had to be supplied with

15 December 2021. **194** Ó Carragáin, *Churches in the Irish landscape*. **195** Ibid., p. 268. **196** O'Neill, *The Irish hand*, pp 3–6. **197** Raghnall Ó Floinn, *Irish shrines and reliquaries of the Middle Ages* (Dublin, 1994).

building materials and the services of skilled builders. Sustenance for small ascetic communities was provided by their own services as confessors and intercessors to the aristocracy, provisions from their own long-standing landholdings, and royal and ecclesiastical patronage. Inis Uasail on Lough Currane, Co. Kerry, in the over-kingdom of Corcu Duibne (sub-kingdom of Áes Irrus Deiscirt), one of Ó Carragáin's examples, consists of a Romanesque church, a burial ground with large recumbent inscribed grave-slabs and a large drystone building which may have had a communal function such as a refectory. Ó Carragáin details what he describes as Inis Uasail's estate, the bulk of which seems to have been located north of Lough Currane with a detached estate at Glanhurkin on the coast around St Finán's Bay.[198] A community such as that of Inis Uasail was probably small and if they adhered in any way to the fundamental tenets of monasticism, especially poverty and eschewing wealth, then these estates were granted to support them, not necessarily as their possessions but as lands belonging to its patron (*érlam*) St Finán, chief saint of the kingdom of Corcu Duibne.[199] Ó Carragáin suggests that two used early medieval millstones located on the shores of Lough Currane in Termons townland, opposite the island, based on their size, may have been stored for use by the community in a mill of greater than average output.[200] As bread was a basic staple of the monastic diet, milling was probably an activity often undertaken by communities, although it could have been supplied from elsewhere. 'The monastery of Tallaght' quotes Elair of Inis Locha Cré (Monaincha) as declaring that the only bread brought onto his island was *arán Ruis Cré* 'the bread of Roscrea', implying that the latter's anchorites were fed from the main ecclesiastical complex 5km away.[201]

Among the other manual activities engaged in by monastic communities – and not many are alluded to either in the 'rules' or in the 'Tallaght dossier' – were gathering apples, splitting wood and brewing.[202] As discussed by Follett, other passages in the 'Tallaght dossier' describe a system of tithes and offerings received from church communities (*muinter*), some produce from church lands worked by tenants (*torad ind érlama*), accepted even if those owning the land or their labourers were impure (*anidan*). One reason for the tenants' waywardness may have been their reluctance to provide for the poor, a matter that is of particular concern in the 'rules' and the 'Tallaght dossier'.[203] The Rule of Ailbe is clear on the subject of wealth and almsgiving:[204]

198 Ó Carragáin, *Churches in the Irish landscape*, pp 88–99, see Figs 73, 86 (maps). **199** Ó Riain, *DIS*, pp 327–31. **200** Ó Carragáin, *Churches in the Irish landscape*, p. 94. **201** Gwynn and Purton, 'The monastery of Tallaght', p. 128 §4. **202** Ibid., pp 145 §49, 148 §55; Gwynn, 'The teaching of Mael Ruain', pp 60–1 §55. **203** Follett, *Céli Dé in Ireland*, pp 89–91. **204** O Neill, 'Rule of Ailbe', pp 108–9 §55. Original: *Dia ndénae-su a n-uile-se, / be ferr asa ferr, / bad for déirc ocus umli / congabthar do chell.*

> If you do all this, you shall be better and better;
> Let it be on alms and humility that your church be founded.

Nor was trading or seeking royal favour to be tolerated according to the 'Rule of Comgall', likely to have been composed in the ninth century:[205]

> Be not given to buying and trafficking.
> Let your piety to Christ be great.
> Beg not of a king in Ireland,
> If you be a client of Mary's Son.

How could this direction be followed in a society in which aristocrats related to kings held offices in the church? For example, the office of abbot of Armagh was hereditary and at times as powerful as that of the king of Ireland, and provincial kings scrambled to be patrons and to influence the ecclesiastical world. The position adopted by medieval mendicants in regard to possessions – in the sense of Latin *possessio*, capital goods such as building and lands – is instructive. Their disavowal of communal possessions meant that bishops, secular clergy and other orders were often handed control over possessions even if the mendicants used them or profited from them.[206] As noted previously, two of the Kells memoranda record rather similar arrangements for the pious pilgrims (*cráibdig*, *deorada*) of the *dísert* of Coluim Cille.[207] Eminent individuals including Máel Sechlainn mac Conchobair Ua Máel Sechlainn, king of Tara and Domnall mac Robartaig, *comarbae* of Colum Cille endowed the *dísert*. The memorandum conferred the blessings of Christ and Colum Cille on those who respected this grant – presumably by not disturbing the pious pilgrims – and a curse was placed on those who acted otherwise.[208] The second memorandum seems closer to the likely arrangement in place for Inis Uasail, as proposed by Ó Carragáin, and many other monastic communities. Tigernán Ua Ruairc, king of Bréifne (d. 1172), granted lands in the vicinity of Kells to God and Colum Cille to support the church of *Int Eidnén* at the time of its consecration by Máel Ciaráin mac Megáin, who died in 1148 as a noble priest of the *reiclés* of *Suide Choluim Cille* ('the seat of Colum Cille') at Kells.[209] This was a royal transaction and the solemnity of the grant was marked by the attendance of Máel Brigte Ua Fairchellaig, *comarbae* of Máedóc in Druim Lethan (Drumlane, Co. Cavan) with the reliquary, the Breac Máedóc. Tigernán Ua Ruairc's intentions were not entirely honourable, even though the particular grant may have been in hope of his salvation, as he was actively undermining the local dynasty, the Uí Máel

205 Strachan, 'An Old-Irish metrical rule', p. 200 §22. Original: *Nírba chreccach cundarthach; / do Chríst ba mór do gaire: / ní foigisríg i nÉre, / diamba chéle Maic Muire.* **206** Neslihan Şenocak, 'The making of Franciscan poverty', *Revue Mabillon* 24 (2013), 5–26, at p. 21. **207** pp 116–19. **208** Mac Niocaill, *Notitiae*, II, 12–17. **209** Ibid., VII, 24–5; AFM.

Sechlainn, by granting away lands in the kingdoms of Brega and Mide to the church, part of his strategy to extend his dominance beyond his own midland kingdom of Bréifne.[210]

The question arises as to who might have administered the estates granted to these small monastic communities, who collected the tithes and organized the agricultural endeavours that supported the monks and hermits? Donnchadh Ó Corráin's valuable study of the Meic Cuinn na mBocht of Clonmacnoise, mentioned earlier, points in the direction of the likely regulation and relationships involved.[211] Between the 950s and 1130s, they variously held the offices of abbots and bishops of Clonmacnoise, in charge of schools and scriptoria, teachers and heads of various institutions in the monastery. As literary men, they were chroniclers, hagiographers, canon lawyers, authors of vernacular texts and professional scribes. In Ó Corráin's estimation, 'they grew wealthy on the emoluments of office and on their income from church lands ... They were ambitious and acquisitive, perhaps rapacious'.[212] They were involved in planning Clonmacoise's architecture and landscape, laying down paved pathways and repairing the stone church.[213] The *Eclais Bec* (Temple Ciarán), the reliquary church, was retained by them as a family church, and two of them Célechair mac Cormaic and Máel Chiaráin mac Cormaic both died on St Ciarán's Bed (*Imdaid Chiaráin*) in 1134.[214] Their importance in the context of monasticism lies in the appellation Conn *na mBocht* 'Conn of the Poor' and Meic Cuinn *na mBocht* 'the descendants of Conn na mBocht'. Who were these *boicht* 'poor'? A number of annalistic entries identify them as communities living in Clonmacnoise or on its lands who were following a distinctive way of life. In 1031:[215]

> Conn na mBocht, superior of the *céli Dé* and of the anchorites of Clonmacnoise, first gathered together a herd for the poor of Clonmacnoise in Ísel Ciaráin and he donated twenty cows of his own to it.

Following Brian Ó Cuív in his understanding of 'the poor' (*na boicht*) of the monastery of Cork mentioned in *Aislinge Meic Con Glinne*,[216] Ó Corráin argues correctly that Conn na mBocht was not providing for a poor house in the sense of a refuge for paupers: 'rather it is a house of monks observing a strict vow of holy poverty, something like the mendicant orders of the later Middle Ages. Their house was propertied as an institution, but they held no property as individuals'.[217] Indeed this is reflected in the appellation *bocht* which was

210 Herbert, *Iona, Kells, and Derry*, p. 96; Denis Casey, *Tigernán Ua Ruairc and a twelfth-century royal grant in the Book of Kells* (Dublin, 2020). **211** Ó Corráin, 'Máel Muire, the scribe'. **212** Ibid., p. 25. **213** AFM 1070, 1104; AClon 1098. **214** AFM. **215** AFM. Original: *Cond na mBocht, ceand Celedh ndhé,7 ancoiri, Cluana Mic Nóis, do chéid tionól airghe do bochtaibh Cluana i nIseal Chiaráin, 7 ro edhbair fiche bó uaidh féin inntí.* **216** Brian Ó Cuív, 'Miscellanea: 1. "Boicht" Chorcaige', *Celtica* 18 (1986), 105–11. **217** Ó Corráin, 'Máel

frequently used in the late medieval period to describe the Franciscan friars as *na bráithre bochta* 'the poor friars'. Ísel Ciaráin seems to have been the ecclesiastical settlement at Bealin/Twyford, location of an inscribed high cross, in the barony of Kilkenny West, Co. Westmeath, in which there was a church and in which the *céli Dé* and the *boicht* of Clonmacnoise – if they were separate communities – lived.[218] That it was protected from marauding and disrespectful activities, as was the *dísert* of Coluim Cille in Kells, is understood from the outrage committed by the king of Mide in 1072:[219]

> A violent quartering of troops by Murchad mac Conchobair in Ísel Ciaráin and on the *céli Dé*. The steward of the poor (*rechtaire na mbocht*) was killed there. On that account, Mag nÚra was granted to the poor.

Here the estates of Ísel Ciaráin were added to by royal grant and it is clear from an annalistic entry in 1093 that Cormac mac Cuinn na mBocht acquired Ísel Ciaráin, its churches and its estates free from the ownership of the Uí Flaithén, another hereditary family, who also had held the office of abbot in Clonmacnoise.[220] Hence whatever material provisions were needed by the monastic communities of Clonmacnoise, particularly those of Ísel Ciaráin, were guaranteed by Meic Cuinn na mBocht, probably in return for the salvation of their souls. That this system operated in other large monasteries is implied by the obit of Colcu Ua hErudáin *cenn bocht* of Armagh in 1077.[221] Another member of Uí Erudáin, Cummascach, died in 1074 as a religious scholar (*suí in ecnai 7 crábuid*) and deposed abbot of Armagh.[222] It is a telling illustration of the workings of Irish monasteries, in which the community committed to a religious life was dependent on and protected by those who governed their monasteries, most likely in the hope of forgiveness of their sins and their future salvation.

Muire', p. 12. **218** SMR no. WM029–008 and WM029–009. **219** AFM, AClon (1069). Ó Corráin, 'Máel Muire', p. 20. Original: *Trén-coinnmhedh la Murchadh mac Conchobhair i n-Isioll Chiaráin, 7 forsna Célibh Dé, go ro marbhadh rechtaire na m-bocht ann, conidh de tuccadh Magh Núra do na bochtaibh.* Ó Corráin argues that Ísel Cíaráin and Bruiden Da Choca, the fictional banqueting-hall in the tale of the same name were the same site, possibly the Dillon Castle in Bryanmore Upper townland (NMS WM023-070- and WM023-070001). **220** Ó Corráin, 'Máel Muire', p. 21. **221** AU, AFM. **222** AU, AFM 1075. See AU, AI, AFM 1059–60.

CHAPTER 9

A new monastic culture flourishes

'ut sciam quid et quantum de terreno meo regno coelestis rex possideat ad opus pauperum suorum monachorum'

'... so that I may know what and how much of my earthly kingdom the king of Heaven may possess for the use of his poor monks'

This statement was made by Muirchertach Mac Lochlainn, king of Cenél nÉogain and claimant to the high-kingship of Ireland in a charter dating to *c.*1157 endowing the newly established Cistercian abbey of Newry.[1] In the charter Muirchertach was allowing kings subject to him to grant other lands to the monks for the welfare of their souls with the caveat that he had to consent to their gifts. As Marie Therese Flanagan has demonstrated, during the twelfth and early thirteenth centuries Irish kings adopted the use of charters to grant lands to foundations of new continental orders, especially the Augustinians and the Cistercians. Indeed, she describes the Newry abbey charter as 'the earliest surviving charter-text formulated in the European Latin tradition that was issued by an Irish king'.[2] This was a significant milestone for many reasons. Irish kings were creating new administrations to rule their kingdoms and in doing so were absorbing long-standing administrative practices from elsewhere. These practices were probably gradually introduced during the eleventh century, gaining momentum through increasing correspondence with external institutions and individuals such as the formidable archbishops of Canterbury, Lanfranc and Anselm, and Irish connections with the Ottonian and papal bureaucracies. The greatest impetus for adopting new administrative practices, at least by the twelfth century, originated in the waves of transformation in the church, not just in Ireland but throughout western Christendom.[3] Hence Flanagan argues, for example, that as elsewhere, the Cistercian monks of Newry drafted the charter-text and then presented it to Muirchertach for his approval and the attachment of his seal. And furthermore, it was drafted by an Irishman with a high level of competence in the Irish language, as evidenced by the accuracy of Irish personal and place-names.[4] The Newry charter also offers a

1 Flanagan, *Royal charters*, pp 291–305. 2 Flanagan, 'Saint Malachy and the introduction of Cistercian monasticism', 11. 3 Giles Constable, *The reformation of the twelfth century* (Cambridge, 1996; repr. 2002). 4 Flanagan, 'Saint Malachy and the introduction of

clue to the nature of Cistercian monasticism in Ireland just after the death of Malachy in 1148. The grant is confirmed 'in honour of the Blessed Mary and of St Patrick and of St Benedict, father and founder of the Cistercian order' (... *et sancti Benedicti patris et fundatoris ordinis Cisterciensis*). Flanagan – interpreting Constance Berman's revision of the origins and growth of the order in an Irish context[5] – regards *ordo Cisterciensis* as not referring to the order as a fully fledged institutional order but to a particular monastic lifestyle and liturgy. She suggests that the reference to St Benedict in this and other Irish charters, which is distinctive, was based on an Irish perception that a distinguishing feature of Cistercian monasticism was its origin in the Rule of Benedict.[6]

The Newry abbey charter and Flanagan's analysis of the text and its associated circumstances provide a critical basis for the discussion of monasticism in Ireland between *c.*1100 and 1215, the date of the Fourth Lateran Council. As ever with this subject, one can take many directions in an analysis of monasticism in Ireland during this period but in an attempt to shift the narrative from the standard one dominated by the chronology of new foundations and their associated styles of art and architecture,[7] this chapter addresses the effect of emerging spiritual and liturgical movements on Irish monasticism, the consequences of greater institutionalization of the Irish church on monastic offices and reaction to these changes, and, finally, the relationship between monasteries and the laity.

TRANSMISSION OF A RENEWED MONASTIC CULTURE TO IRELAND

The dominant 'new' monastic lifestyle to spread through Ireland during the twelfth century emanated from the Arrouasian canons, the Cistercians, and to a lesser extent the Premonstratensians and Benedictines, the first two introduced into the country by Malachy of Armagh.[8] This proliferation of 'new' international orders had been preceded by a Benedictine phase starting with the arrival of Dúnán, the first bishop of Dublin from Cologne to Dublin in *c.*1030 and continued throughout the eleventh century with the appointment as bishops of Irishmen who had been formed in English Benedictine houses. This phase petered out during the twelfth century and later new Benedictine houses such as Fore, Co. Westmeath, endowed by Hugh de Lacy on the site of an earlier

Cistercian monasticism', 12. 5 Constance Hoffman Berman, *The Cistercian evolution. The invention of a religious order in twelfth-century Europe* (Philadelphia, 2000). 6 Flanagan, 'Saint Malachy and the introduction of Cistercian monasticism', 22–3. 7 Roger Stalley, *The Cistercian monasteries of Ireland. An account of the history, art and architecture of the White Monks in Ireland from 1142 to 1540* (London and New Haven, 1987). 8 Flanagan, *Transformation*, pp 118–68.

monastery, were Anglo-Norman foundations.[9] The great pity is that Irish sources narrating the appearance and reception of different monastic and canonical rules and spirituality are meagre and in no way match the large corpus of tracts, sermons and letters that survive from elsewhere. Is it not possible at all to reckon how Arrouaisian and Cistercian canonical and monastic spirituality – bearing in mind the long-standing debate about the differences between them at this time[10] – was received in Ireland, and how their spirituality corresponded with existing monastic culture and spirituality. One approach is to examine the literature concerning leaders of the Irish church produced by major figures such as Anselm of Bec and Canterbury and Bernard of Clairvaux to see how they conveyed their distinct monastic cultures – much as Anselm and Bernard differed in their perspectives[11] – to their Irish confrères. Given the virtual absence of texts on the Irish side, the only possibility by which to measure the extent of their influence in various spheres is to identify themes in surviving literature and in the actions of the leading Irish ecclesiastics of the time.

Of all the monastic literature relating to the Irish church, Bernard of Clairvaux's friendship with Malachy of Armagh generated a sizable corpus of material, including letters, sermons and a *vita*.[12] Bernard's promotion of Malachy as representing a *speculum et exemplum* ('mirror and example') embodying an ideal of abbatial and epsicopal spirituality ensured that he became one of the best-known Irishmen on the Continent during the late medieval and early modern period.[13] If Bernard's letters to Malachy and to his brethren in Ireland following his death in Clairvaux are read as written primarily in a monastic and spiritual idiom,[14] even though they comment on practical issues, then the importance of personal transmission of ideas can be understood. Spiritual friendship was an essential part of twelfth-century Cistercian culture and Bernard's communications with Malachy and his descriptions of him in the *vita* and sermons after his death are replete with the language of loving *amicitia*.[15] In his study of Bernard's 'inner self', Brian Patrick McGuire explains the

9 Ó Clabaigh, 'The Benedictines in medieval and early modern Ireland'; Bhreathnach, 'Benedictine influence in Ireland'. 10 This debate has generated a lot of literature, see Caroline Walker Bynum, *Jesus as mother. Studies in the spirituality of the high Middle Ages* (Berkeley and Los Angeles, 1982); Michel Parisse (ed.), *Les chanoines réguliers. Émergence et expansion (xie-xiiie siècles)* (Saint-Étienne, 2009); Ursula Vones-Liebenstein, 'Similarities and differences between monks and regular canons in the twelfth century' in *CHMM*, pp 766–82. 11 The classic and most intelligible work on monastic culture remains Leclercq, *Love of learning*. 12 Leclercq and Rochais, *Sancti Bernardi opera*, iii, pp 307–78; Jean Leclercq, 'Documents on the cult of St Malachy', *Seanchas Ard Mhacha* 3 (1959), 318–32. 13 Flanagan, 'St Malachy, St Bernard of Clairvaux, and the Cistercian order'. 14 Donnchadh Ó Corráin in his treatment of Malachy and Bernard is unduly harsh, regarding Malachy, among other unpleasant characteristics, as one 'who could dissimulate, and if necessary bully.' In Ó Corráin's estimation, Bernard's image of the shy, withdrawn holy man 'is a pious fiction.' Ó Corráin, *The Irish church*, p. 79. 15 Burton and Kerr, *The Cistercians in the Middle Ages*,

significance of Bernard's promotion of Malachy for his own campaign to spread the *ordo Cisterciensis* in that through Malachy he could envisage the expansion of the *ordo* and especially 'the Clairvaux line of monasteries' in regions of Europe where he considered reformed monasticism had been unknown. But Malachy was not alone in this mission. In Scandinavia, Bernard's agent was Archbishop Eskil of Lund (d. 1177) who led a drive to found Cistercian monasteries not only to embed the *ordo* in that region but also as a means to forge an independent identity from the metropolitan of Hamburg-Bremen.[16] William of Rievaulx (d. 1145), originally from Yorkshire, became a monk of Clairvaux, acted as Bernard's secretary, and was chosen by Bernard to establish a Cistercian community at Rievaulx in Yorkshire, Clairvaux's first daughter-house in England in 1132. Bernard's letters to Malachy written between 1140 and 1142 are concerned with the founding of Mellifont, the first Cistercian monastery in Ireland.[17] (Fig. 27) Clearly, despite Malachy's pressure to train men quickly and send them hastily to Ireland, Bernard was insistent on their being formed properly:[18]

> When they have been instructed in the school of the Holy Ghost, when they are clothed with strength from on high, then they will return to their father to sing the songs of the Lord no longer in a strange land but in their own.

Despite Bernard congratulating Malachy on the spiritual and temporal success of Mellifont, his own monks from Clairvaux must have returned swiftly with more negative reports, as he urged Malachy to be vigilant 'in a new country amongst a people little accustomed to the monastic life and unfamiliar with it', somehow ignoring the fact that Malachy was himself a native of the 'new' country.[19] Given the narrative of this present volume on the continuing tradition of monasticism in Ireland to this period, this was harsh of Bernard but was in tune with his overall view of the Irish church as chaotic and backward – as opposed to Malachy the ideal bishop – and in need of a renewed process of conversion.[20] The letters are specific in their condemnation and requirements for reform, commenting on discipline, liturgy and observance, key elements of following the *ordo*. The monks from Clairvaux had left Mellifont not necessarily for reasons of purely ethnic tensions but because of disputes around monastic cultures:[21]

pp 142–3. **16** Brian Patrick McGuire, *Bernard of Clairvaux. An inner life* (Ithaca and London, 2020), pp 387–95. **17** Bruno Scott James (trans.), *The letters of St Bernard of Clairvaux* (London, 1953; repr. 1967), pp 452–5 nos 383–5. **18** James, *Letters*, p. 453 no. 383. **19** Ibid., p. 454 no. 385. **20** Diarmuid Scully, 'Ireland and the Irish in Bernard of Clairvaux's Life of Malachy: representation and context' in Bracken and Ó Riain-Raedel, *Ireland and Europe*, pp 239–56. **21** James, *Letters*, p. 454 no. 385. My italics.

> But perhaps those natives of your country who are little disciplined and *who found it hard to obey observances that were a little strange to them*, may have been in some measure the occasion of their return.

Even in sending Gilla Críst Ua Conairche[22] back from Clairvaux to become the first abbot of Mellifont in 1142, Bernard was anxious about his capacity to maintain the *ordo*:[23]

> I have sent back to you my very dear son Christian, having instructed him as well as I could *in the observances of our Order*, and I hope that in future he will be more careful about them.

In his final comment to Malachy in the same letter he advises him, again alluding to the observances of the order:[24]

> I would suggest that you persuade those religious who you are hoping will be useful to the new monastery that they should unite with their Order, for this would be very advantageous to the house, and you would be better obeyed.

Malachy was probably recruiting men from among existing monasteries in Ireland whose monastic traditions differed from the *ordo Cisterciensis*. Early in his career when re-founding a monastery at Bangor, according to Bernard's life of Malachy, he brought at Ímar Ua hÁedacáin's command ten brethren with him – presumably from Armagh – and once a wooden oratory had been built 'an Irish work finely wrought', 'from that time was service rendered in it to God as in the old days – the devotion was the same, the numbers were fewer'. Malachy was put in charge of the community by Ímar and he was both their leader and a model in following a committed life *(ipse rector, ipse regula fratrum)*.[25] In other words, Malachy led by example. Leadership was to the fore among the many reformers of the age, the concept of abbots guiding their communities *verbo et exemplo* ('by word and deed') being the fundamental cornerstone of highly influential monasteries such as Bec in Normandy, which boasted equally important abbots including Lanfranc and Anselm, or the later Aelred of Rievaulx (d. 1167) whose authority was felt in royal circles in England and Scotland. As part of the renewal of *RB* and the development of the *ordo Cisterciensis* respectively, they were viewed as living examples of monastic discipline and power.[26] That this message

22 https://www.dib.ie/biography/ua-conairche-christian-gilla-crist-a8730. **23** James, *Letters*, p. 454 no. 385. My italics. **24** Ibid., p. 455 no. 385. My italics. **25** Meyer, *St Malachy the Irishman*, pp 31–2 §VI.14 (Leclercq and Rochais, *Sancti Bernardi opera*, iii, p. 323). **26** Steven Vanderputten, 'Custom and identity at Le Bec'. See also Steven Vanderputten, *Imagining religious leadership in the Middle Ages.*

was acted on in Ireland is manifest from the calibre of church leaders who emerged during the twelfth century. The transformation was not due to Malachy alone. He could not have succeeded without the many individuals who were already working towards it, who worked with him and who succeeded him after his death in 1148. Máire Herbert postulates that the changed approach to episcopal and monastic leadership, especially as now understood in Armagh, is reflected in the twelfth-century homily on the life of St Martin of Tours.[27] Sulpicius Severus's life of Martin was known in Irish monastic circles from at least the days of Adomnán who used it as a model for his life of Columba. It remained in use, particularly in Armagh, through the centuries as evidenced by its inclusion in the early ninth-century Book of Armagh.[28] The twelfth-century vernacular homily was the latest manifestation of devotion to Martin in Armagh, a devotion that was heightened by the belief that Patrick was Martin's nephew. The homily's contemporary message portrays Martin as the ideal bishop 'whose ministry eschewed the trappings of authority and worldly privilege in favour of monastic humility and asceticism'.[29] No one could serve God and the world at the same time:[30]

> Now a multitude of the saints and the righteous of the Lord, both in the Old and New Testament, cast from them service and warfare on behalf of Devil and World and worldly wealth for service of the heavenly king, to wit, God. For no one could serve them both: even as he cast from him the earthly warfare for the heavenly warfare, to wit, the high Saint, noble, venerable, who has a festival and commemoration on the occurrence of this time and this season, holy Martin, high bishop of Tours.

There is a close similarity between the homily's description of Martin's 'inner life' (*a betha inmedónach*) – a life of constant contemplation of God in prayer and reading, his abstinence, moderation and poverty – and Bernard's description of Malachy's 'inner man' and the same moral message is directed towards those in ecclesiastical positions of authority:[31]

27 Máire Herbert, 'The life of Martin of Tours: a view from twelfth-century Ireland' in Michael Richter and Jean-Michel Picard (eds), *Ogma. Essays in Celtic Studies in honour of Proinséas Ní Chatháin* (Dublin, 2002), pp 76–84. One version of the life was edited by Whitley Stokes, 'A Middle-Irish homily on S. Martin of Tours', *Revue celtique* 2 (1873–5), 381–402, 508. **28** TCD MS 52 folios 192r–222v. See www.confessio.ie. **29** Herbert, 'The life of Martin of Tours', p. 82; see also Flanagan, *Transformation*, pp 101–3. **30** Stokes, 'A Middle-Irish homily', 386–7. Original: *Sochaide tra do noemaib 7 do firenaib in choimded etir fetarlaic 7 nufhiadnaïse rolecset uadib fógnum 7 miltnidecht do demun 7 do domun 7 dindmas in tshaegail. arfognam don rig némda .i. do dia. Uair ni coemnacair nech fógnam doib diblínib. Amal ró léic uad in miltnidecht talmanda ar in miltnidecht némda .i. in tardnoem uasal airmitnech diata líth 7 foraithmet inecmong nareesea 7 ina haimsiresea i. sanctus martinus episcopus (.i. noem martain uasal-epscop torindse).* **31** Stokes, 'A Middle-Irish homily', 400–1 §42 Original: *ní suided an*

> Martin: 'he used not to sit in a canopied place as some sit in canopied thrones'
>
> Malachy: 'From the first day of his conversion to the end of his life he lived with nothing of his own … even when he was a bishop. Nothing was appropriated or assigned to his episcopal upkeep from which the bishop might live.'

In practice, what is being reflected here are not monastic ideals that were unknown in the existing Irish monastic tradition but the separation between ecclesiastical authority – the bishop – and the inner man – the monk. One could exercise power in matters of morals, administration and jurisdiction but that power was not to be contaminated by accumulation of wealth, poverty of sanctity or neglect of the soul. For men like Malachy who were engaged in a fairly monumental task of transformation involving clever politics and often tense situations, their committed monastic life may have offered them spiritual confidence at times of turmoil.

In their overview of the Cistercians in the Middle Ages, Janet Burton and Julie Kerr identify key elements in Cistercian spirituality: Marian devotion, devotion to the saints, to cults and relics, the practice of mysticism and mystical experiences. The daily experience of God was to be regarded as a foretaste of the heavenly bliss that awaited the soul in eternity.[32] Monks were 'angels of God' on earth, a most pertinent link to Malachy, who changed his name from Máel Máedóc 'servant of Máedóc' (of Ferns) to Malachias, the Old Testament prophet whose name meant 'messenger' and 'angel'. It was no coincidence then that Bernard in his sermon at the burial of Malachy in Clairvaux declared that they had received him 'as an angel of God'.[33] Of course, this would not have been at all alien to Irish monks. Adomnán in his life of Columba, has many references to angels visiting the saint and certain places within and outside Iona's monastic enclosure being resorted to by angels.[34] Devotion to the Blessed Virgin was not unknown in Ireland and this devotion was part of monastic tradition, epitomized by the hymn *Cantemus in omni die* composed by Cú Chuimne of Iona (d. 747).[35] An Irish version of the *Dormitio* or *Transitus Mariae* was in circulation from around the eighth century and continued to be in use into the late medieval period.[36] As all Cistercian foundations were dedicated to Mary, their most

inad cúmdachta, amal tshuidit araile hi cathairib cumdachtaib; Meyer, *St Malachy the Irishman*, pp 57–8 §XIX.43 (Leclercq and Rochais, *Sancti Bernardi opera*, iii, pp 348–9). 32 Burton and Kerr, *The Cistercians*, pp 125–48. 33 Meyer, *St Malachy the Irishman*, p. 97. 34 Anderson and Anderson, *Life of Columba*, pp 214–17 [iii.22]; Sharpe, *Adomnán of Iona*, pp 208–8 [III 5]; Leclercq, *Love of learning*, pp 57–8. 35 Bernard and Atkinson, *Liber Hymnorum*, i, pp 32–4. For the most detailed study of devotion to the Virgin Mary in Ireland, see Peter O'Dwyer, *Mary: a history of devotion in Ireland* (Dublin, 1988). 36 St John D. Seymour, 'Irish versions of the *Transitus Mariae*', *Journal of Theological Studies* 23 (1921), 36–

immediate influence on Marian devotion in Ireland was to extend this reverence, as evident from the dedications in twelfth-century Irish royal charters.[37] Although no Irish evidence survives it is certain that, as elsewhere, she was accorded a special place in the liturgy of these new monastic foundations. An indication of Cistercian influence on patrons in their devotion to Mary can be understood from the gift of a chalice of gold bestowed on the altar of Mary at Mellifont in 1157 by Derbforgaill, daughter of Murchad Ua Máel Sechlainn and wife of Tigernán Ua Ruairc, who died in the same monastery in 1193.[38] Dedications to native Irish saints, which had proliferated in earlier centuries, were restricted. The Cistercian monastery at Monasterevin (Co. Kildare) was allowed in 1199 by the General Chapter to celebrate the feast of St Eimín, founder of the earlier monastery there. In 1206, St Brendan was added to the celebration of the feast of St Benedict in Irish Cistercian foundations. As both these saints were regarded as eminent monastic fathers and as Brendan was well known on the Continent, this may not have been particularly unusual. In 1255, Mellifont and its daughter-houses in Ireland were permitted to commemorate Malachy during vespers and matins while in 1268, the final sanction was given for the full celebration of his feast day with the lighting of three candles (*lampadibus*) and the preaching of a sermon.[39] The apparent exclusion of native saints, apart from the occasional nod to Patrick, Brigit and Columba, and an increasing promotion of international saints, often caused local saints to be revered at the sites of older monasteries, some of which became cathedrals housing their relics, and in the wider landscape at other monuments (e.g., crosses, lesser churches, oratories) and natural features (e.g., holy wells, rocks, pilgrim paths). It was also one reason why shrines and relics of native saints remained in the possession of hereditary families. St Bernard did not especially encourage popular pilgrimages either to Cistercian monasteries or by monks to pilgrim sites elsewhere. Relics were important to Cistercian communities and patrons endowed new foundations with holy objects.[40] Hence Domnall Ua Briain, king of Thomond, who endowed Holycross Abbey (Co. Tipperary) during the late twelfth century, may not alone have confirmed the dedication in its founding charter, a dedication wholly in line with Cistercian devotion to the Holy Cross, but may have even granted a relic of the True Cross to the abbey.[41] At a later period, Holycross Abbey had at least two reputed relics of the True

43; Herbert and McNamara, *Irish biblical apocrypha*, pp 119–31; Caoimhín Breatnach, 'An Irish homily on the life of the Virgin Mary', *Ériu* 51 (2000), 23–58. **37** Flanagan, *Irish royal charters*, passim. It is interesting to note that the Augustinian foundation in Ferns was also dedicated to Mary but not to St Benedict as in the case of other Cistercian foundations, Flanagan, *Irish royal charters*, pp 284–5. **38** AFM. **39** Geraóid Mac Niocaill, *Na manaigh liatha in Éirinn 1142–*c.*1600* (Baile Átha Cliath, 1959), p. 33. **40** Burton and Kerr, *The Cistercians*, pp 133–40. **41** It should be noted that in 1188 Leopold III of Austria also gifted the Cistercian abbey of Heiligenkreuz, which he had founded in 1133, with a relic of the True Cross.

Cross in its possession, which attracted many pilgrims, and which may have led to its church's restoration to provide a more worthy setting for its relics.[42] The splendid Romanesque portal at Clonfert cathedral was built *c.*1180 (Fig. 28), as has been suggested by Tadhg O'Keeffe, and if it was constructed to give the impression of an ante-church linked iconographically to the celestial city of Jerusalem,[43] then this edifice may have been a physical manifestation of renewal of a long-standing monastic foundation. More significantly, the memory of its origins were not forgotten as inside the church an elaborate Romanesque house-shrine was constructed that may have contained the relics of Bishop Maeinenn/Móenu (d. 572) and of his illustrious successor Cumméne Fota (d. 611/2). The relics were 'removed from the earth by the community (*sámud*) of Brénainn and were enclosed in a protecting shrine (*ro cuireadh scrín cumhdaighthe iompa*)' in 1162, possibly to coincide with the five hundred and fiftieth anniversary of Cumméne's death.[44] This ceremony is one of a suite of translations and enshrinements that took place during the twelfth century, among them the relics of Colmán mac Luacháin of Lynn, Comán of Roscommon, and Manchán of Lemanaghan.[45] As evident elsewhere in Europe at the time, relics, their enshrinement and ritual ceremonies such as processions and maledictions, were potent symbols of both ecclesiastical and royal authority.[46] What is curious about the Clonfert event is that the bishop at the time was Petrus Ua Mórda, a Cistercian who had been abbot of Boyle Abbey (d. 1171). As a Cistercian, his perspective on founders' relics probably differed from that of the *sámud*: theirs was rooted in the authority of the past, the Cistercian bishop's interest was in promoting past holy men to secure his episcopal seat and to sanction Cumméne and Móenu as acceptable twelfth-century saints.[47] Although relics of St Malachy were translated from Clairvaux to Mellifont and other Irish houses, his cult did not flourish in Ireland, unlike on the Continent where he was venerated widely along with St Bernard.[48]

42 Flanagan, *Irish royal charters*, pp 140, 310 n. 10; Stalley, *The Irish Cistercians*, pp 117–19. 43 Tadhg O'Keeffe, 'The Romanesque portal at Clonfert Cathedral and its iconography' in Cormac Bourke (ed.), *From the isles of the north. Early medieval art in Ireland and Britain. Proceedings of the third international conference on insular art held in the Ulster Museum, Belfast, 7–11 April 1994* (Belfast, 1995), pp 261–9. 44 AFM; for a description of a fragment of an elaborate Romanesque shrine from Clonfert see https://field-monuments.galwaycommunity heritage.org/content/archaeology/clonfert-house-shrine accessed 19 May 2020. This ceremony has been linked to the Augustinian canons of St Mary's de Portu Puro at Clonfert. See Christy Cuniffe, 'The canons and canonesses of St Augustine at Clonfert' in Browne and Ó Clabaigh, *Households of God*, pp 103–23, at p. 113, but as is clear from the circumstances above, the canons could not have been involved. 45 AU 1122, ATig, AFM 1170, AFM 1166 respectively. 46 Steven Vanderputten, 'Itinerant lordship. Relic translations and social change in eleventh- and twelfth-century Flanders' in Vanderputten, *Reform, conflict, and the shaping of corporate identities. Collected studies on Benedictine monasticism in medieval Flanders,* c.*1050*–c.*1150* (Zürich and Berlin, 2013), pp 193–214. 47 For the Cistercian view on relics see Burton and Kerr, *The Cistercians* pp 126–40. 48 Flanagan, 'St Malachy, St Bernard of

The idea that the monastery was the heavenly Jerusalem in anticipation, 'a place of waiting and of desire, of preparation for that holy city toward which we look with joy',[49] was a well-established concept in the Irish monastic tradition. In a letter to Malachy, Bernard asks him 'with the wisdom given you by the Lord [to] look for and prepare a site similar to what you have seen here, far removed from the turmoil of the world.'[50] Bernard understood the idea of the monastery as the heavenly Jerusalem 'in anticipation' and expressed it clearly in the following extract addressed to his novices:[51]

> He has become not a visitor who admired the city as a traveler (*sic*), but as one of its devoted inhabitants, one of its authentic citizens, not of the earthly Jerusalem … but of the one above, the free Jerusalem, our mother. And if you must know, I am speaking of Clairvaux. There one can find a Jerusalem associated with the heavenly one through the heart's complete devotion, through the imitation of its life, and through real spiritual kinship.

The monk, and indeed nun, could undergo mystical experiences by living in this earthly Jerusalem in the form of ecstasies and visions of Heaven and heavenly beings but this type of experience was not confined to Cistercians. It was a long-standing part of universal monastic culture, in Ireland as much as elsewhere, nowhere more clearly expressed than in the many episodes narrated by Adomnán about Columba. As so many medieval accounts of monastic ecstasy occur during the elevation of the Eucharist, Columba's visions suggest that such experiences were not an unknown occurrence in monastic Ireland. The problem lies in the absence of historic lived experiences such as survive elsewhere:[52]

> At another time, four holy founders of monasteries crossed over from Ireland, to visit Saint Columba, and found him in the island of Hinba. The names of these illustrious men were Comgall mocu Aridi, Cainnech mocu Dalon, Brénden mocu Alti, Cormac grandson of Léthan. They chose, all with one accord, that Saint Columba should consecrate the sacred mysteries of the Eucharist in the church, in their presence. He obeyed their command, and on the Lord's Day according to custom he entered the church, along with them, after the reading of the Gospel. And there, when the rites of the Mass were being celebrated, Saint Brénden mocu Alti saw (as he afterwards told Comgall and Cainnech) a kind of fiery ball, radiant and very bright, that continued to glow from the head of Saint

Clairvaux', 301, 310–11. **49** Leclercq, *Love of learning*, p. 56. **50** James, *Letters*, p. 453 no. 383. **51** Leclercq, *Love of learning*, p. 55; Burton and Kerr, *The Cistercians*, pp 143–7. **52** Anderson and Anderson, *Life of Columba*, pp 206–7 [iii.17]; Sharpe, *Adomnán of Iona*, p. 219 [III 17].

Columba as he stood before the altar and consecrated the sacred oblation, and to rise upwards like a column, until those holiest ministries were completed.

What may be understood from Bernard's engagement with Malachy and others in Irish monastic circles is that while his 'spiritual' language may have been unusual to some of his audience, most of the concepts were already known. Even his concerns about monastic observances cannot have been completely alien to a monastic audience already acquainted with an ascetic lifestyle. What was different was the introduction of the Cistercian liturgy, architecture and building methods and gradually, the institutionalization of the order that incorporated Irish Cistercian monasteries into an international network ruled by a General Chapter.

MONKS AND BISHOPS AS LEADERS OF THE IRISH CHURCH

A characteristic of the changes implemented in western Christendom between the eleventh and early thirteenth centuries is that they were influenced and in many instances led by monks and regular canons. The transformation of the Irish church was no exception to this paradigm (see Table 6).

TABLE 6: Irish bishops who were monks, canons or influenced by 'new' monastic orders

Name	Diocese	Order	Dates of Episcopacy
Cellach m. Áeda (Celsus)	Armagh	?Benedictine influenced; consecrated chapel (*reiclés*) of SS Peter & Paul in Armagh in 1126; buried in Lismore in 1129	1105–29
Máel Máedóc Ua Morgair (Malachias)	Connor Armagh Down (Ulaid)	Cistercian and/or Arrouaisian	1124–32 1132–6 1136–47
Gilla Meic Liac m. Diarmata (Gelasius)	Armagh	?Cistercian influenced Abbot of Derry	1137–74
Conchobar m. meic Con Caille (Concors)	Armagh	Abbot of chapel/ community (*reiclés*) of SS Peter & Paul in Armagh	1174–5
Tomaltach Ua Conchobair (Thomas)	Elphin Armagh	?Cluniac or Cistercian: see Mac Niocaill, *Manaigh liatha*, p. 23 n. 22	1180–4
Echdonn m. Gilla Uidir (Eugenius)	Armagh	?Augustinian canon Abbot of Bangor	1202–6

Name	Diocese	Order	Dates of Episcopacy
Gilla Críst Ua Morgair (Christianus)	Clogher/Louth (Airgialla)	?Augustinian canon Buried in church of SS Peter and Paul in Armagh	1135–8
Áed Ua Cáellaide (Edanus)	Clogher/Louth (Airgialla)	Arrouaisian canon Prior of Louth	1138–79
Gilla Críst Ua Mucaráin (Christinus)	Clogher/Louth (Airgialla)	?Augustinian canon Abbot of Clones	*c.*1187–93
Máel Ísu Ua Máel Chiaráin	Clogher/Louth (Airgialla)	Cistercian Abbot of Mellifont	1194–7
Gilla Tigernaig m. Gilla Rónáin (Thomas)	Clogher/Louth (Airgialla)	Arrouaisian canon Prior of Louth	1197–1217/18
Máel Pátraic Ua Banáin	Connor	Died on Iona in 1174	?1137–71/2
Gilla Domangoirt m. Cormaic	Down (Ulaid)	Augustinian canon Abbot of Bangor	1175
Máel Ísu Ua hAinmire (Malchus)	Waterford/ Lismore Cashel	Benedictine trained in Winchester	*c.*1096–1111 1111–35
Muirges Ua hÉnna (Mattheus)	Cashel Papal legate	Cistercian	post 1182–1206
Gilla na Náem Ua Muirchertaig (Nehemias)	Cloyne	?Benedictine	d. 1149
Laurentius Ua Súillebáin	Cloyne	?Benedictine Died in Lismore	1201–5
Gilla Áeda Ua Maigín	Cork	?Augustinian canon	1148–72
Gregorius Ua hÁeda	Cork	? Augustinian canon	*c.*1173–82
Mairín Ua Briain(Marianus)	Cork Cashel	Cistercian Died in Inishlounaght monastery	1223–38
Gillebertus	Limerick Papal legate	Unknown if monastic In correspondence with St Anselm At the court of Queen Matilda	*c.*1106–45
Brictius	Limerick	?Benedictine Mentioned in necrology of St James, Würzburg	fl. 1167–89

TABLE 6: Irish bishops who were monks, canons or influenced by 'new' monastic orders (*continued*)

Name	Diocese	Order	Dates of Episcopacy
Gilla Críst Ua Conairche (Christianus)	Lismore Papal legate	Cistercian Abbot of Mellifont Died in Cistercian monastery of Abbeydorney in 1186	1151–*c.*1179
Malachias	Lismore	Cistercian	1203–16
Dúnán (Donatus)	Dublin	Benedictine Formed in Cologne	*c.*1028–74
Donngus Ua hAingliu (Donatus)	Dublin	Benedictine Formed in Canterbury	1085–95
Samuel Ua hAingliu	Dublin	Benedictine Formed in St Albans	1096–21
Lorcán Ua Tuathail (Laurentius)	Dublin	Abbot of Glendalough Became an Arrouaisian canon	1162–80
Ailbe Ua Máel Muaid (Albinus)	Ferns	Cistercian Abbot of Baltinglass	1186–1223
Gilla na Náem Laignech	Glendalough	?Benedictine Died in St James, Würzburg in 1160/1	1152–*c.*1157
Finn Ua Gormáin	Kildare	Cistercian Abbot of Newry	d. 1160
Dúngal Ua Cáellaide (Donatus)	Leighlin	? Arrouaisian canon	d. 1181
John	Leighlin	Cistercian Abbot of Monasterevin	disputed election, 1198–1201
Felix Ua Duib Sláine	Ossory	?Cistercian	1180–1202
Felix Ua Ruanada	Tuam	Augustinian canon Prior of Saul	1202–35
Muirchertach Ua Flaithbertaig	Annaghdown	?founder of Premonstratensian house at Annaghdown	*c.*1202–41
Petrus Ua Mórda	Clonfert	Cistercian Abbot of Grellach dá Iach	*c.*1150–71
Florint Ua Máel Ruanaid	Elphin	Cistercian Abbot of Boyle	*c.*1180–95

This table offers only one dimension of a complex network. A number of these bishops may not have been affiliated to any new order but were influenced by monastic culture through their contacts with religious orders and probably led some form of committed religious lives. Gillebertus of Limerick is a notable example of this category insofar as there is no evidence for a monastic career but sufficient evidence for interaction with monks and their patrons.[53] Some notably belonged to existing ecclesiastical families and this trend continued among regular and secular bishops in Ireland well into the later medieval period. Most notable among them were Cellach mac Áeda of Armagh, Malachy, his brother Gilla Críst Ua Morgair of Clogher/Louth, Áed Ua Cáellaide of Clogher/Louth, Muirges Ua hÉnna of Cashel and Lorcán Ua Tuathail of Dublin. What did their monastic affiliations bring to their episcopal office and to the transformation of the Irish church? It is clear that from the time of Dúnán's appointment as bishop of Dublin in the early eleventh century the Irish church became part of wider conversations within western Christendom. While the literature usually consulted to depict the state of the Irish church from this period onwards – the letters of Lanfranc, St Bernard of Clairvaux's works concerning Malachy or Giraldus Cambrensis's works on Ireland – is highly critical of the state of the Irish church, it ignores a considerable change in the ecclesiastical culture of Ireland from the 1020s onwards. The view that caused historians to regard the Irish church as aberrant, mainly due to its perceived insularity and different culture and society, has changed in recent decades thanks to the assiduous scholarship of Marie Therese Flanagan and others. The narrative of the movement towards the re-organization of the Irish church, as revealed in the affiliations and careers of twelfth-century Irish bishops, was not unusual. Choices were made on the basis of the strong influence of a particular personality and their strategies – mainly prominent abbots, bishops and kings – external campaigns and orders, regional differences, and existing infrastructures. Clearly, in England, for example, powerful Benedictines spearheaded the eleventh- and early twelfth-century changes, and their influence extended into Ireland with the appointment of Benedictines as bishops. Lanfranc and Anselm no doubt had the authority of Canterbury in mind when meddling in the Irish church, but, as former abbots of Bec themselves, they were very much steeped in Benedictine monasticism. No more than those of Bernard of Clairvaux, their letters speak to the ideals and language of intense monastic culture. Their criticism of the peoples among whom they worked or were attempting to lead to salvation was not confined to the Irish. In a letter Lanfranc wrote to Anselm in 1073–4 one finds the customary plea of seeking brotherly support for his difficult mission in England:[54]

53 Aidan Breen (https://www.dib.ie/biography/gilbert-gille-gilla-gilli-a3470#) suggested that Gillebertus was a monk of St Albans 'given that when bishop of Limerick he dedicated chapels and a large cross in that monastery and a church in the adjoining town at the request of the abbot.' 54 Samu Niskanen (ed.), *Oxford medieval texts: epistolae Anselmi Cantuariensis*

> To Anselm, his lord, father, brother and friend, Lanfranc the sinner wishes God's everlasting salvation.
>
> Blessed father, you best know what is good for me. Whether coming to the land of the English or going to Rome, I have disclosed to your holiness everything that I thought my affairs made necessary to disclose at that time. Pray then, and urge your friends and household so to pray, that almighty God may either guide me to better success or lead my soul out of this prison of the flesh through a declaration of His holy name. *The land where we live is daily shaken by so many and such great evils and defiled by such adultery and other filth that virtually no man persists of the sort that would either take care for his soul or at least yearn to hear the wholesome doctrine of how to proceed towards God.*

The sentiments of the final sentence highlighted above in italics, written to describe the English, were also used to condemn the Irish by the same correspondents and others during this period.

When Anselm sent Máel Ísu Ua hAinmire back to Ireland in 1096 to become bishop of Waterford, he was sending a man trained in the Benedictine culture of Winchester under the tutelage of the formidable abbot Walkelin, one of those who acted as an intermediary during the long dispute between Anselm and William Rufus on the relationship between the church and the king.[55] In contrast to Malchus, whose sanctity and learning is acknowledged in Bernard's life of Malachy and in the letter sent by Muirchertach Ua Briain and others to Anselm seeking his appointment as bishop of Waterford, according to Eadmer, Anselm had doubts about Samuel Ua hAingliu, who was consecrated bishop of Dublin at Winchester in 1096.[56] Prior to his consecration, Anselm kept Samuel in his company for some time, carefully instructing him how he ought to walk in the house of God.[57] Anselm's doubts were justified and in 1101–2 he had to send him a letter censuring him among other misdemeanours for expelling the

archiepiscopi: letters of Anselm, archbishop of Canterbury, vol. 1: the Bec letters (Oxford, 2019), pp 70–3: letter i.22. online edition https://www.oxfordscholarlyeditions.com/view/10.1093/actrade/9780199697168.book.1 accessed 28 January 2022. Original: *Domino, patri, fratri, amico Anselmo Lanfrancus peccator perpetuam a Deo salutem. Quid michi expediat, beatitudo uestra optime nouit. In Anglorum enim terram ueniens siue Romam proficiscens omnia sanctitati uestrae reserraui quae reseranda esse tunc temporis pro mearum rerum necessitate iudicaui. Sic ergo orate, sic ab amicis ac familiaribus uestris oratum iri deposcite quatinus omnipotens Deus aut ad meliorem fructum me perducat aut de ergastulo huius carnis animam meam in sui sancti nominis confessione educat. Tot enim tantisque tribulationibus terra ista in qua sumus cotidie quatitur, tot adulteriis aliisque spurcitiis inquinatur, ut nullus fere hominum ordo sit qui uel animae suae consulat uel proficiendi in Deum salutarem doctrinam saltem audire concupiscat.* **55** R.W. Southern (ed.), *The life of St Anselm archbishop of Canterbury by Eadmer* (London etc., 1962), p. 91 n. 5. **56** Meyer, *St Malachy the Irishman*, pp 24–5 §IV.8; Gwynn, *The Irish church*, pp 99–115. **57** Rule, *Eadmeri historia novorum in Anglia*, pp 73–4.

community of monks from the church of the Holy Trinity (Christ Church cathedral) in Dublin (*item audivi quod monachos, qui in ipsa ecclesia ad serviendum Deo congregati erant, expellas et dispergas*).[58] Not only did he send a letter to Samuel but he also sent a copy to the trustworthy Máel Ísu Ua hAinmire to go in person to Dublin to intervene.[59] They were part of a Benedictine network of monks who knew one another and were actively influencing ecclesiastical affairs in Ireland as they were in many other lands. It was no accident that the Uí Briain kings, Toirdelbach and especially his son Muirchertach, in their efforts to modernize the Irish church turned to persuasive individuals from among Benedictines who were at the height of their powers during their reigns. The power of kings and nobles to promote a particular monastic order or to decide on the leaders of a reform cannot be underestimated.

That the 'Le Bec/Canterbury' Benedictine project in Ireland did not progress much beyond the death of Muirchertach Ua Briain in 1119 and certainly the death of Malchus in 1135 was in part due to monastic politics. As explained by Bernard, Malchus played an important part in Malachy's early formation, thus presumably introducing him to a Benedictine form of monasticism. He spent some years with Malchus 'so that in that lapse of time he might drink deeply from his aged breast, being mindful of the proverb: with the ancient is wisdom'.[60] If that was the case, then Malachy came to the *ordo Cisterciensis* already familiar with the Benedictine rule as followed in late eleventh-century England. Furthermore, according to Bernard, Malchus, along with Gillebertus, bishop of Limerick, who was acquainted with English Benedictine and Augustinian connections although he was not necessarily a monk, and who corresponded with Anselm,[61] forced Malachy to submit to their wishes to accept the archbishopric of Armagh, going so far as to threaten him with anathema.[62] The threat of anathema was a tool of coercion used by many prelates, including the dying Anselm in 1109 against Thomas II, archbishop of York, who continued to refuse to swear obedience to Canterbury. Yet Malachy did not take the Benedictine path but chose to introduce the *ordo Cisterciensis* and the customs of the Arrouaisian canons whose mother house was in the diocese of Arras. During the period 1132–8, adoption of the Arrouaisian customs by cathedral chapters was at its peak in Flanders and a small number of foundations were established in England and Scotland.[63] Malachy may have

58 F.S. Schmitt, *Sancti Anselmi Cantuariensis archiepiscopi opera omnia* vol 4 (Edinburgh, 1949), p. 192, letter 278. **59** Schmitt, *Sancti Anselmi opera* vol. 4, p. 191, letter 277. **60** Meyer, *St Malachy the Irishman*, p. 25 §IV.8. **61** Flanagan, *Transformation*, pp 45–6, 51–2. **62** Meyer, *St Malachy the Irishman*, p. 39 §X.20. **63** Brigitte Meijns, 'Les chanoines réguliers dans l'espace flamand' in Parisse, *Les chanoines réguliers*, pp 455–76, at p. 465; John Compton Dickinson, 'English regular canons and the Continent in the twelfth century', *Transactions of the Royal Historical Society* (ser. 5) 1 (1951), 71–89; G.W.S. Barrow, 'Scottish rulers and the religious orders 1070–1153', *Transactions of the Royal Historical Society* 3 (1953), 77–100; Janet Burton, *Monastic and religious orders in Britain, 1000–1300* (Cambridge, 1994; repr. 2000), pp

encountered the Arrouaisian customs as he travelled through Scotland and the north of England, possibly at the court of David I of Scotland, who had brought the canons to the royal burgh of Stirling (Cambuskenneth Abbey) in 1147 or by meeting canons such as David I's stepson, Waldef, grandson of Earl Waltheof of Northumbria.[64] Waldef was formed in the Augustinian house of Nostell, then became prior of Kirkham – both houses located in Yorkshire – and *c.*1143 entered the Cistercians and was elected abbot of Melrose in 1148. In that same year Malachy visited the Augustinian house of Guisborough in Yorkshire, founded by Robert de Brus *c.*1119, because he was aware of the religious men there who were leading a canonical life (*ducentes canonicam vitam*).[65] Waldef's monastic career in a sense mirrors that of Malachy, moving from a version of a *vita apostolica* with Ímar Ua hÁedacáin at Armagh, through a Benedictine education, to gaining an understanding of a more formal Augustinian rule and then the *ordo Cisterciensis*. This was an age of monastic experimentation, and whatever about the politics of gaining ecclesiastical and lay patrons to further church transformation, all these rules borrowed from *RB* and the customaries of Cluny and Cîteaux. The Arrouaisian and especially the Premonstratensian customs were that bit more austere than *RB*, or at least that was the impression put abroad by their adherents.

The most significant use of Arrouaisian customs in Ireland by Malachy was the move of the *sedes episcopalis* from Clogher to Louth and the institution of a cathedral chapter of regular canons there.[66] This decision involved Malachy and his colleagues, particularly Bishop Áed Ua Cáellaide, establishing the ideal *sedes episcopalis*. It is worth quoting the extract relating to Malachy that survives in the thirteenth-century Chartulary of Arrouaise:[67]

> Malachy of holy memory, archbishop of the Irish, making a journey among us, inspecting our customs and approving of them, brought transcriptions of our books and liturgical practice to Ireland, and he ordered almost all the clergy located in cathedral churches (*in episcopalibus sedibus*) and in numerous other places in Ireland, to respect and heed especially our order and habit (*habitus*) and divine office in the church.

52–4; Janet Burton, 'The regular canons and diocesan reform in northern England' in Burton and Stöber, *The regular canons*, pp 41–58; Andrew T. Smith and Garrett B. Ratcliff, 'A survey of relations between Scottish Augustinian canons before 1215' in Burton and Stöber, *The regular canons*, pp 115–44. **64** Meyer, *St Malachy the Irishman*, p. 51 §XV.36. **65** Ibid., p. 51; Flanagan, *Transformation*, p. 122. **66** P.J. Dunning, 'The Arroasian order in medieval Ireland', *Irish Historical Studies* 4 (1945), 297–315; Flanagan, 'St Mary's Abbey, Louth'; Flanagan, *Transformation*, pp 136–44. **67** Dunning, 'The Arroasian order', 300 n. 1; Amiens, Bibliothèque municipale MS 1077 f. 5 https://ccfr.bnf.fr/portailccfr/jsp/index_view_direct_anonymous.jsp?record=eadcgm:EADC:D48020232 accessed 1 February 2022. Original: *Sanctae memoriae Malachias, Hiberniensium archiepiscopus, per nos iter faciens, inspectis consuetudinibus nostris et approbatis, libros nostros et usus ecclesiae transcriptos suam in Hiberniam*

There are many noteworthy aspects to establishing a new *sedes episcopalis*, not least the move from the traditional episcopal seat of the diocese of Airgialla from Clogher to Louth determined by the alliance between Malachy and his brother Gilla Críst who was consecrated bishop of the diocese, Gilla Críst's successor Áed Ua Cáellaide, and Donnchad Ua Cerbaill, king of Airgialla. But why choose Louth as the site of a cathedral church housing canons following Arrouaisian customs and liturgy? Flanagan suggests that it had to do with this powerful alliance and that it is also reflected in the decision to found Mellifont also in the diocese of Airgialla.[68] If this move was planned post-1136 when Malachy was no longer in Armagh, the site could not have been more symbolic. It was not Armagh, where between his resignation in 1136 and the appointment of Gilla Meic Liac (Gelasius) as archbishop, Niall mac Áeda, a member of the dominant hereditary family and brother of the reforming Cellach mac Áeda, had attempted to seize the archbishopric. Yet Louth was closely associated with Armagh as its patron was Mochta, a reputed disciple of Patrick, and the saint's shrine and collection of relics were of some importance. In 818, Cuanu, abbot of Louth, who was exiled into Munster by Áed mac Néill, king of Tara, brought the shrine of Mochta with him. It seems to have been deposited in Lismore.[69] Although no reference is made to Mochta's relics it is possible, given Malachy's close relationship with Lismore, that they were returned to Louth at this time. Other relics, supposedly collected by Mochta in Rome, were translated (*ro togbhadh* AFM; *diar tocbad* AC) at a great chapter held in Louth in 1242 by Albert Suerbeer, archbishop of Armagh, and the abbots of the canons regular in Ireland to honour the order in Louth. Flanagan surmises that this may have been on the occasion of the one hundredth anniversary of the introduction of the Arrouaisian canons to Louth and may even have involved the commissioning of new reliquaries.[70] If that was the context, then a foundation date of 1142 would fit with the dating of St Mochta's house, the stone shrine-chapel at Louth, which, according to Ó Carragáin, would date to the mid-to-late twelfth century based on its architectural features.[71] Would such a 'native'-type building dedicated to an early saint have been appropriate to an Arrouaisian foundation even though its aim was to create a new model in Ireland? Arrouaise itself was established in the late eleventh century beside a tree known as *Tronc Bérenger* which marked the grave of Bérenger, one of three bandits who had killed two early Irish pilgrims Luglius and Luglianus. More importantly, *Tronc Bérenger* marked the boundary between Flanders and the kingdom of France in the late medieval period. Abbot Gautier of Arrouaise included a *vita* of the Irishmen in the abbey's cartulary during the late twelfth century.[72] Augustinians were also attracted to

detulit, et fere omnes clericos in episcopalibus sedibus et in multis aliis locis per Hiberniam constitutos, ordinem nostrum et habitum et maxime divinum in ecclesia officium suscipere et observare praecepit.
68 Flanagan, 'St Mary's Abbey, Louth', 228. **69** AI, AU. **70** Flanagan, 'St Mary's Abbey, Louth', 229. **71** Ó Carragáin, *Churches in early medieval Ireland*, pp 280–2. **72** Léonard

the cult sites of Anglo-Saxon saints such as Guthlac of Repton and Bertelin at Runcorn.[73] Thus Mochta, given his association with Patrick and the existence of relics purportedly from Rome in Louth, would have linked the new *sedes eposcopalis* with an important chapter in Irish church history and with Rome. Added to that was the likelihood that during the 1130s this area (known as a *trícha cét,* later cantred of Louth) became the demesne-land of the regional king, Donnchad Ua Cerbaill.[74]

The monastic career of Áed Ua Cáellaide's contemporary, Lorcán Ua Tuathail, also reflects the progression of monasticism in twelfth-century Ireland. He was trained in Glendalough by an unnamed local bishop who was his master and who taught him *verbo pariter et exemplo*.[75] He became abbot at the age of twenty-five in 1153 and archbishop of Dublin in 1162. His associations with new monasticisms being introduced into Ireland during his career are evident in his witnessing the charters of Diarmait Mac Murchada, king of Leinster who was his brother-in-law, granting lands and freedoms to Cistercians and Augustinians (Arrouaisians and unaffiliated regular canons) and also in the building programmes in the Romanesque style undertaken in Glendalough, most notably the priory of St Saviour's which was an Augustinian foundation, at least from the time of Lorcán's elevation as archbishop of Dublin.[76] (Fig. 29) Once he became archbishop he moved to re-organize the customs of the community in the cathedral of Holy Trinity, which may have transferred from Benedictine monks to secular canons during the twelfth century, to observe the Arrouaisian rule.[77]

Finally, the monastic background of Gillebertus (Gille), bishop of Limerick and author of the only substantial works relating to the twelfth-century re-organization of the Irish church to survive (d. 1145), is worth considering. Little is known about Gillebertus's life but the outline of his experience of monasticism is clear enough to provide a context for the views on monks expressed in his works.[78] His encounters with monasticism were not dissimilar to those of other

Dauphant, 'Frontière idéelle et marqueurs territoriaux du royaume des Quatre rivières (France, 1258–1529)' in Patrick Boucheron, Marco Folin et Jean-Philippe Genet (eds), *Entre idéel et matériel. Espace, territoire et légitimation du pouvoir (v. 1200–v. 1640)* (Paris, 2018), pp 313–28 (figs 3 and 4). https://books.openedition.org/psorbonne/41103?lang=en. **73** Andrew Abram, 'Augustinian canons and the survival of cult centres in medieval England' in Burton and Stöber, *The regular canons*, pp 79–95. **74** Paul MacCotter, *Medieval Ireland. Territorial, political and economic divisions* (Dublin, 2008), p. 236. **75** Grosjean, 'Vie et miracles', 131: lines 16–19; Mac Shamhráin, '*Prosopograpica Glindelachensis*', 86 §A39. **76** Flanagan, *Royal charters*, pp 37–105, 253–90; O'Keeffe, 'Diarmait Mac Murchada and Romanesque Leinster', pp 53–4. **77** This is not certain. It is not clear what happened after Samuel Ua hAingli expelled the monks in the early twelfth century. Flanagan, *Transformation*, p. 144 n. 139 notes that there could have been ambiguity about the role of the bishop's personal household and a separate monastic community. **78** Fleming, *Gille*. Marie Therese Flanagan makes many valuable observations about Gillebertus in both her volumes, *Irish royal*

Irish reformers. If he was appointed bishop of Limerick *c.*1106, it must have been with the acquiescence of Muirchertach Ua Briain who ruled the Hiberno-Norse city during the late eleventh and early twelfth centuries.[79] This must have meant that Gillebertus participated in Muirchertach's ecclesiastical initiatives from early on, and on the evidence of his correspondence with Anselm he was a member of the latter's ecclesiastical circle.[80] He is likely to have become acquainted with diocesan and parochial reforms in Normandy when he met Anselm in Rouen *c.*1106,[81] especially as regards the regular holding of diocesan synods as a means of creating a bond between the bishop and parish priests, and of controlling monasteries in benefitting from parochial dues. While these prescriptions were part of a common strategy of reforming prelates, the bishops of Normandy attempted to enforce their authority (*salvo jure episcopale*) by holding regular synods between 1080 and 1130.[82] Many of these Norman bishops themselves were abbots, and indeed confrères of Lanfranc and Anselm, but that did not deter them from controlling the power of the great Norman abbeys. Gillebertus is clear as to the role of abbots and monks in the church: they are the *oratores* and they were governed by bishops and were not to undertake *cura animarum*. He explains his reasoning in *De statu ecclesiae*:[83]

> The monastery is placed under the second pyramid and it has the abbot, who is himself a priest, at its apex and under him the six grades. Under his care are those who only pray because it is not the task of monks to baptise, to give communion or to minister anything ecclesiastical to the laity unless, in the case of necessity, they obey the command of the bishop. Having left the secular world to be free for prayer, their sole duty is to God.

Gillebertus's presence at the court of Queen Matilda *c.*1115x1118 – once in Westminster assisting at the consecration of her chancellor Bernard as bishop of St Davids and when he was summoned from London to St Albans for the

charters and *Transformation*. 79 See AI 1088, 1093, 1114, 1115, 1116; AU 1088; AFM 1084, 1088, 1101. 80 Schmitt, *Sancti Anselmi opera*, vol. 5, pp 375–6, letter no. 429; Fleming, *Gille*, pp 166–9. 81 Flanagan, *Transformation*, pp 49–50. 82 Grégory Combalbert, 'Le contrôle des clercs paroissiaux vu par les évêques normands (XIe–XIIe siècles)', *Cahier des Annales de Normandie* 35 (2009), 369–96. Gillebertus, for example, lists among the bishop's duties that he hold a synod twice a year for three days, in summer and autumn. By doing so, this brings the bishop and the priests of his diocese together to enable him to examine them in regard to their personal lives and pastoral ministry: Fleming, *Gille*, pp 160–1: lines 254–8. 83 Fleming, *Gille*, pp 148–9: lines 43–9. Original: *Secunda vero piramis subscribitur monasterium et habet in acumine abbatem et sub ipso sex gradus qui ipse sacerdos est atque sub his oratores tantum quoniam non est monachorum baptizare, communicare, aut aliquod ecclesiasticum laicis ministrare nisi forte cogente necessitate imperanti episcopo obediant. Quorum propositum est soli Deo relictis saecularibus in oratione vacare.*

dedication of chapels there – suggests that he was no peripheral bishop.[84] In such circles, Gillebertus would have encountered highly influential prelates, many of them monks and canons, and perhaps, more significantly, the queen herself who with her husband Henry I was an enthusiastic patron of the Augustinians.[85] They were instrumental in founding an Augustinian priory at Carlisle in 1122, which became a cathedral chapter in 1133 when Thurstan, archbishop of York, obtained papal permission for the creation of a new see. It should be remembered that this was a tight knit network. For example, the priory of Nostell appears to have had its origins in a community of hermits joined by the royal chaplain, Ethelwold, who later became the first bishop of Carlisle while retaining the priorate of Nostell. The community of Nostell was encouraged in their mission by archbishop Thurstan, and Henry I was their most senior patron. Robert, the first prior of St Andrews was a canon of Nostell as was Robert I, the first bishop of St Andrews.[86] While Gillebertus's *De uso ecclesiatico* and *De statu ecclesiae* may have been written at an earlier date, as papal legate until the 1130s these various experiences must surely have influenced his guidance of the Irish church.

The circumstances in which the second generation of Irish diocesan bishops found themselves could be regarded fairly as more complex than that of the initial generation of reformers.[87] They had to negotiate their way around multiple networks, be it their own kin, many of whom belonged to hereditary ecclesiastical families, the papacy, a world of increasingly institutionalized international orders, local and provincial Irish kings, recently arrived Anglo-Norman prelates and rulers, and the power of the English crown. The complexity of this world is evident from the many disputes that arose relating to Irish church affairs in the late twelfth and early thirteenth centuries. The career of Muirges (Mattheus) Ua hÉnna (d. 1206), archbishop of Cashel and papal legate is a case in point. Muirges was born into a family steeped in the church. Among his near relatives were the early reforming bishop Domnall Ua hÉnna, bishop of Killaloe (d. 1098) who corresponded with Lanfranc and Anselm and was counsellor to Toirdelbach Ua Briain, king of Munster (d. 1086). Other members of the Uí Énna included Gilla Pátraic, bishop of Killaloe who succeeded Domnall as bishop of Killaloe and was head of the monastery of Cork, Gilla na Náem Ua hÉnna a member of the community of Killaloe (*do muntir Cille Da Lua*) (d. 1095) and Conchobar Ua hÉnna, bishop of Killaloe (d. 1216).[88] As papal legate (1192–8/1201), Muirges had to preside over a church in which cultural and ecclesiastical conflict was rife.[89] He took an active interest in monastic matters. While he may not have been a monk throughout his life, he

84 https://www.dib.ie/biography/gilbert-gille-gilla-gilli-a3470. 85 Burton and Stöber, *Regular canons*, pp 4, 85, 245. 86 I wish to thank Professor Janet Burton for clarifying the chronology of the Augustinians in Carlisle for me. 87 Bhreathnach, 'The world of bishops in religious orders'. 88 Ó Corráin, 'Church and dynasty', 53. 89 Gwynn, *The Irish church*, pp 143–54.

died in Holycross Abbey, the Cistercian foundation whose charter he probably witnessed together with Domnall Ua Briain, king of Thomond and Gilla Críst Ua Conairche, bishop of Lismore and papal legate sometime between 1168 and 1185.[90] He was not loath to demote long-established churches as is evident by his heading the witness list of a charter in which Domnall Ua Briain granted the land of Mungret (Co. Limerick) to Brictius, bishop of Limerick, and the clergy of St Mary's cathedral Limerick.[91] Mungret's decline began during Muirchertach Ua Briain's reign and no doubt intensified as Gillebertus advanced Limerick as the *sedes epsicopalis*, Muirges finally sealing its fate with Brictius and Domnall Ua Briain. He also presided over the more spectacular gradual absorption of the diocese of Glendalough into the diocese of Dublin by the Anglo-Norman archbishop, John Cumin, an exercise that was finally accomplished in 1216 by Henry of London, archbishop of Dublin.[92] As an arbiter of disputes, for example, Muirges negotiated a settlement between John Cumin and the monks of St Mary's Abbey over contested lands.[93] He also arranged with John Cumin for the reburial of Hugh de Lacy's body in Bective Cistercian abbey in 1195, having brought it from the Columban monastery of Durrow where de Lacy had been killed in 1186. Ultimately, after much dispute his body was brought to join his head in 1205 in the Victorine Abbey of St Thomas the Martyr in Dublin.[94] Despite all these skills of negotiation and involvement in the new politics of the Irish church, Muirges was set aside as papal legate and even excommunicated in 1201. One reason for his fall from grace involved his family's interests in the diocese of Killaloe. He expelled a certain Diarmait or Domnall Ua Conaing, a member of a rival hereditary ecclesiastical family, from the diocese of Killaloe and replaced him as bishop with Conchobar Ua hÉnna, no doubt a relative of his. Ua Conaing died in exile in Cork in 1195. Such instances of the entrenched power of these hereditary families led Donnchadh Ó Corráin to question the extent of reform in the Irish church: 'Is this reform in any of the many senses in which the term is used and abused or is it agile professional adaptation to changing circumstances and new styles?'[95] Hopefully this volume has demonstrated that there is no single, straightforward answer to that question; quite the opposite, the situation was extremely complex and ever-shifting.

90 Flanagan, *Royal charters*, pp 136–7, 310–11 n. 13. **91** Ibid., pp 316–17. **92** Gwynn, *The Irish church*, pp 265–70. **93** John T. Gilbert (ed.), *Chartularies of St Mary's Abbey, Dublin* (London, 1884; repr. Cambridge, 2012), i, pp 145–6. **94** John T. Gilbert (ed.), *Register of Abbey of St Thomas, Dublin* (London, 1889; repr. Cambridge, 2012), pp 348–51; Gwynn, *The Irish church*, p. 148. **95** Ó Corráin, 'Church and dynasty', 62–3.

KINGS AND ADVENTURERS AS PATRONS OF THE NEW ORDER

A recent survey of 1,695 large urban churches across northwest Europe dating to between AD 700 and 1500 analysed the economic and social factors that drove peaks and troughs of cathedral building in various regions.[96] Although the evidence and the periods of construction booms do not coincide well with what is known about Irish church building during the same period, nonetheless the study provides valuable indicators for increased ecclesiastical building activity. Among these indicators were the growth of urban centres, the internationalization of trade conducted to the advantage of maritime towns and cities, significant changes in the exploitation of agricultural and human resources, and the stimulus of architectural innovation, especially with the rise of the Gothic style. In addition, state formation or consolidation and energetic ecclesiastical regeneration encouraged church building, while clearly, warfare, disease and natural disasters had the opposite effect.

Two examples, relevant to Ireland, are worthy of note. During the tenth and eleventh centuries the powerful alliance between ecclesiastical and lay lordships in the Rhine–Seine region promoted the founding of proprietary churches (*eigenkirchen*). Increased access to income from tithes and a re-organization of production mobilized substantial capital and labour resources that in turn allowed for major building projects to be undertaken. Such economic and social circumstances need to be incorporated into the Irish narrative. Why were kings such as Flann Sinna in concert with Colmán, abbot of Clonmacnoise, undertaking monumental projects such as erecting the Cross of the Scriptures and building the stone 'cathedral' at Clonmacnoise, the latter probably as an *eigenkirche* for the southern Uí Néill dynasty?[97] Did similar economic and political circumstances prevail in the Irish midlands, admittedly on a vastly smaller scale, as they did in the Rhine–Seine region? The same could be said of the church building programme of the Dál Cais dynasty beginning with Brian Bórama in the later tenth century and culminating with his descendants, especially Muirchertach Ua Briain, in the twelfth century. Despite endemic warfare during their reigns, these kings had the necessary resources to hand, including authority over the Norse towns of Dublin, Limerick and Waterford, to endow the building of stone churches and the enshrinement of saints' relics. The second example from the above-mentioned analysis is that of post-Conquest England where there was a surge in church building from the 1070s to the 1280s, a period of consolidation of Norman and royal power, of changes in land

96 Auke Rijpma, Eltjo Buringh, Jan Luiten van Zanden and Bruce Campbell, 'Church building and the economy during Europe's "age of cathedrals", 700–1500', *Explorations in Economic History* 76 (2020), 101–316. The survey covered Belgium, England, France, Germany, the Netherlands and Switzerland. 97 Ó Carragáin, *Churches in early medieval Ireland*, pp 121–3. 98 Raghnall Ó Floinn, 'Viking and Romanesque influences 1100 AD–

ownership, and also a highly energized church leadership intent on demonstrating their authority through monumental architecture. This surge in building, no more than the promotion of ecclesiastical and societal changes, had an effect on the situation in Ireland, perhaps best illustrated by the emergence and popular acceptance by the church and its lay patrons of Romanesque architecture.

The Romanesque period heralded a surge in activity in Ireland particularly during the twelfth century, manifested in stone sculpture and architecture, metalwork and manuscripts.[98] Stone churches built in the Romanesque style, large and small, urban and rural, are found throughout Ireland with concentrations in the east and southeast, along the Shannon and in the Burren (Co. Clare).[99] On the basis of the rare surviving inscriptions, normally carved on and around doorways, this surge in building resulted from exactly the same circumstances described in relation to the Rhine–Seine region in the eleventh century, that of an alliance between powerful ecclesiastical and lay lords. Eleventh- and twelfth-century Ireland saw a consolidation of power in the hands of provincial kings and as the movement towards church reform advanced, episcopal power increased. In his study of regional variations in church building in Ireland, Ó Carragáin correctly argues that ecclesiastical monuments are often the clearest expression of royal power, and no more so than during the Romanesque period.[100] How did this alliance affect monasticism? Monastic communities, among them eremitical communities, benefited from the surge in Romanesque buildings. Romanesque sculpture occurs both on the sites of existing communities and of new foundations of the continental orders. The building programme supported by Diarmait Mac Murchada, king of Leinster, in alliance with ecclesiastics such as Lorcán Ua Tuathail and Áed Ua Cáellaide, during the mid- to late twelfth century was extensive.[101] This included the small church – possibly even a mortuary chapel – of the Augustinian canons at St Mary's, Ferns, the very elaborate church of St Saviour's Augustinian house at Glendalough and Baltinglass Cistercian abbey, Co. Wicklow. Mac Murchada appears to have followed his episcopal advisers' preference for endowing new orders, as is also evident from his charters.[102] Cashel, Lismore, and possibly Kilmalkedar, Co. Kerry,[103] were endowed by Cormac Mac Cárthaig, king of

1169 AD' in Michael Ryan (ed.), *Treasures of Ireland. Irish art 3000 BC–1500 AD* (Dublin, 1983), pp 58–69; O'Keeffe, *Romanesque Ireland*; Rachel Moss, *The art and architecture of Ireland. Vol. 1:Medieval c.400–1600* (Dublin, New Haven and London, 2014), pp 46–9. **99** O'Keeffe, *Romanesque Ireland,* p. 34 (fig. 5). **100** Tomás Ó Carragáin, 'Regional variation in Irish pre-Romanesque architecture', *The Antiquaries Journal* 85 (2005), 23–56, at pp 25, 30–1. **101** O'Keeffe, 'Diarmait Mac Murchada and Romanesque Leinster'. **102** Flanagan, *Royal charters*, pp 37–105. **103** Richard Gem, 'The Romanesque church of Kilmalkedar in context' in NicGhabhann and O'Donovan, *Mapping new territories*, pp 101–113. Gem suggests that the fine Romanesque church at Kilmalkedar, Co. Kerry, was built around the early to mid-1130s, modelled on Cormac's Chapel at Cashel, its patron possibly being Cormac Mac

Munster and his allies, resulting in some of the finest Romanesque architecture in Ireland.[104] Romanesque architecture did not bypass smaller existing, and most likely eremitical, communities, many of them the *dísert* churches of larger monasteries. Examples include Clone, Co. Wexford, Friars Island, Co. Clare, Inchagoill, Co. Galway, Inisfallen, Co. Kerry, Inis Uasail, Co. Kerry and Monaincha, Co. Tipperary. Far from being in decline, therefore, these communities were vibrant enough during the twelfth century to have substantial, decorative churches built on their sites. Of course, their status may have been bolstered by bishops making claims for their own dioceses, as likely was the case of Inchagoill (Tuam), Inis Uasail (Ardfert) and Monaincha (Roscrea), where much larger Romanesque churches and other monuments were being erected as powerful displays of ecclesiastical authority.[105] While Irish kings and bishops were revitalizing existing monastic complexes during the twelfth century, at the same time they were building extensive complexes for the new orders, and in particular for the Cistercians. What might be regarded as the first phase of Cistercian foundations between 1142 and 1200 heralded a new era in Irish architecture supported mainly by Irish patrons. Of the surviving remains, Romanesque and/or early Gothic features are still evident at Mellifont, Co. Louth (1142: Uí Cherbaill, Uí Máel Sechlainn); Monasteranenagh, Co. Limerick (1148: Uí Briain); Inislounaght, Co. Tipperary (1148: Uí Briain, Uí Fáeláin); Baltinglass, Co. Wicklow (1148: Meic Murchada); Boyle, Co. Roscommon (1161: Meic Diarmata); Jerpoint, Co. Kilkenny (*c.*1160x1180: Meic Gilla Pátraic); Holycross (1180: Uí Briain); Abbeyknockmoy, Co. Galway (*c.*1190: Uí Chonchobair and Uí Chellaig); Corcomroe, Co. Clare (1194/5: Uí Briain, Uí Lochlainn).

The custom of patrons endowing a variety of monastic communities and orders was widespread in Ireland as elsewhere and it was based not alone on prominent lay individuals gaining status in society for their endowments but on the belief that the power of monastic prayer was effective when calling for divine intervention. While intercessory prayer has often been portrayed as a form of gift exchange between monasteries and the powerful laity which ultimately led to corruption, the position was far more complex. Renie S. Choy argues for an intersection between the interior prayer – the monk striving for *puritas cordis* –

Cárthaig's ally, Mathgamain Ua Conchobair, king of Ciarraige and Corcu Duibne (d. 1138). **104** Tadhg O'Keeffe, 'Lismore and Cashel: reflections on the beginnings of Romanesque architecture in Munster', *Journal of the Royal Society of Antiquaries of Ireland* 124 (1994), 118–52. **105** Roger Stalley, 'The Romanesque sculpture of Tuam' in Alan Borg and Andrew Martindale (eds), *The vanishing past. Studies of medieval art, liturgy and metrology presented to Christopher Hohler* BAR International Series 111 (Oxford, 1981), pp 179–95; Jessica Cooke, 'The Annaghdown doorway and King Ruaidrí Ua Conchobair: loyalty and patronage in twelfth-century Connacht', *Journal of the Royal Society of Antiquaries of Ireland* 150 (2020), 182–200.

and intercessory prayer as part of the functional world of relationships.[106] The monk's interior prayer has been discussed in Chapter 7 and here its extension to wider society is considered based on Irish evidence. Hagiography points towards the continuation in Ireland of the power of the *vir Dei* 'the man of God' – Peter Brown's 'holy man'[107] – and an increasing reliance on communal prayer. Saints' lives include many instances of miraculous interventions made on behalf of royalty and the poor alike. Even in lives that were revised in the twelfth and thirteenth centuries, of which there are many, the *vir Dei* predominates. On the other hand, the earliest Irish royal charters are examples of the role of monastic prayer in the relationship between donors and beneficiaries, that, as Flanagan explains, were not simply 'one-off acts' but were ongoing relationships 'that were supposed to last in perpetuity and to link him or her [the donor] indirectly to God, the Virgin Mary, or a specific saint.'[108] Land grants and building of churches gifted in exchange for intercessory prayers were intended to lend stability to the social order promoted by Gillebertus of Limerick (among many others at the time), that of those who prayed, those who worked and those who fought. The significance of these charters is not only that the recipients belonged to a new ecclesiastical phenomenon in Ireland, the continental orders, but that we come close for the first time to the individual voice of any Irish king. They may be formulaic texts that were drawn up by monastic or royal officials but they express the universal wishes of kings pleading for the remission of their sins, the salvation of their own and their family's souls. The charter issued by Diarmait Mac Cárthaig, king of Desmond to the church of St John the Apostle and Evangelist in Cork *c.*1167x1175, is more effusive than the rest in recording the grant to the church 'having experienced the fleeting nature of human memory and the unstable pomp of a transitory world' (*Labilem experti mortalium memoriam et labentis mundi pompam instabilem*). As Flanagan points out this is a somewhat old-fashioned pious prologue (*arenga*) that had been abandoned in Anglo-Norman charters but had survived to the twelfth century in German imperial charters.[109]

THE DEMISE OF THE OLD MONASTIC TRADITION?

The conflicting strategies of Irish kings, diocesan bishops, new monastic orders, Anglo-Norman adventurers and Angevin kings during the twelfth and thirteenth centuries made for a turbulent period for monasticism in Ireland. Reforming bishops and orders have been portrayed by Ó Corráin as asset stripping existing

106 Choy, *Intercessory prayer and the monastic ideal*, p. 20. **107** Peter Brown, 'Holy men' in Averil Cameron, Bryan Ward-Perkins and Michael Whitby (eds), *The Cambridge history of ancient history. Volume 14: Late antiquity: empire and successors, AD 425–600* (Cambridge, 2008), pp 781–810. **108** Flanagan, *Royal charters*, pp 242–3. **109** Ibid., pp 179, 334–5.

churches and monasteries of their lands and their tithes.[110] This is too simplistic a conclusion for a situation that was changing constantly and varied enormously from one locality to the next. It is a hugely important subject that needs detailed consideration in a future project but in the context of this volume, the fate of existing monastic communities might offer a hypothetical model for the greater project. How were the *dísert*-type monastic communities of *cráibdig* or *deorada Dé* assimilated into the re-organized church? How were they affected by new monastic foundations? Did the majority of them adopt some form of Augustinian rule? Did any of them survive to follow their traditional monastic lifestyle beyond the early thirteenth century? What happened to such communities elsewhere may be compared with Ireland. Kenneth Veitch's study of the reform of a number of existing native Scottish religious communities during the twelfth and thirteenth centuries is particularly applicable.[111] The study dealt with Loch Leven (Perth and Kinross),[112] Inchaffray (Strathearn, Perthshire),[113] Monymusk (Aberdeenshire)[114] and Abernethy (Perth and Kinross).[115]

The *céli Dé* of St Serf's, the island monastery on Loch Leven, like their brethren in St Andrews, were given a choice *c.*1150 by David I, king of Alba (d. 1153), and Bishop Robert of St Andrews (d. 1159) to become canons of the Augustinian house that they had founded there or be expelled. Their charter confirming the grant is instructive:[116]

> [David I] had given and granted to the canons of St Andrews the island of Loch Leven, that they might establish canonical order there; and the *céli Dé* who shall be found there, if they consent to live as regulars, shall be permitted to remain in society with, and subject to, the others; but should any of them be disposed to offer resistance, his will and pleasure is that such should be expelled from the island.

Unlike some of the *céli Dé* at St Andrews who held out for a lengthy period, the handover of St Serf's to the canons appears to have been accomplished without resistance. Veitch suggests that one reason may have been that unlike other *céli*

110 Ó Corráin, *The Irish church*, *passim*. **111** Kenneth Veitch, 'The conversion of native religious communities to the Augustinian rule in twelfth- and thirteenth-century Alba', *Records of the Scottish Church History Society* 29 (1999), 1–22. **112** People of Medieval Scotland 1093–1371 (PoMS database) PoMS, no. 616 (https://www.poms.ac.uk/record/person/616/ accessed 2 March 2022). **113** https://www.poms.ac.uk/record/person/1115/ accessed 2 March 2022). **114** PoMS, no. 8492 (https://www.poms.ac.uk/record/person/8492/ accessed 2 March 2022). **115** PoMS, no. 977 (https://www.poms.ac.uk/record/person/977/ accessed 2 March 2022). **116** Veitch, 'Conversion of native religious communities', 2, quoting from Archibald Campbell Lawrie (ed.), *Early Scottish charters prior to AD 1153* (Glasgow, 1905), p. 187 no. 232. Original: *Sciatis me concessisse et dedisse canonicis Sanctae Andreae, insulam de Lochleuen ut ipsi ibi instituant ordinem canonicalem et Keledei qui*

Dé communities such as those in Abernethy, the *céli Dé* on Loch Leven may have been ruled by an abbot in orders and not a lay abbot. Dubthach, abbot of Loch Leven is described in a document *c.*1128 as *Duftah sacerdos et abbas.*[117] As part of the foundation, Bishop Robert provided the canons with a basic set of books: a pastoral, a gradual, a missal, a lectionary, the Gospels, the Acts of the Apostles, some works of Origen (?) and Prosper, the *Sententiae* of St Bernard, treatises on the sacraments, the Bible, the Book of Solomon and the Song of Songs, the Book of Genesis, a collection of religious maxims and ecclesiastical rules.[118] Even if no evidence of such a collection survives from Ireland, at least the Loch Leven list furnishes us with some idea of the suite of books that were necessary for an Augustinian community, and indeed for many other communities of the period.[119]

There is no mention of *céli Dé* at Inchaffray. The community dedicated to St John the Evangelist is described as consisting of *fratres* and *hermites.* It would seem that *c.*1200 this community under the direction of a certain Máel Ísu, most likely a member of the community, and in accordance with the wishes of their patrons Gilla Brigte, earl of Strathearn and his wife Matilda d'Aubigny, and the bishops of Dunblane and Dunkeld, became Augustinian canons.[120] In return, they were granted authority over five existing churches, which Veitch surmises may have been part of Gilla Brigte's strategy of accelerating a process 'whereby the brethren were adopting a more pastoral role and thus ensuring the parochialization of his earldom was undertaken by loyal, local clergy'.[121]

As at St Andrews, the *céli Dé* of Monymusk fell foul of William de Malveisin, bishop of St Andrews (d. 1238) which led to a papal judgement *c.*1210 x 1211 about their rights which was agreed amicably between the parties. The judgement offers a valuable cameo of the community and the accommodation between it and the bishop, including the uneasy relationship between the two:[122]

ibidem inventi fuerint si regulariter vivere voluerint in pace cum eis et sub eis maneant et si quis illorum ad hoc resistere voluerit volo et praecipio ut ab insula ejiciatur. **117** Lawrie, *Early Scottish charters*, pp 66–7 no. 80. Interestingly, one of the jurors involved in the case outlined in the document was Muiredach the venerable old Irishman (*Morrehat vir venerandae senectutis et hiberniensis*). It is not clear from the witness list if Muiredach was a member of the *céli Dé* community or or a lay juror or clerk. **118** Lawrie, *Early Scottish charters*, pp 210 no. 263. Original: *Et cum his libris, id est cum pastorali, graduali, missali, origine, sententiis abbatis Claruallensis, tribus quaternionibus de sacramentis, cum parte bibliotecae, cum lectionario, cum Actibus Apostolorum, textu evangeliorum Prospero, tribus libris Salomonis, glosis de canticis canticorum, interpretationibus dictionum, collectione sententiarum, expositione super Genesim, exceptionibus ecclesiasticarum regularum.* **119** For an idea about Irish foundations, see Colmán Ó Clabaigh, 'Community, commemoration and confraternity', pp 240–3. **120** Veitch, 'Conversion of native religious communities', 5–10; William Alexander Lindsay, John Dowden and John Maitland Thomson (eds), *Charters, bulls and other documents relating to the Abbey of Inchaffray* (Edinburgh, 1908), pp 6–8 no. 9. PoMS, no. 1115 (https://www.poms.ac.uk/record/person/1115/ accessed 3 March 2022. **121** Veitch, 'Conversion of native religious communities', 10. **122** www.poms.ac.uk/record/source/3980/ accessed 3 March 2022

> The bishop granted that the *céli Dé* may have, henceforth, one refectory and one dormitory and one oratory without a cemetery. They shall receive the bodies of the *céli Dé* and of clerics or laymen staying with them, into the cemetery of the parish church of Monymusk where they shall be buried, just as they are accustomed to being buried, saving all rights to the mother church. Twelve *céli Dé* shall be there and Brice shall be the thirteenth, who the *céli Dé* shall present to the bishop of St Andrews so that he may be their master or prior. At their resignation or death, the *céli Dé* shall elect three from their fellow *céli Dé*, by their common assent, and they shall present whoever to the bishop of St Andrews, so that by his wish, from the three, he may choose one as prior or master. *The céli Dé shall not be permitted to the livelihood or order of monks or of regular canons without the assent of the same bishop, or his successors*, [and] neither to exceed the named number of *céli Dé*. At the resignation or death, any of the *céli Dé* can substitute anyone up to the stated number. Whoever the *céli Dé* present to the bishop of St Andrews to be deputy shall swear that he will hold and serve this composition faithfully and without deceit or evil trickery.

The sentence highlighted in the above passage is significant in that it underlines again the key role of bishops in controlling the number, size and type of monastic foundations in their dioceses. It would appear that the *céli Dé* in Monymusk went through a period of transition as they are referred to in some documents as *Keledei sive canonici* ('*céli Dé* or canons') or *canonici qui Keledei dicuntur* ('canons who are called *céli Dé*').[123] Their conversion to canons was achieved by May 1245 when Pope Innocent IV issued a bull addressing it to the prior and convent of Monymusk of the order of St Augustine.[124]

Abernethy's structure was similar to that of many Irish monasteries with lay abbots, priests, lectors and *céli Dé* in charge of the economic, liturgical, learning and spirituality of the church. The *céli Dé* community at Abernethy lasted until *c.*1239 but had disappeared by 1273.[125] One factor in the eclipse of Abernethy, which is again relevant to Ireland, was the rise further north of the Tironensian abbey of Arbroath founded by William I, king of the Scots, in 1178 with the bishops of St Andrews to the east constantly expanding their authority.[126]

What happened in Scotland, and indeed in England where hermitages were often converted into Augustinian priories or taken over by bishops and other

translation from *Liber cartarum Prioratus Sancti Andree in Scotia* (Edinburgh, 1841), p. 371. I have not included the original here due to the length of the text. **123** Veitch, 'Conversion of native religious communities', 12. **124** Ibid., 15 (www.poms.ac.uk/record/source/3244/ accessed 3 March 2022); *Liber cartarum Prioratus Sancti Andree*, pp 372–3. **125** Veitch, 'Conversion of native religious communities', 16–17. PoMS, no. 4249 (www.poms.ac.uk/record/person/4249/ accessed 3 March 2022). **126** PoMS, no. 41 (www.poms.ac.uk/record/person/41/ accessed 3 March 2022).

religious orders[127] and in Wales where the existing culdee (*céli Dé*) hermitages linked to larger communities (*clasau*) were also transformed into Augustinian communities,[128] corresponds to the myriad of monastic transformations that happened in twelfth- and thirteenth-century Ireland. I have argued elsewhere that the common perception of an Augustinian takeover from *c.*1140 is based on a simplistic reading of Gwynn and Hadcock's invaluable volume (*MRHI*) and an over-reliance on the evidence of Sir James Ware and Mervyn Archdall's works on Irish monasticism. This approach has misinterpreted a far more complicated picture,[129] that can be understood only by a systematic study of the fate of individual pre-Norman monastic communities during the twelfth and thirteenth centuries. What follows here is merely an illustration of what occurred at some places drawing on the Scottish – and English and Welsh – parallels and on the comparatively few documents that survive from Ireland. In the absence of documents, archaeological and architectural evidence functions as a vital resource to our understanding of the prevailing circumstances. These changes are worth tracing between the Synod of Kells (1152) and the Fourth Lateran Council (1215), which among other decrees curtailed the establishment of new religious orders.

In Armagh, the abbey of SS Peter and Paul emerges as the primary monastic community with obits of abbots recorded in 1174 (AU, ATig, AFM), 1175 (AU, AFM), 1203 (AFM) and 1255 (AFM). When originally founded by Ímar Ua hÁedacáin in the early twelfth century there is no indication that it was an Augustinian house but a papal confirmation of 1245 regards the community as following the Augustinian rule.[130] The church of SS Peter and Paul was apparently at the heart of the ecclesiastical complex at Armagh. According to AU, Armagh was burned in 1166 'up to the Cross of the door of the Close and all the Close with its churches – except the monastery of [SS] Paul and Peter and a few of the houses besides – and a street towards the Close to the west'.[131] While the term 'close' used by the translators is usually associated with English cathedral towns such as Norwich,[132] what may be implied from use of the term *ráith*

127 Jane Herbert, 'The transformation of hermitages into Augustinian priories in twelfth-century England' in William J. Sheils (ed.), *Monks, hermits, and the ascetic tradition.* Studies in Church History 22 (Oxford, 1985), pp 131–45; Janet Burton, 'The eremitical tradition and the development of post-Conquest religious life in northern England' in Nicole Crossley-Holland (ed.), *Eternal values in medieval life. Trivium,* 26 (Lampeter, 1991), pp 18–39; Tom Licence, 'The Benedictines, the Cistercians and the acquisition of a hermitage in twelfth-century Durham', *Journal of Medieval History* 29 (2003), 315–29. **128** Karen Stöber and David Austin, 'Culdees to canons: the Augustinian houses of north Wales' in Janet Burton and Karen Stöber (eds), *Monastic Wales. New approaches* (Cardiff, 2013), pp 39–54. **129** Bhreathnach, '*Vita apostolica*'. **130** Sheehy, *Pont. Hib.*, ii, pp 114–18 no. 273. **131** AU. Original: *co Crois doruis Ratha 7 in Raith uile co n-a templaibh – cenmotha recles Poil 7 Petair 7 uaiti do taighibh archena – 7 sreith fri Raith aníar.* **132** Roberta Gilchrist, *Norwich cathedral close. The evolution of the English cathedral landscape* (Woodbridge, 2005). For an interpretation

annalistic entry is that by 1166 a number of the features of a cathedral and monastic landscape – cathedral, monastery, lesser churches, crosses, cemeteries, streets divided into sections (*trian*) – existed within a precinct in twelfth-century Armagh. SS Peter and Paul did not escape later depredations. It was burned in 1196 and plundered in 1199,[133] presumably necessitating its consequent restoration. The 1245 papal confirmation of possessions affirms that the abbey of SS Peter and Paul held a substantial amount of land and some churches in modern counties Armagh and Tyrone.[134] On the basis of late medieval evidence, the surprising survival of the *céli Dé* community (transmogrified into *Colidei*) in Armagh can be compared with their counterparts in St Andrews (*Keledei*).[135] After numerous skirmishes with bishops, canons and kings, the *Keledei* in St Andrews settled into what G.W.S. Barrow described as a small college of highly placed secular clerks closely connected with the bishop and the king, living off what had been left to them of their original income. They were not *céli Dé* in the original sense but they acted as a useful counterbalance for bishop and king to the powerful regular canons of the Augustinian priory.[136] Armagh may not have been that dissimilar to St Andrews during the twelfth and thirteenth centuries with various institutions competing against one another as a different ecclesiastical organization emerged. The *céli Dé* at Armagh do not appear in the records between 921 and 1366 by which time they had become part of the cathedral's establishment. In Armagh, they were the equivalent of the vicars choral, consisting of a *precentor* (the person who led the office) and five brethren, and came third in precedence after the dean and cathedral chapter and the regular canons of SS Peter and Paul. Some priors were priests, some proficient in music and theology and others were masters of works in charge of the upkeep of buildings.[137] It is not clear that they followed a particular rule and none of them held the title of *fer léiginn*, an office that seems to have disappeared from Armagh on the death of Martain Ua Brolaigh (*aird-eccnaidh Gaoidheal 7 fer leighinn Arda Macha*) in 1188.[138]

Derry was one of the few monasteries in which the office of *fer léiginn* survived into the thirteenth century. It was ruled by Flaithbertach Ua Brolcháin

of Richard Bartlett's 1602 map of Armagh and its depiction of the abbey of SS Peter and Paul see Paul Logue, 'Reinterpreting Richard Bartlett's image of Armagh', *Ulster Journal of Archaeology* 74 (2017–18), 220–30, at pp 226 (fig. 2), 227 (fig. 4). **133** AU, AFM. **134** Sheehy, *Pont. Hib.*, pp 115–16 no. 273. **135** For the most detailed documentation of both communities see Reeves, *Culdees*, pp 10–19, 33–41. On St Andrews, see G.W.S. Barrow, 'The cathedral chapter at St Andrews and the Culdees in the twelfth and thirteenth centuries', *The Journal of Ecclesiastical History* 3:1 (1952), 23–39; G.W.S. Barrow, *Kingdom of the Scots. Government, church and society from the eleventh to the fourteenth century* (London, 1973; repr. 2003), pp 187–202 (2nd ed.); Simon Taylor, 'From *Cinrigh Monai* to *Civitas Sancti Andree*: a star is born' in Michael H. Brown and Katie Stevenson (eds), *Medieval St Andrews. Church, cult, city* (Woodbridge, 2017), pp 20–34, at pp 31–3. **136** Barrow, *Kingdom of the Scots*, p. 195; Taylor, 'From *Cinrigh Monai*', p. 32. **137** Reeves, *Culdees*, pp 13–14. **138** AU, AFM.

as *comarbae Choluim Chille* from 1150 to 1175 with authority over all the Columban monasteries. Flaithbertach followed the traditional custom of visitations to all regions in Ireland with the exception of Munster.[139] He was also active along with the northern king Muirchertach Ua Lochlainn – patron of the Cistercian monastery of Newry – in building works and in re-organizing the ecclesiastical landscape.[140] In 1162, AU records:

> Total separation of the houses from the churches (*ó templuibh*) of Daire was made by the successor of Colum Cille (namely, Flaithbertach) and by the king of Ireland, that is, by Muircertach Ua Lochlainn; where were demolished eighty houses, or something more. And the stone wall of the centre was likewise built (*dénam caisil in erláir*) by the successor of Colum Cille and malediction [pronounced] upon him who should come over it forever.

Having cleared the centre of the settlement, in 1164, they built the Teampull Mór ('the great church'):[141]

> The great church of Daire was built by the successor of Colum Cille, that is, by Flaithbertach, son of the bishop Ua Brolchain and by the community (*sámud*) of Colum Cille and by Muirchertach Ua Lochlainn, high-king of Ireland. And the [top] stone of that great church, wherein there are ninety feet [in length], was completed within the space of forty days.

In the same year a delegation visited Flaithbertach from Iona seeking to bestow the abbacy of Iona on him but this was prevented by Gilla Meic Liac, archbishop of Armagh and Muirchertach Ua Lochlainn. Whatever about the politics of this episode, the description of Iona's delegation gives a fairly accurate account of a pre-reform community and is comparable with the officials listed in the praise poem to Áed Ua Forréid:[142]

139 AFM 1150, 1151, 1153, 1161, AU 1161. **140** AU 1162. Original: *Errscardugh na taighi o thempluibh Daire do denum la comarba Coluim Cille (.i., Flaithbertach) 7 la righ Erenn, idon, la Muircertach hUa Lochlainn; dú in ro tógbadh ochtmoga taighi, no ni is uilliu. Ocus denam caisil in erlair la comarba Coluim Cille beos 7 mallacht ar inti ticfa tairis do gres.* Notably, in 1162 the Cistercian monastery at Newry was burned with all its books and furniture and the yew tree that Patrick had planted there (AFM). **141** AU 1164. Original: *Tempull mór Dairi do denum la comarba Coluim Cille, idon, la Flaithbertach, mac in espuic hUi Brolcain 7 ra samudh Coluim Cille 7 la Muircertach hUa Lochlainn, la hairdrigh nErenn. Ocus tairrnic cloch in tempaill moir sein Daire, i faelet nocha traighed, fri ré cethorchat laa.* **142** AU 1164. Original: *Maithi muinnteri Ia, idin, in sacart mor, Augustin 7 in fer leiginn (idon, Dub Sidhe) 7 in disertach, idon Mac Gilla Duibh 7 cenn na Ceile nDe, idon, Mac Forcellaigh 7 maithi muinnteri Ia arcena do thiachtain ar cenn comarba Coluim Cille, idon, Fhlaithbertaich hUi Brolcain, do gabail abdaine Ia a comairli Somarlidh 7 Fer Aerther Gaidhel 7 Innsi Gall, co roastaei comarba Patraic 7 ri*

> Select members of the community of Ia, namely, the chief priest (*in sacart mór*), Augustin and the lector (*fer léiginn*) (that is, Dubsidhe) and the hermit (*dísertach*), Mac Gilladuib and the head of the *céli Dé* (*cenn na Céile nDé*), namely, Mac Forchellaig and select members of the community (*muinter*) of Ia besides came requesting the successor of Colum Cille, namely, Flaithbertach Ua Brolcháin, to accept the abbacy (*abdaine*) of Ia, on the advice of Somharlidh and of the Men of Airthir Gaedhel and of Insi Gall; but the successor of Patrick and the king of Ireland, that is, Ua Lochlainn and the nobles of Cenél Éogain prevented him.

Even after Flaithbertach's death, Derry continued to function as a major church with its lesser churches and various traditional officials and to be the scene of constant disputes and killings among the competing dynasties in the northwest. This environment is best illustrated by a series of events recorded in AU 1214:[143]

> Tomás son of Uchtrach and Ruaidhrí son of Raghnall, plundered Doire completely and took the treasures of the community (*muinter*) of Doire and of the north of Ireland besides from out the middle of the church of the *reiclés*.
>
> Ua Catháin and the Fir Craíbhe came to Doire to seize a house against the sons of Mac Lochlainn, so that between them they killed the great cellarer (*cellóir*) of the *reiclés* of Doire. But God and Colum Cille wrought a great miracle therein: the man that assembled and mustered the force, namely, Mathgamain Mag Aithne, was killed in reparation to Colum Cille immediately, at the door of the *reiclés* of Colum Cille.
>
> Ainmire Ua Cobhthaigh, abbot of the *reiclés* of Doire, eminent cleric select for piety, for disposition, for meekness, for magnanimity, for benevolence, for great charity, for every goodness besides, after most excellent penance entered the way of all flesh in the *Dubreiclés* of Colum Cille.

These annalistic entries, and many others besides, attest to the central importance of the *Dubreiclés* in Derry. It housed the monastery's treasures and senior ecclesiastics and nobles died or were laid out there, hoping no doubt to

Erenn, idon, Ua Lochlainn 7 maithi Ceneoil Eogain e. 143 AU 1214. Original: *Tomás, mac Uchtraigh 7 Ruaidhri, mac Raghnaill, do argain Dairi go huilidhi 7 do breith shet muinntere Daire 7 Tuaisce[i]rt Erenn archena do lár tempaill in reiclesa ímach. hUa Catha[i]n, 7 Fir na Craibhe do thiachtain co Daire do ghabail taighi 'mo macaibh Meg Lachlainn, co romarbsat celloir mor reiclesa Daire ettora. Dorona Dia 7 Coluim Cille tra mírbail moir annsein: idon, in fer tinoil 7 tochastail, idon, Mathgamain Mag Aithne, do marbadh i neinech Coluim Cille fo cetoir i ndorus in dubreiclesa Coluim Cille. Ainmire hUa Cobhthaigh, ab reiclesa Daire, uasal cleirech togaidhe ar crabadh, ar duthchus, ar mine, ar mordhacht, ar midhcaire, ar mórdérch, ar ecnai, ar gach maithius archena, post optimam penitentiam ingressus est uiam uniuersae carnis i n-dubreicles Coluim Cille.*

ensure salvation surrounded by relics associated with Colum Cille. No more than dying on Ciarán's bed in the *Eclais Bec* at Clonmacnoise, the practical circumstances of such deaths in the *Dubreiclés* are not clear. Did it involve a special watch over the dying person and did it consist of a chapel and a hospice? The hospice might just hark back to the *céli Dé*'s caring for the sick that Haggart and Ó Corráin suggested on the basis of evidence from Armagh and Clonmacnoise.[144] Twelfth-century papal confirmations of the possessions of St Andrews include the transfer of the hospital there, which catered for beggars, guests and pilgrims and which seems to have been run by the *céli Dé*, to the regular canons.[145] Derry's *Dubreiclés* was also transferred to the regular canons as Bishop Colton's description in his 1397 visitation of the diocese of Derry was brought *ad monasterium Canonicorum Regularium, vocatum Cella Nigra de Deria*.[146]

The fate of the *cráibdig* in the *dísert* of Kells was probably similar to that of the *céli Dé* of Loch Leven in that they were given the choice of becoming regular canons or at least face an existence on the margins of monastic life in an Anglo-Norman settlement. In the mid-twelfth century their property was already being encroached upon when the head of the most powerful ecclesiastical family in Kells, the Uí Bresléin, bought some of their land for his sons, one of whom is described as a *deorad*, presumably a member of the monastic community.[147] More land was lost to the Augustinian foundation of St Mary's Abbey that was endowed in the 1180s/90s by Hugh de Lacy I and confirmed by John, lord of Ireland, in 1192.[148] Maurice Sheehy noted correctly that the grant of *Rosbindig* and Ard Mín to the canons were lands that had been granted previously to the *dísert* by Tigernán Ua Ruairc, king of Bréifne,[149] for the upkeep of *Int Eidnén* on the occasion of the consecration of the church there.[150] Aubrey Gwynn argued that St Mary's was separate from the 'Columban monastery of the old Irish rule' on the basis that later descriptions of Kells located the abbey outside Cannon Gate and therefore outside the original monastic precinct.[151] However, the original *dísert* may also have been outside the precinct and replaced by de Lacy's foundation. While difficult to prove, de Lacy had a track record of replacing existing hermitages with canons regular, as he did with the hermitage at Ewias/

These events are also recorded in AFM and ALC. **144** See above p. 242. **145** Reeves, *Culdees*, pp 156–7; www.poms.ac.uk/record/source/3741/ accessed 11 March 2022. **146** William Reeves (ed.), *Acts of Archbishop Colton in his metropolitan visitation of the diocese of Derry* AD *MCCCXCVII; with a rental of the see estates at that time* (Dublin, 1850), p. 20. There appears to have been an ongoing dispute during the late medieval period about the authority of the abbot of SS Peter and Paul, Armagh over the Cella Nigra in Derry (see Reeves, *Colton visitation,* p. 84; *MRHI*, pp 168–9). **147** Mac Niocaill, *Notitiae*, pp 32–4 (XI). **148** Ibid., pp 38–9; https://www.dib.ie/biography/lacy-hugh-de-a4631. **149** https://www.dib.ie/biography/ua-ruairc-tigernan-a8754. **150** Sheehy, *Pont. Hib.*, ii, pp 106–7 no. 267 n. 1. **151** Aubrey Gwynn, 'Some notes on the history of the Book of Kells', *Irish Historical*

Llanthony Prima in Wales against the wishes of the existing community.[152] In Ireland, de Lacy and his knights granted generous tithes and benefices to Llanthony Prima and Secunda, chief among them Duleek and the church of Dysart (Dísert Tóla), barony of Delvin, Co. Westmeath.[153] Duleek is a particularly good example of the takeover of a pre-Norman ecclesiastical complex. It had ambitions towards becoming an episcopal seat and was designated as such at the Synod of Ráith Bresail in 1111 but lost out to Clonard at the Synod of Uisnech in the same year.[154] The layout of the site with its enclosure and various churches replicates so many other large pre-Norman settlements. These included, according to a 1381 extent, the shrine chapel of the founder saint, St Cianán 'the human remains of which same saint lie on the northern side of the chancel', where the canons and other clergy 'celebrate divine service daily in a loud voice in the church'.[155] This was an appropriation of St Cianán whose relics were translated, probably by William St Leger, bishop of Meath (1349–52), into a new tomb. The translation is celebrated in the late medieval office of Cianán that can be traced to a Llanthony source.[156] If so, the Llanthony depiction of the saint's relics lying on the northern side of the chancel with canons and others singing the Divine Office there suggests that if a new tomb was erected, it may have imitated the *foramina* type of tomb-shrine found over saints' graves in churches in western Christendom from the twelfth century onwards.[157] In addition to St Cianán's church at Duleek, there was also a church dedicated to St Patrick and an oratory dedicated to St Corbán that was situated

Studies 9 (1954), 131–61. **152** Herbert, 'Transformation of hermitages', p. 143. **153** Arlene Hogan, *The Priory of Llanthony Prima and Secunda in Ireland, 1172–1541. Lands, patronage and politics* (Dublin, 2008), pp 97, 101–3. **154** *MRHI*, p. 93. **155** Hogan, *Llanthony Prima and Secunda*, pp 102, 351 (charter 98). Original Latin text from Eric St John Brooks (ed.), *The Irish cartularies of Llanthony Prima & Secunda* (Dublin, 1953): *in qua idem sanctus, in parte boriali in cancella humaniter requiescit … ubi habent unum vel duos de confratibus suis eorundem procuratores qui dicte ecclesie deseruiunt ac ipsi et duo parochiales capellani et quatuor clerici in eadem cotidie alta voce divina celebrant*, p. 295 (Charter no. 98). **156** Kathleen Hughes, 'The offices of S. Finnian of Clonard and S. Cianán of Duleek', *Analecta Bollandiana* 73 (1955), 342–72, at pp 355–6, 363: *In translatione dicatur sic: Qua exultauit presulem, Willelmus pastor Midie, immensam reddens gratiam.* **157** John Crook, *English medieval shrines* (Woodbridge, 2011), pp 191–212. I am grateful to Raghnall Ó Floinn for this information. John Bradley and Anngret Simms (the appendix by John Bradley), 'The geography of Irish manors: the example of the Llanthony cells of Duleek and Colp in county Meath' in John Bradley (ed.), *Settlement and society in medieval Ireland. Studies presented to F.X. Martin, o.s.a.* (Kilkenny, 1988), pp 291–326, at p. 317 refers to a description of the shrine of St Cianán in the 1381 Llanthony extent (Hogan, *Llanthony Prima and Secunda*, p. 351) as 'having a hole through which the faithful could place their hand in order to touch the relics of the saint within' but I have been unable to locate this text. Bradley may have had in mind the episode in *Félire Óengusso* (p. 244.45) in which Colum Cille put his hand through the side of Cianán's *membra* 'shrine' and the dead saint held his hand in a sign of unity (*óentu*). This shrine might have been a tomb-shaped shrine which anticipated the *foramina*-type shrines of the later period. I am grateful to Cormac Bourke for providing me with this likely explanation of Bradley's

next to the cemetery of St Cianán,[158] both of which were placed in the possession of the Llanthony canons. Any local supervision over these churches, and indeed the survival of Muirchertach Ua Cellaig's twelfth-century foundation of St Mary's, Duleek, appear to have been restricted by the Llanthony canons who, with the de Lacys, de Verduns and other families along with the bishops of Meath, developed a thoroughly Anglo-Norman manor that included their own house (St Michael's), a parish church (St Cianán's), a motte, a gatehouse and possibly town walls. As in many cases throughout Ireland, however, the imprint of the original pre-Norman enclosure can be traced in the modern street patterns of Duleek.[159] Finally, the case of the *céli Dé* of Devenish is worth noting. Their community appears to have lasted to the early seventeenth century, seemingly sharing the island with a community of Augustinian canons, both of them led by two hereditary ecclesiastical families, the Uí Flannacáin and the Uí Chorcráin.[160]

The survival of early monastic communities unaltered from the mid-twelfth century onwards was unusual. Irish patrons moved away from endowing them in favour of houses of the new orders. Anglo-Norman knights, such as Hugh de Lacy I and John de Courcy, encouraged major foundations in their own English and Welsh lordships to found daughter-houses in Ireland. Both Anglo-Norman and Irish bishops appropriated lands that had been set aside to support monastic communities, and it is likely that individuals who had been attached to these communities were subsumed into the new ecclesiastical structure as canons of cathedral chapters, as regular canons or as monks in new foundations. The Uí Gormáin of Armagh, Louth and Termonfeckin, who were presumably kinsmen, exemplify this shift from old to new.[161] Flann (Florint) Ua Gormáin (d. 1174) was chief scholar (*aird-fher léiginn*) of Armagh directing the schools of Ireland for twenty-one years, having spent twenty-one years previously among the Franks and the English.[162] Máel Muire Ua Gormáin (*fl. c.*1170) was abbot of the Arrouasian house at Knock, Co. Louth, and author of *Félire Uí Gormáin* ('The Martyrology of Ua Gormáin'),[163] while Máel Cáemgin Ua Gormáin (d. 1164) was for a time abbot of the canons of Termonfeckin and master (*maighistir*) of

comments. **158** Brooks, *Cartularies of Llanthony*, p. 221 (Charter no. 20). Original: *oratorium sancti Karbarii [Karbany] situm iuxta cimiterium sancti Kenani apud Duuelec*. Hogan, *Llanthony Prima and Secunda*, pp 101–2 (42n), 258 (Charter 20). Although Hogan (71n) suggests that the name is best translated as Cairbre as in this text, the other versions in the Llanthony cartularies – *Carban*, *Karban*, *Kerban* – would suggest that the dedication is to a saint Corbán or Cerbán. Ó Riain, *DIS*, p. 224 suggests that he is to be identified possibly with Corbán of Naas but given the close association between St Patrick and St Cianán, the oratory may have been dedicated to Cerbán (Cerpanus), for whom, according to Tírechán, Patrick wrote the alphabet, at a place near Tara (Bieler, *Patrician texts*, pp 132–3 §13(1), 162–3 §51(1). Another possibility, suggested by John Bradley, is that this oratory commemorated Corban, abbot of Duleek (d. 754). Bradley, 'The geography of Irish manors', p. 318. **159** Simms, 'The geography of Irish manors'. **160** *MRHI* pp 33, 169. **161** Flanagan, *Transformation*, pp 149, 153, 169. **162** AU, ALC, AFM, ATig. **163** *DIB*: https://www.dib.ie/biography/ua-gormain-

Louth.[164] Flanagan notes the use of the title *maighistir* derived from Latin *magister*, which becomes more common in the annals, as opposed to the traditional *fer léiginn*, and surmises that it is suggestive of an education in a continental cathedral school or embryonic university in a useful discipline, at least in the case of Flann Ua Gormáin.[165] The decision taken at the Synod of Clane in 1162 that no one should be a *fer léiginn* in an Irish church unless an alumnus (*dalta*) of Armagh must partially explain the virtual disappearance of the office of *fer léiginn* from the annalistic record.[166] In addition, in 1169 Ruaidrí Ua Conchobair, king of Ireland, granted an endowment to the *fer léiginn* of Armagh in honour of St Patrick to teach the students of Ireland and Alba.[167] Even though the annals use the term *fer léiginn* of Armagh, the number recorded as holding this office reduces considerably. *Fir léiginn* are recorded in Armagh (1167, 1169, 1188), Iona (1164), Clonmacnoise (1169) and Derry (1185, 1189, 1220). The language of monastic scholarship changed and although the terms *suí* (*saoi*) and *ecna* (*eagna*) continue to be used *maighistir* appears more frequently and canons and monks are associated with expertise in specialist disciplines. An entry in the Annals of the Four Masters in 1230 represents what emerges as a complex amalgam of old and new offices and titles, no doubt reflecting the precarious transition when one ecclesiastical structure supplanted another:

> *Giolla Iosa Ua Cléirigh* ***epscop Luighne****, Ioseph Mac Techedain* ***epscop Conmaicne****, Mac Raith Mag Serraigh* ***epscop Conmaicne****, Rool Petit* ***epscop na Midhe*** *Riaglóir tocchaidhe, 7 milidh Criost, Giolla Coimdeadh Ua Duilennáin* ***comharba Feichin, 7 ab reicclésa cananach Eassa Dara****, Muiredhach Ua Gormghaile* ***prióir Innsi Mic nErin****, Maol Muire Ua Maol Eóin* ***comarba Ciaráin Cluana Mic Nóis****, Giolla Cartaigh Ua hEilgiusáin* ***canánach 7 angcoire****, Donn Slebhe Ua hIonmainen* ***manach naomhtha 7 ard-maighistir saoir Mainistre na Buille*** *d'écc.*
>
> Giolla Íosa Ua Cléirigh, bishop of Luighne; Ioseph Mac Techedáin, bishop of Conmaicne; Mac Raith Mag Serraigh, bishop of Conmaicne; Rool Petit (Rodolphus Petit), bishop of Meath, a fine regulator and soldier of Christ; Giolla Coimdeadh Ua Duilennáin, coarb of St Feichín and abbot of the church of the canons at Easdara (Ballysadare); Muiredhach Ua Gormghaile, prior of Inis-mac-nerin (Church Island, Lough Key); Maol Muire Ua Maol Eóin, coarb of St Ciarán of Clonmacnoise; Giolla Cartaigh Ua hEilgiusáin, a canon and anchorite; and Donn Slébhe Ua hIonmainén, a holy monk and the chief master of the carpenters of the monastery of Boyle, died.

mael-muire-a8739 accessed 16 March 2022. **164** AFM. **165** Flanagan, *Transformation*, p. 169. **166** AU, AFM. **167** AU, AFM.

Of the old structure, the title of *comarbae* (coarb) remained a feature of late medieval Ireland, as did many of the hereditary families such as the Uí Máel Eóin family of Clonmacnoise. The Uí Gormghaile took over the church at Inis Mac n-Erin and held onto it until the fifteenth century.[168] Gilla in Coimded Ua Duilennáin's holding the offices of *comarbae* of St Feichín and abbot of the Augustinian house at Ballysadare, Co. Sligo, illustrates the likely position of many ecclesiastics who decided to combine the old and new structure, presumably for practical reasons such as avoiding loss of income, land and patronage. The region around Ballysadare, Co. Sligo, was a highly contested territory at the time between the Uí Eaghra lords and the newly arrived de Berminghams. As is the case with the majority of Irish Augustinian houses, Ua Duilennáin's obit in 1230 is the only indication that the canons were in Ballysadare before the fifteenth century.[169] This may be due to lack of documentation or that the presence of canons was intermittent and community numbers were consistently low. They probably serviced the great church of St Feichín (*tempaill moir Fechin i ndEs Dara*),[170] the remains of which survive in the form of a Romanesque doorway and other architectural features.[171] Donn Sléibe Ua hInmainéin, a Cistercian monk in Boyle abbey, may also have been a member of a hereditary family of skilled craftsmen. Cú Duilig Ua hInmainéin with his sons or apprentices (*cona maccaib*) covered the Shrine of St Patrick's Bell possibly working in Dublin *c.*1100.[172] (Fig. 30) Among all these Irish names in the AFM 1230 entry is Ralph Petit, one of the early Anglo-Norman bishops of Meath (1227–30) and a testament to the intrusion, primarily in the east of Ireland, of a new community into the Irish church with its own cultural and political outlook.

Many hereditary ecclesiastical families availed of the opportunities generated by the re-organization of the Irish church and succeeded in clinging on to power by holding bishoprics and abbacies into the thirteenth century and even later. Hence, for example, families such as the Uí Briain, Uí Énna and Uí Longargáin were variously bishops of Cloyne, Killaloe and Cashel, the Uí Máel Eoin of Clonmacnoise, the Uí Dubthaig of Clonfert, Cong, Mayo and Tuam and the Uí Selbaig of Cork. Some of these bishops were also monks or canons. Muirges (Mattheus) Ua hÉnna (d. 1206) and Donnchad Ua Longargáin (d. 1216) were archbishops of Cashel and Cistercians. Áed Ua Máel Eoin, bishop of Clonmacnoise, was also a Cistercian who died in the monastery of Kilbeggan in 1237.[173] This phenomenon of holding onto offices was essential during this period of turmoil as ecclesiastical lands were beginning to be divided into

168 *MRHI*, p. 179. **169** *MRHI*, pp 160–1. **170** AC, AFM 1261. **171** www.archaeology.ie (SL020109001); https://www.crsbi.ac.uk/ view-item?i=13744 (The corpus of Romanesque sculpture in Britain and Ireland) accessed 17 March 2022. **172** Bourke, *Early medieval hand-bells*, p. 309. **173** Sheehy, *Pont. Hib.*, ii, p. 62 no. 222 n. 1.

episcopal estates, parochial benefices, lands remaining with hereditary *airchinnig*, and endowments to new monastic foundations. In addition, there was a constant uncertainty about the stability of diocesan borders as both ecclesiastical and lay authorities sought to redraw boundaries and to downgrade or upgrade dioceses.

One of the most acrimonious cases of rivalry between dioceses was that between Lismore and Waterford which lasted until 1363 when the two were united.[174] This dispute, which was referred to the papacy on a number of occasions, was a complex case that involved a land grab by the smaller urban diocese of Waterford from the well-endowed pre-Norman diocese of Lismore that was exacerbated by tension between Anglo-Norman bishops of Waterford and Irish bishops of Lismore, especially in the first decades of the thirteenth century.[175] It may have prompted those in Lismore to compile or at least revise the life of their founder Mochutu (alias Cárthach) as a way of claiming ownership of their extensive lands but in the end this effort was unsuccessful. As late as 1166, Lismore had been the location of a synod attended by the bishops of Leth Moga (the southern half of Ireland) with Gilla Críst Ua Conairche, bishop of Lismore and papal legate, presiding and at which the new cathedral was consecrated.[176] When Christianus died in 1186, the monastic presence of Lismore simply faded into the background, following a similar fate to Glendalough after its union with Dublin. Ardmore, on the coast south of Lismore, a monastery likely to have been founded during the conversion period – whose patron was St Déclán – had failed to be granted diocesan status at the Synod of Kells in 1152. (Fig. 31) Nonetheless, with the support of the local Uí Fáeláin dynasty and its ambitious clerics, notably the priest Máel Étaín Ua Duib Rátha and Bishop Eugenius, Ardmore had a brief period of splendour during which the cathedral and magnificent round tower were probably built.[177] The Annals of Inisfallen records the death of Ua Duib Rátha in 1203, noting that he had finished building the church (*teampall*) at Ardmore. He may have belonged to a hereditary family as the death of Gilla Pátraic Ua Duib Rátha *fer léiginn* of Killaloe and *suí Muman* ('scholar of Munster') is recorded in 1110.[178] More notable was the career of Eugenius, bishop of Ardmore, who appears to have signed a charter dating to 1172 in which Diarmait Mac Cárthaig, king of Desmumu (Desmond) endowed the church of St John the Apostle and Evangelist in Cork. While there is some doubt as to his status in that charter there is no doubt that he was a bishop. He acted as suffragan bishop of Lichfield in 1184/5 due to a vacancy between episcopacies there and probably died in the late 1180s.[179] Once the Uí Fáeláin dynasty declined in the early thirteenth

174 *MRHI*, pp 91–2, 100–1. 175 P.J. Dunning, 'Pope Innocent III and the Waterford-Lismore controversy 1196–1218', *The Irish Theological Quarterly* 28:3 (1961), 215–32. 176 AI. 177 Dónal O'Connor, 'Bishop Eugene of Ardmore revisited', *Decies* 63 (2007), 23–33. 178 AI, AFM. 179 Flanagan, *Irish royal charters*, pp 198–9.

century, in part following the intrusion of the Anglo-Norman Robert le Poer into their kingdom, Ardmore's status also diminished to the point that it is recorded only as a simple church belonging to the diocese of Lismore in the 1302–7 papal taxation of Irish dioceses.[180] All its architectural splendour came to nought due to the complex politics of the period and Ardmore's main claim to fame reverted to the renown of its founder whose life is likely to have been compiled as part of its campaign to gain diocesan status.

The effect of so many changes in church organization on island and lakeshore communities varied. Inis Cealtra, which on the basis of its archaeological and architectural remains was vibrant until the late twelfth century mainly due to Uí Briain patronage, did not attract any new order and became something of a backwater as evidenced by a series of fifteenth-century papal letters.[181] Like many of these 'old' sites its importance was revived in the post-Reformation period when it became one of Ireland's most popular pilgrimage sites, in the words of John Rider, reformed bishop of Killaloe (d. 1632):[182]

> … there are divers Abbies or Monasteries dissolved in my Dioces, wherein yet ye people do bury theyr dead out of ye ordinary place of christian buriall to ye contempt of religion and maintenance of theyr superstition. And besides that, to these places many ffriars and Priests doe ordinarily resort and sometimes in ye yeare great concourse of people publickely: as in … Inishgealtragh or ye Iland of Seven Altars …

What of the fate of the most famous of all eremitical communities, Skellig, from the twelfth century onwards? Contrary to the received narrative,[183] Skellig's community – if any community existed post-1200 – did not become Augustinian nor was the island a hugely popular pilgrimage site. The Augustinian priory at Ballinskelligs was founded in 1210 from Ratoo in north Kerry and paid tithes to the bishop of Ardfert.[184] The canons took over possession of Skellig but despite references to them in the Calendar of Papal Letters,[185] nothing is said about them inhabiting the island, operating a pilgrimage or receiving any income from

180 *CDI 1302–1307* (London, 1886), p. 305. **181** *CPL* VI, 33, 68; VII, 265. **182** Philip Dwyer, *The diocese of Killaloe from the Reformation to the close of the eighteenth century* (Dublin, 1878), p. 101. See also the very detailed description of Inis Cealtra's archaeology, architecture and history at https://www.clarecoco.ie/services/planning/publications/inishcealtra/inish-cealtra-appendix-2-detailed-support-material-26764.pdf accessed 18 March 2022. **183** Peter Harbison, *Pilgrimage in Ireland. The monuments and the people* (London, 1991); Louise Nugent, *Journeys of faith. Stories of pilgrimage from medieval Ireland* (Dublin, 2020), pp 24, 126, 127–8. **184** *MRHI*, p. 192. Gwynn and Hadcock (pp 195, 404) suggest that the early community became canons and that there may have been hermits on Skellig in this later period but there is no evidence for these suggestions. For a detailed description of the Ballinskelligs priory complex see Crowley and Sheehan, *The Iveragh peninsula*, pp 347–51. **185** See Skelligs, St Michael's Mount (de Rupe) on British History Online (BHO)

pilgrims. Medieval claims about miraculous wells on Skellig and St Michael rising out of the island to assist St Patrick in banishing snakes and reptiles from Ireland may have been based on local traditions or more likely invented to promote the island's reputation.[186] The hazardous nature of the voyage and landing on the island as well as the necessity to have the right type of boat to navigate the rough crossing from the mainland is mentioned in the mid-thirteenth century text known as the *Libellus de fundacione ecclesie Consecrati Petri* composed in the Schottenkloster in Regensburg[187] and in John Lynch's seventeenth-century *De Praesulibus Hiberniae*.[188] Even at this late stage the voyage would have been undertaken only by the most adventurous pilgrims. Interestingly, according to the *Libellus* pilgrims visited the island between the feast day of SS Philip and James (1 May) and the feast day of St Michael the archangel (29 September). The indulgence granted by Pope Paul V to the nobles and people of Ireland in 1607 lists Skellig among the places that were frequented by pilgrims. Each site is associated with a particular feast day or days, Skellig with the apparition of St Michael (8 May) and the dedication of St Michael (29 September).[189] Skellig is also listed among the pilgrimage sites which a certain Heneas MacNichill visited in 1541 as penance imposed by the dean of Armagh for strangling his own son. He was absolved of his sin by the primate of Armagh for undertaking this onerous pilgrimage.[190] The paucity of descriptions of Skellig, even in later visitors' journals – which might mention it in passing – adds to the impression that while pilgrims visited, they did not come in hordes.

These are but a handful of examples of the effect that the re-organization of the Irish church and the arrival of Anglo-Norman adventurers accompanied by their avaricious ecclesiastics had on existing monastic communities. Many moved with the times but equally many either became quiet backwaters revered locally and possibly served by a small number of priests or simply slipped into oblivion.

VEILED WOMEN AND ABBESSES: WOMEN RELIGIOUS IN A CHANGING CHURCH

The role of religious women in Ireland throughout this period of transformation is no clearer than it is for previous centuries.[191] The dedication of so many

https://www.british-history.ac.uk/cal-papal-registers/brit-ie/vol1. **186** O'Meara, *Gerald of Wales*, p. 80. **187** Pádraig A. Breatnach, 'Medieval traditions from West Munster', *Studia Hibernica* 17–18 (1977–8), 58–70, at p. 61. **188** John Francis O'Doherty (ed.), John Lynch *De Praesulibus Hiberniae*, 2 vols (Dublin, 1944), ii, pp 150–1. **189** John Hagan, 'Miscellanea Vaticano-Hibernica, 1580–1631', *Archivium Hibernicum* 3 (1914), 227–365, at p. 264. **190** Laurence P. Murray, 'A calendar of the register of Primate George Dowdall, commonly called the "Liber Niger" or "Black Book"', *Journal of the County Louth Archaeological Society* 6:3 (1927), 147–58, at pp 148, 152. **191** Major studies in this field include Hall, *Women and*

churches to holy women has been interpreted as evidence for the proliferation of female foundations in early Ireland. As explained in Chapter 2, the evidence for this belief is fairly thin. While there is somewhat more clarity from the thirteenth century onwards, a similar element of over-estimation of female communities has been suggested for the twelfth century. Even in cases where it is likely that a female community existed, their affiliations are vague or seem to have fluctuated, as demonstrated by Yvonne Seale in relation to the early thirteenth-century foundation of Ballymore-Loughsewdy, Co. Westmeath, which has over the centuries been linked to all the major international orders of the period.[192] Similarly, the convent of Kilcreevanty, Co. Galway, founded by Cathal Croibhdhearg Ó Conchobhair *c.*1200, fluctuated between the Benedictine, Augustinian and Cistercian rules, causing tension with the archbishop of Tuam. An agreement was reached in 1223 that finally designated the convent as Arrouasian.[193] Marie Therese Flanagan has discussed the concern demonstrated by both Gillebertus and Malachy for the status of women religious, living communally (*moniales* and *sanctimoniales*), arguing that a convent of nuns existed at Termonfeckin, Co. Louth, and formed part of Malachy's plan for his new Louth diocese.[194] She draws attention to an encomium to Donnchad Ua Cerbaill, king of Airgialla, added to a fifteenth-century antiphonary from Armagh, in which he is praised for the restoration of the monasteries of monks, canons and nuns. Notably, the nuns are described as *caillech n-dubh* [sic] 'a black nun', probably alluding to Arrouasian canonesses. Special notice is given to the monasteries of monks on the banks of the Boyne (Mellifont) and of canons and nuns at Termonfeckin.[195] Various documents have been frequently used as evidence for the establishment of a wave of female communities as part of the 'reform' of the Irish church. For example, two papal confirmations of the dependencies and possessions of the Augustinian nunneries of Clonard (1195) and Kilcreevanty, Co. Galway (1223) have been drawn upon as proof for numerous 'co-located' communities (canons and canonesses living on the same site) existing in twelfth and thirteenth-century Ireland.[196] The evidence is often sketchy and is based on a scenario set out by Gwynn and Hadcock in relation to many of these putative houses. Their entry on the nunnery at Annaghdown is representative of Gwynn and Hadcock's tentative descriptions:[197]

the church, pp 63–6; Collins, *Female monasticism*, pp 28–58. Browne et al., *Brides of Christ*. **192** Yvonne Seale, 'Putting women in order: a comparison of the medieval women religious of Ballymore-Loughsewdy and Prémontré' in Browne et al., *Brides of Christ*, pp 85–99, at pp 86–92. **193** Sheehy, *Pont. Hib.*, i, p. p. 240 no. 154 n. 1. **194** Flanagan, *Transformation*, pp 70–3, 149–53. **195** TCD MS 77 f. 48v: https://digitalcollections.tcd.ie/concern/works/6q182t51n?locale=en. **196** Hall, *Women and the church*, pp 70–4, 75–8; Collins, *Female monasticism*, pp 79–80, 104–10. **197** *MRHI*, p. 312. I have highlighted a number of words.

> St Brendan (d. *c.*578) established nuns here under his sister, Briga: *Ware*. The church of St Mary *Evachdun, cum villa Kelgel*, is among the dependencies confirmed to the Arroasian canonesses of Clonard in 1195 …, and St Mary, *Eanchduyn* was confirmed to those of Kilcreevanty *c.*1223 and again in 1400 … At Annaghdown, the nuns **may** have become Arroasian soon after Clonard, *c.*1144, and the abbey of regular canons **appears** to be of that period: its dedication to St Mary (de Portu Patrum) **suggests** that one church was shared by the canons and nuns, each having separate residential buildings as at other double monasteries, or there **may** have been only a small community of nuns attached to the almonry. The nuns, as Arroasian canonesses, **would** have been subject to Clonard, as head house of that order in Ireland, till *c.*1223, when Kilcreevanty became head house for Connacht. The confirmation of 1400 **seems** to have been merely repeating the entries in the previous bull of 1223–4. In that case, the nuns were **possibly** transferred from Annaghdown to Inishmaine *c.*1223–4 …

A house of canonesses may have existed at Annaghdown by the late twelfth century as it is listed among the dependencies of the Augustinian nunnery at Clonard in 1195, although this is not definite.[198] The surviving architecture on the site consists of a Transitional church of a continental-style Augustinian abbey built post-1180.[199] Tracy Collins has suggested that a rectangular structure and possibly later tower may have been the nunnery at Annaghdown, although this is by no means certain.[200] By *c.*1223, St Mary's Annaghdown was subject to the nunnery at Kilcreevanty, Co. Galway, as was St Mary's in Clonfert. The existence of these nunneries depends on accepting that the churches dedicated to St Mary were served by female communities. What the papal confirmations validate and protect are the possessions and the tithes of the nunneries at Clonard and Kilcreevanty, and in particular the income from a list of churches dedicated to Mary:[201]

> *Clonard's possessions dedicated to St Mary*: St Mary's Lusk with ten fields granted as alms by John archbishop of Dublin, St Mary's of Dublin with the farms of Ballinsgellan, St Mary's Duleek with the farm of Ballimleochid (?Calliaghstown, barony Skreen, Co. Meath), St Mary's Termonfeckin with the farm of Achadersamid (?Callystown, barony Ferrard, Co. Louth), St Mary's Skreen with the nearby plain of Dumdonnuil (Calliaghstown, barony Skreen, Co. Meath), St Mary's Trim,

198 Sheehy, *Pont. Hib.*, p. 84 no. 29. 199 Cooke, 'The Annaghdown doorway', p. 195. 200 SMR GA069-001007; Collins, *Female monasticism*, p. 211. 201 Sheehy, *Pont. Hib.*, i, p. 84 no. 29 (Pope Celestine III, 1196: Clonard); p. 240 no. 154 (Pope Honorius, 1223:

> St Mary's Kells with its house in that town and the farm of Disnirthirechan (Castlekeeran, Co. Meath), St Mary's Fore with the farm of Kellarthalgach (?Collinstown/Calliaghstown, barony Fore, Co. Westmeath), St Mary's Durrow, St Mary's Clonmacnoise to the east with the farm of Kellogainechair, St Mary's to the west [?of Clonmacnoise] with the farm of Drumalgach, St Mary's Annaghdown with the farm of Kelgel.
>
> *Kilcreevanty's possessions dedicated to St Mary*: St Mary's Clonmacnoise, St Mary's Roscommon, St Mary's Derrane with a mill, St Mary's Ardcarne, St Mary's Cloonoghil, St Mary's Annaghdown, St Mary's Clonfert, St Mary's Killinmulroney, St Mary's Drumgalgagh.

Although quite late, the surrender by Margaret Shyke, the abbess of St Brigit's Odder (Co. Meath) – where the nuns of Clonard had moved to *c.*1380–4 – more or less confirms that most of these were farms owned by the nuns, and not convents:[202]

> 1547 – Surrender of the convent of Saint Brigide of Odder, of the Order of Saint Augustine, in the county of Meath, by Margaret Shyke, Abbess, with the consent of the Convent; and of the church, belfry, and cemetery, and all its possessions; the lands of Odder, Callaghton, near Fowyr, and near Kells; the Nuns Park, Skryne, Callaghton, near Clonard, and the rectory of Odder, in the County of Meath.

The grant of the lands of Kilcreevanty to the earl of Clanricarde in 1570 is equally informative as it mirrors the 1223 papal confirmation in many instances but it also supplies a few details about possible dependent cells. St Mary's Clonmacnoise is described as 'the Chapel', 'the ruinous chapel or house called Teaghfin near the Abbey of Cong', 'the cell of nuns of Ardcarne'. In a pattern similar to Clonard's possessions, some lands are signified by the place-name element *caillech* (*callagh*, *calliagh*): Ballynagalliagh and Killnegallagh, Co. Sligo.[203] Although not nunneries, many of these places, on the basis of onomastic evidence, were associated with women religious. They may have housed solitary women or a small group of women whose lives were dedicated to the church, occasionally reclusive or possibly serving the clergy in some capacity but under the authority of an abbess.[204]

Kilcreevanty). **202** *CPR* i, p. 134 [1547]. **203** Hubert Thomas Knox, *Notes on the early history of the dioceses of Tuam Killala and Achonry* (Dublin, 1904), pp 280–5, 386–7. **204** For an account of the many forms of medieval women religious in the late medieval period, see Colmán Ó Clabaigh, 'Marginal figures? Quasi-religious women in medieval Ireland' in Browne et al., *Brides of Christ*, pp 118–35.

If Gwynn and Hadcock's assumption that a network of Augustinian nunneries existed in late twelfth-century Ireland is set aside, in parallel with their assumption about the foundation of many houses of regular canons at the same time, what emerges is closer to Vanderputten's 'ambiguous identity of female monasticism' than a standard narrative of enclosed women following a rule under the authority of an abbess whose power was contained by an abbot, bishop or prior. That is not to deny the existence of such foundations. St Mary de Hogges in Dublin and Killone, Co. Clare, were probably such houses. However, a more nuanced approach to female monasticism in twelfth-century Ireland is necessary and, as elsewhere, different and fluctuating models need to be addressed before the narrative of the thirteenth century is reflected backwards into the previous century.[205] The fate of early Irish monasteries that incorporated female communities is also worth considering. The most prominent, Kildare, was subject to on-going dynastic rivalries to the detriment of the office of abbess. The annals record constant burnings and dynastic killings. Abbesses belonged to the dynasties who contended for the provincial kingship of Leinster, the Uí Dúnlaing, Uí Chennselaig and Uí Chonchobair Failgi.[206] The last recorded abbess, Sadb daughter of Glúniarn Mac Murchada, related to the provincial king Diarmait Mac Murchada, died in 1171. There is no further evidence for either an abbess or a female community, if one even existed in the pre-Norman period, at Kildare except for Giraldus Cambrensis's description of the fire that was never extinguished and that was tended by nineteen nuns, the twentieth being Brigit herself.[207] Killevy may have continued to exist through the late medieval period, probably as an Augustinian community, although, as ever, the records are scant.[208]

The personal names of two twelfth-century abbesses allude to some form of female religious life in their use of the term *caillech* (*calliagh*), already noted above as a place-name element of lands owned by nuns. Caillech of Killevy 'a pious excellent senior' (*senóir cráibhdhech toghaidhe*) died in 1150 while Caillech Domnaill, abbess of Clonbroney, Co. Longford, and *comarbae* of the founder saint Samthann died in 1163.[209] As Máirín Ní Dhonnchadha has shown, the term *caillech* has a wide range of meanings both lay and religious.[210] *Caille* 'veil' is derived from Latin *pallia* and hence the interpretation of *caillech* as 'a veiled one' or nun. *Caillech*, however, can mean 'a spouse, married woman', 'a spouse of

205 Katharine Sykes, 'New movements of the twelfth century: diversity, belonging, and order(s)' in Kim Curran and Janet Burton (eds), *Medieval women religious* c.*800*–c.*1500. New perspectives* (Woodbridge, 2023), pp 43–60. **206** AU: 1112, 1132, 1171, AFM: 1112, 1167, 1171. **207** O'Meara, *Gerald of Wales*, pp 81–4. This tale is hardly evidence for the existence of a twelfth- or thirteenth-century nunnery and is a description that might hark back to the origins of the sanctuary, although this is open to debate. **208** Aubrey Gwynn, *The medieval province of Armagh, 1470–1545* (Dundalk, 1946), pp 103–4. **209** AFM. **210** Ní Dhonnchadha, '*Caillech* and other terms for veiled women'.

Christ, virgin, nun', 'an old woman', 'a supernatural being' and 'a housekeeper'. In addition, *caillech aithrige* means 'a penitent spouse' (Latin *clientella*). *Fedb*, from Latin *uidua* 'a widow' can be a synonym for *caillech aithrige*. In the case of Caillech of Killevy, she was both a nun and an old woman. Caillech Domnaill belonged to a family of hereditary abbesses as her kinswoman, Cocrích, *comarbae* of Clonbroney, died in 1108.[211] In 1159, Annad mac Nóennenaig Ua Cerbaill and his brother are listed among the kings of Uí Briúin Bréifne who were slain at the battle of Áth Firdiad (Ardee, Co. Louth) in which Ruaidrí Ua Conchobair, king of Connacht and Tigernán Ua Ruairc, king of Bréifne were heavily defeated by Muirchertach Ua Lochlainn, king of Cenél Éogain and contender for the kingship of Ireland. What can be gathered then about Caillech Domnaill is that she held the abbacy of Clonbroney as a member of a hereditary family whose women held the abbacy and who were nobles of Uí Briúin Bréifne. Her name would suggest that the use of *caillech* signifies that she was the widow of Domnall and not the devotee of Domnall, as there is no obvious saint of that name. Other personal names with the element *caillech*, however, imply that it was an indicator of women following a committed religious life. There are two instances of Caillech Dé 'the veiled one of God': Caillech Dé daughter of Ua hEidin of Aidne was the mother of Ruaidrí Ua Conchobair, king of Ireland (d. 1198) and his sister Mór (d. 1190). As their father Toirdelbach Ua Conchobair had a number of wives, it is possible that Caillech Dé entered religion, possibly as a vowess, when she was set aside by her husband.[212] Interestingly, one of Ruaidrí Ua Conchobair's daughters was also named Caillech Dé (d. 1211), perhaps after her grandmother. She may also have been a vowess.[213] Another personal name formation that suggests stronger evidence for women who were devotees of saints, possibly living in or close to a monastic community, is the use of names such as Caillech Finnéin ('the veiled one/devotee of St Finnéin') daughter of Sitriuc, king of Dublin, who died in the same year as her father, in 1142.[214] She may have resided in Clonard. Caillech Fináin daughter of Bran mac Maíl Mórda, deposed king of Leinster who died in Cologne in 1052, had three sons and a daughter by one Ugaire Ua Domnaill of the Uí Chennselaig dynasty. Given her Leinster connections and the connection between Cologne and St Brigit, it is likely that the saint to whom she was a devotee was Finán Lobar who is associated with Swords, Kildare and Clonmore, Co. Carlow.[215] Although not a Leinster woman, Caillech Cóemgin (devotee of Cóemgen), mother Ruaidrí na Saide Buí Ua Conchobair may have had connections with Glendalough.[216] She was the daughter of Ócán Ua Fallamain, king of Clann Uatach in Connacht and it is possible that she retreated into religion following a series of unsavoury events in 1092. Ruaidrí was blinded by Ua Flaithbertach, king of west Connacht,

211 AFM. **212** Dobbs, 'Ban-shenchus', 191, 234. **213** AFM. **214** ATig, AFM. **215** Ó Riain, *DIS*, p. 330. **216** Dobbs, 'Ban-shenchus', 190.

thus depriving him of the provincial kingship of Connacht. This is followed in the annals by a reference to the drowning in Loch Cairgin of *In cráibdech* ('the pious one') Fiachra Ua Fallamain, a priest of Connacht, as a result of being cursed by Ruaidrí. It is possible that Fiachra was Caillech Cóemgin's brother.

As noted elsewhere, retirement to a monastery was common among the aristocracy, male and female. For example, a number of senior Uí Chonchobair women followed this path during the twelfth century. In 1151, Derbforgaill daughter of Domnall Ua Lochlainn, king of Cenél nÉogain, and contender for the kingship of Ireland, and wife of Toirdelbach Ua Conchobair, king of Connacht and also contender for the kingship of Ireland, died *ina h-ailithri* ('on her pilgrimage') at Armagh.[217] Nuala, daughter of Ruaidrí Ua Conchobair, styled 'queen of Ulaid' (*banrígan, bantigerna*) as she was married to Ruaidrí mac Duinn Sléibe (d. 1201), died in Cong and according to the annals was buried honourably in the canons' church of Cong (*a h-adhnacal go h-onórach i t-teampall canánach Conga*).[218] Nuala's father died in Cong in 1198 but was buried in Clonmacnoise, the family's traditional mausoleum, while her brother/half-brother Muirghius Canánach and sister/half-sister Finnghuala died in Cong in 1224 and 1247. Muirghius, who was a canon, is praised for his learning, his singing and his poetry.[219] The only woman among the Uí Chonchobair who possibly was a nun was Duibessa, another one of Ruaidrí Ua Conchobair's daughters, who was married to Cathal Mac Diarmata, king of Mag Luirg, and who is recorded as dying 'a black nun' (*ina caillech dhuibh*) in 1230.[220]

There is no doubt that In Caillech Mór 'the great abbess' Agnes Ua Máel Sechlainn of the royal family of Mide (d. 1196) was a canoness. She is described in the *Banshenchas* ('the Lore of Women') as *ceann caillech Érend* 'head of the nuns of Ireland', abbess of Clonard.[221] Clonard was a dynastic family foundation controlled by the midland dynasty of Uí Máel Sechlainn that appears to have been 'transformed' by female members of the extended dynastic family. By the twelfth century the Uí Máel Sechlainn were a very fractious dynasty riven by internal rivalries whose kingdom, which technically stretched from the eastern coast (modern Co. Meath) into modern Co. Westmeath was constantly under pressure from competing provincial kings. These kings favoured one Ua Máel Sechlainn faction over another and having divided the kingdom between east and west Mide, attempted to control the Ua Máel Sechlainn kingship. The church was implicated in this complex dynastic rivalry. This is most clearly reflected in the fluctuation of the diocesan divisions of the kingdom of Mide, from the two sees of Duleek and Clonard of the Synod of Ráith Bresail in 1111 to the two sees of Clonard and Clonmacnoise of the rival Synod of Uisnech that was convened by Murchad Ua Máel Sechlainn and the abbot of Clonmacnoise

217 AFM. **218** AFM, ALC, AC. **219** AFM, ALC, AC. Original (AFM): *aon bá dearscnaighthi do Ghaoidhelaibh i l-legionn, i c-canntaireacht, 7 a n-dénamh uérsa.* **220** ALC. **221** Dobbs, 'Ban-shenchus', 234; ALC.

in 1111 to 'correct' the Ráith Bresail synod's decision. This was despite the best efforts of the early 'reforming' bishop Máel Muire Ua Dúnáin, who had strong personal links with Clonard and Mide but who became an advisor to Muirchertach Ua Briain, king of Munster, in his attempts at establishing an agreed diocesan structure in Ireland in the early twelfth century.[222] In addition, Murchad Ua Máel Sechlainn's wife was Mór, daughter of Muirchertach Ua Briain.[223] Understanding Murchad and the ecclesiastical and political connections of the Ua Máel Sechlainn women is essential to explaining the background to the endowment of a female Arrouasian foundation in Clonard in the mid-twelfth century. During his career Murchad, who always had a precarious hold on his kingship, was both protected and censured by the church. In 1144, he was protected from Toirdelbach Ua Conchobair, king of Connacht, by 'an extensive array of relics and ecclesiastical guarantors', but was censured in 1150 by the 'successor of Patrick', Gilla Meic Liac, archbishop of Armagh.[224] On that occasion, the kingdom of Mide was divided in three parts by more powerful regional kings. If Murchad endowed the Cistercian foundation at Bective, Co. Meath, the first daughter-house of Mellifont – and this is not certain – he may have done so in the mid-to late 1140s while under the protection of leading ecclesiastics or as reparation for his misdeeds in 1150. He died in Durrow, Co. Offaly, in 1153. His wife Mór also died in Durrow in 1137, as did his son Máel Sechlainn who was poisoned in 1155.[225] Durrow was both a royal caput and an eminent church. Clonard also held this status as annalistic entries record the deaths there of nobles such as Ben Mide daughter of Conchobar Ua Máel Sechlainn in 1137 and in 1139, Cú Chonnacht, chief *ollam* in poetry.

Turning to the Ua Máel Sechlainn women, their patronage of the church was as complex as that of their male relatives, and there is no indication that they lived cloistered lives in any new foundation. In 1167, Derbail daughter of Donnchad Ua Máel Sechlainn died in Clonmacnoise 'after a victory of will and confession', suggesting that like many other noble women she retreated to an ecclesiastical settlement at the end of her life. In the same year her kinswoman Derbforgaill daughter of Murchad Ua Máel Sechlainn was involved in the completion or furnishing of the 'Nuns' Church' at Clonmacnoise.[226] She had already donated gold, a chalice and altar-cloths to Mellifont in 1157, and she died there in 1193.[227] The most notorious episode in Derbforgaill's life was her

222 Ó Corráin, 'Mael Muire Ua Dúnáin', p. 50. Máel Muire Ua Dúnáin finally died in retirement in Clonard in 1117. **223** Dobbs, 'Ban-shenchus', 232. **224** AClon [1139]; Flanagan, *Transformation*, pp 181–3. **225** AFM entries *sub anno*. **226** AFM. For a detailed consideration of the date of this impressive Romanesque building and Derbforgaill's involvement in its construction, see Jenifer Ní Ghrádaigh, '"But what exactly did she give?": Derbforgaill and the Nuns' Church at Clonmacnoise' in Heather King (ed.), *Clonmacnoise Studies* 2 (Dublin, 2003), pp 175–207. **227** AU, ALC, AFM; Flanagan, *Transformation*, p. 201.

kidnapping (voluntarily or otherwise) in 1152 by Diarmait Mac Murchada, king of Leinster and arch-rival of her husband, Tigernán Ua Ruairc, king of Bréifne. Notwithstanding her father Murchad's role in endowing new foundations, her association with Mac Murchada and Ua Ruairc, two royal patrons of the church, must have had an influence on her. Ua Ruairc granted lands to the community of Kells, Co. Meath,[228] as well as apparently granting lands to an Augustinian community at Navan, Co. Meath.[229] Mac Murchada endowed one of the earliest houses of women following the Arrouaisian observance, St Mary de Hogges in Dublin. Confirmation of grants made by him to the convent were endorsed by the papal legate to Ireland Cardinal John Paparo in 1152,[230] suggesting that this foundation was the first Augustinian house endowed by Mac Murchada. Flanagan has suggested on the basis of the prior of Louth having first say in the election of the abbess of Odder – the site to which the Clonard convent transferred *c.*1380 – that the abbess of Clonard may have been dependent on St Mary's Louth.[231] A further vital connection between Diarmait Mac Murchada and the Uí Máel Sechlainn was that his sister Dubcablach was wife of Muirchertach Ua Máel Sechlainn and, more significantly, mother of Agnes 'the great abbess'.[232] The latter was related to Derbforgaill, probably a first cousin. It was from within this network that the Augustinian convent at Clonard was founded.

Who were the female religious of Clonard and what was their form of monastic life? We have no detailed evidence regarding their way of life except that they were somehow affiliated to the Arrouaisian observance, which, if genuinely followed could have meant a strict observance of the Divine Office and rules concerning their habits, their food and their work. Evidence from elsewhere suggests that some women, the *sorores*, were involved in manual labour or worked in hospitals, while others, possibly the wealthier women, produced items such as altar-cloths and vestments.[233] In this context, Derbforgaill's gift of cloth for the nine altars in the church at Mellifont could have been made in a female foundation, possibly even Clonard. If the list of Clonard's possessions confirmed in the papal confirmation of 1195 is a genuine reflection of the foundation's lands and churches for which it was responsible,[234] it raises issues about the role of women such as Agnes Ua Máel Sechnaill as both ecclesiastical administrators and heads of communities of holy women. Was she, *In Caillech Mór* 'the great abbess', similar to the early abbesses in Kildare, because of her secular or spiritual authority? Certainly, she and her cousin Derbforgaill lived

228 Mac Niocaill, *Notitiæ*, pp 24–6 (VII). **229** Eric St John Brooks (ed.), 'A charter of John de Courcy to the abbey of Navan', *Journal of the Royal Society of Antiquaries of Ireland* 3 (1933), 38–45, at p. 39. **230** Flanagan, *Irish royal charters*, pp 384–5. **231** Flanagan, 'St Mary's Abbey, Louth', 231–33. **232** ALC. **233** Alexis Grélois, 'Les chanoines réguliers et la conversion des femmes aux XIIe siècle' in Parisse, *Les chanoines réguliers*, pp 233–64, at pp 245–6. **234** Sheehy, *Pont. Hib.*, i, pp 83–6 no. 29.

through a violent era during which fierce dynastic and regional wars were fought, while at the same time those involved in these wars contributed hugely to a church in the process of transformation. And notably, both women seem to have outlasted their menfolk and lived long lives. And if there was transformation, existing practices did not end. The Uí Máel Sechlainn and families subject to them kept the Clonard community in their grasp until the late fourteenth century when the last abbess of a 'Mide' family died. Thereafter, the office was held by local Anglo-Norman women until the dissolution.[235]

TOWARDS A NEW MONASTICISM

From the late 1220s a new international monastic phenomenon was introduced into Ireland in the form of the mendicant orders, and most especially the Dominicans and the Franciscans. In their initial phase, they founded houses in the emerging Anglo-Norman towns and they were supported by the English crown and by increasingly powerful Anglo-Normans prelates and lords.[236] Their impact on the old monastic tradition is difficult to gauge due to the absence of detailed sources but what is known suggests that Irish patrons did not turn to endowing the mendicants until the mid-thirteenth century. Among the earliest was Domhnall Cairbreach Ó Briain who is said to have founded a Dominican house in Limerick and was reputedly buried there in 1241.[237] He was also the reputed founder of the Franciscan friary in Ennis, a house that continued to be associated with the Uí Briain until its dissolution in the sixteenth century. A more definite example of Irish endowment of mendicants is that of Feidhlimid Ó Conchobhair, king of Connacht, who founded St Mary's Dominican priory in Roscommon in 1253 and was buried there in 1265.[238] Roscommon had been the location of an important earlier monastery to which Feidhlimid's ancestor, Toirdelbach, had presented a piece of the true cross in 1123 which was encased in the shrine later known as 'The Cross of Cong'.[239] St Mary's Roscommon became one of the Dominicans' most important houses in Ireland during the late medieval period.[240] The early monasteries of Lismore and Ardmore fell foul of more successful episcopal seats such as Waterford and Cloyne but from the mid-thirteenth century must have also been in competition for both manpower

235 Hall, 'Towards a prosopography of nuns', 4–5. The community transferred to Odder, Co. Meath, *c.*1380. **236** Ó Clabaigh, *The friars in Ireland*, pp 1–29. **237** *MRHI*, pp 226–7. **238** Ó Clabaigh, *The friars in Ireland*, p. 10. **239** Griffin Murray, *The Cross of Cong. A masterpiece of medieval Irish art* (Sallins, 2014). **240** Not a great distance away, the Uí Mocháin held the abbacy of the Cistercian abbey of Boyle on three occasions: Aodh Ua Mocháin (fl. *c.*1150), Domhnall Ó Mocháin (*c.*1434–*c.*1442), Conchobhar Ó Mocháin, bishop of Achonry (*c.*1444–6). Benedict Ó Mocháin (d. 1361) was *airchinnech* of the old church of Killaraght, Co. Sligo: Mac Niocaill, *Na manaigh liatha*, pp 172–3.

and assets with the new orders including the Dominicans and Franciscans who both had foundations in Youghal. Youghal developed into a burgeoning borough at the mouth of the river Blackwater mainly due to the patronage of the Anglo-Norman Fitzgeralds.[241] In addition, the riverine early monastery of Molana (Dairinis) nearby was renewed during the same period by Augustinian canons who built a substantial monastery on the site.[242] These, then, eclipsed the older monasteries of Lismore and Ardmore.

Hereditary ecclesiastical families crop up among the few named thirteenth-century Irish friars. Two of the bishops of Clonmacnoise who were Franciscans seem to have belonged to long-established families who had already been affiliated to that monastery. Tomás Ó Cuinn (alias O'Quinn), bishop of Clonmacnoise (1252–78), may have been a descendant of the family of Conn na mBocht mentioned previously. His popular and vivid preaching tours are mentioned in the Irish *Liber exemplorum*, a thirteenth-century compilation originating in an Anglo-Irish Franciscan milieu.[243] The family of Domhnall Ó Bráein, Franciscan bishop of Clonmacnoise (*c.*1302), were associated with Clonmacnoise and Roscommon, where they were the *comarbai* of St Comán until the 1230s. Tipraide Ó Bráein died as *comarbae* of Comán in 1232 on the island of Inis Clothrann, Co. Longford. He is praised for his learning in theology, history and law (*saoí cléircechta, sencusa, 7 breithemhnassa*).[244] No more than the Augustinians and the Cistercians, the mendicant orders must have attracted members of families already attached to the church and also from among patrons' families, and did so throughout the late medieval period. While the Fourth Lateran Council curtailed the establishment of new religious orders as well as enforcing discipline in relation to simony and possessions, papal letters throughout the later medieval period indicate that while the structure of early Irish monasticism did not survive, many individuals and families adapted to the new monastic disposition and made their own of it.

It cannot be denied that the twelfth and early thirteenth centuries were transformational and tumultuous periods in Ireland. In the monastic world, a stable existing tradition founded on the universal precepts of monasticism within a particular regional culture gave way to a greater international and gradually centralized movement. The Irish aristocracy and newly arrived Anglo-Norman lords both enthusiastically embraced this changing form of monasticism. But what of those who were already committed to a religious life in long-established monasteries or those who wished to commit themselves to a particular spiritual way of life? They were caught between the 'old' and the 'new' and in many

241 Anne-Julie Lafaye, 'Reconstructing the landscape of the mendicants in east Munster: the Franciscans' in Eamonn Cotter (ed.), *Buttevant. A medieval Anglo-French town in Ireland* (Rathcormac, 2013), pp 67–82. **242** Eamonn Cotter, 'Molana abbey – a fortified house?', *Archaeology Ireland* 29:4 (Winter, 2015), 22–5, at pp 22–3. **243** Ó Clabaigh, *The friars in Ireland*, pp 31, 286. **244** AFM.

instances they probably straddled both until by the mid-thirteenth century it was no longer possible to do so. The traditional structure of an Irish monastery, spiritual and temporal, divided into new components. The diocese, the parish, the monastery, the friary, the priory, the nunnery were theoretically hived off from the *airchinnig* and their hold on ecclesiastical lands and relics, and from those learned in native history and law. While this division was not as clear-cut as often portrayed, it is true that for those following a committed monastic life, the choice of lifestyle was now confined to membership of international monastic and mendicant orders.

Conclusion

The exceptionalist approach to monasticism in early medieval Ireland has meant that its traditions and institutions have yet to be fitted into the wider context of the development of western monasticism from its early centuries. It is as if monasticism in Ireland flourished during the sixth and seventh centuries and then in its pristine state returned to Britain and the Continent, leaving a static form of monasticism, diminished by increasing secularization, to take root in the great monasteries of Ireland. Scholars have clung to two periods of 'progress'. The *céli Dé* movement promoted a renewed lifestyle of asceticism from the eighth century onwards. Ireland's first encounter with 'normalized' Benedictine monasticism and ecclesiastical reform came in the letters and admonitions of Lanfranc and Anselm to Irish kings and bishops. Recent scholarship has shown, however, that Irish kings and clerics were in contact with the Ottonian church and travelling on pilgrimages to Rome, and that Dúnán (Donatus), the first bishop of Dublin (d. 1074) was probably trained in a Benedictine milieu in Cologne.[1] From a methodological perspective, viewing Ireland's monasticism as somewhat exotic and not part of the normalized 'reformed' monasticism of elsewhere by the eleventh century is to underestimate the complexity of monasticism in western Christendom between 900 and 1250. The general narrative has been dominated over many years by events such as the drawing up and instituting of the *Regularis Concordia* in Anglo-Saxon England by bishops Dunstan (d. 988), Æthelwold (d. 984) and Oswald (d. 992) with King Edgar (d. 970) and Queen Ælfthryth (d. 1000/1), the Lotharingian reforms centred in Gorze and Metz, and the rise of the Cluniac network during the tenth to twelfth centuries.[2] In the past historians interpreted episodes of the imposition of discipline on monastic houses as necessary to revive monasticism (normally categorized as 'Benedictine') plagued by internal decline and external attacks and as the beginning of an incremental process of reform that culminated in

1 Bethell, 'English monks and Irish reform'; Pádraig Ó Riain, *A martyrology of four cities: Metz, Cologne, Dublin, Lund*; Ó Floinn, 'The foundation relics of Christ Church cathedral'; Dagmar Ó Riain-Raedel, 'New light on the beginnings of Christ Church cathedral, Dublin' in Seán Duffy (ed.), *Medieval Dublin XVII* (Dublin, 2019), 63–80. 2 There is extensive literature on these subjects.See the comprehensive bibliography on the history of monasticism in late antiquity and the early Middle Ages compiled by Albrecht Diem, Syracuse University http://www.earlymedievalmonasticism.org/bibliographymonasticism.htm accessed on 22 May 2020. Note the works of Giles Constable and in particular his review of Cluniac studies, 'The future of Cluniac studies', *The Journal of Medieval Monastic Studies* 1 (2012), 1–16.

'revival'. This narrative, however, requires nuance and has been subjected to much scrutiny in the past decade. In his study of the 'reform' of female religious communities in the Lotharingian dioceses of Metz and Toul during the mid-tenth century,[3] Steven Vanderputten argues that the renewal of a stricter 'Benedictine' regime was often to the detriment of these women's independence, and most importantly from an Irish perspective, 'reforms' marked the beginning of an intolerance towards 'ambiguous' non-Benedictine observances.[4]

The acknowledgement by scholars of the existence of 'ambiguous' or 'hybrid' forms of monasticism throughout Europe allows for monasticism in Ireland to fit into the recent emerging narrative of medieval *monasticisms*.[5] The idea that a standard form of Benedictine monasticism existed in the church from the time of Louis the Pious and Benedict of Aniane in the ninth century has been challenged by the greater emphasis now placed on local and regional studies such as those undertaken by Steven Vanderputten and others. Even the idea of Cluny as a monolithic institution is now questioned. In the words of Giles Constable, one of the most authoritative scholars on medieval monasticism, 'Cluny did not speak with a single voice ... It certainly had great influence in monastic affairs, which formed part of medieval society generally, but it was not the only centre of monastic reform and must be studied in relation to other monasteries, not in isolation, and as part of the larger religious scene of the time'.[6] Ireland's location on the periphery of Europe tends to validate scholars' – and more so the popular – view of its distinct early medieval culture, a culture that sought to adhere to the remnants of a 'pagan' Celtic culture. Hence its monastic tradition must have been different and exotic. A parallel so-called 'Celtic' monastic and spiritual tradition is extended also to Scotland and Wales where the old churches, *clasau*, in Wales or the *céli Dé* foundations in Scotland,[7] were 'reformed' by the Augustinian canons and Cistercians during the twelfth and thirteenth centuries. Forms of monasticism that did not fit into a normalized Benedictine rule – such as it was – were not, however, confined to the western Atlantic 'Celtic' lands. Indigenous practices and customs and a diversity of monastic lifestyles can be detected in other regions. For example, Valerie Ramseyer, draws attention to the complexity of monasticism in southern Italy and Sicily where forms of monasticism were practised by 'wandering ascetics, cloistered monks, household religious, solitary hermits, and cave monasticism'.[8] This monastic tradition,

3 Steven Vanderputten, *Dark age nunneries. The ambiguous identity of female monasticism, 800–1050* (Cornell, 2018), p. 88. 4 Vanderputten, *Dark age nunneries*, p. 89. 5 Vanderputten, *Medieval monasticisms*. 6 Constable, 'The future of Cluniac studies', p. 12. 7 Thomas Owen Clancy, 'Iona, Scotland and the Céli Dé' in Barbara E. Crawford (ed.), *Scotland in dark age Britain. The proceedings of a day conference held on 18 February 1995* (St Andrews, 1996), pp 111–30; Veitch, 'Conversion of native religious communities'; Nancy Edwards (ed.), *The archaeology of the early medieval Celtic churches* (London, 2009); Karen Stöber, 'The regular canons in Wales' in Burton and Stöber, *The regular canons*, pp 97–114. 8 Valerie Ramseyer, 'Questions of monastic identity

which was open to Greek and Latin influences, and subject to transformations emanating from elsewhere, nevertheless maintained its unique regional characteristics well into the twelfth century.[9] The same could be said for Irish monasticism at that time. If the Irish tradition is included with the many forms of monasticism prevalent elsewhere, it can be accommodated in the greater narrative not as an exotic outlier but as part of another example of 'ambiguous' and 'hybrid' monasticism.

In his reassessment of the early Irish church, Richard Sharpe posed the fundamental question: 'How monastic was the monastic church, and what was its relationship to the church among the laity?'[10] The response among scholars to date tends to echo Sharpe's own response: 'It is a mistake to treat monasticism as the be-all and end-all of Irish ecclesiastical organization'.[11] Pastoral care functioned under the jurisdiction of bishops and a secular clergy, although diocesan and proto-parish formation was organized to take account of a kin-based society and the interests of large corporate churches.[12] What became pervasive, however, were the concepts and vocabulary of monasticism which were used to describe so much of ecclesiastical life. All scholars agree that the term *manach* (< *monachus*) was applied to a range of people: true monks, tenants of monastic lands, servile retainers and aristocratic penitents. Indeed, the term *fír* or *glan manaig* ('true monks') was used at times to distinguish true monks from *túathmanaig* 'lay tenants', although *manach* could be used to denote both.[13] Depending on the source and its date, the terms *abb/abbas*, *airchinnech*, *comarbae*, *princeps* and *principatus* could signify the head of a committed religious community or the lay and often hereditary lord of a monastic estate. As in so many instances, the Irish situation may not have been as unusual as perceived, as the offices of *airchinnech* and *comarbae* in their lay sense were not that dissimilar from the lay advocates that ruled monastic estates elsewhere. Dunstan (d. 988), for example, as abbot of Glastonbury appointed his brother Wulfric as *prepositus* 'with full authority to see to the business of his estates outside the monastery precinct thus making sure that neither he himself [Dunstan] nor any professed monk should have to trouble himself with the senseless bustle of this world'.[14] Wulfric's son Ælfwine succeeded his father as *prepositus* but later became a professed monk. The term *prepositus* is explained by Winterbottom and Lapidge, as 'a sort of reeve, or, in Benedictine terminology, a 'prior'; what in modern parlance would be called an 'estates bursar''.[15] During his lifetime, Wulfric acquired a substantial amount of land from the Anglo-Saxon kings Edmund (d. 946) and Eadred (d. 955) which ultimately came into Glastonbury's

in medieval southern Italy and Sicily (*c*.500–1200)', in *CHMM*, pp 399–414, at p. 319. 9 Ramseyer, 'Monastic identity', pp 412–14. 10 Sharpe, 'The organization of the church in early medieval Ireland'. 11 Ibid., 270. 12 Ó Corráin, 'The early Irish churches'; Breatnach, *Córus Bésgnai*. 13 Etchingham, *Church organisation*, p. 328 (quoting *CIH*, 918.12–17). 14 Winterbottom and Lapidge, *St Dunstan*, p. xxvii §18.1. 15 Ibid., p. xxvii.

possession. *Pr(a)epositus* is used both in ecclesiastical and secular contexts in Irish sources and is often equated with *rechtaire*, normally a royal steward,[16] not unlike Wulfric's position in Glastonbury.

As for historians' assessment of regulated monasticism in early Ireland, the usual approach has been to examine a particular set of sources: ecclesiastical canons and penitentials, secular laws, hagiography, and the 'Tallaght dossier' associated with the *céli Dé*. The greatest concentration of scholarship has been in the period of the major monastic foundations during the late sixth/early seventh centuries to the appearance of the *céli Dé* in the late eighth century. For Kathleen Hughes, the *céli Dé* spearheaded a spiritual reform of an increasingly secularized church and in comparing them to the so-called contemporary Carolingian reforms judged that 'Irish ascetic practice lacked the discipline of the Benedictine rule or the uniformity of Carolingian reform. Anchorites might meet for discussion, but there was no emperor to enforce their decisions, not even a metropolitan to keep them in mind'.[17] And that only came when the ascetic temper of the influential minority in traditional Irish monasticism turned, under the new régime, to the Cistercian rule. 'Here was a way of life with the physical austerity, the spiritual devotion, and total commitment of the early Irish ascetics, together with the organization which twelfth-century opinion recognized as necessary'.[18] In his outline survey of monasticism 'in its primary sense', which he acknowledged was not a comprehensive reassessment of monastic practice and spirituality, but related to 'aspects of ecclesiastical organization, jurisdiction and mission', Etchingham concluded that a 'cenobitic variety of monasticism is of the essence throughout the period studied [AD 650–1000]'.[19] The sources signal that the unregulated self-appointed holy man – and presumably woman, although little is said of these – was viewed unfavourably, while the authorized anchorite was highly regarded, so much so that in certain circumstances they could be appointed to head a church or to act as judge. Not many lived totally solitary lives, and they mainly existed within or in proximity to an ecclesiastical community who often supplied them with their upkeep. On occasion, they were elevated to high office and could retreat from the main community to do penance. Diversity in strictness would appear to have been a hallmark of early Irish monasticism.[20]

How far has this volume answered Richard Sharpe's question 'How monastic was the monastic church, and what was its relationship to the church among the laity?'. How far has it progressed the study of early Irish monasticism beyond Donnchadh Ó Corráin's last comments on the subject:[21]

16 *DIL s.v.* In the Penitential of Columbanus, the *praepositus* is a monastic superior (Ludwig Bieler (ed.), *The Irish penitentials* (Dublin, 1963), pp 96–8 §§9–12. See Etchingham, *Church organisation*, pp 91, 324. 17 Hughes, *Church in early Irish society*, p. 183. 18 Ibid., p. 271. 19 Etchingham, *Church organisation*, p. 361. 20 Ibid., p. 362. 21 Ó Corráin, *The Irish church*, p. 15.

> The nature of these religious houses [early Irish monasteries] has caused historians many difficulties. They were not Benedictine houses (whatever meaning we may attach to that wider term), and their senior members are more likely to resemble well-endowed secular canons, whose communal and individual wealth maintained within them different kinds of coenobitic communities of varying severity, houses of mendicants (as in Clonmacnoise), houses of Céli Dé, and cultural institutions – scriptoria, libraries and schools of Latin and Irish learning.

Both Sharpe and Ó Corráin queried the degree to which the early Irish church was monastic and both were very aware of the complex nature of that institution. In a sense, Ó Corráin's assessment is correct in that he identified the various strands that existed in at least the larger Irish monasteries. They consisted of various constituencies: economic, religious and temporal. In turn, the religious constituency consisted of bishops, priests, monks, hermits, nuns and vowesses, scholars and scribes. Very few were completely detached from the main settlement but some chose to live a more ascetic life in hermitages that were either close by, even within the main settlement, or in more extreme cases in isolated places such as on lakes and coastal islands. Among the male religious, not all were ordained priests, many probably were not. Those who were may have followed lives more like canons, especially as the concept of the *vita apostolica*, exemplified by Augustinian canons, became more widespread from the eleventh century onwards. Coenobitic communities were under the authority of their own religious superior, but were also subject to the rule of a bishop – who may have been one and the same – the head of the temporal constituency and his family, and sometimes a local or provincial dynasty. This was a mutually beneficial relationship as the temporal authorities sustained the monastic communities with their basic needs through providing them with a habitation (often called a *dísert*), a church, a school and supplies. This must have been the case also for even the most isolated hermitages. In return, they no doubt expected their monastic communities to intercede with God and the monastery's founder saint for the salvation of their souls. The impression gained throughout the literature is that communities were small, even in the large monasteries. How many such monastic communities existed at any one time cannot be estimated but it would appear that they became increasingly concentrated in middle-ranking and large monasteries so that by the eleventh century, most of them were in places such as Armagh, Clonmacnoise, Derry, Emly, Glendalough, Kells and Lismore. Of course, this may be a somewhat skewed view of the situation, as the vast bulk of sources that survive emanated from the larger monasteries. Apart from hermitages located outside the monastic enclosure, how extensive monasticism was in lesser churches is not clear, although it was not at all as widespread as popularly believed. Not every medieval church ruin in the Irish landscape was a monastery or hermitage. The likely local ecclesiastical structure involved a variety of institutions, mainly a priest or priests administering pastoral care to the laity, some celibate, some not, some living the *vita apostolica* and following a committed religious life similar to later canons. It cannot be ruled out that ordained monks, even those in minor orders, interacted to varying degrees with the laity. The sources, especially those emanating from *céli Dé* spheres, suggest that they were involved particularly with penitents, many of whom seem to have been lay aristocrats. Craig Haggart's theory that the *céli Dé* became the custodians of hospices, likely only in Armagh or Clonmacnoise, might have been linked to their role as confessors (*anmchairde*) to nobles, senior clerics and religious who ended their lives in great monasteries. Nor were religious communities ignorant of temporal affairs, be it in the monastery itself or outside. So many monasteries and churches were subject to endemic raiding by Irish and Norse kings involved in dynastic and territorial conflicts that those in the *dísert* must have witnessed and suffered due to this violence. In 923, for example, Dublitir, priest of Armagh, was killed when the Vikings of Carlingford Lough, raided the female foundation at Killevy, Co. Armagh.[22] Although the annals do not elaborate, one wonders if the nuns of Killevy were taken by the raiders and sold on the slave market. Yet it seems that violence against monks and hermits may have been rare enough, normally occurring at the hands of the Vikings. Étgal, abbot of Skellig Michael, died of hunger at the hands of the Vikings in 824,[23] while Abel, a scribe, was killed by the Vikings along with many others on the Great Saltee Island in 922.[24] And yet, at the same time, the Vikings – contrary to the normal perception of them as murderers of monks – on occasion recognized the distinction between the inhabitants of the *dísert* and hospice and the rest, and spared them. The description of the raid by Gothfrith son of Ímar and the Vikings of Dublin on Armagh in 921 not only hints at this phenomenon but also offers a glimpse of the range of inhabitants living in the monastery at the time:[25]

> Ard Macha was invaded by the foreigners of Áth Cliath, i.e. by Gothfrith grandson of Ímar, with his army, on the fourth of the Ides *10th* of November, the Saturday before the feast of Martin, and the prayer-houses with their complement of *céli Dé* and sick he spared from destruction, and also the church, save for a few dwellings which were burned through carelessness.

Armagh was a crowded settlement located on and around a hill and there are sufficient references to its buildings to provide a fairly complete account of its

22 AU, AFM [921]. 23 AI. 24 AFM [920]. 25 AU. Original: *Indredh Aird Macha h-i.iiii. Id. Nouembris o Gallaibh Atha Cliath, .i. o Gothbrith oa Imhair, cum suo exercitu, .i. h-isint Sathurn ria feil Martain, & na taigi aernaighi do anacal lais cona lucht de cheilibh De & di*

layout (Fig. 32).[26] Among the buildings and structures mentioned between 900 and 1266 were the great stone church (*in damliac mór*), bell towers, other stone and wooden chapels dedicated to Brigit and Colum Cille, a building/church called *in tSaball* 'the barn',[27] the church of the burial mounds (*Tempall na Ferta*)), the abbot's house, its close (*ráith*) and twenty houses around it, among them houses of elders (*tech srotha*), a house in which kings resided, a library (*tech screbtra*), schoolmasters' houses (e.g., *tech Fethgna*), ?the house/church of the elect or of the silent (*damliac na toga*, *damliac na tóe*), students' houses, a guest house (*lis óiged*), a kitchen, three districts (*Trían Mór* 'the large third', *Trían Masáin* 'Masán's third', *Trían Saxan* 'the Saxon third'), streets, the cemetery of the kings, ramparts, crosses dedicated to Brigit, Colum Cille, bishops Éogan and Sechnall and a sanctuary/sacred grove (*fid nemed*). The great church was built in 995 and restored with a shingle roof in 1125. The church dedicated to SS Peter and Paul was erected in 1126. It would appear that Cellach, abbot and bishop and associate of Malachy and Ímar Ua hÁedacáin, undertook a re-organization of Armagh, probably as part of his attempt to transform the monastery. In 1266/8, the primate Giolla Pátraic Ó Scannail commenced the building of a new cathedral (*teampall mór*), presumably replacing the earlier church. He also built a new dyke or moat (*díc* borrowed from French *digue* or OE *díc*) around Armagh in 1264.

Armagh has the full complement of buildings required for all the activities carried out there comparable to the buildings named on the Plan of St Gall. It might be conjectured that the monastic or ascetic quarter in Armagh was to the southeast of the main church where Damliac in tSabaill and Damliac na Tóe – perhaps a hospice or guesthouse and church of the anchorites – stood, and to the south of them, the late medieval priory of the *céli Dé* which possibly stood on an earlier foundation. It may also be significant that the busier end of the settlement around the abbot's house was located on the other side of the great church, as was the twelfth-century abbey of SS Peter and Paul. Was this an indication that Ímar Ua hÁedacáin's community did not wish to be closely associated with the established monastic community, and that they regarded themselves as following the *vita apostolica* like canons? The location of St

lobraibh, & in ceall olcheana, nisi paucis in ea tectis exaustis per incuriam. **26** For all references to Armagh, see Catherine McCullough and W.H. Crawford, *Irish Historic Towns Atlas no. 18 Armagh* (Dublin, 2007), pp 12–13 and p. 2 (fig. 1). https://www.ria.ie/irish-historic-towns-atlas-online-armagh. **27** *Saball* is a borrowing from Latin *stabulum* and means 'a barn, stable'. It is also found in the place-name Saball Pátraicc (Saul, Co. Down) and is usually interpreted as referring to a barn-shaped church. However, *stabulum* is glossed by the word *midachthech* in BL MS Harley 1023, a term which could mean 'the house of a physician'. If this has any merit, it might imply that the *Saball* was Armagh's hospice (Robin Flower, *Catalogue*, p. 433, l. 4). It might also be noted that one of Cluny's dependent communities in the early fourteenth century was the Nigrum Stabulum (Alexandre Bruel, 'Visites des monastères de l'ordre de Cluny de la province d'Auvergne en 1286 et 1310', *Bibliothèque de*

Saviour's at Glendalough, an Arrouasian foundation of the mid-twelfth century, a fair distance from the main settlement, was a more extreme statement of a newly formed community separating itself from the old. At the even more extreme scale of asceticism, as at Monaincha or Skellig, communities were living isolated but organized lives. These were not hermits in a 'Celtic' wilderness following an aberrant tradition unrelated to universal monasticism. They were normally associated with larger monasteries and they followed the fundamental ideology of monasticism encapsulated in concepts such as *amor et timor Dei*, *opus Dei*, *laus perennis*. It is likely that these communities were respected and regarded as an elite group, based on their piety and their learning.

One indication in the annals of someone who may have followed a committed religious life is reference to them as bishop, anchorite and scribe or an expert in some branch of learning in their obit. And as chastity was not always a requirement, many belonged to hereditary families, in line with other professional classes in society. Chastity may have been practised often in later life. Those more likely to have followed regulated, celibate and more ascetic lives from the eighth to the twelfth century were the *céli Dé* ('clients of God'), *deorada Dé* ('exiles of God') and the *cráibdig* ('pious people'). The *céli Dé* and the *cráibdig* appear to have formed part of a national network, many living in dedicated communities in larger monasteries, whose interests were in monastic regulation, liturgy and learning. The *deorada Dé* appear mainly in legal sources where the impression is gained of them as highly regarded and trustworthy because of their sanctity. To what extent all of these communities and individuals interacted with the laity depended on where they resided and what the local customs were in relation to *cura animarum*. *Céli Dé* sources suggest that they regarded themselves as involved in the salvation of souls, probably acting mainly as *anmchairde* 'confessors' to the aristocracy. The tension between a *vita activa* and a *vita contemplativa* is evident in saints' lives as saints often withdrew from the world to the wilderness only to be pursued by their followers or those seeking succour. Cóemgen of Glendalough had to be ordered by an angel to return to the main monastery, which he was seen to be neglecting.[28] Moving beyond the early monastic founders to the so-called 'Tallaght dossier' produced during the eighth and ninth centuries, although the *céli Dé* and their leaders were concerned with a stricter way of life, in origin their structure was based on a small network of coenobitic communities who exercised influence beyond their enclosures. In fact, Máel Ruain of Tallaght is seen to dislike some anchorites. When he sent Cornán, an anchorite and musician, a gift of fellowship (*caradrad*) of prayer, he rejected Cornán's offer to play him music saying that his ears would prefer the music of Heaven.[29] He was even more critical of an anchorite in Clonard who wore

l'École des chartes 38 (1877), 114–27, at p. 120 §17). **28** Plummer, *BNnÉ*, i, 127–8 (x: 20); ii, 123–4 (x: 20). **29** Gwynn, 'The teaching of Máel Ruain', pp 30–1 §50.

himself out with excessive daily genuflections. Máel Ruain predicted that before his death he would not be able to genuflect at all and thus the unfortunate anchorite became crippled and was unable to make a single genuflection.[30] One of the dominant characteristics of the *céli Dé*, that is often overlooked, is that most of its prominent adherents in the eighth and ninth centuries are recorded as holding senior ecclesiastical offices as bishops, abbots and scribes.[31] Their manifest concern for pastoral care and penance – to quote Westley Follett –[32] meant that they could not withdraw completely from the world and that their capacity to direct not just their own communities but to upgrade clerical education and liturgy in Ireland was enhanced by their status as bishops, whatever the geographical or geo-political extent of their jurisdictions. From the end of the ninth century onwards, however, it would seem that the way of life and functions of the *céli Dé* changed and that they may have concentrated on being carers of guests, the poor and the sick.[33] This meant that they did not necessarily follow a committed religious life, and certainly that many of them were active in their wider monastic communities and among the laity. Others, however, continued to practise the asceticism of their founders, sometimes identified as *céli Dé*, or as *deorada Dé* and *cráibdig*.

The warnings in regulatory texts to *anmchairde* not to accept gifts from the laity but to disperse them among the poor suggests that even the religious elite could succumb to greed.[34] Ownership of possessions and property is frowned upon in the regulatory texts and the term *na boicht* 'the poor' is occasionally used to describe monastic communities. The *Hibernensis* stipulate that worldly possessions were to be dispensed with, as cenobites lived 'communally in emulation of the family of the apostles' (*qui in commone uiuunt in instar apostolorum familiæ*). This stipulation is echoed in later texts such as the Rule of Ailbe:[35]

> When reward is being shared out to each according to his measure, give to the brother yonder who needs it most.

The Kells memoranda, the relationship between the Meic Cuinn na mBocht, the eminent family at Clonmacnoise and its *boicht* and *céli Dé*, and the evidence of late medieval episcopal land holdings, demonstrate that these communities avoided dealing with material matters by depending on those in charge of temporal matters for their upkeep.

30 Ibid., pp 60–1 §103. **31** These include Máel Ruain of Tallaght (d. 792), Caínchomrac of Finglas (d. 791), Dublitter of Finglas (d. 796), Eochaid of Tallaght (d. 812), Flann of Finglas (d. 812), Mac Riaguil of Birr (d. 822), Bran of Finglas (d. 838), Flaithnia of Birr (d. 853), Robartach of Finglas (d. 867), Torpaid of Tallaght (d. 874) and Máel Petair of Terryglass (d. 895). **32** Follett, *Céli Dé in Ireland*, p. 213. **33** Haggart, 'A reassessment'. **34** Gwynn, 'The teaching of Mael Ruain', pp 18–19 §30. **35** O Neill, 'Rule of Ailbe', pp 102–3 §27[d].

The monastic tradition of the early founders, exemplified by Columba and Columbanus, established a monastic culture of intense asceticism in Ireland that continued as a core element of Irish monasticism to the twelfth century. Even on the Continent, as happened in the Ottonian Empire especially during the eleventh century, Irish monks brought with them some of their more severe practices which, if Denis Bethell was correct, was possibly accepted in the rather conservative intellectual centres of the Roman Empire.[36] The monk and anchorite (*inclusus*), Marianus Scotus (Máel Brigte) left Ireland at the request of his superior, Tigernach Bairrcech, abbot of Moville and chief confessor of Ireland (*ard-anmchara Érenn*) (d. 1061).[37] He began his life as a *peregrinus* for some misdemeanour that had caused Tigernach's displeasure. His career from *c.*1056 was spent in the Ottonian Empire, first in the monastery of St Martin in Cologne, then via Würtzburg he went to Fulda where he became a recluse in 1059. At the request of Siegfried, archbishop of Mainz and abbot of Fulda (d. 1086), Marianus came to Mainz and in 1069 was enclosed again, this time in the chapel of St Bartholomew in the monastery of St Martin in that city, where he remained until his death in 1082.[38] Marianus Scotus was not alone in being banished from Ireland to the Continent for transgressing a monastic rule. In his chronicle at 1043, he records the death of an Irishman Animchadus, monk and *inclusus*, in the monastery of Fulda. Lights could be seen and psalms could be heard emanating from Animchadus's grave, and it is possible that Marianus was successor to the saintly recluse. Animchadus had been expelled by his senior, Corcrán, from his community on the island of Inis Cealtra, as he had shown lack of humility in giving some brethren more drink than had been permitted by the abbot.[39] The conflict between Animchadus and Corcrán on the dispensing of drink to his brethren finds an echo in 'The teaching of Máel Ruain'. Máel Ruain's control over his community is illustrated in an anecdote about allowing them to drink on certain festivals. Dublitir of Finglas sought to convince Máel Ruain to relax his rule in Tallaght but Máel Ruain replied sternly:[40]

> 'So long', said he, 'as they are under my control and keep my commands, they shall drink no drop that causes them to forget God in this place [Tallaght].'

Original: *In tan fondailter fochall / do chách iarna mes, / tabair-siu don bráthir thall / as mó ricc a les.* 36 Bethell, 'English monks and Irish reform', p. 114. 37 Despite being accorded this lofty title along with being described as an anchorite Tigernach Bairrcech was not celibate as he was succeeded in the abbacy by his son Flaithbertach. Ó Riain, *DIS*, p. 574. 38 Bartholomew MacCarthy, *The Codex Palatino-Vaticanus, No. 830* (texts, translations and indices). Todd Lectures Series 3 (Dublin, 1892), pp 4–7. 39 MacCarthy, *Codex Palatino-Vaticanus*, pp 31–2. 40 Gwynn, 'The teaching of Mael Ruain', pp 24–5 §40. Original: '*An feadh', ar se, 'beid fam chumhachtaibh-si 7 choimheadfas siad mh'aithne, ní ibaid bráon dermaid De san bhaili-si.*'

Neither Animchadus nor Marianus are mentioned in the Irish annals while Corcrán Clérech ('the cleric') is lauded in his obit as 'head of religious life of Ireland' (*cenn crábuid na h-Érenn*).[41]

If Marianus and Animchadus were treated harshly by their superiors in Ireland, they did not seek an easy life on the Continent. Marianus reports that Elias, otherwise Ailill of Muckno (Co. Monaghan), whose death is recorded in 1042 as head of the Irish in Cologne, and who was abbot of the monasteries of St Martin and St Panthaleon in that city, clashed with Piligrinus, archbishop of Cologne (d. 1036), an ardent pro-Cluniac cleric, about the strict regime followed by him and his Irish brethren. Elias's response to the bishop's attempts to oust the Irish from St Panthaleon is worth mentioning, even if it likely to be apocryphal: 'If Christ be for pilgrims, Bishop Piligrinus should not return from that place [the royal court] alive to Cologne'.[42] And Elias's alleged prophecy was fulfilled as Piligrinus died suddenly during the wedding of Henry III and Gunhilda of Denmark in Nijmegen. The Irish may not have been the direct cause of his death as he was involved in other more international controversies and negotiations but they may have added to the bishop's woes. Marianus's chronicle is a valuable testimony as it bridges two apparently separate monastic worlds, that of his native land and that of an increasingly formalized Ottonian Benedictine way of life. Marianus's own personal journey raises fundamental questions. What was the nature of monasticism in Ireland in the eleventh century and had it remained unchanged since monasticism spread to the island during the conversion process, sometime during the fifth and sixth centuries? Do the apparently extreme views and actions of abbots Corcrán and Tigernach in Ireland, Elias in Cologne, and the *inclusi* Animchadus and Marianus in Fulda and Mainz suggest that the Irish maintained a monastic tradition that was harsher than that pertaining elsewhere? An interesting marginal note in Middle Irish written into an eleventh-century codex from the Bavarian Benedictine monastery of Oberaltaich (Munich MS Clm 9550) reads *Impede Mauritii cum sociis et Sancti Emmerammi martiri imdilgiud dona helehrechib trogaib se ule* ('The intercession of Mauritius with his companions and of St Emmeram, martyr, for forgiveness on behalf of all these miserable pilgrims'). This gloss has been interpreted by Pádraig A. Breatnach as indicating that Benedictine monasteries such as that at Oberaltaich and those Irish foundations in Regensburg were giving shelter to groups of Irish pilgrims.[43] While undoubtedly Irish pilgrims occasionally sought accommodation in these houses, the use of the term *ailithrech tróg* 'wretched pilgrim' to describe a community is more likely to refer

41 AI 1040. 42 MacCarthy, *Codex Palatino-Vaticanus*, p. 32. Original: *si Christus in ipsis fuit peregrinis, ne umquam omnino ad Coloniam vivus venisset de curte episcopus Piligrinus.* 43 Pádraig A. Breatnach, 'The origins of the Irish monastic tradition at Ratisbon (Regensburg)', *Celtica* 13 (1980), 58–77, at pp 70–1.

to a group of *cráibdig* or *deorada Dé* in this context. This likelihood is corroborated by other marginalia in manuscripts originating from Regensburg. Marianus Scottus, scribe and founder of the Irish monastery of Weih-Sankt-Peter (d. *c.*1080),[44] described himself as *Muredach tróg macc Robartaig*[45] while his confrere Johannes signed himself as *Eoin tróg imnedach*.[46] Both were seeking intercession as *tróig* 'ones in need of mercy' and were members of a community of pilgrims in the sense of *deorada Dé*, not just exiles from their own land but exiles from the world. This transfer of an existing monastic concept appears to be clear from the scribal colophon in Latin included in Princeton MS Garrett 70 folio 86r which reads:[47]

> Holiest virgin of virgins, Mary mother of God, and all the saints and elect of God intercede on behalf of the poor miserable priest Johannes and on behalf of his fellow pilgrim brothers, so that their souls may rest in perpetual peace. Amen. That Johannes, namely, who wrote this little work for his brothers in the sixth year of his pilgrimage and of the Incarnation of the Lord, the 1082nd, in the reign of Henry the Fourth.

Marianus also referred to his confreres in the same terms, dedicating his work to his brother pilgrims (*Marianus Scottus scripsit hunc librum suis fratribus peregrinis*).[48] These intercessory formulae suggest that both the Irish in eleventh-century Cologne and eleventh-century Regensburg were attracted to the Benedictine tradition as pertained in the Ottonian world but that they did not necessarily let go of their own strict monastic traditions either.

As explored throughout the volume, it is clear that the fundamental ideology of monasticism as articulated by early writers, John Cassian, Pope Gregory the Great and others, was adhered to in Ireland. It did not follow a Benedictine tradition, if there was such a coherent tradition before the tenth century, but was probably a survival of earlier monastic traditions that flourished in Britain and

44 Marianus Scottus (Muiredach son of Robartach): DIB https://www.dib.ie/biography/marianus-scottus-muiredach-son-robartach-a5449 compiled by Aidan Breen. 45 Breatnach, 'Irish monastic tradition at Ratisbon', p. 63: preserved in Oesterreichische National-bibliothek Vienna MS cod. Lat. 1247. 46 Breatnach, 'Irish monastic tradition at Ratisbon', pp 63–4: Princeton University Library, MS Garrett 70. For a detailed discussion of the linguistic aspects of these intercessory formulae see Elliott Lash, 'Princeton MS Garrett 70 (1081–82) and other Regensburg manuscripts as witnesses to an Irish intercessory formula and the linguistic features of late-eleventh-century Middle Irish', *Peritia* 31 (2020), 165–92. 47 Lash, 'Princeton MS Garrett 70', pp 167–8. Original: *Sanctissima uirgo uirginum dei genetrix maria et omnes sancti et electi dei pro misero iohanne indigno presbitero et pro suis comperegrinis fratribus intercedite ut illorum animę in pace perpetua requiescant. Amen. Qui uidelicet iohannes hoc opusculum fratribus suis scripsit anno peregrinationis sue vi° dominice autem incarnationis milessimo octuogessimo secundo. Regnante quarto Henrico.* 48 Breatnach, 'Irish monastic tradition at Ratisbon', p. 75 n. 74.

Gaul, and even further to north Africa and the Middle East during the fifth and sixth centuries. Its regulatory texts, many of which are in the vernacular, are closer to the exhortatory format of the 'Sayings of the Desert Fathers' (*Apophthegmata Patrum*) than to the Rule of St Benedict or the Rule of the Master. It is possible that the Irish church preferred the format of penitentials to impose discipline on monastic communities, a format that was imposed also on the rest of the clergy and on the laity. This less defined format of exhortatory regulations is transformed in the 'Tallaght dossier', linked in particular to Máel Ruain of Tallaght (d. 792) and the *céli Dé* movement, into somewhat more codified rules and customs in the vernacular. These appear to have included customs associated with particular founders, and to have been addressed to the general clergy and lay penitents as well as the *céli Dé* themselves. The manuscript tradition of the 'Tallaght dossier' is complex as versions only survive in late medieval manuscripts and were subject to revision by late scribes, but it would seem that they are a fairly accurate representation of how many monastic communities were governed until the twelfth century. How far changes imposed on monastic communities elsewhere, especially in England and Germany, from the tenth century onwards influenced the Irish tradition is difficult to gauge. Echoes of the Benedictine rule occur occasionally in Irish texts, in the *Navigatio Sancti Brendani*, for example, although this does not amount to evidence of its use in Ireland. From the tenth century onwards, however, the island was open to many cultural contacts, through the church and the expanding trade of the Norse towns with a very extensive Scandinavian world. For example, it is likely that Dúnán of Dublin (d. 1074), probably a monk trained in a Benedictine milieu in Cologne, and his successors, trained as Benedictines in English monastic cathedrals, brought new customs and liturgy with them to their urban diocese. The monastery at Lismore became increasingly influential throughout the eleventh century and was the residence of Máel Ísu Ua hAinmere, first bishop of Waterford and a Benedictine trained in Winchester. On the other hand, Irish manuscripts of the period such as the Southampton Psalter, the Psalter of Caimín and the two copies of the *Liber Hymnorum* represent a monastic culture bound to an existing tradition of commentaries and hymnology. The Psalter of Caimín, for example, is textually old-fashioned, yet its artwork is in the contemporary Hiberno-Norse Ringerike style. Similarly, all the hymns in *LH*, both in Latin and in the vernacular, can be dated to earlier than the ninth century while they are also illuminated in the Hiberno-Norse Ringerike style. This relatively easy coexistence of old and new traditions is evident in other sources and only turned into a cultural conflict during Malachy's lifetime, exaggerated to a certain extent by external forces such as Lanfranc, Anselm and Bernard of Clairvaux. The outcome of the transformations that happened during the twelfth-century heralded considerable changes to this coexistence. The personnel *in situ* were not all banished since members of hereditary ecclesiastical families became bishops in the new dioceses and abbots in the foundations of new orders. The same families retained custody of church lands, albeit reduced in scale, shrines and relics, old manuscripts, while vernacular traditional history and learning moved into spheres divided between the lord's castle, professional schools and some of the new orders.[49] The survival of early texts depended on continual transmission by professional compilers and scribes, the most enthusiastic among them Uilliam Mac an Leagha (d. *c*.1475), a member of a medical family with a particular interest in religious texts.[50] Ó Corráin's fervent argument that the generation of Irish bishops who had to deal with Henry II and his episcopal and papal allies was diplomatically naive, if not gullible, is overly critical. He claims that they 'took the dramatic decision [at the Council of Cashel in 1171/2] to turn their backs on their own church, on its traditional usages and inherited pieties, on its long and distinguished history, on its newly reformed structure put in place, with great public ceremony and papal approval, at the Synod of Kells as recently as 1152'.[51] This statement denies the acumen of twelfth- and thirteenth-century Irish bishops, many of whom were monks or canons, to navigate the complex world of negotiations with the papacy and the Angevin kings, especially Henry II and his son John, a narrative documented in detail by Marie Therese Flanagan.[52]

The greatest gap in early medieval monastic Irish studies has been a lack of interest in the ideology of those committed to monasticism. There may be no normalized rules, no personal correspondence or reflections but there are enough sources to bring us close to the monastic mind. There are few surprises in what emerges from these prayers, didactic poems, hymns and commentaries on the psalms and canonical hours. The psalter is at the heart of life, whether reciting the full cursus of 150 psalms, an abbreviated version or concentrating on the much loved *Beati* (Psalm 118). This may have depended on the levels of literacy in a given community and also on the degree of asceticism being practised. The likelihood is that communities living in a *dísert* dedicated their days to constant prayer. The eight vices – gluttony, avarice, anger, lust, dejection, listlessness, self-esteem and pride – were the great challenges facing the hermit and the monk according to John Cassian and this was also part of the Irish monastic tradition. The canonical hours were the antidote to the vices, shields that could protect the wavering monk supported by the strength of his community's psalmody. If alone in an hour of need, the monk could resort to Cassian's monologistic prayer, repetition of the name of Jesus or a line from a psalm, to avoid sinning. 'Grant me tears, O Lord,/to blot out my sins': with tears

49 Edel Bhreathnach, 'The mendicant orders and vernacular learning in the late medieval period', *Irish Historical Studies* 37 (2010–11), 357–75. 50 DIB: https://www.dib.ie/biography/mac-lega-uilliam-iollann-a4990. 51 Ó Corráin, *The Irish church*, pp 109, 114. 52 See, for example, Marie Therese Flanagan, 'Hiberno-papal relations in the late twelfth century', *Archivium Hibernicum* 34 (1976–7), 55–70.

and compunction (*compunctio*) the sins of the eight vices could be washed away. And in the words of the poem known as 'Cormac's Rule' once cleansed 'the food that is after the extinction of desire, Christ's body with the blood of Mary's son' (*bíad bís iar ndíbdud toile, corp Críst la fuil Maic Maire*).[53] Chant and performance were also essential to a monastic community's life. No musical notation survives from Ireland but manuscripts such as the two copies of the *Liber Hymnorum* include echoes of communal and responsorial singing. An unusual telling of the origins of chant explained in a Middle Irish poem suggests knowledge of Guido of Arezzo's Harmonic Hand and of St Dunstan's supposed musical reputation. The cycle of hymns, as reflected mainly in *LH*, consisted of universal hymns such as *Hymnum dicat turba fratrum* attributed to Hilary of Poitiers and Latin and vernacular hymns all of which probably pre-date the ninth century. Some are attributed to the early founders, Columba being most prominent, and many are in praise of native and universal saints: Mary, Michael, the apostles, Patrick, Brigit, Columba and more. The divergence from the contents of Anglo-Saxon and Frankish hymnals and the continued use of many early hymns composed in an Irish milieu is yet another indication of an attachment to an existing tradition along with a strong cultural independence – what had been transmitted from earlier generations was cherished and not to be cast aside hastily. If this was the situation when a different liturgical tradition was introduced from the eleventh century onwards, the tussle between old and new that underlies some of the commentary about Arrouaisian and Cistercian liturgies in the lives of Malachy and Lorcán Ua Tuathail is unsurprising. The old hymns almost disappear from the liturgy, although some continue to be used in late medieval manuscripts. The *LH* hymn in honour of St Patrick *Ecce fulget* is included with notation in the fifteenth-century Antiphonary of Kilmoone (TCD MS 80, f. 122r) as a vesper hymn.[54]

Female monasticism in early Ireland is dominated by the royal monastery at Kildare and its founder, St Brigit. There is no doubt that it was originally a female foundation under the jurisdiction of a bishop, and that a male foundation also existed. Its abbess was a powerful figure in the province of Leinster, and Brigit's cult was widespread in Ireland, Britain and on the Continent. Many of the early abbesses were members of Brigit's people, the Fothairt, reflecting their original custodianship of Kildare and its surrounding ceremonial landscape.[55] By the tenth century, however, the office was increasingly held by women whose dynasties either held the kingship of Leinster or aspired to do so. Hence, it was transformed from a potent ceremonial and religious office into a contested

53 Strachan, 'Cormac's rule', p. 66, lines 12c–d. **54** Patrick V. Brannon, 'Medieval Ireland: music in cathedral, church and cloister', *Early Music* 28:2 (2000), 193–202, at pp 195–6. **55** Edel Bhreathnach, '1500th anniversary of St Brigit's death. But who was she?', *History Ireland* 32/2 (March/April, 2024), 14–17.

political office. Despite the abbess of Kildare's importance, there is little evidence for a thriving female monastic community in Kildare by this later period and no continental order established a convent there in the twelfth century or afterwards. Killevy, with its links to Armagh, may have survived as a more successful female community than Kildare if the sources memorializing its founder Monenna are credible. Her life attributed to Conchubranus, which may date to the eleventh century, seems to be addressed to a community of sisters, and the hymns in her honour, which appear in the same manuscript as Conchubranus's life, resemble a dossier prepared for an existing community. Other forms of female monasticism, alluded to in the *Hibernensis*, included women withdrawing from the world to follow a religious life. They might be widows or women whose husbands agreed to this new direction in their wives lives. Obits in the annals suggest that this practice was relatively common among aristocratic women especially during the eleventh and twelfth centuries. Most prominent among the monasteries housing these penitent women, some who may have gone to them in old age or due to illness, were Armagh, Clonmacnoise, Derry, Glendalough and Lismore. It is notable that apart from the deaths of its abbesses, there is no record of other noble women dying in Kildare. Female monasticism during the twelfth century was dominated by the endowments of royal families both to existing monasteries and to new foundations. The women of the midlands Ua Máel Sechlainn dynasty were particularly active in Clonmacnoise, the Arrouaisian foundation at Clonard and in Mellifont. This enthusiasm is a mirror of their menfolk who like many other Irish kings, became keen patrons of the new orders. As a result of their patronage, and of the patronage of Anglo-Norman lords, female communities became somewhat more visible, although caution is needed not to overstate the number of foundations that came into existence.

The great change to Irish monasticism witnessed during the twelfth and thirteenth centuries with the introduction of the new orders, monastic and mendicant, into Ireland, and the gradual demise, or more correctly absorption, of the existing monastic tradition, was far from smooth and successful. The history of the Cistercians during that period is replete with tensions both between Irish houses, their mother houses in Britain, with Clairvaux, and with the General Chapter.[56] Much has been made of the comments of Stephen of Lexington about racial tensions,[57] but as Brendan Smith has demonstrated in relation to the so-called 'conspiracy' of Mellifont, the main cause of the lengthy dispute that endured from 1216 to 1231 was the conflict for authority and territory at the heart of appointments to the primacy of Armagh and the

56 Mac Niocaill, *Na manaigh líatha*, pp 20–44, 77–101. 57 Barry W. O'Dwyer, *The conspiracy of Mellifont, 1216–1231. An episode in the history of the Cistercian order in medieval Ireland* (Dublin, 1970).

bishopric of Clogher/Louth which involved local Irish kings, Anglo-Norman lords and rival contenders, a number of whom were abbots of Mellifont.[58] Malachy and Áed Ua Cáellaide's Louth experiment fell apart and the Cistercians of Mellifont became embroiled in the consequent disorder. Stephen of Lexington's visitation to Mellifont in 1228 can only be understood in the context of the monastery's role in the Armagh–Clogher dispute. This was a power struggle that transcended the racial divide.[59] This interpretation of the 'Mellifont Conspiracy' is a valuable lesson in demonstrating the futility of imposing a strict division between pre- and post-1169 in Irish history. Great changes occurred during the twelfth century, including to the monastic tradition, but these changes were heralded long beforehand, and their effect seeped well into the thirteenth century. That later narrative is yet to be written.

58 Brendan Smith, 'The Armagh–Clogher dispute and the 'Mellifont Conspiracy': diocesan politics and monastic reform in early thirteenth-century Ireland', *Seanchas Ard Mhacha* 14:2 (1991), 26–38. **59** Smith, 'The Armagh–Clogher dispute', 37.

Bibliography

Note: Works preceded by an asterisk (*) are primary texts either original and/or in translation

Abram, Andrew, 'Augustinian canons and the survival of cult centres in medieval England' in Burton and Stöber, *The regular canons*, pp 79–95.

*Africa, Dorothy (trans.), 'Life of the holy virgin Samthann' in Thomas Head (ed.), *Medieval hagiography. An anthology* (New York, 2000), pp 97–110.

Alciati, Roberto, 'The invention of western monastic literature: texts and communities' in *CHMM*, pp 144–61.

*Anderson, Alan Orr and Marjorie Ogilvie Anderson (eds), *Adomnán's life of Columba* (Oxford, 1991 revised ed.).

*Archdall, Mervyn, *Monasticon Hibernicum. Or, a history of the abbeys, priories, and other religious houses in Ireland* (Dublin, 1786); edited with additional notes by Patrick F. Moran. 3 vols (Dublin, 1873).

*Atkinson, Robert (ed.), *The passions and the homilies from Leabhar Breac. Text, translation, and glossary.* Todd Lecture Series vol. 2 (Dublin, 1887).

Barrow, G.W.S., 'The cathedral chapter at St Andrews and the Culdees in the twelfth and thirteenth centuries', *The Journal of Ecclesiastical History* 3:1 (1952), 23–39.

Barrow, G.W.S., 'Scottish rulers and the religious orders 1070–1153', *Transactions of the Royal Historical Society* 3 (1953), 77–100.

Barrow, G.W.S., *Kingdom of the Scots. Government, church and society from the eleventh to the fourteenth century* (London, 1973; repr. 2003).

*Bartlett, Robert (ed. and trans.), *Geoffrey of Burton. Life and miracles of St Modwenna.* Oxford Medieval Texts (Oxford, 2002).

Bartlett, Robert, *Why can the dead do such great things? Saints and worshippers from the martyrs to the reformation* (Princeton, 2013).

Beach, Alison I. and Isabelle Cochelin (eds), *The Cambridge history of medieval monasticism in the Latin West* [*CHMM*] (Cambridge, 2020).

Beach, Alison I., and Andra Juganaru, 'The double monastery as a historiographical problem (fourth to twelfth century)' in *CHMM*, pp 561–78.

Berman, Constance Hoffman, *The Cistercian evolution. The invention of a religious order in twelfth-century Europe* (Philadelphia, 2000).

*Bernard, John Henry and Robert Atkinson (eds and trans), *The Irish Liber Hymnorum*. 2 vols. Henry Bradshaw Society 13 and 14 (London, 1898).

*Best, Richard Irvine (ed.), 'The Lebar Brecc tractate on the canonical hours' in Osborn J. Bergin and Carl Marstrander (eds), *Miscellany presented to Kuno Meyer* (Halle, 1912), pp 142–66.

*Best, Richard Irvine, 'An early monastic grant in the Book of Durrow', *Ériu* 10 (1926–8), 135–42.

*Best, Richard Irvine, and Hugh Jackson Lawlor (eds), *The martyrology of Tallaght: from the Book of Leinster and MS 5100–4 in the Royal Library, Brussels.* Henry Bradshaw Society 68 (London, 1931).

Bethell, Denis, 'The lives of St Osyth of Essex and St Osyth of Aylesbury', *Analecta Bollandiana* 88:1–2 (1970), 75–127.

Bethell, Denis, 'English monks and Irish reform in the eleventh and twelfth centuries' in T. Desmond Williams (ed.), *Historical Studies VIII* (Dublin, 1971), pp 111–35.

Bhreathnach, Edel, 'The *seanchas* tradition in late medieval Ireland' in Bernadette Cunningham and Edel Bhreathnach (eds), *Writing Irish history. The Four Masters and their world* (Dublin, 2007), pp 17–23.

Bhreathnach, Edel, 'The mendicant orders and vernacular learning in the late medieval period', *Irish Historical Studies* 37 (2010–11), 357–75.

Bhreathnach, Edel, 'Benedictine influence in Ireland in the late eleventh and early twelfth centuries: a reflection', *The Journal of Medieval Monastic Studies* 1 (2012), 63–91.

Bhreathnach, Edel 'Who controlled Roscrea in the twelfth century?' in Harbison and Hall, *A carnival of learning*, pp 33–40.

Bhreathnach, Edel, 'Observations on the Book of Durrow memorandum' in John Carey, Kevin Murray and Caitríona Ó Dochartaigh (eds), *Sacred histories. A festschrift for Máire Herbert* (Dublin, 2015), pp 14–21.

Bhreathnach, Edel, 'The world of bishops in religious orders in medieval Ireland, 1050–1230' in Karen Stöber, Julie Kerr and Emilia Jamroziak (eds), *Monastic life in the medieval British Isles. Essays in honour of Janet Burton* (Cardiff, 2018), pp 71–88.

Bhreathnach, Edel, 'The nature of pre-"reform" Irish monasticism' in Bhreathnach, Krasnodębska and Smith, *Monastic Europe*, pp 21–43.

Bhreathnach, Edel, 'The *Vita Apostolica* and the origin of the Augustinian canons and canonesses in medieval Ireland' in Browne and Ó Clabaigh, *Households of God*, pp 1–27.

Bhreathnach, Edel, 'Saints' dedications and the ecclesiastical landscape of Hiberno-Norse Dublin: Irish, Scandinavian and others' in Seán Duffy (ed.), *Medieval Dublin XVIII* (Dublin, 2020), pp 143–68.

Bhreathnach, Edel, 'The saintly mothers and virgins of early Ireland. A diverse group remembered in places, personal names and genealogies' in Alf Tore Hommedal, Åslaug Ommundsen and Alexander O'Hara (eds), *St Sunniva. Irsk dronning, norsk vernehelgen. Irish queen, Norwegian patron saint* (Bergen, 2021), pp 138–53.

Bhreathnach, Edel, 'Skellig Michael, Co. Kerry: a lonely island hermitage at the edge of the world?', *Journal of Medieval Monastic Studies* 11 (2022), 35–49.

Bhreathnach, Edel, '1500th anniversary of St Brigit's death. But who was she?', *History Ireland* 32:2 (2024), 14–17.

Bhreathnach, Edel, Malgorzata Krasnodębska-D'Aughton and Keith Smith (eds), *Monastic Europe. Medieval communities, landscapes, and settlement* (Turnhout. 2019).

Bhreathnach, Edel and Ger Dowling, 'Founding an episcopal see and an Augustinian foundation in medieval Ireland: the case of Ferns, Co. Wexford', *Proceedings of the Royal Irish Academy* 121C (2021), 191–226.

*Bieler, Ludwig (ed.), *The Irish penitentials* (Dublin, 1963).

*Bieler, Ludwig (ed.), *The Patrician texts in the Book of Armagh* (Dublin, 1979).

*Bieler, Ludwig (ed.), *Libri epistolarum sancti Patricii episcopi*. Clavis Patricii II (Dublin, 1993).

*Binchy, Daniel A. (ed.), '*Bretha Crólige*', *Ériu* 12 (1938), 1–77.

*Binchy, Daniel A., 'Secular institutions' in Myles Dillon (ed.), *Early Irish society* (Dublin, 1954), pp 52–65.

*Binchy, Daniel A. (ed.), 'Irish law tracts re-edited. I. *Coibnes uisci thairidne*', *Ériu* 17 (1955), 52–85.

Binchy, Daniel A., 'The passing of the old order' in Brian Ó Cuív (ed.), *Proceedings of the International Congress of Celtic Studies held in Dublin, 6–10 July 1959* (Dublin, 1962), pp 119–32.

*Binchy, Daniel A. (ed.), *Corpus iuris Hibernici* 6 vols (Dublin, 1978) [*CIH*].

Bitel, Lisa, 'Sex, sin, and celibacy in early Christian Ireland', *Proceedings of the Harvard Celtic Colloquium* 7 (1987), 65–95.

Bitel, Lisa M., *Isle of the saints. Monastic settlement and Christian community in early Ireland* (Ithaca and London, 1990).

Bitel, Lisa, Review of Harrington, *Women in a Celtic church*, *The Catholic Historical Review* 89:4 (2003), 749–51.

Blom, Alderik H., *Glossing the psalms. The emergence of the written vernaculars in western Europe from the seventh to the twelfth centuries* (Berlin and Boston, 2017).

Boazman, Gill, 'Hallowed by saints, coveted by kings: Christianisation and land tenure in Rathdown, *c*.400–900' in Tomás Ó Carragáin and Sam Turner (eds), *Making Christian landscapes in Atlantic Europe. Conversion and consolidation in the early Middle Ages* (Cork, 2016), pp 22–53.

Boswell, James, *Rediscovering gay history. Archetypes of gay love in Christian history* (London, 1982).

Bourke, Cormac, *The early medieval hand-bells of Ireland and Britain* (Dublin, 2020).

Bourke, Edward, Alan R. Hayden and Ann Lynch, *Skellig Michael, Co. Kerry: the monastery and the South Peak. Archaeological stratigraphic report: excavations, 1986–2010* (Dublin, 2011). Available online only at https://www.worldheritageireland.ie/fileadmin/user_upload/documents/SkelligMichaelExcavations_07Feb.pdf

Bowen, Judith Margaret, 'Serving the greater cause: aspects of the religious thinking of Prosper Guéranger (1805–75)' (PhD, University of York, 2004) https://etheses.whiterose.ac.uk/21049/1/415181.pdf

Boyle, Alexander, 'The list of abbesses in Conchubranus' life of St Monenna', *Ulster Journal of Archaeology* 34 (1971), 84–6.

*Boyle, Elizabeth, 'Lay morality, clerical immorality, and pilgrimage in tenth-century Ireland: *Cethrur macclérech* and *Epscop do Gáedelaib*', *Studia Hibernica* 39 (2013), 9–48.

Boyle, Elizabeth, 'Eschatological themes in Lebor na hUidre' in Ó hUiginn, *Lebor na hUidre*, pp 115–30.

Boyle, Elizabeth, 'Sacrifice and salvation in Echtgus Úa Cúanáin's poetic treatise on the Eucharist' in Mullins, Ní Ghrádaigh and Hawtree, *Envisioning Christ on the cross*, pp 181–94.

Boyle, Elizabeth, 'Eschatology and reform in early Irish law: the evidence of Sunday legislation' in Matthew Gabriele and James T. Palmer (eds), *Apocalypse and reform from late antiquity to the Middle Ages* (Abingdon, 2018), pp 121–38. http://thecelticist.ie/wp-content/uploads/2020/02/Cain-Domnaig.pdf

Boyle, Elizabeth, 'The afterlife in the medieval Celtic-speaking world' in Pollard, *Imagining the medieval afterlife*, pp 62–78.

Boyle, Elizabeth, *History and salvation in medieval Ireland* (Abingdon and New York, 2021).

Boyle, Elizabeth and Deborah Hayden (eds), *Authorities and adaptations. The reworking and transmission of textual sources in medieval Ireland* (Dublin, 2014).

Boyne, Patricia, *John O'Donovan (1806–1861). A biography* (Kilkenny, 1987).

Boynton, Susan, 'Eleventh-century continental hymnaries containing Latin glosses', *Scriptorium* 53:2 (1999), 200–51.

Boynton, Susan, 'Latin glosses on the office hymns in eleventh-century continental hymnaries', *Journal of Medieval Latin* 11 (2001), 1–26.

Boynton, Susan, 'Prayer as liturgical performance in eleventh- and twelfth-century monastic psalters', *Speculum* 82 (2007), 896–931.

Boyton, Susan, 'Monastic liturgy, 1100–1500: continuity and performance' in *CHMM*, pp 958–74.

Bracken, Damian, and Dagmar Ó Riain-Raedel (eds), *Ireland and Europe in the twelfth century. Reform and renewal* (Dublin, 2006).

Bradley, John and Anngret Simms (appendix by John Bradley), 'The geography of Irish manors: the example of the Llanthony cells of Duleek and Colp in county Meath' in John Bradley (ed.), *Settlement and society in medieval Ireland. Studies presented to F.X. Martin, o.s.a.* (Kilkenny, 1988), pp 291–326.

Bradley, John, 'Toward a definition of the Irish monastic town' in Catherine E. Karkov and Helen Damico (eds), *Aedificia nova. Studies in honor of Rosemary Cramp* (Kalamazoo, 2008), pp 325–60.

Brannon, Patrick V., 'Medieval Ireland: music in cathedral, church and cloister', *Early Music* 28:2 (2000), 193–202.

Bray, Dorothy Ann, '*Secunda Brigida*: Saint Ita of Killeedy and Brigidine tradition', *North American Congress of Celtic Studies* 2 (1992), 27–38.

Bray, Dorothy Ann, 'The manly spirit of St Monenna' in Ronald Black, William Gillies and Roibeard Ó Maolalaigh (eds), *Celtic connections. Proceedings of the 10th international congress of Celtic studies* (East Linton, 1999), pp 171–81.

*Breatnach, Caoimhín, 'An Irish homily on the life of the Virgin Mary', *Ériu* 51 (2000), 23–58.

Breatnach, Liam, 'Canon law and secular law in early Ireland: the significance of *Bretha Nemed*', *Peritia* 3 (1984), 439–59.

*Breatnach, Liam, *Uraicecht na ríar. The poetic grades in early Irish law* (Dublin, 1987).

*Breatnach, Liam, 'The first third of *Bretha Nemed Toísech*', *Ériu* 40 (1989), 1–40.

Breatnach, Liam, *A companion to the Corpus iuris Hibernici* (Dublin, 2005).

Breatnach, Liam, 'A verse on succession to ecclesiastical office' in Breatnach et al., *Lobháin*, pp 32–41.

*Breatnach, Liam (ed.), '*Cinnus atá do thinnrem:* a poem to Máel Brigte on his coming of age', *Ériu* 58 (2008), 1–35.

*Breatnach, Liam (ed.), *Córus Bésgnai. An Old Irish law tract on the church and society* (Dublin, 2017).

Breatnach, Liam, '*Ríagail na Manach Líath* "The Rule of the Grey Monks": a late medieval fabrication', *Celtica* 32 (2020), 77–100.

Breatnach, Pádraig A., 'Medieval traditions from West Munster', *Studia Hibernica* 17–18 (1977–8), 58–70.

Breatnach, Pádraig A., 'The origins of the Irish monastic tradition at Ratisbon (Regensburg)', *Celtica* 13 (1980), 58–77.

Breatnach, Pádraig A., Caoimhín Breatnach and Meidhbhín Ní Urdail (eds), *Léann lámhscríbhinní Lobháin. The Louvain manuscript heritage* (Dublin, 2007).

Breay, Claire and Joanna Story (eds), *Anglo-Saxon kingdoms. Art, word, war* (London, 2018).

*Brooks, Eric St John, 'A charter of John de Courcy to the abbey of Navan', *Journal of the Royal Society of Antiquaries of Ireland* 3 (1933), 38–45.

*Brooks, Eric St John (ed.), *The Irish cartularies of Llanthony Prima & Secunda* (Dublin, 1953).

Brown, George H., 'The psalms as the foundation of Anglo-Saxon learning' in Nancy van Deusen (ed.), *The place of the psalms in the intellectual culture of the Middle Ages* (New York, 1999), pp 1–24.

Brown, Peter, *The body and society. Men, women, and sexual renunciation in early Christianity* (New York, 1988; repr. 2008).

Brown, Peter, *The rise of western Christendom. Triumph and diversity, AD 200–1000* (Chichester, 1996; repr. 10th anniversary revised edition, 2013).

Brown, Peter, 'Holy men' in Averil Cameron, Bryan Ward-Perkins and Michael Whitby (eds), *The Cambridge history of ancient history. Volume 14: Late antiquity: empire and successors, AD 425–600* (Cambridge, 2008), pp 781–810.

Brown, Peter, *The ransom of the soul. Afterlife and wealth in early western Christianity* (Cambridge Mass. and London, 2015).

Browne, Martin and Colmán Ó Clabaigh (eds), *The Irish Benedictines. A history* (Dublin, 2005).

Browne, Martin and Colmán Ó Clabaigh (eds), *Households of God. The regular canons and canonesses of Saint Augustine and of Prémontré in medieval Ireland* (Dublin, 2019).

Browne, Martin, Tracy Collins, Bronagh Ann McShane and Colmán Ó Clabaigh (eds), *Brides of Christ. Women and monasticism in medieval and early modern Ireland* (Dublin, 2023).

Bruel, Alexandre, 'Visites des monastères de l'ordre de Cluny de la province d'Auvergne en 1286 et 1310', *Bibliothèque de l'École des chartes* 38 (1877), 114–27.

Bruun, Mette B., 'Jean Mabillon's Middle Ages: on medievalism, textual criticism, and monastic ideals' in Alicia C. Montoya, Sophie van Romburgh and Wim van Anrooij (eds), *Early Modern medievalisms. The interplay between scholarly reflection and artistic production* (Leiden, 2010), pp 427–44.

Bunge, Gabriel (translated by Michael J. Miller), *Earthen vessels. The practice of personal prayer according to the patristic tradition* (San Francisco, 2002).

*Burgess, Glyn S. and Clara Strijbosch (eds), *The Brendan legend. Texts and versions.* The Northern World vol. 24 (Leiden and Boston, 2006).

Burton, Janet, 'The eremitical tradition and the development of post-Conquest religious life in northern England' in Nicole Crossley-Holland (ed.), *Eternal values in medieval life. Trivium* 26 (Lampeter, 1991), pp 18–39.

Burton, Janet, *Monastic and religious orders in Britain, 1000–1300* (Cambridge, 1994; repr. 2000).

Burton, Janet, 'The regular canons and diocesan reform in northern England' in Burton and Stöber, *The regular canons*, pp 41–58.

Burton, Janet and Julie Kerr (ed.), *The Cistercians in the Middle Ages* (Woodbridge, 2011).

Burton, Janet and Karen Stöber (eds), *The regular canons in the medieval British Isles* (Turnhout, 2012).

Bynum, Caroline Walker, *Jesus as mother. Studies in the spirituality of the high Middle Ages* (Berkeley and Los Angeles, 1982).

Bynum, Caroline Walker, 'Fast, feast, and flesh: the religious significance of food to medieval women', *Representations* 11 (1985), 1–25.

Byrne, Francis John, '*Senchas*: the nature of Gaelic historical tradition' in J.G. Barry (ed.), *Historical Studies* IX (Belfast, 1974), pp 137–59.

Byrne, Paul, 'The community of Clonard from the sixth to the twelfth centuries', *Peritia* 4 (1985), 157–73.

Campbell, Ewan and Adrián Maldonado, 'A new Jerusalem "at the ends of the earth": interpreting Charles Thomas's excavations at Iona Abbey 1956–63', *The Antiquaries Journal* 100 (2020), 33–85.

Canny, Nicholas, *Imagining Ireland's pasts. Early modern Ireland through the centuries* (Oxford, 2021).

Carey, John, *The Irish national origin-legend: synthetic pseudohistory.* Quiggin Pamphlets on the Sources of Mediaeval Gaelic History 1 (Cambridge, 1994).

Carey, John, 'The three things required of a poet', *Ériu* 48 (1997), 41–58.

*Carey, John (trans.), *King of mysteries. Early Irish religious writings* (Dublin, 2000).

Carey, John, *Lebor Gabala Erenn. Textual history and pseudohistory.* Irish Texts Society subsidiary series 20 (Dublin, 2009).

*Carey, John (ed. and trans.), *In tenga bithnua. The ever-new tongue.* Apocrypha Hiberniae II (Turnhout, 2009).

*Carey, John (ed.), 'The two clerical students and the next life' in Carey et al., *The end and beyond*, pp 139–43.

*Carey, John, Emma Nic Cárthaigh and Caitríona Ó Dochartaigh (eds), *The end and beyond. Medieval Irish eschatology* 2 vols (Aberystwyth, 2014).

*Carney, James (ed.), 'A Chrínóc, cubaid do cheól', *Éigse* 4 (1945), 280–4.

*Carney, James (ed.), 'A Chrínóc, cubaid do cheól. To an old psalm-book', *Medieval Irish lyrics* (Dublin, 1967), pp 74–9.

Casey, Denis, *Tigernán Ua Ruairc and a twelfth-century royal grant in the Book of Kells* (Dublin, 2020).

Charles-Edwards, Gifford, 'The Springmount Bog tablets: their implications for insular epigraphy and palaeography', *Studia Celtica* 36 (2002), 27–45.

Charles-Edwards, T.M. (Thomas Mowbray), 'The social background to Irish *peregrinatio*', *Celtica* 11 (1976), 43–59.

Charles-Edwards, T.M., *Early Irish and Welsh kinship* (Oxford, 1993).

Charles-Edwards, T.M., 'A contract between king and people in early medieval Ireland? *Críth Gablach* on kingship', *Peritia* 8 (1994), 107–19.

Charles-Edwards, T. M., *The early mediaeval Gaelic lawyer*. E.C. Quiggin Memorial Lectures 4 (Cambridge, 1999).

Charles-Edwards, T.M., *Early Christian Ireland* (Cambridge, 2000).

Charles-Edwards, T.M. '*Érlam*: the patron-saint of an Irish church' in Alan Thacker and Richard Sharpe (eds), *Local saints and local churches in the early medieval West* (Oxford, 2002), pp 267–90.

Charles-Edwards, T.M., 'The monastic rules ascribed to Columbanus' in Sébastien Bully, Alain Dubreucq and Aurélia Bully (eds), *Colomban et son influence: moines et monastères du haut Moyen Âge en Europe* (Rennes, 2018), pp 295–304.

Chitty, Derwas J., *The desert a city. An introduction to the study of Egyptian and Palestinian monasticism under the Christian empire* (New York, 1966; repr. 1995).

Choy, Renie S., *Intercessory prayer and the monastic ideal in the time of the Carolingian reforms* (Oxford, 2016).

Claffey, John A., 'A very puzzling Irish missal', *Journal of the Galway Archaeological and Historical Society* 55 (2003), 1–12, with corr. vol. 56, 245.

Clancy, Thomas Owen, 'Saint and fool: the image and function of Cummíne Fota and Comgán Mac Da Cherda in early Irish literature' (PhD, University of Edinburgh, 1991) http://hdl.handle.net/1842/7381

Clancy, Thomas Owen, 'Iona, Scotland and the Céli Dé' in Barbara E. Crawford (ed.), *Scotland in dark age Britain. The proceedings of a day conference held on 18 February 1995* (St Andrews, 1996), pp 111–30.

Clancy, Thomas Owen (ed.), *The triumph tree. Scotland's earliest poetry AD 550–1350* (Edinburgh, 1999).

Clark, James G., 'Monks and the universities, *c.*1200–1500' in *CHMM*, pp 1074–92.

Clark, James G., 'The rule of Saint Benedict' in Krijn Pansters (ed.), *A companion to medieval rules and customaries* (Leiden, 2020), pp 37–76.

Clarke, Howard B., 'Quo vadis? Mapping the Irish "monastic town" ' in Seán Duffy (ed.), *Princes, prelates and poets in medieval Ireland. Essays in honour of Katharine Simms* (Dublin, 2013), pp 261–78.

Clarke, Howard B., Máire Ní Mhaonaigh and Raghnall Ó Floinn (eds), *Ireland and Scandinavia in the early Viking age* (Dublin, 1998).

*Clover, Helen and Margaret Gibson (eds), *The letters of Lanfranc, archbishop of Canterbury* (Oxford, 1979).

Clyne, Miriam, 'The founders and patrons of the Premonstratensian houses in Ireland' in Burton and Stöber, *The regular canons*, pp 145–72.

Cochelin, Isabelle, 'Monastic daily life (*c.*750–1100): a tight community shielded by an outer court' in *CHMM*, pp 542–60.

*Colgan, John, *Acta sanctorum veteris et maioris Scotiae sev Hiberniae sanctorum insulae* (Louvain, 1645).

*Colgan, John, *Triadis Thaumaturgæ seu divorum Patricii Columbae et Brigidae … acta* (Louvain, 1647).

Collins, Tracy, '"The other monasticism". Killone nunnery, Co. Clare'. *Archaeology Ireland. Heritage Guide* 38 (Dublin, 2007).

Collins, Tracy, *Female monasticism in medieval Ireland. An archaeology* (Cork, 2021).

Combalbert, Grégory, 'Le contrôle des clercs paroissiaux vu par les évêques normands (XIe–XIIe siècles)', *Cahier des Annales de Normandie* 35 (2009), 369–96.

*Comyn, David (ed. and trans.), *Foras feasa ar Éirinn le Seathrún Céitinn, DD. The history of Ireland by Geoffrey Keating, DD*, vol. I (London, 1902).

*Connolly, Seán, 'Vita Prima Sanctae Brigitae: background and historical value', *Journal of the Royal Society of Antiquaries of Ireland* 119 (1989), 5–49.

*Connolly, Seán and Jean-Michel Picard, 'Cogitosus's *Life of St Brigit*: content and value', *Journal of the Royal Society of Antiquaries of Ireland* 117 (1987), 5–27.

Constable, Giles, '*Nudus nudum Christi sequi* and parallel formulas in the twelfth century. A supplementary dossier' in Frank Forrester Church and Timothy George (eds), *Continuity and discontinuity in church history. Essays presented to George Huntston Williams on the occasion of his 65th birthday* (Leiden, 1979), pp 83–91.

Constable, Giles, *The reformation of the twelfth century* (Cambridge, 1996; repr. 2002).

Constable, Giles, 'The future of Cluniac studies', *The Journal of Medieval Monastic Studies* 1 (2012), 1–16.

*Constable, Giles and Bernard S. Smith (eds), *Libellus de diversis ordinibus et professionibus qui sunt in aeclessia (revised edition)* (Oxford, 2003).

Cooke, Jessica, 'The Annaghdown doorway and King Ruaidrí Ua Conchobair: loyalty and patronage in twelfth-century Connacht', *Journal of the Royal Society of Antiquaries of Ireland* 150 (2020), 182–200.

Coon, Lynda L., 'The architecture of the ascetic body' in Kaczynski, *Oxford handbook of Christian monasticism*, pp 51–65.

Cotter, Eamonn, 'Molana abbey – a fortified house?', *Archaeology Ireland* 29:4 (Winter, 2015), 22–5.

Crook, John, *English medieval shrines* (Woodbridge, 2011).

Crowley, John and John Sheehan (eds), *The Iveragh Peninsula. A cultural atlas of the Ring of Kerry* (Cork, 2009)

Crowley, John and John Sheehan (eds), *The book of the Skelligs* (Cork, 2022).

Cuniffe, Christy 'The canons and canonesses of St Augustine at Clonfert' in Browne and Ó Clabaigh, *Households of God*, pp 103–23.

Cunningham, Bernadette, *The world of Geoffrey Keating. History, myth and religion in seventeenth-century Ireland* (Dublin, 2000).

Cunningham, Bernadette, *The Annals of the Four Masters. Irish history, kingship and society in the early seventeenth century* (Dublin, 2010).

Cunningham, Bernadette and Edel Bhreathnach (eds), *Writing Irish history. The Four Masters and their world* (Dublin, 2007).

Dauphant, Léonard, 'Frontière idéelle et marqueurs territoriaux du royaume des Quatre rivières (France, 1258–1529)' in Patrick Boucheron, Marco Folin et Jean-Philippe Genet (eds), *Entre idéel et matériel. Espace, territoire et légitimation du pouvoir (v. 1200–v. 1640)* (Paris, 2018), pp 313–28. https://books.openedition.org/psorbonne/41103?lang=en

Davies, Wendy E., 'Clerics as rulers: some implications of the terminology of ecclesiastical authority in early medieval Ireland' in Nicholas P. Brooks (ed.), *Latin and the vernacular languages in early medieval Britain* (Leicester, 1982), pp 81–97.

Davies, Wendy, 'Local priests in northern Iberia' in Steffen Patzold and Carine van Rhijn (eds), *Men in the middle. Local priests in early medieval Europe* (Berlin and Boston, 2016), pp 125–44.

de Bhaldraithe, Eoin, 'Obedience: the doctrine of the Irish monastic rules', *Monastic Studies* 14 (1983), 63–84.

de Brún, Pádraig, Seán Ó Coileáin and Pádraig Ó Riain (eds), *Folia Gadelica. Essays presented by former students to R.A. Breatnach on the occasion of his retirement from the professorship of Irish language and literature at University College, Cork* (Cork, 1983).

de Vogüé, Adalbert, 'Aux origines de l'habit monastique (IIIe–IXe siècle)', *Studia Monastica* 43:1 (2001), 7–20.

de Vogüé, Adalbert, 'The Master and St Benedict: a reply to Marilyn Dunn', *The English Historical Review* 107 (1992), 95–103.

de Vogüé, Adalbert and Joël Courreau (eds), *Rule for nuns. Sources Chrétiennes*, vol. 345, (Paris, 1988), pp 170–272.

Dickinson, John Compton, 'English regular canons and the Continent in the twelfth century', *Transactions of the Royal Historical Society* (ser. 5) 1 (1951), 71–89.

Diem, Albrecht, 'Disimpassioned monks and flying nuns. Emotion management in early medieval rules' in Christina Lutter (ed.), *Funktionsräume, Warhnehmungsräume, Gefühlsräume. Mittlealterliche Lebensformen zwischen Kloster und Hof* (Vienna and Munich, 2011), pp 17–40.

Diem, Albrecht, 'The limitations of asceticism' in Walter Pohl and André Gingrich (eds), *Medieval worlds. Comparative and interdisciplinary studies* 9: *Monasteries and sacred landscapes and Byzantine connections* (Vienna, 2019), pp 112–38. https://www.medievalworlds.net/0xc1aa5576%200x003abd5b.pdf

Diem, Albrecht and Philip Rousseau, 'Monastic rules (fourth to ninth century)' in *CHMM*, pp 162–94.

Dillon, Gavin David, 'Betha Cholmáin maic Luacháin: an ecclesiastical microcosm of the twelfth-century Irish midlands' (PhD, University College Cork, 2013). Copyright Gavin Dillon https://cora.ucc.ie/bitstream/handle/10468/1253/Full%20Text%20E-thesis.pdf?sequence=5

*Dillon, Myles (ed. and trans.), 'The taboos of the kings of Ireland', *Proceedings of the Royal Irish Academy* 54C (1951–2), 1–6, 8–25, 27–36.

*Dimock, James F. (ed.), *Giraldi Cambrensis opera*. 8 vols. Vol. 5 (London, 1867).

*Dinneen, Patrick S. (ed. and trans.), *Foras feasa ar Éirinn le Seathrún Céitinn, DD. The history of Ireland by Geoffrey Keating, DD*, vol. III (London, 1908).

*Dobbs, Margaret (ed.), 'The Ban-shenchus [part 2]', *Revue celtique* 48 (1931), 163–234.

Doherty, Charles, 'Exchange and trade in early medieval Ireland', *Journal of the Royal Society of Antiquaries of Ireland* 110 (1980), 67–89.

Doherty, Charles, 'Some aspects of hagiography as a source for Irish economic history', *Peritia* 1 (1982), 300–28.

Doherty, Charles, 'The monastic town in early medieval Ireland' in Howard Clarke and Anngret Simms (eds), *The comparative history of urban origins in non-Roman Europe. Ireland, Wales, Denmark, Germany, Poland and Russia from the ninth to the thirteenth century*. BAR International Series 255 (Oxford, 1985), i, pp 45–75.

Doherty, Charles, 'The transmission of the cult of St Máedhóg' in Próinséas Ní Chatháin and Michael Richter (eds), *Ireland and Europe in the early Middle Ages: texts and transmission/ Irland und Europa im früheren mittelalter. Texte und űberlieferung* (Dublin, 2002), pp 268–83.

Doherty, Charles, 'Was Sulien at Glendalough?' in Doherty, Doran and Kelly, *Glendalough. City of God*, pp 261–77.

Doherty, Charles, Linda Doran and Mary Kelly (eds), *Glendalough. City of God* (Dublin, 2011).

*Dooley, Ann and Harry Roe (trans.), *Tales of the elders of Ireland. A new translation of Acallam na Senórach* (Oxford, 1999).

Doran, Linda, 'Medieval communication routes through Longford and Roscommon and their associated settlements', *Proceedings of the Royal Irish Academy* 104C (2004), 57–80.

Doyle, Ian W., 'Mediterranean and Frankish pottery imports in early medieval Ireland', *The Journal of Irish Archaeology* 18 (2009), 17–62.

Doyle, Ian W., 'Early medieval E ware pottery: an unassuming but enigmatic kitchen ware?' in Bernice Kelly, Niall Roycroft and Michael Stanley (eds), *Fragments of lives past. Archaeological objects from Irish road schemes* (Dublin, 2014), pp 81–93.

Duffy, Seán (ed.), *Medieval Ireland. An encyclopedia* (New York, 2005).

Duffy, Seán, *Brian Boru and the battle of Clontarf* (Dublin, 2013).

Duffy, Seán, 'See Rome and die: the burial-place of Donnchad mac Briain', *History Ireland* 22:2 (2014), 6–7.

Duggan, Eddie, 'A game on the edge: an attempt to unravel the Gordian Knot of *tafl* games', *Board Game Studies Journal* 15 (2020), 99–132.

Dumville, David N., *Councils and synods of the Gaelic early and central Middle Ages*. Quiggin Pamphlets on the Sources of Mediaeval Gaelic History 3 (Cambridge, 1997).

Dumville, David N., 'The origins and early history of insular monasticism: aspects of literature, christianity, and society in Britain and Ireland, AD 400–600', *Kansai Institutional Repository* 30 (1997), A85–A107. https://www.kansai-u.ac.jp/Tozaiken/publication/asset/bulletin/30/85david.pdf

Dumville, David N., '*Félire Óengusso*: problems of dating a monument of Old Irish', *Éigse* 33 (2002), 19–48.

Dunn, Marilyn, 'Monastic rules and their authors in the early medieval West', *The English Historical Review* 105 (1990), 567–94

Dunn, Marilyn, 'The Master and St Benedict: a rejoinder', *The English Historical Review* 107 (1992), 104–11.

Dunn, Marilyn, *The emergence of monasticism. From the Desert Fathers to the early Middle Ages* (Malden, Oxford and Victoria, 2000; repr. 2007).

Dunne, Tom, 'Towards a national art? George Petrie's two versions of the last circuit of pilgrims of Clonmacnoise' in Murray, *George Petrie*, pp 126–36.

Dunning, P.J., 'The Arroasian order in medieval Ireland', *Irish Historical Studies* 4 (1945), 297–315.

Dunning, P.J., 'Pope Innocent III and the Waterford-Lismore controversy 1196–1218', *The Irish Theological Quarterly* 28:3 (1961), 215–32.

Dwyer, Philip, *The diocese of Killaloe from the Reformation to the close of the eighteenth century* (Dublin, 1878).

Earls, Maurice, 'Lost connections', *Dublin Review of Books* 118 (August 2015) https://www.drb.ie/essays/lost-connections

Edwards, Nancy (ed.), *The archaeology of the early medieval Celtic churches* (London, 2009).

*Elrington, Charles Richard (ed.), *The whole works of the Most Rev. James Ussher, DD, lord archbishop of Armagh and primate of all Ireland*, vol. iv (Dublin, 1864).

Empey, Mark, ' "Value-free" history? The scholarly network of Sir James Ware', *History Ireland* 20:2 (2012), 20–3.

*Esposito, Mario (ed.), 'Conchubrani vita sanctae Monennae', *Proceedings of the Royal Irish Academy* 28C (1910), 202–51.

Esposito, Mario, 'The sources of Conchubranus' life of St Monenna', *English Historical Review* 35 (1920), pp 71–8.

Etchingham, Colmán, *Church organisation in Ireland AD 650 to 1000* (Naas, 1999).

Etchingham, Colmán, 'Episcopal hierarchy in Connacht and Tairdelbach Ua Conchobair', *Journal of the Galway Archaeological and Historical Society* 52 (2000), 13–29.

Etchingham, Colmán, 'Pastoral provision in the first millennium: a two-tier service?' in FitzPatrick and Gillespie, *The parish in medieval and early modern Ireland*, pp 79–90.

Etchingham, Colmán, 'The Irish "monastic town": is this a valid concept?', *Kathleen Hughes Memorial Lectures* 8 (Cambridge, 2010).

Etchingham, Colmán, 'The organization and function of an early Irish church settlement: what was Glendalough?' in Doherty et al., *Glendalough. City of God*, pp 22–53.

Fagnoni, Anna Maria, 'Oriental eremitical motifs in the *Navigatio Sancti Brendani*' in Burgess and Strijbosch, *The Brendan legend*, pp 53–79.

Fahey, Jerome, 'Kilmacduagh and its ecclesiastical monuments', *Journal of the Royal Society of Antiquaries of Ireland* 34 (1904), 220–33.

FitzPatrick, Elizabeth and Raymond Gillespie (eds), *The parish in medieval and early modern Ireland. Community, territory and building* (Dublin, 2006).

*Fitzsimons, Henry, *Catalogus præcipuorum sanctorum Hiberniæ* (Liège, 1619).

Flanagan, Marie Therese, 'Hiberno-papal relations in the late twelfth century', *Archivium Hibernicum* 34 (1976-7), 55–70.

Flanagan, Marie Therese, 'St Mary's Abbey, Louth, and the introduction of the Arrouaisian observance into Ireland', *Clogher Record* 10:2 (1980), 223–34.

Flanagan, Marie Therese, *Irish society, Anglo-Norman settlers, Angevin kingship. Interactions in Ireland in the late twelfth century* (Oxford, 1989).

Flanagan, Marie Therese, 'John de Courcy, the first Ulster plantation and Irish church men' in Brendan Smith (ed.), *Britain and Ireland 900–1300. Insular responses to medieval European change* (Cambridge, 1999), pp 154–78.

Flanagan, Marie Therese, *Irish royal charters. Texts and contexts* (Oxford, 2005).

Flanagan, Marie Therese, 'Saint Malachy and the introduction of Cistercian monasticism to the Irish church: some suggestive evidence from Newry Abbey', *Seanchas Ard Mhacha* 22:2 (2009), 8–24.

Flanagan, Marie Therese, *The transformation of the Irish church in the twelfth century* (Woodbridge, 2010).

Flanagan, Marie Therese, 'St Malachy, St Bernard of Clairvaux, and the Cistercian order', *Archivium Hibernicum* 68 (2015), 294–311.

*Flechner, Roy *The Hibernensis. A study and edition.* 2 vols (Washington, 2019).

*Fleming, John, *Gille of Limerick (c.1070–1145). Architect of a medieval church* (Dublin, 2001).

*Fleming, Patrick, *Collectanea Sacra seu S. Columbani Hiberni Abbatis … seu Hibernia antiqorum Sanctorum ACTA ET OPUSCULA & &* (Louvain, 1667).

Fletcher, Christopher, '«Sire, uns hom sui ». Transgression et inversion par rapport à quelle(s) norme(s) dans l'histoire des masculinités médiévales?', *Micrologus Library* 78 (2017), 23–50.

Flower, Robin (ed.), *Catalogue of Irish manuscripts in the British Library [formerly British Museum]* Vol. II (London, 1926).

Flower, Robin, *The Irish tradition* (Oxford, 1947; repr. Dublin, 1993).

Follett, Westley, 'The Divine Office and extra-Office vigils among the culdees of Tallaght', *The Journal of Celtic Studies* 5 (2005), 81–96.

Follett, Westley, *Céli Dé in Ireland. Monastic writing and identity in the early Middle Ages.* (Woodbridge, 2006).

Follett, Westley, 'Cassian, contemplation, and medieval Irish hagiography' in Gernot R. Wieland, Carin Ruff and Ross G. Arthur (eds), *Insignis sophiae arcator. Medieval Latin studies in honour of Michael W. Herren on his 65th birthday* (Turnhout, 2006), pp 87–105.

*Follett, Westley, '*Archangelum mirum magnum*: an Hiberno-Latin hymn attributed to Máel Rúain of Tallaght', *The Journal of Medieval Latin* 19 (2009), 106-29.

*Follett, Westley, 'The veneration of St Michael at Tallaght: the evidence of *Archangelum mirum magnum*', *Cambrian Medieval Celtic Studies* 66 (Winter, 2013), 37–56.

Ford, Alan, 'James Ussher and the creation of an Irish protestant identity' in Brendan Bradshaw and Peter Roberts (eds), *British consciousness and identity. The making of Britain, 1533–1707* (Cambridge, 1998), pp 185–212.

Forsyth, Katherine (ed.), *Studies on the Book of Deer* (Dublin, 2008).

Freeman, Elizabeth, 'The Fourth Lateran Council of 1215, the prohibition against new orders, and religious women', *Journal of Medieval Religious Cultures* 44:1 (2018), 1–23.

*Fry, Timothy (trans.), *The Rule of St Benedict in English* (Collegeville, 1981; repr. 2018).

Gardiner, Eileen, '*The Vision of Tnugdal*' in Pollard, *Imagining the medieval afterlife*, pp 247–63.

Gem, Richard, 'The Romanesque church of Kilmalkedar in context' in NicGhabhann and O'Donovan, *Mapping new territories*, pp 101–113.

*Gilbert, John T. (ed.), *Chartularies of St Mary's Abbey, Dublin*. 2 vols (London, 1884; repr. Cambridge, 2012).

*Gilbert, John T. (ed.), *Register of Abbey of St Thomas, Dublin* (London, 1889; repr. Cambridge, 2012).

Gilchrist, Roberta, *Norwich cathedral close. The evolution of the English cathedral landscape* (Woodbridge, 2005).

Gilchrist, Roberta and Barney Sloane, *Requiem. The medieval monastic cemetery in Britain* (London, 2005).

Gillespie, Raymond, 'Scribes and manuscripts in Gaelic Ireland, 1400–1700', *Studia Hibernica* 40 (2014), 9–34.

Gittos, Helen, *Liturgy, architecture, and sacred places in Anglo-Saxon England* (Oxford, 2013).

Godfrey, Aaron W., 'The rule of Isidore', *Monastic Studies* 18 (1998), 7–29.

Gougaud, Louis, 'Inventaire des règles monastiques irlandaises', *Révue Bénédictine* 25 (1908), 167–84, 321–33; 28 (1911), 86–9.

Gougaud, Louis, *Ermites et reclus. Études sur d'anciennes formes de vie religieuse*. Moines et Monastères 5 (Ligugé, 1928).

*Greene, David (ed.), *Fingal Rónáin and other stories* Medieval and Modern Irish series 16 (Dublin, 1955; repr. 1993).

Greene, David, 'Varia I', *Ériu* 33 (1986), 161–4.

Grélois, Alexis, 'Les chanoines réguliers et la conversion des femmes aux XIIe siècle' in Parisse, *Les chanoines réguliers*, pp 233–64.

*Grosjean, Paulus (transcription), 'Catalogus codicum hagiographicorum latinorum bibliothecarum Dubliniensium: vita sancti Flannani', *Analecta Bollandiana* 46 (1928), 81–148.

*Grosjean, Paul, 'Two religious pieces', *Zeitschrift für celtische Philologie* 18 (1930), 299–303.

*Grosjean, Paul, 'Textes hagiographiques irlandais', *Études celtiques* 2:4 (1937), 269–303.

*Grosjean, Paul, 'Édition du *Catalogus praecipuorum sanctorum Hiberniae* de Henry Fitzsimon' in John Ryan (ed.), *Féil-sgríbhinn Eóin Mhic Néill. Essays and studies presented to Professor Eoin MacNeill on the occasion of his seventieth birthday, May 15th 1938* (Dublin, 1940; repr. 1995), pp 335–93.

Grosu, Emanuel, '*Navigatio Sancti Brendani abbatis*: allegory of the characters', *Philobiblon. Transylvanian Journal of Multidisciplinary Research in the Humanities* 22:1 (2017), 7–18.

*Guglielmetti, Rossana E. and Giovanni Orlandi (eds and trans), *La navigazione di San Brendano. Navigatio sancti Brendani* (Firenze, 2018).

Guldentops, Guy, Christian Laes and Gert Partoens (eds), *Felici curiositate. Studies in Latin literature and textual criticism from antiquity to the twentieth century. In honour of Rita Beyers* (Turnhout, 2017).

Gwynn, Aubrey, *The medieval province of Armagh, 1470–1545* (Dundalk, 1946).

Gwynn, Aubrey, 'Some notes on the history of the Book of Kells', *Irish Historical Studies* 9 (1954), 131–61.

Gwynn, Aubrey, 'Tomaltach Ua Conchobair coarb of Patrick (1181–1201): his life and times', *Seanchas Ard Mhacha* 8:2 (1977), 231–74.

Gwynn, Aubrey [Gerard O'Brien (ed.)], *The Irish church in the eleventh and twelfth centuries* (Dublin, 1992).

Gwynn, Aubrey and Dermot F. Gleeson, *A history of the diocese of Killaloe*. Part 1 (Gwynn) (Dublin, 1962).

* Gwynn, Edward J. (ed.), 'An Irish penitential', *Ériu* 7 (1914), 121–95.

*Gwynn, Edward J. (ed. and trans.), 'The rule of Tallaght', *Hermathena* 44 (1927), 2nd supplement. Contains the 'Rule of the Céli Dé' and the 'Teaching of Mael Ruain'.

*Gwynn, Edward J., and Walter J. Purton (eds and trans), 'The monastery of Tallaght', *Proceedings of the Royal Irish Academy* 29C (1911–12), 115–79.

*Hagan, John, 'Miscellanea Vaticano-Hibernica, 1580–1631', *Archivium Hibernicum* 3 (1914), 227–365.

*Hagen, John J. (trans.), *The jewel of the church. A translation of* Gemma ecclesiastica *by Giraldus Cambrensis* (Leiden, 1979).

Haggart, Craig, 'The *céli Dé* and the early medieval Irish church: a reassessment', *Studia Hibernica* 34 (2006–7), 17–62.

Haight, Roger, Alfred Pach and Amanda Avile Kaminski (eds), *Western monastic spirituality. Cassian, Caesarius of Arles, and Benedict. Past light on present life* (New York, 2022).

Hall, Dianne, 'Towards a prosopography of nuns in medieval Ireland', *Archivium Hibernicum* 53 (1999), 3–15.

Hall, Dianne, *Women and the church in medieval Ireland,* c.*1140–1540* (Dublin 2003; repr. 2008).

Hamlin, Ann Elizabeth (Thomas R. Kerr (ed.)), *The archaeology of early Christianity in the north of Ireland.* BAR British Series 460 (Oxford, 2008).

Hamp, Eric P., 'Varia VII.1. *Fer Diad*', *Ériu* 33 (1982), p. 178.

Hanmer, Meredith, *The chronicle of Ireland. Collected by Meredith Hanmer in the years 1571* (Dublin, 1633; repr. Dublin, 1809).

Harbison, Peter, *Pilgrimage in Ireland. The monuments and the people* (London, 1991).

Harbison, Peter, *The high crosses of Ireland. An iconographical and photographic survey*. 3 vols (Bonn, 1992).

Harbison, Peter and Valerie Hall (eds), *A carnival of learning. Essays to honour George Cunningham and his 50 conferences on medieval Ireland in the Cistercian Abbey of Mount St Joseph, Roscrea, 1987–2012* (Roscrea, 2012).

Harney, Lorcan, 'Fasting and feasting on Irish church sites: the archaeological and historical evidence', *Ulster Journal of Archaeology* 73 (2015–16), 182–97.

Harrington, Christina, *Women in a Celtic church. Ireland 450–1150* (Oxford, 2002).

Haverty, Martin, *The Aran Isles; or, A report of the excursion of the ethnological section of the British Association from Dublin to the western islands of Aran, in September 1857* (Dublin, 1859).

Hawkes, Jane (ed.), *Making histories. Proceedings of the sixth international conference on insular art, York 2011* (Donington, 2013).

*Heist, W.W. (ed.), *Vitae sanctorum Hiberniae ex codice olim Salmanticensi nunc Bruxellensi* (Brussels, 1965).

Helms, Mary W., 'Sacred landscape and the early medieval European cloister. Unity, paradise, and the cosmic mountain', *Anthropos* 97:2 (2002), 435–53.

Helms, Mary W., 'Before the dawn. Monks and the night in late antiquity and early medieval Europe', *Anthropos* 99:1 (2004), 177–91.

Helvétius, Anne-Marie et al., 'Re-reading monastic traditions: monks and nuns, east and west, from the origins to *c*.750' in *CHMM*, pp 40–72.

Hen, Yitzhak, 'The nature and character of the early Irish liturgy' in *L'irlanda e gli irlandesi nell'alto medioevo: Spoleto, 16–21 aprile 2009* (Spoleto, 2010), pp 353–77.

Hennig, John, 'The historical work of Louis Gougaud', *Irish Historical Studies* 3 (1942), 180–6.

Hennig, John, 'Studies in the Latin texts of the Martyrology of Tallaght, of *Félire Oengusso* and *Félire húi Gormáin*', *Proceedings of the Royal Irish Academy* 69C (1970), 45–112.

Henry, Françoise, 'Remarks on the decoration of three Irish psalters', *Proceedings of the Royal Irish Academy* 61 (1960–1), 23–40.

Henry, Françoise, *Irish art during the Viking invasions (800–1020 AD)* (London, 1967).

Henry, Françoise, *Irish art in the Romanesque period (1020–1170 AD)* (London, 1970).

Henry, Françoise and G.L. Marsh-Micheli, 'A century of Irish illumination (1070–1170)', *Proceedings of the Royal Irish Academy* 62C (1961–3), 101–66 + 44 plates.

Herbert, Jane, 'The transformation of hermitages into Augustinian priories in twelfth-century England' in William J. Shiels (ed.), *Monks, hermits, and the ascetic tradition.* Studies in Church History 22 (Oxford, 1985), pp 131–45.

Herbert, Máire, *Iona, Kells, and Derry. The history and hagiography of the monastic* familia *of Columba* (Oxford, 1988; repr. Dublin, 2002).

Herbert, Máire, 'Charter material from Kells' in Felicity O'Mahony (ed.), *The Book of Kells. Proceedings of a conference at Trinity College Dublin, 6–9 September 1992* (Aldershot, 1994), pp 60–77.

Herbert, Máire, '*Caithréim Cellaig*: some literary and historical considerations', *Zeitschrift für celtische Philologie* 49–50 (1997), 320–33.

Herbert, Máire, 'The life of Martin of Tours: a view from twelfth-century Ireland' in Michael Richter and Jean-Michel Picard (eds), *Ogma. Essays in Celtic Studies in honour of Proinséas Ní Chatháin* (Dublin, 2002), pp 76–84.

Herbert, Máire, 'Before charters? Property records in pre-Anglo-Norman Ireland' in Marie Therese Flanagan and Judith A. Greene (eds), *Charters and charter scholarship in Britain and Ireland* (Basingstoke, 2005), pp 107–19.

Herbert, Máire, 'Review of Pádraig Ó Néill, *Exegetica: Psalterium Suthantoniense*', *Études celtiques* 40 (2014), 341–2.

Herbert, Máire, 'A praise-poem from eleventh-century Armagh' in Caoimhín Breatnach, Méibhín Ní Urdail and Gordon Ó Riain (eds), *Lorg na leabhar. A festschrift for Pádraig A. Breatnach* (Dublin, 2019), pp 139–48.

*Herbert, Máire and Martin McNamara (eds), *Irish biblical apocrypha. Selected texts in translation* (Edinburgh, 1989).

*Herbert, Máire and Pádraig Ó Riain (eds), *Betha Adamnáin: The Irish life of Adamnán* (Cork, 1988).

Hiley, David, *Western plainchant. A handbook* (Oxford, 1993).

Hodne, Lasse, 'The turtledove: a symbol of chastity and sacrifice', *IKON: Journal of Iconographic Studies* 2 (2009), 159–66.

*Hogan, Arlene, *The Priory of Llanthony Prima and Secunda in Ireland, 1172–1541. Lands, patronage and politics* (Dublin, 2008).

Holland, Martin, 'On the dating of the Corpus Irish missal', *Peritia* 15 (2001), 280–301.

Holland, Martin, 'The twelfth-century reform and Inis Pátraic' in MacShamhráin, *The island of St Patrick*, pp 150–78.

Holmes, Stephen Mark, 'Catalogue of liturgical books and fragments in Scotland before 1560', *The Innes Review* 62:2 (2012), 127–212.

Houlihan, James W., *Adomnán's Lex Innocentium and the laws of war* (Dublin, 2020).

*Howlett, David (ed.), 'Three poems about Monenna', *Peritia* 19 (2005), 1–19.

*Hudson, Benjamin T. (ed.), *Prophecy of Berchán. Irish and Scottish high-kings of the early Middle Ages* (Westport, Connecticut and London, 1996).

Hughes, A.J. and William Nolan (eds), *Armagh history and society. Interdisciplinary essays on the history of an Irish county* (Dublin, 2001).

Hughes, Kathleen, 'The offices of S. Finnian of Clonard and S. Cianán of Duleek', *Analecta Bollandiana* 73 (1955), 342–72.

Hughes, Kathleen, *The church in early Irish society* (London, 1966; repr. 1980).

Hughes, Kathleen, *Early Christian Ireland. Introduction to the sources* (London, 1972; repr. 2008).

Hughes, Kathleen and Ann Hamlin, *Celtic monasticism. The modern traveller to the early Irish church* (New York, 1977; repr. Dublin, 2004).

*Hull, Vernam (ed. and trans.), 'Apgitir chrábaid: the alphabet of piety', *Celtica* 8 (1968), 44–89.

Izzo, Kathryn Alyssa, 'The Old Irish hymns of the Liber Hymnorum: a study of vernacular hymnody in medieval Ireland' (PhD, Harvard University, 2007).

*Jackson, Kenneth Hurlstone, *Aislinge Meic Con Glinne* (Dublin, 1990).

*James, Bruno Scott (trans.), *The letters of St Bernard of Clairvaux* (London, 1953; repr. 1967).

Jamroziak, Emilia, 'The historiography of medieval monasticism: perspectives from northern Europe' in Steinunn Kristjánsdóttir (ed.), *Medieval monasticism in northern Europe. Religions* 12:7 (Basel, 2021), pp 1–13. https://doi.org/10.3390/rel12070552

Jasper, Kathryn and John Howe, 'Hermitism in the eleventh and twelfth centuries' in *CHMM*, pp 684–96.

Jefferies, Henry, 'Erenaghs in pre-plantation Ulster: an early seventeenth-century account', *Archivium Hibernicum* 53 (1999), 16–19.

Jeffery, Peter, 'Eastern and western elements in the Irish monastic prayer of the hours' in Margot E. Fassler and Rebecca A. Baltzer (eds), *The Divine Office in the Latin Middle Ages. Methodology and source studies, regional developments, hagiography* (Oxford, 2000), pp 99–143.

Jeffery, Peter, 'Psalmody and prayer in early monasticism' in *CHMM*, pp 112–27.

Jenkins, David, *'Holy, holier, holiest'. The sacred topography of the early medieval Irish church* (Turnhout, 2010).

Johnston, Elva, 'Transforming women in Irish hagiography', *Peritia* 9 (1995), 197–220.

Johnson, Elva, 'Íte: patron of her people?', *Peritia* 14 (2000), 421–8.

Johnston, Elva, *Literacy and identity in early medieval Ireland* (Woodbridge, 2013).

Johnson, Elva, 'Locating female saints and their foundations in the early medieval Irish martyrologies' in Martin Browne et al., *Brides of Christ*, pp 22–36.

Kaczynski, Bernice M. (ed.), *The Oxford handbook of Christian monasticism* (Oxford, 2020).

Kehnel, Annette, *Clonmacnois. The church and lands of St Ciarán: change and continuity in an Irish monastic foundation (6th to 16th century)*. Vita regularis 8 (Münster, 1997).

*Kelly, Fergus (ed.), *Audacht Morainn* (Dublin, 1976; repr. 2010).

Kelly, Fergus, *A guide to early Irish law* (Dublin, 1988).

Kelly, Fergus, *Early Irish farming* (Dublin, 1997).

Kelly, Mary, 'Twelfth-century ways of learning: from Worcester or Cologne to Glendalough', *Journal of the Royal Society of Antiquaries of Ireland* 141 (2011), 47–65.

Kenney, James F., *The sources for the early history of Ireland. An introduction and guide* vol. 1 (New York, 1929; repr. Dublin, 1993).

Keynes, Simon, 'King Athelstan's books' in Michael Lapidge and Helmut Gneuss (eds), *Learning and literature in Anglo-Saxon England. Studies presented to Peter Clemoes on the occasion of his sixty-fifth birthday* (Cambridge, 1985), pp 143–201.

Knowles, Michael David, 'Great historical enterprises II. The Maurists', *Transactions of the Royal Historical Society* 9 (1959), 169–87.

*Knowles, David and C.N.L. Brooke (eds), *The monastic constitutions of Lanfranc*. Oxford medieval texts (Oxford, 1951; repr. 2002).

Knox, Hubert Thomas, *Notes on the early history of the dioceses of Tuam Killala and Achonry* (Dublin, 1904).

Kristjánsdóttir, Steinunn, 'No society is an island: Skriðuklaustur monastery and the fringes of monasticism', *The Journal of Medieval Monastic Studies* 4 (2015), 153–72.

Kristjánsdóttir, Steinunn, *Monastic Iceland* (Abingdon, 2022).

Lafaye, Anne-Julie, 'Reconstructing the landscape of the mendicants in east Munster: the Franciscans' in Eamonn Cotter (ed.), *Buttevant. A medieval Anglo-French town in Ireland* (Rathcormac, 2013), pp 67–82.

Lambkin, Brian, 'Blathmac and the céili Dé: a reappraisal', *Celtica* 23 (1999), 132–54.

Lanigan, John, *An ecclesiastical history of Ireland, from the first introduction of Christianity among the Irish, to the beginning of the thirteenth century*. 4 vols (Dublin, 1822–9).

Lapidge, Michael, 'The cult of St Indract at Glastonbury' in Whitelock, McKitterick and Dumville, *Ireland in early mediaeval Europe*, pp 179–212.

*Lapidge, Michael and James L. Rosier (eds), *Aldhelm. The poetic works* (Cambridge, 1985).

Lash, Elliott, 'Princeton MS Garrett 70 (1081–82) and other Regensburg manuscripts as witnesses to an Irish intercessory formula and the linguistic features of late-eleventh-century Middle Irish', *Peritia* 31 (2020), 165–92.

Lash, Ryan, et al., '"Differing in status, but one in spirit": sacred space and social diversity at island monasteries in Connemara, Ireland', *Antiquity* 92 (2018), 437–55.

Lauwers, Michel (trans. Matthew Mattingly), 'Constructing monastic space in the early and central medieval west (fifth to twelfth century)' in *CHMM*, pp 317–39.

*Lawlor, Hugh Jackson (ed.), *St Bernard of Clairvaux's life of St Malachy of Armagh* (London and New York, 1920).

*Lawlor, Hugh Jackson and Richard Irvine Best (eds), *The martyrology of Tallaght from the Book of Leinster and MS. 5100–4 in the Royal Library, Brussels,* Henry Bradshaw Society 68 (London, 1931).

Lawrence, Frank, 'What did they sing at Cashel in 1172?: Winchester, Sarum and Romano-Frankish chant in Ireland', *Journal of the Society for Musicology in Ireland* 3 (2007–8), 111–25.

*Lawrie, Archibald Campbell (ed.), *Early Scottish charters prior to AD 1153* (Glasgow, 1905).

Leclercq, Jean, 'Documents on the cult of St Malachy', *Seanchas Ard Mhacha* 3:2 (1959), 318–32.

Leclercq, Jean, *The love of learning and the desire for God. A study of monastic culture* (trans. Catharine Misrahi, New York, 1982). (Original French version: *L'amour des lettres et le désir de Dieu* (Paris, 1957; repr. 1990).

*Leclercq, Jean and H. M. Rochais, *Sancti Bernardi Opera vol III* (Rome, 1963), pp 295–378 [Bernard of Clairvaux's Life of Malachy].

Ledwich, Edward and James Ford, *The antiquities of Ireland* (Dublin, 1790; repr. 1804).

Leerssen, Joep, 'Petrie: polymath and innovator' in Murray, *George Petrie*, pp 7–11.

L'Hermite-Leclerq, Paulette, 'Reclusion in the Middle Ages' in *CHMM*, pp 747–65.

*Levison, Wilhelm (ed.), 'Vita Albarti archiepiscopi Cassellensis' in Bruno Krusch and Wilhelm Levison (eds), *Passiones vitaeque sanctorum aevi Merovingici* VI (Hannover and Leipzig, 1913), pp 21–3.

Leyser, Conrad, *Authority and asceticism from Augustine to Gregory the Great* (Oxford, 2000).

Licence, Tom, 'The Benedictines, the Cistercians and the acquisition of a hermitage in twelfth-century Durham', *Journal of Medieval History* 29 (2003), 315–29.

Licence, Tom, 'Anchorites, wise folk and magical practitioners in twelfth-century England', *History. The Journal of the Historical Association* (December 2021). Online at https://doi.org/10.1111/1468-229X.13227.

Lifshitz, Felice, 'The historiography of central medieval western monasticism' in *CHMM*, pp 365–81.

*Lindsay, William Alexander, John Dowden and John Maitland Thomson (eds), *Charters, bulls and other documents relating to the abbey of Inchaffray* (Edinburgh, 1908).

Lionard, Pádraig and Françoise Henry, 'Early Irish grave-slabs', *Proceedings of the Royal Irish Academy* 61 (1960–1), 95–169.

Logue, Paul, 'Reinterpreting Richard Bartlett's image of Armagh', *Ulster Journal of Archaeology* 74 (2017–18), 220–30.

Long, Chris, 'Clonfeacle, an early monastic site', *Seanchas Ard Mhacha* 20:2 (2005), 23–33.

*Love, Rosalind C. (ed.), *Goscelin of Saint-Bertin. The hagiography of the female saints of Ely.* Oxford medieval texts (Oxford, 2004).

Lutter, Christina, '*Vita communis* in Central European monastic landscapes' in Eirik Hovden, Christina Lutter and Walter Pohl (eds), *Meanings of community across medieval Eurasia. Comparative approaches* (Leiden, 2016), pp 362–87.

Lynn, C.J., 'Some fragments of exotic porphyry found in Ireland', *The Journal of Irish Archaeology* 2 (1984), 19–32.

Mac Airt, Seán and Nollaig Ó Muraíle, 'Ecclesiastical affairs in Armagh in the ninth and tenth centuries', *Seanchas Ard Mhacha* 25:2 (2015), 225–38.

Macalister, R.A.S., *Corpus inscriptionum Insularum Celticarum.* 2 vols (Dublin, 1945–9).

Mackley, Jude S., *The legend of St Brendan. A comparative study of the Latin and Anglo-Norman versions* (Leiden, 2008).

*MacCarthy, Bartholomew, *The Codex Palatino-Vaticanus, No. 830* (texts, translations and indices) Todd lecture series 3 (Dublin, 1892).

MacCotter, Paul, *Medieval Ireland. Territorial, political and economic divisions* (Dublin, 2008).

MacDonald, Aidan, 'Adomnán's monastery of Iona' in Cormac Bourke (ed.), *Studies in the cult of Saint Columba* (Dublin, 1997), pp 24–44.

Mac Eoin, Gearóid, 'The date and authorship of *Saltair na Rann*', *Zeitschrift für celtische Philologie* 28 (1960–1), 51–67.

*Mac Eoin, Gearóid S. (ed. and trans.), 'A poem by Airbertach Mac Cosse', *Ériu* 20 (1966), 112–39.

Mac Mathúna, Séamus, '*The Irish life of Saint Brendan*: textual history, structure and date' in Burgess and Strijbosch, *The Brendan legend*, pp 117–58.

*MacNeill, Eoin (trans.), 'Ancient Irish law: the law of status or franchise', *Proceedings of the Royal Irish Academy* 36C (1921–4), 265–316.

Mac Niocaill, Geraóid, *Na manaigh liatha in Éirinn 1142–* c.*1600* (Baile Átha Cliath, 1959).

*Mac Niocaill, Gearóid (ed.), *Notitiæ as Leabhar Cheanannais 1033–1161* (Baile Átha Cliath, 1961).

*Mac Niocaill, Gearóid (ed.), 'Fragments d'un coutumier monastique irlandais du viiie–ixe siècle', *Scriptorium* 15:2 (1961), 228–33.

Mac Shamhráin, Ailbhe S., '*Prosopgraphica Glindelachensis*: the monastic church of Glendalough and its community sixth to thirteenth centuries', *Journal of the Royal Society of Irish Antiquaries* 119 (1989), 79–97.

Mac Shamhráin, Ailbhe S., 'The "unity" of Cóemgen and Ciarán: a covenant between Glendalough and Clonmacnois in the tenth to eleventh centuries' in Ken Hannigan and William Nolan (eds), *Wicklow, history and society. Interdisciplinary essays on the history of an Irish county* (Dublin, 1994), pp 139–50.

Mac Shamhráin, Ailbhe, *Church and polity in pre-Norman Ireland. The case of Glendalough* (Maynooth, 1996).

MacShamhráin, Ailbhe (ed.), *The island of St Patrick. Church and ruling dynasties in Fingal and Meath, 400–1148* (Dublin, 2004).

McCafferty, John, 'Brigid of Kildare: stabilizing a female saint for early modern Catholic devotion', *Journal of medieval and early modern studies* 50:1 (2020), 53–73. https://read.dukeupress.edu/jmems/article-pdf/50/1/53/735141/0500053.pdf

McCone, Kim, 'Werewolves, cyclopes, *díberga* and *fianna*: juvenile delinquency in early Ireland', *Cambridge Medieval Celtic Studies* 12 (Winter, 1986), 1–22.

McCullough, Catherine and W.H. Crawford, *Irish Historic Towns Atlas no. 18: Armagh* (Dublin, 2007): https://www.ria.ie/irish-historic-towns-atlas-online-armagh.

*McDonald, John Paul, *Treatise on monastic studies – 1691– Dom Jean Mabillon* (Lanham, 2004).

McGinn, Bernard, 'Medieval visions of the end: the Irish contribution' in Carey et al. *The end and beyond*, vol. I, pp 11–36.

McGuire, Brian Patrick, *Friendship and community. The monastic experience, 350–1250* (Michigan, 1988; repr. Ithaca, 2010).

McGuire, Brian Patrick, *Bernard of Clairvaux. An inner life* (Ithaca and London, 2020).

McKitterick, Rosamund, 'Kathleen Winifred Hughes 1926–1977' in Whitelock, McKitterick and Dumville, *Ireland in early mediaeval Europe*, pp 1–18.

*McLaughlin, Róisín (ed.), 'A Latin-Irish text on fasting in the *Leabhar Breac*', *Ériu* 60 (2010), 37–80.

*McLaughlin, Róisín (ed.), 'A text on almsgiving in RIA MS 3 B 23 and the *Leabhar Breac*', *Ériu* 62 (2012), 113–83.

*McLeod, Neil, *Early Irish contract law* (Sydney, 1992).

McLeod, Neil, 'Brehon law' in Duffy, *Medieval Ireland. An encyclopedia*, p. 42.

McManus, Damian, 'A chronology of the Latin loan-words in early Irish', *Ériu* 34 (1983), 21–71.

McNamara, Martin, *The apocrypha in the Irish church* (Dublin, 1975).

McNamara, Martin (ed.), *Biblical studies. The medieval Irish contribution.* Proceedings of the Irish Biblical Association I (Dublin, 1976).

McNamara, Martin, *The psalms in the early Irish church* (Sheffield, 2000).

McNamara, Martin, 'Five Irish psalter texts', *Proceedings of the Royal Irish Academy* 109C (2009), 37–104.

McNamara, Martin, 'End of an era in early Irish biblical exegesis: Caimin psalter fragments (11th–12th century) and the Gospels of Máel Brigte (1138 AD)', *Proceedings of the Irish Biblical Association* 33–4 (2010–11), 76–121.

McNamara, Martin, *The Bible and the apocrypha in the early Irish church (AD 600–1200).* Collected essays (Turnhout, 2015).

McNamara, Martin, 'The "*Leabhar Breac* gospel history" against its Hiberno-Latin background' in Guldentops et al., *Felici curiositate*, pp 23–53.

Maddox, Melanie C., 'Finding the City of God in the lives of St Kevin: Glendalough and the history of the Irish celestial civitas' in Doherty et al., *Glendalough. City of God*, pp 1–21.

Maddox, Melanie C., 'Re-conceptualizing the Irish monastic town', *Journal of the Royal Society of Antiquaries of Ireland* 146 (2016), 21–32.

Magnani, Eliana, 'Female house ascetics from the fourth to the twelfth century' in *CHMM*, pp 213–31.

Malone, Sylvester, *Life of Flannan, patron of Killaloe diocese* (Dublin, 1902).

Manning, Conleth, *Clonmacnoise, Co. Offaly* (Dublin, 1998 2nd ed.).

Manning, Conleth, 'References to church buildings in the annals' in Smyth, *Seanchas*, pp 37–52.

Manning, Conleth, 'Rock shelters and caves associated with Irish saints' in Tom Condit and Christiaan Corlett (eds), *Above and beyond. Essays in memory of Leo Swan* (Bray, 2005), pp 109–20.

Manning, Conleth, 'Teampall Bhreacáin, Aran, its five phases and obscured doorway' in NicGhabhann and O'Donovan, *Mapping new territories*, pp 115–28.

Manning, Conleth, 'The decline of the settlement at Clonmacnoise' in Victoria L. McAlister and Linda Shine (eds), *Rethinking medieval Ireland and beyond. Essays in honor of T.B. Barry* (Leiden and Boston, 2023), pp 175–88.

Márkus, Gilbert, 'Dewars and relics in Scotland: some clarifications and questions', *The Innes Review* 60:2 (2009), 95–144.

Mattingly, Matthew (ed.), 'The *Memoriale Qualiter*: an eighth century monastic customary', *The American Benedictine Review* 60:1 (2009), 62–75.

Meijns, Brigitte, 'Les chanoines réguliers dans l'espace flamand' in Parisse, *Les chanoines réguliers*, pp 455–76.

Melville, Gert, 'Inside and outside. Some considerations about cloistral boundaries in the central Middle Ages' in Steven Vanderputten and Brigitte Meijns (eds), *Ecclesia in medio nationis. Reflections on the study of monasticism in the central Middle Ages* (Leuven, 2011), pp 167–82.

*Messingham, Thomas, *Florilegium insulae sanctorum, seu vitae et acta sanctorum Hiberniae* (Paris, 1624).

Mews, Constant J., 'Gregory the Great, the Rule of Benedict and Roman liturgy: the evolution of a legend', *Journal of Medieval History* 37:2 (2011), 125–44.

Mews, Constant J., 'The flight of Carthach (Mochuda) from Rahan to Lismore: lineage and identity in early medieval Ireland', *Early medieval Europe* 21:1 (2013), 1–26.

*Meyer, Kuno (ed.), 'Maelisu's hymn to the archangel Michael', *The Gaelic Journal. Irisleabhar na Gaedhilge* 4:36 (1890), 56–7.

*Meyer, Kuno (ed.), *Aislinge Meic Conglinne. The vision of MacConglinne* (London, 1892).

*Meyer, Kuno (ed.), *Hibernica minora, being a fragment of an Old-Irish treatise on the Psalter with translation, notes and a glossary and an appendix containing extracts hitherto unpublished from MS. Rawlinson, B512 in the Bodleian Library*. Anecdota Oxonienesia. Mediæval and Modern Irish Series 8 (Oxford, 1894).

*Meyer, Kuno (ed. and trans.), 'Anecdota from Irish MSS XV: Regula Mochutu Rathin', *Gaelic Journal* 5:12 (1895), 187–8.

*Meyer, Kuno (ed. and trans.), 'Stories and songs from Irish manuscripts: VI. Colcu ua Duinechda's Scúap Chrábaid, or Besome of Devotion', *Otia Merseiana* 2 (1900–1), 92–105.

*Meyer, Kuno, 'Mitteilungen aus irischen Handschriften: Die Midianiterschlacht', *Zeitschrift für celtische Philologie* 3 (1901), 23–4.

*Meyer, Kuno, 'Mitteilungen aus irischen Handschriften: II Aus Rawlinson B. 512. Von den Todsünden', *Zeitschrift für celtische Philologie* 3 (1901), 24–8.

*Meyer, Kuno, 'Mitteilungen aus irischen Handschriften: *Regula Choluimb Chille*', *Zeitschrift für Celtische Philologie* 3 (1901), 28–30.

*Meyer, Kuno (ed. and trans.), 'Comad Manchín Léith', *Ériu* 1 (1904), 38–40.

*Meyer, Kuno, 'Mitteilungen aus irischen Handschriften: Siebenteilung aller geistlichen und weltlichen Rangstufen', *Zeitschrift für celtische Philologie* 5 (1905), 498–9.

*Meyer, Kuno (ed. and trans.), 'The duties of a husbandman', *Ériu* 2 (1905), 172.

*Meyer, Kuno (ed.), *The triads of Ireland.* RIA Todd lecture series 13 (London, 1906).

*Meyer, Kuno (ed.), 'A medley of Irish texts: VI. The adventures of Ricinn, daughter of Crimthann mac Lugdach', *Archiv für celtische Lexicographie* 3 (1907), 308–9.

*Meyer, Kuno (ed.), 'A medley of Irish texts: X. Incipit Regula Mucuta Raithni', *Archiv für celtische Lexicographie* 3:4 (1907), 312–20.

*Meyer, Kuno, 'Mitteilungen aus irischen Handschriften: Ermahnung den Leib zu kasteien', *Zeitschrift für keltische Philologie* 6 (1908), 264–6.

*Meyer, Kuno, 'Mitteilungen aus irischen Handschriften: Die acht Horen zur Bekämpfung der Todsünden', *Zeitschrift für celtische Philologie* 6 (1908), 271.

*Meyer, Kuno, 'Mitteilungen aus irischen Handschriften: Hinterlassenschaft eines Mönches', *Zeitschrift für keltische Philologie* 6 (1908), 271.

*Meyer, Kuno, 'Mitteilungen aus irischen Handschriften: *Anmchairdes Mancháin Léith so*' *Zeitschrift für celtische Philologie* 7 (1910), 310–12.

*Meyer, Kuno (ed. and trans.), *Betha Colmáin maic Lúacháin. Life of Colmán son of Lúachan.* Todd lecture series XVII (Dublin, 1911).

*Meyer, Kuno (trans.), *Selections from ancient Irish poetry* (London, 1911).

*Meyer, Kuno (ed.), 'Ein Gedicht aus Additional 30,512, fol. 34b2 [*Is saoth lem in t-aos léigind*]', *Zeitschrift für Celtische Philologie* 9 (1913), 470.

*Meyer, Kuno, 'Mitteilungen aus irischen Handschriften: Mochutta cc.', *Zeitschrift für celtische Philologie* 10 (1915), 43–4.

*Meyer, Kuno (ed. and trans.), *Bruchstücke der älteren Lyrik Irlands* (Berlin, 1919).

*Meyer, Kuno, 'Ord prainni 7 prainntighi inn so sís', *Zeitschrift für celtische Philologie* 13 (1921), 27–30.

*Meyer, Robert T. (trans.), *Bernard of Clairvaux. The life and death of Saint Malachy the Irishman* (Kalamazoo, 1978).

Miles, Brent, 'The *Sermo ad reges* from the Leabhar Breac and Hiberno-Latin tradition' in Boyle and Hayden, *Authorities and adaptations*, pp 141–58.

Milfull, Inge B., *The hymns of the Anglo-Saxon church. A study and edition of the 'Durham Hymnal'* (Cambridge, 1996).

Morley, Vincent, *Ó Chéitinn go Raiftearaí. Mar a cumadh stair na hÉireann* (Baile Átha Cliath, 2011; athchló, 2017).

Morris, Richard, *Churches in the landscape* (London, 1989).

Moss, Rachel, *The art and architecture of Ireland. Vol. 1: Medieval c. 400–1600* (Dublin, New Haven and London, 2014).

*Mulchrone, Kathleen (ed.), *Caithréim Cellaig*. Mediaeval and Modern Irish Series 24 (Dublin, 1933; repr. 1971).

*Mulchrone, Kathleen (ed.), *Bethu Phátraic. The tripartite life of Patrick* [I. Texts and sources] (Dublin, 1939).

Müller, Cornelia et al. (eds), *Body-language-communication: an international handbook on multimodality in human interaction.* Vol. 1 (Berlin and Boston, 2013).

Mullins, Juliet, 'Preaching the Passion: *imitatio Christi* and the passions and homilies of the Leabhar Breac' in Mullins et al., *Envisioning Christ on the cross*, pp 195–213.

Mullins, Juliet, Jenifer Ní Ghrádaigh and Richard Hawtree (eds), *Envisioning Christ on the cross: Ireland and the early medieval west* (Dublin, 2013).

Murdoch, Brian, 'Preaching in medieval Ireland: the Irish tradition' in Alan J. Fletcher and Raymond Gillespie (eds), *Irish preaching 700–1700* (Dublin, 2001), pp 40–55.

Murphy, Donald, 'Excavations of an early monastic enclosure at Clonmacnoise' in Heather A. King (ed.), *Clonmacnoise Studies* 2 (Dublin, 2003), 1–33.

*Murphy, Gerard (ed.), 'A poem in praise of Aodh Úa Foirréidh, bishop of Armagh (1032–1056)' in Sylvester O'Brien (ed.), *Measgra i gcuimhne Mhichíl Uí Chléirigh. Miscellany of historical and linguistic studies in honour of Brother Michael Ó Cléirigh O.F.M., chief of the Four Masters, 1643–1943* (Dublin, 1944), pp 140–64.

*Murphy, Gerard (ed. and trans.), *Early Irish lyrics: eighth to twelfth century* (Oxford, 1956).

Murray, Emily, 'The faunal remains' in Bourke et al., *Skellig Michael excavations*, pp 426–30.

Murray, Emily and Finbar McCormick, 'Environmental analysis and food supply' in Jenny White Marshall and Claire Walsh (eds), *Illaunloughan Island. An early medieval monastery in County Kerry* (Bray, 2005), 67–80.

Murray, Griffin, *The Cross of Cong. A masterpiece of medieval Irish art* (Sallins, 2014).

Murray, Griffin and Kevin O'Dwyer, *Saint Manchan's shrine. Art and devotion in twelfth-century Ireland* (Tullamore, 2022).

Murray, Laurence P., 'A calendar of the register of Primate George Dowdall, commonly called the "Liber Niger" or "Black Book"', *Journal of the County Louth Archaeological Society* 6:3 (1927), 147–58.

Murray, Peter, *George Petrie (1790–1866). The rediscovery of Ireland's past* (Cork, 2004).

Murray, Peter, 'The Tara paper controversy and the round towers essay' in Murray, *George Petrie*, pp 103–7.

Nagy, Joseph Falaky, *Conversing with angels and ancients. Literary myths of ancient Ireland* (Dublin, 1997).

*Ní Bhrolcháin, Muireann (eag.), *Maol Íosa Ó Brolcháin* (Maigh Nuad, 1986).

Ní Bhrolcháin, Muireann, 'Maol Íosa Ó Brolcháin: an assessment', *Seanchas Ard Mhacha* 12:1 (1986), 43–67.

Ní Bhrolcháin, Muireann, 'Maol Íosa Ó Brolcháin: his work and family', *Donegal Annual* 38 (1986), 3–19.

Ní Dhonnchadha, Máirín, '*Caillech* and other terms for veiled women in medieval Irish texts', *Éigse* 28 (1995), 71–96.

*Ní Dhonnchadha, Máirín (trans.), 'Rícenn and Cairech Dercáin' in Angela Bourke et al. (eds), *The Field Day anthology of Irish writing vol. IV: Irish women's writing and traditions* (Cork, 2002), pp 129–30.

Ní Ghrádaigh, Jenifer, 'But what exactly did she give?': Derbforgaill and the Nuns' Church at Clonmacnoise' in Heather King (ed.), *Clonmacnoise Studies* 2 (Dublin, 2003), pp 175–207.

Nic Aongusa, Bairbre, 'The monastic hierarchy in twelfth century Ireland: the case of Kells', *Ríocht na Midhe* 8:3 (1990–1), 3–20.

NicGhabhann, Niamh, *Medieval ecclesiastical buildings in Ireland, 1789–1915* (Dublin, 2015).

NicGhabhann, Niamh and Danielle O'Donovan (eds), *Mapping new territories in art and architectural histories: essays in honour of Roger Stalley* (Turnhout, 2021).

*Niskanen, Samu (ed.), *Oxford medieval texts: epistolae Anselmi Cantuariensis archiepiscopi: letters of Anselm, archbishop of Canterbury, vol. 1: the Bec letters* (Oxford, 2019).

Nooij, Lars B,. 'The Irish material in the Stowe Missal revisited', *Peritia* 29 (2018), 101–9.

Nugent, Louise, *Journeys of faith. Stories of pilgrimage from medieval Ireland* (Dublin, 2020).

O'Brien, Elizabeth, *Mapping death. Burial in late Iron Age and early medieval Ireland* (Dublin, 2020).

Ó Carragáin, Éamonn, 'High crosses, the sun's course, and local theologies at Kells and Monasterboice' in Colum Hourihane (ed.), *Insular and Anglo-Saxon art and thought in the early medieval period* (Princeton, 2011), pp 149–73.

Ó Carragáin, Éamonn, 'Recapitulating history: contexts for the mysterious moment of resurrection on Irish high crosses' in Hawkes, *Making histories*, pp 246–61.

Ó Carragáin, Tomás, 'Regional variation in Irish pre-Romanesque architecture', *The Antiquaries Journal* 85 (2005), 23–56.

Ó Carragáin, Tomás, 'Church building and pastoral care in early Ireland' in FitzPatrick and Gillespie, *The parish in medieval and early modern Ireland*, pp 91–123.

Ó Carragáin, Tomás, *Churches in early medieval Ireland. Architecture, ritual and memory* (London and New Haven, 2010).

Ó Carragáin, Tomás, 'Rebuilding the "city of angels": Muirchertach Ua Briain and Glendalough, *c.* 1096–1111' in John Sheehan and Donnchadh Ó Corráin (eds), *The Viking Age: Ireland and the West. Papers from the proceedings of the fifteenth Viking Congress, Cork, 18–27 August 2005* (Dublin, 2010), pp 258–70.

Ó Carragáin, Tomás, 'Recluses, relics and corpses: interpreting St Kevin's House' in Doherty, Doran and Kelly, *Glendalough. City of God*, pp 64–79.

Ó Carragáin, Tomás, 'The view from the shore: perceiving island monasteries in early medieval Ireland', *Hortus Artium Medievalium. Journal of the International Research Centre for Late Antiquity and Middle Ages* 19 (2013), 21–33.

Ó Carragáin, Tomás, 'Altars, graves and cenotaphs: *leachta* as foci for ritual in early medieval Ireland' in Nic Ghabhann and O'Donovan, *Mapping new territories* , pp 129–46.

Ó Carragáin, Tomás, *Churches in the Irish landscape AD 400–1100* (Cork, 2021).

Ó Carragáin, Tomás and John Sheehan, 'The early medieval archaeology of Skellig Michael' in Crowley and Sheehan, *The book of the Skelligs*, pp 99–114.

Ó Clabaigh, Colmán, 'The Benedictines in medieval and early modern Ireland' in Browne and Ó Clabaigh, *The Irish Benedictines*, pp 79–121.

Ó Clabaigh, Colmán, *The friars in Ireland, 1224–1540* (Dublin, 2012).

Ó Clabaigh, Colmán, 'Community, commemoration and confraternity: the chapter office and chapter books in Irish Augustinian foundations' in Browne and Ó Clabaigh, *Households of God*, pp 235–51.

Ó Clabaigh, Colmán, 'Marginal figures? Quasi-religious women in medieval Ireland' in Browne et al., *Brides of Christ*, pp 118–35.

O'Connor, Dónal, 'Bishop Eugene of Ardmore revisited', *Decies* 63 (2007), 23–33.

O'Connor, Dónal, 'Did bishop Malchus of Waterford resign because of the Synod of Raithbreasail?', *Decies* 68 (2012), 1–16.

O'Connor, Ralph, *The destruction of Da Derga's hostel. Kingship and narrative artistry in a mediaeval Irish saga* (Oxford, 2013).

Ó Corráin, Donncha, 'Dál Cais – church and dynasty', *Ériu* 24 (1973), 52–63.

Ó Corráin, Donnchadh, 'The education of Diarmait Mac Murchada', *Ériu* 28 (1977), 71–81.

Ó Corráin, Donnchadh, 'The early Irish churches: some aspects of organisation' in Donnchadh Ó Corráin (ed.), *Irish antiquity. Essays and studies presented to Professor M.J. O'Kelly* (Cork, 1981), pp 327–41.

Ó Corráin, Donnchadh, 'Foreign connections and domestic politics: Killaloe and the Uí Briain in twelfth-century hagiography' in Whitelock, McKitterick and Dumville, *Ireland in early mediaeval Europe*, pp 213–31.

Ó Corráin, Donnchadh, 'Mael Muire Ua Dúnáin (1040–1117), reformer' in de Brún, Ó Coileáin and Ó Riain, *Folia Gadelica*, pp 47–53.

Ó Corráin, Donnchadh, 'Early Irish hermit poetry?' in Donnchadh Ó Corráin, Liam Breatnach and Kim R. McCone (eds), *Sages, saints and storytellers. Celtic studies in honour of Professor James Carney* (Maynooth, 1989), pp 251–67.

Ó Corráin, Donnchadh, 'Máel Muire, the scribe: family and background' in Ó hUiginn (ed.), *Lebor na hUidre*, pp 1–28.

Ó Corráin, Donnchadh, *The Irish church, its reform and the English invasion* (Dublin, 2017).

Ó Corráin, Donnchadh, Liam Breatnach and Aidan Breen, 'The laws of the Irish', *Peritia* 3 (1984), 382–438.

Ó Cróinín, Dáibhí, 'A tale of two rules: Benedict and Columbanus' in Browne and Ó Clabaigh, *The Irish Benedictines*, pp 11–24.

*Ó Cuív, Brian (ed.), 'Some early devotional verse in Irish', *Ériu* 19 (1962), 1–24.

Ó Cuív, Brian, 'Miscellanea: 1. "Boicht" Chorcaige', *Celtica* 18 (1986), 105–11.

*Ó Cuív, Brian, 'St Gregory and St Dunstan in a Middle-Irish poem on the origins of liturgical chant' in Nigel Ramsay, Margaret Sparks and Tim W. T. Tatton-Brown (eds), *St Dunstan: his life, times and cult* (Woodbridge, 1992), pp 273–97.

*Ó Cuív, Brian, *Catalogue of Irish language manuscripts in the Bodleian Library at Oxford and Oxford college libraries. Part I: descriptions* (Dublin, 2001).

Ó Dochartaigh, Caitríona, 'Questions of orality, performance and transmission in relation to medieval Irish prayer' in Gisbert Hemprich (ed.), *Festgabe für Hildegard L.C. Tristram. Überreicht von Studenten, Kollegen und Freunden des ehemaligen Faches Keltologie der Albert-Ludwigs-Universität Freiburg* (Berlin, 2009), pp 69–79.

Ó Dochartaigh, Caitríona, 'Homiletic texts and the transmission of eschatological apocrypha in a medieval Irish context', *Apocrypha: International Journal of Apocryphal Literatures* 23 (2012), 141–53.

*O'Doherty, John Francis (ed.), John Lynch *De Praesulibus Hiberniae*, 2 vols (Dublin, 1944).

*Ó Domhnaill, Mághnus (ed.), *Beatha Gillasius Ardmachanus* (Baile Átha Cliath, 1939)

*Ó Domhnaill, Mághnus (ed.), *Beatha Naoimh Maolmhodhaigh* (Baile Átha Cliath, 1940).

O'Dwyer, Barry W., *The conspiracy of Mellifont, 1216–1231. 1. An episode in the history of the Cistercian order in medieval Ireland* (Dublin, 1970).

O'Dwyer, Peter, *Céli Dé. Spiritual reform in Ireland 750–900* (Dublin, 1981).

O'Dwyer, Peter, *Mary: a history of devotion in Ireland* (Dublin, 1988).

Ó Fiaich, Tomás, 'The church of Armagh under lay control', *Seanchas Ard Mhacha* 5:1 (1969), 75–127.

Ó Flaithearta, Mícheál, 'The etymologies of (Fer) Diad' in Brian Ó Catháin and Ruairí Ó hUiginn (eds), *Ulidia 2. Proceedings of the second international conference on the Ulster Cycle of tales, National University of Ireland, Maynooth, 24–27 June 2005* (Maynooth, 2009), pp 218–25.

Ó Floinn, Raghnall, 'Viking and Romanesque influences 1100 AD–1169 AD' in Michael Ryan (ed.), *Treasures of Ireland. Irish art 3000 B.C.–1500 AD* (Dublin, 1983), pp 58–69.

Ó Floinn, Raghnall, *Irish shrines and reliquaries of the Middle Ages* (Dublin, 1994).

Ó Floinn, Raghnall, 'The foundation relics of Christ Church cathedral and the origins of the diocese of Dublin' in Seán Duffy (ed.), *Medieval Dublin VII* (Dublin, 2006), pp 89–102.

Ó Floinn, Raghnall, 'Bishops, liturgy and reform. Some archaeological and art historical evidence' in Bracken and Ó Riain-Raedel, *Ireland and Europe in the twelfth century*, pp 218–38.

Ó Floinn, Raghnall, 'Personal belief in Hiberno-Norse Dublin' in Anne Pedersen and Søren M. Sindbæk (eds), *Viking encounters. Proceedings of the eighteenth Viking Congress, Denmark, August 6–12, 2017* (Aarhus, 2020), pp 235–48.

*O'Grady, Standish Hayes (ed. and trans.), *Silva Gadelica (I-XXXI): a collection of tales in Irish with extracts illustrating persons and places.* 2 vols (London, 1892).

O'Halloran, Clare, *Golden ages and barbarous nations. Antiquarian debate and cultural politics in Ireland, c.1750–1800* (Cork, 2004).

O'Hara, Alexander and Faye Taylor, 'Aristocratic and monastic conflict in tenth-century Italy: the case of Bobbio and *Miracula sancti Columbani*', *Viator* 44:3 (2013), 43–62.

*Ó hInnse, Séamus (ed. and trans.), *Miscellaneous Irish annals (AD 1114–1437)* (Dublin, 1947).

*O'Keeffe, J.G. (ed.), 'Mac Dá Cherda and Cummaine Foda', *Ériu* 5 (1911), 18–44.

O'Keeffe, Tadhg, 'Lismore and Cashel: reflections on the beginnings of Romanesque architecture in Munster', *Journal of the Society of Antiquaries of Ireland* 124 (1994), 118–52.

O'Keeffe, Tadhg, 'The Romanesque portal at Clonfert Cathedral and its iconography' in Cormac Bourke (ed.), *From the isles of the north. Early medieval art in Ireland and Britain. Proceedings of the third international conference on insular art held in the Ulster Museum, Belfast, 7–11 April 1994* (Belfast, 1995), pp 261–9.

O'Keeffe, Tadhg, 'Diarmait Mac Murchada and Romanesque Leinster. Four twelfth-century churches in context', *Journal of the Royal Society of Antiquaries of Ireland* 127 (1997), 52–79.

O'Keeffe, Tadhg, *Romanesque Ireland. Architecture and ideology in the twelfth century* (Dublin, 2003).

*Olden, Thomas (ed. and trans.), 'On the geography of Ros Ailithir', *Proceedings of the Royal Irish Academy* 2nd ser. 2 (1879–88), 219–52.

O'Leary, Aideen, 'The identities of the poet(s) Mac Coisi: a reinvestigation', *Cambrian Medieval Celtic Studies* 38 (Winter, 1999), 53–71.

O'Loughlin, Thomas, *Celtic theology. Humanity, world and God in early Irish writings* (London and New York, 2000).

O'Loughlin, Thomas (ed.), *Adomnán at Birr, AD 697. Essays in commemoration of the Law of Innocents* (Dublin, 2001).

O'Loughlin, Thomas, 'The monastic Liturgy of the Hours in the *Nauigatio sancti Brendani*: a preliminary investigation', *Irish Theological Quarterly* 71(2006), 113–26.

O'Loughlin, Thomas, 'Review of Catherine Thom, *Early Irish monasticism. An understanding of its cultural roots* (London, 2007)', *New Blackfriars* 90: 1030 (November 2009), 740–1.

*Ó Maidín, Uinseann (trans.), *The Celtic monk. Rules and writings of early Irish monks.* Cistercian Studies series 162 (Kalamazoo, 1996).

*O'Meara, John J. (trans.), *The voyage of Saint Brendan. Journey to the Promised Land* (Dublin and New Jersey, 1976–8).

*O'Meara, John J. (trans.), *Gerald of Wales. The history and topography of Ireland* (London, 1982; repr. 1988).

*Ó Muraíle, Nollaig (ed. and trans.), *Leabhar Mór na nGenealach. The great book of Irish genealogies compiled (1645–66) by Dubhaltach Mac Fhirbhisigh.* 5 vols (Dublin, 2003).

Ó Muraíle, Nollaig, 'O'Donovan, John (1806–1861)', *Oxford dictionary of national biography* (Oxford, 2004). www.oxforddnb.com/view/article/20561

*O Neill, Joseph (ed.), 'The rule of Ailbe of Emly', *Ériu* 3 (1907), 92–115.

*Ó Néill, Pádraig P. (ed. and trans.), 'Airbertach mac Cosse's poem on the Psalter', *Éigse* 17 (1977–9), 19–46.

Ó Néill, Pádraig, 'The date and authorship of *Apgitir Chrábaid*: some internal evidence' in Próinséas Ní Chatháin and Michael Richter (eds), *Irland und die Christenheit: Bibelstudien und Mission. Ireland and Christendom: the Bible and the missions* (Stuttgart, 1987), pp 203–15.

Ó Néill, Pádraig P., 'An Irishman at Chartres in the twelfth century: the evidence of Oxford, Bodleian Library, MS Auct.F.III.15', *Ériu* 48 (1997), 1–35.

Ó Néill, Pádraig, 'Glosses to the psalter of St Caimín: a preliminary investigation of their sources and their function' in Breatnach et al., *Lobháin*, pp 21–31.

*Ó Néill, Pádraig P. (ed.), *Exegetica: Psalterium Suthantoniense.* Corpus Christianorum 240 (Turnhout, 2012).

Ó Néill, Pádraig P., 'Old wine in new bottles: the reprise of early Irish psalter exegesis in Airbertach Mac Cosse's poem on the psalter' in Boyle and Hayden, *Authorities and adaptations*, pp 121–40.

O'Neill, Pamela, 'When onomastics met archaeology: a tale of two Hinbas', *The Scottish Historical Review* 87:1 (2008), 26–41.
O'Neill, Timothy, *The Irish hand. Scribes and their manuscripts from the earliest times* (Cork, 2014 (reprint)).
*O'Rahilly, Cecile (ed.), *Táin Bó Cúailnge Recension 1* (Dublin, 1976).
O'Reilly, Jennifer, 'The Hiberno-Latin tradition of the evangelists and the gospels of Mael Brigte', *Peritia* 9 (1995), 290–309.
O'Reilly, Jennifer, 'The wisdom of the scribe and the fear of the Lord in the Life of Columba' in Dauvit Broun and Thomas Owen Clancy (eds), *Spes Scotorum. Hope of the Scots* (Edinburgh, 1999), pp 159–211.
O'Reilly, Jennifer, 'Seeing the crucified Christ: image and meaning in early manuscript art' in Mullins et al., *Envisioning Christ on the cross*, pp 52–82.
O'Reilly, Myles, *Lives of the Irish martyrs and confessors* (New York, 1878).
*Ó Riain, Pádraig (ed.), *Cath Almaine.* Mediaeval and Modern Irish Series 25 (Dublin, 1978).
Ó Riain, Pádraig, 'Cainnech alias Columcille, patron of Ossory' in de Brún, Ó Coileáin and Ó Riain, *Folia Gadelica*, pp 20–35.
*Ó Riain, Pádraig (ed.), *Corpus genealogiarum sanctorum Hiberniae* (Dublin, 1985).
Ó Riain, Pádraig, 'The Tallaght martyrologies, redated', *Cambridge Medieval Celtic Studies* 20 (Winter, 1990), 21–38.
Ó Riain, Pádraig, 'Dublin's oldest book? A list of saints 'made in Germany'' in Seán Duffy (ed.), *Medieval Dublin V* (Dublin, 2004), 52–72.
Ó Riain, Pádraig, *Feastdays of the saints. A history of Irish martyrologies.* Subsidia hagiographica 86, Société des Bollandistes (Bruxelles, 2006).
*Ó Riain, Pádraig, *A martyrology of four cities: Metz, Cologne, Dublin, Lund.* Henry Bradshaw Society 118 (London, 2008).
Ó Riain, Pádraig, 'The Louvain achievement II: hagiography' in Edel Bhreathnach, Joseph MacMahon and John McCafferty (eds), *The Irish Franciscans 1534–1990* (Dublin, 2009), pp 189–200.
Ó Riain, Pádraig, 'The medieval story of Saint Crónán of Roscrea' in Harbison and Hall, *A carnival of learning*, pp 158–62.
Ó Riain, Pádraig, Diarmuid Ó Murchadha and Kevin Murray (eds), *Historical dictionary of Gaelic placenames. Foclóir stairiúil áitainmneacha na Gaeilge fasc. 1 (Names in A –).* Irish Texts Society (Dublin, 2002).
Ó Riain, Pádraig, Diarmuid Ó Murchadha and Kevin Murray (eds), *Historical dictionary of Gaelic placenames. Foclóir stairiúil áitainmneacha na Gaeilge fasc. 2 (Names in B –).* Irish Texts Society (London, 2005).
Ó Riain-Raedel, Dagmar, 'The question of the "pre-Patrician" saints of Munster' in Michael A. Monk and John Sheehan (eds), *Early medieval Munster. Archaeology, history and society* (Cork, 1998), pp 17–22.
Ó Riain-Raedel, Dagmar, 'New light on the beginnings of Christ Church cathedral, Dublin' in Seán Duffy (ed.), *Medieval Dublin XVII* (Dublin, 2019), 63–80.
O'Scea, Ciaran, 'Erenachs, erenachships and church landholding in Gaelic Fermanagh, 1207–1609', *Proceedings of the Royal Irish Academy* 112C (2012), 271–300.
O'Sullivan, Anne, 'The colophon of the Cotton Psalter (Vitellius F XI)', *Journal of the Royal Society of Antiquaries of Ireland* 96 (1966), 179–80.
O'Sullivan, Jerry and Tomás Ó Carragáin, *Inishmurray. Monks and pilgrims in an Atlantic landscape* (Cork, 2008).
O'Sullivan, William, 'A finding list of Sir James Ware's manuscripts', *Proceedings of the Royal Irish Academy* 97 (1997), 69–99.
Ó hUiginn, Ruairí (ed.), *Lebor na hUidre. Codices Hibernenses Eximii 1* (Dublin, 2015).

Pansters, Krijn, 'Medieval rules and customaries reconsidered' in Krijn Pansters (ed.), *A companion to medieval rules and customaries* (Leiden, 2020), pp 1–36.

Parisse, Michel (ed.), *Les chanoines réguliers. Émergence et expansion (xie–xiiie)* (Saint Étienne, 2009)

Patterson, Helen, 'The Antiphonary of Bangor and its musical implications'. A PhD thesis (Toronto, 2013) https://tspace.library.utoronto.ca/bitstream/1807/70131/3/Patterson_Helen_201311_PhD_thesis.pdf.%20%5B1.2.2%5D.pdf

Pettiau, Hérold, 'The officials of the church of Armagh in the early and central Middle Ages, to AD 1200' in Hughes and Nolan, *Armagh history and society*, pp 121–86.

Petrie, George, *The ecclesiastical architecture of Ireland, anterior to the Anglo-Norman invasion; comprising an essay on the origin and uses of the round towers of Ireland* (Dublin, 1845).

Petrie, George, *Christian inscriptions in the Irish language* ed. Margaret Stokes, 2 vols (Dublin, 1872–8).

Pfaff, Richard, *The liturgy in medieval England. A history* (Cambridge, 2009).

*Pfeil, Brigitte, *Die 'Vision des Tnugdalus' Albers von Windberg* (Frankfurt am Main, 1999) https://celt.ucc.ie/published/L207009/index.html

Phelan, Owen M., *The formation of Christian Europe. The Carolingians, baptism, and the Imperium Christianum* (Oxford, 2014).

Picard, Jean-Michel, 'Structural patterns in early Hiberno-Latin hagiography', *Peritia* 4 (1985), 67–82.

Picard, Jean-Michel, '*Princeps* and *principatus* in the early Irish church: a reassessment' in Smyth, *Seanchas*, pp 146–60.

*Plummer, Charles (ed.), *Vitae sanctorum Hiberniae, partim hacentus ineditae*. 2 vols (Oxford, 1910; repr. 1968).

*Plummer, Charles (ed.), 'Vie et miracles de S. Laurent, archevêque de Dublin', *Analecta Bollandiana* 33 (1914), 121–86.

*Plummer, Charles (ed.), *Bethada náem nÉrenn. Lives of Irish saints.* 2 vols (Oxford, 1922; repr. 1968).

*Plummer, Charles (ed.), *Irish litanies. Text and translation*. Henry Bradshaw Society 62 (London, 1925).

Pollard, Richard Matthew (ed.), *Imagining the medieval afterlife* (Cambridge, 2020).

Pulsiano, Phillip, and Elaine Treharne (eds), *A companion to Anglo-Saxon literature* (Oxford and Malden, MA, 2001).

*Radice, Betty (trans.) (revised by M.T. Clanchy), *The letters of Abelard and Heloise* (London, 2003 (revised ed.)).

Raftery, Joseph, 'A stone figure from Co. Mayo', *Journal of the Royal Society of Antiquaries of Ireland* 14 (1944), 87–90.

*Ramsey, Boniface (trans.), *John Cassian. The conferences* (New York, 1997).

*Ramsey, Boniface (trans.), *John Cassian. The institutes* (New York, 2000).

Ramseyer, Valerie, 'Questions of monastic identity in medieval southern Italy and Sicily (*c*.500–1200)' in *CHMM*, pp 399–414.

Rapp, Claudia, *Brother-making in late antiquity and Byzantium. Monks, laymen, and Christian ritual* (Oxford, 2016).

*Reeves, William (ed.), *Acts of Archbishop Colton in his metropolitan visitation of the diocese of Derry AD MCCCXCVII; with a rental of the see estates at that time* (Dublin, 1850).

Reeves, William, 'Irish Library – No. 2: Fleming's *Collectanea Sacra*', *Ulster Journal of Archaeology*, 1st series 2 (1854), 253–61.

Reeves, William, *The culdees of the British Islands, as they appear in history, with an appendix of evidences* (Dublin, 1864; repr. Felinfach, 1994).

Reeves, William, 'On the Céli-Dé, commonly called Culdees', *Transactions of the Royal Irish Academy* 24 (1873), 119–263.

Reeves, William and Eugene O'Curry, 'On an Irish MS of the Four Gospels in the British Museum', *Proceedings of the Royal Irish Academy* 1st series 5 (1850–3), 45–67.

Reilly, Eileen, 'The insect remains' in Bourke et al., *Skellig Michael excavations*, pp 399–413.

Reisenweaver, Anna, 'Guido of Arezzo and his influence on music learning', *Cederville University: Musical Offerings* 3:1 Article 4 (2012): https://digitalcommons.cedarville.edu/ musicalofferings/vol3/iss1/4.

Rijpma, Auke, Eltjo Buringh, Jan Luiten van Zanden and Bruce Campbell, 'Church building and the economy during Europe's "age of cathedrals", 700–1500', *Explorations in Economic History* 76 (2020), 101–316: https://www.sciencedirect.com/science/article/abs/pii/S0014498319302268

Ritari, Katja, 'Holy souls and a holy community: the meaning of monastic life in Adomnán's *Vita Columbae*', *Journal of Medieval Religious Cultures* 37:1 (2011), 129–46.

Ritari, Katja, *Pilgrimage to Heaven. Eschatology and monastic spirituality in early medieval Ireland* (Turnhout, 2016).

Ritmueller, Jean, 'The Hiberno-Latin background of the Leabhar Breac homily "In Cena Domini"', *Proceedings of the Harvard Celtic colloquium* 2 (1982), 1–10.

Ritmueller, Jean, 'The gospel commentary of Máel Brigte ua Máeluanaig and its Hiberno–Latin background', *Peritia* 2 (1983), 185–214.

*Ritmueller, Jean (ed.), 'Matthew 10: 1–4: the calling of the Twelve Apostles: the commentary and glosses of Máel Brigte úa Máeluanaigh (Armagh 1138) (London, British Library, Harley 1802, fol. 25v-26v). Introduction, edition, translation' in Guldentops et al., *Felici curiositate*, pp 55–69.

*Riyeff, Jacob (trans.), *The Old English Rule of Saint Benedict with related Old English texts* (Collegeville, 2017).

Robson, Michael, *St Francis of Assisi. The legend and the life* (London and New York, 1997).

*Rochford, Robert (Fr B.B.), *The life of the glorious bishop S. Patricke, apostle and primate of Ireland together with the lives of the holy virgin S. Bridgit and of the glorious abbot Saint Columbe, patrons of Ireland* (St Omer, 1625).

Roe, Helen M., 'The orans in Irish Christian art', *Journal of the Royal Society of Antiquaries of Ireland* 100 (1970), 212–221.

Roling, Bernd, 'Phoenician Ireland: Charles Vallancey (1725–1812) and the oriental roots of Celtic culture' in Karl A.E. Enenkel and Konrad Adriann Ottenheym (eds), *The quest for an appropriate past in literature, art and architecture* (Leiden, 2018), pp 750–70.

*Rule, Martin (ed.), *Eadmeri historia novorum in Anglia*. Rolls series 81 (London, 1884; repr. Cambridge, 2012).

*Rule, Martin (ed.), *The missal of St Augustine's Abbey Canterbury* (Cambridge, 1896; repr. 2017).

Rumsey, Patricia, 'Tensions over time: conflicting understanding of monastic prayer in late-eighth-century Armagh', *Seanchas Ard Mhacha* 25:2 (2015), 29–49.

Ryan, John, *Irish monasticism. Origins and early development* (Dublin, 1931; repr. 1992).

Ryan, Michael, Kevin Mooney, Frank Prendergast and Barry Masterson, 'Church Island: a description' in MacShamhráin, *The island of St Patrick*, pp 106–24.

Ryan, Salvador, 'Steadfast saints or malleable models? Seventeenth-century Irish hagiography revisited', *The Catholic Historical Review* 91:2 (2005), 251–77.

Saak, Eric Leland (ed.), *Catechesis in the later Middle Ages I. The exposition of the Lord's Prayer of Jordan of Quedlinburg, OESA (d. 1380). Introduction, text and translation* (Leiden and Boston, 2015).

Salmon, Pierre, 'La composition d'un *Libellus precum* à l'époque de la réforme grégorienne', *Benedictina* 26 (1979), 285–322.

Sargent, Andrew, 'A misplaced miracle: the origins of St Modwynn of Burton and St Eadgyth of Polesworth', *Midland History* 41:1 (2016), 1–19 https://core.ac.uk/download/pdf/43762774.pdf

*Schmitt, F.S., *Sancti Anselmi Cantuariensis archiepiscopi opera omnia* vol. 4 (Edinburgh, 1949).

*Scott, A.B. and F.X. Martin (ed. and trans.), *Expugnatio Hibernica. The conquest of Ireland by Giraldus Cambrensis* (Dublin, 1978).

Scully, Diarmuid, 'Ireland and the Irish in Bernard of Clairvaux's Life of Malachy: representation and context' in Bracken and Ó Riain-Raedel, *Ireland and Europe*, pp 239–56.

Seale, Yvonne, 'Putting women in order: a comparison of the medieval women religious of Ballymore-Loughsewdy and Prémontré' in Browne et al., *Brides of Christ*, pp 85–99.

Seaver, Matt, Conor McDermott and Graeme Warren, 'A monastery among the glens', *Archaeology Ireland* 32:2 (Summer, 2018), 19–23.

*Selmer, Carl (ed.), *Navigatio Sancti Brendani abbatis from early Latin manuscripts* (Notre Dame, 1959; repr. Dublin, 1989).

Şenocak, Neslihan, 'The making of Franciscan poverty', *Revue Mabillon* 24 (2013), 5–26.

Seymour, St John D., 'Irish versions of the *Transitus Mariae*', *Journal of Theological Studies* 23 (1921), 36–43.

Sharpe, Richard, 'Hiberno-Latin *laicus*, Irish *láech* and the devil's men', *Ériu* 30 (1979), 75–92.

Sharpe, Richard, 'Some problems concerning the organization of the church in early medieval Ireland', *Peritia* 3 (1984), 230–70.

Sharpe, Richard, 'Dispute settlement in medieval Ireland: a preliminary enquiry' in Wendy Davies and Paul Fouracre (eds), *The settlement of disputes in early medieval Europe* (Cambridge, 1986), pp 169–89.

Sharpe, Richard, *Medieval Irish saints' lives. An introduction to* Vitae sanctorum Hiberniae (Oxford, 1991).

Sharpe, Richard (trans.), *Adomnán of Iona. Life of St Columba* (London, 1995).

Sheehan, John, 'Early medieval Iveragh, AD 400–1200' in Crowley and Sheehan, *The Iveragh Peninsula*, pp 113–21.

Sikora, Maeve, 'Steinfigur eines Geistlichen' in Christoph Stiegemann, Martin Kroker and Wolfgang Walter (eds), *Credo. Christianisierung Europas im Mittelalter. Band II: Katalog* (Petersberg, 2013), pp 236–7 no. 198.

Simms, Katharine, *Gaelic Ulster in the Middle Ages. History, culture and society* (Dublin, 2020).

Simpson, Linzi, 'Forty years a-digging: a preliminary synthesis of archaeological investigations in medieval Dublin' in Seán Duffy (ed.), *Medieval Dublin I* (2000), pp 11–68.

Simpson, Linzi, 'Fifty years a-digging: a synthesis of medieval and archaeological excavations in Dublin city and suburbs' in Seán Duffy (ed.), *Medieval Dublin XI* (2011), pp 9–112.

Smith, Andrew T. and Garrett B. Ratcliff, 'A survey of relations between Scottish Augustinian canons before 1215' in Burton and Stöber, *The regular canons*, pp 115–44.

Smith, Brendan, 'The Armagh-Clogher dispute and the "Mellifont Conspiracy": diocesan politics and monastic reform in early thirteenth century Ireland', *Seanchas Ard Mhacha* 14:2 (1991), 26–38.

Smyth, Alfred P. (ed.), *Seanchas. Studies in early and medieval Irish archaeology, history and literature in honour of Francis J. Byrne* (Dublin, 2000).

*Southern, R.W. (ed.), *The life of St Anselm archbishop of Canterbury by Eadmer* (London etc., 1962).

*Sperber, Ingred (ed.), 'The life of St Monenna or Darerca of Killevy' in Hughes and Nolan, *Armagh history and society*, pp 63–97.

Stacey, Robin Chapman, *Dark speech. The performance of law in early Ireland* (Philadelphia, 2007).

Stalley, Roger, 'The Romanesque sculpture of Tuam' in Alan Borg and Andrew Martindale (eds), *The vanishing past. Studies of medieval art, liturgy and metrology presented to Christopher Hohler.* BAR International Series 111 (Oxford, 1981), pp 179–95.

Stalley, Roger, *The Cistercian monasteries of Ireland. An account of the history, art and architecture of the White Monks in Ireland from 1142 to 1540* (London and New Haven, 1987).

Stalley, Roger, *Early Irish sculpture and the art of the high crosses* (New Haven and London, 2020).

Steckel, Sita, 'Satirical depictions of monastic life' in *CHMM*, pp 1154–70.

Stevens, Paul, 'For whom the bell tolls: the monastic site at Clonfad 3, Co. Westmeath' in Michael Stanley, Ed Danaher and James Eogan (eds), *Creative minds. Production, manufacturing and invention in ancient Ireland* (Dublin, 2010), pp 85–98.

Stevenson, Jane, 'Altus Prosator', *Celtica* 23 (1999), 326–68.

Stewart, Columba, *Cassian the monk* (New York and Oxford, 1998).

Stewart, Columba, 'The practices of monastic prayer: origins, evolution, and tensions' in Philip Sellew (ed.), *Living for eternity. The White Monastery and its neighbourhood. Proceedings of a symposium at the University of Minnesota, Minneapolis, March 6–9, 2003* (Minneapolis, 2009 internet version), pp 97–108. http://egypt.cla.umn.edu/eventsr.html

Stewart, Columba, 'Monastic space and time' in Hendrik W. Dey and Elizabeth Fentress (eds), *Western monasticism* ante litteram. *The spaces of monastic observance in late antiquity and the early Middle Ages* (Turnhout, 2011), pp 43–51.

Stewart, Columba, 'The literature of early western monasticism' in Kaczynski, *Oxford handbook of Christian monasticism*, pp 85–100.

Stifter, David, 'Brendaniana, etc.', *Keltische Forschungen* 1 (2006), 191–214.

Stöber, Karen, 'The regular canons in Wales' in Burton and Stöber, *The regular canons*, pp 97–113.

Stöber, Karen and David Austin, 'Culdees to canons: the Augustinian houses of north Wales' in Janet Burton and Karen Stöber (eds), *Monastic Wales. New approaches* (Cardiff, 2013), pp 39–54.

*Stokes, George T. (ed.), *Pococke's tour in Ireland in 1752* (Dublin and London, 1891). https://celt.ucc.ie//published/E750002-001.html

*Stokes, Whitley, 'A Middle-Irish homily on S. Martin of Tours', *Revue celtique* 2 (1873–5), 381–402, 508.

*Stokes, Whitley (ed. and trans.), *The tripartite life of Patrick, with other documents relating to that saint.* 2 vols (London, 1887).

*Stokes, Whitley (ed.), *Lives of saints from the Book of Lismore*. Anecdota Oxoniensia 5 (Oxford, 1890).

*Stokes, Whitley (ed.), *Félire Huí Gormáin. The martyrology of Gorman*. Henry Bradshaw Society 9 (London, 1895).

*Stokes, Whitley (ed.), 'Acallamh na Senórach' in Ernst Windisch and Whitley Stokes (eds), *Irische Texte* 4 (Leipzig, 1900), pp 1–438.

*Stokes, Whitley (ed.), *Félire Óengusso Céli Dé. The martyrology of Oengus the Culdee*. Henry Bradshaw Society 29 (London, 1905; repr., Dublin, 1984).

Stokes, Whitley and John Strachan (eds), *Thesaurus paleohibernicus. A collection of Old-Irish glosses, scholia, prose, and verse*. 2 vols (Cambridge, 1901–3; repr. Dublin, 1975 and 1987).

Stokes, William, *The life and labours in art and archaeology of George Petrie LL.D.* (London, 1868).

*Strachan, John (ed.), 'An Old-Irish metrical rule', *Ériu* 1 (1904), 191–208.

* Strachan, John (ed.), 'Addenda to Ériu 1, 191 *sq.*', *Ériu* 2 (1905), 58–9.

*Strachan, John (ed.), 'Cormac's rule', *Ériu* 2 (1905), 62–8.

*Strachan, John, 'Two monastic rules', *Ériu* 2 (1905), 227–9.

Swift, Catherine, 'Forts and fields: a study of "monastic towns" in seventh and eighth century Ireland', *Journal of Irish Archaeology* 9 (1998), 105–25.

Swift, Catherine, Review of Harrington, *Women in a Celtic church*, *Irish Economic and Social History* 30 (2003), 128–9.

Swift, Catherine, 'Early Irish priests within their own localities' in Fiona Edmonds and Paul Russell (eds), *Tome: studies in medieval Celtic history and law in honour of Thomas Charles-Edwards* (Woodbridge, 2011), pp 29–40.

Swift, Catherine, 'Religion (as a factor in Irish town formation)' in Howard B. Clarke and Sarah Gearty (eds), *More maps and texts. Sources and the Irish Historic Towns Atlas* (Dublin, 2018), pp 67–86.

Swift, Catherine, 'Soul sisters: two Irish holy women in their late antique context' in Browne et al., *Brides of Christ*, pp 37–55.

Sykes, Katharine, 'New movements of the twelfth century: diversity, belonging, and order(s)' in Kim Curran and Janet Burton (eds), *Medieval women religious c. 800–c. 1500. New perspectives* (Woodbridge, 2023), pp 43–60.

*Symons, Thomas (ed.), *Regularis Concordia Anglicae nationis monachorum sanctimonialiumque. The monastic agreement of the monks and nuns of the English nation* (London, 1953).

Taylor, Simon, 'From *Cinrigh Monai* to *Civitas Sancti Andree*: a star is born' in Michael H. Brown and Katie Stevenson (eds), *Medieval St Andrews. Church, cult, city* (Woodbridge, 2017), pp 20–34.

Thacker, Alan T., 'Æthelwold and Abingdon' in Barbara Yorke (ed.), *Bishop Æthelwold. His career and influence* (Woodbridge, 1988; repr. 1997), pp 43–64.

Thibodeaux, Jennifer D., *The manly priest. Clerical celibacy, masculinity, and reform in England and Normandy, 1066–1300* (Philadelphia, 2015).

Thomas, Charles, 'Topographical notes: III. *Rosnat*, *Rostat*, and the early Irish church', *Ériu* 22 (1971), 100–6.

Thomas, Colleen M., 'Missing models: visual narrative in the insular Paul and Antony panels' in Hawkes, *Making histories*, pp 77–89.

Thomas, Kate H., *Late Anglo-Saxon prayer in practice. Before the Books of Hours* (Berlin and Boston, 2020).

Thompson, John, 'William Reeves and the medieval texts and manuscripts at Armagh', *Peritia* 10 (1996), 363–80.

*Thornton, Andrew (trans.), *Grimlaicus: rule for solitaries* (Collegeville, 2011). *Project MUSE* muse.jhu.edu/book/46747

*Thorpe, Benjamin (ed.), *The homilies of the Anglo-Saxon church. The Sermones Catholici or homilies of Ælfric*. Vol I (London, 1844).

Tracey, Liam, 'Celtic mists: the search for a Celtic rite' in Ann Buckley (ed.), *Music, liturgy, and the veneration of saints of the medieval Irish church in a European context* (Turnhout, 2017), pp 291–304.

Treharne, Elaine and Phillip Pulsiano, 'An introduction to the corpus of Anglo-Saxon vernacular literature' in Pulsiano and Treharne, *A companion to Anglo-Saxon literature*, pp 1–10.

Trout, Dennis E., 'Augustine at Cassiciacum: *otium honestum* and the social dimensions of conversion', *Vigiliae Christianae* 42:2 (1988), 132–46.

*Turner, Andrew J. and Bernard J. Muir (eds), *Eadmer of Canterbury. Lives and miracles of Saints Oda, Dunstan, and Oswald*. Oxford medieval texts (Oxford, 2006).

*Ulster Society for Medieval Latin Studies (eds), 'The life of St Monenna by Conchubranus [Part 1]', *Seanchas Ard Mhacha* 9:2 (1979), 250–73; [Part II] 10:1 (1980–1), 117–41; [Part III] 10:2 (1982), 426–54.

*Ussher, James, *Britannicarum ecclesiarum antiquitates* (Dublin, 1639).

Valdez del Álamo, Elizabeth, 'The cloister, heart of monastic life' in Bhreathnach, Krasnodębska-D'Aughton and Smith, *Monastic Europe*, pp 171–94.

Valente, Mary, 'Reassessing the Irish "monastic town"', *Irish Historical Studies* 31 (1998), 1–18.

*Vallancey, Charles, *Collectanea de rebus Hibernicis* vol. 3 (Dublin, 1786).

Vanderputten, Steven, 'Itinerant lordship. Relic translations and social change in eleventh- and twelfth-century Flanders' in Vanderputten, *Reform, conflict, and the shaping of corporate identities. Collected studies on Benedictine monasticism in medieval Flanders, c.1050–c.1150* (Zürich and Berlin, 2013), pp 193–214.

Vanderputten, Steven, *Imagining religious leadership in the Middle Ages. Richard of Saint-Vanne and the politics of reform* (Ithaca, 2015).

Vanderputten, Steven, *Dark age nunneries. The ambiguous identity of female monasticism, 800–1050* (Ithaca and London, 2018).

Vanderputten, Steven, 'Custom and identity at Le Bec' in Benjamin Pohl and Laura L. Gathagan (eds), *A companion to the Abbey of Le Bec in the central Middle Ages (11th–13th centuries)* (Leiden and Boston, 2018), pp 228–47.

Vanderputten, Steven, *Medieval monasticisms. Forms and experiences of the monastic life in the Latin west* (Berlin and Boston, 2020).

Veitch, Kenneth, 'The conversion of native religious communities to the Augustinian rule in twelfth- and thirteenth-century Alba', *Records of the Scottish Church History Society* 29 (1999), 1–22.

*Vendryes, Joseph, 'Trois historiettes irlandaises du manuscrits de Paris', *Revue celtique* 31 (1910), 300–11.

*Vendryes, Joseph (ed. and trans.), 'L'aventure de Maelsuthain', *Revue celtique* 35 (1914), 203–11.

Vendryes, Joseph, 'Étymologies. II. – GALLOIS *afwyn* et *afn*; BRETON *aven*', *Études celtiques* 4:2 (1948), 327–34.

Verbist, Peter, 'Reconstructing the past. The chronicle of Marianus Scotus', *Peritia* 16 (2002), 228–334.

Verheijen, Luc (ed.), *Nouvelle approche de la Règle de Saint Augustin*. 2 vols (Bégrolles en Mauges, 1980; Louvain, 1988).

*Vivian, Tim, Kim Vivian and Jeffrey Burton Russell (eds), *The lives of the Jura fathers. The life and rule of the holy fathers Romanus, Lupicinus, Eugendus, abbots of the monasteries in the Jura mountains* (Kalamazoo, 1999).

*Volmering, Nicole, 'The second vision of Adomnán' in Carey et al., *The end and beyond*, vol. 2, pp 647–81.

*Volmering, Nicole, 'A bibliography of medieval Irish eschatology and related sources' in Carey et al., *The end and beyond*, vol. 2, pp 855–912.

Vones-Liebenstein, Ursula, 'Similarities and differences between monks and regular canons in the twelfth century' in *CHMM*, pp 766–82.

Waddell, John, 'An archæological survey of Temple Brecan, Aran', *Journal of the Galway Archæological and Historical Society* 33 (1972–3), 5–27.

*Wagner, Albrecht (ed.), *Visio Tnugdali*. Lateinisch und Altdeutsch (Erlangen, 1882; repr. Hildesheim and New York, 1989).

Wakeman, William Frederick, *Archaeologica Hibernica. A hand-book of Irish antiquities, pagan and Christian, especially of such as are of easy access from the Irish metropolis* (Dublin, 1848).

*Walker, G.S.M. (ed.), *Sancti Columbani opera*. Scriptores Latini Hiberniae 2 (Dublin, 1957; repr. 1970).

*Ward, Benedicta, *The sayings of the Desert Fathers. The alphabetical collection* (Kalamazoo, 1975).

*Ware, James, *Librorum manuscriptorum in bibliotheca Jacobi Waraei equitis aurati catalogus* (Dublin, 1648).

*Ware, James, *De Hibernia et Antiquitatibus ejus, Disquisitiones* (London, 1654).

*Ware, James, *De praesulibus Hiberniae commentarius* (Dublin, 1665).

*Warner, George F. (ed.), *The Stowe missal. MS.D.II.3 in the library of the Royal Irish Academy, Dublin.* Henry Bradshaw Society 31 and 32 (London, 1906, 1915).

*Warren, Frederick Edward (ed.), *The manuscript Irish missal belonging to the President and Fellows of Corpus Christi College, Oxford* (London, 1879).

*Warren, Frederick E., *The liturgy and ritual of the Celtic church* (Oxford, 1881; repr. Woodbridge, 1987 (with introduction by Jane Stevenson)).

*Warren, Frederick E., and W. Griggs, *Antiphonary of Bangor. An early Irish manuscript in the Ambrosian Library at Milan.* 2 vols (London, 1893–5).

Webber, Teresa, 'Reading in the refectory. Monastic practice in England, *c.* 1000 – *c.* 1300', London University annual John Coffin memorial palaeography lecture 18 February 2010 (revised text, 2013): https://www.academia.edu/9489001/Reading_in_the_Refectory_Monastic_Practice_in_England_c._1000-c.1300.

West, Máire, 'Aspects of *díberg* in the tale *Togail Bruidne Da Derga*', *Zeitschrift für celtische Philologie* 49–50 (1997), 950–64.

Whitelock, Dorothy, Rosamund McKitterick and David Dumville (eds), *Ireland in early mediaeval Europe. Studies in memory of Kathleen Hughes* (Cambridge, 1982).

Williams, Hannah, 'Authority and pedagogy in Hermann of Reichenau's *De Octo Vitiis Principalibus*'. PhD University of Manchester (2006). British Library EThOS online dissertation no. 693454 (https://ethos.bl.uk/).

Williamson, Paul, 'Acquisitions of sculpture at the Victoria and Albert Museum 1986–1991: supplement', *The Burlington Magazine* 133 (1991), 876–80.

Wilmart, André, 'La Trinité des Scots à Rome et les notes du *Vat. Lat. 378*', *Revue Bénédictine* 41 (1929), 218–30.

Wilmart, André, 'Finian parmi les moines romains de la Trinité des Scots', *Revue Bénédictine* 44 (1932), 359–61.

*Winterbottom, Michael and Michael Lapidge (eds and trans), *The early lives of St Dunstan.* Oxford medieval texts (Oxford, 2011).

*Winterbottom, Michael and Rodney M. Thomson (eds), *William of Malmesbury: saints' lives: lives of SS Wulfstan, Dunstan, Patrick, Benignus and Indract* (Oxford, 2002).

Yorke, Barbara (ed.), *Bishop Æthelwold. His career and influence* (Woodbridge, 1988; repr. 1997).

Zakharine, Dmitri, 'Medieval perspectives in Europe: oral culture and bodily practices' in Cornelia Müller et al. (eds), *Body-language-communication. An international handbook on multimodality in human interaction* vol. 1 (Berlin and Boston, 2013), pp 343–64.

Zatta, Jane, 'The "Vie Seinte Osith": hagiography and politics in Anglo-Norman England', *Studies in Philology* 96:4 (1999), 367–93.

Zimmerl-Panagl, Victoria (ed.), *Monastica 1: Donati Regula, Pseudo-Columbani Regula Monialium (frg.).* Corpus scriptorum ecclesiasticorum Latinorum 98 (Berlin, Munich and Boston, 2015).

ELECTRONIC RESOURCES

Biographies in Irish:
www.ainm.ie

Bibliographies:
https://www.vanhamel.nl/codecs
https://bill.celt.dias.ie/

British History Online:
https://www.british-history.ac.uk/

British Library Catalogue:
http://www.bl.uk/catalogues/illuminatedmanuscripts/

The Corpus of Romanesque Sculpture in Britain and Ireland:
https://www.crsbi.ac.uk/

Dictionary of Irish biography:
https://www.dib.ie

Dublin Institute for Advanced Studies (Celtic Studies) Monasticon Hibernicum database:
https://monasticon.celt.dias.ie/

Excavation reports Ireland:
https://excavations.ie/

George du Noyer drawings:
http://rsai.locloudhosting.net/exhibits/show/du-noyer-volumes/about

The Henry Bradshaw Society, London:
https://henrybradshawsociety.org/history

Historic Environment Scotland:
https://www.historicenvironment.scot/visit-a-place/places/
https://canmore.org.uk/

Inis Cealtra Report Appendix (Clare County Council)
https://www.clarecoco.ie/services/planning/publications/inishcealtra/inish-cealtra-appendix-2-detailed-support-material-26764.pdf.

Irish Place Names Commission:
www.logainm.ie

Irish Script on Screen:
https://www.isos.dias.ie/

Middle English dictionary:
https://quod.lib.umich.edu/m/middle-english-dictionary/

Monasticism bibliography (compiled by Albrecht Diem):
http://www.earlymedievalmonasticism.org/bibliographymonasticism.htm

National Monuments of Ireland Historic Viewer:
www.archaeology.ie

Oxford Grove Music Dictionary online:
https://www.oxfordmusiconline.com/grovemusic/

People of Medieval Scotland 1093–1371 (PoMS database):
https://www.poms.ac.uk/

Pontificale Romanorum:
http://www.liturgialatina.org/pontificale/

Royal Irish Academy: eDIL – electronic dictionary of the Irish language
http://dil.ie

Royal Irish Academy: Historical Irish Corpus 1600–1926:
http://corpas.ria.ie/

Royal Irish Academy: Irish Historic Towns Atlas:
https://www.ria.ie/research-projects/irish-historic-towns-atlas

Saints in Scottish place-names:
https://saintsplaces.gla.ac.uk/

TCD MS Digital Collections:
https://digitalcollections.tcd.ie/

UCD School of Archaeology Glendalough Project:
https://www.ucd.ie/archaeology/research/glendalough

Index